The Origin & Evolution of Man

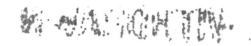

Thomas Y. Crowell Company   New York   Established 1834

The Origin & Evolution of Man

Readings in Physical Anthropology

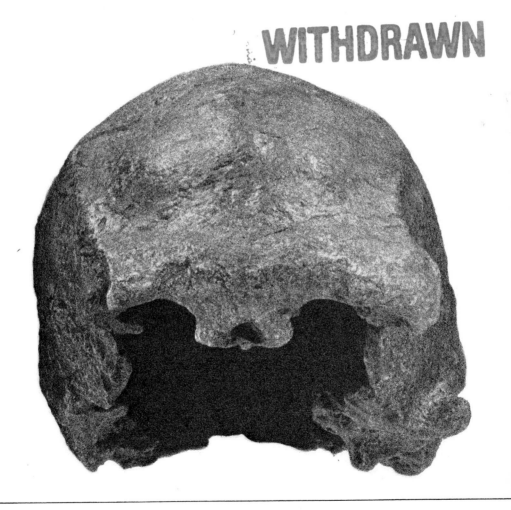

Edited by Ashley Montagu

Library of Congress Cataloging in Publication Data

MONTAGU, ASHLEY, 1905–   comp.
   The origin & evolution of man.

   Includes bibliographical references.
   1. Somatology.—Addresses, essays, lectures.
2. Human evolution.—Addresses, essays, lectures.
I. Title.
GN60.M62   573.2   73-3351
ISBN 0-690-60081-X

Typography and cover design by Hermann Strohbach

Manufactured in the United States of America

1 2 3 4 5 6 7 8 9 10

TO THE MEMORY OF HELMUTH CORDS

PREFACE

Anthropology is, surely, the most enthralling and humanizing of studies. It is a study which stands in immediate relation to virtually every aspect of humanity—a view which I first found stated by Thomas Henry Huxley in a letter written to a young man, in 1889, who had asked him for advice about making anthropology his life work. Huxley wrote, "I know of no department of natural science more likely to reward a man who goes into it thoroughly than anthropology. There is an immense deal to be done in the science pure and simple, and it is one of those branches of inquiry which brings one into contact with the great problems of humanity in every direction."

The young man was Alfred Cort Haddon (1855–1940) who, taking Huxley's advice, subsequently went on to become one of the distinguished founding fathers of anthropology, cultural and physical in England, and a notable contributor to the development of the science. As his biographer wrote of him, "His Anthropology might be called Philanthropology. His great service to Science, for which he will always be famous, was to lay the foundations and to build the framework of Anthropology well and truly on sound scientific principles; his service to humanity was to show that 'the proper study of Mankind' is to discover Man as a human being, whatever the texture of his hair, the colour of his skin or the shape of his skull." [1]

As happens with the development of every science, the gray shadow of specialization is now falling over anthropology, and especially physical anthropology which now demands such detailed and profound study of the most careful kind. It is, therefore, more than ever necessary, in this proliferation of specialties, to keep always in sight the basic core and main purpose of anthropology. That main purpose, at least as I have always conceived it, is the understanding of man as a whole. How, in all his varieties, living and extinct, both culturally and physically, he got to be the way he is now.

The achievement of this understanding is rather a large order and therefore demands the coverage and investigation of a great many different fields, all of which are related to the main purpose of throwing light on the nature of man. This approach to the study of anthropology cuts across the humanities as well as the sciences, and renders rather sterile the arguments of some writers that the subject belongs exclusively either in one field or the other. There is scarcely an area of knowledge over which anthropology does not cast its net.

It has always seemed to me that students of physical anthropology should be well trained in cultural anthropology so they may always remain sensitive to the principal referent of their interest and to the role that culture has played in the physical evolution of man, and that as anthropologists we should always remember that anthropology is not only about man, but should also be *for* man. May Sarton has put it beautifully in one of her poems:

> Never forget this when the talk is clever:
> Wisdom must be born in the flesh or wither,
> And sacred order has been always won
> From chaos by some burning faithful one

[1] A. Hingston Quiggin, *Haddon The Head-Hunter* (Cambridge: Cambridge University Press, 1942) 152.

Whose human bones have ached as if with fever
To bring you to these high triumphant places,
Forget the formulas, remember men.*

In the present volume of readings I have endeavored to provide the student with a broad conspectus of the field of physical anthropology,—or, as some are beginning to call it, biological anthropology,—with special emphasis where the subject touches the borderlands of other fields. In this way I hope the student will obtain a good view not only of the length and breadth of the subject, but also of its depth. There is scarcely an area of life upon which anthropology does not touch, and this is as true of physical as it is of cultural anthropology. With this in mind the student will increasingly come to understand that anthropology, and especially physical anthropology, has an important practical use, and is not merely the "academic" subject it was once considered to be.

I first commenced the study of anthropology more than fifty years ago. I knew most of the founding "fathers" and "mothers" of the subject, and have witnessed the growth and development

of the subject from a few practitioners to literally thousands of actively engaged teachers, researchers, and students. My growing up with the subject is to some extent reflected in the choice of contributions to this volume. Included are a number of contributions which I regard as of classical and enduring importance, but which have generally been overlooked or slighted. Ultimately the collection reflects the experiences and preferences of the editor:

> What do you need to make an anthology?
> *Scissors and paste.*
> But what gives the book its flavor then?
> *The scissorman's taste.*   [Anon.]

The longest segment of the volume is devoted to a subject that is currently, and will long continue to be, a most important arena of knowledge in which the anthropologist must be involved. This is "race." I make no apologies for this seeming overweighting of a volume of readings on physical anthropology. It is a matter which continues to be of the most serious social and political importance, and it is one upon which the anthropologist must always have the last word.

A. M.

Princeton, N.J.
13 March 1973

---

* May Sarton, from the poem "The Sacred Order," *The Lion and the Rose,* by May Sarton (New York: Rinehart Co., 1959). Reprinted by permission of the author and the publisher.

CONTENTS

THIRTEEN · RACE

The Origin & Evolution of Man

ONE • PHYSICAL ANTHROPOLOGY

1 • THE STRATEGY OF PHYSICAL ANTHROPOLOGY

Sherwood L. Washburn

As Washburn discusses at length in the following article, the main obstacle to progress in physical anthropology up to the middle of the twentieth century consisted of the addiction to description and the ritualistic worship of measurement. The touching faith of anthropologists in caliper measurement had to be witnessed to be believed. The feeling was that if one accumulated a sufficient number of measurements and coined an adequate number of "scientific" terms like "tapeinocephalic" or "hypereuryprosopic" (which, incidentally, no one ever used), somehow one could cast these anthropological spells upon the material, put the measurements through a calculating machine, and make significant answers appear. There were people who held professorships who actually believed this. One may recall Goethe's sterling words, "Where an idea is wanting, a word can always be found to take its place,"—especially when the word is a scientific term.

Measurement will always be a tool of the physical anthropologist's, but it will never again constitute the major part of his methodology. For the most part the value of measurement in physical anthropology has been replaced by the biological approach—in fact, this designation would be preferable for physical anthropology itself, with the emphasis on the broad application of analytic biology rather than physical measurement and description. But the scope of physical anthropology is even wider than that, for it now involves the study of behavior and its effects upon the evolution of man. As Washburn points out, the objective continues to be the understanding and interpretation of human evolution.

SOURCE: A. L. Kroeber, ed., *Anthropology Today* (Chicago: University of Chicago Press, 1953), pp. 714–27. Copyright 1953 by the University of Chicago. Reprinted by permission of the publisher.

Washburn properly emphasizes the role of theory as a methodology in physical anthropology. Theory, one should always remember, is the lifeblood of science, but it is not the point at which to remain content. Theory is the stage between the problem which generated it and the inquiry calculated to throw light on the problem, and thus should serve as a stimulus to that inquiry.

Washburn emphasizes the amount one must really know about his whole field in order to be able to interpret the value of an explanation in any specific area whatever. The techniques designed to help solve a problem must be based on a fairly full understanding of those factors which have been shown by other researchers to be involved—mere reliance on traditional methods of measurement is unlikely to yield useful results. This makes it mandatory for anyone undertaking research on any problem in physical anthropology to make himself as fully acquainted with the relevant literature as possible. It requires a thoroughgoing acquaintance with the procedure of "looking up the literature," a skill which should be part of the training of every student preparing for a career in this field, rather than one left to him to pick up in his own way. The results are too often spectacularly distressing.

Finally, Washburn brings out the need for an understanding of the history and function of culture as well as a dynamic biology. He underscores the importance of the role of culture in addition to that of biological factors in the shaping of evolutionary history.

The strategy of a science is that body of theory and techniques with which it attacks its problems. All sciences have their traditional ways of marshaling and analyzing data, and the effectiveness of a science may be judged by the way its strategy actually solves problems and points the way to new research. For many years physical anthropology changed little and was easy to define. Physical anthropologists were those scientists, interested in human evolution and variation, who used measurements as their primary technique. The main training of a physical anthropologist consisted in learning to make a small number of measurements accurately, and one of the great concerns of the profession has been to get agreement on how these measurements should be taken. The assumption seems to have been that description (whether morphological or metrical), if accurate enough and in sufficient quantity, could solve problems of process, pattern, and interpretation.

It was essential to get a general appreciation of the varieties of primates, including man, before the problems of evolution could be understood. As knowledge of the primates increased, the kinds of problems to be solved became more and more defined. Is man's closest living relative an arboreal ape or a tiny tarsier? By what methods could such a problem be attacked? Should as many characters as possible be compared, or would a few critical ones settle the matter? Should adaptive characters be stressed, or does the solution of the problems of phylogeny lie in nonadaptive features? Does the body evolve as a unified whole, or may different parts change at different times?

The general understanding of the primates and of human races proceeded rapidly and productively in the nineteenth century. The classifications of Flower and Lydekker (1891) and Deniker (1900) are remarkably close to those of today. The principal progress since that time has been in the discovery of fossils, and the quantity and quality of descriptive materials has increased greatly. Many small problems have been clarified, but the main outlines of the classification of the primates were clear more than fifty years ago.

During the last fifty years, although excellent descriptive data were added, techniques improved, and problems clarified and defined, little progress was made in understanding the process and pattern of human evolution. The strategy of physical anthropology yielded diminishing returns, and, finally, application of the traditional method *by experts* gave contradictory results. After more than a century of intensive fact-finding, there is less agreement among informed scientists on the relation of man to other primates than there was in the latter part of the nineteenth century. (Schultz, 1936, 1950*a*, *b*; Simpson, 1945; and Straus, 1949, have recently summarized many of these conflicting views and the evidence for them.) With regard to race, agreement is no greater, for some recognize a few races based on populations, while others describe a great number, many of which are types and refer to no populations at all.

Difficulties of this sort are by no means confined to physical anthropology but are common in many parts of descriptive zoölogy. The dilemma arises from continuing the strategy which was appropriate in the first descriptive phase of a science into the following analytic phase. Measurements will tell us which heads are long, but they will not tell us whether longheaded people should be put into one biological category. A photograph may show that a person is fat, but it gives no clue to the cause of the fat, and a grouping of fat people may be as arbitrary as one of longheads.

It is necessary to have a knowledge of the varieties of head form, pigmentation, body build, growth pattern, etc., before the problems of evolution, race, and constitution can be clearly stated. But all that can be done with the initial descriptive information is to gain a first understanding, a sense of problem, and a preliminary classification. To go further requires an elaboration of theory and method along different lines. Having passed through its initial descriptive phase, physical anthropology is now entering into its analytic stage. Change is forced on physical anthropology partially by the fact that its own strategy has ceased to yield useful results but, far more, by the rise of modern evolutionary theory. . . . The meeting of genetics, paleontology, and evolutionary zoölogy created the new systematics (neozoölogy), just as the impact of the new evolutionary theory is creating a new physical anthropology. Anthropologists are fortunate that their problems are logically and methodologically similar to those which have been debated and largely solved in zoölogy. Therefore, their task is far simpler than that which confronted taxonomists fifteen years ago. The anthropologist may simply adopt the new evolutionary point of view, and his task is primarily one of adapting to this intellectual environment and devising techniques suitable to his particular needs. The nature and implication of the changes will be made clearer by considering the contrast between the old and the new systematically, under the headings of purpose, theory, technique, and interpretation. These comparisons will be made briefly in Table 1, and then each will be considered in some detail. It should be remembered in making the comparisons that the differences are in degree only and that brief contrasts, especially in a table, make them appear unduly sharp. As Stewart (1951) has rightly pointed out, the new physical anthropology has evolved from the old, and there is a real continuity. However, a great change is taking place in a short time. If this is called "evolution," it is evolution of a quantum type. It is a burst of acceleration on the part of a species which had been quiescent for a long period of time. Actually, the physical anthropology of 1950 will seem much more like that of 1900 than it will like that of 1960. Since the transition described in this paper is still taking place, it would be very difficult to discern its magnitude from the anthropological literature. The remarks in this paper are based heavily on the discussions which have been held at the Wenner-Gren summer seminars for physical anthropologists, and those reading only current American physical anthropology would get little

Table 1

	OLD	NEW
Purpose	Primarily classification	Understanding process
	Problems solved by classification and correlation	Classification a minor part, and the *cause* of differences critical
	Description of difference enough	
Theory	Relatively little and unimportant; facts speak for themselves	Theory is critical, and the development of consistent, experimentally verified hypotheses a major objective
Technique	Anthropometry 80 per cent, aided by morphological comparison	Measurement perhaps 20 per cent, supplemented by a wide variety of techniques adapted to the solution of particular problems
Interpretation	Speculation	The primary objective of the research is to prove which hypotheses are correct; the major task begins where the old left off

idea of the size or importance of these changes. Since the transition in zoölogy is now general and international, that in anthropology soon will be, and it is hoped that the extent and nature of the changes now taking place in other countries may be discussed at length at this conference.

Purpose

In commenting on the contrasts between the new and the old physical anthropology outlined in Table 1, it should be stressed that the area of interest or ultimate purposes of the field are the same. The understanding and interpretation of human evolution remains the objective. However, the immediate purpose of most scientific investigations will be but a small step toward the final goal. The investigator will be concerned with race, constitution, fossil man, or some similar problem. In the past the primary purpose of the majority of investigations of this sort was classification rather than the interpretation of any part of the phenomenon being investigated.

This point can be made clear by examples. It has long been known that browridges vary in size and form. Cunningham (1909) gave a classification into which the majority of browridges can be fitted. The classification of browridges by this or similar schemes is a standard part of traditional physical anthropology. But what do the differences mean, and to what are they related? The classification gives no answers to these problems. To say that one fossil has browridges of Type II and another of Type III does not give any information on the significance of the difference, nor does it allow any inference to be made concerning relationship. In general, big browridges are correlated with big faces, but the appearance of size is also dependent on the size and form of the braincase. Microcephals appear to have large ridges, but this is due solely to the small size of the brain. In such an extreme case everyone would interpret the dif-

ference as being due to the change in size of the brain, but how much of the difference between the browridge of Java man and modern man is due to the difference in the face, and how much to a difference in the brain? In the literature a phylogeny of browridges is presented (Weidenreich, 1947). This can be interpreted only if the ridges are sufficiently independent in size and form that tentative conclusions may be drawn from the classification and historical sequence. No one doubts the validity of the descriptive statements, but there is very real doubt that any conclusions can be drawn from this sort of table. This is because the ridge is anatomically complex and because the same general form of ridge may be due to a diversity of different conditions. For example, the central part of the divided type of ridge may be due to a large frontal sinus, acromegaly, a deposit of mechanically unoriented bone, or highly oriented bone. The general prominence of the region may be due to a large face or a small brain; but probably, with faces of equal mass, those associated with long cranial bases and large temporal muscles have larger browridges than those which are associated with shorter bases and larger masseter muscles. The description of the differences between an Australian Aboriginal and a Mongoloid can be done by the traditional methods, but it can be interpreted only if the anatomical causes lying behind the differences are analyzed. The description offers no technical difficulty, but analysis is possible only by the use of a variety of methods which have not been part of the equipment of anthropology. . . .

This example shows the way in which classification was the aim and tool of physical anthropology. As viewed traditionally, if one was interested in browridges, the procedure was to classify the structures and then to draw conclusions on the interrelations of races or fossil men. That is, the classification gave a tool to be used in the analysis of evolution and variation. It was, in this sense, final knowledge. But in a different sense the classification merely outlined the problems to be investigated. No description of the types of brow-ridges gives understanding of the reasons for any of them. The classifications show what kinds exist, under what circumstances they are found, and so pose a series of problems which need investigation. To traditional physical anthropology, classification was an end, something to be used. To the new physical anthropology, classifications merely pose problems, and methods must be devised to solve them.

The traditional reliance on classification as a method of analysis produced two of the characteristics of traditional zoölogy taxonomy and physical anthropology. (1) If classification is the primary aim and tool, then agreement on method is all-important. Therefore, the efforts of physical anthropologists have been to get agreements on how to take measurements and observations. Introductions to physical anthropology are largely instructions on how to take measurements, with little or no indication of what it is that the measurements are supposed to mean. International congresses have ended with pleas for uniformity, so that classification might continue. One may hope that this congress will break with the traditions of the past and urge that undue emphasis on uniformity is undesirable and will stress the need for new techniques for the solution of particular problems. (2) The second result of the emphasis on classification is that, when difficulties arise, they are met by making the classifications more complicated. This may be illustrated in the study of race. By the early part of the nineteenth century, several simple classifications of races existed, and causal explanations had been offered. Races were due to climate, isolation, etc. In the meantime, classifications of races have become vastly more numerous, and many are extremely complex, but explanations of cause and process have remained much as they were. Dobzhansky (1950) points out that the principal task of the anthropologist now should be to try to understand the causes and process of race

formation. Dobzhansky's clear and eloquent plea should be read by all anthropologists, and I have only one qualification, or rather explanation. Traditional anthropologists thought that they were dealing with cause and process much more than Dobzhansky thinks they were. The difference really lies in the attitude toward classification. The traditional physical anthropologist thought that classification, if done in sufficient detail, would give the clues to problems of cause and process. Classifications were accompanied by remarks on how they were explained by hybridization, environment, etc. If one believes that classifications alone give understanding, then one will make the classifications more and more complicated, just as anthropologists have been doing. However, if one thinks that classification can do no more than map the results of process, then one will be content with a very rough mapping until the processes have been analyzed. The new physical anthropology is separated from the old, not by any difference in the desire to know causes, but by a very real difference in belief as to the extent to which classification can reveal causes.

Some classification is a necessary first stage in ordering the data in an area of knowledge, but its meaning depends on understanding the processes which produce the variety of form. After the first stage of preliminary description, scientists must turn to problems of process or face an era of futile elaboration of classifications which cannot be interpreted for lack of adequate techniques and theories.

It is a characteristic of the first stage of a science that theory is not considered important. If classification can solve problems and if it can be reached by marshaling enough facts, then theory need be of little concern. However, as knowledge increases and problems are more precisely formulated, theory becomes of great importance. For a considerable time after the idea of organic evolution had been accepted, comparisons were made without any general theoretical concern, other than that the parts compared should be homologous. Later, anthropology was particularly disturbed by the controversy as to whether deductions concerning relationship should be made on the basis of adaptive or nonadaptive characters. This, in turn, raised the question of whether it was better to compare many features, or whether the comparison of a few critical ones might not give more reliable results. Parallel evolution became recognized as a complicating feature, but, on the whole, physical anthropology continued to operate without any great concern for its theoretical foundations. It should be stressed that this general point of view was characteristic of much of historical zoölogy, ethnology, and archeology. Theoretical issues were not absent, but they were not deemed very important, and the major effort went into collecting specimens and data and describing facts. The realization has been growing for some years that facts alone will not settle the problems and that even the collection of the "facts" was guided by a complex body of unstated assumptions.

Theory

The necessary guiding theories have been recently set forth by numerous zoölogists, and the new zoölogy states simply that evolution is the history of genetic systems. Changes in isolated populations are due to mutation, selection, and accidents of genetic sampling (drift). The major cause of change is selection, which is a simple word covering a vast number of mechanisms (Dobzhansky, 1951). The implications of this theory for physical anthropology are numerous and complicated. The basic issue may be stated as follows: If evolution is governed primarily by adaptation, the demonstration of the nature and kind of adaptation is the principal task of the anthropologist. Evolution is a sequence of more effective behavior systems. To understand be-

havior, live animals must be studied first, and then, when fossils are found, the attempt can be made to interpret the differences by a knowledge of the living forms. It is necessary to remember that fossils were alive when they were important. They were the living, adapted forms of their day, and they must be understood in that setting. In so far as the record is fragmentary, the task is full of uncertainty; but this is a difficulty inherent in the kind of material and does not alter the logical problem.

Traditional physical anthropology was based on the study of skulls. Measurements were devised to describe certain features of the bones, and, when the technique was extended to the living, the measurements were kept as close to those taken on the skeleton as possible. From a comparative and classificatory point of view this was reasonable, and for a while it yielded useful results, but it brought the limitations of death to the study of the living. Whereas the new physical anthropology aims to enrich the study of the past by study of the present, to understand bone in terms of function and life, the old tried to reduce the living to a series of measurements designed to describe bones. Similarity in measurements or combinations of measurements was believed to show genetic affinity. Although it is true that humans of similar genotype are metrically similar, it is not true that similar measurements necessarily mean genetic similarity. Boyd (1950) has discussed this in detail. However, the point is so important that one example will be given here. Straus (1927) has shown that the ilium is approximately the same length in males and females, but the upper part is longer in males, and the lower longer in females. It is only an accident that the two different parts happen to give approximately the same total length. The descriptive statement that the ilium length is the same in male and female is correct and could be proved beyond doubt with elaborate statistics. However, the conclusion that the bones are anatomically or genetically similar would be wrong. The basis for dividing the ilium into upper and lower parts is that these have different functions. The upper is concerned primarily with muscle origin and sacral articulation. The lower ilium is an important segment of the pelvic inlet, which grows rapidly at puberty (Greulich and Thoms, 1944), making the large female inlet suitable for childbirth. The understanding of the ilium which leads to the division into upper and lower segments is based on an appreciation of its function in the living, on the different adaptive nature of the two parts. It is in this sense that the understanding of the living enriches and brings life to the study of the bones. The metrical discrimination is based on anatomical understanding which can be partially expressed metrically and given deeper meaning by statistics. But the original discrimination is based on an appreciation of an adaptive complex. After the choice to measure upper and lower ilium has been made, measurements help by showing the degree of difference, the variability and the correlation of parts, and prove that the anatomical judgment was justified. *But no statistical manipulation will make a discrimination which is not inherent in the original measurements.* Statistics may bring out relations which are there but which are not obvious to the investigator, as shown by Howells (1951).

If a measurement is regarded as genetically determined, nonadaptive, and not correlated with others, it might then be used in the comparison of races without further question. This seems to have been the approximate working hypothesis of traditional physical anthropology. However, if traits are anatomically complex, adaptive, and correlated, they will be useful for description, but comparisons will not automatically yield solutions to problems of affinity. Present genetic and evolutionary theory suggests that characters are, for the most part, complex and adaptive, but this does not give information about any particular situation. The theory that the measurements were nonadaptive allowed one to work blindly and with confi-

dence. The traditional measurements, accurately taken and treated with proper statistics, *gave certain answers.* The belief that traits are complex and adaptive means that the metrical comparisons *pose problems,* which must then be investigated by other methods. Measurements tell us that roundheads have become more common (Weidenreich, 1945), but they do not tell us that roundheads are genetically similar or why roundheads have become more common. From an anatomical point of view, is brachycephalization due to changes in the brain, dura, sutures, or base of the skull? From an evolutionary point of view, is the change due to adaptation or genetic drift? It should be stressed that, although all seem agreed that selection is the most important factor in evolution, there is no agreement on the importance of genetic drift (Carter, 1951; Dobzhansky, 1951) or the extent to which traits of little or no adaptive importance exist or spread.

In the past, investigators have assumed that characters were adaptive or nonadaptive, but this is the very question which needs investigation (as discussed by Dobzhansky, 1950). Further, it should be stressed that it is not a question of one or the other, but of selective pressures varying from very little to very great. Some characteristic features of a race may be due to drift, others to strong selection, others to mild selection, still others to mixture due entirely to cultural factors. Whether a particular trait or gene frequency is highly adaptive or of little importance can be settled only by research, and the answer will surely differ at different times and places.

Closely related to the idea of nonadaptation is the concept of orthogenesis. If evolution is *not* caused by selection, then the long-term changes must be due to some other cause, and change may be accounted for by some inner irreversible force. This general concept has been very common in anthropology. For example, it has been maintained that, since man's arms are shorter than apes', man could not be descended from an ape, as this would reverse the course of evolution. According to the theory that evolution is adaptive, there is no reason why man's ancestors may not have had much longer arms. When selection changed, arms may have become shorter. (Actually, the difference is small; Schultz, 1950*a*.) According to the irreversible orthogenetic-force theory, man could not be descended from an ape, and a few measurements settle the matter. According to the theory of natural selection, man could be descended from an ape, but the theory does not prove that he was. All it does is indicate the kind of adaptive problem which must be understood before the data of comparative anatomy and the fossil record can be interpreted. Certainly, one of the reasons why the theory of orthogenesis, irreversibility, and the importance of nonadaptive characters was popular is that it allowed conclusions to be drawn by a few rules based on little evidence. The theory of selection offers no simple answers but merely points the direction in which answers must be sought. The successive adaptive radiations of the primates must be understood in terms of the evolution of more efficient behavior. The elucidation of the adaptive mechanisms will require all the help which paleontology, anatomy, archeology, and experiment can give. Far more work will be done to reach less definitive conclusions, but an understanding of the pattern and process of primate evolution will be gained. The belief that selection is the major cause of evolution alters the way evolution should be studied. In so far as anthropological conclusions have been based on the concepts of orthogenesis, irreversibility, and the use of nonadaptive traits, the conclusions need re-examination. Parallelism needs to be interpreted as the result of similar selection on related animals rather than be used as a way of discounting resemblances.

Aside from the concept of selection, there are two other aspects of evolutionary theory which are of the utmost importance for anthropology. These are, first, that descriptions should be based on

populations and, second, that genes, or traits, may vary independently. Taken together, these two facts mean that the anthropological concept of type is untenable, and refusal to accept this fact is the main reason why some anthropologists have been reluctant to adopt genetic concepts. Both these points have been elaborated by numerous authors. . . . The implications for anthropology of the concept of population and independence of genes are best understood by the history of the concept of race (Count, 1950). In the earlier racial classifications a race was a group of people living in one part of the world who were obviously different from other people in physical characters. Thus the peoples of Europe, Africa south of the Sahara, eastern Asia, Australia, and the Americas were early recognized as races. How the peoples of India should be treated was always a problem, for a variety of reasons which lie beyond the scope of this essay. In the main, this classification is the same as that which Boyd (1950) gives on the basis of gene frequencies. Even the difficulty with regard to India is present in Boyd's classification. As knowledge increased, the larger areas were subdivided, and groups such as the Bushmen or Polynesians were recognized. The division of the world into areas occupied by more or less physically distinct groups was completed before 1900. The genetic study of race seems to be substantiating a large part of this general classification of mankind, although parts will surely be changed.

After 1900, to an increasing extent, a fundamentally different kind of "race" came to be used. In this race the group described was not a breeding population but a segment of such a population sorted out by various criteria. This second kind is called "type." Originally the Australoid race meant the populations of aboriginal Australia. By extension, the Australoid type was any skull, whether found in South Africa or America, which had certain morphological features common in the population of Australia. Similarly, the Mongoloid, or Negroid, race applies to groups of populations which have already been found to have genetic individuality. But there is no suggestion that the Mongoloid or Negroid types can be substantiated genetically.

The difficulty with the typological approach has been recognized by many (especially Huxley and Haddon, 1936; Benedict, 1940; Dahlberg, 1942), who pointed out that the more unrelated characters are used for sorting, the more races (types) there will be. Weidenreich (1946) objected to adding the blood groups to the traditional anthropological characters, on the ground that this would make the theoretical total of races 92,780! With the typological approach, the more that is known, the more types there will be; but, no matter how much is known, the number of populations remains unchanged. However much is ultimately known about the genetics and anatomy of the Australian aborigines, there are still the same tribes living on the same continent. Populations are reproductive groups which are defined by the ethnologist or archeologist, or deduced from the way skeletons are found. The intensity of anatomical and genetical investigation does not increase the number of populations.

A "race" is a group of genetically similar populations, and races intergrade because there are always intermediate populations. A "type" is a group of individuals who are identical in those characters (genetic or phenotypic) by which the type was sorted (but *not* in other features!). The race concept and the type concept are fundamentally different, and modern zoölogical theory is compatible only with the race concept.

If anthropologists should adopt current zoölogical practice, several of the classifications of human races would be discarded, and the strategy of some schools of thought would be entirely abandoned. However, the change may be less than it appears at first sight. The reason for this is that most physical anthropologists simply were not interested in theory. In the majority of classifications, exemplified by that of Hooton (1946), some

of the races refer to populations and others to types. Even the type descriptions usually contain data on the whole series, prior to the type analysis. At present *there is no anthropological theory of race*, but two old, incompatible concepts carried along side by side. One of the primary tasks in developing a new physical anthropology is systematically to apply the modern zoölogical concept of race, to discard the types, and to put the traditional information into the form in which it will be most useful for the understanding of race formation.

In summarizing the contrast between the old and the new physical anthropology with regard to theory, the main point to emphasize is that the application of a consistent, experimentally verified, evolutionary theory is the first task of the physical anthropologist. Since investigators were not interested in theory and since there is great diversity in actual practice, no useful purpose would be served by trying to discuss the implications of the new evolutionary theory in more detail. In the past, all the useful ideas were present in traditional physical anthropology, but so were the useless ones.

Boyd (1950) has stressed the break with the past, and Stewart (1951) the continuity with the past. Actually, physical anthropology is in a period of rapid transition in which both continuity and great change are important. At such a time disagreements are to be tolerated and major changes of personal opinion expected. For example, in 1940 Boyd criticized anthropologists for using adaptive characters when he maintained that they should use only nonadaptive ones. In 1950 he was equally vehement in his criticism of anthropologists for not seeking to use adaptive traits. At neither time were anthropologists as a profession doing either consistently, and at both times the real issue was to try to demonstrate which traits were adaptive, an issue which can be settled only by research.

Agreement is needed on the following points:

(1) physical anthropology needs a consistent, proved, theoretical framework; (2) the necessary evolutionary and genetic theories are available and should be applied to the problems of human evolution; (3) untenable concepts should be abandoned; (4) a time of transition should be *welcomed* in which great differences in personal opinion are to be expected. These differences should be settled by research and not allowed to become personal or national issues.

Technique

A successful scientific strategy depends on theories and techniques adequate to solve problems. As theories change, techniques must alter also, as they exist only to solve problems and not as ends in themselves. Traditional physical anthropology was committed to the view that description alone would solve its problems, and, in practice, description of a very limited kind. The same measurements were applied to the solution of problems of the classification of the primates, relations of fossil men, description of race, human growth, and constitution. The technical training of a physical anthropologist was primarily indoctrination in the measurements of a particular school. In spite of the vast progress in biology, the practices of the physical anthropologist remained essentially the same for over one hundred years, although modified in detail and refined. As pointed out earlier, these techniques were an efficient part of the strategy of a descriptive science. They helped to outline the classification of the primates, fossil men, and races. The problems of interpreting human evolution and variation were clarified, but the traditional techniques failed to solve the problems of process. There are more different theories of man's origin and differentiation now than there were fifty years ago, and in this sense the strategy of physical anthropology failed. This was due partly to the theoretical dilemmas outlined before and partly to inadequacy of the techniques.

The reasons why the traditional anthropometric measurements are inadequate to do more than they already have done, that is, outline a rough classification and indicate problems, can be made clear by an example. A variety of measurements and observations are traditionally taken on the nose (length, breadth, shape of profile, form of lower margin). Then these data are compared, on the basic assumption that *nose* is an independent entity which has been described and whose attributes may be compared. But the concept of adaptation suggests that the middle part of the face should be viewed in a very different way. Benninghoff (1925) and recently Seipel (1948) have shown by the use of the split-line technique that the face is highly organized in response to the stresses of mastication. The margins of the piriform aperture are thick in stressed, and thin in unstressed, forms. Further, the breadth of the aperture corresponds approximately to the intercanine distance, or breadth, of the incisor teeth. In man the incisors develop in the subnasal area, and, as Baker (1941) has shown, developing teeth exert a positive force increasing the size of the surrounding bone. Gans and Sarnat (1951) have shown that the growth in the region of the maxillary-premaxillary suture is accelerated at the time of eruption of the permanent canine tooth. This supplements the observations of Seipel (1948) on the way the erupting canine causes the reorganization of a large area of the face in the chimpanzee. Far from being an independent structure which can be described by itself, the nose is an integrated part of the face, and variations in its form can be interpreted only as a part of the functioning face. The form of the nose is the result of a variety of factors. Just how many and how they are interrelated can be discovered only by research, but it seems clear that the most important ones, as far as gross form is concerned, are the teeth and forces of mastication. But these are not included in the traditional descriptions of the nose, nor will looking at skulls or measuring them give this kind of information.

Since the problem of interpreting the form of the nose is part of the problem of understanding the functioning pattern of the face, the methods needed to interpret this form must describe the pattern. The traditional measurements will not do this, and they must be supplemented by techniques which are appropriate to this particular problem. Such methods are the split-line technique of Benninghoff, alizarin vital stain, experimental removal of teeth, marking sutures, etc. Some of these techniques can be applied directly to man. Others require experimental animals, but at least this much is necessary to understand what is done when a simple measurement is taken across the nasal aperture. There is no way of telling in advance what methods, in addition to measurement, will be needed, as these depend on the particular problem to be solved. What is needed in research and in education is an elastic approach, showing the problems which have arisen from the traditional classifications and techniques and encouraging every attempt to develop new and more efficient methods.

Interpretation

The traditional method of interpretation in physical anthropology primarily was speculation. Races, for example, have been attributed to endless mixtures, hormones, minerals, climate, adaptation, isolation, and chance, but little effort has been devoted to proving any of the theories. Similarly, measurements have been claimed to be adaptive or nonadaptive, but detailed proof substantiating either point of view is lacking. Actually, all dimensions of the human body serve functions, and the practical issue is to show what, in an anatomical sense, is being measured and what genetic or environmental factors may modify it. The face as

a whole may be highly adaptive, and its main course in human evolution determined by selection, but small differences between races may be due to genetic drift. What is needed is *proof* of adaptation or drift in particular cases.

The point may be made clearer by returning to the example of the nose. It has often been suggested that big noses appear when faces become small. But this theory has many exceptions and gives no idea of the factors actually involved. Since the split-line technique shows that the nasal bones are actually stressed by the forces of mastication, would it be reasonable to suppose that these bones would be bigger if the forces were reduced? If one nasal bone of a rat is removed on the first day of life, the other nasal bone grows to approximately one and a half times normal size. Further comparable removal of interparietal and parietal bones shows that these also grow large if free to do so. It seems to be a general rule that cranial roofing bones will grow bigger if forces normally stopping growth are removed. Schaeffer (1920) pictures skulls in which the nasal bones are entirely absent and the roof of the nose is formed by the maxillae. Piecing these lines of evidence together, it appears that the answer is again a question of pattern. Other th'ngs being equal, less pressure may result in more growth of nasal bone, but the actual proportions will depend on the interrelations of the size of the nasals, frontal processes of the maxillae, and the pressures.

Instead of relating nose form to selection or climate, it is necessary to insert an intermediate step, the analysis of the nose. Rather than saying that the pigmy's broad nose is an adaptation to the tropics, it may be that the nose is the result of a short face with large incisor teeth. The short face may be correlated with small total size (stature?), and the big teeth need explanation. Not enough is known about the form of the face to be sure that the racial differences of the nose should be correlated with climate at all.

Perhaps the relation of speculation, proof, and the importance of new methods can be best illustrated by theories concerning race mixture. It has become customary in physical anthropology to account for most of the races of the world by mixture. Of the four interrelated causes of difference recognized by zoölogists (mutation, selection, drift, and migration), only one has been regarded as the principal source of new varieties of man. The absence of evidence for three primary races has been pointed to by Boyd (1950) and numerous others, and it is probably only rarely that mixture has been a major cause of race formation. The differentiation of races, for whatever reasons, must be accounted for on other grounds, as mixture can only make gene frequencies more alike.

If the Indians are a result of Mongoloid and Australian mixture, then they should have high blood group N, and considerable B. Actually they have the least N in the world, and B only among the Eskimo. In other words, the postulated mixture does not explain the facts known about the Indians. The more complicated hypotheses work no better. If Negroids are an important element in the mixture, then Rh° should appear in the Indian, and it does not. If European elements are there, A2 and Rh negative should be present. It is clear that mixture alone will not explain the American Indian blood groups. Drift and/or selection must have operated also to change the gene frequencies, because what is found in the American Indian is something new, not found in the Old World or derivable from Old World frequencies by any mixtures. In spite of all the work that was done by traditional methods, it was possible for competent investigators to hold a number of divergent views as to the origin of the American Indian. The advent of a technique which made it possible to deal with the theories in objective, quantitative terms clearly shows that much of the speculation was unfounded and the role of mix-

ture, as opposed to differentiation, exaggerated. The blood groups provide precise techniques for measuring mixture, provided that the mixture is relatively recent, as Carbon 14 suggests in the case of the American Indian (Johnson, 1951).

In summary, the traditional physical anthropologist thought that his task was finished when he had classified and speculated. This era is past, and there are enough classifications and speculations. Now methods must be developed that will prove which speculations were on the right track. The best of the past should be combined with new techniques to bring proof in the place of speculation.

Conclusion

The attempt has been made to consider under the headings of purpose, theory, technique, and interpretation the changes now taking place in physical anthropology. The strategy of the traditional descriptive investigations has been contrasted with the developing analytic strategy, with its emphasis on theory, process, and experiment. The whole change is precisely parallel to that which has taken place in systematics.

The new strategy does not solve problems, but it suggests a different way of approaching them. The change from the old to the new affects the various parts of physical anthropology very differently. In studies of growth and applied anthropology, where the knowledge of dimensions is directly useful, changing theories make little difference. In evolutionary investigations the theoretical changes are of the greatest importance, and much of the anthropological work on race and constitution is eliminated by the rejection of the concept of type. However, one of the main implications of the new point of view is that there is a far more detailed interrelationship between the different parts of anthropology than under the old strategy. A dynamic analysis of the form of the jaw will illuminate problems of evolution, fossil man, race, growth, constitution, and medical application. The unraveling of the process of human evolution and variation will enrich the understanding of other mammalian groups, whereas the detailed description of a fossil has a much more limited utility. By its very nature, the investigation of process and behavior has a generality which is lacking in purely descriptive studies. The problems of human evolution are but special cases of the problems of mammalian evolution, and their solution will enrich paleontology, genetics, and parts of clinical medicine.

But some of the problems of human evolution are unique to man. In so far as man has adapted by his way of life, the study of human evolution is inseparably bound to the study of archeology and ethnology. It is because of the importance of the cultural factor that a separate study of human evolution is necessary. Human migrations, adaptations, mating systems, population density, diseases, and ecology—all these critical biological factors become increasingly influenced by the way of life. If we would understand the process of human evolution, we need a modern dynamic biology and a deep appreciation of the history and functioning of culture. It is this necessity which gives all anthropology unity as a science.

L I T E R A T U R E   C I T E D

BAKER, L. W. 1941. "The Influence of the Formative Dental Organs on the Growth of the Bones of the Face," *American Journal of Orthodontics,* XXVII, 489–506.

BENEDICT, R. 1940. *Race: Science and Politics.* ("Modern Age Books.") New York: Viking Press.

BENNINGHOFF, A. 1925. "Spaltlinien am Knochen, eine Methode zur Ermittlung der Architektur platter Knochen," *Anatomischer Anzeiger,* LX, 189–205.

BOYD, W. C. 1950. *Genetics and the Races of Man.* Boston: Little, Brown & Co.

CARTER, G. S. 1951. *Animal Evolution.* London: Sidgwick & Jackson.

COUNT, E. W. 1950. *This Is Race.* New York: Henry Schuman.

CUNNINGHAM, D. J. 1909. "The Evolution of the Eyebrow Region of the Forehead, with Special Reference to the Excessive Supraorbital Development of the Neanderthal Race," *Transactions of the Royal Society, Edinburgh,* XLVI, 283–311.

DAHLBERG, G. 1942. *Race, Reason, and Rubbish.* New York: Columbia University Press.

DENIKER, J. 1900. *The Races of Man.* New York: Charles Scribner's Sons.

DOBZHANSKY, T. 1950. "Human Diversity and Adaptation," *Cold Spring Harbor Symposia on Quantitative Biology,* Vol. XV: *Origin and Evolution of Man,* pp. 385–400. Cold Spring Harbor, Long Island, N.Y.: Biological Laboratory.

———. 1951. *Genetics and the Origin of Species.* 3d ed. New York: Columbia University Press.

FLOWER, W. H., and LYDEKKER, R. 1891. *Mammals Living and Extinct.* London: Adam & Charles Black.

GANS, B. J., and SARNAT, B. G. 1951. "Sutural Facial Growth of the *Macaca rhesus* Monkey," *American Journal of Orthodontics,* XXXVII, 827–41.

GREULICH, W. W., and THOMAS, H. 1944. "The Growth and Development of the Pelvis of Individual Girls before, during, and after Puberty," *Yale Journal of Biology and Medicine,* XVII, 91–97.

HOOTON, E. A. 1946. *Up from the Ape.* Rev. ed. New York: Macmillan Co.

HOWELLS, W. W. 1951. "Factors of Human Physique," *American Journal of Physical Anthropology,* n.s., IX, 159–91.

HUXLEY, J. S., and HADDON, A. C. 1936. *We Europeans.* New York: Harper & Bros.

JOHNSON, F. 1951. *Radiocarbon Dating.* ("Memoirs of the Society for American Archaeology," No. 8.)

SCHAEFFER, J. P. 1920. *The Nose, Paranasal Sinuses, Nasolacrimal Passageways, and Olfactory Organ in Man.* Philadelphia: Blakiston's Son & Co.

SCHULTZ, A. H. 1936. "Characters Common to Higher Primates and Characters Specific for Man," *Quarterly Review of Biology,* XI, 259–83, 425–55.

———. 1950a. "The Physical Distinctions of Man," *Proceedings of the American Philosophical Society,* XCIV, 428–49.

———. 1950b. "The Specializations of Man and His Place among the Catarrhine Primates," *Cold Spring Harbor Symposia on Quantitative Biology,* Vol. XV: *Origin and Evolution of Man,* pp. 37–52. Cold

Spring Harbor, Long Island, N.Y.: Biological Laboratory.

SEIPEL, C. M. 1948. "Trajectories of the Jaws," *Acta odontologica Scandinavica,* VIII, 81–191.

SIMPSON, G. G. 1945. *The Principles of Classification and a Classification of Mammals.* (American Museum of Natural History Bull. 85.) New York.

STEWART, T. D. 1951. "Three in One: Physical Anthropology, Genetics, Statistics," *Journal of Heredity,* XLII, 255–56, 260.

STRAUS, W. L. 1927. "The Human Ilium: Sex and Stock," *American Journal of Physical Anthropology,* XI, 1–28.

———. 1949. "The Riddle of Man's Ancestry," *Quarterly Review of Biology,* XXIV, 200–223.

WEIDENREICH, F. 1945. "The Brachycephalization of Recent Mankind," *Southwestern Journal of Anthropology,* I, 1–54.

———. 1946. *Apes, Giants, and Man.* Chicago: University of Chicago Press.

———. 1947. "The Trend of Human Evolution," *Evolution,* I, 221–36.

TWO • HISTORY OF OUR KNOWLEDGE OF THE APES

2 • EARLY CONCEPTS OF THE ANTHROPOMORPHA

C. D. O'Malley & H. W. Magoun

The history of our discovery of and growing acquaintance with the great apes is set out most informatively by O'Malley and Magoun in the following contribution. Dr. O'Malley was an historian of science, among whose many outstanding contributions is the definitive biography of Vesalius.[1] Dr. Magoun is a neuroanatomist who has made fundamental contributions to our understanding of the nervous system.

As the authors show, it is quite remarkable how late the western world was in becoming acquainted with the three great apes, the chimpanzee, the orang-utan, and the gorilla, for the first was not described until 1640, the second not until 1658, and the third only from a skull in 1847. In 1851 Isidore Geoffrey-Saint-Hilaire announced to his colleagues, and a year later published, his discovery of two preserved specimens of the young gorilla. His drawings of the external features of these specimens were excellent.[2] But the description of a living gorilla was not published until 1861, by Paul Du Chaillu in his *Explorations & Adventures in Equatorial Africa* (London: John Murray).

It was in that same book that Paul Du Chaillu bequeathed to the nineteenth and twentieth centuries the lurid view of "the ferocious gorilla," in his over-dramatization of encounters with that creature and his highly colored versions of its behavior. Such a view of the gorilla fitted that era's views of nature as "red in tooth and claw," and Du Chaillu made much of that theme in his lectures and several of his other books. It was an utterly false view of the nature of the gorilla, and, indeed, of all the great apes, to which the character of ferocity was extended as it was to virtually all "wild beasts." It was a very damaging view—damaging to the apes, and impoverishing and diminishing to men. As long ago as 1699 Edward Tyson had commented on the gentleness of his juvenile chimpanzee; but it was not until George Schaller's field report (1963) on the mountain gorilla that the "amiability" of that creature's nature was first made unequivocally clear.[3] Jane Lawick-Goodall has since shown how happily friendships may be established with "wild" chimpanzees in their native habitat.[4] It is no accident that this was accomplished by a young woman, either, for habitually men have not approached "wild" animals with affection. We speak of anthropoid apes as our "near relations"; perhaps it should be the anthropologist who follows this up by doing whatever he can to see that these near relations of ours are protected from those members of our species who are at present engaged in rapidly effecting their extermination.[5]

The best account of the history of our knowledge of the great apes, and also the best general account of them, is Robert M. Yerkes and Ada W. Yerkes, *The Great Apes: A Study of Anthropoid Life* (New Haven: Yale University Press, 1929). See also Ramona and Desmond Morris, *Men and Apes* (New York:

---

[1] C. D. O'Malley, *Andreas Vesalius of Brussels 1514–1564* (Berkeley: University of California Press, 1964).

[2] Isidore Geoffrey-Saint-Hilaire, "Note sur le Gorille," *Ann. Sci. nat.*, Paris, XVI (1851), 154–158; "Sur le Gorille," *Compte-Rendu des Académie des Sciences*, Paris, XXXIV (1852), 81–84.

[3] George B. Schaller, *The Mountain Gorilla* (Chicago: University of Chicago Press, 1963); George B. Schaller, *The Year of the Gorilla* (Chicago: University of Chicago Press, 1964).

[4] Jane Lawick-Goodall, *In the Shadow of Man* (Boston: Houghton Mifflin Co., 1971).

[5] For the perilous state of the orang-utan see Barbara Harrisson, *Orang-Utan* (New York: Doubleday & Co., 1963).

McGraw-Hill, 1966), and Vernon Reynolds, *The Apes* (New York: E. P. Dutton & Co., 1967).

The recent centennial celebration (1959) of the publication of Darwin's *Origin of Species by Natural Selection or the Preservation of Favoured Races in the Struggle for Life* evoked widespread interest in exploration of the pre-Darwinian development of concepts of evolution. Most of these studies have been concerned with problems of general biological significance, probably because of the broad orientation of the *Origin of Species*. None of them has devoted specific emphasis to the background of thinking related to the evolution of that species to which the greatest interest of all of us is attached, namely, to the origin of man.

Darwin himself made brief but explicit reference to this in the concluding paragraph of the *Origin of Species* when he wrote: "By this means light will be thrown on the origin of man and his history," a prophecy later elaborated in his *Descent of Man* (1871). In the meantime Huxley, Darwin's protagonist, had presented an excellent survey, *Man's Place in Nature* (1863),[1] discussing the relation of the great apes to the evolution of man, while earlier outstanding accounts, to which reference will be made later, were those of Tyson (1699) and Buffon (1739). In more recent times the work of Elliot (1913)[2] and Yerkes (1929)[3] have been of special merit.

Since the source material is scattered and some of the syntheses are themselves difficult to obtain, it has seemed worthwhile to prepare a compilation of translations of original descriptions, together with a reproduction of the fascinating iconography which has accumulated around this topic.[4] As arranged below, the material commences with brief reference to accounts from early travelers, passes to the initial studies upon apes brought to Europe, and then to the more elaborate accounts of the early systematists and natural historians. Finally, because most of this early material was concerned with the chimpanzee, reference is made for the sake of completeness to the initial descriptions of the Orang-outang and Gorilla.

Accounts of Early Travelers

The first account is derived from antiquity, that of Hanno, a Carthaginian navigator of about 500 B.C., who appears to have ventured southward along the Africa coast beyond Sierra Leone and possibly as far as Cape Palmas. According to Hanno's report:[5]

We arrived at a bay called the Southern Horn; at the bottom of which lay an island . . . having a lake, and in this lake another island, full of savage people, the greater part of whom were women, whose bodies were hairy, and whom our interpreters called Gorillas (Γόριλλαι). Though we pursued the men, we could not seize any of them, but all fled from us, escaping over precipices, and defending themselves with stones. Three women were however taken; but they attacked their conductors with their teeth and hands, and could not be prevailed on to accompany us. Having killed them, we flayed them, and brought their skins with us to Carthage.

The next traveler's account of any significance, some two millennia later, was written by Duarte

---

SOURCE: *"Physis"—Rivista di Storia della Scienza* vol. 4 (Florence, Italy: Casa Editrice Leo S. Olschki, 1962): 39–63. Reprinted by permission of the publisher.
[1] 14, pp. 9–70.
[2] 10.
[3] 25.
[4] The idea for this paper developed in the course of an evening spent in the library of Dr. Robert Moes.
[5] 12, pp. 13–15.

Lopez, a Portuguese who visited the Congo region in 1578 and reported: [6]

Apes, Monkeyes, and such other kinde of beastes, small and great of all sortes there are many in the Region. . . . Some of them are very pleasant and gamesome, and make good pastime, and are used by the Lordes there for their recreation and to show them sport. For although they be unreasonable Creatures, yet will they notably counterfait the countenances, the fashions, and the actions of men.

Succeeding the account of Lopez is that of Andrew Battell who had been taken prisoner by the Portuguese in South America and in 1591 transported to Angola where he was forced to remain for a number of years. Finally having escaped and returned to England he gained the acquaintance of Samuel Purchas, who published Battell's account in 1625.[7] Battell identified two apes, the greater of which was called Pongo and the lesser Engesco, remarking:

The *Pongo* is in all proportions like a man, but that he is more like a giant in stature than a man; for he is very tall, and hath a man's face, hollow-eyed, with long hair upon his brows. His face and ears are without hair, and his hands also. His body is full of hair, but not very thick, and it is of a dunnish colour. He differeth not from a man but in his legs, for they have no calf. He goeth always upon his legs, and carryeth his hands clasped upon the nape of his neck when he goeth upon the ground. They sleep in the trees, and build shelters from the rain. They feed upon fruit they find in the woods and upon nuts, for they eat no kind of flesh. They cannot speak, and have no more understanding than a beast.

The people of the country, when they travel in the woods, make fires when they sleep in the night. And in the morning, when they are gone, the *Pongoes* will come and sit about the fire till it goeth out, for they have no understanding to lay the wood together. They go many together, and kill many negroes that travel in the woods. Many times they fall upon the elephants, which come to feed where they be, and so beat them with their clubbed fists and pieces of wood that they will run roaring away from them.

Those *Pongoes* are never taken alive, because they are so strong that ten men cannot hold one of them, but yet they take many of their young ones with poisoned arrows. The young *Pongo* hangeth on his mother's belly, with his hands clasped fast about her, so that when the country people kill any of the females, they take the young one which hangeth fast upon his mother. When they die among themselves, they cover the dead with great heaps of boughs and wood, which is commonly found in the forests.

The first depiction of an ape, albeit of somewhat fabulous appearance, is that published by Conrad Gesner in his *Historia Animalium* in 1554. In his accompanying text Gesner wrote: [8]

There is a Cercopithecus of unusual form, in the size and shape of a man; indeed, in regard to its limbs, virile member and face you may say it is a wild man because it is wholly covered with hair. No animal except man stands for so long; it loves children and women just like the men of its region, and when it has fled its chains attempts openly to lie with them, as we have seen. Furthermore, although it is a wild animal, yet so industrious that you may say it has more talent than some men, not, indeed, ours but those barbarous ones who live in very inclement regions as the Ethiopians, Numidians and Lapps. . . . We shall speak below of the Satyrs, by which name recent writers have called those hairy animals to which it is similar in shape and wantonness. Here I have presented an illustration of that kind of ape (Fig. 1, right), borrowed from a German book [9] describing the Holy Land.

---

[6] 16, p. 89.
[7] 4, p. 54.
[8] 11, p. 970.

[9] Bernhard von Breydenbach. *Peregrinationes in Terram Sanctam*, Mainz. 1486.

 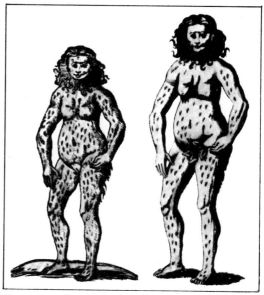

Figure 1: A rare form of Cercopithecus, from Gesner 1586), right, and Aldrovandi (1645), left, possessing a long tail in spite of its erect posture and other semblance to man. This figure was copied from a book of *Travels to the Holy Land* which may account for the animal's cane or staff.

In the early seventeenth century, Ulisse Aldovandi cited and gave Gesner's account together with an illustration redrawn and differing in unimportant details (Fig. 1, left).[10]

In a posthumously published work (1658) Jakob de Bondt, or Bontius, gave an account of a female orang-outang, or *Homo Sylvestris,* from Borneo where he had resided for a number of years. According to Bontius: [11]

Although not even children believe in satyrs with goat's hoofs, sphinxes and butting fauns, yet this amazing monster with its human visage, human manner of groaning and shedding tears, does exist. . . . I saw several of each sex walking erect and in particular one female Satyr of which I give an illustration here (Fig. 2, left),

Figure 2: The female Orang-outang from Bontius (1658), left, whose reputed modesty caused Tyson (1699) to add "to his figure what becomes that character" (right).

hiding her face with great shyness from strange men, who wept copiously, groaned and expressed other human emotions so that you might say that no other human characteristic was lacking to her except speech. The Javanese say that they can speak, but do not choose to do so lest they be compelled to work, but that is ridiculous. They are called Orang-outang which means man of the forest, and it is said that they are born of the lust of women of the Indies who mate with apes and monkeys to satisfy their detestable desires.

Tyson was to write later of Bontius' figure: "I confess I do mistrust the whole *Representation.* But because he hath express'd that this Creature hath so much Modesty, I have added to his *Figure* what becomes that Character." [12] (Fig. 2, right). While the figure is admittedly fanciful, considerable significance can be attached to Bontius' ac-

[10] 1, pp. 245, 249.
[11] 5, p. 284.

[12] 24, p. 19.

count, for, as we know today, the Orang-outang is the only ape resident in Borneo. Bontius should, therefore, be credited both with its initial description and its name, from the Javanese term for "man of the woods." This name, Orang-outang, was applied indiscriminately to apes, until Camper (1799), whose specimens were also obtained from the Dutch East Indies, differentiated it from other species.

Initial Studies in Europe

A generation after Battell, the first of the man-like apes was brought to Europe and studied there, and in 1640, Rembrandt's anatomist, Nicolaus Tulp, a Dutch physician, provided the following account: [13]

. . . the Indies' Satyr which, as I recall, was brought from Angola and presented to Frederick Henry, Prince of Orange. Although this Satyr was a quadruped, yet because of its resemblance to the human species it is called Orang-outang, or man of the forest. . . . It had the height of a child of three and the thickness of one of six.

Its body was neither fat nor slender but squarish, very vigorous and agile. Its joints were so compact and its muscles so enormous that it accomplished whatever it ventured. Its anterior body was wholly without hair but the posterior was hirsute and covered with black hair. Its face counterfeited that of man, but with the indented nostrils of the ape and wrinkled like that of a toothless old woman.

The ears were not different in shape from the human as was likewise true of the chest, equipped on each side with a pretumid breast— for it was a female. The belly had a very deep

umbilicus, and the upper and lower limbs had an exact likeness to those of man, as much as one egg is like another. Nor did it lack the necessary joint at the elbow, the arrangement of the fingers of the hand, the human shape of the thumb, the calf of the leg or the support of the heel of the foot. This suitable and well-formed arrangement of the limbs was the reason that it often walked erect and without difficulty and could support and carry a burden of great weight.

When about to drink, it grasped the handle of the tankard with one hand, the other supporting the bottom of the vessel. Thereafter it wiped the remaining drops from its lips no less skillfully than you might see done by some polished courtier. It displayed that same dexterity whenever it lay down, inclining its head on the couch, properly covering and enveloping itself with the blankets just as if a very graceful man were lying down.

Furthermore, the King of the Sambaceni once told Samuel Blomart, a relative of mine, that on the island of Borneo these Satyrs, especially the males, had such boldness of spirit and such strong muscular structure that they not infrequently attacked armed men, not to mention girls and women of the timid sex. Sometimes they are overcome by such strong desire for women that not infrequently they ravish those they have seized. They are extremely inclined to venery—which characteristic they have in common with the lustful Satyrs of the ancients. Indeed, they are so shamelessly lustful that the women of the Indies avoid the lairs and paths in which these shameless animals lurk, as worse than those of dog or serpent.

Tulp's young female Chimpanzee is depicted in modest pose with downcast eyes and hands shielding the genital region (Fig. 3, left). Opposite to this is Thomas Bartholin's figure of a Cercopithecus which displays the contrasting qualities of the

---

[13] 23, p. 270 ff. A second representation of the animal was made for William Grotius, brother of the celebrated Hugo, which was dispatched to friends in Paris. It was on the basis of this drawing, which was never published, and information supplied from The Hague, that the French philosopher and natu-

ralist Claude Peiresc declared that the animal's ability to understand Flemish, to laugh and to cry, placed it in a middle category between monkey and human.—E. T. Hamy, *Documents inédits sur l'Homo Sylvestris rapporté d'Angola en 1630.* "Bull. Mus. Hist. nat.," Paris, 1897, 3:277–82.

male (Fig. 3, right). Bartholin wrote of the animal: [14]

A Cercopithecus endocus which had died of a disease in the royal citadel, was dissected in the home of Henricus Jakobus Scriberius, Royal Surgeon. It has the head of a swine, hairless buttocks and a reddish color. Its shape was unlike that of any described by those who write on natural history. One may suspect that because this Cercopithecus was depicted by no one that it is a monster or an animal hitherto not seen or depicted by others. Whatever the case may be, Scriberius invited me to the anatomy of this animal together with Caspar Bartholin, my son, and others.

The most remarkable of all accounts of the anthropomorpha appeared in the year 1699 and was dedicated by its author to John Sommers, Lord High Chancellor of England and President of the Royal Society, in the fulsome manner of the time: "The Animal of which I have given the Anatomy, coming nearest to Mankind; seems the Nexus of

Figure 3: A female chimpanzee described by Tulp (1640, left), shown in modest pose. At the right is Bartholin's (1673–80) figure of a Cercopithecus, depicting the aggressive virility of the male.

---

[14] 3, 1, pp. 67–8, 313, Fig. 1.
[15] 24, pp. 7–8.
[16] 24, p. 30.
[17] 24, p. 25.

the Animal and the Rational, as your Lordship, and those of your High Rank and Order for Knowledge and Wisdom, approaching nearest to that kind of Beings which is next above us; Connect the Visible, and Invisible World." This was Edward Tyson's monograph, *Orang-outang, sive Homo Sylvestris: or The Anatomy of a Pygmie Compared with that of a Monkey, an Ape, and a Man.* The specimen was an immature, male chimpanzee, brought to England in a debilitated condition as the result of an infected jaw suffered from a fall on shipboard. Tyson wrote as follows:

Our *Pygmie* was . . . the most gentle and loving Creature that could be. Those that he knew aboard he would come and embrace with the greatest tenderness, opening their Bosoms, and clasping his Hands about them; and . . . tho' there were *Monkeys* aboard he would never associate with them, and as if nothing a-kin to them, would always avoid their Company.
After our *Pygmie* was taken, and a little used to wearing Cloaths, it was fond enough of them; and what it could not put on himself, it would bring in his Hands to some of the Company to help him to put on. It would lie in a Bed, place his Head on the Pillow, and pull the Cloaths over him, as Man would do; but was so careless and so very a Brute as to do all Nature's Occasions there.[15]
What chiefly our *Pygmie* affected, when *Wild*, I was not informed of; after it was taken, and made tame, it would readily eat any thing that was brought to the Table; and very orderly bring its Plate thither, to receive what they would give him. Once it was made Drunk with *Punch.* . . . But it was observed, that after that time, it would never drink above one Cup, and refused the offer of more than what he found agreed with him.[16]

Tyson heard his Pygmie "*Cry* like a *Child*; and he hath been often seen to kick with his feet, as Children do, when either he was pleased or angered." [17] Dissection showed his larynx to be exactly like that of man, and Tyson declared that: "If there was any farther advantage for the form-

Figure 4: The chimpanzee of Tyson (1699), in front and rear view. The animal was dying when Tyson first saw him, and the staff reflects his feebleness and need for support.

ing of *Speech,* I can't but think our *Pygmie* had it. But upon the best Enquiry, I was never informed, that it attempted any thing that way." [18]

Of the animal's appearance (Fig. 4), Tyson wrote:

In my first *Figure* I represent him as weak and feeble and bending; for when I first saw him, he was dying.[19] . . . Being weak, the better to support him, I have given him a Stick in his Right-Hand, But our *Figure* being made after he was dead, the *Head* seems to have fallen in between the Shoulders.[20]

In the dissection of the inward parts, Tyson remarked:

We come now to describe the *Testes* . . . the Skin which inclosed them, was not so dilated, as to hang down like a *Cod;* but contracted them up nearer to the Body of the *Penis;* which seemed to me seems a wise Contrivance of

Nature. For hereby these Parts are less exposed to injuries, they might otherwise receive in climbing Trees, or other accidents in the Woods. . . . But whether the *Testes* being thus closely pursed up to the Body, might contribute to that great *salaciousness* this *Species of Animals* are noted for, I will not determine: Tho' 'tis said, that these *Animals,* that have their *Testicles* contained within the Body, are more inclined to it, than others. That the whole *Ape*-kind is extreamly given to *Venery,* appears by infinite Stories related of them. And not only so, but different from other Brutes, they covet not only their *own Species,* but to an *Excess* are inclined and sollicitous to those of a *different,* and are most *amorous* of fair *Women.*[21]

In his evaluation Tyson concluded of his Pygmie: "I take him to be wholly a *Brute,* tho', in the formation of the *Body,* and in the *Sensitive* or *Brutal* Soul, it may be, more resembling a Man, than any other *Animal:* so that in this *Chain* of the *Creation,* as an intermediate Link between an *Ape* and a *Man,* I would place our *Pygmie.*" [22]

While Tyson had provided the classic description of the Chimpanzee, the name itself, from the native African *Quimpezes,* first appeared in English in 1738 as the title of an engraving prepared by Gerard Scotin for Sir Hans Sloane, President of the Royal Society (Fig. 5, left). The legend accompanying the figure states: [23]

This Creature was brought over by Captain Henry Flower in the Ship Speaker from Angola on the Coast of Guinea in August 1738. It is of the Female kind & is two feet four inches high, walks erect, drinks tea, eats her food & sleeps in a human way, was 21 Months old when this Picture was drawn. She has a Capacity of understanding and great Affability, has muscular Arms & Legs of great strength. The Males when at full growth do force women and dare attack an Armed Man as the Mother of this Creature frequently did,

---

[18] 24, p. 51.
[19] 24, p. 82.
[20] 24, p. 16.

[21] 24, p. 42.
[22] 24, p. 5.
[23] 22.

Figure 5: The first use of the term chimpanzee in England, in an engraving by Scotin (1738, left), with the copy of this figure reproduced the following year in Germany (right).

who was upwards of 5 feet high & was shot by a Negro ere he could take this from her.

In the middle of the title, below the figure, can be seen a drinking vessel with a cup-like cover removed beside it. The animal is shown holding this cup, presumably of tea, part way to its lips. This figure was redrawn and reproduced a year later in the *Nova Acta Eruditorum* under the title: *A Brief Description of a very rare Animal, called the Chimpanzee, brought to London from the Kingdom of Angola.*[24] According to the accompanying text:

We display here for our readers an illustration [Fig. 5, right] of a very ferocious animal of astonishing and forbidding appearance, but resembling the human in shape and stature. It has scarcely ever been seen by our people, although perhaps heard of by a very few. It is from Angola, an African kingdom, from whose inhabitants it received the name Chimpanzee. It was brought from these shores to London by Henry Howe [*sic*], Captain of the ship Speaker,

in August 1738. It is a female two feet four inches tall and walks with body erect; strong and muscular, some parts of its limbs are hirsute. It seeks nourishment from its dung, but it also likes tea, which it drinks from a vessel like a human. In sleep, moreover, it imitates him, and is not lacking in cleverness; in its voice there is a human chattering. When the males become adult they lustfully seek human women and challenge even armed men to battle. The same was done very often by the mother of this one depicted on copper. It was five feet tall and had not a Moor killed it with a weapon, it is hardly likely that its offspring would have been present here. Scotin, an expert artisan, skillfully engraved the likeness of this one, twenty-one months old, in London, following the advice, if our suspicion is correct, of John [*sic*] Sloane, President of the Royal Society, to whose name we see ascribed whatever has been written of this strange monster. Having recently obtained a copy of this illustration, we have sought to copy it as closely as possible so that it might enlighten the story of the animal kingdom.

In this view (Fig. 5, right) the drinking vessel is omitted, and the animal is seen holding a cup just below its breast.

Twenty years later, in his *Gleanings of Natural History*, George Edwards, naturalist, painter and librarian to the Royal College of Physicians of London, wrote of the *Man of the Woods*[25]:

This animal, which is one of the first of the genus of Monkies, is supposed to come the nearest in its outward shape to man. The old ones are said, by many of our voyagers to Africa and India, to be near six feet high, when standing or walking erect.
The subject from which this figure was drawn (Fig. 6, left), is now preserved in the British Museum, in London. It was a young one, and about two feet and a half high when it died: it was first soaked in spirits of wine, then dried, and set up in the action I have given it, the draught being taken before its parts were too much dried or fallen in. Its shape resembled most others of the Monkey kind; its hands and feet the same. It differed from the generality

---

[24] 2, Vol. 8, pp. 564–65.
[25] 9, Pt. 1, pp. 6–8, pl. 213.

in having no tail, or callous skin behind,
to sit on, as most monkies have; and in having
the head rounder, and more human-like than
most of its kind; the forehead was high
and rising, the nose flat, the teeth much
resembled those of men; the hair from the neck
inclined upwards round to the forehead, and hung
down a little over the forehead and the sides
of the face, which was without hair; the ears were
also naked, and much of the human make.
It had two nipples, situated as in man; the face
and naked parts of the paws were of a swarthy
flesh-colour; the body and limbs were covered
with a loose, shaggy, reddish-brown hair,
thicker on the hinder parts, and thinner before:
the hair from the hand to the elbow inclined
towards the elbow.

About fifty years ago was published an
anatomical description, by Edward Tyson, M.D.,
of this same animal, which he calls the Pigmy . . .
and since him, A.D. 1738, a figure was published
of one that was brought from the coast of
Africa, called Chimp-anzee. But . . . these prints
were not satisfactory to me, who had seen
the above-described, which was a female, with
one other (a male) now in my hands; both
agreeing exactly in every part, but what
distinguished the sexes: for which reason I have
published this figure, the original whereof was with
great care done by me, to be preserved amongst
the drawings of animals, in the Museum of
the late Sir Hans Sloane, Bart., now in the
British Museum. I believe them all to be natives
of Africa; though there are voyagers to India
that describe something like them.

Early Systematists

This was the material available then to Linnaeus
who in his *Systema Natura*, published in 1735,[26]
first classed man with the apes under the general
heading, Anthropomorpha. Of the apes, Linnaeus
differentiated the Orang-outang, Troglodyte and
Homo norturnus, each "four-footed, mute and

---

[26] 15.
[27] 14, p. 22.
[28] 13, Vol. 6, p. 63 ff.

Figure 6: Figures of the chimpanzee from Edwards
(1758, left) and Buffon (right), each with a staff,
following the then established tradition.

hairy." He also described the Satyrus as "caudate,
hirsute, bearded, resembling the human body,
strongly given to gesticulations, and very sala-
cious." It is probable, as Huxley noted,[27] that
"Linnaeus knew nothing of his own observations
of the man-like apes of either Africa or Asia, but
a dissertation of his pupil, Hoppius, may be regarded as embodying his views respecting these
animals."

Christian Emanuel Hopp, or Hoppius, of St.
Petersburg, presented his thesis entitled *Anthropomorpha* under the chairmanship of Linnaeus at
Uppsala, September 6, 1760. It was published in
1764.[28] After lengthy introductory remarks, Hoppius continues by remarking:

Of all those things which the terrestrial and
aqueous globe has provided, nothing is more like
the human race than the race of apes. . . .
Perhaps they are unable to speak, but the manner
of their conversation resembles ours and differs
from that of the brutes. Often they walk erect
only on their hind feet; they take food in
their hands and carry it to the mouth; with palms
concave, they drink and, when water is lacking,
dig wells with their hands. Like us, they are
omnivorous. . . . By nature they are malicious
with a tendency to mischief, much given to theft,
very libidinous, always impudent, but at the

Figure 7: The reproduction by Hoppius (1764) of the figures (left to right) from: Bontius, Aldrovandi, Scotin (mislabelled Tulp) and Edwards.

same time modest defecators. . . . They dread crocodiles, serpents and, what is astonishing, contagious fevers. I shall say only a few things of our neighbors, or of those of the race of apes, which, like us, walk erect, stand on two feet, and are very much like us in physiognomy. There are four of these of which I have made note.

Hoppius then goes on to depict (Fig. 7) and discuss the Pygmy of Edwards, the Satyr of Tulp and Scotin, the Lucifer of Aldrovandi, and the Troglodyte of Bontius. The engraving by Scotin (Fig. 5, left) is used for the Satyr although Tulp's figure (Fig. 3, left) would have served as well, for Hoppius remarks: "It is especially distinguished by the size of the abdomen, which is swollen despite its virgin character, and it is especially in this that it differs from the reed-like girls of our race." He also notes that Scotin's Satyr "grasped a drinking vessel with one hand and removed the cover with the other, drank half,

wiping its mouth with its palm." In the reproduction (Fig. 7), the hand is shown half way to the mouth, but the cup unfortunately was omitted, giving the animal an appearance of proferring its breast to view. The modesty of the female ape would have proscribed such a gesture, and the difficulties with this figure, attributable to an engraver's omission, recall the proverbial slip 'twixt cup and lip.

Hoppius concludes his discussion with the following generalization: "No race of brutes so closely approaches man as the apes, and especially the anthropomorpha, in which not only are we amazed at the great likeness of stature to ours, but by the very similar customs." In short, "how very like us is that shameful beast, the ape."

The figure included from Buffon was drawn from life (Fig. 6, right). The animal, which lived for one summer in Paris and died in London the following winter, was about 2½ feet high and did not exceed two years in age. Of it, Buffon wrote: [29]

He was very fond of dainties, which every body gave him: and, as his breast was diseased, and he was afflicted with a teazing cough, this quantity of sweetmeats undoubtedly contributed to shorten his life.

[29] 6, Vol. 10, pp. 46–7.

As to the identity of the animal, Buffon re-marked:

> The Jocko, or small Orang-outang . . .
> which have been brought to Europe, were all,
> perhaps, young animals, who had acquired
> only a part of their growth. . . . Hence it is
> probable, that . . . if possessed of liberty in
> their own climate, [they] would have acquired
> with age the same height and dimensions
> which travellers have ascribed to the great
> Orang-outang . . . till better information be
> received, we must regard these two animals as
> constituting but one species.

Orang-outang

The Orang-outang was first identified as a species distinct from the Chimpanzee by the Dutch anatomist, Peter Camper, who, in 1779, reported his dissection of five specimens. The first was received in 1770 from a physician in Batavia (Fig. 8): "I have drawn this Orang," wrote Camper, "with great exactitude, although it was hardened and shrivelled by spirits of wine." Each of his specimens was very young, had a dull red coat, and resembled the others perfectly. "The true Orang-outang of Asia or Borneo," Camper concluded, "is an animal of a distinct species." [30]

In Lord Monboddo's treatise *Of the Origin and Progress of Language*, which appeared in 1773, a concern with man's natural state and evolutionary relationship to the ape tended to minimize the absence of speech in the Orang-outang.[31] A complementary interest in the subject led his friend, Sir John Pringle, then President of the Royal Society, to appeal to Camper to dissect the vocal apparatus in his specimens. Camper's obliging *Account of the Organs of Speech in the Orang-outang*, submitted to the "Philosophical Transac-

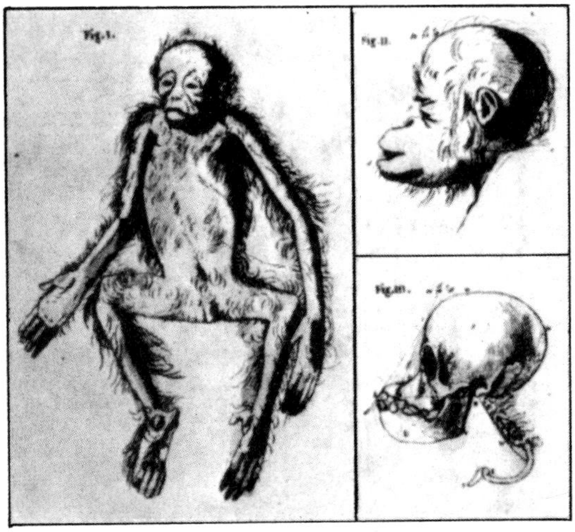

Figure 8: The first scientific figures of the Orang-outang by Camper (1779). The distorted appearance of the animal is explained by its preservation in spirits of wine.

tions of the Royal Society" in 1779,[32] reported that the massive laryngeal ventricles which he had discovered made speech impossible in this form.

Gorilla

The culminating step of anthropoid speciation, the belated differentiation of the Gorilla as "a new species of Orang," was made entirely from skeletal material (Fig. 9) by Thomas S. Savage,

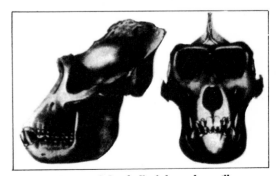

Figure 9: Views of the skull of the male gorilla, representing the first identifiable figures of this animal. From Savage and Wyman (1847).

[30] 7, 1, pp. 5–196.
[31] 18, pp. 270–313.
[32] 8, Vol. 69, pp. 139–59.

an American missionary returning from Africa in 1847 and by Jeffries Wyman, Professor of Anatomy at Harvard University, who helped in the study of its osteology. Neither had seen an intact specimen, but from native accounts, the Reverend Savage assembled the following information: [33]

> While on a voyage home from Cape Palmas, I was unexpectedly detained in the Gaboon River . . . and the month of April (1847) was spent at the house of the Rev. J. L. Wilson, Senior Missionary of the American Board of Commissioners for Foreign Missions to West Africa. Soon after my arrival Mr. Wilson showed me a skull, represented by the natives to be that of a monkey-like animal, remarkable for its size, ferocity and habits. From the contour of the skull, and the information derived from several intelligent natives, I was induced to believe that it belonged to a new species of Orang. . . . I did not succeed however, in obtaining the animal, but several crania of the two sexes and of different ages, with other important parts of the skeleton were received.

> . . . . .

> The river is visited for the purpose of trade in ivory, ebony and dye-woods by vessel from different parts of America and Europe. In view of this fact, it may seem surprising that the animal should be unknown to science, and without its proper place in systems of Zoology. But this is accounted for by the fact that its immediate habitat is back some distance from the coast, and its habits and ferocity such that it is not often encountered. The natives stand greatly in fear of it, and never attempt its capture except in self-defense.

> . . . . .

> They live in bands, but are not so numerous as the Chimpanzée's; the females generally exceed the other sex in number . . . but one adult male is seen in a band . . . when the young males grow up, a contest takes place for mastery, and the strongest, by killing and driving out the others, establishes himself as the head of the community. The silly stories about their carrying off women from the native towns, and vanquishing

> the elephants, related by voyagers and widely copied into books, are unhesitatingly denied. . . .

> Their dwellings, if they may be so called, are similar to those of the Chimpanzée, consisting simply of a few sticks and leafy branches supported by the crotches and limbs of trees; they afford no shelter, and are occupied only at night.

> . . . . .

> It is said that when the male is first seen he gives a terrific yell that resounds far and wide through the forest . . . prolonged and shrill. His enormous jaws are widely opened at each expiration, his underlip hangs over the chin, and the hairy ridge and scalp is contracted upon the brow, presenting an aspect of indescribable ferocity. The females and young at the first cry quickly disappear; he then approaches the enemy in a great fury, pouring out his horrid cries in succession.

> . . . . .

> It is said that this animal exhibits a degree of intelligence inferior to that of the Chimpanzée; this might be expected from its wider departure from the organization of the human subject. . . . Here, as at all other points on the coast, the orangs are believed by the natives to be human beings, members of their own race, degenerated. Some few, who have put on a degree of civilization above the mass, will not acknowledge their belief in this affinity; such profess to view them as embodied spirits, the belief in transmigration of souls being prevalent. . . . The majority however, fully believe them to be men, and seem to be unaffected by our arguments in proof of the contrary. This is especially true of the tribes in the immediate vicinity of the locality. They believe them to be literally "wild men of the woods."

Comment

It is remarkable how consistently these early accounts were concerned with those aspects of the anthropomorpha which continue to attract attention today, i.e., with the degree to which ape and man resemble, or are distinct from, one another. Hanno made reference to the Gorillas as "savage people" and mentioned their use of stones in defense. Lopez and later Tulp were struck by the

---

[33] 21, Vol. 5, pp. 419–43.

extent to which the apes "counterfait the countenances, the fashions, & the actions of men," a feature responsible for the verb "to ape." Although Battell pointed out that his Pongos walked erect, built shelters and buried their dead, he noted their inability to use fire, even when attracted to it, and concluded: "They cannot speak, and have no more understanding than a beast."

On the other hand, the names "Orang-outang" and "Chimpanzee," each meaning "man of the woods," were given the apes by the natives both of Asia and Africa, and these terms appear to have been applied with literal interpretations. As Bontius pointed out: "The Javanese say that they [the Orang-outangs] can speak but do not choose to do so lest they be compelled to work." Later, Savage remarked of Africa: "Here . . . the orangs are believed by the natives to be human beings, members of their own race, degenerated. Some few, who have put on a degree of civilization above the mass, will not acknowledge their belief in this affinity. . . . The majority however, fully believe them to be men, and seem to be unaffected by our arguments in proof of the contrary. . . . They believe them to be literally "wild men of the woods."

One may even infer from Tyson that the Chimpanzee considered its own relationship as closer to man than to other simians. "Our *Pygmie* was . . . the most gentle and loving Creature that could be. Those that he knew aboard [ship] he would come and embrace with the greatest tenderness, opening their Bosoms, and clasping his Hands about them; and . . . tho' there were *Monkeys* aboard he would never associate with them, and as if nothing a-kin to them, would always avoid their Company."

With the domestication of apes and their importation into Europe in the seventeenth century, more elaborate analogies to man's behavior were drawn. Their feeding, and particularly their habits of drinking, received special attention. Tulp remarked of the Chimpanzee: "When about to drink, it grasped the handle of the tankard with one hand, the other supporting the bottom of the vessel. Thereafter it wiped the remaining drops from its lips no less skillfully than you might see done by some polished courtier." Tyson's Pygmie was once "made Drunk with *Punch.* . . . But it was observed, that after that time, it would never drink above one Cup, and refused the offer of more than what it found agreed with him." The Chimpanzee sketched for Sir Hans Sloane "seeks nourishment from its dung, but it also likes tea, which it drinks from a vessel with one hand and removed the cover with the other, drank half, wiping its mouth with its palm." Further testimony for the interest in this function is provided by Scotin's original sketch, together with its first copy, which shows this animal with a cup part way to its lips, though in Hoppius' later version the cup was accidentally omitted.

Other habits of the ape similarly aroused interest. Thus Tulp wrote: "It displayed that same dexterity whenever it lay down, inclining its head on the couch, properly covering and enveloping itself with the blankets just as if a very graceful man were lying down." Tyson's Pygmie "would lie in a Bed, place his Head on the Pillow, and pull the Cloaths over him, as Man would do; but was so careless and so very a Brute as to do all Nature's Occasions there." Hoppius simply made reference to the anthropomorpha as being "at the same time, modest defecators."

An even more pronounced interest explored the sexual proclivities of the anthropomorpha. Like the Satyrs of legend, a remarkably wanton and aggressively lascivious behavior was attributed to the male. The male, according to Gesner, "loves women and, when it has escaped its chains, attempts openly to lie with them." According to Tulp, the males "have such boldness of spirit and . . . sometimes they are overcome by such strong desire for women that not infrequently they ravish those they have seized. They are extremely inclined to venery . . . indeed, they are so shamelessly lustful that the women of the Indies avoid the lairs and paths in which these shameless animals lurk." "The whole *Ape*-kind," Tyson concurred, "is extreamly given to *Venery*. . . . And not only so, but different from other Brutes, they covet not only their *own Species,* but to an *Excess* are inclined and sollicitous to those of a *different,* and are most *amorous* of fair *Women.*"

In sharp contrast, a modest timidity was attributed to the feminine sex. Bontius' female "hid her face with great shyness from strange men," and "because [Bontius] hath express'd that this Creature hath so much Modesty," Tyson, "added to his *Figure* what becomes that Character." The female depicted by Scotin was "cloathed with a thin silk vestment and shewed a great discontent at the opening of her gown to discover her sex." [34]

The behavior of the gorilla was remarkably anticipatory of Darwin's later generalizations concerning sexual selection. According to Savage: the animals "live in bands . . . the females generally exceed the other sex in number . . . but one adult male is seen in a band . . . when the young males grow up, a contest takes place for mastery, and the strongest, by killing and driving out the others, establishes himself as the head of the community. The silly stories about their carrying off women from the native towns . . . related by voyagers and widely copied into books, are unhesitatingly denied."

With sex providing but limited distinction, it was then with respect to speech that the differentiation between apes and man came finally to be drawn. Battell reported: "they cannot speak"; and Bontius described their reputed verbal ability as "ridiculous." They displayed a lively capacity for emotional vocalization, however, and Bontius' "female Satyr . . . wept copiously, groaned and expressed other human emotions so that you might say that no other human characteristic was lacking

to her except speech." Tyson heard his Pygmie cry "like a *Child,*" and his dissection showed its larynx to be exactly like that of man. "And if there was any farther advantage for the forming of *Speech,* I can't think our *Pygmie* had it. But upon the best Enquiry, I was never informed, that it attempted any thing that way."

To the eighteenth-century primitivists, this failure of the apes to speak did not imply that they were incapable of it, nor oppose their close relationship to man.[35] In his *Discourse upon the Origin and Foundation of the Inequality among Mankind,* Rousseau wrote: [36]

All these Observations on the Varieties, which a thousand Causes can produce and have in fact produced in the Human Species, make me doubt if several Animals, which Travellers have taken for Beasts, for Want of examining them properly . . . or merely because these Animals did not speak, were not in fact true Men, (though in a savage State,) whose Race early dispersed in the Woods never had any Opportunity of developing its virtual Faculties, and had acquired no Degree of Perfection, but still remained in the primitive State of Nature.

Description of these pretended Monsters [shows] very striking Conformities with the Human Species, and smaller Differences than may be pointed out between one Man and another. We cannot discover by these Passages, what Reasons the Writers had for refusing to the Animals in question the Name of wild Men; but we may easily guess, that it was on account of their Stupidity and Want of Speech; weak Arguments for those who know, that, though the Organs of Speech are natural to Man, it is otherwise with Speech itself, and are aware to what a Pitch the Perfectibility of the Human Species may have exalted civil Man above his original condition.

It is evident that the Monkey does not belong to the Human Species, not only because he wants the Faculty of Speech, but above all because his Species has not the Faculty of improving, which is the specifick Characteristic of the Human Species. But it does not appear that the same Experiments have been made with the *Pongos* and the *Orang-outang* carefully enough to afford the same Conclusion.

---

[34] 19, p. 247.
[35] 17.
[36] 20, pp. 221 ff.

Lord Monboddo's interest in *The Origin and Progress of Language* led him to point out that, although:

Buffon has formed to himself a definition of man by which he makes the faculty of speech a part of his essence of nature, it is a clear case that we do not speak in that state which, of all others, best deserves the appellation of natural; I mean when we are born, nor for a considerable time after; and even then we learn but slowly and with a great deal of labor and difficulty. . . .

If ever men were in that state which I call natural, it must have been in such a country and climate as Africa, where they could live without art upon the natural fruits of the earth. If this be so, then the short history of man is, that the race having begun in those fine climates and having, as is natural, multiplied there so much that the spontaneous products of the earth could not support them, they migrated into other countries, where they were obliged to invent arts for their subsistence and with such arts language, in process of time, would necessarily come. Must the orang-outangs still be accounted brutes because they have not yet fallen upon the method of communication by articulate sounds?

Three-quarters of a century earlier, Tyson had answered of his Pygmie, "I Take him to be wholly a *Brute*, tho' in the formation of the Body, and in the *Sensitive* or *Brutal* Soul, it may be, more resembling a Man, than any other *Animal:* so that in this *Chain* of the *Creation*, as an intermediate Link between an *Ape* and a *Man*, I would place our *Pygmie.*" [37]

BIBLIOGRAPHY

1. ALDROVANDI, ULISSE, *De Quadrupedibus Digitatis Viviparis*, Bologna, 1695.

2. *Animalis Rarioris, Chimpanzee dicti, ex Regno Angola Londinum advecti, brevior Descriptio*, "Nova Acta Eruditorum," Leipzig, 1739.

3. BARTHOLIN, THOMAS, *Anatome Cercopitheci* Mamonet *dicti*, "Acta Medica & Philosophica Hafniensia," Copenhagen, 1673–80.

4. BATTELL, ANDREW, *The Strange Adventures of Andrew Battell of Leigh, in Angola and the adjoining Regions.* Reprinted from "Purchas his Pilgrimes," ed. with notes by E. G. Ravenstein, London, 1901.

5. BONDT (BONTIUS), JACOB DE, *De Medicina Indorum*, in *Opuscola Selecta Neerlandicorum de Arte Medica*, vol. X, Amsterdam, 1931.

6. BUFFON, GEORGES LOUIS LECLERC, COMPTE DE, *Natural History General and Particular . . . The History of Man and Quadrupeds*, trans. William Smellie, London, 1812.

7. CAMPER, PETER, *De l'Orang-outang et de quelques autres espèces de Singes, in Oeuvres de Pierre Camper, qui ont pour object l'Histoire naturelle, la Physiologie et l'Anatomie comparée*, Paris, 1803.

8. CAMPER, PETER, *Account of the organs of speech of the Orang-outang*, "Philosophical Transactions of the Royal Society," London, 1779.

9. EDWARDS, GEORGE, *Gleanings of Natural History*, London, 1758.

10. ELLIOT, DANIEL GIRAUD, *A Review of the Primates*, New York, 1913. (Monographs of the American Museum of Natural History, I–III).

11. GESNER, CONRAD, *Historia Animalium liber secundus qui est de Quadrupedibus*. Frankfurt, 1586.

12. HANNO, *The Voyage of Hanno translated and accompanied by the Greek text*, by Thomas Falconer, London, 1797.

13. HOPP (HOPPIUS), CHRISTIAN EMANUEL, *Anthropomorpha*, "Caroli Linnaei Amoenitates Academicae," Leyden, 1764.

14. HUXLEY, THOMAS H., *Man's Place in Nature*, Ann Arbor, Michigan, 1959.

15. LINNÉ (LINNAEUS), CHARLES, *Systema Natura*, Leyden, 1735.

16. LOPEZ, DUARTE, *A Reporte of the Kingdom of Congo . . . drawen out of the writinges and discourses of Odoardo Lopes a Portingall, by Philippo Pigafetta. Trans. out of the Italian by Abraham Hartwell*, London, 1597.

17. LOVEJOY, ARTHUR O., *Essays in the History of Ideas*, New York, 1960, pp. 144–37. The Supposed Primitivism of Rousseau's *Discourse on Inequality*," pp. 38–61, "Monboddo and Rousseau."

[37] For additional information on primates, see: Ruch, T. C., *Bibliographia Primatologica; a Classified Bibliography of the Primates Other Than Man.* C. C. Thomas, Springfield, Illinois, pt. 1, 1941.

18. MONBODDO, LORD JAMES BURNET, *Of the Origin and Progress of Language,* 2 ed., Edinburgh, 1774.

19. MONTAGU, ASHLEY, *Edward Tyson, M.D. . . . and the Rise of Human and Comparative Anatomy,* Philadelphia, 1943.

20. ROUSSEAU, JEAN JACQUES, *A Discourse upon the Origin and Foundation of the Inequality among Mankind,* London, 1761.

21. SAVAGE, THOMAS S., *Notice of the External Characters and Habits of Troglodytes Gorilla, a New Species of Orang from the Gaboon River; Osteology of the same by Jeffries Wyman,* "Boston J. of Natural History," 1847.

22. SCOTIN, GERARD, "Chimpanzee, Scotin sculp. A.D. 1738." A copy of the original engraving is in the Print Department of the British Museum.

23. TULP, NICOLAUS, *Observationum Medicarum libri tres,* Amsterdam, 1640, p. 270 ff.

24. TYSON, EDWARD, *Orang-Outang, sive Homo Sylvestris: or, The Anatomy of a Pygmie compared with that of a Monkey, an Ape, and a Man,* London, 1699.

25. YERKES, ROBERT M., and ADA W., *The Great Apes, a Study of Anthropoid Life,* New Haven, 1929.

THREE • APES AND MEN

3 • THE RECENT HOMINOID PRIMATES

Adolph H. Schultz

In this admirable survey Schultz, the world's leading primatologist, gives us an authoritative account of the morphological differences and likenesses between apes and men. A lifetime of experience, devoted to increasing our knowledge of the comparative anatomy of apes and man, is here afforded the reader. A special contribution of Schultz's to his field has always been his skill with pen and pencil, as is well illustrated in this article. Schultz's publications have always served to emphasize the fundamental importance of learning to draw, particularly as a part of the training of a physical anthropologist. The visual impact of Figure 2, for example, tells us more about the comparative size and proportions of the great apes and man than, literally, volumes could. The same is true for most of Schultz's drawings.

Special attention should be given to Schultz's observations on the primate thumb, especially to the reduction of the size of the hand in man. Of equal interest is his assertion that the smallness of the face in man is due not so much to its reduction from the prognathic face of the ape, but rather that the latter has undergone an enormous development, while man's has retained its childlike form. There are those, including the editor of this volume, who believe that the form of the hominid face, together with many other cranial features, represents the expression of a neotenous process. Schultz does not, I believe, subscribe to this view, although most zoologists, if not most physical anthropologists, find neoteny a very

satisfactory explanation of the retention of the small face and jaws in man. Table 3, which shows the average number of hairs per square centimeter in hominoids, calls attention to the reduced body and head hair in Mongoloids in comparison to other hominoids, suggesting the neotenous character of this trait, together with other neotenous traits such as their large brain and head, large trunk, and short legs. Schultz's comments on the variations in skin color in the chimpanzee—white, brown, and black—should, perhaps, suggest some fruitful ideas for the evolution of the varieties of skin color in man. In this connection it may be of interest to note that many years ago on the head of a six-month-old female gorilla I observed the presence of black, brown, and red hairs.

The importance of morphology for an understanding of function is especially brought out in Schultz's description of the skeleton. Here the "dry bones" truly speak; for bones are, in fact, anything but "dry," they have only been made so by dryasdust osteologists.

The significant conclusion which Schultz draws from his studies is that a separate hominid branch appeared on the hominid family tree before any of the branches leading to the recent great apes had diverged from one another, and not later, as many authorities have believed.[1]

Preface

During the hundred years following Huxley's (1863) epochal publication of "Evidence as to man's place in nature" the comparative-anatomical and palaeontological study of the primates most similar to men progressed at a rapidly increasing rate. In an attempt to survey the great mass of accumulated new evidence for man's evolutionary history Prof. Heberer had in 1962 invited some

SOURCE: Adolph H. Schultz, "Die Renzenten Hominoidea," Adolph S. Schultz, trans. and Gerhard Heberer, ed., *Menlische Abstammungslehre* (Stuttgart: Gustav Fischer Verlag, 1965). Reprinted by permission of the publisher.
[1] For his general survey of the primates see Adolph H. Schultz, *The Life of the Primates* (New York: Universe Books, 1969).

of his colleagues to contribute reviews of their respective fields of research for a volume centered upon our present views on man's place among the primates, entitled *Menschliche Abstammungslehre, 1863–1964*. The writer had been assigned the chapter on the living anthropoid apes, with special emphasis on their morphology and with the understanding that the fossils, dentition, skull, brain, and historical aspects are to be dealt with in separate chapters by other authors. With this general orientation, including the condition that the book is intended for the "educated layman" and should go into print very quickly, the writer had assembled and turned in his manuscript in 1962, but eventually it did not appear until three years later. For the latter reason the writer was glad to have been asked to translate and revise his chapter in German for a new publication in English. The necessary consent of the editor of the original German edition was readily and generously given by Prof. Heberer when Prof. Washburn and the writer discussed this matter with him during the international congress of primatology in Frankfurt a. M. in 1966. It was also agreed that the writer would be free to make alterations in his text according to his latest views and to change or add such illustrations as seem desirable.

A brief description of the distinguishing characters of the recent man-like apes gains most of its interest through comparisons between these specializations and the corresponding conditions of lower primates on one side and of man on the other. The enormous amout of relevant information which has become available in widely scattered publications can no longer be surveyed completely in a review of limited size. It seems justified, therefore, to deal here chiefly with such topics which have received comparatively little attention in most of the many summarizing accounts of the higher primates by other authors and to select some of the subjects which have been of particular interest to the writer. With these se-

lections it will be possible to demonstrate not only the outstanding evolutionary trends, common to all hominoids, but also some of the more significant specializations characterizing the different families and genera. The particular conditions in the latter often represent simply different stages of perfection along the same general trends or reveal the comparatively late diverging innovations acquired by single genera or species. To include in addition a critical discussion of our latest knowledge of the brain, teeth, chromosomes, hemoglobins, parasites, and so on of the living higher primates would require today the cooperation of many specialists, without as yet leading to general and close agreement in phylogenetic conclusions regarding the precise interrelations of the hominoids.

The detailed classification of primates and parts of its nomenclature are being continually changed in numerous more or less significant respects and hence are not used in the literature in a uniform and generally understood manner. It will be necessary, therefore, to begin with some brief introductory explanations of the system and names preferred by the writer. These follow mainly the scholarly taxonomic chapter by Fiedler (1956) in the first volume of the well-known handbook of primatology, which can be consulted for a full discussion of this matter and, incidentally, also for a great deal of further information and literature on hominoids, contributed by many other specialists.

Introduction

The suborder Simiae of the primates is clearly divided in two ancient groups according to some of their anatomical characters, which differ consistently. One of these main groups is found exclusively in America and the other ranges through Africa and the southern part of Asia and in times past also Europe. The simian primates of the Old World, the so-called catarrhines, can be subdivided quite sharply into the superfamilies of Cercopithecoidea, or catarrhine monkeys, and of Hominoidea. To the latter are assigned all man-like apes as well as man and his close forerunners, which are often and rightly referred to as the higher primates. Of this formerly larger superfamily of Hominoidea survive only three families of which the Hylobatidae contain the gibbons and siamangs, the Pongidae the three types of great apes and the Hominidae recent man. Only the last-named has gained world-wide distribution and by far the largest population of all primate species.

The smallest of the recent hominoids, the hylobatids, are still more numerous and more widely ranging than the great apes of today and have developed two generically distinct types (*Hylobates* and *Symphalangus*) and a total of six or possibly seven good species. In contrast to this the orang-utans (*Pongo*) and gorillas (*Gorilla*) are each represented by only one species and the chimpanzees (*Pan*) by two. A great many additional species of recent apes had been proposed and described under a confusing variety of names during the first few decades of our century, but all of these are today regarded as at most mere local races, if not as manifestation of the exceptionally great variability of the pongids in particular.

In the single species of siamangs [1] the Sumatran animals are generally somewhat larger than the Malayan ones and in the also single species of orang-utans the hair color is as a rule slightly darker in Bornean individuals than in those from their last refuge area in Sumatra, where they still survive. With such very limited differences one can merely justify expected geographic races, but not separate species. The best-known chimpanzee

species (*Pan troglodytes*) seems to have become more or less clearly differentiated into three subspecies, of which two live in West-Africa, *P. t. verus* occurring toward the north and *P. t. troglodytes* farther south, while *P. t. schweinfurthi* ranges through parts of Central Africa. A second and much later discovered species of chimpanzees (*Pan paniscus*) is isolated on the left side of the Congo river and tends to be slightly smaller and to have certain other distinctive features, but the commonly used name of "pygmy chimpanzee" is hardly warranted in view of the fact that the individual variations in body size of both species overlap extensively (Schultz 1954). Among gorillas one can also distinguish different types on the basis of a number of minor features (Schultz 1934), particularly the two subspecies of the so-called "lowland" and "mountain" gorillas, which should be more appropriately named western and eastern gorillas, since their respective ranges, though smaller than those of chimpanzees, are not at all restricted to low coastal zones or else mountainous ones.

In this review of the recent hominoids it can merely be mentioned that the great variety of fossil ones provides very tempting evidence for a provisional reconstruction of the general phylogenetic relationships within this entire superfamily. These fossils, however, are still inadequate for plotting the exact places and ages of divergence in the evolutionary pathways leading to the living types. From fossil finds we have learned that from a common ancestral stock of all later higher primates there have evolved more families than survive, such as the Oreopithecidae and Pliopithecidae, which seem to have died out in Pliocene time. We have no fossils, however, to trace any of the modern apes far back into the past. Of the African apes not a single tooth has ever been found to indicate their appearance and distribution during the Pleistocene period, and of gibbons and orang-utans we can merely demonstrate their much wider distribution during the

---

[1] The gibbons which are isolated in the Mentawi Islands, west of Sumatra, had formerly been regarded as a separate species of "dwarf siamangs," but for numerous reasons are more properly assigned to the genus *Hylobates* in which they have been placed in a subgenus *Brachitanytes* (Schultz 1932; 1933).

same brief period, but all preceding lines of connection with earlier forms remain hypothetical. These remarks are inserted here to point out that the determination of the phylogenetic interrelations of the modern hominoids and, particularly, of man's place among them still rests mainly on comparative studies of the living forms which offer endless possibilities for obtaining morphological, biochemical, behavioral and still further evidence.

Body Size and Proportions

The body size of the living hominoids differs at least as widely as did that of the fossil ones. Gibbons are mere dwarfs alongside gorillas, among which some old males can attain a weight of over 200 kg., representing the extreme of all recent primates and one reached by only few of the past, such as *Gigantopithecus* or *Megaladapis*. Intraspecifically body size can also vary to a remarkably high degree not only in man, but in the man-like apes as well. For instance, in a series of 80 adult gibbons from a small area the fresh body weight was found to range from 3.8 to 7.3 kg. (Schultz 1944). That longitudinal dimensions have an equally high variability can here be indicated only by the following data: The length of the humerus varies among 145 perfectly normal, adult, male, western gorillas between 389 and 500 mm. according to measurements by Schultz (1937) and by Randall (1943–1944) (32 of the 84 specimens of the latter author had already been used by the former author and have naturally been counted only once).

The average sex difference in body weight is negligible in some hominoid genera, but extremely great in others, as shown by the data in Table 1. In orang-utans and gorillas this sex difference is fully marked as, for example, in baboons or proboscis monkeys, whereas in gibbons it is barely recognizable with many individual females equal-

Table 1: Average body weights (kg.) of adult female and male hominoids according to data by the author and those collected by him from the literature. Since reliable weights of adult gorillas have rarely been recorded the present averages are merely approximate ones. The figures for man represent rough general averages of data for different races.

	FEMALES	MALES	FEMALE AVER. IN PERCENT MALE AVER.
Gibbon (*H. lar*)	5.3	5.7	93
" (*H. concolor*)	5.8	5.6	103
" (*H. hoolock*)	6.6	6.9	96
" (*H. klossii*)	6.5	6.2	105
Siamang	10.2	11.1	92
Orang-utan	37	75	49
Chimpanzee	42	48	88
Gorilla	85	175	48
Man	58	65	89

ling or even surpassing males in size, as is so often the case also among platyrrhines.

The body proportions of all higher primates are in various respects very distinct from those of monkeys, and this not only in consequence of their different modes of locomotion but also due to common specializations, shared by all recent hominoids. Table 2 lists the averages of some of the most significant proportions, based on the author's measurements of the outer bodies of numerous fully adult apes and men. The corresponding averages for adult macaques (*Macaca mulatta*) must suffice here for representing these conditions in Old World monkeys, among which most of these relative measurements are comparatively uniform (Schultz 1956). From the first four indices of the table it is evident that the trunk of higher primates is without exception very much stouter and particularly broader than that of macaques and all the many other Cercopithecoidea whose proportions have been determined so far. This striking and consistent difference between the higher and the lower catarrhines

Table 2: Averages of some body proportions of adult hominoids and macaques based upon strictly corresponding measurements by the author (for further data on more proportions and in additional primates see Schultz 1956). Number of specimens in parentheses. Relative Head Size = (Length + Breadth + Height of Brain Part): 3 in percent of Trunk Length. Relative Ear Size = Height × Breadth of Outer Ear in percent of Head Length times Total Head Height. For all other details of the absolute and relative measurements see Schultz 1929.

PROPORTION	MACAQUE (28)	GIBBON (80)	SIAMANG (9)	ORANG (13)	CHIMP. (30)	GORILLA (5)	MAN (25)
Chest Girth : Trunk Length	104	152	170	187	165	217	160
Shoulder Breadth : Trunk Length	34	53	52	62	57	70	65
Hip Breadth : Trunk Length	34	43	47	50	52	66	61
Chest Breadth : Chest Depth	88	117	125	126	127	138	128
Lower Limb Length : Trunk Length	100	148	131	116	127	124	169
Upper Limb Length : Trunk Length	113	243	233	200	172	172	148
Upper Limb Length : Lower Limb Length	112	165	178	172	136	138	88
Foot Length : Trunk Length	44	52	52	62	50	47	48
Hand Length : Trunk Length	29	59	51	53	49	40	37
Thumb Length : Trunk Length	16	31	28	23	23	22	25
Head Size : Trunk Length	21	26	26	26	26	29	30
Total Face Height : Trunk Length	21	19	23	30	27	28	24
Upper Face Height : Head Size	74	52	62	86	77	72	50
Relative Ear Size	14	13	8	3	17	4	5

manifests itself also in the relative width of the hipbones and of the sternum, as well as in the shape of the thorax, the curvature of the ribs, and so on, as will be shown in the discussion of the skeleton. With the widening of the chest in all hominoids the shoulderblades have been shifted to the broad back from their lateral position, typical for all quadrupedal monkeys, prosimians and most other mammals (Fig. 1). The shoulder-joints of the apes and man have come to lie in one frontal plane with the spinal column and no longer in one plane with the sternum, and they face laterally instead of ventrally, as in monkeys.

From the data in Table 2 it is seen also that this important and general increase in the relative girth and breadth of the trunk in all hominoids has advanced more in siamangs than in gibbons and has become much more extreme in gorillas than in man. The latter difference is clearly apparent in Fig. 2, where it should also be noticed that the height of the trunk of the man-like apes

is accentuated by the high position of their shoulders. Even with the arms hanging down freely the clavicles of the apes diverge steeply toward the high shoulders, whereas those of man are directed almost horizontally, except in early fetal life, when the shoulders still lie well above the sternoclavicular joints (Schultz, 1926). Externally man is the only hominoid with a clearly-formed neck, deserving that name, because in the full-grown apes the anatomical neck is hidden laterally behind the high shoulders, in front by the large face and dorsally by the powerful nuchal musculature, reaching to the high shoulders, as also shown in Fig. 2.

The proportionate lengths of the limbs surpass in all recent hominoids those of catarrhine monkeys according to the relative indices in Table 2. The total lower limb length (from great trochanter to sole of foot) in its percentage relation to the trunk length (suprasternal notch to upper edge of pubic symphysis) varies but little around 100

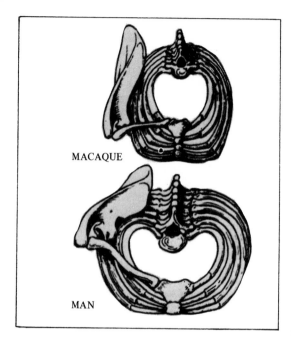

MACAQUE

MAN

Figure 1: Cephalic view of thorax and right shoulder girdle of adult macaque and man. (*From Schultz 1957*)

in adult Old World monkeys, and among the apes it has increased least in orang-utans with their exceptionally weak legs and most in gibbons. The variations of this proportion range in 80 adults of *Hylobates lar* from 132 to 166 and in 30 adult chimpanzees from 114 to 150, with the highest values of both series clearly surpassing the lowest ones among normal human beings. For instance, in a series of only 25 adult bodies from several human races the author obtained corresponding range of 141 to 179. It can be stated, therefore, that it is merely on an average that man has acquired the relatively longest lower extremities and that some gibbons and even chimpanzees can have proportionately longer legs than have some men at the completion of growth. Incidentally, the highest of all values for this same index are found in certain prosimians, particularly those specialized for leaping, such as

tarsiers, sifakas, and so on. It should also be mentioned that the great average relative leg length of man is ontogenetically a remarkably late acquisition, since at birth it still averages only about 110, a value which is not at all outstanding among newborns of other primates.

The relative total length of the upper limb (from acromion to the tip of the longest finger in percentage of trunk length) surpasses even in man all the corresponding values for Old World monkeys, reaching in some races maximum figures of 188. The latter fall well within the ranges of variations of adult chimpanzees (157 to 200) and gorillas (148 to 187). Among all primates this relative arm length has increased by far the most in the Asiatic apes, particularly in the gibbons, whose arms measure individually up to 274 percent of their trunk length and in upright posture reach clear to the ground in spite of the high shoulders and comparatively long legs. This specialization in the length of the arms of the best brachiators is far more extreme than the increase in the length of the legs of bipedal man. It is specially the forearm which has become so extraordinarily lengthened in the Asiatic apes, as shown by the following averages of the brachial index (radius length in percent of humerus length): Gibbons = 113, siamangs = 111, orang-utans = 100, chimpanzees = 93, gorillas = 80, man = ca. 76 (Schultz 1937). The increased length of the lower limb of man, however, has not affected one segment more than the other, because the analogous crural indices (tibia length in percent of femur length) differ but little among the hominoids, averaging 87 in gibbons and siamangs, 92 in orang-utans, 83 in chimpanzees, 80 in gorillas, and 83 to 89 in the various races of man (Schultz 1937).

The intermembral index, which expresses the total length of the upper limb in percentage of that of the lower one, is one of the few proportions of adults which distinguishes man from the

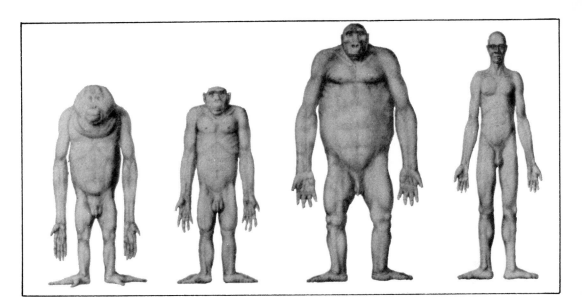

Figure 2: The body proportions of an adult orangutan, chimpanzee, gorilla, and man, reduced to the same scale and drawn without hair and with straightened lower limbs and feet turned laterally facilitate comparisons. (*From Schultz 1933*)

apes even if the ranges of individual variations are taken into consideration. In all adult catarrhines the upper limbs surpass the lower ones in length, except in man, in whom the legs become postnatally longer than the arms, as they do also in many prosimians (Schultz 1954; 1956). The distinction of this important and intraspecifically quite constant proportion is in man not nearly as marked as it is in siamangs, whose average intermembral index of 178 has changed much more from the corresponding average of 112 for macaques, which represents roughly an unspecialized condition. An intermembral index without the inclusion of hand and foot, which has been obtained from measurements of the long limb bones of many very large series of adult skeletons, also separates man from the apes, but not from all other primates, as shown by the following few data: The length of humerus + radius in percentage of the length of femur + tibia varies in a total of 753 skeletons of different human races between 64 and 79 and averages 128 in gibbons, 148 in siamangs, 144 in orang-utans, 107 in chimpanzees, and 117 in gorillas. The same index varies among catarrhine monkeys between 75 and 100, thus reaching occasionally just below the highest figures of man. The lowest of all these intermembral indices are found in the prosimian genera of *Tarsius, Propithecus* and *Galago* with values very near 50 (Schultz 1937; 1954).

The hand-like grasping ability of the feet of most monkeys and apes, in contrast to the lack thereof in our feet, had led Schreber (1775) to propose a radical separation between man and the nonhuman primates known at that time. Blumenbach (1791) followed this with the formal division of Linné's preceding single order of Primates in the two orders of Bimana and Quadrumana, the former being reserved exclusively for man. This naive classification according to one highly overrated distinction persisted in some quarters for a surprisingly long time. Nevertheless the feet and hands of primates are of outstanding interest because they have generally retained original pentadactyl conditions with much more

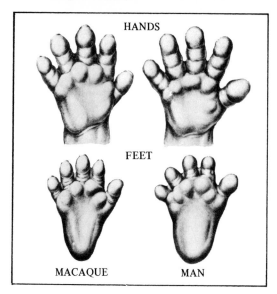

HANDS

FEET

MACAQUE   MAN

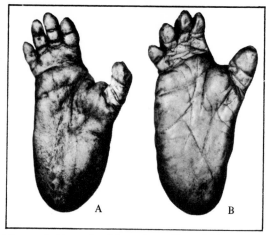

Figure 4: Feet of adult male gorillas: (A) western, (B) eastern subspecies. (From Schultz 1931)

Figure 3: (Above) hands and (Below) feet of (Left) a fetus of a macaque and (Right) of a man with sitting heights of 24 mm. (From Schultz 1957)

limited modifications than they have in so many other mammals.

In early stages of fetal development the feet of man are far more similar to those of monkeys than they are to their own, final condition in adult life. As shown in Fig. 3, the human fetal foot has a relatively short, abduced first toe and relatively long phalangeal parts of the other toes among which the middle one is the longest. The primitive touch pads are well formed and so are the cutaneous interdigital webs, particularly between the second and third toes, where they are retained throughout life in some chimpanzees, occasional men and gibbons, and nearly all siamangs, the last having gained their name of *Symphalangus syndactylus* from that feature.

Such ontogenetic findings leave no doubt that the foot of adult man with all its specializations for bipedal walking has been transformed from the prevailing type of primate feet, adapted chiefly to grasping and climbing. That such transformations have primarily resulted from modifications in the rates of growth of different parts of the feet, has been shown by detailed studies of the individual development of different primates (Schultz 1956).

The eastern gorilla, discovered only at the beginning of our century and hence unknown when all apes had been assigned to the "Quadrumana," resembles man most closely in regard to the outer form of its foot (Fig. 4). The grasping ability of the first toe is decidedly more limited than in typical western gorillas and the other toes appear to be remarkably short and better suited for terrestrial than arboreal life.[2] In the gibbons, siamangs, and orang-utans the toes II to V are exceptionally long and together serve as a perfect climbing-hook for their life in the trees. The opposite extreme exists in the foot of terrestrial man, whose lateral toes have become shortened not only externally, but also in their entire phalangeal portions, to a much more marked

---

[2] In walking on flat ground the first toe is abduced, but not rotated. The separate, distal parts of the other toes are extremely short on account of thick plantar padding which extends far distally, but the total length of the phalanges is only moderately shortened as indicated in the foot of an eastern gorilla in Fig. 5.

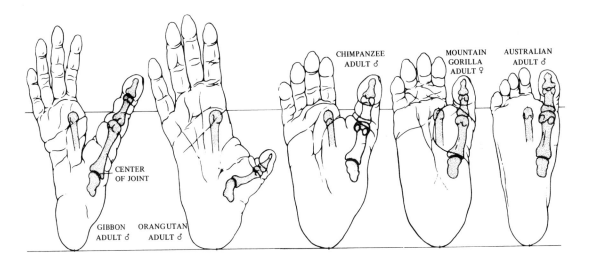

Figure 5: Feet of adult hominoids showing the exact relation between the outer form and some skeletal parts of the same specimens, all reduced to equal length from heel to second metatarso-phalangeal joint. (*From Schultz 1950*)

degree than in any other primate (Fig. 5). The first toe, which is so uniform and thumb-like in all adult monkeys, has become specialized in widely different ways among the hominoids. In the Hylobatidae this digit is remarkably long and nearly to its base free of the sole, giving it a great mobility, but only moderate strength. This unique condition corresponds to that of the thumb in the same apes, which is also comparatively long and free of the palm for most of its metacarpal segment. In eastern gorillas and in man only the distal part of the phalangeal portion of the great toe really reaches beyond the plantar pillow. In all orang-utans the permanently abduced first toes have clearly degenerated as in no other primate. Not only is this digit relatively short and exceptionally far proximal, but in more than half of all orang-utans it also contains only one phalanx instead of the normal two,[3] as shown by the example in Fig. 5. This elimination of a phalanx is analogous to the reduction of the short fifth toe of man, in which the middle phalanx is quite commonly lacking, or to the nearly universal suppression of the outer thumbs of *Ateles* and of *Colobus*, or of the outer second fingers of *Arctocebus* and *Perodicticus*. That the entire feet of orang-utans have become one-sidedly specialized as extremely long hooks is evident also from their enormous proportionate length, which surpasses that of all other higher primates according to the data in Table 2. When standing upright on flat ground orang-utans have to support themselves awkwardly on the lateral edges of their outwardly twisted feet with the long and curved phalanges of the digits II to V tightly flexed as in a fist.

---

[3] Tuttle and Rogers (1966) have recently reported this congenital bilateral lack of a terminal phalanx in the first toes of orang-utans in 60 percent of 30 animals from the Yerkes Primate Center with a surprisingly unequal distribution in both sexes, namely in 87 percent of females, whereas in only 33 percent of males. According to the writer's former (1941; 1956) and latest records on a total of 121 other orang-utans of known sex, the same condition existed in 62 percent of all specimens, females alone showing it in 73 percent, but males in only 49 percent of the cases. In a few additional orang-utans this reduction was present on one side only.

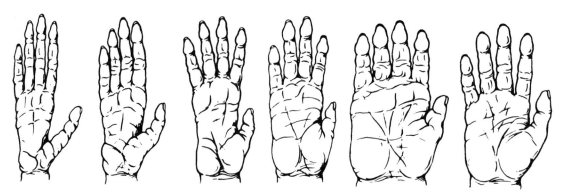

Figure 6: Hands of adult hominoids, reduced to same total length. (*From left to right*) Gibbon, siamang, orang-utan, chimpanzee, gorilla, and man. (*From Schultz 1965*)

The total length of the hand in relation to the trunk length has its maximum average among all hominoids in gibbons and its minimum in man, as shown by the data in Table 2. The hand is also most slender in the former, though broadest not in man, but in gorillas (Fig. 6). The proportionate length of the phalangeal and metacarpal parts of the fingers has remained remarkably uniform in all higher primates. In the middle digit, for example, this relation equals approximately 3:2 in the long-handed gibbons as well as in the great apes and even in man with his short hands (Schultz 1930). In contrast to this, the corresponding proportion of the hominoid feet shows very marked generic differences, since the lengths of the phalangeal and metatarsal parts of the toes have evidently changed independently of each other.

The thumb is of particular interest as a vital aid for most arboreal primates in securing good holds on branches and on account of its gradually perfected usefulness for many additional purposes. The thumb of all hominoids is longer in relation to their size, as represented by trunk length, than it is in any monkeys and reaches its maximum relative length in gibbons, while man and the great apes have very similar, smaller averages,

according to Table 2. Only in its relation to the greatest hand length is the thumb of man longer than that of the apes and thereby reaches beyond the palm, as shown in Fig. 6. This, however, does not support the frequent claim that the human thumb has become longer, because it is the length of the other fingers of man and even the size of his entire hand which are comparatively small and may possibly have become reduced only after man's hands had become freed from their former functions of support and locomotion. The free part of the thumb branches from the palm much nearer the wrist in all catarrhines than in any New World monkeys and at the same time it has become very much rotated to face the other digits for effective opposability. As shown by the examples in Fig. 3, these conditions are not yet present in early fetal life when the thumb still branches from near the base of the second finger and is as yet not the least rotated. This stage of development remains practically unchanged in platyrrhines, whereas in all catarrhines the thumb shifts and rotates during later fetal development as it did in its evolutionary specialization (for details see Schultz 1926; 1949; 1956).

As a unique specialization of chimpanzees and gorillas is to be mentioned that they support themselves in quadrupedal posture on the knuckles of their fingers II to V, since these digits become automatically flexed with the slightest dorsal extension of the hand on account of the

MACACA
NEMESTR

MAN

CHIMPANZEE

GORILLA

Figure 7: Different positions of the hands in quadrupedal posture in some catarrhines. (*Drawn from photographs*)

relatively short flexor muscles of the fingers. Undoubtedly in closest connection therewith the skin on the dorsal side of the middle segments of these fingers has developed regular dermatoglyphics, which are not present in any other primates (Biegert 1961). This support on the knuckles in standing quadrupedally raises the level of vision and the mechanical finger flexion is of advantage in hanging under branches as well as in carrying objects during bipedal walk. These specializations are not clearly developed in orang-utans and totally lacking in man, gibbons and all other catarrhines (Fig. 7).

The last four indices in Table 2 express some

proportions of the head in an exact numerical manner. The percentage relation between the mean head diameter and the trunk length is significantly greater in all hominoids than in macaques and other monkeys. This, however, shows the corresponding difference in relative brain size in only a very approximate, general way, because the outer dimensions of the brain part of the head are much influenced by the development of the supraorbital arch and the thickness of the temporal muscles as well as the existence of cranial crests. In gorillas the head height can furthermore be greatly increased by the frequent thick subcutaneous pad of connective tissue near the vertex (Straus 1942) (see Fig. 12).

The size of the face in its relation to that of the trunk is much larger in the pongids than in the other hominoids and surpasses even in man that of gibbons. According to the relation between the upper face height and the mean head diameter the three great apes are again distinguished by the largest averages and man and the gibbon by the smallest ones, with the siamang bridging the gap. From these and various other relative measurements, representing the proportionate size of the face, it has become very evident that it is not the face of man which has become exceptionally small, but the faces of the great apes and most of all those of male orangutans and gorillas, which have evolved to an

Figure 8: Female white-handed gibbon with its young of 2 months. (*Photographed by J. Klages, from Schultz 1965*)

enormous size. Not only gibbons, but a variety of monkeys have proportionately just as small, or even smaller, faces than man, and this not for allometric reasons alone (see Figs. 8, 30, 31).

Characters of the Outer Body

The pigmentation of skin and hair can vary very extensively not only in man, but also in all manlike apes and, furthermore, can change with age at least as much in the latter as in the former. For instance, many chimpanzees have as light a skin color as Europeans, while others acquire regionally brown or black skin sooner or later, often extending even to the palms and soles. As in some colored human beings, the epithelial lining of the gums and palate of apes often show dark pigment in irregular distribution. The hair color of *Hylobates lar* varies even within local populations to a surprising degree between nearly white, brown, and black, except for the always white hands, feet, and brows (Fig. 9). Among chimpanzees rare individuals also can have very light or reddish hair, and in some young gorillas the hair is gray or chestnut-brown instead of nearly black. The hair on the back of old male gorillas turns very light so that they well deserve their name of "silver-back." Full-grown orang-utans often develop hair of record length, measuring at times more than 70 cm. on the back and shoulders. The density of hair is another variable feature of hominoids, as shown by the data in Table 3. As a rule this density is most marked on the head and much smaller on the ventral than on the dorsal side of the trunk. In male gorillas the entire wide chest becomes practically bare with advancing age. Gibbons have by far the densest hair of all catarrhines and the difference between their extreme hair density and the very moderate density of the great apes is much more pronounced than the difference between the latter and that of man. It is of interest also that the siamang re-

Figure 9: An old male orang-utan in the London Zoo.

sembles the pongids more nearly than the gibbons in regard to its hair density, as in many other features. Many adult orang-utans develop remarkably conspicuous moustaches and/or beards which usually are of lighter color than their other hair. They occur only in occasional

Table 3: The average numbers of hairs per square centimeter of skin on the vertex, back, and chest of adult primates (from Schultz 1931, and some later data).

	VERTEX	BACK	CHEST
Macaques	650	480	70
Gibbons	2100	1720	600
Siamangs	715	430	260
Orang-utans	158	175	105
Chimpanzees	185	100	70
Gorillas	410	145	4
Europeans	330	0	3
Negroes	305	0	0
Mongolians	128	0	0

Figure 10: Head of another old male orang-utan with strong moustache and beard and differently formed cheek pads. (*Drawn from a photograph*)

females and can be totally absent in a minority of even fully-grown males. Similarly striking individual variations without close sex-linkage exist also in the unique cheekpads of adult orang-utans (Figs. 9 and 10). These puzzling formations are never exactly alike in any two specimens, they can be lacking in some few males and fairly well formed in rare females. They are already indicated in fetuses by perpendicular skin folds and in newborns by faint ridges of converging hairs, but any further development appears only after puberty (Schultz 1941; 1956).

All catarrhine monkeys and all gibbons and siamangs have in common sharply bordered horny callosities, covering directly the ischial tuberosities and thus serving as hard pads in sitting. Ontogenetically, however, these structures differ significantly in the Cercopithecoidea and Hylobatidae since they appear early in the prenatal development of the former, whereas not until the time of birth or even later in the latter, when they replace the preceding lanugo hair of the corresponding region (Schultz 1933; 1937; 1956). Many individuals of the great apes can also acquire such cornified callosities of considerable size and thickness, but only gradually during postnatal growth. In man alone has nothing like it ever been recorded, evidently because the gluteal musculature is interposed between skin and bone.

The volar sides of the hands and feet of all primates are covered by highly specialized, tactile skin, bearing complicated ridge patterns of so-called dermatoglyphics which appear already on the embryonic touchpads and retain their detailed arrangement throughout life. The systematic and very comprehensive investigation of these structures by Biegert (1961) supports convincingly the assumption of a common origin of all recent hominoids and the conclusion that the three families must have evolved in diverging directions, because their differently specialized ridge patterns can all be derived from generally more primitive conditions of lower catarrhines, from which man has not deviated the most in all respects.

All simian primates have normally only two mammary glands left which develop near the second or third ribs where they usually remain permanently. In man alone do they migrate caudally during growth, to become centered at about the fourth intercostal space. In orang-utans and some species of monkeys the nipples lie far laterally near the axillae, but in the hylobatids and African great apes they have come practically as close together as in man. The glandular tissue of the breasts is widely spread out over the chest with little difference in its thickness in typical monkeys, but among the hominoids it is much more limited in extent while increasing in depth

during lactation until many female apes develop similarly protruding or even hanging breasts as exist in women.

Among external features may here also be mentioned the throat pouches which are most conspicuous in adult siamangs and orang-utans. In old males of the latter species these pouches can reach all the way to the axillae and hold more than 6 liters of air when fully extended. The laryngeal pouches of gorillas can extend equally far, but are usually less voluminous. Among chimpanzees the corresponding sacs are as a rule of very modest size, but some remarkably large ones have been described, including a record one of an old female, which appeared like a huge goitre (Yerkes 1943). The exact function of these laryngeal formations, which have been thoroughly reviewed by Starck and Schneider (1960), cannot yet be satisfactorily explained. They are not simply secondary sex characters, even though they are usually best developed in old males. Their supposed role as a resonating apparatus is also unconvincing in view of the fact that gibbons and siamangs can call equally loud, but only the latter have and make use of pouches with an effective volume.

The external genital organs of the hominoids have been dealt with in a voluminous literature, which has recently been reviewed by Hill (1958). For the purposes of this paper it must suffice to discuss briefly the most interesting generic differences in these structures. The male genitalia and, particularly, the testes are exceptionally small in gorillas, whereas comparatively large in chimpanzees, as shown by the following data: The testicular weight in percentage of body weight averages among adults 0.27 in chimpanzees, 0.08 in man and gibbons, 0.05 in orang-utans (Schultz 1938) and only about 0.02 or even less in gorillas (Wislocki 1942, Hall-Cragg 1962). The permanent descent of the testes takes place some time before birth in man,

Figure 12: Head of an adult male gorilla. (*Drawn from a photograph*)

Figure 11: Heads of a female and a male chimpanzee at different ages. (*From Schultz 1940*)

whereas usually not until during infancy in the apes. The scrotum of all pongids lies behind the penis, as in man, but in the Hylobatidae the paired scrotal sacs are situated on both sides or even toward the front of the penis. A so-called baculum or penis bone occurs in all male hominoids, except man, but is proportionately much smaller in the apes than in many monkeys. Of the external female genitalia it is specially noteworthy that those of the gibbons resemble the human condition more closely than do those of the great apes, whose labia majora tend to disappear during early growth. Important generic differences exist also in regard to the cyclic swelling of the female pudendal region which reaches an enormous size in mature chimpanzees during each menstrual period, is barely indicated in

gorillas, occurs only toward the end of pregnancy in orang-utans, and is totally lacking in gibbons and man. An excellent and detailed discussion of these sex swellings, which are found also in a great variety of Old World monkeys, has been published by Harms (1956).

Among the external features of the head one may mention the remarkable existence of deep wrinkles in the skin of chimpanzees and gorillas, present already in older fetuses and becoming most marked on and below the eyelids, the cheeks and the region of the mouth. The numerous oral wrinkles are undoubtedly connected with the great mobility of the large lips (Figs. 11 and 12). The shape and size of the outer nose differs enormously among hominoids, even though the noses of all are supported by the same few cartilages, as shown by the examples in Fig. 13. The septum cartilage of the apes projects very little

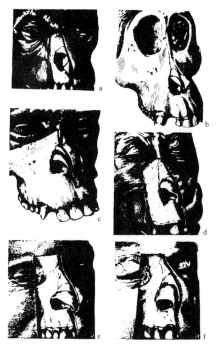

Figure 13: Noses and nasal cartilages of (a), a siamang, (b), orang-utan, (c), chimpanzee, (d), gorilla, (e), Negro, and (f), European. (*From Schultz 1935*)

beyond the bony aperture, corresponding to their flat outer noses, and the roof cartilage forms only a small continuation of the nasal bones, especially in gorillas. The wing cartilages are also not nearly as large in the apes as they are in man, not even those in the excessively broad and thick nasal wings of gorillas. In the captive adult male gorilla "Gargantua" the author found a roof cartilage of less than 1 cm² and paper-thin alar cartilages, limited to the nasal center and not extending into the huge wings, which were mere

pads of fat. In contrast to this, the prominent nose of man is far more extensively supported by cartilage, which closely determines its shape. While the nearly immobile nasal wings of the apes consist of little more than skin and fat, the thin and mobile wings of human noses are extensively stiffened by cartilage to keep them from being sucked shut with every inhalation.

The outer ears of the hominoids differ widely in their relative size, as shown by the last index in Table 2. Orang-utans are distinguished by the proportionately smallest ears of all primates, whereas chimpanzees by nearly the largest ones among the Simiae. No functional reasons can be given for this extreme difference between these pongids, of which one has its ears atrophied and the other excessively overdeveloped in individually variable degrees. Ontogenetically this is a direct result of very different rates of growth, since small ears simply increase their size far less than large ones, particularly postnatally, inasmuch as newborn orang-utans still have relatively larger ears than adults. The edge of the helix shows in hominoids a strong tendency to become rolled-in not only on top, but also posteriorly, where this occurs rarely and then as a mere indication among the lower catarrhines (Fig. 14). Clearly pointed ears, commonly called "satyr ears," are among monkeys typical for only macaques and baboons and do not occur in any hominoids, not even in early stages of development.[4] There is no justification, therefore, to interpret the occasional "Darwinian tubercles" on human ears as an atavistic manifestation of ancestral, pointed ears (Lasinski 1960). True ear lobules, free of cartilage, exist not only in most human beings, but also in the African apes and some monkeys, while they are absent in gibbons and nearly all orang-utans (Fig. 14). The extrinsic ear musculature of the hominoids is poorly developed in comparison with that of monkeys,

---

[4] The pointed form of the ear of the fetus of supposedly an orang-utan, pictured by Darwin (1874), is clearly due to accidental distortion through having been preserved in a tight container. Furthermore this specimen is certainly not an orang-utan, but in the writer's opinion a gibbon.

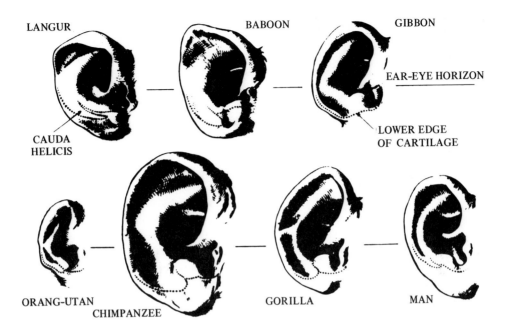

LANGUR   BABOON   GIBBON

EAR-EYE HORIZON

CAUDA
HELICIS

LOWER EDGE
OF CARTILAGE

ORANG-UTAN   GORILLA   MAN
CHIMPANZEE

Figure 14: The outer ears of some adult catarrhines with the lower border of the cartilage shown by the dotted lines. (*From Schultz 1950*)

whose ears are correspondingly more mobile.

Among the superficial characters there are finally to be mentioned the interesting palatine ridges, or rugae, which have been retained even by man as utterly useless remnants. These transverse folds of the lining of the hard palate exist in nearly all mammals and appear already at early stages of intrauterine development. As a rule they aid the newborn in firmly holding the maternal nipple and later in life they not only lead food to the grinding teeth, but, when cornified, are also helpful in crunching food. Many mammals have their entire hard palates covered with dense rows of parallel rugae of considerable and very effective height. In all prosimians they are also well developed, though not as numerous as in most ungulates. The great majority of monkeys still possess from 6 to 10 of these transverse folds, extending mostly back to the last molars, as shown by the example of the macaque in Fig. 15. In the higher primates one can recognize a clear trend to limit these ridges to the anterior part of the palate and to interrupt and ramify these, now low, folds into more or less irregular and asymmetrical patterns. According to the numerous data, collected by the writer (1958), gibbons, siamangs, and orang-utans have as rough averages 8 pair of rugae, which still often reach as far back as the second molars. A quite complicated pattern is characteristic for chimpanzees, among which the highest numbers of rugae have been found. These numbers varied between 5 and 15 in 46 chimpanzees, between 3 and 10 in 16 gorillas, and between 2 and 8 in 519 human beings. These folds, which retain their number throughout life, extend only to the first molars in the African apes and often to merely the posterior premolars in man. It is of interest to note that with advancing degeneration of these structures they have become specially variable in most of their details.

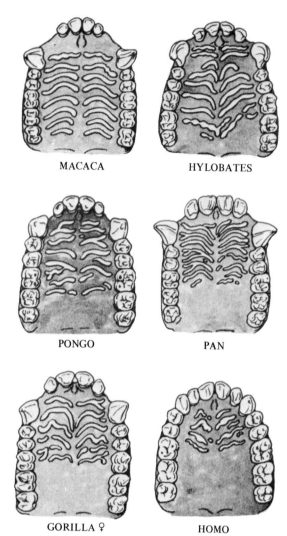

MACACA   HYLOBATES

PONGO   PAN

GORILLA ♀   HOMO

Figure 15: Typical palatine ridges of adult hominoids and of a macaque. (*From Schultz 1958*)

Skeleton

Of all bodily parts of the recent man-like apes the skeleton has become best known because it is available in our collections in numbers adequate for a full consideration of its important intraspecific variability. That the latter is of great

interest in the study of phylogenetic problems can here be shown by the example of the numerical variations of the vertebrae. With only few highly specialized exceptions all mammals possess normally 7 cervical vertebrae. For primates it can also be confidently assumed that this same number has remained unchanged, because 6 or 8 of these vertebrae have been found in only very rare cases. In striking contrast to this high stability of the phylogenetically constant number of cervical vertebrae, there have occurred extremely great changes, accompanied by very marked variability, in the number of vertebrae in the tails of primates, which ranges from 0 to 35! In all recent hominoids the tail has become extremely reduced, except for its brief appearance in embryonic life before it is overgrown by adjoining tissues and its more numerous segments have been resorbed or fused. In adults the rudimentary coccygeal vertebrae have been found to vary between 3 and 5 and to average 4.2 in a total of 745 human skeletons. In the man-like apes this reduction has generally progressed even farther, namely to averages between only 2.2 in siamangs and 3.3 in chimpanzees, with a total range of individual variations for apes from 0 to 6 (Schultz 1930; 1961).

The combined number of thoracic and lumbar vertebrae is a clear expression for the important segmental position of the pelvic ring on the vertebral column. This number fluctuates among primates between 15 and 24, with values above 20 occurring only in certain prosimians and a few exceptional platyrrhines. Among all Old World monkeys these vertebrae number as a rule 19 and vary merely between 18 and 20. The recent hominoids are the only primates showing a pronounced reduction in this number and hence a clear trend to shift the pelvis in a cranial direction. As is evident from the data in Table 4, this specialization has progressed most in orang-utans and also more in the other pongids than it has in man. The relevant marked difference between gibbons and siamangs is of interest as showing

Table 4: Percentage distribution of variations in the number of thoracic + lumbar vertebrae and of sacral vertebrae and average numbers of these vertebrae in hominoids and macaques (from Schultz 1961). To limit this table to the most significant data, all cases of transitional vertebrae have here been included with the nearest lower variations. Numbers of skeletons examined are listed in parentheses.

	NUMBER OF VERTEBRAE	MACAQUE (216)	GIBBON (319)	SIAMANG (29)	ORANG (127)	CHIMP. (162)	GORILLA (81)	MAN (125)
THORACIC + LUMBAR	15	—	—	4	19	—	—	—
	16	—	—	10	74	29	43	7
	17	—	5	48	7	68	56	91
	18	5	72	38	—	3	1	2
	19	91	23	—	—	—	—	—
	20	4	—	—	—	—	—	—
	Average	19.0	18.2	17.3	15.9	16.8	16.6	17.0
SACRAL	2	3	—	—	—	—	—	—
	3	93	3	—	—	—	—	—
	4	4	42	38	3	1	1	3
	5	—	51	55	59	36	36	72
	6	—	4	7	36	55	56	24
	7	—	—	—	2	8	6	1
	8	—	—	—	—	1	1	—
	Average	3.0	4.6	4.7	5.4	5.7	5.7	5.2

again a closer approach to the great apes in the latter than in the former, which are the only hominoids which still have occasionally 19 thoracic + lumbar vertebrae. This reduction of the number of presacral segments took place mainly at the expense of the lumbar region. The great majority of catarrhine monkeys has retained the original number of 7 lumbar vertebrae, combined with 12 thoracic ones, but in all recent hominoids the lumbar region has been shortened by at least one segment and usually by several. On an average gibbons and man possess 5 lumbar vertebrae, siamangs 4.4, orang-utans 4.0, and both the African apes 3.6 with only 3 existing in more than a third of the cases (for details see Schultz 1961). Due to the extremely short lumbar region of the great apes and the fact that also their extremely long iliac blades can reach high above the lumbosacral border, the iliac crests approach the last pair of ribs so exceptionally closely that the lateral flexibility of the trunk has become far more re-

stricted in the pongids than in man, the Hylobatidae and, of course, the lower catarrhines. This is very evident from the examples in Figs. 16, 17, and 18, and explains the necessarily close correspondence in the transverse direction and curvature of the ilia and the lower part of the thorax in the great apes.

The original number of vertebrae, fused in the sacrum, was most likely only 3 and this has been retained practically unchanged by the great majority of lower primates. A significant increase in this number of sacral vertebrae has taken place quite independently in two groups, namely in the lorisoid prosimians, which have as many as 9 such segments, and in all the hominoids, as shown in Table 4. This phylogenetic trend to enlarge the solid sacral wedge between the hipbones has progressed least among the higher primates in gibbons and most in the great apes, agreeing thereby with the degrees of specialization in the reduction of presacral vertebrae. That the addition of verte-

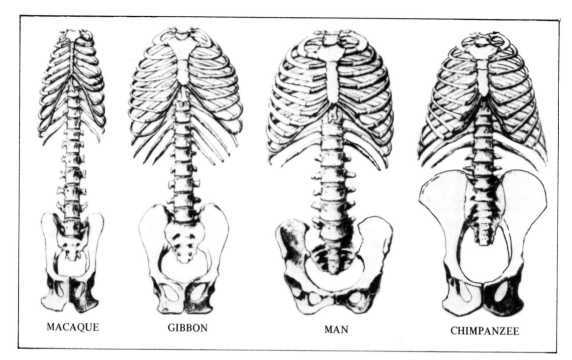

MACAQUE   GIBBON   MAN   CHIMPANZEE

Figure 16: Exact drawings of ligamentous trunk skeletons of four adult female primates, reduced to same total length. (*From Schultz 1950*)

brae to the hominoid sacrum has not yet become stabilized, is shown by the remarkable range of numerical variations of the sacral segments in gorillas and chimpanzees, which extends over 5 figures, whereas in monkeys at most over only 3. "Unilateral variations," represented by asymmetrical transition-vertebrae, with typical lumbar characters on one side and sacral ones on the other, are also exceptionally frequent in all apes, as has been demonstrated in a special publication by the author (1961).

The proportional length of the different regions of the vertebral column depends not only on the number of segments but often also on other factors, as is very evident, for example, by the extremely different lengths of the neck in giraffes and in elephants in spite of both containing 7 cervical vertebrae. In primates the relatively longest necks belong to the hominoids whose cervical re-

gions equal always more than 20 percent of the entire length of the presacral spine in contrast to the considerably shorter neck length of all lower catarrhines. Man and the man-like apes are dis-

Table 5: Average length of the cervical region of the vertebral column in percentage of the trunk length and average lengths of the cervical, thoracic, and lumbar regions in percentage of the total presacral spine length (with the wet intervertebral discs) in adult hominoids and macaques (after Schultz 1961).

	TRUNK LENGTH	PRESACRAL SPINE LENGTH		
	CERVICAL REGION	CERVICAL REGION	THORACIC REGION	LUMBAR REGION
Macaque	17.2	16.6	40.8	42.6
Gibbon	21.7	21.0	48.7	30.3
Siamang	23.5	20.8	50.1	29.1
Orang-utan	24.2	24.5	50.9	24.6
Chimpanzee	22.5	23.5	53.5	23.0
Gorilla	24.2	24.2	51.2	24.6
Man	25.3	22.0	45.1	32.9

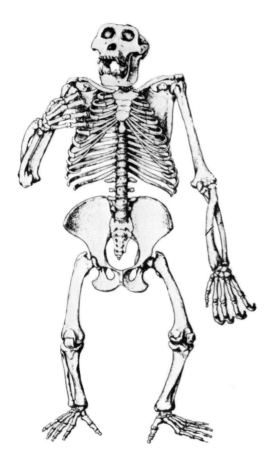

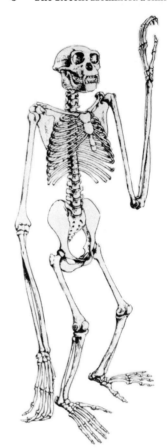

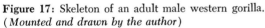

Figure 17: Skeleton of an adult male western gorilla. (*Mounted and drawn by the author*)

Figure 18: Skeleton of an adult siamang.(*Mounted and drawn by the author*)

tinguished from all other catarrhines by their relatively longer thoracic and much shorter lumbar regions, as shown in Table 5 and by many more data in a former publication by the author (1961). As a rule the lumbar region is actually longer than the thoracic one in the Old World monkeys, whereas much shorter in all higher primates and this even more so in the apes than in man.

The thickness and, particularly, the breadth of the bodies of the thoracic and lumbar vertebrae is relatively much greater in hominoids than in monkeys (Schultz 1953). This difference can only in part be due to the different body weight, carried by the spinal column, because the small gibbons as

well as the large gorillas surpass the cercopithecoids in this respect. The largest relative breadth of the lumbar vertebrae exists in man, most likely as a result of his erect posture which has changed the vertebral column from what is functionally a carrying beam in quadrupeds into the only true upright *column* with a thickness gradually increasing toward the base, as in the trunk of a tree.

Among the many other characteristics of the hominoid vertebrae there are some of particular interest because they have become most highly specialized in man, or else decidedly less so than in the apes. For instance, the dorsal spines of the cervical vertebrae of all great apes have acquired

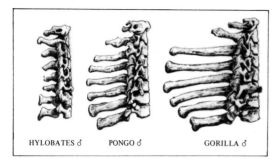

Figure 19: Side views of the first eight vertebrae of adult male gibbon, orang-utan, and gorilla. (*From Schultz 1961*)

an exceptional length to support their powerful nuchal musculature, needed in carrying the heavy and very poorly balanced head (Fig. 19). Cervical spines of such great length occur among all other primates only in the prosimian pottos in which they protrude on the surface and serve for protection when the head and neck are much flexed. In other mammals one often finds similarly overdeveloped vertebral spines, but only in the anterior part of the thoracic region and in a few ungulates also on the seventh cervical vertebra. Since recent and fossil man have as short dorsal spines on the vertebrae of their necks as have gibbons and all monkeys, it can be concluded that only the pongids have become highly specialized in this respect. Especially in full-grown male orang-utans and gorillas, these spines attain such an excessive length that the movability of their necks is very restricted. In the lateral processes of the cervical vertebrae exist also marked differences among the hominoids, especially in the formation of the foramina transversalia, through most of which pass the vertebral arteries. These openings between the true transverse processes and the vestigial costal elements are very rarely missing in even the seventh vertebra of man, but in the other primates it is rare to find corresponding foramina in this segment. In gibbons, for example, real foramina are lacking in the seventh ver-

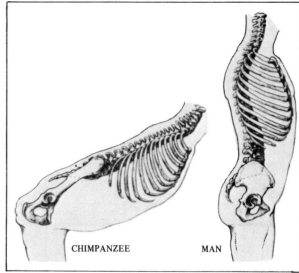

Figure 20: The curvature of the vertebral column and the position and size of the hip bone in an adult ape and man. (*From Schultz 1957*)

tebra in two thirds of the cases and in orang-utans even in all cases. The latter are distinguished by the frequent absence of transverse foramina in also the sixth and fifth vertebrae of the neck, which bear at best mere notches in place of holes (Schultz 1961).

The longitudinal axis of the vertebral column in a position of rest deviates from a straight line much more in man than in the nonhuman primates. The regionally alternating curves of the human spine, shown in Fig. 20, increase the springiness of the perpendicular presacral column. The most marked change from a straight continuation of the row of vertebrae exists in man at the lumbo-sacral border, where the sacrum is so abruptly bent back that it forms a striking promontory with the lumbar region. Man, however, is not the only primate possessing such a promontory, as has often been claimed, but he is the one whose sacrum has become dorso-flexed most extremely in connection with other unique specializations in his entire pelvis. As shown by the

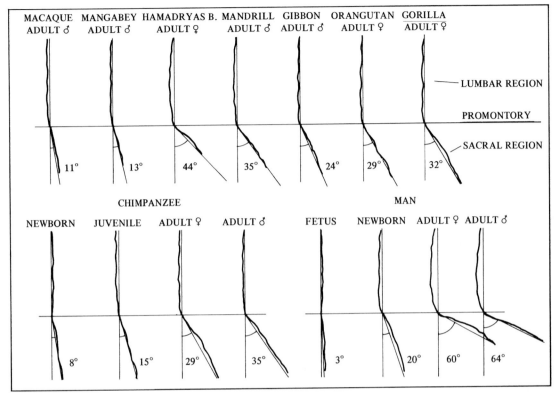

Figure 21: Exact ventral profiles of the lumbar and sacral vertebral regions and angles between their different directions in some catarrhine primates. (*From Schultz 1961*)

examples in Fig. 21, all man-like apes have also acquired unmistakable promontories as adults, though not nearly as marked ones as that of man. The angle between the ventral profiles of the lumbar and of the sacral region increases during growth in all higher primates; in man it is as yet barely indicated in the middle of fetal life, reaches about 20° at birth and somewhere between 60° and as much as 80° in adults. In apes the same angle appears later and increases more slowly to values between 22° and 38° of adults according to the author's data for a great many specimens. In most monkeys the sacrum deviates but little from the general direction of the spinal column even in adults, but in baboons the caudal end of

the sacrum tends to be bent far dorsally to provide a sufficiently wide pelvic passage-way for the unusually large heads of their full-term fetuses (Schultz, 1961, Fig. 17). With the erect presacral part of the human spinal column transmitting its load onto only the anterior end of the sharply tilted sacrum, man has acquired a mechanically precarious articulation at his promontory. It is at this place that the last lumbar vertebra is apt to slip forward and produce a condition known as spondylolisthesis of varying severity, which is not at all rare in man (Taillard 1957), but has never been found in other primates.

As has already been mentioned, the trunk of all hominoids has become extremely broad. In consequence the transverse diameter of the thorax has also come to surpass the sagittal one in length (Fig. 22). At the same time the vertebral column of the higher primates has migrated ventrally in

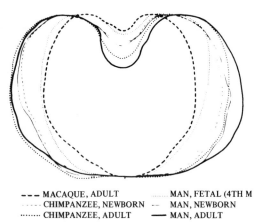

--- MACAQUE, ADULT   .... MAN, FETAL (4TH M
----- CHIMPANZEE, NEWBORN   -- MAN, NEWBORN
.... CHIMPANZEE, ADULT   —— MAN, ADULT

Figure 22: Superimposed tracings of plaster casts of eviscerated thoracic cavities, cut perpendicular to thoracic spine at level of ventral ends of sixth ribs, reduced to same sagittal diameter. (*From Schultz 1956*)

contrast to the condition typical for all quadrupedal monkeys whose vertebrae hardly protrude into the chest cavity. As shown by the outlines of chest cavities in Fig. 22, this hominoid distinction appears only gradually during growth and becomes most pronounced in adult man. The latter extreme represents undoubtedly an adaptation for the advantageous distribution of the load around the upright column which has closely approached the center of gravity. It is of great interest, therefore, that this condition has also developed in all the apes, though not as an equally marked departure from the dorsal position of the vertebrae in monkeys. In direct connection with this specialization of hominoids the ribs had to become much more strongly bent at their dorsal ends than in monkeys, as shown by the examples in Fig. 23. The transverse diameters of the thorax increase steadily in a cranio-caudal direction in all the great apes, which possess a funnel-shaped thorax, while in gibbons and man it is normally more barrel-shaped, as shown in the Figs. 16, 17, and 18, and most clearly in the X-ray photograph

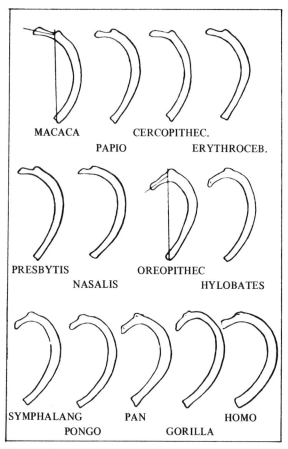

Figure 23: Tracings of second ribs of some adult catarrhines, reduced to same straight length of corpus. (*From Schultz 1960*)

of the trunk of an orang-utan, published by the author in 1961.

Together with the entire trunk the sternum of all higher primates has also become much broader than that of the Cercopithecoidea, so that the former had sometimes been referred to as *Latisternalia*. The data for the length–breadth relation of the corpus sterni in Table 6 show this striking difference between lower and higher primates and also that in this respect chimpanzees have become least specialized, whereas siamangs and orang-utans most specialized. Intraspecifically this

Table 6: Breadth of corpus sterni in percentage of its length in a total of 300 adult catarrhines (Schultz 1930; 1961, and 11 new data). The length was always measured from the level of attachment of the second ribs, even if the manubrium extended to the third ribs.

	RANGE OF VARIATIONS	AVERAGE
Cercopithecus	9–14	10.6
Macaca	8–14	12.2
Hylobates	25–56	35.1
Symphalangus	49–58	53.3
Pongo	43–92	56.8
Pan	16–37	23.9
Gorilla	31–62	45.0
Homo	25–49	35.8

proportion is characterized by an enormous variability in the higher primates, as are so many of their other distinguishing features. The uppermost part of the sternum—the manubrium—is unusual in the Hylobatidae inasmuch as it extends as one single bone to the third ribs in nearly all specimens (Figs. 16 and 18), a condition only occasionally seen in orang-utans and gorillas and as very rare exceptions in man. The longest part of the sternum—the corpus—consists in all monkeys of a row of bony segments which normally never fuse, in contrast to the conditions in all apes and man, whose sternebrae tend to become united with advancing age and this in a caudo-cranial sequence. This typically hominoid specialization of fusing the segmental ossification centers for the corpus sterni into one single bone occurs ontogenetically earlier in man than in the apes in which this process is usually not completed until old age. Detailed findings of this sort, which can be explained only as resulting from shared evolutionary trends, are convincing proofs of the common origin of all hominoids.

The shoulder girdle of the higher primates has also been greatly influenced by the general broadening of the trunk which has led to a lengthening of the collar bones and to the already mentioned shifting of the shoulder blades from the sides to the back. The clavicles of monkeys measure only about 15 or 16 percent of their trunk lengths, but those of all hominoids from anywhere between 26 and 35 percent, having to reach from the ventral manubrium to the dorsal and often far cranially situated acromion (see Fig. 1 and Table 7). As is

Table 7: Averages of the length of the clavicle in percentage of the trunk length in adult catarrhines. As a rule these averages are slightly larger in males than in females, but in chimpanzees and gorillas they are alike in both sexes.

GENUS	SPECIMENS	AVERAGE
Cercopithecus	10	15.1
Macaca	20	16.2
Hylobates	20	32.4
Symphalangus	3	34.5
Pongo	8	35.3
Pan	15	26.8
Gorilla	10	26.0
Homo	20	29.9

to be expected, this relative clavicular length has attained its extreme in the expert brachiators—the Asiatic apes—but it is surprisingly larger in man than in the African apes, even though the human clavicles are horizontally directed instead of steeply diverging upward as in the apes.

The shoulder blades are built quite uniformly in the Old World monkeys, roughly as in the macaque in Fig. 24, but among the hominoids they have developed remarkably different shapes, as shown by the examples in the same figure. The bony plates above and below the scapular spine serve exclusively for the attachment of muscles and as levers for muscular actions and hence have highly variable and often even asymmetrical forms and proportional sizes, conditioned by corresponding differences in muscular development. Orangutans and gorillas represent opposite extremes in the relation in size between the fossae supraspinata and infraspinata. As is also indicated in Fig. 24, the acromial process is much longer and broader in all higher primates than in monkeys according

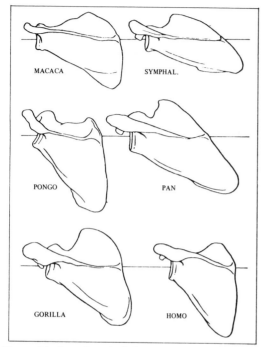

Figure 24: Scapulae of adult macaque and hominoids, oriented according to their morphological lengths. (*From Schultz 1965*)

to exact measurements on many specimens (Schultz 1930).

In the pelvic girdle of the hominoids one can again recognize the influence of the general widening of the entire trunk and this most clearly in the significantly broader iliac blades than in any of the other primates (Figs. 16, 25, and 26). To be more precise, it is the fossa iliaca which has become so much enlarged and this even more in the gorilla than in man, while the great total width of the human ilium is largely due to the uniquely increased sacral surface, that is, its dorsal part which had to become strengthened with the acquisition of the erect posture with which a larger share of the body weight is transmitted from the spinal column to the hip bones than in quadrupeds or brachiators. By exact measurements it was found that the area of the sacro-iliac joint is just

twice as large per kilogram of body weight in man than in the great apes (Schultz 1961). For the same reason the hip joint has also become exceptionally large in bipedal man. The ilia of the pongids have not only increased their width, but also their length. Individually the greatest iliac length amounts to as much as 42 percent of the trunk length in some apes, whereas never more than 25 percent in man. In the cercopithecoids this index is not much larger than in man, with averages fluctuating between only 23 and 28, but in gibbons the average has increased to about 33, in orang-utans to 36 and in the African great apes to 38 (Schultz 1950).

As is shown most clearly in Fig. 20, the weight of the trunk is transferred in apes from the sacro-iliac joints by the long iliac levers to the far caudally situated hip joints, whereas in upright man these joints lie in one perpendicular plane and also much nearer together on account of the shortness of the human ilium which has telescoped the sacrum into the pelvic outlet (Fig. 26). The pelvis of man has become distinguished in many further respects. In nonhuman primates the sacrum lies always high above the pubic symphysis, but in man it has sunk down to a position practically opposite the symphysis, to which it has to remain parallel to keep the birth canal open all the way (Fig. 20). The transverse diameter of the latter vital passage is in man fully as wide as the sagittal diameter (Fig. 37). This is due not only to the low position of the promontory, but also to the fact that the human sacrum is extraordinarily wide and thus wedges the hipbones far apart (Fig. 26). The greatest breadth of the sacrum equals well over 90 percent of the pelvic inlet breadth in man, whereas only somewhere between 70 and 85 percent in the apes (Schultz 1961). The already mentioned, extreme tilting of the pelvic axis, the rotation of the ventral part of the ilium from a frontal to a sagittal direction and the comparative shortness of the ischium, together with the shifting of its tuberosity toward the enlarged

Figure 25: Medial views of right hip bones of adult macaque, gorilla and man, reduced to same trunk length and with symphysion at same level: (A) highest point of acetabulum, (B) highest ventral midsagittal point of sacrum, (C) lowest midsagittal point of sacrum. (*From Schultz 1936*)

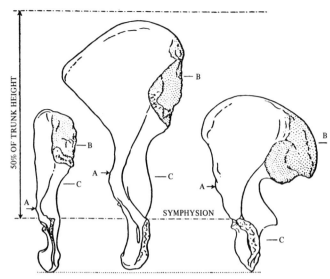

Figure 26: Cephalic and dorsal views of pelves of adult macaque, gorilla and man, reduced to comparable sizes. (*From Schultz 1961*)

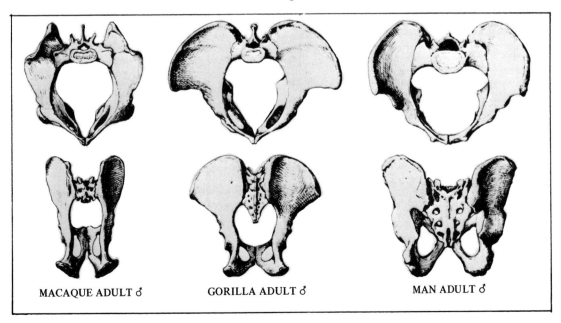

MACAQUE ADULT ♂   GORILLA ADULT ♂   MAN ADULT ♂

acetabulum, are additional specializations of the human pelvis which represent functional adaptations for the altered muscular requirements of perfected bipedal locomotion. That most of these numerous, unique features of man's pelvis are already quite clearly established during fetal development (Rickenmann 1957; Olivier 1962) tends to support the view of an early acquisition of the erect posture in hominoids.

The most significant proportions in the length of the limb bones correspond very closely to those obtained with measurements on the outer body, which have already been discussed. Not only the relative length but also the relative thickness of the long bones shows enormous differences among the hominoids, the latter depending chiefly on body size and relative limb length. As is to be expected, the heavy gorillas have extremely plump bones and the small gibbons very slender ones. The great elongation of the arm bones of the latter required no additional thickness so that they appear especially gracile alongside the robust and relatively short arm bones of gorillas.[5] The middle girth of the ulna surpasses that of the radius in all hominoids, but in the cercopithecoids this relation is reversed with the radius being thicker than the ulna. The long bones of the higher primates are furthermore distinguished by the comparatively great thickness of the fibulae, especially in relation to their trunk length. Among the recent hominoids man is characterized by remarkably thin arm bones, combined with thick leg bones, and the orang-utan by unusually slender leg bones considering the large body size of these primates. These particular distinctions in regard to the degrees of robusticity of the long limb bones are in close agreement with the relative weights of these

bones, which have also been determined in large series of primate skeletons (Schultz 1953; 1962) and are undoubtedly due to the very different and highly specialized use of the limbs in man and in orang-utan.

The foot skeleton of the higher primates is of great interest on account of its widely diverging specializations for different usage. As has already been mentioned . . . and as shown in Fig. 5, there exist remarkably great differences in the relative lengths of the toes among the adult hominoids. For instance, the total length of the phalanges of the middle toe in percentage of the combined length of tarsus and metatarsus III averages only 24 in man, whereas 77 in orang-utans and even up to 90 in some prosimians (see also Fig. 28). The extremely low index of man appears only gradually during growth, equalling 54 at the beginning of fetal life and still 30 at birth. The tarsus has become greatly enlarged not only in bipedal man, but also in the heavy gorilla, being in both of practically equal size in relation to their trunk lengths (Fig. 27). The tarsal length forms 50 percent of the total length of the foot skeleton in man, 40 in gorilla, 34 in chimpanzee, and only between 26 and 28 in orang-utan and hylobatids. The metatarsus and tarsus together constitute the two-armed lever with which the body can be lifted at the ankle joint. The mechanically decisive proportion between the proximal power arm and the distal load arm of this lever differs very widely among primates, as shown by the examples in Fig. 28. The power arm amounts to only 18 percent of the load arm in gibbons, 19 in orang-utans, 27 in chimpanzees, 39 in man, and even 44 in gorillas. In all Old World monkeys these percentage relations are remarkably constant, fluctuating only a little around 23 (Schultz 1963). The strength required of the calf muscles when lifting the body naturally diminishes with an elongation of the power arm, but a relatively great length of the latter, with a consequently distal fulcrum, is disadvantageous for jumping

[5] For instance, the middle circumference of the humerus in percentage of its length averages in male gorillas 26, whereas in gibbons only 13 and in macaques of very similar body weight as the gibbons, but with far shorter humeri, 25.

because the correspondingly short load arm gives only a limited lift to the body.

The first toes of chimpanzees, gorillas and man have become much thicker and stronger than the other toes in contrast to this condition in all monkeys. Only in man does the "great toe" reach about as far as his much shortened other toes. However, the total length of the first digit (with its metatarsus) is not specially great, because it equals roughly half of the total length of the entire foot skeleton in not only man, but also in chimpanzees and gibbons, and in relation to the length of the foot lever the first ray is even much shorter in man than in the hylobatids, as shown by Fig. 28. The first toe of man has become adapted to terrestrial locomotion through the lack of ontogenetic rotation, typical for most other primates, and the loss of metatarsal, but not phalangeal, movability. That the great toe of man developed from an opposable first digit, typical for other primates, is evident from the shape of the joint between the hallux and the first cuneiform bone, which is still not entirely flat, but slightly convex, and not directed transversely, but somewhat medially, in spite of the loss of abductability (Fig. 27). The difference in the exact formation of this joint between man and particularly the eastern gorilla is insignificant in comparison with the corresponding difference between the latter and the chimpanzee (Schultz 1930). The typical simian foot skeleton, designed for climbing and grasping, has in man become altered also through the development of marked sagittal and transverse arches, which act as shock-absorbing springs in his unique mode of locomotion. The distribution of the load over the whole foot corresponds closely to that of the African apes, and even man's degenerated phalanges of the lateral toes are normally still flexed as in most other primates.

The hand skeletons of the hominoids have remained much more uniform than their foot skeletons, differing chiefly in the relative length of the fingers, which has already been discussed. That the

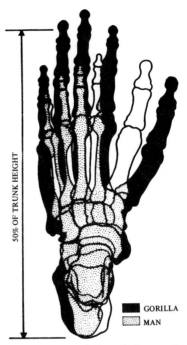

50% OF TRUNK HEIGHT

GORILLA
MAN

Figure 27: Superimposed foot skeletons of an adult gorilla and a man, both reduced to same trunk length. (*From Schultz 1936*)

human hand is surprisingly gracile in comparison with the hands of apes is best shown by the weight of the hand bones in percent of the total skeletal weight (without the caudal vertebrae). These percentages average only 2.7 in man, whereas consistently more in monkeys and much more in the apes, especially in gibbons (6.1) and orangutans (6.0), according to the data collected by the author (1962). The carpus of some of the hominoids contains a specialization which has often been overrated in its phylogenetic significance. It concerns the small central bone which is an old and widely distributed carpal element of vertebrates and which is supposedly lacking among the Simiae in only man, gorilla and chimpanzee. Early in development, however, a separate *centrale* still appears in these primates, but normally it fuses with the *naviculare* and this in man already in the third month of intrauterine life, in chim-

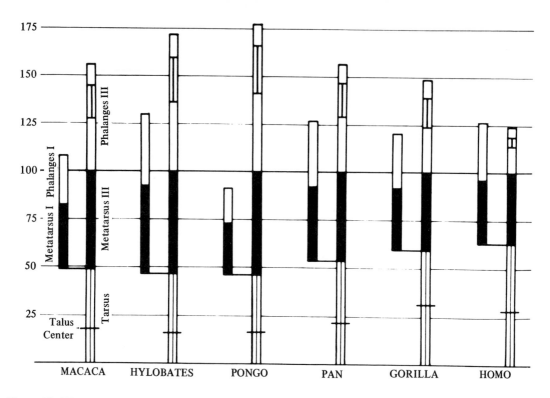

Figure 28: Diagrammatic representation of the average relative lengths of the main parts of the foot skeleton in adult macaques and hominoids, all reduced to same tarsal + metatarsal length (= 100). (*From Schultz 1963*)

panzees about at the time of birth and in gorillas during infantile growth. Exactly the same fusion has also been found repeatedly in some evidently old orang-utans, siamangs, and gibbons, showing that a trend to eliminate a separate *centrale* has been acquired by all hominoids, but differs widely in regard to the ontogenetic stage at which it manifests itself (Schultz 1936; 1956). Even the very early disappearance of the *centrale* of man

does not occur in all individuals since in rare instances it still can persist as a separate carpal element to adult life.

Since the skulls of all recent hominoids have been so frequently described and illustrated in the literature,[6] it will suffice to discuss here only a few examples of the many cranial specializations of these primates. The extremely large human brain had aroused intense interest also in the size of the skull cavity for the brain, especially after Owen (1868) had assigned man to a separate class of animals—the *Archencephala*—to emphasize the sharp distinction between man and all other primates in regard to brain size. By means of later

---

[6] Among the innumerable publications dealing with the skulls of the recent Pongidae the following may be specially mentioned as being based on exceptionally large series: The old but still exemplary monographs by Selenka (1898; 1899) on the skulls of all three great apes, the well-illustrated study by

Coolidge (1929) on subspecific differences in the skulls of gorillas and the report by Allen (1925) on cranial variability in chimpanzees. Large series of hylobatid skulls have been used by the writer in two detailed papers (1933; 1944).

discoveries of fossils it became possible to demonstrate that this extraordinary size of the human brain has been a comparatively late development. At the same time it has also been recognized that brain size is primarily dependent upon its allometric relation to body size. Thus it can be readily understood why the cranial capacity of, for example, the small *Saimiri* monkeys is larger in relation to body weight than is the corresponding relation in man (Schultz 1941).

Table 8 lists first of all the absolute sizes of the cranial capacities in adult higher primates and the surprisingly great ranges of individual variations of these measurements. The recently found maximum capacity of 752 cm³ among all apes (Schultz, 1962) stands much nearer to the minimum value of *Homo erectus* than to that of adult gorillas, which equals only 340 cm³ in females and 420 cm³ in males. The last column in Table 8 shows

the important, but only approximate, relative cranial capacity. In this respect the small gibbons come nearest to man, as is to be expected for reasons of allometry, which also explain the sex differences in this index. The latter are most marked in orang-utans and gorillas simply because the sexes of these apes differ also most in regard to their general body size. The relative cranial capacity undergoes very marked changes during growth on account of the precocious development of the brain, which increases in size more rapidly than the body in general during early stages and more slowly during postnatal life. As shown by the growth curves for the *relative* capacity in Fig. 29, this index drops with increasing body weight from way above 10 in the smaller fetuses to less than 2 in large adult men and to less than 1 in all great apes of more than 45 kg. weight. It is of interest also that the curve for man flattens out more grad-

Table 8: The cranial capacities (cm³) of adult hominoids according to data from the literature and those of the author (1933; 1940; 1941; 1944; 1962; 1965). The figures in the last column express the average capacities in percentage of the corresponding body weights (g.) as listed in Table 1. For the gibbons the weights and capacities could be determined by the author in 82 of the same specimens, but the weights of siamangs and great apes are based on much smaller series than their capacities, so that the *relative* capacities for these apes are only approximate. All data for man are merely rough, general averages, gained from published reports on many different races.

	SEX	SKULLS	RANGE OF VARIATIONS	AVERAGE	RANGE IN PERCENT OF AVERAGE	CAPACITY IN PERCENT OF WEIGHT
Gibbon	Female	85	82–116	101	34	2.0
(*H. lar*)	Male	95	89–125	104	35	1.9
Siamang	Female and Male	40	100–152	125	42	1.2
Orang-utan	Female	111	276–494	366	60	1.0
	Male	96	320–540	424	52	0.6
Chimpanzee	Female	63	275–455	355	51	0.9
	Male	70	322–500	396	45	0.9
Gorilla	Female	173	340–595	458	56	0.5
	Male	400	420–752	535	62	0.3
Man	Female	hundreds	1000–1600	1300	46	2.2
	Male	hundreds	1100–1700	1400	43	2.1

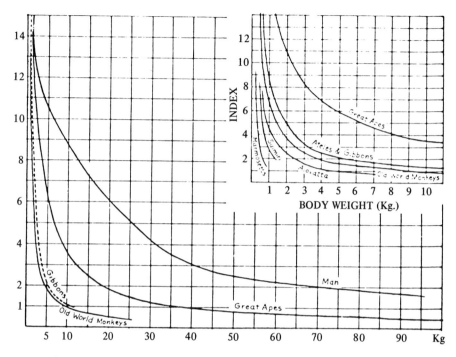

Figure 29: Curves showing the relation between body weight (kg.) and relative cranial capacity (capacity in cm.³ in percentage of body weight in g.), constructed from the author's data for 445 specimens. (*From Schultz 1956*)

ually than do those for the apes, indicating a longer continued postnatal brain growth in the former. At birth the cranial capacity equals in man only about 25 percent of its final size in adults, whereas in the apes anywhere between 35 and 61 percent, according to the writer's latest study (1965). From Fig. 29 it is also evident that this hominoid trend to enlarge the cranial capacity and brain beyond what might be expected from body size is already apparent in gibbons (as among platyrrhines in spider monkeys), has farther progressed with equal intensity in all great apes, and has reached its extreme in recent man. These different steps in the evolution of brain size appear remarkably early in ontogeny.

The size of the eye and of the orbit is, like that of the brain, allometrically dependent upon body size, and in its relation to the latter it decreases with advancing age more evenly than does brain size. For instance, the orbital volume in percent of body weight equals among adults 0.21 in a small marmoset, weighing 0.7 kg., 0.15 in a gibbon of 5.4 kg., 0.06 in a chimpanzee of 44 kg., 0.04 in a man of 66 kg., and 0.03 in a gorilla of 142 kg. (Schultz 1940, and new figure for gorilla). In newborns of the great apes and man the orbital volume has reached already one fifth of its final size in adults, whereas the total body size not nearly that much (Schultz 1965). On an average adult male chimpanzees surpass adult male gibbons 7.9 times in body weight, but only 2.6 times in the orbital volume, showing again that gibbons possess strikingly large orbits (and eyes) in relation to their small body size without, of course, having on that account better visual ability than the great apes. From Figs. 30 and 31 it is readily seen that the height of the orbit in its percentage relation to the height of the face (nasion–prosthion) differs widely among the hominoids and

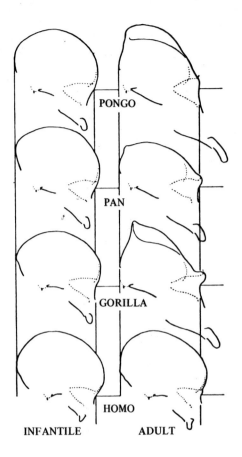

PONGO

PAN

GORILLA

HOMO

INFANTILE   ADULT

Figure 30: Midsagittal sections of infantile and adult skulls of apes and man with superimposed sagittal sections of orbit and occipital condyle and with part of the midsagittal endocranial profile of the frontal bone. All skulls are oriented in the nasion-basion horizon and reduced to same distance from nasion to projection of opisthocranion. (*From corresponding sections of many more primates, see Schultz 1955*)

that the relative size of the suborbital portion of the face must also differ enormously among the hominoids and this chiefly due to the varying sizes of the dental apparatus. The figures 30 and 31 serve also to demonstrate the ontogenetic migration of the orbits, which is so extremely marked in the great apes. In early infants of all monkeys, apes, and man the orbits lie entirely underneath the brain cavity, but in at least all catarrhine monkeys and all man-like apes they shift later far forward, to project in adults to a large extent in front of the brain. This necessitates the formation of a bony roof over the orbits, often strengthened by a thick torus, and leads directly to the postorbital constriction of the skull immediately behind the projecting orbital funnels. The width of this constriction can actually become smaller in adults than in juveniles, being closely correlated with the degree of the orbital migration during the later stages of growth. The life-long retention of a subcerebral position of the orbits is not unique in recent man, but exists also in some platyrrhine monkeys.

During the long continuing development of the dentition with the accompanying great expansion of the entire masticatory apparatus, as well as during the ontogenetically also late changes in the relative size and position of the orbits and the paranasal sinuses, the face changes postnatally far more than the brain-part of the skull. The striking enlargement of the face and its increasing protrusion can be seen by comparing the infantile and adult cranial sections in the Figs. 30, 31, and 32, which also show that these growth changes are most marked in orang-utans and gorillas, especially in males with their largest of all hominoid dentitions. It should be noted also that the facial part of the skull of recent man can hardly have become reduced in size to such an exceptional degree, as is commonly assumed, since it is relatively larger than in gibbons and many monkeys. For instance, according to the author's (1960; 1962) data on large series of primates the height of the face (nasion–prosthion) in percentage of the

undergoes very striking changes during postinfantile growth. This relative measurement averages in adults 66 in gibbons, 41 in orang-utans, 39 in chimpanzees, 35 in gorillas, and 50 in man (Schultz 1960; 1962). From these very significant differences, which greatly influence the construction of the entire face part of the skull, it follows

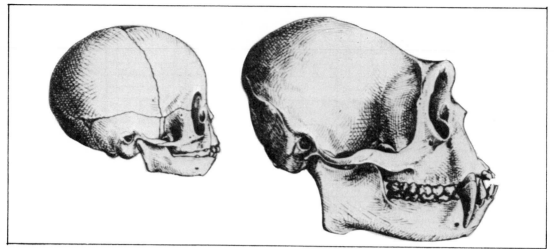

Figure 31: Skulls of a very young infantile and an adult gibbon, reduced to same scale. Centers of occipital condyles marked by perpendicular lines. (*From Schultz 1944*)

length of the skull base (basion–nasion) has in adults of both sexes the following rough averages: gibbons = 55, capuchin monkeys = 58, man = 69, chimpanzees = 87, gorillas = 93, and orang-utans = 100. In relation to the trunk length is the face height of man also significantly larger than that of the gibbon and than those of most

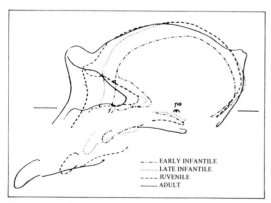

EARLY INFANTILE
LATE INFANTILE
JUVENILE
ADULT

Figure 32: Superimposed midsagittal sections and sagittal sections through middle of orbit of four female western gorilla skulls, reduced to same scale and oriented in ear-eye horizon with coinciding porion points (= po.). (*From Schultz 1956*)

Cercopithecoidea (see Table 2). It appears, therefore, that there is really nothing remarkable about the moderate size of the human face, but that the faces of the great apes are the ones which have become distinguished by their outstandingly large relative size in comparison with other catarrhines, except chiefly the baboons which have also acquired specialized large dentitions, jaws and entire faces.

The construction of the skull of adult hominoids shows an extraordinary tendency for extensive pneumatization which reaches its extreme development in the pongids. Old male gorillas and orang-utans possess enormous paranasal sinuses and the sinus formations of the skull base are also larger than in man. The maxillary sinuses of orangutans can extend all the way into the frontal bone, where they correspond topographically to the huge frontal sinuses of the African apes. In many chimpanzees the right and left maxillary sinuses meet above the hard palate, giving the nasal cavity a double floor (Fig. 33). From the comparative studies of Cave and Wheeler Haines (1940), Wegner (1956) and Cave (1961) it appears that the paranasal sinuses of the hominoids do not only share common general characters, but have also acquired certain specializations, typical for each genus. To the pneumatic cranial parts belong furthermore the mastoid processes, which attain their

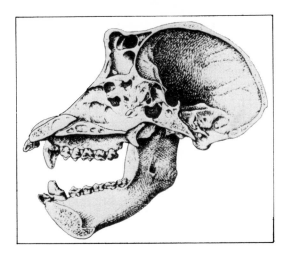

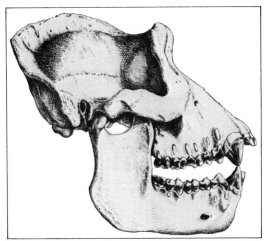

Figure 33: Midsagittally cut skull of an adult chimpanzee showing some of the large sinuses and the proportionate size of the jaws and teeth.

Figure 34: Skull of an adult male western gorilla with exceptionally large teeth and powerful zygomatic arches, but moderate sagittal crest. (*From Schultz 1964*)

large size in recent man at a comparatively early age. In the great apes these processes develop much later, but can become just as large as in man in really old animals (Schultz 1952). Gibbons and monkeys lack clear-cut mastoid processes even in old specimens.

In all mammals, except tarsiers, monkeys, apes, and man, the joint between the skull and the vertebral column lies at the very end of the head at all stages of development. In the entire suborder of the Simiae this joint, and hense also the foramen magnum, are situated much farther forward in fetal and infantile life, to move subsequently toward the rear in widely differing degrees in the various genera (Schultz 1955). As shown by the examples in Figs. 30 and 31, this relative position of the occipital condyles is still very similar in all infantile hominoids, but changes with later growth most in gorillas and orang-utans and least, if at all, in man. This striking difference is due to the fact that in the apes the postinfantile cranial growth in length takes place almost entirely in the precondylar parts, as is clearly evident from Fig. 32. In man, on the other hand, the fetal position of the condyles, only a little behind the center

of gravity of the head, persists practically unchanged throughout growth and thus permits man's greatly reduced nuchal musculature to balance the head in his erect posture. The mechanically disadvantageous location of the occipital joint of adult apes requires such powerful nuchal muscles that their area of cranial attachment has usually to be enlarged with the addition of occipital crests. If the entire heads of adult apes are placed in the ear-eye horizon and supported on the occipital condyles, it has been determined experimentally that to balance the head in that position takes a weight, attached at the inion, which greatly surpasses the weight of the head itself, whereas in adult man such a weight averages only about one fifth of the head weight (Schultz 1942). Incidentally, in its relation to the entire body weight the head weighs more in most adult apes than it does in man in spite of the marked difference in brain weight.

Besides the above mentioned occipital crests apes often develop also sagittal ones to provide an enlarged surface for the attachment of the temporal muscles (Fig. 34). The height of these

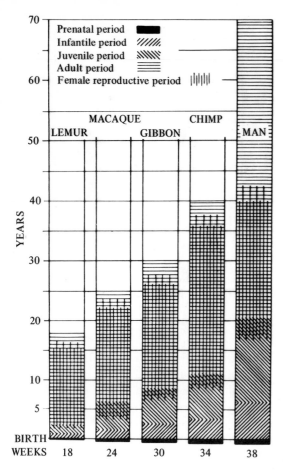

Figure 35: The approximate average duration of the main periods of life in some lower and higher primates. The limits of the infantile and juvenile periods are based upon comparable stages of dental development. (*From Schultz 1966*)

sagittal crests is directly influenced by the size of the jaws in relation to the surface area of the cranial vault. The crests start their development only with the fully completed eruption of the permanent dentition and can continue to grow for a long time thereafter. They are always present in old male gorillas, though very variable in size. Sagittal crests develop also in the majority of adult male orang-utans, rarely in male chimpanzees and least frequently in male gibbons. Since females

have on an average the smaller dentitions and temporal muscles they do not acquire these crests nearly as often as do males, but small crests have been found in some females of all apes.

Age Changes

That the phylogenetic specializations of the hominoids can frequently be traced back to modifications in their ontogenetic processes has already been shown by various examples. Some features, typical for the higher primates, reach their distinct condition only with the completion of growth. Besides these there exist many other important age changes which influence the finished bodily form very little, if at all, and which hence have not yet been discussed. Among the latter none are of greater interest than the prolongation of the various life periods, which represents a general hominoid trend, clearly recognized through comparisons with lower primates (Schultz 1949; 1956). Prenatal life lasts only about 6 weeks in the most primitive primates—the treeshrews—18 weeks in lemurs, 24 weeks in the intensely studied macaques and most likely not significantly longer in other monkeys. In gibbons this period has become prolonged to 30 weeks, in chimpanzees to nearly 34 weeks, and in orang-utans as well as gorillas, according to the few reliable records available so far, to about 38 weeks, that is, to as much as on an average in man. The postnatal life periods show this trend of prolongation to an even more pronounced degree with man representing the extreme of this specialization. All three great apes have practically the same tempo of development which forms a stage between that of gibbons on one side and that of man on the other, as seen in Fig. 35. Even the Hylobatidae differ from the lower primates by having acquired a longer period of growth and a later onset of sexual maturity. This general slowing down of development, which has begun in monkeys, as compared with prosimians, has become greatly accentuated in all apes and has

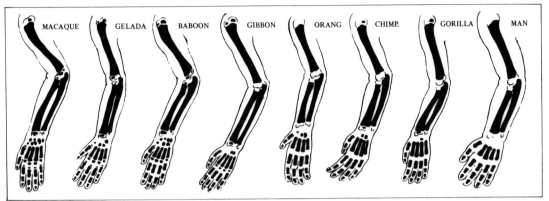

MACAQUE   GELADA   BABOON   GIBBON   ORANG   CHIMP.   GORILLA   MAN

Figure 36: Ossification of the upper extremities of some newborn catarrhines, as shown by X-ray photographs. (*From Schultz 1966*)

progressed most in man regarding postnatal life, has had undoubtedly many profound consequences which can here be merely indicated in a few sentences. The prolongation of infantile dependency and of sexual immaturity has necessitated various adaptations in social behavior, has increased the time for learning and has brought about longer intervals between succeeding generations. The latter implies a reduction of the potential rate of population growth as well as of the tempo of possible evolutionary change in a given time-span. The also greatly increased average longevity of the hominoids has not been accompanied by a corresponding improvement of the durability of all organs. For instance, since the dental tissues have not become strengthened to endure more years of usage, not only man but also the apes commonly experience the extensive break-down of their misnamed "permanent" teeth during the final stages of their allotted life-spans (Schultz 1956).

The diagram in Fig. 35 shows also the approximate duration of fertility in females which, like the other main life periods, has not only increased in the hominoids, but begins and ends much later than in any of the lower primates. It is in regard to the upper limit of the reproductive period in its relation to the total life-span that modern man has come to differ strikingly from the nonhuman primates, inasmuch as a relatively early menopause seems to be a human distinction. This conclusion is supported by a growing number of recent reports on surprisingly long continued ovulatory cycles and even pregnancies of captive monkeys and apes of known old age, which can now be kept in much better health than formerly. The unique lengthening of recent man's life-span beyond the age of female reproduction appears in this light more than ever as a result of our cultural advances.

In spite of the prolonged gestation periods of the higher primates their maturity at birth has not progressed nearly as much as it has in all monkeys. This is very evident from the different state of ossification in newborns, of which typical examples are shown in Fig. 36. It will be noted that the full-term fetuses of hominoids have as yet not nearly as many ossification centers in the carpal elements and in the epiphyses of the other limb bones as have newly born macaques and baboons. The closure of the fontanelles and the development of the teeth and hair have also advanced far more in viable newborn monkeys than in newborns of the higher primates. While macaques and guenons can usually sit and even stand up quite readily within a few days after birth, all hominoids remain very helpless for many weeks and develop far more slowly than any normal Cercopithecoidea. The detailed re-

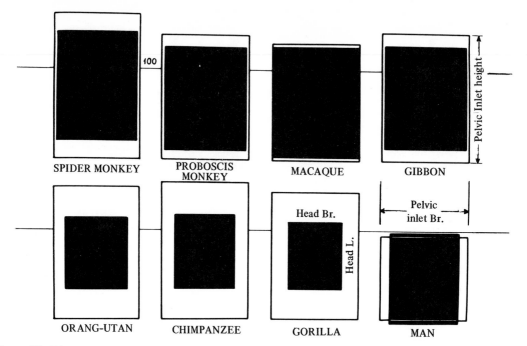

Figure 37: Diagrammatic representation of the relation in size between the average diameters of the pelvic inlet in adult females and the average head length and breadth of newborns of the same species. (*From Schultz 1919*)

port on the physiological maturation of infant chimpanzees by Riesen and Kinder (1952) and the recent opportunities to follow the development of captive-born gorillas leave no doubt that the differences in this respect between these apes and man are insignificant in comparison with the far greater differences between monkeys and apes.

With an average birth weight of nearly 3.5 kg. man surpasses all other primates, since newborns of even the great apes usually weigh hardly 2 kg. In percentage of the maternal body weight that of the newborn equals anywhere between at least 5 and more than 10 in monkeys, 7.5 in gibbons, usually 5.5 in man, but only between 2.4 and 4.1 in the great apes (Schultz 1960). The full-term fetuses of the latter, therefore, are extraordinarily small,[7] a fact which shows itself also in their relation in size to the pelvic birth canal of the mother. This remarkable peculiarity of the pongids is illustrated in Fig. 37 where it is very evident that the head of the newborn has ample room to pass through the wide pelvic inlets of great apes in contrast to the shockingly crowded conditions for the delivery of monkeys, gibbons and man. This explains the usually easy and rapid birth of the pongids and the often very prolonged and difficult labor in other simian primates, including man (Harms 1956).

Of all the manifold postnatal developmental

---

[7] The curves of the intrauterine growth in length and in weight of chimpanzees fall below those of man for only the last few weeks (Schultz 1956). In the writer's experience all newborn pongids have far less subcutaneous fat than develops during the last stage of fetal life in man to become a distinguishing character of the great majority of human newborns.

changes those of the dentition have been studied in particularly large series of primates, because they are well suited for determining the relative ages of specimens. The eruption of the deciduous teeth begins in monkeys as a rule at or very soon after birth with the middle incisors. These teeth are also the first to appear in the higher primates, but not until about the age of three months in the pongids and even later in man. The central incisors are followed by the lateral ones, then by the anterior milk molars and somewhat later by the canines and last of all by the posterior milk molars in all Old World monkeys, gibbons, and man. The pongids alone form an exception to this rule inasmuch as their deciduous canines erupt after all milk molars have appeared. The first permanent molars are added to the deciduous dentition only after a considerable resting period in the process of eruption, namely in the middle of the second year in macaques, toward the end of the third year in the great apes, and not until after the completed sixth year in Europeans. Shortly after these ages there usually follows the first replacement of deciduous teeth with the eruption of the permanent middle incisors. The next replacement is that of the lateral incisors, which is succeeded by the addition of the second permanent molars and then by the replacement of the milk molars through premolars. The canines are not exchanged until about the time the last permanent molars are added, the exact sequence varying somewhat according to species and to sex. This order of eruption of the second dentition, expressed by the formula M1–I1–I2–M2–(P P)–(C M3), represents the general rule for all catarrhines, except recent man. In the latter there has appeared a trend to replace the milk teeth before the addition of all permanent molars, so that the following altered formula is now commonly found at least in Europeans: (I1 M1)–I2–(P C P)–M2–M3, with the teeth enclosed in parentheses erupting often in rapid and variable sequence. Due to the greatly prolonged growth of recent man it has obviously become a selective advantage to replace the delicate milk teeth as soon as possible in preference to the addition of all permanent molars which are no longer indispensable for masticating the prepared food of civilization. The primitive order of dental eruption, which has been retained by some prosimians and at least one platyrrhine (*Aotus*), has the formula M1–M2–M3–I1–I2–C–(P P P), showing that the addition of all permanent molars precedes the process of replacement and quickly gives these rapidly maturing primates long rows of grinding teeth for their early start in chewing solid food (Schultz 1935; 1956; 1960).

In Europeans the dentition is not fully erupted until all the epiphyseal lines of the long limb bones have become obliterated and growth in length has ceased in these bones. As shown by the comparisons in Fig. 38, this particular relation between dental and skeletal development represents an extreme retardation in the former in contrast to the process of epiphyseal closure. In all lower primates, studied so far, and in the Asiatic apes even the last molars are fully erupted when only the epiphyses of the elbow region have fused with the adjoining diaphyses. In chimpanzees and gorillas dental eruption is not completed until epiphyseal closure has progressed much farther at the approximate age of 11 years, but not nearly as far as in any of the races of man for which the relevant data have been collected. From Fig. 38 it can also be concluded that the sequence of epiphyseal obliteration is remarkably uniform among these different primates and certainly far more so than the order of dental eruption.

The closure of the main cranial sutures occurs among the recent great apes much sooner and more rapidly than in man and can even begin before the termination of dental eruption. In most platyrrhines these sutures remain open to old age,

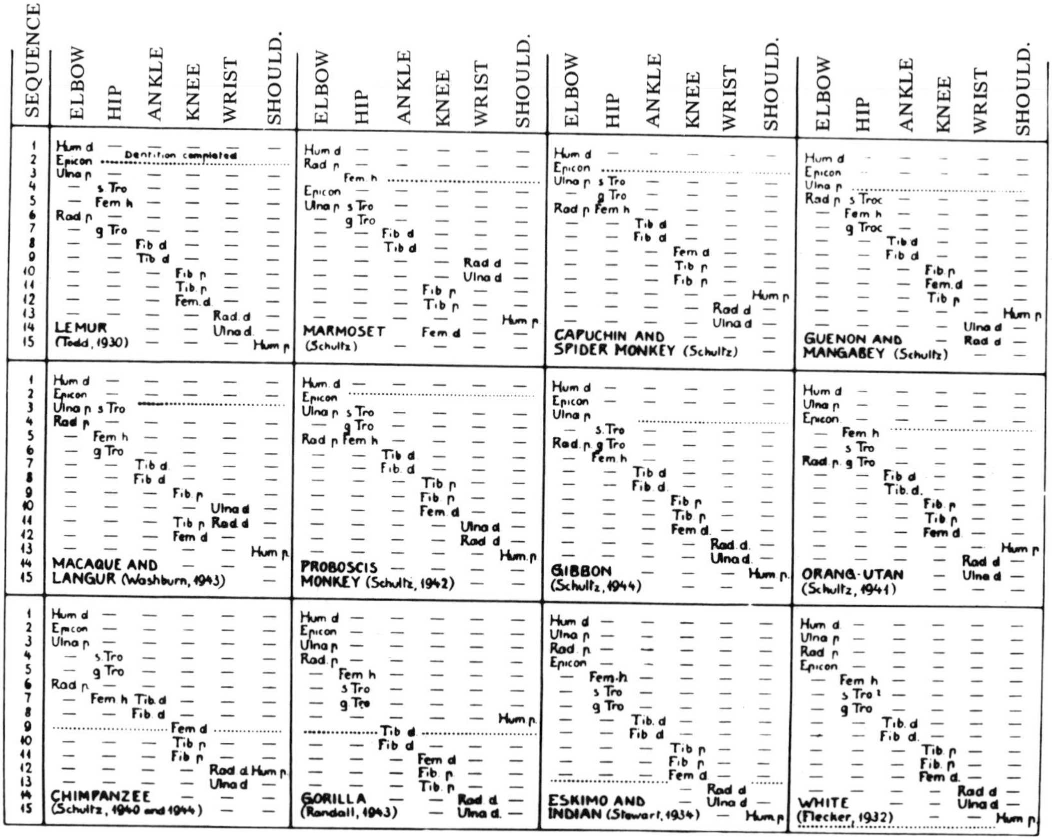

Figure 38: Sequence of epiphyseal union in the long bones of the limbs according to the literature and the author's data. The stage at which the permanent dentition becomes completed is shown by horizontal dotted lines. (p) proximal, (d) distal, (s) small, (g) great. (*From Schultz 1956*)

Band 1

SEQUENCE	| ELBOW	HIP	ANKLE	KNEE	WRIST	SHOULD.	| ELBOW	HIP	ANKLE	KNEE	WRIST	SHOULD.	| ELBOW	HIP	ANKLE	KNEE	WRIST	SHOULD.	| ELBOW	HIP	ANKLE	KNEE	WRIST	SHOULD.
1	Hum d	— Dentition completed —	—	—	—	—	Hum d	—	—	—	—	—	Hum d	—	—	—	—	—	Hum d	—	—	—	—	—
2	Epicon	·········	—	—	—	—	Rad p	—	—	—	—	—	Epicon	·········	—	—	—	—	Epicon	—	—	—	—	—
3	Ulna p		—	—	—	—	Epicon	Fem h	·········	—	—	—	Ulna p	s Tro	—	—	—	—	Ulna p	—	—	—	—	—
4		s Tro	—	—	—	—	Epicon		—	—	—	—		g Tro	—	—	—	—	Rad p	s Troc	—	—	—	—
5		Fem h	—	—	—	—	Ulna p	s Tro	—	—	—	—	Rad p	Fem h	—	—	—	—		Fem h	—	—	—	—
6	Rad p		—	—	—	—		g Tro	—	—	—	—			Tib d	—	—	—		g Troc	—	—	—	—
7		g Tro	—	—	—	—			Fib d	—	—	—			Fib d	—	—	—			Tib d	—	—	—
8			Fib d	—	—	—			Tib d	—	—	—				Fem d	—	—			Fib d	—	—	—
9			Tib d	—	—	—					Rad d	—				Tib p	—	—				Fib p	—	—
10				Fib p	—	—					Ulna d	—				Fib p	—	—				Fem d	—	—
11				Tib p	—	—				Fib p	—	—						Hum p				Tib p	—	—
12				Fem d	—	—				Tib p	—	—					Rad d	—						Hum p
13					Rad d	—						—						—						—
14	LEMUR		Ulna d			—	MARMOSET	Fem d	—	—	—	—	CAPUCHIN AND		Ulna d	—		—	GUENON AND		Ulna d	—		—
15	(Todd, 1930)					Hum p	(Schultz)	—	—	—	—	—	SPIDER MONKEY (Schultz)				Rad d	—	MANGABEY (Schultz)				Rad d	—

Band 2

SEQUENCE	| ELBOW	HIP	ANKLE	KNEE	WRIST	SHOULD.	| ELBOW	HIP	ANKLE	KNEE	WRIST	SHOULD.	| ELBOW	HIP	ANKLE	KNEE	WRIST	SHOULD.	| ELBOW	HIP	ANKLE	KNEE	WRIST	SHOULD.
1	Hum d	—	—	—	—	—	Hum d	—	—	—	—	—	Hum d	—	—	—	—	—	Hum d	—	—	—	—	—
2	Epicon	—	—	—	—	—	Epicon	·········	—	—	—	—	Epicon	—	—	—	—	—	Ulna p	—	—	—	—	—
3	Ulna p	s Tro	·········	—	—	—	Ulna p	s Tro	—	—	—	—	Ulna p	—	—	—	—	—	Epicon	—	—	—	—	—
4	Rad p		—	—	—	—		g Tro	—	—	—	—		s Tro	·········	—	—	—		Fem h	—	—	—	—
5		Fem h	—	—	—	—	Rad p	Fem h	—	—	—	—	Rad p	g Tro	—	—	—	—		s Tro	—	—	—	—
6		g Tro	—	—	—	—			Tib d	—	—	—		Fem h	—	—	—	—	Rad p	g Tro	—	—	—	—
7			Tib d	—	—	—			Fib d	—	—	—			Tib d	—	—	—			Fib d	—	—	—
8			Fib d	—	—	—				Tib p	—	—			Fib d	—	—	—			Tib d	—	—	—
9				Fib p	—	—				Fib p	—	—				Fib p	—	—				Fib p	—	—
10						Ulna d				Fem d	—	—				Tib p	—	—				Tib p	—	—
11				Tib p	Rad d	—					Ulna d	—				Fem d	—	—				Fem d	—	—
12				Fem d	—	—					Rad d	—					Rad d	—					Rad d	—
13						Hum p						—					Ulna d	—					Ulna d	—
14	MACAQUE AND		—	—	—	—	PROBOSCIS	—	—	—	—	—	GIBBON					Hum p	ORANG-UTAN		—	—	—	—
15	LANGUR (Washburn, 1943)					—	MONKEY (Schultz, 1942)	—	—	—	—	—	(Schultz, 1944)					—	(Schultz, 1941)				Hum p	—

Band 3

SEQUENCE	| ELBOW	HIP	ANKLE	KNEE	WRIST	SHOULD.	| ELBOW	HIP	ANKLE	KNEE	WRIST	SHOULD.	| ELBOW	HIP	ANKLE	KNEE	WRIST	SHOULD.	| ELBOW	HIP	ANKLE	KNEE	WRIST	SHOULD.
1	Hum d	—	—	—	—	—	Hum d	—	—	—	—	—	Hum d	—	—	—	—	—	Hum d	—	—	—	—	—
2	Epicon	—	—	—	—	—	Epicon	—	—	—	—	—	Ulna p	—	—	—	—	—	Ulna p	—	—	—	—	—
3	Ulna p	—	—	—	—	—	Ulna p	—	—	—	—	—	Rad p	—	—	—	—	—	Rad p	—	—	—	—	—
4		s Tro	—	—	—	—	Rad p	—	—	—	—	—	Epicon	—	—	—	—	—	Epicon	—	—	—	—	—
5		g Tro	—	—	—	—		Fem h	—	—	—	—		Fem h	—	—	—	—		Fem h	—	—	—	—
6	Rad p	—	—	—	—	—		s Tro	—	—	—	—		s Tro	—	—	—	—		s Tro	—	—	—	—
7		Fem h	Tib d	—	—	—		g Tro	—	—	—	—		g Tro	—	—	—	—		g Tro	—	—	—	—
8			Fib d	—	—	—						Hum p			Tib d	—	—	—			Tib d	—	—	—
9	·········		Fem d	·········	—	—			Tib d	—	—	—			Fib d	—	—	—			Fib d	—	—	—
10				Tib p	—	—			Fib d	—	—	—				Fib p	—	—				Tib p	—	—
11				Fib p	—	—				Fem d	—	—				Tib p	—	—				Fib p	—	—
12					Rad d	Hum p				Fib p	—	—				Fem d	—	—				Fem d	—	—
13						—				Tib p	—	—					Rad d	—					Rad d	—
14	CHIMPANZEE		Ulna d	—	—	—	GORILLA				Rad d	—	ESKIMO AND				Ulna d	—	WHITE				Ulna d	—
15	(Schultz, 1940 and 1944)					—	(Randall, 1943)				Ulna d	—	INDIAN (Stewart, 1934)					Hum p	(Flecker, 1932)					Hum p

and in catarrhine monkeys and the hylobatids they disappear generally at earlier relative ages than in typical platyrrhines and in man, but much later than in the great apes. As a rule the occipito-sphenoid suture becomes closed before the sutures of the vault except in the great apes in which the latter sutures often begin to obliterate before even the basal one does. A supposed lack of intermaxillary bones had long ago been regarded as a clear morphological distinction of man. This widely held view was abandoned only after Goethe's famous demonstration of its fallaciousness.[8] The very minor specialization in man's intermaxillaries actually consists merely in their

[8] Even slightly before that time there had also appeared a little-known, but very noteworthy book on the skeleton of primates by Josephi (1787) which contains a detailed chapter on the intermaxillary, including the following historically interesting statement: "Man nimmt diese *ossa intermaxillaria* mit als ein Hauptunterscheidungszeichen der Affen vom Menschen an; indess, meinen Beobachtungen nach, hat der Mensch ebenfalls solche *ossa intermaxillaria*, wenigstens in den ersten Monaten seines Seyns, welche aber gewöhnlich schon früh, und zwar schon im Mutterleibe mit den wirklichen Oberkiefern vorzüglich nach aussen verwachsen. . . ."

early prenatal fusion with the maxillaries on the facial side, preventing the appearance of corresponding sutures, which exist in all other primates. These sutures tend to become closed in particularly their alveolar parts much sooner in the great apes than in monkeys, in which they are often even among the very last sutures to disappear. Such great differences in the relative ages, at which one or another suture closes, are not at all uncommon in primates. For instance, the internasal suture usually becomes obliterated well before birth in macaques and many chimpanzees, whereas in man it never closes, except in rare old individuals (Schultz 1956; Chopra 1957).

Secondary Sex Differences and Variability

More or less striking sex differences in the color, pattern or length of hair and in other superficial features of most often the face are very common in primates and seem to serve mainly for recognizing, impressing or threatening purposes. Really great differences in size and strength of the body and of the canine teeth, by which males become effective defenders, are comparatively rare and almost entirely limited to catarrhines, such as baboons, most macaques, some species of langurs, proboscis monkeys, orang-utans, and gorillas. This minority is by no means composed of only terrestrial or large-bodied forms, as has been claimed, but embraces a wide variety of small and large species with very different modes of life. Species characterized by moderate sex differences in body build also include arboreal as well as terrestrial ones, namely man, chimpanzee, and a great many monkeys of the Old and New World. The least body differentiation according to sex exists in the majority of prosimians and of platyrrhines, besides the Hylobatidae. Among the recent hominoids sex differences in the body size of adults are on an average exceed-

ingly small in gibbons and extremely large in orang-utans and gorillas, as has already been shown in Table 1. Such sex differences do become much more marked with advancing growth, being as yet barely indicated at birth, if recognizable at all by well-founded averages. It can be concluded, therefore, that either the rates of postnatal growth or its duration can differ in the two sexes. That both these factors can also act in combination has been demonstrated for macaques, chimpanzees and man, whose curves of growth for females fall below those for males during late juvenile life and cease to rise at a somewhat earlier age (Schultz 1956). The sexes can differ also in regard to some of their body proportions. The relative circumference of the chest, for example, averages 203 in adult male orang-utans and only 171 in adult females, but in gibbons both sexes are practically alike in this respect. The relative hip breadth is the only index which surpasses in females that of males in consequence of the marked widening of the female pelvis after puberty (Schultz 1949; 1956). A pronounced sexual dimorphism frequently develops also in the face part of the skull, which becomes higher and more protruding in adult males of particularly orang-utans and gorillas in connection with the corresponding difference in the size of the entire dental apparatus (Schultz 1962). It is well known that in the majority of primates the canines of males are strikingly large in comparison with those of females of the same species. This rule, however, has exceptions among widely different primates, lacking a noteworthy sex difference in this respect, such as man, all Hylobatidae and various Callithricidae. Among the recent Pongidae a sexual difference in the size of the canines is not nearly as great and constant in chimpanzees as it is in the two other genera.

Further secondary sex characters of the hominoids have already been mentioned . . . as representing purely quantitative differences. In orang-utans, for example, beards and cranial crests

Table 9: Most frequent combination of variations in the number of precaudal vertebrae (= statistical norm) in some catarrhine genera. The number of cervical vertebrae is not included because it is 7 with extremely rare exceptions (from Schultz 1957 and 1961 with a few additions).

GENUS	SKELE-TONS	NORM THOR.	NORM LUMB.	NORM SACR.	PERCENTAGE OCCUR-RENCE
Macaca	216	12	7	3	73
Cercopithecus	59	12	7	3	72
Presbytis	122	12	7	3	86
Hylobates	319	13	5	5	36
Pongo	127	12	4	5	43
Pan	162	13	4	6	27
Gorilla	84	13	4	6	28
Homo	493	12	5	5	71

are merely more frequent in males and their crests and throat pouches become larger than in females. In adult gorillas there are fewer and shorter hairs on the chests of males than of females, and the supraorbital torus of the former becomes more strongly developed in adults. The typical amount and kind of sex differentiation in man varies considerably according to race, but always remains exceedingly moderate in comparison with the great differences in some other catarrhine primates.

It has already been pointed out repeatedly above that the man-like apes are distinguished by a remarkably great intraspecific variability in regard to most of their characters. This often not duly appreciated fact can here be demonstrated by a few more examples. Man is supposed to have 12 thoracic, 5 lumbar, and 5 sacral vertebrae according to all textbooks, but actually this combination of the numbers of segments in these spinal regions exists in only 71 percent of human beings and in the remaining 29 percent there occur several other less frequent combinations of numerical variations. As shown by Table 9, the most frequent vertebral formula is found in from 72 to 86 percent of catarrhine monkeys, that is, their constancy in this respect is only a little more marked than it is in man. Contrasting with this the statistical norms of all the man-like apes occur in far smaller percentages of specimens, the great majority having different vertebral formulae with frequencies below that of the norm. It is of interest that the already discussed extreme specializations of the apes in their regional numbers of vertebrae are accompanied by this extraordinary lack of intraspecific stability.

In a formerly much discussed book on the "Hallmarks of Mankind" Wood Jones (1948) had supported his theory of a separate human descent

Table 10: Percentage frequencies of variations in the relations between the ethmoid and sphenoid in the cranial base and between the ethmoid and lacrimal or the frontal and maxillary in the medial orbital wall of simian primates (from Schultz 1950; 1965).

	SKULLS	SPHENO-ETHMOID SUTURE	FRONTO-BASILAR SUTURE	ORBITS	LACRIMO-ETHMOID SUTURE [*]	FRONTO-MAXILLARY SUTURE
Platyrrhina	63	23	77	250	100	0
Cercopithecoidea	341	0.3	99.7	1050	100	0
Hylobatidae	48	0	100	144	100	0
Pongo	94	99	1	310	100	0
Pan	86	77	23	374	63	37
Gorilla	62	50	50	262	49	51
Homo	1016	97	3	1470	99	1.2

[*] Includes the few cases in which all four bones meet in a point.

from tarsier-like ancestors with various claims regarding the topographic relations between the ethmoid bone and its adjoining cranial elements, but evidently without having investigated the variability of these features in adequate series of primate skulls. According to the just-named author a junction of the right and left frontals behind the ethmoid, with the formation of a fronto-basilar suture, is a "catarrhine specialization" which is missing only in man (besides the orang-utan). From the writer's extensive data, shown in Table 10, however, it is evident that one is dealing here with merely a quantitative distinction since the fronto-basilar suture is found only in about one fourth of chimpanzees and half of all gorillas, as well as in 3 percent of human beings (Fig. 39). That these are hereditary variations appears very probable in view of the fact that this suture existed in 10 percent of negro skulls, whereas in only 0.4 percent of European skulls. Here it is of special interest that this is a feature in regard to which chimpanzees and gorillas are much more variable than all the other catarrhines.

The exact formation of the medial orbital wall had also been used by Wood Jones in support of his denial of any close relationship between man and the apes in the belief that the ethmoid and lacrimal meet in the former, while in the latter they are separated by the interposition of the frontal and maxillary. As is shown by the data on very extensive series in the right half of Table 10, a contact between the ethmoid and lacrimal bones actually exists not only in all hylobatids and orang-utans but also in nearly half of the gorillas and in even almost two thirds of the chimpanzees. The ethmoid and lacrimal bones are wedged apart through processes, extending from the frontal and maxillary bones, exclusively in 37 percent of chimpanzees, 51 percent of gorillas, and 1.2 percent of human orbits (Fig. 39), but not in any of the other hominoids nor in any monkeys. Even though this feature is 100 percent constant in the great majority of simian

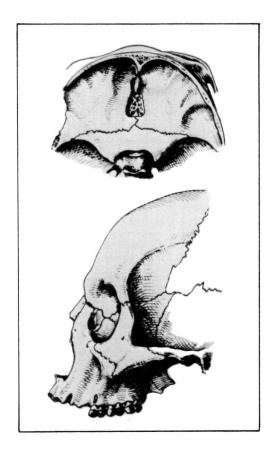

Figure 39: Skulls of two adult Papuas, (above) floor of cranial cavity with a fronto-basilar suture; (below) medial orbital wall with a fronto-maxillary suture. (*From Schultz 1952*)

primates, it evidently can change easily since the fronto-maxillary suture behind the lacrimal was found in 13 out of 14 *Pan paniscus* examined by the writer and hence far more frequently than in *Pan troglodytes*.

The extraordinary variability of the man-like apes in their cranial proportions can here be indicated by only the following few examples: The length-breadth index of the brain-case (without crests) was found to range from 68 to 86 in a series of 248 adult *Hylobates lar* (Schultz 1944), from 70 to 92 in a series of 105 adult orang-utans (Schultz 1941), from 57 to 79 in a series of 80 adult western gorillas (Schultz 1962), and even from 69 to 98 in another series of 311 fully grown western gorillas, measured with a somewhat different technique by Randall (1943–1944). These remarkably large ranges of variations surpass those of most comparable series of human skulls. For instance, the same index fluctuated only between 61 and 78 among 328 skulls of adult Greenland Eskimos (Fürst and Hansen 1915). The variability of the face-part of the skull is as a rule even more marked than that of the brain-part, a distinction which is particularly pronounced in the great apes, as clearly shown by the skulls of chimpanzees in Fig. 40. These three examples of perfectly normal apes differ in so many details that formerly they might have been described as separate species, but today they can readily be fitted within the ranges of variations of large collections of chimpanzee skulls from limited regions. The teeth of the apes are also distinguished by an astonishingly great variability in their absolute and relative size, et cetera, as has been clearly demonstrated with very many and careful data by chiefly Remane (1954; 1961). This quite unusual lack of intraspecific stability in so many different characters of the recent man-like apes has unfortunately not always been taken into consideration in the interpretation and classification of fossil hominoid fragments.

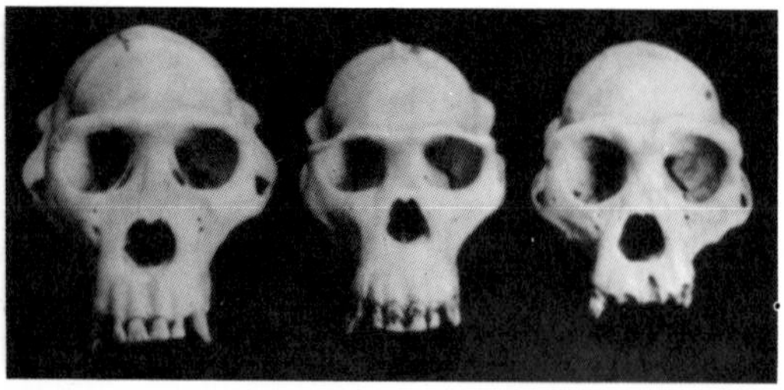

It may finally be mentioned also that asymmetries, which in a sense represent bilateral variations, are by no means limited to man. It has been found, however, that in man the long bones of the upper limbs are roughly twice as asymmetrical as are those of the lower limbs, whereas in monkeys and all apes there exist no significant differences in the degrees of asymmetry of the upper and the lower limb bones, as is shown by the condensed data in Table 11. It seems most

Table 11: Averages of the relative asymmetries of the humerus, radius, femur, and tibia of adult catarrhines (length of larger bone minus length of smaller bone in percentage of the latter, including symmetrical cases) (from Schultz 1937; 1944; 1965).

| | | AVERAGE RELATIVE ASYMMETRY | |
	SKELETONS	Upper Limb	Lower Limb
Macques	118	0.61	0.60
Gibbons	212	0.57	0.59
Orang-utans	69	0.69	0.63
Chimpanzees	88	0.69	0.65
Gorillas	127	0.69	0.73
Different Races of Man	735	1.20	0.63

probable that the liberation of man's arms from participating in locomotion has somehow favored an exceptionally marked degree of asymmetry in his arm bones.

Summary and Conclusions

Among the manifold conditions of the recent Hominoidea, which have been dealt with in this survey, nearly all have been found to differ significantly from the corresponding conditions of the lower catarrhines and to represent distinguishing characters, acquired from a common origin and adapted to often diverging modes of life. The most noteworthy and consequential of these

Figure 40: Skulls of wild adult male chimpanzees from West Africa. (*From Schultz 1963*)

hominoid specializations are the reductions in the number of presacral and caudal segments combined with the greater number of vertebrae fused in the sacrum, the striking widening of the entire trunk with its many correlated alterations, the increased relative length of the upper limbs, the great enlargement of the brain in its allometric relation to body size, and the prolongation of the various main periods of life together with the numerous changes in relative age, speed or duration of developmental processes, especially the reduced state of maturity at birth. An endless variety of further anatomical, physiological, and ontogenetic conditions, which have here not been mentioned at all, could be enumerated in support of the today generally accepted conclusion that man and all of the man-like apes belong in one and the same natural group of primates. That the recent hominoids can readily be divided into three clearly differentiated and roughly equivalent subgroups has also been demonstrated with the evidence derived from a great variety of features.

The Hylobatidae have in general remained less specialized than have the great apes and man and represent in some ways transitional stages between Cercopithecoidea and the Pongidae, with the siamang having approached the latter more closely than have the gibbons. The differences between the gibbons and the larger siamang are not merely allometric ones, as has been rashly concluded by some students with very inadequate material, but consist also of numerous conditions which have nothing to do with body size, such as vertebral variations, density of hair, et cetera. Furthermore, the diploid number of chromosomes equals 44 in gibbons of all species studied so far, whereas 50 in the siamang, besides cer-

tain additional chromosomal peculiarities distinguishing the latter from the former (Hamerton et al. 1963; Chiarelli 1966). Even though the hylobatids still possess regularly well-formed ischial callosities and have made only modest progress in the enlargement of the brain, the changes in regional numbers of vertebrae, the widening of the iliac bones, and the retardation of growth and development, they have nevertheless gained some extreme and even unique specializations, such as the long canines of females, the greatest relative length of the arms and many distinguishing features of their hands, feet, sternum, hair, et cetera. In considering all of these conditions of the recent Hylobatidae it seems well justified to assume that they had followed their own course of evolution ever since they had begun to diverge from the same early ancestral stock of catarrhines which had also given rise to the other hominoids.[9]

The numerous, closely corresponding, phylogenetic trends of specialization, which have been shared by all recent great apes, force us to conclude that they must have had one common origin and that they still fit well into the same subfamily of Ponginae. The modern proposals of radical changes in this classification on the basis of similarities in certain details of chromosome morphology or of blood chemistry seem premature and remain unconvincing as long as no thorough attempt is made to correlate such isolated findings with the vast mass of other pertinent evidence. The close relationship between all three types of the recent great apes is demonstrated beyond doubt by the remarkable agreement in all their significant developmental processes as well as in the great majority of their anatomical characters. Exceptions can readily be explained as limited specializations, acquired after the phylogenetic division of the three genera. Considering the great spatial and, most likely, chronological separation between the Asiatic and African pongids, it is to be expected that cor-

---

[9] Recent investigations have at least cast serious doubts on the formerly widely held theory that the fossil *Pliopithecus* represents an early form of hylobatids (for further comments see Schultz 1966).

responding differences in the degrees of similarity had developed, particularly that chimpanzees and gorillas stand much closer to one another than either does to the orang-utan. Regardless, however, of what importance we may choose to assign to the many different bodily adaptations, which have resulted from the various modes of life of the great apes, there still remains the only justifiable conclusion that even the Asiatic and African ones have not become nearly as much separated as all three types are removed from recent man. Accordingly it seems far more likely that a separate hominid branch had appeared on the hominoid family tree before any of the branches leading to the recent pongids had clearly diverged from each other and not later, from only the lines ending in *Gorilla* and *Pan,* as has been assumed by Gregory (1934), Vallois (1955) and other authors.

While the Asiatic apes had evolved into the most highly perfected brachiators, the hominids had become extreme cruriators, as Keith (1934) had called them. The many profound specializations of man are chiefly those which had appeared as direct adaptations for, or as indirect consequences of erect posture, which was the first and most decisive change. To these first acquisitions was added the later great development of the brain with the correlated cranial transformations. The undoubtedly much more recent, extreme prolongation of the postnatal life periods also belongs to the outstanding innovations of human evolution.

As has been repeatedly emphasized here, a great many specializations of all hominoids are very closely correlated with their posture and locomotion. In this connection it is to be mentioned first of all that the man-like apes can and do stand and walk bipedally much more easily than can the lower catarrhines. This ability had been prepared by the typically hominoid cranial migration of the pelvis, the ventral shift of the spinal column, the dorsal translocation of the shoulder blades, as well as the manifold and mechanically advantageous modifications in the pelvis and the feet. Upright walking and running has thus become easily possible for gibbons and even more so for siamangs. Chimpanzees and gorillas can also walk erect on the ground without difficulty, whereby they naturally carry the center of gravity of the body perpendicularly above the feet. Orang-utans in captivity are frequently seen to stand and sometimes to walk bipedally, but in an awkward fashion on account of their long feet, specialized for grasping limbs and unsuited for flat ground. The change from the occasional erect locomotion of apes to a permanent one in early man was far more readily accomplished with a hominoid bodily construction than with that of Old World monkeys.

The extreme specializations for two-armed locomotion seem not to have appeared until rather late in evolution according to what can be learned from fossil finds (Zapfe 1960 a. o.). Among all catarrhines the ability to brachiate has become most highly perfected in the recent Hylobatidae which can move by their arms alone with such amazing agility and speed that they can propel themselves through space for incredible distances without using their legs at all. The heavy orang-utans do not use brachiation nearly as often nor as gracefully, being by comparison slow and cautious in most of their movements, though otherwise as well adapted to an almost exclusively arboreal life as their small cousins, the gibbons. Chimpanzees can brachiate as easily as and more speedily than orang-utans, but in general they spend much more daytime on the ground than in the trees and prefer quadrupedal locomotion if they do not carry food or newborns in their hands. The heavy adult gorillas can also move by their arms underneath branches, but hardly any better than well-trained boys are able to do, and usually they live on the ground rather than in trees (Schaller 1963). As is very evident from Fig. 41, the plump body build of full-grown

Figure 41: Adult male gorilla of the middle Congo. Note face hanging far below the high shoulders, the "saddle back" and the broad hips. (*From Schultz 1965. After a film, courtesy of 20th Century-Fox*)

gorillas is not at all suited for nimble quadrupedal locomotion, such as distinguishes the slender guenons. With its broad trunk, concave back, high shoulders, and stout legs the gorilla cannot rely for protection on speed, but rather on the strength of its powerful arms, which are freed for defense with the easily possible assumption of the upright posture.

It may be mentioned here also that the extremely arboreal existence of the Asiatic apes entails dangers which play not nearly as prominent a role in the terrestrial life of the African apes and man. This claim is based on the fact that repaired fractures, occurring in all parts of the skeleton, have been found among the former in up to 50 percent of old animals and as being more common at all ages than in the latter (Schultz 1956; 1961). It is quite certain that fatal accidents, which in tropical jungles rarely become known, are also specially frequent in the most arboreal and most commonly brachiating hominoids.

The preferred use of the upper limbs in the locomotion of brachiators could not transfer new functions to their lower limbs, but remained a limited specialization in comparison with the adaptations and consequences of bipedalism. With the latter the arms and specially the hands, freed from serving in locomotion, were enabled to take over new tasks, beginning with the carrying of objects and leading to the manufacture of tools.

Among nature's exceptionally diverse experiments with the original stock of the hominoids the hylobatids were assigned the one-sided and restricted path to an extreme arboreal existence, the pongids had followed a very similar direction in Asia, while in Africa they had hesitated between life on the ground and in the trees, preferring the one or the other in varying degrees. By abandoning the forest and specializing in bipedal walk the hominids had been selected for the most successful experiment and could even remain more conservative in some ways than the great apes while acquiring other unique and decisive specializations.

REFERENCES

ALLEN, J. A., 1925, Primates collected by the American Museum Congo Expedition. *Bull. Amer. Mus. Nat. Hist.*, 47:283–499.

BIEGERT, J., 1961, Volarhaut der Hände und Füsse. *Primatologia*, 2, Liefer. 3:1–326 (Karger, Basel).

BLUMENBACH, J. F., 1791, *Handbuch der Naturgeschichte.* 4te Aufl. (Göttingen).

CAVE, A. J. E., and R. WHEELER HAINES, 1940, The paranasal sinuses of the anthropoid apes. *J. Anat.*, 74:493–523.

———, 1961, The frontal sinus of the gorilla. *Proc. Zool. Soc. London*, 136:359–373.

CHIARELLI, B., 1966, Marked chromosome in catarrhine monkeys. *Folia primatologica*, 4:74–80.

CHOPRA, S. R. K., 1957, The cranial suture closure in monkeys. *Proc. Zoolog. Soc. London*, 128:67–112.

COOLIDGE, H. J., JR., 1929, A review of the genus *Gorilla. Memoirs Mus. Comp. Zool.* Harvard College, 50:291–381.

DARWIN, C., 1874, *The descent of man, and selection in relation to sex.* 2nd ed. (London).

FIEDLER, W., 1956, Uebersicht über das System der Primaten. *Primatologia*, 1:1–266 (Karger, Basel).

FÜRST, C. M., and F. C. C. HANSEN, 1915, Crania Groenlandica. (Höst & Son, Copenhagen).

GREGORY, W. K., 1934, *Man's place among the anthropoids.* (Clarendon Press, Oxford).

HALL-CRAGG, E. C. B., 1962, The testis of *Gorilla gorilla beringei. Proc. Zoolog. Soc. London,* 139: 511–514.

HAMERTON, J. P., KLINGER, H. P., MUTTON, D. E., and LANG, E. M., 1963, The somatic chromosomes of Hominoidea. *Citogenetics,* 2:240–263.

HARMS, J. W., 1956, Fortpflanzungsbiologie. *Primatologia,* 1:561–600 (Karger, Basel).

——, 1956, Schwangerschaft und Geburt. *Primatologia,* 1:661–722 (Karger, Basel).

HILL, W. C. O., External genitalia. *Primatologia,* 3. T. 1:630–704 (Karger, Basel).

JOSEPHI, W., 1787, *Anatomie der Säugethiere.* 1. Band (Knochenlehre der Affen). (J. C. Dieterich, Göttingen).

KEITH, A., 1934, *The construction of man's family tree.* Forum Series No. 18 (Watts & C., London).

LASINSKI, W., 1960, Aeusseres Ohr. *Primatologia,* 2, T. 1, Liefer. 5:41–74 (Karger, Basel).

OLIVIER, G., 1962, *Formation du squelette des membres chez l'homme* (Vigot Frères, Paris).

OWEN, R., 1868, On the anatomy of vertebrates. Vol. III, *Mammals* (Longmans, Green & Co., London).

RANDALL, F. E., 1934–1944, The skeletal and dental development and variability of the gorilla. *Human Biol.,* 15:236–254, 307–337, 16:23–76.

REMANE, A., 1954., Methodische Probleme der Hominoiden-Phylogenie, II. *Z. f. Morphol. u. Anthropol.,* 46:225–268.

——, 1961. Probleme der Systematik der Primaten. *Z. f. wissensch. Zool.,* 165:1–34.

RICKENMANN, E., 1957, *Beiträge zur vergleichenden Anatomie insbesondere des Beckens bei Catarrhinen.* Diss. Univ. Freiburg (Switzerland).

RIESEN, A. H. and E. F. KINDER., 1952, *Postural development of infant chimpanzees.* (Yale Univ. Press, New Haven).

SCHREBER, J. C. D., 1775, *Die Säugethiere in Abbildungen nach der Natur mit Beschreibungen.* (Walther, Erlangen).

SCHULTZ, A. H., 1926, Fetal growth of man and other primates. *Quart. Rev. Biol.,* 1:465–521.

——, 1929, The technique of measuring the outer body of human fetuses and of primates in general. Carnegie Inst. Wash. Publ. 394, *Contrib. to Embryol.,* 20:213–257.

——, 1930, The skeleton of the trunk and limbs of higher primates. *Human Biol.,* 2:303–438.

——, 1931, Man as a primate. *Scientific Monthly,* 1931:385–412.

——, 1931, The density of hair in primates. *Human Biol.,* 3:303–321.

——, 1932, The generic position of *Symphalangus klossii. J. Mammal.,* 13:368–369.

——, 1933, Observations on the growth, classification and evolutionary specialization of gibbons and siamangs. *Human Biol.,* 5:212–255, 385–428.

——, 1933, Die Körperproportionen der erwachsenen catarrhinen Primaten, mit spezieller Berücksichtigung der Menschenaffen. *Anthropol. Anz.,* 10: 154–185.

——, 1934, Some distinguishing characters of the mountain gorilla. *J. Mamm.,* 15:51–61.

——, 1935, Eruption and decay of the permanent teeth in primates. *Amer. J. Phys. Anthropol.,* 19: 489–581.

——, 1935, The nasal cartilages in higher primates. *Amer. J. Phys. Anthropol.,* 20:205–212.

——, 1936, Characters common to higher primates and characters specific for man. *Quart. Rev. Biol.,* 11:259–283, 425–455.

——, 1937, Proportions, variability and asymmetries of the long bones of the limbs and the clavicles in man and apes. *Human Biol.,* 9:281–328.

——, 1938, The relative weight of the testes in primates. *Anat. Rec.,* 72:387–394.

——, 1940, The size of the orbit and of the eye in primates. *Amer. J. Phys. Anthropol.,* 26:389–408.

——, 1941, The relative size of the cranial capacity in primates. *Amer. J. Phys. Anthropol.,* 28:273–287.

——, 1941, Growth and development of the orang-utan. Carnegie Inst. Wash. Publ. 525, *Contrib. to Embryol.,* 29:57–110.

——, 1942, Conditions for balancing the head in primates. *Amer. J. Phys. Anthropol.,* 29:483–497.

——, 1944, Age changes and variability in gibbons. *Amer. J. Phys. Anthropol.,* n. s. 2:1–129.

——, 1949, Ontogenetic specializations of man. *Arch. Julius Klaus-Stift.,* 24:197–216.

——, 1949, Sex Differences in the pelves of primates. *Amer. J. Phys. Anthropol.,* n. s. 7:401–424.

——, 1950, Morphological observations on gorillas. Henry Cushier Raven Memorial Vol.: *The Anatomy of the Gorilla,* 227–253 (Columbia Univ. Press, New York).

——, 1950, The physical distinctions of man. *Proc. Amer. Philos. Soc.,* 94:428–449.

————, 1952, Ueber das Wachstum der Warzenfortsätze beim Menschen und den Menschenaffen, *Homo,* 3:105–109.

————, 1952, Vergleichende Untersuchungen an einigen menschlichen Spezialisationen, *Bull. Schweiz. Ges. f. Anthrop. u. Ethnol.,* 28:25–37.

————, 1953, The relative thickness of the long bones and the vertebrae in primates. *Amer. J. Phys. Anthropol.,* n. s. 11:277–311.

————, 1954, Bemerkungen zur Variabilität und Systematik der Schimpansen. *Säugetierkundl. Mitteil.,* 2:159–163.

————, 1954, Studien über die Wirbelzahlen und die Körperproportionen von Halbaffen. Vierteljahrsschr. Naturfor. Ges. Zürich, 99:39–75.

————, 1955, The position of the occipital condyles and of the face relative to the skull base in primates. *Amer. J. Phys. Anthropol.,* n. s. 13:97–120.

————, 1956, Postembryonic age changes. *Primatologia,* 1:887–964 (Karger, Basel).

————, 1956, The occurrence and frequency of pathological and teratological conditions and of twinning among nonhuman primates. *Primatologia,* 1:965–1014 (Karger, Basel).

————, 1957, *Die Bedeutung der Primatenkunde für das Verständnis der Anthropogenese.* Ber. 5te Tagung D. Ges. f. Anthropol., 13–28.

————, 1957, Past and present views of man's specializations. *Irish J. Med. Science,* 1957:341–356.

————, 1958, Palatine ridges. *Primatologia,* 3, T. 1: 127–138. (Karger, Basel).

————, 1960, Einige Beobachtungen und Masse am Skelett von *Oreopithecus. Z. Morphol. u. Anthropol.,* 50:136–149.

————, 1960, Age changes and variability in the skulls and teeth of the Central American monkeys *Alouatta, Cebus* and *Ateles. Proc. Zool. Soc. London,* 133:337–390.

————, 1960, Age changes in primates and their modifications in man. *Human Growth,* 1–20 (Pergamon Press, London).

————, 1961, Some factors influencing the social life of primates in general and of early man in particular. *Viking Fund Publ. in Anthropol.,* 31:58–90.

————, 1961, Vertebral column and thorax. *Primatologia,* 4, Liefer. 5:1–66 (Karger, Basel).

————, 1962, The relative weights of the skeletal parts in adult primates. *Amer. J. Phys. Anthropol.,* n. s. 20:1–10.

————, 1962, Die Schädelkapazität männlicher Gorillas und ihr Höchstwert. *Anthropol. Anz.,* 25:197–203.

————, 1962, Metric age changes and sex differences in primate skulls. *Z. Morphol. u. Anthropol.,* 52: 239–255.

————, 1963, Relations between the lengths of the main parts of the foot skeleton in primates. *Folia primatologica,* 1:150–171.

————, 1963, Age changes, sex differences, and variability as factors in the classification of primates. *Classification and Human Evolution* (S. L. Washburn, ed.), 85–115. Chicago.

————, 1964, A gorilla with exceptionally large teeth and supernumerary premolars. *Folia primatologica,* 2:149–160.

————, 1965, Die rezenten Hominoidea. *Menschliche Abstammungslehre* (G. Heberer, ed.), 56–102. Stuttgart.

————, 1965, The cranial capacity and the orbital volume of hominoids according to age and sex. Homenaje a Juan Comas, II:337–357. Mexico.

————, 1966, Changing views on the nature and interrelations of the higher primates. Yerkes Newsletter (Emory University), 3:15–29.

SELENKA, E., 1898, Rassen, Schädel und Bezahnung des Orangutan. *Studien über Entwickelungsgesch.,* Heft 6, Menschenaffen. (Wiesbaden).

————, 1899, Schädel des Gorilla und Schimpanse. *Studien über Entwickelungsgesch.,* Heft 7, Menschenaffen. (Wiesbaden).

STARCK, D., and R. SCHNEIDER, 1960, Larynx. *Primatologia,* 3. T. 2:423–587 (Karger, Basel).

STRAUS, W. L., JR., 1942, The structure of the crownpad of the gorilla and of the cheek-pad of the orang-utan. *J. Mammal.,* 23:276–281.

TAILLARD, W., 1957, *Les Spondylolisthesis.* (Masson et Cie., Paris).

TUTTLE, R. H. and ROGERS, C. M., 1966, Genetic and selective factors in reduction of the hallux in *Pongo pygmaeus. Amer. J. Phys. Anthropol.,* 24:191–198.

VALLOIS, H., 1955, Ordre des Primates. *Traité de Zoologie,* 17:1854–2206. (Paris).

WEGNER, R. N., 1956, *Studien über Nebenhöhlen des Schädels,* Wissensch. Z. Univ. Greifswald, 5, Mathem.-naturwiss. Reihe, 1.

WISLOCKI, G. B., 1942, Size, weight and histology of the testes in the gorilla. *J. Mammal.,* 23:281–287.

WOOD JONES, F., 1948, *Hallmarks of mankind.* (Williams & Wilkins, Baltimore).

YERKES, R. M., 1943, *Chimpanzees: A laboratory colony.* (Yale Univ. Press, New Haven).

ZAPFE, H., 1960, Die Primatenfunde aus der miozänen Spaltenfüllung von Neudorf an der March, Tschechoslowakei. *Schweiz. Palaeontol. Abhdl.,* 78:1–293.

FOUR • PROBLEMS OF CLASSIFICATION

4 • THE MEANING OF TAXONOMIC STATEMENTS

George Gaylord Simpson

The author of this contribution, a leading paleontologist and distinguished author of *The Meaning of Evolution* and many other seminal works, offers here the best discussion available of taxonomic procedures for the anthropologist. Simpson underscores the point, too often overlooked by amateur taxonomists and others, that the meaning of the name bestowed upon a specimen, even though that name may have been coined in order to reflect its status and affinities, does not in fact tell us anything about either the status or affinities of the specimen, but simply represents the taxon to which the nomen was first attached. For instance, the name "Pithecanthropus" was intended by its discoverer, Eugene Dubois, to reflect the "apeman" status and affinities of this first of the pithecanthropines. "Pithecanthropus" did, in fact, communicate the "apeman" notion; unfortunately, too, for it influenced and prejudiced thinking in an unsound direction. "Pithecanthropus" was not an "apeman," but a man, *Homo,* and is today so recognized by all authorities, but for many years the name "Pithecanthropus" served to impede recognition of that fact.

In general it would be a good idea to avoid endowing the remains of fossil primates with names purporting to describe their status and affinities. Perhaps "Homo sapiens" is one of the worst examples of a "meaning name." As that distinguished student of man, Oscar Wilde, once remarked, Linnaeus' name for man is perhaps the most premature ever bestowed upon any taxon. A name such as *Dryopithecus,* although a "meaning name," is preferable to "a status

SOURCE: Sherwood L. Washburn, ed., *Classification and Human Evolution* (Chicago: Aldine Publishing Company, 1963), pp. 1–31. Copyright © by Wenner-Gren Foundation for Anthropological Research, Inc., 1963. Reprinted by permission of the author and Aldine-Atherton, Inc.

and affinities" name. "Dryopithecus" merely indicates an ape who lived in an oak forest—apart from the "pithecus" it implies no taxonomic judgment.

That taxa are always *populations* is, as the author emphasizes, too often forgotten when an individual species is being described. Insufficient experience of the great variability common to all mammalian forms, especially to hominoid forms, constitutes one of the principal factors in the proliferation of claims to new species and even genera in the paleoanthropological literature. Certain common human frailties, such as ego-involvement, emotional investment, prestige, even "national honor," have not surprisingly often been involved.

In Part II Simpson provides an excellent case history of the fossil primate *Oreopithecus,* showing that principally as a result of a detailed study of the teeth, while it may be recognized as a hominoid, it cannot possibly be included among the Hominidae.

Introduction

Everyone who deals with evolution has occasion to use and to understand statements in the special language of taxonomy and classification. Communication is impeded by the facts that not all who use that language speak it fluently and that those fluent in it do not all speak the same dialect. In our conference on classification in relationship to human evolution we were talking this language much of the time. The main function of this contribution was to discuss the grammar and semantics of a reasonably standard dialect of the language. Centering the discussion on hominoid classification brings up and may clarify certain crucial points. This chapter is not, how-

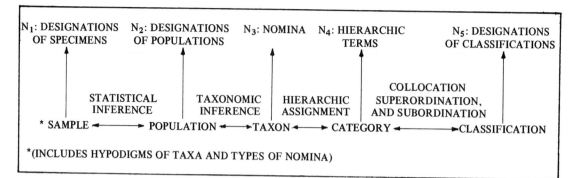

Figure 1: Schema of processes (arrows), name sets (N), and referents (capitals) in taxonomy. Vertical arrows all represent the process of designation or symbolization. The processes represented by horizontal arrows proceed logically from left to right, but in practice no one operation can be carried out without reference to the others. These arrows are therefore drawn pointing both ways.

ever, concerned with expressing opinions about human classification and evolution, but with discussing how such opinions are or should be expressed. I have recently covered theoretical aspects of animal taxonomy in some detail (Simpson, 1961), and mere repetition of parts of that book is here avoided.

Classification, Terminology, and Nomenclature

Taxonomic language involves not only a very large number of different designative words (names, terms) but also several different *kinds* of designations. The things or concepts designated by these words, technically their referents,[1] are also of different kinds, and the meanings or semantic implications are likewise diverse.

It is therefore essential that they be clearly distinguished. One way to do this is to consider the main operations involved in classification and the points or levels where special designations are required, as shown schematically in Figure 1.

The process starts with observation of the specimens in hand, the objective materials. The specimens studied and believed to be related in some biologically relevant way are a *sample*. If they are believed to represent a definite taxon (as determined at another level of inference), they constitute a *hypodigm*. Unequivocal designations of the specimens must refer to them as concrete, discrete objects; they are not designated by any name of the population or taxon to which they are supposed to belong. The ideal designation, practically universal in zoology but unfortunately not in anthropology, is by a collection or repository symbol and a catalogue number uniquely associated with each specimen. This is one kind of designation, one set of names (symbols of some sort, not necessarily or usually in words), and may be called the N_1 naming set.[2]

Observations and specimens, no matter how numerous, have no scientific significance purely per se. They acquire significance only when they are considered as representative of a larger group, or population, of possible observations or of individuals united by some common principle or relationship. The population may be abstract, for instance as symbolized in the equation for gravitation, applicable to a potentially infinite number

---

[1] A psycholinguistic term also useful in zoological taxonomy. See Brown (1958).

[2] Recognizing different sets of taxonomic designations and distinguishing them in this way is due to Gregg (1954), although I do not follow him in detail.

of events but derived from a finite series of experimental observations. In zoological taxonomy the population is finite and concrete: a set of organisms existing (now or formerly) in nature. The existence and characteristics of that population are inferred from the sample drawn (we hope at random) from the population. The methods of inference are statistical by definition, which does not mean that any particular procedure of mathematical statistics is necessarily used although, of course, that is often appropriate and useful. A population is obviously not the same as the specimens actually studied, a sample drawn from the population.

At the next step in the process, all populations belong to taxa and all taxa are composed of populations. However, the two are not necessarily coextensive. It is often necessary to recognize and designate a local population that is a part of a taxon but does not in itself comprise a whole taxon. For some populations a different set of names or symbols, N_2, may therefore be required. Populations are in fact sometimes given distinct designations in zoological systematics, commonly by specification of their geographic location, but there is no established and uniform system. It may be sufficient to designate a population either as that from which a given sample was drawn (hence by extension of an N_1 designation) or as identical with that of a given taxon (hence by an N_3 designation).

A taxon is a group of real organisms recognized as a formal unit at any level of a hierarchic classification (Simpson, 1961, which see also for definitions and more extended discussions of hypodigms, categories, and heirarchies). A taxon is therefore a population, although the over-all population of one taxon may include many distinct populations of lesser scope. A taxon is created by inference that a population (itself statistically inferred from a sample which now becomes a hypodigm) meets a definition adopted for units in an author's classification. The set of designations for

taxa, N_3 names, are those of formal, technical zoological nomenclature, e.g. *Homo*, the name of a taxon in primate classification. The word "name" is used in many different ways, both in the vernacular and in technical discussion, and this has engendered confusion. I propose that technical Neo-Linnaean names in the N_3 set be called *nomina* (singular, *nomen*). Vernacular names ("lion," "monkey," "Neanderthal man") are in the N_3 set if they designate taxa, but they are not nomina.

Each taxon is assigned to (considered as a member of) a category, which has a defined rank in hierarchic classification. A category is a set, the members of which are all the taxa placed at a given level in such a classification. Categories are distinct from taxa, do not have populations as members, and are not represented by samples. They have their own set of names, N_4, which are the relatively few terms applied to levels of the Neo-Linnaean system: basically phylum, class, order, family, genus, and species, with various combinations in super-, sub-, and infra-, and occasionally such additional terms as cohort or tribe.

Finally the various taxa of assigned categorical rank are collocated, superordinated, and subordinated among themselves and so form a hierarchic classification. This is done in terms of the N_3 (nomina) and N_4 (hierarchic terms) names. The added implications are conveyed less by nomenclatural than by topological means, primarily by arrangement and not consistently by verbal or related symbolization. Designations of classifications, N_5, are normally bibliographic references to their authors and places of publication.

What, now, are the meanings or implications of the various sets of designations? N_1 designations refer to particular objects. They imply only that a given specimen exists. They assure that when the same designation is used, the same object is meant. N_2 and N_3 designations both refer to groups that are considered to be populations related in some way. An author using such designations must make clear, explicitly or implicitly, the kind of relationship he has in mind. In modern zoology unless some other usage is definitely stated, it is generally understood that the relationship is genetic, that is, that it reflects evolutionary relationships. Concepts of what constitutes evolutionary relationships, how they are to be determined, and how reflected in classification become difficult and complex, but that is a different point.

Besides the implication that a population, usually genetic in relationship, is designated, nomina, N_3 names, further imply that the unit designated is given a definite rank in classification, that it is associated with an N_4 term. Under the International Code the forms of some nomina reflect the categorical rank of the corresponding taxa. For example, nomina ending in -idae (e.g. Hominidae) name families, and italicized, capitalized single words (e.g. *Homo*) name genera.

Most nomina, however, lack implications as to superordination, and *none have any implications beyond those mentioned.* For instance, nomina have no implications as to relationships among taxa at the same categorical level (e.g. *Homo* and *Tarsius*) or among taxa at any levels with etymologically distinct names (e.g. *Gorilla* and Pongidae). Further implications, which may be numerous and intricate as will be illustrated later, are inherent in the arrangement of nomina in a classification and not in the nomina themselves.

Discussion at the conference repeatedly illustrated the need for employing and distinguishing the different naming sets. The ambiguity and clumsiness of usual references to particular specimens and populations were especially evident. For example no clear and simple way was found for designating the various specimens from Olduvai Bed I that are believed not to belong to the taxon called *Zinjanthropus boisei* by Leakey. Presumably they will eventually be placed in taxa with distinct nomina (in the N_3 set), but that will not solve the problem of referring to the specimens themselves or to the populations inferred from them without ambiguity and without prejudice as to their taxonomic interpretation. As another example, no one maintains that *Telanthropus* is a valid taxon at the generic level, but no way has been found to refer to the specimens in question except as *Telanthropus,* an N_3 designation that necessarily implies a taxonomic conclusion agreed to be incorrect.

It must be emphasized that one of the greatest linguistic needs in this field is for clear, uniform, and distinct sets of N_1 and N_2 designations, applied to specimens and to local populations as distinct from taxa. Just what form such designations should take is a matter for proposal and agreement among those directly concerned with the specimens and their interpretation. It suffices here to stress that they *must not* have the form of Neo-Linnaean nomina. (The catalogue now being compiled by Oakley and Campbell may opportunely provide designations for specimens of fossil Hominidae.)

The Chaos of Anthropological Nomenclature

Men and all recent and fossil organisms pertinent to their affinities are animals, and the appropriate language for discussing their classification and relationships is that of animal taxonomy. When anthropologists have special purposes for which zoological taxonomic language is not appropriate, they should devise a separate language that does not duplicate any of the functions of this one and that does not permit confusion with its forms. There is, I believe, no reason for use of an additional language when what is being discussed is in fact the taxonomy of organisms. This language has been developed over a period of hundreds of years by cumulative experience and thought and has been thoroughly tested in nonanthropological use. It is admittedly imperfect, but for its purpose it is the best instrument available. Its imperfections call rather for improvement than for replacement. The most important needed improvement, with particular reference to anthropology, is that all those who use it should speak it well and in accordance with the best established current usages.

It is notorious that hominid nomenclature, particularly, has become chaotic. It is ironical that some of those who have most complained of the chaos have been leading contributors to it. A recent proposal that an international commission be formed to deal with the chaos refuses to recognize the appropriate code and the appropriate commission already set up. The author then proceeds to compound the confusion that he condemns.

Insofar as the chaos is merely formal or grammatical, it could be cleared up by knowledge of and adherence to the International Code of Zoological Nomenclature (Stoll et al., 1961), supplemented, if necessary, by whatever action might be proposed to and endorsed by the International Commission for Zoological Nomenclature. Much of the complexity and lack of agreement in nomenclature in this field does not, however, stem from ignorance or flouting of formal procedures but from differences of opinion that cannot be settled by rule or fiat. For example, when Leakey inferred from an Olduvai specimen (which he made a hypodigm) the existence of a taxon that he called *Zinjanthropus boisei* he was using correct taxonomic grammar to express the opinion that the taxon was distinct at both specific and generic categorical levels from any previously named. In equally grammatical expression of other opinions many other nomina, such as *Paranthropus boisei*, *Australopithecus robustus boisei*, or *Homo africanus boisei*, might have been proposed and might now be used. Or the specimen might have been and

might now be referred to (or added to the hypodigm of) some previously named taxon such as *Paranthropus crassidens*. Any of those alternatives accord equally with the Code and would have equal status before the Commission. Decision among them is a zoological, not a nomenclatural or linguistic question, and it will be made by an eventual consensus of zoologists qualified in this special field.

Insofar as the chaos is due to faulty linguistics rather than to zoological disagreements, it stems either from ignorance or from refusal to follow rules and usages.[3] This must be almost the only field of science in which those who do not know and follow the established norms have so frequently had the temerity and opportunity to publish research that is, in this respect, incompetent.

An overt reason sometimes given for refusal to follow known nomeclatural norms is that some nomen is, in the opinion of a particular author, inappropriate. For example, some choose to rename *Australopithecus* as *Australanthropus*, thus adding another objective synonym to the chaos, on the grounds that the Greek *anthropos* more nearly expresses their opinion as to the affinities of the genus than does *pithekos*. The argument is completely irrelevant. *Australopithecus* does not mean "southern ape." Its meaning (defined by its referent) is simply the taxon to which the nomen was first attached and to which it was the first nomen attached. *Palaeolumbricus* or *Jitu* would have served just as well. The generic nomen does not, in itself, express any opinion as to the affinities of the taxon, and if nomina were changed in accord with every shade of opinion on affinities the chaos would be even worse than it is.[4]

---

[3] Mayr, Linsley, and Usinger (1953) provide an excellent introduction to the rules and basic taxonomic usages. The promulgation of a later code (Stoll *et al.*, 1961) must, however, now be taken in account.

[4] It is true that when the system was being developed, from 200 to 250 years ago, the then relatively few nomina were usually intended to be etymologically

descriptive. The experience of two centuries has, however, conclusively demonstrated that as a general principle this is absolutely unworkable. Except for the occasional mnemonic value, it is unfortunate that nomina do often have ostensible etymological meanings in addition to their real, taxonomic meanings.

Another reason for the chaos is the previously mentioned failure to develop and use consistently different designations for specimens, populations, and taxa, that is, distinct N_1, N_2, and N_3 name sets. A truly eminent anthropologist insisted on using the (N_3) nomen *Sinanthropus pekinensis* for specimens and a population although he concluded that this nomen does not designate a *taxon* specifically distinct from *Pithecanthropus erectus* or indeed from *Homo sapiens*. The example is far from unique.

Probably no one has ever admitted this, but it seems almost obvious that nomina (N_3) have sometimes been given to single specimens just to emphasize the importance of a discovery that could and should have been designated merely by a catalogue number (N_1). Of course no two specimens are alike, and it is always possible to fulfill the formal requirement that ostensible definition of a taxon must accompany proposal of a nomen. However, and again I would say obviously, the "definition" has often been only a description of an individual "type" with no regard for or even apparent consciousness of the fact that taxa are *populations*. This is not just a matter of exaggerating the taxonomic difference between specimens. It is a much more fundamental misunderstanding of what taxonomy is all about, of what nomina actually name. It is a relapse into pre-evolutionary typology, from which (I must confess) even the nonanthropological zoologists have not yet entirely freed themselves. Nomina have types, but not in the old typological sense. The types are not the referents of the N_3 nomina but are among the referents of N_1 designations. The referents of nomina are taxa—certain kinds of populations.

It is of course also true that the significance of differences between any two specimens has almost invariably come to be enormously exaggerated by one authority or another in this field. Here the fault is not so much lack of taxonomic grammar as lack of taxonomic common sense or experience. Many fossil hominids have been described and

named by workers with no other experience in taxonomy. They have inevitably lacked the sense of balance and the interpretive skill of zoologists who have worked extensively on larger groups of animals. It must, however, be sadly noted that even broadly equipped zoologists often seem to lose their judgment if they work on hominids. Here factors of prestige, of personal involvement, of emotional investment rarely fail to affect the fully human scientist, although they hardly trouble the workers on, say, angleworms or dung beetles.

It is not really my intention to read an admonitory sermon to the anthropologists. You are all well aware of these shortcomings—in the work of others. I must pass on to matters more positive in value.

Species and Genera

The undue proliferation of specific and generic nomina is in part a semantic problem. The proposal of such nomina is rarely accompanied by an appropriate definition of the categories (as distinct from the taxa) involved, but ascribing specific or generic status to slightly variant specimens can be rationalized only on a typological basis. Whether consciously or not, taxa are evidently being defined as morphological types and statistical-taxonomic inferences from hypodigm to population to taxon (see Fig. 1) are being omitted. But in modern biology taxa are populations and the following two nonconflicting definitions of the species are widely accepted:

Species are groups of actually or potentially interbreeding populations, which are reproductively isolated from other such groups.

An evolutionary species is a lineage (an ancestral–descendant sequence of populations) evolving separately from others and with its own unitary evolutionary role and tendencies. (Quoted from Simpson, 1961, where sources are cited and the definitions are further discussed.)

The naming of a species either should imply that the taxon is believed to correspond with one or both of those definitions or should be accompanied by the author's own equally clear alternative definition.

Evidence that the definition is met is largely morphological in most cases, especially for fossils. The most widely available and acceptable evidence is demonstration of a sufficient level of statistical confidence that a discontinuity exists *not* between specimens in hand but *between the populations inferred from those specimens.* The import of such evidence and the semantic implication of the word "species" are that populations placed in separate species are either

(1) in separate lineages (contemporaneous or not) between which significant interbreeding does not occur, or

(2) at successive stages in one lineage but with intervening evolutionary change of such magnitude that populations differ about as much as do contemporaneous species.

In dealing with the incomplete fossil record the information at hand commonly cannot establish the original presence or absence of a discontinuity. Allowance must be made for probabilities that further discovery will confirm or confute the existence of an ostensible discontinuity. Those probabilities depend on various circumstances. If populations are approximately contemporaneous, only moderately distinctive, and separated by a large geographic area from which no comparable specimens are known, there is considerable possibility that discovery of intervening populations would eliminate discontinuity. That is, for example, the situation regarding the original hypodigms of *Pithecanthropus erectus* and *Atlanthropus mauritanicus.* In my opinion the possibility that the Trinil

population and the Ternifine population belong to the same species is such that different specific (a fortiori, generic) nomina are not justified at present.

If, on the other hand, populations being compared are of markedly different ages, decision to give them different specific nomina should depend on judgment whether such nomina would be justified if it turned out that they belong in successive segments of the same lineage. That would apply, for example, to the Mauer population as compared with the late Pleistocene European neanderthaloid population, and I should think would justify different specific nomina in this example.[5] Still a third situation arises when samples indicate populations that were approximately contemporaneous and living in the same region (synchronous and sympatric) as may be true, at least in part, for the Kromdrai, Swartkrans, Makapan, and Sterkfontein populations. In such cases allowance hardly has to be made for possible discoveries of populations living at other times and in different places. The degree of statistical confidence generated by the samples actually in hand may be taken as definitive of the probability of an original discontinuity, for instance between *Australopithecus africanus* and *A. robustus.*

The category genus is necessarily more arbitrary and less precise in definition than the species. A genus is a group of species believed to be more closely related among themselves than to any species placed in other genera. Pertinent morphological evidence is provided when a species differs less from another in the same genus than from any in another genus. When in fact only one species of a genus is known, that criterion is not available, and judgment may be based on differences comparable to those between accepted genera in the same general zoological group. There is no absolute criterion for the degree of difference to be called generic, and it is particularly here that experience and common sense are required.

It must be kept in mind that a genus is a *differ-*

---

[5] I am not suggesting what those nomina should be. Among many other possibilities they might be *Homo heidelbergensis* and *Homo neanderthalensis,* or *Homo erectus* and *Homo sapiens.*

ent category from a species and that it is in principle a *group* of species. Much of the chaos in anthropological nomenclature has arisen from giving a different generic nomen to every supposed species, even some clearly not meriting specific rank. In effect no semantic distinction has been made between genus and species, and indeed the number of proposed generic nomina for hominids is much greater than the number of validly definable species. Monotypic genera are justified when, and only when, a single, isolated known species is so distinctive that the probability is that it belongs to a generic group of otherwise unknown ancestral, collateral, or descendant species. No one can reasonably doubt that this is true, for example, of *Oreopithecus bambolii* and that in this case the (at present) monotypic genus is justified. It is, however, hard to see how the application of more than one generic name to the various presently known australopithecine populations can possibly be justified, whatever the specific status of those populations may be.

Phylogeny and Resemblance

As most biologists understand modern taxonomic language, its implications are primarily evolutionary, but there is some persisting confusion even among professional taxonomists. It is not possible for classification directly to *express,* in all detail, opinions either as to phylogenetic relationships or as to degrees of resemblance. As a rule with important exceptions, degrees of resemblance tend to be correlated with degrees of evolutionary affinity. Resemblance provides important, but *not the only,* evidence of affinity. Classification can be made consistent with, even though not directly or fully expressive of, evolutionary affinity, and its language then has appropriate and understandable genetic implications. Classification cannot, at least in some cases, be made fully consistent with resemblance, and any implications as to resemblance

are secondary and not necessarily reliable. These relationships can be explored by consideration of several hypothetical models or examples, set up so as to be simplified parallels of real problems in the use of taxonomic language to discuss human origins and relationships.

Classification and taxonomic discussion of related but distinct contemporaneous groups, such as the living apes and living men, involves a pattern of evolutionary divergence. That will first be discussed by means of a model. Discovery of related fossils almost always complicates the picture by revealing other groups divergent from both of those primarily concerned. It may, however, also reveal forms that are ancestral or that are close enough to the ancestry to strengthen inferences about the common ancestor and the course of evolution in the diverging lineages. In general the characters of two contemporaneous groups as compared with their common ancestry will tend to fall into the following classes, exemplified by characters of recent Pongidae and Hominidae:

A. Ancestral characters retained in both descendent groups. E.g. absence of external tail, pentadactylism, dental formula.
B. Ancestral characters retained in the first descendent group but divergently evolved in the second. E.g. quadrupedalism, grasping pes.
C. Ancestral characters retained in the second but divergent in the first group. E.g. undifferentiated lower premolars.
D. Characters divergently specialized in both. E.g. brachiation versus bipedalism.
E. Characters progressive but parallel in both. E.g. increase in average body size.
F. Convergent characters. I know of none between pongids and hominids, a fact which (if it is a fact) greatly simplifies judgment as to their affinities.

Different numbers of characters will fall into different categories. For instance in pongid-hom inid comparison there are certainly many more A characters than any others and more B than C characters. (The given example of a C character is dubious.) Many characters do not simply and absolutely fall into one category or other. Retention of ancestral characters is usually relative and not absolute; some changes generally occur and "retained" usually means only "less changed." In constructing the simplest possible model on this basis, further simplifying postulates are that characters evolve at constant rates and that characters in the same group (e.g. D or E) evolve at the same rates. Those postulates are certainly never true in real phylogenies, and more realistic but also much more complicated models can be constructed by taking varying rates of evolution into account. The simplest possible limiting case, although unrealistic in detail, nevertheless more clearly illustrates valid and pertinent matters of principle. Such a model, analogous to pongid-hominid divergence, is illustrated in Figure 2. Numbers preceding the category designations symbolize relative numbers of characters in the corresponding categories. Exponents symbolize progressive change: a-b-c-, or in a different direction x-y-z. It is assumed that in this example there are no F (convergent) characters. Roman numerals represent taxa: IV and V the two contemporaneous groups being compared, and I their common ancestry, ancestral to IV through II and to V through III.

From such data a comparison matrix can be formed. . . . For present purposes a . . . sufficient method is to tabulate step differences between taxa. Change from C to C^a, for instance, is

one step and from C^a to C^c is two more. These are multiplied by the number of characters in the category, 1 for C characters. The matrix for the model in Figure 2 is given in Table 1. In this form of comparison, the smaller the number the greater the similarity. In this model I and II are most and IV and V least alike.

Table 1: Comparison Matrix for Data of the Model in Fig. 2

	I	II	III	IV	V
I	0	6	9	18	29
II	6	0	12	12	32
III	9	12	0	24	19
IV	18	12	24	0	36
V	29	32	19	36	0

Let us suppose now that classification were to be based *entirely* on degrees of resemblance, as has been proposed by some taxonomists, and that classificatory language was therefore understood to be directly and solely expressive of resemblance. In building up higher taxa one would of course start by uniting I and II. If I and II are species, they would be placed in one genus; if genera, in one family. The maximum difference within the higher taxon would be 6. If no greater difference were allowed, all other lower taxa, III, IV, and V, would have to be placed in separate, monotypic higher taxa, an arrangement with nearly minimal significance, indicating no more than the close resemblance of I and II. If a difference of 12 were allowed in the higher taxon, II would be united with I and II, but IV should now also go with II, from which its difference is also 12. However, a taxon including IV and I would have to allow a difference of 18 and one including IV and III a difference of 24. But now V must also be added, for its difference from III is only 19. Thus *all* the lower taxa must go in a single taxon of next higher rank, an arrangement that indicates nothing of resemblances or relationships among any of those taxa. Insertion, or in actual examples discovery, of

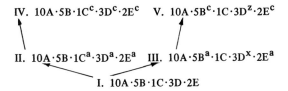

IV. $10A \cdot 5B \cdot 1C^c \cdot 3D^c \cdot 2E^c$ V. $10A \cdot 5B^c \cdot 1C \cdot 3D^z \cdot 2E^c$

II. $10A \cdot 5B \cdot 1C^a \cdot 3D^a \cdot 2E^a$ III. $10A \cdot 5B^a \cdot 1C \cdot 3D^x \cdot 2E^a$

I. $10A \cdot 5B \cdot 1C \cdot 3D \cdot 2E$

Figure 2: A model of simple evolutionary divergence. Symbols are explained in the text.

additional taxa, say between II and IV, would only compound the difficulties and lead still more inevitably to equally unsatisfactory alternatives.

I believe that the conclusion from the model is quite general for analogous real cases. In such situations the use of classificatory language as direct expression of degrees of resemblance commonly tends to produce one of two extremely inexpressive results: (1) one higher taxon includes the two most similar lower taxa and all other higher taxa are monotypic; or (2) one higher taxon includes all the lower taxa, no matter how numerous.[6]

Now let us agree that classificatory language is to have primarily evolutionary significance. For the moment degrees of resemblance need not be considered at all. It is clear from consideration of characters in categories B, C, and D that II can be ancestral to IV but not to III or V, and that III can be ancestral to V but not to II or IV. In actual instances the conclusions are neither so simple nor so obvious, but probabilities are readily established by the same categories of evidence. On this basis, I and IV can be placed in one higher taxon and III and V in another of the same categorical rank. That arrangement expresses the opinion, postulated as true in the model, that II and IV are phylogenetically related to each other and that III and V are also related in more or less the same way and degree. The arrangement is also consistent with but does not express the opinion, also postulated as true, that II is ancestral to IV and III to V.

In completion of this arrangement there are two alternatives as regards I. It could be placed in a third higher taxon ancestral to both of the two already formed, or it could be placed in the same higher taxon as II and IV, because it is phylogenetically closer to II than to III. Degree of resemblance here enters in as evidence for the latter inference.

Those are not the only classifications that would be consistent with the postulated evolutionary history. It would also be consistent to put I, II, and III in one higher taxon and IV and V in two others, or I, II, III, and IV in one and V in another. The implications on affinity would be somewhat different in each case but not conflicting: all are consistent with the postulates of the model. Choice would depend in part on what implications one wanted especially to bring out, since not all can be expressed in one classification. It would also depend on other considerations such as not changing previous classifications unnecessarily and conveying as much significant information as possible. (The last alternative mentioned above is the least informative.)

The model also illustrates the tendency, which is open to exception, for degree of resemblance to correlate with nearness of common ancestry. II and III are nearer their common ancestry than are IV and V, and they resemble each other more closely. The same is true of III and IV or of II and V as against IV and V. Such relationships are not directly implicit in the classification, but they are important in arriving at the judgments of affinity that are implicit in it.

Another important point illustrated in the model is that II and III resemble each other much more closely than III resembles its descendant V. It is realistic to expect an early—say Miocene—ancestor of *Homo* to be more like an ancestral ape than like modern man. It is unrealistic to expect the Miocene ancestors of either (or both) groups *necessarily* to have any of the specialized features that are diagnostic between *recent* members of the two families.

---

[6] Even extremists who would classify by resemblance *only,* usually admit that the biological significance of such classification may be confused by differential rates of evolution and by convergence. Note that in our simplified model both of those admitted sources of confusion have been eliminated by postulation, and that biologically significant classification from the numerical data alone still is impossible.

Taxonomic Language: Hominidae as Example

The Hominidae may be taken as an example of different principles (e.g. typological versus evolutionary) of classification and of the classificatory implications of different interpretations of data. For purposes of exemplification the data are postulated to be as in Figure 3A. Postulated ranges of variation of known specimens are indicated by the stippled areas, and in order to simplify the subsequent diagrams parts of those ranges are labeled A–F. X is a postulated individual specimen to be classified; it does not represent a specimen actually known. This arrangement is not presented as a realistic summary of what is, in fact, known. It is greatly simplified in several respects. Some known fossils do not fit clearly into the stippled areas, and some parts of those areas are not clearly represented by known fossils. Structure does not, in fact, follow a linear, one-dimensional scale and could be realistically indicated only by a (quite impractical) *n*-dimensional scale. Nevertheless this is the general *kind* of pattern, however grossly over-simplified, that the data do present.

Typological interpretation, Figure 3B, takes into account morphology only. It ignores temporal sequence and makes no phylogenetic interpretations. It abstracts an arbitrary number of fixed, distinctive types in the morphogenetic field and exercises subjective judgment as to whether a given, concrete specimen belongs to one type or another. Types may be hierarchically divided into sub-types, but variation is then ignored in the sub-types, and genetical or evolutionary considerations do not enter in at any categorical level. As previously mentioned, this basis for classification has been largely abandoned in modern taxonomy. Nevertheless hominid classification started out on this basis, and even some of the most recent work in that field is at least covertly typological. The classificatory and nomenclatural expression of the typological arrangement in the diagram could take several forms, depending on the categorical level assigned to differences between types, for example:

I   *Homo africanus—Australopithecus africanus*

II   *Homo erectus—Pithecanthropus erectus*

III   *Homo neanderthalensis—Homo neanderthalensis*

IV   *Homo sapiens—Homo sapiens*

Figures 3C and D represent two possible kinds of phylogenetic interpretations of the same postulated data. Here temporal and genetic relationships are taken into account, and classification is based in principle on inferences as to evolutionary affinity. The differences between Figures 3C and D do not involve any difference in taxonomic principle but only in opinion as to probable evolutionary relationships. Both kinds of interpretation (with many differences in detail as to the particular placing of actual specimens) are currently supported by different students. Choice between them will depend on the accumulation of more data, and the ultimate arrangement will probably not be entirely of either kind in a clear-cut way but will involve elements of both. It will certainly be more complex than either of my diagrams.

Figure 3C diagrammatically represents the interpretation that hominids have been represented by only one interbreeding population since the early Pleistocene, at least. On this interpretation there is only one lineage or evolutionary species and only one genetical species at any one time. In that case, the species would have been highly variable, and even more so during much of past time than *Homo sapiens* is at present. At some time around the middle Pleistocene it might have varied all the way from what in purely morphological (or typological) terms could be called marginal australopithecoid through pithecanthropoid to marginal neanderthaloid. Such variation would be improbable within a single deme or local population. It would be less improbable among

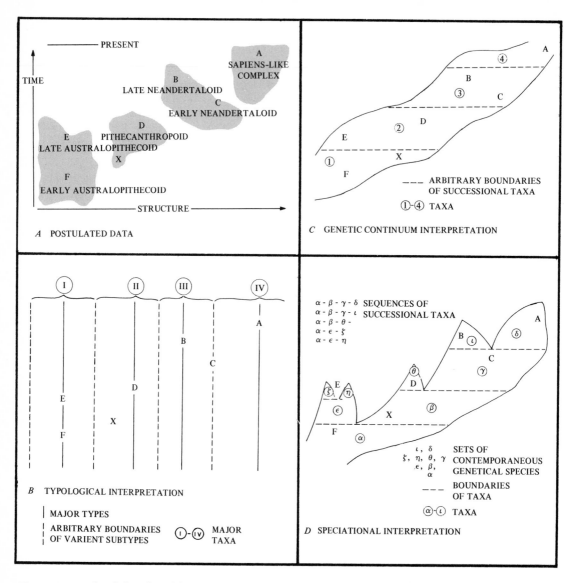

Figure 3: Postulated data (simplified and generalized) and three possible taxonomic interpretations of known hominids. Further explanation in text.

geographically separate (allopatric) populations or sub-species. Such geographic semi-isolates would of course be variable in themselves, but some might, for instance, vary about a more australopithecoid modal morphology and others about a more neanderthaloid mode. Discovery that fossil hominids fall into such modally distinct, synchronous but allopatric groups would favor this interpretation. Whether current data do or do not tend to follow such a pattern I leave to the specialists in such matters.

The over-all ranges and modes of morphology change greatly from earlier to later parts of the phylogeny as postulated in Figure 3*C*, as they also do from early Pleistocene to now in the data actually known. It is useful, if not absolutely necessary, to take this into account in classification. The only possible way to do this (adhering to evolutionary taxonomic principles and accepting the interpretation as one genetic continuum) is to divide the lineage arbitrarily into successional taxa, as also exemplified in the diagram. The placing of the arbitrary boundaries and the ranks given the taxa will depend on judgment as to categorization of morphological differences and also, in practice, on where incomplete knowledge happens to make a morphological gap coincide more or less with a time line, as occurs between C and D in my postulated data. Again several different classifications would be consistent with the given phylogenetic interpretation, among them these two:

1. *Homo africanus—Australopithecus africanus*
2. *Homo erectus—Pithecanthropus erectus*
3. *Homo neanderthalensis—Homo neanderthalensis*
4. *Homo sapiens—Homo sapiens*

The same nomina are used here as in the typological interpretation, but the diagrams show that their meanings are different in the two. That is further shown by the fact that specimen X here falls into *africanus* but in Figure 3*B* into *erectus*.

Figure 3*D* represents an interpretation with speciation occurring within the Pleistocene hominid group so that there is not a single lineage but successive branching giving rise to two or more distinct, contemporaneous species, of which only one of the two last to arise has survived. The sets of contemporaneous species are separated by natural gaps (noninterbreeding) and are not arbitrary. Successive species in a lineage like α-δ-γ-δ are arbitrary as regards that lineage, alone, but in the whole pattern their boundaries are also fixed by the (hypothetically) nonarbitrary points

of splitting of the lineage into two species. The probability of this kind of pattern would be supported by discovery of contemporaneous (synchronous) populations with overlapping geographic distribution (sympatric) that did not intergrade and hence were probably not interbreeding significantly. (The existence of two or more distinct species does not, however, depend on their being sympatric.) Again I leave to the appropriate specialists whether data actually in hand do support such an interpretation.

One of several possible nomenclatures consistent with this pattern would be:

ζ *Australopithecus robustus*
η *Australopithecus africanus*
ϑ *Pithecanthropus erectus*
ι *Homo neanderthalensis*
δ *Homo sapiens*

It is not clear what actual specimens might fall into the hypothetical species α, δ, γ, and ε, and I therefore suggest no nomenclature for them. It is clear, in any event, that some, at least, of the same nomina as used under the interpretations in Figure 3*B* and *C* are also applicable in *D* but again have different significance and contents. Specimen X, for example, is now neither in *africanus* nor in *erectus* but in unnamed hypothetical species β.

If identical nomina in Figures 3*C* and *D* referred to the same populations, there would be no ambiguity. Unfortunately, however, this is not likely to be the case. Population C in Figure 3*C* would probably be placed in the same taxon and referred to by the same specific nomen as population B. In Figure 3*D* population C would probably be placed in a different taxon and given a different nomen from population B. The ambiguity resides not in the taxonomic system but in the imperfection of our data and lack of agreement in their zoological interpretation. When such ambiguity persists, clarity demands that an author specify the populations included in his taxa, for example by adequate designation of their hypodigms. In the present example a possible clarifying device (if it accorded with an accepted zoological interpretation) would be to place populations B and C in separate subspecies. The placing of those subspecies in species would then clearly show different placing of the corresponding populations by different students.

Taxonomic Language: *Oreopithecus* as Example

The currently debated classification of *Oreopithecus* may be taken as another example of the use of classificatory language and its implications for phylogeny. Simply for purposes of the example, the following postulates are accepted:

1. Pongidae and Hominidae are distinct families of common ancestry and are united in the superfamily Hominoidea. This is now the usual conclusion and classification.
2. *Oreopithecus* had a common ancestry with both Pongidae and Hominidae at a time when the hominoid ancestry was distinct from that of any other recognized superfamily (e.g. Cercopithecoidea). This is not established, but some, probably most, recent students consider it probable.
3. *Oreopithecus bambolii* is at least generically distinct from any other known species. This is universally accepted.

Table 2 gives four phylogenetic opinions (not the only ones possible) consistent with these postulates and gives for each two classifications consistent with that opinion and also consistent with further opinion as to the lesser or greater difference between *Oreopithecus* and forms considered allied to it according to the respective phylogenetic opinions.

Classifications B and C appear more than once

Table 2: Some Possible Opinions as to the Phylogeny and Distinctiveness of Oreopithecus, and Some Classifications Consistent with Those Opinions

OPINIONS AS TO PHYLOGENY OF OREOPITHECUS	OPINIONS AS TO DISTINCTIVENESS OF OREOPITHECUS	
	a. Lesser	b. Greater
I. In or near hominine ancestry.	A. Hominoidea Hominidae Homininae *Oreopithecus*	B. Hominoidea Hominidae Oreopithecinae *Oreopithecus*
II. Divergent from early hominids after separation from pongids.	B. Hominoidea Hominidae Oreopithecinae *Oreopithecus*	C. Hominoidea Oreopithecidae *Oreopithecus*
III. Divergent from early pongids after separation from hominids.	D. Hominoidea Pongidae Oreopithecinae *Oreopithecus*	C. Hominoidea Oreopithecidae *Oreopithecus*
IV. Divergent from common stem of pongids and hominids.	C. Hominoidea Oreopithecidae *Oreopithecus*	E. Oreopithecoidea Oreopithecidae *Oreopithecus*

in the table. Each is consistent with more than one opinion as to phylogeny. That is also true of all the other classifications, which are consistent with different phylogenetic opinions not distinguished in the table. For instance, A is consistent both with the view that *Oreopithecus* is directly ancestral to *Homo* and that it is a little-differentiated side branch from the direct ancestry. C appears three times in the table, but even that is not exhaustive: C is also consistent with several other possible opinions as to phylogeny. This forcefully illustrates the principle that classification is not intended to be an adequate expression of phylogeny but only to be consistent with conclusions as to evolutionary affinities.

Nevertheless each classification does have quite definite implications as to phylogeny; it is consistent with some and not with other opinions. Classification B, for instance, is definitely inconsistent with phylogenetic opinion III. In this sense a classification does express opinion on phylogeny in a broad or somewhat loose way. B does not express opinion as to whether *Oreopithecus* is a remote ancestor of *Homo,* an ancient hominid sidebranch, or a rapidly evolved hominine sidebranch, but it does express the opinion that *Oreopithecus* had a common ancestry with the hominids after hominids and pongids were distinct. C, which is the arrangement I personally prefer on present evidence, expresses the opinion that my postulate 2, above, is probable, and further that *Oreopithecus* is markedly differentiated from both pongids and hominids, but that the degree of distinctiveness is not so great as to warrant categorization as a superfamily. The basis for this preference is outlined in a following comment written after the conference and most of the evidence is summarized in Straus's paper. . . .[7]

---

[7] William L. Straus, Jr., "The Classification of Oreopithecus," in *Classification and Human Evolution,* Sherwood L. Washburn, ed. (Chicago: Aldine Press, 1963), pp. 146–177.

Conclusion

Classification is not an exact science and is not likely soon to become one. In order for its language to become completely unambiguous and uniform it would be necessary to have adequate samples of all pertinent populations, to reach universal agreement as to their affinities, and similarly to agree on just how to translate those affinities into formal classification.

Added Notes

Aspects of Definition and Diagnosis

Attention has been given to the definition of man and his distinction, at various taxonomic levels, from his nonhuman or less fully human relatives. It may clarify matters to point out that the problem of definition is a complex with several different aspects. All are related and all intergrade, but ambiguity is introduced if no distinction is made among these aspects. The most essential distinctions may be illustrated by comparison of *Homo sapiens* and *Pan troglodytes,* the phylogenetic relations of which are represented in Figure 4 as a simple splitting of one ancestral lineage into two and the subsequent divergent evolution of the latter into the present terminal species named. That there were also other splittings and other lineages is a complication that can be ignored for purposes of the example.

The terminal species are completely discrete and, as living populations, completely accessible biological and taxonomic units. The diagnosis of living man with respect to the chimpanzee, symbolized by A in the diagram, is simple and unambiguous, and it may be made in almost any terms we like, for example by the presence of different proteins in the blood, by the non-overlapping frequency distributions of premolar structure or brain size, by the differences in

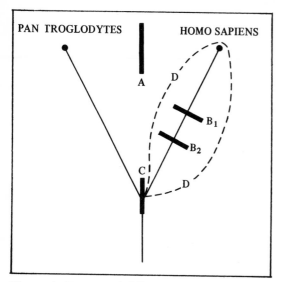

Figure 4: Diagram of different aspects of diagnosis between chimpanzee and man, and between living and fossil man. Further explanation in text.

locomotion, or by the absence in one and presence in the other of true language. Diagnosis of *Homo sapiens* with respect to his own ancestry, represented by B in the diagram, will theoretically involve some but not all of the same criteria as the A-diagnosis. It will involve such diagnostic characters as evolved within the human ancestry since the separation from the chimpanzee lineage, but will exclude characters of the common ancestry preserved in *Homo* and not in *Pan*. An operational B-diagnosis must also exclude characters not determinable in the available fossils, because it is the fossils, only, to which the diagnosis must be applied in practice. The origin of such A-diagnosis characters as language, self-awareness, human social structure and the like is of greatest evolutionary interest, but simply is not pertinent to the practical classification of actual fossil specimens.

In principle a B-diagnosis involves drawing a more or less arbitrary line across what was in nature a continuum. In practice these lines are commonly placed where there are gaps in knowl-

edge. There are at present no known specimens unequivocally recognizable as intermediate between *Homo sapiens* and *H. erectus* or between *Homo* and *Australopithecus*, but it is reasonably certain that such creatures existed and probable that specimens of them will eventually be found. In the meantime our ignorance of them permits unambiguous diagnoses between those specific and generic taxa. Campbell . . . has pointed out that successive taxa may be naturally separated at peaks of evolutionary rates, and it is also likely that such peaks may correspond with gaps in present knowledge. At present, however, and for purposes of practical classification, we cannot definitely place such peaks or even be quite sure that they did exist, and in any event a *precise* diagnostic boundary would still be an arbitrary line in a continuum.

It is clear that different characters and character-complexes (e.g. the locomotory, masticatory, and central nervous system complexes) have evolved at different rates and accelerated at different times. The possible B-diagnoses are therefore multiple and will involve different characters or complexes at different times, as symbolized by the separation of B_1 and B_2 in the diagram. As total change is gradual and cumulative, it will also be ranked at different categorical levels at different points. Such ranking is not completely arbitrary because it can be more or less coordinated with current categorical ranking of taxa separated by A-diagnosis. That agreement on such ranking can be reached is evident by unanimity in the contributions to this book that *Homo sapiens* and *H. erectus* differ only specifically but that *Australopithecus africanus* is generically distinct from both. Some disagreement exists at higher levels, but only by one hierarchic substep, e.g. as between superfamily and family or family and subfamily.

Another aspect of definition is symbolized by C in the diagram, representing the difference between the ancestors of *Pan* and *Homo* when they first separated. At the very time of the separation, this distinction was (with high probability if not complete certainty) at the specific level only. As Dobzhansky pointed out, it is further likely that the initially differentiating characters of *both* groups occurred together as simple variants in a single species ancestral to the two. The actual characters involved are likely to be (in simplest, incipient form) some but certainly not all of those eventually involved in the A-diagnosis. I can see no reliable way of judging a priori just which of those characters do in fact stem from the C-differentiation, and indeed it is possible in principle that the C-diagnosis will be by characters not present in either *Pan* or *Homo*. The C-diagnosis does not depend on the characters entirely in themselves or on the magnitude of the difference at the time of separation, but on our knowledge (or opinion) as to the taxonomic significance of the *subsequent* divergence of the lineages involved. The categorical level is assigned *ex post facto*: in the Miocene our ancestor was probably one of several species of a genus of Pongidae but now that same species, if definitely identified, might properly be classified in a quite distinct genus of Hominidae.

Finally, it is desirable that the whole evolutionary unit enclosed in the broken line marked D in the diagram should also be recognized and named as a taxon. Its definition would ideally involve all the differentiating aspects of A, B, and C.

The Dentition of *Oreopithecus*

The dentition of *Oreopithecus*, which is completely known from a large number of specimens and which I have been able to study in detail through the courtesy of Dr. J. Hürzeler, is extremely distinctive. It differs more from either pongid or hominid dentitions than living pongids and hominids, together, differ among themselves. The pro-

portions of canines and premolars are indeed hominid-like, but the morphology of those teeth, which I take to be far more significant than a simple matter of proportions, is decidedly non-hominid, as is also that of all the other teeth. I completely agree with Dr. Hürzeler's conclusion, strongly reinforced by the study presented . . . by Dr. William L. Straus, Jr., that *Oreopithecus* is not a cercopithecoid and that it is morphologically a hominoid. I cannot, however, support reference to the Hominidae. This negative conclusion is based not only on the great differences of the teeth of *Oreopithecus* from those of any sure hominid (the genera *Homo* and *Australopithecus*, both *sensu lato,* or known Homininae and Australopithecinae) but also on the following considerations:

1. There are known forms (notably *Ramapithecus* and *Kenyapithecus*) approximately contemporaneous with *Oreopithecus* that have much more hominid-like dentitions.

2. The peculiarities of the *Oreopithecus* cheek teeth (e.g., specialized protoconule region and course of the crista obliqua on the upper molars; presence of a mesoconid and of a peculiar paraconid or, more likely, pseudo-paraconid on the lower molars) are all present in incipient or fully developed form in *Apidium,* an early Oligocene genus. (Dr. E. L. Simons, and earlier Dr. W. K. Gregory have pointed out this resemblance, which is also mentioned in Straus's paper. . . . Dr. Simons has several very important new specimens of *Apidium* which have not yet been described in print but which I have seen through his courtesy.)

3. No Anthropoidea have yet been definitely identified before the early Oligocene. Comparison of all known Anthropoidea and of conceivably ancestral earlier prosimians strongly suggests that the anthropoid ancestry in general and the hominoid ancestry in particular

lacked peculiarities of dentition already present in *Apidium* and emphasized in *Oreopithecus*.

These considerations seem to me to indicate that the lineage leading to *Oreopithecus* was already distinct near the very base of hominoid differentiation and that its dental differences from both pongids and hominids are not on the whole primitive but are at least in large part divergent with respect to the ancestry of those groups. If that is correct, the placing of *Oreopithecus* (and *Apidium*) in a family Oreopithecidae of the superfamily Hominoidea, for which a preference is expressed above, becomes almost obligatory. It is further highly improbable that the important skeletal resemblances of *Oreopithecus* to the Hominidae, as listed by Straus, are primitive for the Hominoidea. They would therefore appear to be the result of parallelism or convergence to a degree that is noteworthy but not inherently improbable. The total result is a peculiar adaptive type quite unlike that of either the Pongidae or the Hominidae.

This example also illustrates two points of general taxonomic principle. First, the varying significance of different characters and character complexes for classification requires that they be weighted in the light of the whole biological and evolutionary picture as far as it is known. Second, there are often, as in this case, considerations highly pertinent to biological classification and yet difficult or impossible to reduce to simple numerical form and to include in a computer program for obtaining a (likewise highly pertinent) coefficient of similarity or distance function.

Affinities and Classification of the Hominoidea

Within the last few years data for classification of the hominoids have been greatly enriched in breadth and depth: discovery of new pertinent fossils; continued anatomical investigation; studies of serology, hemoglobins, and chromosomes; more detailed behavioral observations of nonhuman hominoids, particularly under natural conditions. Since almost every conceivable view (along with some rather inconceivable ones) has been upheld at one time or another, this new information is useful not so much in giving us a new pattern of affinities as in enabling us to choose more surely among the many already proposed and to gain more confidence in various points of detail. Without reviewing evidence or arguments, in this note I shall briefly state how the probabilities look to me now. I shall also briefly sketch some of the main, different family-group (superfamily, family, subfamily) classifications that would be consistent with those probabilities and indicate my own preference among them.

GIBBONS

On fossil evidence, the gibbon ancestry was probably distinct from that of other apes when hominoids first appear in the fossil record, early Oligocene, and was certainly so in the Miocene. Recent karyological and serological evidence, presented . . . by Klinger and by Goodman, respectively, also indicates strong divergence of living gibbons from all other living hominoids. No evidence suggests special affinities with orangs, on one hand, or with the chimpanzee–gorilla group on the other. Special affinity with *Homo* is out of the question. It is probable that these three groups did not diverge among themselves until after the gibbon ancestry had already split off. On the other hand, the gibbons have not diverged radically from other apes either morphologically or adaptively. What is distinctive in their facies is largely due to their having remained smaller than other hominoids and to their specialized locomotion, which in turn seems to require the first peculiarity. Miocene fossils (demonstrated to members of the 1962 conference by Professor Zapfe in Vienna) suggest that the locomotory specialization evolved comparatively late. Although gibbons, strictly speaking, and siamangs are usually placed in different genera, they are manifestly very closely related and I now prefer to place them all in *Hylobates*.

ORANGS

Morphologically and to some extent also adaptively *Pongo* is not markedly unlike the living chimpanzees and, to less extent, gorillas. This has long, although not quite unanimously, been considered evidence of rather close relationship. Schultz, whose knowledge of orangs is unexcelled, continued to uphold that view in the conference. On the other hand, karyological (Klinger) and serological (Goodman) evidence seems to separate *Pongo* from *Pan* (and *Gorilla*) as sharply as *Hylobates*. Fossil orangs have not been identified before the Pleistocene, but there is no evident reason why the ancestry of *Pongo* may not be found near that of *Pan* in the dryopithecine complex. On balance, it still seems probable that *Pongo* is especially related to the African apes, but that the split was far enough back to permit considerable, more or less clandestine molecular and chromosomal divergence. Morphological divergence has been less, probably because of retention of somewhat similar adaptation.

GIGANTOPITHECUS

When known only from isolated molars, this Chinese Pleistocene genus was claimed to be a hominid. Later finds of lower jaws and dentitions, not yet adequately described as far as I know, seem clearly to exclude it from the Hominidae. It seems to be a terminal specialization not very close to any living form. During the 1962 conference Leakey suggested special affinity with *Pongo*, and that is a possibility. On present very inadequate evidence I would, however, prefer to place

it only as Pongidae *incertae sedis*, and I omit it from further consideration.

AFRICAN APES

A consensus has always considered gorillas and chimpanzees as especially and rather closely related, and all the recent evidence, including that of serology and karyology, confirms that view. They are of course sharply distinct species, at a point of divergence where experienced taxonomists may well waver between giving only specific or also generic weight to that divergence. Merely listing characters that demonstrate the self-evident fact of their distinctness does not necessarily suffice to maintain the time-honored generic separation, and at present I prefer to consider both chimpanzees and gorillas as species of *Pan*. Whether *P. paniscus* is a valid third species, closer to *P. troglodytes* than to *P. gorilla*, is still moot. Placing all the African apes in *Pan* permits classification to express the clear fact that they are much more closely related to each other than to any species of other genera, and henceforth I shall use the nomen *Pan* in this sense.

It has long been the virtually universal opinion that *Pan* is anatomically and adaptively rather close first to *Pongo* and then to *Hylobates*. Recent studies, while also confirming that these are quite distinct groups well separated at a generic level, at least, agree with the old conclusion that the three genera belong together in a natural taxon at some higher level. Nevertheless, as noted above, newer subanatomical evidence suggests that separation of the ancestors of the three genera within that higher taxon is ancient. The situation is complicated only by comparisons with the Hominidae, summarized below.

No explicit and particular connection of *Pan* with a Tertiary ancestry has yet been found or, at least, clearly recognized. It is, however, probable that in a general sense the ancestry occurred somewhere in known or unknown members of what is here called the dryopithecine complex.

THE DRYOPITHECINE COMPLEX

The Miocene and Pliocene of Africa, Europe, and Asia have produced many specimens clearly apelike and distinct from contemporaneous closer relatives of *Hylobates* (notably *Pliopithecus* and the closely allied, perhaps not generically distinct, *Limnopithecus*). They are otherwise highly diverse and clearly represent a greater number of lineages than the four or perhaps five recent species that might possibly have arisen from this complex (*Pongo pygmaens, Pan troglodytes,* perhaps *Pan paniscus, Pan gorilla,* and *Homo sapiens*). Many or most of the dryopithecine–complex lineages have therefore become extinct, and it is the opposite of surprising to find that some of them (e.g. *Proconsul*) have combinations of characters not found in taxa as diagnosed primarily on the basis of living species.

With the sole exception of *Proconsul*, the members of this complex are known only from very incomplete remains, largely single teeth or unassociated upper and lower jaws with partial dentitions. Their classification and nomenclature are unsatisfactory and almost chaotic within the group. This situation could surely be improved by a revision even of the already known fragments, and I consider such revision plus a really systematic search for better specimens the greatest desideratum of primate paleontology at present. Some of these forms, such as *Dryopithecus* itself, may be rather near the ancestry of the living great apes, *Pan* and perhaps also *Pongo*. Others, such as *Ramapithecus,* and possibly *Kenyapithecus,* may belong near the ancestry of *Homo*. Still others, as already mentioned, are doubtless more or less terminal in lineages not close to any living forms. If or when more probable affinities with later groups are established, it should be possible to place some of the dryopithecine-complex species and genera in taxa, e.g. in

subfamilies, currently based primarily on living species. It is, however, my opinion that the present unsatisfactory stage of study and incompleteness of sampling do not establish such connections at a sufficient level of probability.

OREOPITHECUS

Elsewhere in this chapter I have sufficiently expressed the opinion that *Oreopithecus* probably represents a lineage separate from near the base of hominoid differentiation, with limited parallelism with the Hominidae, but culminating in an extinct terminal form adaptively very unlike either the great apes or any hominids.

AUSTRALOPITHECUS

Despite earlier polemics, it is now perfectly clear that among other sufficiently known genera *Australopithecus* (*sensu lato,* including *Paranthropus* and *Zinjanthropus*) is most closely allied to *Homo*. Late *Australopithecus,* at least, is almost certainly contemporaneous with early *Homo* (including *Pithecanthropus,* etc.) and hence not ancestral to it. Present evidence does not exclude, and may be taken to favor, the possibility that early *Australopithecus,* or an unknown genus close to it, was such a direct ancestor. Although *Australopithecus* greatly strengthens the opinion that *Homo* had an apelike ancestor in common with the living great apes, it does not at present seem to me to give additional clear evidence as to precisely which apes, among living forms or the dryopithecine complex, are most nearly related to *Homo*.

HOMO

Since the 19th century it has been the usual, although by no means the universal, opinion that among living mammals *Homo* is most closely allied to *Pan*. That conclusion, based originally on classical anatomical grounds, is strongly supported by all the new evidence, anatomical, karyological, biochemical, and behavioral, presented at recent conferences. It now seems to me so probable that other alternatives need no longer be seriously considered. It should, however, be strongly emphasized that *Homo* represents an anatomical and adaptive complex very radically different from that of any other known animal and (with the partial exception of *Homo's* close ally *Australopithecus*) differing far more from other living or adequately known fossil hominoids than they differ among themselves. Seemingly contradictory evidence (e.g. that of the haemoglobins as reported by Zuckerkandl . . .) indicates merely that in *certain* characters *Homo* and its allies retain ancestral resemblances and that *these* are not the characters involved in their otherwise radical divergence—a common and indeed universal phenomenon of evolution.

AFFINITIES, ADAPTIVE RADIATION, AND PHYLOGENY

Figure 5 shows, by combination of a dendrogram and an adaptive grid, my present views as to the affinities and the adaptive or structural-functional relationships of the living hominoids. Interpretation of probable closeness of genetic connection is indicated by depth of branching, although it is to be emphasized that such a diagram is not a phylogenetic tree and has no time dimension. Adaptive or ecological (and corresponding structural-functional-behavioral) resemblances and differences are approximated by horizontal distances between the terminal points.

Figure 6 shows in schematic form the combined phylogenetic inferences reviewed above for various groups of hominoids.

CLASSIFICATION

Evolutionary classification takes into account: degrees of homologous resemblance in *all* available

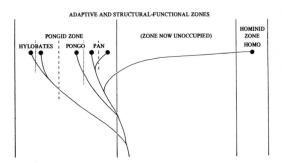

Figure 5: Dendrogram of probable affinities of recent hominoids in relationship to their radiation into adaptive-structural-functional zones. The two major adaptive zones are bordered by solid lines. Pongid radiation into sub- and sub-sub-zones is schematically suggested by broken and dotted lines. A dendrogram of this sort has no time dimension and does not indicate lineages, but it is probable that divergences of lines showing affinities are topologically similar to the phylogenetic lineage pattern.

respects; the most probable phylogenetic inferences from all data (including the foregoing resemblances plus evolutionary analysis and weighting of the various characteristics); and also the practical needs of discussion and communication.

It now seems perfectly clear and is all but universally recognized that the animals here called

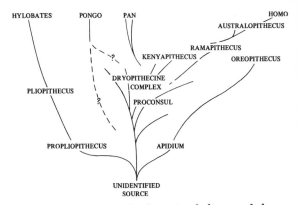

Figure 6: Tentative and schematic phylogeny of the Hominoidea. Most of the individual fossil genera are omitted, and lineages as drawn are meant to be impressionistic and diagrammatic (especially in and around the dryopithecine complex) rather than representing all or particular generic or specific lines.

hominoids (in anticipation of a conclusion) form a natural evolutionary unit that should be recognized and named as a taxon. When the whole order Primates is taken into account, the categorical level of this taxon should clearly be no higher than infraorder and no lower than family. A case could be made out for either extreme of those rankings, but in my opinion the intermediate ranking, that of superfamily, is best in balance and convenience. It also accords with the recent consensus, and thus with the principle that communication is best served if nomenclature is not changed unnecessarily. The current and nomenclaturally correct nomen for this superfamily is Hominoidea.

At the next lower level, I have already expressed the opinion that the apparent lineage *Apidium-Oreopithecus* is at present best ranked as a family, because of its ancient separation plus its marked divergence from any other group now usually given family rank. In view especially of Straus's analysis . . . , the only reasonable alternative is to rank this lineage as a subfamily of Hominidae on balance of anatomical resemblance alone. That is not wholly excluded by present evidence, but its phylogenetic implications seem to me extremely improbable. (Unless *Pongo, Pan,* and all the dryopithecine complex were also placed in the Hominidae it would be definitely inconsistent with the phylogeny of Figure 6.)

Because of the clear and ancient separation of *Hylobates* and its fossil allies from other hominoids, those forms are now frequently, probably usually, given family status. On the other hand, *Hylobates* almost certainly had a common hominoid ancestry with *Pongo* and *Pan,* and its evolutionary divergence from those genera and their fossil allies is decidedly less than that of either *Homo* or *Oreopithecus.* That would justify placing the *Hylobates* group as a subfamily of a family also containing *Pongo, Pan,* and some, at least, of the dryopithecine complex. Both arrangements

are consistent with reasonable interpretations of the available data, and choice becomes a matter of personal judgment and convenience. I continue to prefer the second alternative, partly as a matter of linguistic convenience. One frequently wants to distinguish humans and apes (plus or including gibbons) and this is most conveniently done at the family level. The secondary distinction between gibbons and (other) apes is convenient at the subfamily level.

If the gibbons are given family rank, an analogous argument can be made for also giving *Pongo* separate family rank, since it cannot be *demonstrated* to have split off more recently from the *Pan* ancestry and since it now proves to be serologically about equally distinct. This is nevertheless still largely an argument from ignorance, and the most extensive positive evidence we have, that of anatomy, still suggests closer affinities between *Pongo* and *Pan.* Certainly if *Hylobates* and *Pan* are in one family, *Pongo* belongs in the same family and the alternatives involve subfamilies. Of the five possible subfamily arrangements of the three genera (and their fossil allies), only placing *Hylobates* in one subfamily and *Pongo* and *Pan* in another or placing each in a separate subfamily seem worthy of consideration on present knowledge. Both can be defended, but I continue tentatively to favor the former, because I believe that *Pongo* and *Pan* probably are more closely related than *Hylobates* and *Pongo* and because I think monotypic subfamilies should be as few as possible.

For the dryopithecine complex, there are three possibilities: (1) all could be put in the same subfamily as *Pongo* and *Pan;* (2) they could all be placed in a subfamily or family of their own; (3) those clearly related to *Pongo, Pan,* or *Homo* could be put in family-group taxa with those genera and the others in one or more separate subfamilies or families. The first could be justified on grounds of general resemblance and of probability that *part* of this complex is near the ancestry of *Pan*, perhaps also of *Pongo*. The second arrangement makes a horizontal grouping that is phyletically complex and to some extent artificial, but is justifiable *faute de mieux* in our present lack of almost any good knowledge of detailed relationships in this group, and pending withdrawal of particular genera if their affinities with other established taxa are later demonstrated. The third arrangement is definitely preferable and should ultimately be adopted, but as indicated above present knowledge seems inadequate to follow it with sufficient probability. I now waver between (1) and (2), but hesitantly continue to follow (2) simply because there seem to be insufficient grounds for changing it until this complex is better understood.

It is now virtually established that the affinities of *Homo* with *Pan* are closer than with *Pongo* or *Hylobates*. That suggests the possible desirability of placing *Pan* in the Hominidae and *Pongo* and *Hylobates* in one or two other families, an arrangement supported by Goodman and by Klinger. . . . In fact, as noted above, this view as to affinities is an old one and has been held for two or three generations by students who nevertheless all excluded *Pan* from the Hominidae. The new data increase confidence in the conclusion as to affinities but do not, in my opinion, either require or justify the proposed change in classification. The question involves the whole complex of taxonomic principles and cannot be argued in detail here. The following, in briefest form, are among the principal reasons for continuing to exclude *Pan* from the Hominidae:

1. *Pan* is the terminus of a conservative lineage, retaining in a general way an anatomical and adaptive facies common to all recent hominoids *except Homo* (and probably to all adequately known fossil ones except *Australopithecus* and the very different *Oreopithecus*). *Homo* is both anatomically and adaptively the most radically distinctive of all hominoids, divergent to a degree considered familial by all primatologists.

2. *Pan* is obviously not ancestral to *Homo*. The common ancestor was almost certainly more *Pan*-like than *Homo*-like, which suggests not that *Pan* should go in the Hominidae but that the common ancestor should be in a separate family with *Pan* (or in still another ancestral family).

3. When a younger family arises from an older, the situation is frequently or usually similar to that of the *Pan* and *Homo* lineages: one of several lineages of the older family splits into two or more, *one* of which diverges (and/or diversifies) until its descendants warrant family status. If the lineages that did *not* diverge are also placed in the later family on the basis of more recent common ancestry, carrying this process on down will eventually require inclusion of all descendants of earlier splittings also in the latest family—eventually the whole animal kingdom would be in the Hominidae on this principle. An arbitrary division must be made in practical classification, and the obvious place to make it is where the lineage *later* reaching family status split off—in this instance where the ancestors of *Homo* split from those of *Pan* and other pongids. Classification cannot be based on recency of common ancestry *alone*.

4. Both arrangements are equally consistent with our present understanding of hominid phylogeny, but the proposed new arrangement is less consistent with other evolutionary considerations, notably that of adaptive divergence. Therefore the change is neither required nor warranted. That radical change of nomenclatural usage would also create great confusion in discussion of hominoid relationships.

Subfamily separation of *Australopithecus* and *Homo* became usual at the time when placing of

Australopithecus in the Pongidae (as here used) or Hominidae (also of present usage) was disputed and the australopithecines were claimed to include several genera. Now that there is essential agreement that *Australopithecus* belongs in the Hominidae, I see no sufficient reason for having two subfamilies, especially as each has only one known genus as I and, I believe, most others now define the genera. "Australopithecine" and "hominine" may still be used as strictly vernacular terms for structural levels, although there is little need for such terms as long as we know only one genus at each level.

Finally, Leakey suggested at the conference a possible alternative classification that requires comment. (I do not know whether he himself considers the alternative preferable and proposes to use it.) He pointed out that the Hominoidea of my classification could be reduced to family rank and that my families and subfamilies, with some reassignment of genera, could be considered subfamilies (plus another subfamily for *Proconsul*, which I give only generic rank). The supporting phylogeny looked rather different from mine, but was topologically almost identical. Aside from minor points, either classification was consistent with either phylogeny. Without going into detail, I here only say that at the very best I do not think his classification an improvement justifying so many departures from current usage. The reasons are mostly implicit or explicit in the preceding comments.

The following is the outline classification that I now favor, with all accepted recent genera included but a number of fossil genera omitted:

Superfamily Hominoidea
Family Pongidae
   SUBFAMILY HYLOBATINAE
    Pliopithecus
    Hyolobates
   SUBFAMILY DRYOPITHECINAE
    Dryopithecus and other genera of the dryopithecine complex, *tentatively* includ-
ing *Proconsul, Ramapithecus,* and *Kenyapithecus.*
   SUBFAMILY PONGINAE
    Pongo
    Pan
Family Hominidae
    Australopithecus
    Homo
Family Oreopithecidae
    Apidium
    Oreopithecus

(Placing Oreopithecidae at the end and next to Hominidae has no special significance; as Darwin noted over a century ago, you cannot put organisms in one linear evolutionary sequence or show their true affinities on a sheet of paper. Putting *Australopithecus* in the Hominidae and adding the Oreopithecidae are the only essential changes from my 1945 classification, which I believe *in general* to be consistent with the mass of more recent information. Unfortunately that is less true of some of the nonhominoid primates.)

BIBLIOGRAPHY

BROWN, R. 1958. *Words and things.* Glencoe, Ill.: Free Press.

CLARK, W. E. LE G. 1959. *The antecedents of man.* Chicago: Quadrangle Books.

COLD SPRING HARBOR SYMPOSIA ON QUANTITATIVE ZOOLOGY 1950. *Origin and evolution of man.* C. S. H. Symposia Vol. XV. [Especially Mayr, pp. 109–118.]

GENOVÉS, T. S. 1960. "Primate taxonomy and *Oreopithecus.*" *Science,* 133:760–761. [A recent example of misunderstanding of taxonomic language, corrected by Straus (1960).]

GREGG, J. R. 1954. *The language of taxonomy.* New York: Columbia Univ. Press.

HEBERER, G. 1961. "Abstammung des Menschen." In Bertalanffy and Gessner, *Handbuch der Biologie.* [Incomplete; classification, disagreeing with my concepts of taxonomic language, especially in Lieferung 117/118, pp. 287 and 307.]

MAYR, E., ED. 1957. *The species problem.* Amer. Assoc. Adv. Sci., Pub. No. 50.

MAYR, E., E. G. LINSLEY, and R. L. USINGER. 1953. *Methods and principles of systematic zoology.* New York: McGraw-Hill.

SIMONS, E. L. 1959. An anthropoid frontal bone from the Fayum Oligocene of Egypt: the oldest skull fragment of a higher primate. Amer. Mus. Novitates, No. 1976.

SIMPSON, G. G. 1945. *The principles of classification and a classification of mammals.* Bull. Amer. Mus. Nat. Hist., 85:i–xvi, 1–350. [Primate classification now requiring much updating but still illustrative of the method.] 1961. *Principles of animal taxonomy.* New York: Columbia Univ. Press. 1962. *Primate taxonomy and recent studies of nonhuman primates.* New York Acad. Sci., Conference on Relatives of Man. [Contains material pertinent to the present topic and not repeated here.]

STOLL, N. R., *et al.* 1961. *International code of zoological nomenclature.* London: Internat. Trust for Zool. Nomencl.

STRAUS, W. L., JR. 1960. "Primate taxonomy and *Oreopithecus.*" *Science,* 133:760–761. [Correction of misuse of taxonomic language by Genovés. (1960).]

5 · SOME FALLACIES IN THE STUDY OF HOMINID PHYLOGENY

Elwyn L. Simons

In the past the tendency of physical anthropologists has been to confer a new taxonomic status upon a newly discovered hominoid skull or even a postcranial bone. The practice of paleontologists and zoologists of presenting a detailed account of the morphological grounds for the creation of a new taxon has been almost invariably ignored by most anthropological writers. In most cases what they have done has been to create the new taxon, report it without detailed description, and then later, if at all, to attempt to justify their classificatory efforts. This, as Simons shows in this cogent critique, is both an unscientific and a confusing procedure; indeed, one that has obfuscated and retarded the study of man's origins, and is therefore one to be strongly discouraged.

Taxonomy is no longer the post-prandial exercise it was earlier in the century, when field-workers were few and finds even fewer, and every discovery of a fossil hominid skull was hailed as both unique and epoch-making. On those occasions it seemed fitting to the describer to bestow a taxonomic name upon the find worthy of the status to which he considered it entitled; hence the proliferation of names like *Pithecanthropus erectus, Sinanthropus pekinensis, Ramapithecus, Kenyapithecus, Australopithecus africanus, Zinjanthropus boisei,* and the like, to mention only a few. It should have been fairly obvious to anyone comparing them that *Pithecanthropus* and *Sinanthropus* belonged in the single genus *Homo,* and in the single species *erectus,* but apparently it was not. *Ramapithecus* and *Kenyapithecus,* as Simons has shown, belong in the same genus. *Australopithecus* and *Zinjanthropus* likewise belong together in the single genus *Australopithecus.*

By "fairly obvious" I mean that if the requirements for the exercise of taxonomic ingenuity had been as rigorous as they are in other branches of paleontology, characterized by less millennial ardor than is common in anthropology, such errors of classification could have been avoided. In fairness to earlier workers, however, it should be pointed out that in most cases they had very few specimens with which to make comparisons. When Dubois named the skullcap he had discovered in 1891/92 *Pithecanthropus erectus,* it was

114 Elwyn L. Simons

a legitimate enough name to bestow upon such an apparently apeman-like form.

The strong tendency in paleoanthropological taxonomy has been toward "splitting." This seems to be true for the early history of most attempts at classification. It is a problem to be aware of and to guard against, a problem best handled by requiring more rigorous evidence for any new taxon than has been demanded in the past.

The century-long search for documentation of the fossil record of man's ancestry, which was particularly stimulated by publication of Darwin's *Origin of Species* in 1859, has by now brought in relatively abundant evidence concerning the major stages of man's lineage during the Pleistocene epoch. Accelerated discovery during the past few years confirms the view that the mainstream of human evolution in Pleistocene times evidently passed through a species of *Australopithecus* and then through *Homo erectus* and men of Neanderthaloid type to the modern varieties of *Homo sapiens*.[1] These comparatively new findings have shifted fundamental research somewhat away from the *Australopithecus-Homo sapiens* lineage, which most students consider a plausible sequence, toward the problem of the nature and distribution of pre-*Australopithecus* hominids and hominoids.[2] It is in this area that all new discoveries of the major stages in human phylogeny will come. Generally speaking, study of the Pleistocene section of human phylogeny has been carried out by anatomists and anthropologists, while the Miocene-Pliocene portion of the story has been investigated mainly by paleontologists. There have been, and perhaps there will continue to be, good reasons for this dichotomy. The study of Tertiary Mammalia (including nonhuman Primates) requires a more extensive background in stratigraphy, in field methods, and particularly in comparative osteology and mammalian taxonomy than is often possessed by students of man. Another factor has slowed progress in this area—the idea, expressed by some vertebrate paleontologists, that the evolution of higher Primates, and of man in particular, is too controversial and confused a subject to be worth much serious attention. If this view remains common among those best equipped to interpret fossil species, such lack of interest will only prolong the controversy.

In spite of the fact that there are almost no members of the Dryopithecinae of Miocene-Pliocene age for which reasonably comprehensive osteological remains are known, the actual number of specimens of this period that have been discovered is considerable (about 550), and the geographic range of the specimens is extensive. Moreover, advances in geochronometric dating techniques (potassium-argon analysis in particular) now, or shortly, will enable us to make a far more accurate temporal arrangement of man's pre-Pleistocene relatives than we have had. Many of these relatives fall taxonomically within the pongid subfamily Dryopithecinae. Although the

SOURCE: *Science* vol. 141 (September 6, 1963): 879–89. Copyright © 1963 by the American Association for the Advancement of Science. Reprinted by permission of the publisher and the author.
[1] W. E. LeGros Clark, *Proc. Am. Phil. Soc.* 103, 159 (1959).
[2] A few taxonomic terms used in this article may require definition for the general reader: Dryopithecinae, a subfamily of pongids which includes several species of Miocene-Pliocene "apes"; Hominidae, the family of man and his immediate forerunners; Hominoidea (hominoids), a superfamily which includes the great apes and man, living and fossil, but excludes monkeys; Pongidae, the family of the fossil and living great apes. The term "Primates" is capitalized when the order Primates, as a major mammalian subdivision, is intended: "primates" (not capitalized) means some, but not all, members of this order.

fossil record for most dryopithecines is scanty, restudy of this osteologically limited material has now become imperative, because it is adequate to clarify the evolutionary succession of pongids and hominids.

I wish to state initially that I have carefully examined the view that *Proconsul*, from the East African Miocene, should be placed in a different subfamily from Eurasian dryopithecines and have found it unconvincing. Actually, there is hardly any morphological basis for separating Dryopithecinae (*Dryopithecus, Proconsul, Sivapithecus,* and related genera) from Ponginae (*Pongo, Pan, Gorilla*). Through the proper application of modern taxonomic principles, even without recovery of specimens more complete than those we now have, much more can be said about evolutionary relationships among the so-called dryopithecines than has been said to date. Dobzhansky [3] recently summed up the pertinence of good taxonomy as it applies to fossil man. His point is equally relevant to the taxonomy of earlier hominoids.

"Does it really matter what Latin name one bestows on a fossil? Unfortunately it does. It flatters the discoverer's ego to have found a new hominid genus, or at least a new species, rather than a mere new race. But generic and specific names are not just arbitrary labels; they imply a biological status. Living men constitute a single species: *Homo sapiens*. Now, *Homo sapiens* can be descended from only one ancestral species living at any given time in the past. To be sure, some plant species arise from the hybridization of two ancestral species, followed by a doubling of the complement of chromosomes, but it is most unlikely that mankind could have arisen by such a process. It follows, then, that if two or several hominid species lived at a given time in the past, only one of them can possibly be our ancestor.

All other species must be assumed to have died out without leaving descendants."

Undoubtedly a much more lucid picture of the Tertiary antecedents of man could be drawn on the basis of existing evidence were it not for the questionable nomenclatural practices of past years. Clearly, and regrettably, the taxonomic significance of the new systematics has been slower in gaining wide acceptance among anthropologists and paleontologists than among most biologists studying modern taxa. Of course, paleontologists have recognized for many years that the type individual of a fossil species is merely a specimen acquired through chance circumstances of fossilization and discovery from a population of variable organisms of which it may not even be a typical member. Types of fossil origin are thus chosen primarily as name-bearers for postulated species groups.[4] Apparently it was less generally understood, until comparatively recently, that when one makes a specimen the type of a new species, or of a new genus and species, there is an obligation laid on the proposer of the new taxon to present a good deal of morphological or other evidence of probable genetic separation from any previously described species. This point applies particularly to Hominoidea, in which there is greater variability in dental pattern and relative tooth size than there is in many other mammal groups. Distinctions in dentition in a hominid specimen, sufficient to warrant designation of the specimen as the type for a new species, must be at least as great as the distinctions that occur between species of the closest living relatives of the fossil form.

Speciation

In order to understand what fossil species were and are, it is necessary to comprehend the processes of speciation and to be familiar with modern methods of species discrimination among living

[3] T. Dobzhansky, *Sci. Am.* 208, 169 (1963).
[4] G. G. Simpson, *Am. J. Sci.* 40, 413 (1940).

animals. Thus, in the case of the dryopithecines, in order to distinguish two fossil species of a given genus, one should be able to demonstrate that forms which are roughly contemporaneous show characters that fall outside the extreme range of morphological variability to be noted in comparable parts of all subspecies of present-day pongids, such as *Pan troglodytes* or *Gorilla gorilla*. High physical and dental variability in given species of man and apes has long been known,[5] but it is clear that this has not been taken into account by the majority of past and recent describers of fossil hominoids. Beginning with Mayr[6] in 1950, or slightly earlier, several experienced taxonomists have drawn attention to the extreme oversplitting of the known varieties of Pleistocene hominids. Since the late 19th century this erroneous approach to taxonomy has produced approximately 30 genera and almost countless species. At the other extreme from this taxonomic prolixity stand such workers as Mayr and Dobzhansky, who, drawing on their knowledge of modern speciation, have adduced evidence for a single line of but a few species, successive through time, in this particular lineage.[7] To alter their view it would only be necessary to demonstrate the occurrence of two distinguishable species of hominids in a single zone of one site, but, despite much discussion of possible contemporaneity, in my opinion such contemporaneity has not been satisfactorily established. There is fair morphological evidence that there were two species of *Australopithecus* (*A. africanus* and *A. robustus*), but their synchronous existence has not been confirmed by finds of both at the same level in one site. Although the concept of monophyletic hominid evolution during the Pleistocene is now widely accepted, certain fallacies continue to affect thinking on probable pre-Pleistocene forms in this subfamily.

In the discussion that follows I attempt to outline and to clarify some of these fallacies. Changes in the taxonomy of fossil hominoids are suggested, on the basis of my direct observation of relevant original materials in America, Europe, East Africa, and India during the past 10 years.[8] Among those acquainted with the traditional atmosphere of controversy that has surrounded the question of hominid origins there is often some reluctance to set forth an up-to-date survey of the implications of recent research on the subject. Clearly, all the points made here cannot be extensively supported by documentary evidence in this brief review. Nevertheless, it seems advisable to set some of the newer conclusions before the public at this stage.

Oversplitting of Fossil Species

Apart from the widespread temptation to be the author of a new species or genus, there are three primary causes of the oversubdivision of many extinct taxa (in the case under consideration, fossil Pongidae and Hominidae). These are, (i) uncertainties resulting from incompleteness of the available fossils; (ii) doubts concerning the identity and relative age of species (whether two or more given "types" are time-successive or contemporaneous); and (iii) questions relative to the possible, or probable, existence in the past of ecologic barriers that could perhaps have brought

[5] A. Remane, *Arch. Naturgeschichte* 87, 1 (1922); A. Remane, in *Primatologia,* Hofer, Schultz, Starck, Eds. (1960), vol. 3, p. 637; W. K. Gregory and M. Hellman, *Anthropol. Papers Am. Museum Nat. Hist.* 28, 1 (1926); A. Schultz, *Am. J. Phys. Anthropol.* 2, 1 (1944).

[6] E. Mayr, *Cold Spring Harbor Symp. Quant. Biol.* 15, 109 (1950).

[7] E. Mayr, *Am. Naturalist* 74, 249 (1940); T. Dobzhansky, *Am. J. Phys. Anthropol.* 2, 251 (1944).

[8] My conclusions are documented [further] in a monographic analysis of dryopithecines now in preparation.

about speciation between populations widely separated geographically.

In view of these and other sources of uncertainty, taxonomists of fossil Primates have generally sidestepped the question of reference of new finds to previously established species, maintaining that it is unwise to assign later discoveries to species named earlier when finds are not strictly comparable or when they consist only of fragments of the whole skeleton; they frequently describe as separate species specimens which appear to come from clearly different time horizons; and they usually draw specific or generic distinctions when materials are recovered from sites that are widely separated geographically, particularly if these sites are on different continents. With continued advances in the dating of past faunas by geochemical means, and with advances in paleogeography, it becomes increasingly possible to improve procedures and practices in the taxonomy of extinct Primates, and to resolve many of the above-mentioned problems.

Generic and specific distinctions of imperfectly known forms. In the past it has sometimes happened that a taxonomist proposing a new species or genus of fossil vertebrate has maintained that, although no characteristics that would, of themselves, warrant separation of the new fossil specimen (B) from a previously known type (A) could be observed, the recovery of more complete osteological data would show the forms concerned to be different. This sort of anticipation is poor scientific practice, and such an argument should never be used in an effort to distinguish a new taxon unless (i) there is clear evidence of a marked separation in time between the previously described species A and the putative "new" form B, or (ii) there is definite geological

evidence of geographic or ecologic separation—for example, evidence of a seaway or a desert—which would greatly reduce or eliminate the possibility of morphologically similar specimens A and B being members of one widespread, variable, but interbreeding, population. Some students would not grant even these two exceptions but believe that morphological distinctions must be demonstrated. Generally, some small distinctions occur as a result of individual variation and can be misused as evidence of species difference. Therefore it is best to rely mainly on differences which can be shown to be probable indicators of distinctly adapted, and consequently different, species.

Abundant data on Recent and late Tertiary mammals show that many of the larger species were, and are, distributed in more than one continent, particularly throughout Holarctica. Moreover, the belief that there were fairly close faunal ties between Africa and Eurasia during Miocene-Recent times has been confirmed by the recovery and description, during the past 3 years, of new samples of continental vertebrates of this period from Kenya, Tanganyika, and the Congo.[9,10] Several of the mammals in these localities show close morphological similarity to Eurasian forms, and while many African species of the period do not show extra-African ties, the types which the two land masses have in common do show that increased intercommunication was possible. The fact that some stocks did not range outside Africa cannot offset the clear evidence that many of the same genera and even of the same species occurred in both Eurasia and Africa at this time.

Taxonomic uncertainty deriving from temporal differences. Many hominoid species were proposed in the past mainly on the strength of a posited time separation from a nearly identical but presumably earlier (or later) "species." Most of the "species" designated on this basis should be reinvestigated in an effort to determine their

[9] L. S. B. Leakey, *Ann. Mag. Nat. Hist.* 13, 689 (1962).
[10] D. A. Hooijer, *Ann. Musee Roy. Afrique Central, Tervuren,* in press.

true temporal position and taxonomic affinities. A "new look" is needed because of recent improvements in the potassium-argon method of dating, and in other geochemical dating methods [11,12] which should ultimately enable students of past species to discuss them in terms of an absolute time scale. Like other kinds of scientific evidence, dates obtained by the potassium-argon method can of course be misapplied. For instance, it must be demonstrated that dated sediments come from (or bracket) the same zones as the faunas they are supposed to date. There are other well-known sources of error in geochemical dating, but in my experience the strongest criticisms of this method come from persons relatively unacquainted with the analytical techniques involved.

One example of the application of geochemical dating techniques to the study of fossil hominoids will suffice to show what wide application such information may have. Simons [13] has proposed that, on morphological grounds, the primitive gibbon-like genera *Pliopithecus* and *Limnopithecus* can no longer be considered distinguishable. Newly recovered materials of *Pliopithecus* [subgenus *Epipliopithecus*] from Miocene Vindobonian deposits of Europe are closely similar, both in dentition and in postcranial structure, to "*Limnopithecus*" from the Rusinga Island beds of Kenya, East Africa. The fauna associated with this East African primate was regarded, at the time of Hopwood's proposal that a genus "*Limnopithecus*" be established, as being of earliest Miocene age and, therefore, older than the European *Pliopithecus* materials. In his fullest discussion

of the generic characteristics of "*Limnopithecus*," Hopwood [14] was able to list only a few slight features of distinction between the tooth rows, then known, of *Pliopithecus* and of "*Limnopithecus*." These are dental variations of a degree which have repeatedly been shown to occur even within members of one small population of such living pongids as *Pongo pygmaeus* and *Gorilla gorilla*. Hopwood further bolstered establishment of his new genus by remarking that additional bases for distinguishing the genera concerned "are the various ages of the deposits in which they are found and their widely separated localities." But he did comment, "apart from convenience neither reason [for placing the African species in a new genus] is particularly sound. . . ." The point I stress here is that taxonomic separations such as Hopwood proposed are not "convenient," for they create complexity where it does not exist.

Recently, Evernden and his associates [12] have reported a date of 14.9 ± 1.5 million years obtained by the potassium-argon technique from biotite samples of tufaceous sediments in the Rusinga Island series. Admittedly this is only a single datum, but if this sample is truly satisfactory for dating by the potassium-argon method, and if it does come from the same horizons as the "*Proconsul* fauna," it shows that the fauna which contains "*Limnopithecus*" *legetet* and "*L.*" *macinnesi* could be contemporary with the European Vindobonian materials. Nevertheless, more dating of this fauna will be necessary before we have proof that it is as young as this. If this younger age becomes established, species of "*Limnopithecus*" may well fall entirely within the known temporal distribution of European members of *Pliopithecus*. Evernden and his co-workers also state that the evidences from relative faunal dating suggest a middle or late, rather than an early, Miocene age for the Rusinga fossils. In my opinion this view is supported by close similarities between three other Rusinga primate

[11] K. P. Oakley, *Advan. Sci.* 18, 415 (1962).
[12] J. F. Evernden, D. E. Savage, G. H. Curtis, G. T. James, *Am. J. Sci.*, in press.
[13] E. L. Simons, *Genetic and Evolutionary Biology of the Primates* (Academic Press, New York, in press), chap. 2.
[14] A. T. Hopwood, *J. Linnean Soc. Zool.* 38, 31 (1933).

species (which I discuss later) and forms which occur in the Siwalik deposits of India, of probable middle or late Miocene age.

Finally, it should be stressed that Hopwood did exhibit considerable foresight in recognizing the basic unsoundness of attempting to reinforce a taxonomic separation by the argument of possible (but not proved) temporal difference. The foregoing example, and others which could be noted, show the danger of using the temporal argument when separating closely similar fossil specimens taxonomically. Moreover, it has been demonstrated that many extant mammalian genera have time ranges greater than the entire Miocene epoch, as estimated at present. Numerous instances of genera with long time ranges could be adduced. For instance, the perissodactyl genera *Tapirus* and *Dicerorhinus* in all probability extend back to the early Miocene or late Oligocene, about 25×10^6 years ago; members of some genera of carnivores (*Ursus, Bassariscus, Lutra, Felis,* and others) have all been described from deposits of late Miocene or early Pliocene age (10 to 15×10^6 years ago). Of course, we do not know that any hominoid genera survived as long as the genera in these categories, but most hominoid genera probably endured for at least 3 to 7 million years without much change of form. Consequently, even if it were known that European and East African *Pliopithecus* differed in absolute age by 4 or 5 million years, taxonomic separation at the generic level could not safely be based on this fact alone.

Migration, paleogeography, and past restrictions of species ranges. One of the most widespread assumptions in the study of the antecedents of man is that at some early period (Miocene, Pliocene, or "Villafranchian," depending on the author concerned) the species ancestral to *Homo sapiens* was restricted to a comparatively small geographic area. This restriction is taken by many scientists to account for the supposed "failure" to find pre-Pleistocene human forerunners. Such an assumption may be referred to as the "Garden of Eden illusion." Insofar as this widespread view is held as a scientific theory by some persons interested in the evolutionary history of man, it appears to be based on analogy with the restricted ranges of various recent mammal species, particularly, in this case, of higher Primates with limited distributions, such as orangutan (*Pongo pygmaeus*) or mountain gorilla (*Gorilla g. beringei*).

Place of Man's Origin

Some people believe that the place of hominid or human origin has not been discovered; conjectures, by others, as to its location have followed shifting vogues. Thus, when the first materials of "*Meganthropus*" were recovered in Java from levels lower stratigraphically than those at which "*Pithecanthropus*" remains were recovered, many students favored the view that differentiation of the ancestral stock of mankind occurred in Southeast Asia. Later, with the realization that *Australopithecus* finds from the Transvaal were hominid remains, a case was made for initial hominid differentiation in South Africa.[15] Now, new additions to our knowledge of early Hominidae, made in East Africa by Leakey and his associates, have shifted attention northward to that quadrant of the African continent.

It should be obvious that the oldest *known* localities of occurrence of human tools, or of given species of higher Primates, are probably not the first places where these technical developments or species arose. In order to report with confidence the exact regions of origin of the human species and of earliest cultural items, we would need 100 times the archeological and paleontological evidence that we now have, with absolute dates for all sites.

---

[15] D. M. S. Watson, *Am. Scientist* 41, 427 (1953).

There are a number of possible reasons for the persistence of the "Garden of Eden" concept among scientists, but here I mention only a few of the misconceptions through which this point of view appears to have been initiated and sustained. Students who believe that ancestral species occurred in restricted areas may have in mind four well-known kinds of diffusion from local centers: (i) spreading of cultural items from specific places of invention; (ii) wandering of tribes, both historic and prehistoric, over great distances; (iii) spreading of advantageous gene mutations from individuals or local populations outward throughout an entire species population; and (iv) intercontinental faunal migrations across land bridges at various times in the past.

All these, and other, similar concepts, while pertinent in their own right, do not in my opinion validate the illusion that, through time, each species, as a unit, wanders widely from one region to another. Such a picture is particularly inaccurate in the case of Late Tertiary land-mammal species, such as species among the dryopithecines, whose main area of distribution was the tropical and warm-temperate portion of the Old World. Of course, given sufficient time, species ranges, particularly among the large Mammalia, do expand and contract, and do occasionally shift from one continent to another in response to environmental change. Nevertheless, movement of subpopulations is much greater than the range shifts of an entire species. Even within an evolving species lineage, time-successive species apparently do not appear from one of several populations of the antecedent species; in general, all populations of a single species tend to evolve together, the species changing as a whole because, as the environment changes, newly advantageous genes originating in various sections of the group spread through the species. Of course, if these streams of gene flow are broken for sufficiently long periods, speciation will ultimately occur. A single species, however, *is* a single species just because gene flow through-

out all its members is (or recently has been) taking place.

Range of Large Mammal Species

Now, in applying these ideas to the evolution of large mammals in the Miocene-Recent period, primarily to mammals of the tropical and warm-temperate regions of Palearctica, certain points extremely relevant to the interpretation of dryopithecine evolution emerge. The first of these is illustrated in Fig. 1, which shows a hypothetical model of the range of a large mammal species-series at three periods in the earth's history. The diagram is given as an abstraction because limitations in the distribution of sites yielding fossil land mammals (limitations that result from erosion of sediments or from non-deposition) are such that exact species ranges for past forms cannot now be drawn (and probably never can be). Nevertheless, this is the sort of distribution which recovered fossils indicate was characteristic, during the period with which we are concerned, of certain species of groups such as elephants, hyenas, the

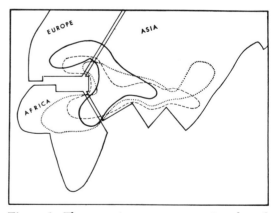

Figure 1: Three species ranges, successive through time, of a hypothetical lineage of a large mammal, as they might have appeared in (dashed lines) the late Miocene, (dotted lines) the early Pliocene, and (solid lines) the late Pliocene.

big cats, and ruminants. In this context it should be pointed out that the early supposition that many surviving species of large mammals have diminished ranges owing primarily to climatic fluctuations during the Pleistocene and to the activity of human hunters has, by now, been abundantly confirmed. Two examples, taken from dozens, illustrate this point. The lion, *Felis leo*, is now extinct in Eurasia except for a few small surviving populations in India. However, 15,000 to 20,000 years ago, *Felis leo* occurred widely in Europe and the Near East and was, presumably, then abundant in the Indian subcontinent and perhaps even further east. Ewer [16] has reported fossil remains closely resembling *Felis tigris* (but from a mammal slightly larger than the largest of modern tigers) from Olduvai Gorge in Tanganyika. Today, of course, the tiger exists only in Asia.

In the sort of species succession through time that is diagramed in Fig. 1, is it not possible to say where the paleontological "species" came from—the population during, for example, the late Pliocene did not come *from* any one place and, strictly speaking, does not have a known place of origin. As nearly as can at present be determined, from the literature and from direct study of the relevant fossils in East Africa and in India in Miocene-Pliocene times, Eurasia and Africa had over 35 genera of land mammals in common. These included insectivores, anthracotheres, rodents, ruminants, monkeys, apes, hyracoids, hyenas, felids, mastodonts, deinotheres, and several other groups of mammals. Members of over 15 additional mammalian genera that now occur in Africa but have not yet been found in fossil sites on that continent have been found in Pliocene deposits of the Indian

Siwalik Hills.[17, 18] This total figure of half-a-hundred genera stands in spite of the early tendency to separate, at the generic level, African mammals from allied forms found elsewhere, just because they are of African provenance. Nevertheless, there are some distinct differences in African and Eurasian faunas of Miocene and Pliocene times.

Although numerous groups do appear to have been prevented from crossing between the two areas, there is now evidence that certain mammal species had no difficulty in getting across whatever partial ecological barriers may have existed between the two regions in Pliocene times. One of these is the proboscidean species *Trilophodon angustidens*, which has been found as far east as Baluchistan, occurs in the Kenya Miocene, and has recently been reported by Hooijer from the Congo.[10] There are enough such occurrences to indicate to me that there was reasonably free faunal interchange between these two major regions of the Old World at some time in the Miocene. I see no reason why certain species of dryopithecines or early hominids, or both, could not have participated in this interchange.

Nevertheless, one may ask whether higher Primates ever had range distributions as extensive as those of such later Tertiary Mammalia as I have mentioned. Clearly, the range distribution of most present-day great apes is a restricted or relict distribution, but the fossil record of the pongids for the Miocene through the Villafranchian, as it now stands, is ample indication that certain varieties of these animals had much wider range distributions formerly than they have now. This also appears to be true for many animals of the later Pleistocene. For instance, *Pongo pygmaeus*, now restricted to the islands of Borneo and Sumatra, was then present in South China, and if the Siwalik Pliocene fossils reported by Pilgrim[19] are truly ancestors of this species, it probably had, at an earlier date, an extended range through the Malay Peninsula and Burma into India. Probable antece-

[16] R. F. Ewer, *Advan. Sci.* 18, 490 (1962).
[17] A. T. Hopwood and J. P. Hollyfield, *Fossil Mammals of Africa*, Brit. Museum (*Nat. Hist.*) 8, 1 (1954).
[18] E. H. Colbert, *Trans. Am. Phil. Soc.* 26, 376 (1935).
[19] G. E. Pilgrim, *Records Geol. Surv. India* 45, 1 (1915).

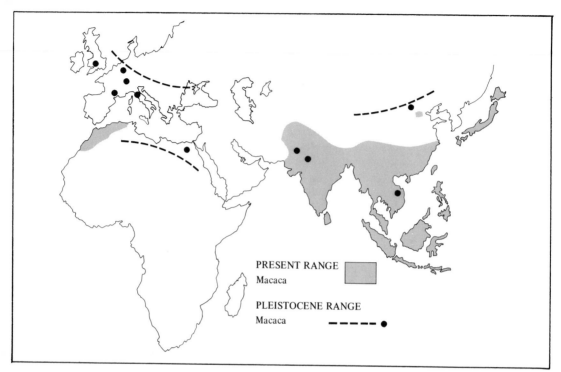

PRESENT RANGE
Macaca

PLEISTOCENE RANGE
Macaca

Figure 2: Recent and fossil distribution of the species of *Macaca*.

dents of the gibbons (*Pliopithecus*) are known from several scattered localities throughout Europe and northern and eastern Africa; at one time they must have been distributed (in suitable habitats) between these areas and the present range of members of this genus, in Southeast Asia. Evidently the ranges of modern species of great apes have dwindled greatly as a result of environmental changes in the relatively recent past. Among such changes was shrinking of the type of forest cover that was necessary for their existence. In certain populations, such as those of *Pongo* in South Asia, extermination or restriction of isolated enclaves on offshore islands surely came about as a result of hunting by human beings.

One of the varieties of primates least affected by these types of constriction are the present-day species of the genus *Macaca*. Distribution of mem-

bers of this genus (Fig. 2) illustrates the extremes of geographic range which members of a single stock of a prehominoid grade of partly arboreal primates have been able to achieve. It need not be assumed that man's ancestors had limited species range until they became terrestrial bipeds. In late-Pliocene and Villafranchian times, *Macaca* was nearly twice as widespread geographically as it is today. An acceptable evolutionary interpretation of this distribution would be that the ancestors of present-day *Macaca* reached the present extremes of their range (Japan, Gibraltar, and so on) when continental shelves were exposed during one of the Pleistocene glaciations, and that the far-flung present-day populations are descendants of perhaps no more than one widespread species that existed 1 to 3 million years ago. Of course, this species could have been already differentiating into genetically diverse populations (subspecies), with only moderate gene exchange between them,

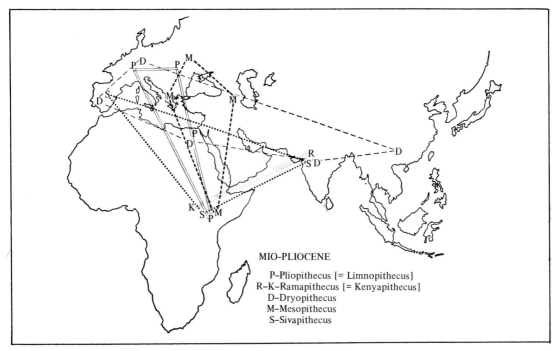

MIO-PLIOCENE

P–Pliopithecus [= Limnopithecus]
R–K–Ramapithecus [= Kenyapithecus]
D–Dryopithecus
M–Mesopithecus
S–Sivapithecus

Figure 3: Occurrence and range distribution of some Miocene-Pliocene Hominoidea.

before and while the total range of the species was approaching its greatest extent. But it seems more probable that such species distinctions as exist in *Macaca* came about through relatively recent cessation of gene flow between various populations within the entire genus range.[20] This would be particularly the case for populations isolated on islands since the last glaciation, or separated by late disappearance of suitable habitat, as between the western population of North Africa and its eastern allies. Members of *Macaca* appear

to have been able to achieve such broad distribution mainly because its species have been ecologically plastic. Some varieties, such as the Japanese monkey, have remained relatively arboreal, while others, like the Barbary ape of Gibraltar, are almost entirely terrestrial. Conceivably, from the late Miocene on, the earliest hominids were at least as capable of extending their range as the species of *Macaca* evidently were at a somewhat later date.

Thus, it can no longer be argued with confidence that the reason no pre-Pleistocene forerunners of man have been discovered is that these pre-hominids lived only in a limited geographical area of the Old World, and in a region (perhaps of tropical forests) which has yielded no fossil remains. It is now quite clear that the early hominoids as we know them from fossil remains ranged widely in the Old World in Miocene and Pliocene times. In Fig. 3 the scattered occurrences of the hominoid genera are connected by straight lines,

[20] Although several present-day species of *Macaca* surely must be valid—that is, genetically isolated—it is of some interest to observe that most of these living "species" of the genus *Macaca* have not been shown by cross-breeding experiments to be distinct species [see A. P. Gray, *Mammalian Hybrids* (Commonwealth Bureau of Animal Breeding and Genetics, Edinburgh, 1953)].

forming rough approximations to range diagrams. Particulars of the sites and species upon which Fig. 3 is based can be found in Piveteau.[21] In spite of three contrary factors—the rarity of fossil Primates, the enthusiasm of certain taxonomists for subdividing at the generic level, and failure to discover fossil-bearing localities in relevant areas—each of several "generic" units among Anthropoidea of this period have now been reported from at least two Old World continents, and some have been discovered in all three. That ancestors of man are not included among these extensive materials is, in my opinion, no longer an easily defended viewpoint. Moreover, the idea is equally controverted on morphological grounds. Some dryopithecines do show hominid features. The argument that human antecedents lived during pre-Pleistocene times in a restricted area which remains undiscovered has another rather unlikely consequence. This assumption implies that apes and even some monkeys (*Dryopithecus, Pliopithecus, Macaca*), although largely or partly arboreal, were able to spread their range widely, while the forerunners of man were somehow unable to do this. We are here concerned with a stock which, by the early Pliocene, was probably experimenting with terrestrial living and bipedal locomotion. If, at this time, man's predecessors were not able to distribute themselves as readily as their contemporaries among the monkeys and apes could, then it becomes necessary to conclude that man's evolutionary emergence from his pre-human past was truly explosive. This conclusion becomes all the more necessary if we assume that our supposedly poorly distributed antecedents suddenly outdistanced their more "primitive" contemporaries in the matter of species-range extension.

[21] J. Piveteau, *Traite Paleontol.* 7, 167 (1957).
[22] J. F. de V. Comella and M. C. Pairo, *Bol. Inst. Geol. Espan.* 91, 1 (1947).
[23] Personal communication, and Yale Peabody Museum records.

Species Distinctions

It should be noted that, although the particular specimens assigned by one or more competent authorities to the genera indicated in Fig. 3 are adequately known for purposes of generic placement, students cannot tell definitely whether the specimens assigned to a genus were members of the same or of different species. The common practice has been to regard European, Asian, and African finds of later Tertiary fossil Mammalia as belonging to different species, presumably in part because of the tacit assumption that ecologic barriers would, in nearly all cases, have prevented members of a species from reaching all three areas. Nevertheless, since these fossil forms are known primarily from fragmentary dentitions, it remains as difficult to prove that members of populations discovered in different continents represent distinct species as to demonstrate that they are members of the same species. Consequently, it will not be possible to test the validity of species distinctions among many such extinct mammals until much greater numbers of fossils of particular groups are known. In the case of these fossil "apes," for instance, when enough material has been recovered, statistical methods may be used in making species distinctions.

In connection with Fig. 3, it should also be pointed out that leading taxonomists of fossils differ as to the generic assignment of some of the species represented. For instance, after initial assignment of certain Spanish dryopithecine remains to the genus *Sivapithecus* [22] (an assignment followed here), this material was later referred elsewhere. On the other hand, Lewis [23] believes that materials currently assigned to *Dryopithecus* from the Miocene of Czechoslovakia should be placed in the genus *Sivapithecus*.

Consequently, I doubt that it has been established that *Sivapithecus* does not occur in Europe. Conversely, Fig. 3 does not indicate a range extension of *Pliopithecus* into Southeast Asia, but it seems entirely possible that the very fragmentary type of *"Hylopithecus"* from the Siwalik "series" may represent a primitive gibbon, perhaps assignable to *Pliopithecus*. With reference to this specimen, it seems instructive to quote what must be one of the most amazing passages in the history of bad taxonomic practice. This remark occurs as a conclusion to the description of the type species of *"Hylopithecus"*: [24] "In preference to leaving the tooth now described without a generic name and so increasing the difficulty of reference I am giving it the name of *Hylopithecus*, although I am conscious that my material is quite insufficient for diagnosis."

Origin of the Hominidae

In 1910 Pilgrim was ready to state that Hominidae are descended from *Sivapithecus*.[25] Later, in 1922, W. K. Gregory observed [26] "that man is a late Tertiary offshoot of the *Dryopithecus-Sivapithecus* group. . . ." Discoveries of hominoids during the half century which has elapsed since Pilgrim's writing have reinforced his viewpoint. Entirely apart from morphological considerations, such conclusions gain strength in the light of the taxonomic procedures and zoogeographic examples that I have discussed. It is curious that, in spite of numerous suitably cautious demonstrations in paleontological papers that the origins of man lay among the dryopithecines, it is still widely held by experts that next to nothing of definite value is known about the pre-Pleistocene forerunners of man.[27] One is reminded of a possibly apocryphal comment said to have been made in 1860 by the wife of the Bishop of Worcester. On learning from her husband that T. H. Huxley had then recently argued that man had ape-like ancestors, she observed: [28] "Descended from apes! My dear, let us hope that it is not true, but if it is let us pray that it will not become generally known." Although the fact of human evolution is no longer doubted, the phyletic sequence before the Pleistocene has never been elucidated during the more than 100 years which separate us from the pronouncements of T. H. Huxley.

Briefly, the following relevant facts as to the origin of the family of man are known. Fossil "apes" of the *Dryopithecus-Sivapithecus* type have now been recovered from deposits distributed throughout a vast area of warm-climate regions of the Old World, including sites in Spain, France, central Europe, Turkey, Georgia, the U.S.S.R., Egypt, Kenya, Uganda, Pakistan, India, and China. Without undertaking a taxonomic revision of these forms at this juncture, but assuming for the moment that all these occurrences do in fact pertain to dryopithecines, I must point out that far too many genera have been proposed for them.[29] Some of the genera which have been named are *Ankarapithecus*, *Austriacopithecus*, *Bramapithecus*, *Griphopithecus*, *Dryopithecus*, *Hylopithecus*, *Indopithecus*, *Kenyapithecus*, *Neopithecus*, *Paidopithex*, *Proconsul*, *Paleosimia*, *Ramapithecus*, *Rhenopithecus*, *Sivapithecus*, *Sugrivapithecus*, and *Udabnopithecus*.[29, 30]

Such a large number of distinct genera implies an extensive adaptive radiation of sudden appearance in the early or middle Miocene, but in the

[24] G. E. Pilgrim, *Mem. Geol. Surv. Ind.* 14, 12 (1927).

[25] G. E. Pilgrim, *Records Geol. Surv. Ind.* 40, 63 (1910).

[26] W. K. Gregory, *Origin and Evolution of the Human Dentition* (Williams and Wilkins, Baltimore, 1922), vol. 1, p. 548.

[27] F. C. Howell, *Science* 130, 831 (1959).

[28] M. F. Ashley Montagu, in T. H. Huxley, *Man's Place in Nature* (Univ. of Michigan Press, new ed., 1959), intro.

[29] I am currently engaged in a taxonomic revision of Dryopithecinae, based on direct study of nearly all known European, African, and Indian materials.

[30] W. K. Gregory, M. Hellman, G. E. Lewis, *Carnegie Inst. Wash. Publ.* 495 (1938), p. 1; E. L. Simons, *Postilla* 57, 1 (1961).

case of the dryopithecines this diversification probably occurred more on paper than in reality. Direct study of nearly all of the original specimens of these Primates suggests to me that the dryopithecines should probably be assigned to only three or four distinct genera, perhaps even fewer.

Species of four of these "genera" (*Dryopithecus, Sivapithecus, Proconsul,* and *Ramapithecus*) are now fairly well known. To date, however, no student has adequately dealt with the possibility that not even all of these genera may be separable from each other. This is an important issue, for it now appears that the direct hominid lineage passed through members of at least two of these taxa.

Starting with the more *Australopithecus*-like of these forms and working backward through time, we can now draw some fairly clear inferences about the evolutionary appearance of Hominidae. *Ramapithecus brevirostris,* of probable early Pliocene (Pontian) age, from the Nagri zone of the Siwalik Hills of India, has long been known to possess several characters in the upper dentition and maxilla which significantly approach the dental conformation of Pleistocene species of tool-making man. Briefly, these characters, which distinguish the forms from typical pongids and suggest hominid ties, are a parabolic (not U-shaped) dental arcade, an arched palate, a canine fossa, low-crowned cheek teeth, small incisors and canines, a low degree of prognathism, and a short face. Separately, almost all of these features can be found among pongids, but their occurrence in combination in *R. brevirostris* is a strong indication of hominid ties. Recently, Leakey has described a new East African primate specimen, "*Kenyapithecus wickeri,*" probably from about the same period or a little earlier, which is exactly like *R. brevirostris* in these and other features. In fact, in my opinion, not one *significant* character of difference exists between the two specimens

(both are maxillae). This being so, the new form from Kenya should be assigned tentatively to *R. brevirostris,* at least until such a time as further material provides a basis for demonstrating that the two are different species. The conclusion that these two specimens are at least of the same genus has recently been supported by Frisch, who has also studied them directly.[31] Perhaps the most extraordinary thing about Leakey's Fort Ternan, Kenya, specimen is its extreme similarity to the type specimen of *R. brevirostris*—an important and very significant fact that "generic" splitting only obscures. Greater differences than are to be noted here typically occur among members of a single-family social group within nearly all species of present-day hominoids. These two specimens indicate to me a considerable probability that in early Pliocene or latest Miocene times, or both, a single species of progressive (?) dryopithecine ranged all the way from northern India to East Africa, and perhaps farther. Personal examination of the specimens concerned also indicates that a third individual of this species, from the Nagri zone of the Siwalik Hills, in the Haritalyangar area, is represented by Pilgrim's specimen No. D185—the right maxilla of "*Dryopithecus punjabicus*"—in the Indian Museum, Calcutta. This specimen agrees with the other two in significant details of dental morphology, and in the possession of a much-reduced rostrum and an extremely short canine root (alveolus). These three specimens of *Ramapithecus* strongly reinforce each other in indicating a valid species group. Moreover, all three specimens come from a stratigraphic level higher than that at which most of the more generalized dryopithecine remains are found.

The transitional nature of these specimens of itself raises the question of arbitrariness in separating the families Pongidae and Hominidae—a problem which has also been posed recently in connection with another event, the discovery of close biochemical similarities between man and

---

[31] J. E. Frisch, *Anthropol. Anz.* 25, 298 (1962).

the apes, in particular the African apes.[32] Nevertheless, there do seem to be fairly good reasons for continuing to view the Pongidae and the Hominidae as distinct enough to be considered separate families. What I want to stress is the fact that the transitional nature of the *Ramapithecus* materials is such that they cannot be placed with finality in either group. Personally I do not see that it very much matters whether members of this genus be regarded as advanced pongids or as primitive hominids, but perhaps considerations of morphology slightly favor placement among the hominids. There is certainly no need to produce a new, higher category for such links—an alternative which has sometimes been resorted to in the past when a fossil taxon was determined to be roughly intermediate between two others.

Two Series of Dryopithecines

To date, the most extensive series of dryopithecines come from two main areas, the Rusinga Island and Fort Ternan beds of Kenya and the Siwalik Hills of India and Pakistan. A primary difficulty in understanding the actual significance of these two series of Primates arises from the fact that the Indian dryopithecines were studied and described primarily in the period between 1910 and 1937, while the dryopithecines of Kenya have been dealt with mainly since 1951. No one has ever published the results of extensive comparative study of the two sets of materials. Lewis, in the most recent taxonomic treatment of the Siwalik "apes," in 1937, reduced the number of genera to four (*Bramapithecus, Ramapithecus, Sivapithecus, Sugrivapithecus*), with ten contained species.[33] Members of the first two of these genera

[32] E. Zuckerkandl, R. T. Jones, L. Pauling, *Proc. Natl. Acad. Sci. U.S.* 46, 1349 (1960); M. Goodman, *Ann. N.Y. Acad. Sci.* 102, 219 (1962).
[33] G. E. Lewis, *Am. J. Sci.* 34, 139 (1937).

he regarded as more manlike than members of the other two; *Sivapithecus* and *Sugrivapithecus* he regarded as being closer to the present-day great apes. Unfortunately, there was a lack of associations between upper and lower dentitions in the Siwalik material, and knowledge of some of these genera—such as *Bramapithecus*, known only from jaw fragments containing the last two molars—was very limited. There were no whole or nearly complete dentitions in which to study the range of variability. This situation has now changed, because of the recovery in Africa (1948–1962) of relatively complete portions of skulls, maxillae, and mandibles of several individual dryopithecines, together with postcranial bones and, in some cases, associated upper and lower jaws. Comparison of these two series of data indicate the following problems.

1) In both the Kenyan and the Indian sites (in the lower part of the section, in particular) is found a large form with large snout, protruding incisors, slicing anterior premolars, and rather high-crowned teeth. In the East African material the lingual molar cingula are more pronounced, but otherwise, characters of dentition, snout, and jaw do not differ significantly. Mainly, these Miocene varieties have been called *Sivapithecus indicus* (Siwaliks), and *Proconsul major* (Rusinga). May it not be that these two sets of fossils represent a single species that ranged fairly widely, and perhaps over a long period, but which in known populations (even from far-flung portions of its range) is not particularly variable? This large-snouted type of ape is temporally distributed from early or middle Miocene (Rusinga; Chinji, in the Siwaliks) to latest Miocene or early Pliocene (Fort Ternan; Nagri, in the Siwaliks), as is evidenced by a very large upper canine recovered at Fort Ternan, at the same level as *"Kenyapithecus,"* reported by Leakey;[9] perhaps by other teeth found at Fort Ternan, that have not been described; and by several discoveries in the Nagri Zone. Differences in the molar-crown patterns of

the two populations are about as great within each area as between the two groups. A few successive species may be indicated by this material, or only a single species may be involved. This species could well be ancestral to the gorilla and chimpanzee. Ancestors of the African apes certainly need not always have been restricted to that continent.

2) A second primate form common to the Kenya and Indian areas in the Miocene is represented by the *Sivapithecus africanus* material (Kenya) and the "species" *Sivapithecus sivalensis* (India). In this group the teeth, particularly the canines, are relatively smaller than in "*S.*" *indicus,* and lingual cingula on upper molars apparently occur less frequently. The possibility remains high that other East African and Siwalik species, of the 15 accepted as valid in the more recent literature, will fall into synonymy with these two species as new data are recovered, or as a result of a fuller comparative study now in progress. The main distinction in dentition (and almost the only difference in known parts) between some *Sivapithecus* and modern *Pongo* is the higher degree of crenulation of the crowns of cheek teeth in *Pongo.* Several specimens of Indian *Sivapithecus* show rather crenulate molar crowns, and this may be assumed to indicate something about the origin of the orangutan. Such crenulations are particularly developed in the upper molar described by Pilgrim as "*Paleosimia,*" which may be a valid genus. In view of these crenulate teeth, it appears probable that a species that differentiated toward the Bornean great ape is represented in the Siwalik material, but this form has not been fully distinguished in taxonomic work to date. The probability that *Proconsul* cannot be separated generically from

Dryopithecus is worth mentioning here. Both these genera, if indeed they are two rather than one, appear to be restricted to the Miocene. *Sivapithecus* apparently crosses the Mio-Pliocene boundary but is not easily separated from *Ramapithecus,* a conclusion indicated by Leakey's report on the East African materials [9] and by my own studies on the Indian dryopithecines.

Conclusion

In concluding it seems advisable to make several observations as to the current state of knowledge of the origins of advanced hominoids.

The fossil hominoids of the Miocene of Kenya do not now appear to belong to the early part of that epoch, as had been previously believed, but may be of middle or, less probably, late Miocene age. Similarities between hominoids of the Miocene in India and Kenya, together with resemblances in other members of the two faunas, suggest that the Chinji Zone of the Siwaliks may be middle or late Miocene, as originally suggested by several early workers (see footnote 18). At this time the "radiation" which produced the great apes of today and man seems barely to have begun. The possible occurrence of *Dryopithecus* in early Miocene equivalents of Egypt requires further investigation.[34] There is now nearly universal agreement among those most competent to judge that *Oreopithecus* does not stand in the ancestral line of later pongids and hominids, although it is related to them.[35] In view of these conclusions, the origins of man and of the great apes of Africa and Borneo are seen to lie directly among the dryopithecines. This conclusion supports the extensive discussions of Gregory as to the significance for human phylogeny of the *Dryopithecus* molar pattern and LeGros Clark's analysis of the morphological evidences favoring the occurrence of secondary canine reduction in the ancestry of Hominidae.[36]

[34] R. Forteau, *Ministry of Finance, Survey Department, Cairo* (1920), vol. 1.
[35] W. L. Straus, Jr. *Clin. Orthopaed.* 25, 9 (1962).
[36] W. E. LeGros Clark, *The Fossil Evidence for Human Evolution* (Univ. of Chicago Press, Chicago, Ill., 1955).

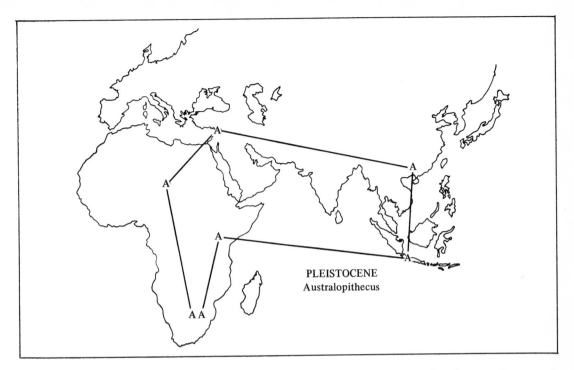

Figure 4: Reported range of *Australopithecus* species.

There is now adequate fossil evidence to indicate, (i) that, from about middle Miocene times, a few widely distributed species of the larger hominoids were present in both Eurasia and Africa and that successive differentiation of these species, through time, has occurred, with little branching or radiation; (ii) that the primary center of speciation among these animals was outside of Europe; (iii) that some dryopithecines in known parts entirely close the slight morphological gap between Hominidae and Pongidae; and (iv) that, if reports as to localities of *Australopithecus* [37] by several serious students be accepted, the data now show that this earliest generally accepted antecedent of man was widely distributed in tropical regions of the Old World in the early Pleistocene (Fig. 4). Present archeological evidence does suggest that the use of tools may have occurred first in Africa, but this is not the same as to suppose that the initial species of man differentiated there, unless man be defined solely as a tool-manufacturing primate. To date, the latter supposition is an inference primarily supported by negative evidence—namely, the scanty recovery of australopithecines

---

[37] In addition to major finds in Olduvai Gorge, Tanganyika, and the Transvaal, South Africa, the reported assignments of fossils to the Australopithecinae and specifically to *Australopithecus* (subgenera *Australopithecus* and *Paranthropus*) are as follows. (i) Stekelis *et al., Bull. Res. Council Israel Sect. G* 9, 175 (1960), teeth found in association with a Villafranchian fauna at Tell Ubeidiya, Jordan Valley, Israel; (ii) Y. Coppen, *Compt. Rend.* 252, 3851 (1961), *Australopithecus* cranial fragment found near Largeau, Lake Chad, North Africa; J. T. Robinson, *Am. J. Phys. Anthropol.* 11 (1953), transfer of Javan "*Meganthropus*" to *Australopithecus* (subgenus *Paranthropus*); G. H. R. von Koenigswald, *Koninkl. Ned. Akad. Wetenschap. Proc.* B60, 153 (1957), description of *Australopithecus* (= *Hemianthropus*) *peii*, from China.

and of pebble tools in Southeast Asia and China. It must be remembered that one creditable occurrence is all that is needed to demonstrate the early presence of *Australopithecus* in the East. Such an occurrence apparently has now been confirmed by von Koenigswald, through his description of about a dozen teeth, assigned by him to a new genus, *"Hemianthropus,"* in materials recovered from Chinese drugstores.[37] In my opinion these teeth are from members of the Australopithecinae assignable to the sub-genus *Paranthropus,* but Woo [38] suggests that some of these teeth could belong to *Gigantopithecus.*[39]

6 • SOME PROBLEMS OF HOMINID CLASSIFICATION

D. R. Pilbeam & Elwyn L. Simons

In this contribution the authors are concerned with clarifying some traditional ways of thinking about the phylogeny of man. Instead of asking the usual question "How *Homo*-like is *Australopithecus?*" they suggest asking "How australopithecine-like is *Homo?*" The answer they give is that *Australopithecus* is very much like *Homo,* and therefore deserves to be placed in the genus to which some authors believe he belongs.[1]

Another important point is the recognition of the fact that, since man's Pliocene ancestors more closely resembled men than they did apes, therefore an early separation of the lines must have led to man on the one hand and the apes on the other, as established by the fossil record, instead of the view sometimes bruited that man's separation from the ape stem occurred within the Pleistocene or Plio-Pleistocene boundary. The traditional way of thinking about these matters has greatly influenced both morphological reconstructions and classificatory procedures. For example, Boule's reconstruction of Neanderthal man as a bull-necked, chinless, low-foreheaded, knock-kneed, pileated monster was based not only on an inadequate knowledge of elementary human anatomy, but upon the preconceived notion that "primitive man" [2] ought to look ape-like. In spite of many protests against this view of Neanderthal man, and the final demolition of it by Straus and Cave,[3] the notion of his "bestial apelike" appearance and alleged aggressive conduct is widespread among laymen and those who should know better. The word "Neanderthal" has become a synonym for every kind of brutishness. Years ago I protested this kind of libel and misrepresentation in a communication to the *New York Times.*[4] The general

[38] J.-K. Woo, *Palaeontol. Sinica* 146, 1 (1962).
[39] I thank the Wenner-Gren Foundation of New York and the board of the Boise fund of Oxford University for financial support in the preparation of this article. I also thank W. E. LeGros Clark, A. L. McAlester, B. Patterson, C. L. Remington, M. C. McKenna, and W. L. Straus, Jr., for critical reading of the manuscript. Illustrations were prepared by Mrs. Martha Erickson.
[1] C. Loring Brace and Ashley Montagu, *Man's Evolu-* tion (New York: The Macmillan Co., 1965).
[2] Ashley Montagu, Ed., *The Concept of the Primitive* (New York: The Free Press, 1968).
[3] W. L. Straus, Jr., and A. J. E. Cave, "Pathology and Posture of Neanderthal Man," *Quarterly Review of Biology,* XXXII (1957), 348–363. See pp. 216–232 of the present volume.
[4] Ashley Montagu, "Unmaking a Scapegoat: On the Neanderthal Man and His Mind, A Defense," *New York Times,* 20 July 1941, p. E7.

response was that such a defense was eccentric.

Pilbeam and Simons present many challenging ideas in this contribution, and all of them are reasonable and solidly based on the evidence. Full familiarity with their ideas is fundamental for the student of physical anthropology.

The early 1950's were years of controversy in human paleontology; argument, discussion, and sometimes polemic were focused on the relationship to other primates of the genus *Australopithecus*, primates sometimes called near-men or man-apes. These were known mainly, at that time, from finds made in the Transvaal, South Africa. Although the species of *Australopithecus* are now considered hominid, many students were reluctant at first to accept such a status, believing that small brain volume and "imperfect" adaptation to upright posture prevented their assignment to the Hominidae, the taxonomic family which includes living man. Instead, these creatures were regarded as aberrant apes.

Subsequently, it was realized that it is not possible to exclude species from the Hominidae on account of small brain size; the ancestors of modern man must obviously, at some stage, have had smaller brains. The "imperfections" of the *Australopithecus* pelvis were also overstressed; there is good reason to believe that the species of *Australopithecus* were now habitual and efficient bipeds. The concept that different functional systems may evolve independently and at varying rates (mosaic evolution), has also been assimilated by most anthropologists, and, in addition, it is no longer

SOURCE: D. R. Pilbeam and Elwyn L. Simons, "Some Problems of Hominid Classification," *American Scientist* vol. 53 (New Haven, Conn., 1965): 98–120. Reprinted by permission of the author and the publisher.

considered reasonable to discriminate taxa on the basis of a few characters alone.

Another sort of misunderstanding derives from one's reference point in studying hominid evolution. Perhaps we have been looking down the wrong end of the telescope, so to speak, trying to understand the evolution of man by looking backward through time "from the vantage point of the Recent" (Patterson, 1954). If *Homo* species evolved from the species *Australopithecus africanus,* as many believe, we should expect that these species would have many features in common. Those characters in which they differ, however, should be regarded as specializations of *Homo,* not as peculiarities of *Australopithecus.* One must not ask "How *Homo*-like is *Australopithecus?*" but rather the opposite.

Origin of the Hominidae

Washburn has stated recently that "most of the characters of *Homo* seem to have evolved well within the Pleistocene, and there is no need to postulate an early separation of man and ape" (1963: 203). But the fossil record, although limited, instead seems to indicate a pre-Pliocene separation. Our Pliocene ancestors evidently were socially and adaptively more like man than great apes. By the early Pleistocene, except in the matter of brain-size, man's relatives (men or near-men) were almost as different morphologically from both living and extinct great apes as are men today. *Australopithecus* in fact resembles *Homo* far more than either resembles the African apes, man's closest living relatives.

Ever since the nineteenth-century inception of human paleontology, the comparison of early man with living apes, the only other well-known hominoids, has been overemphasized. This tendency has led, on the one hand, to stressing supposedly ape-like features in late forms of fossil man (Boule's classic studies of European Neander-

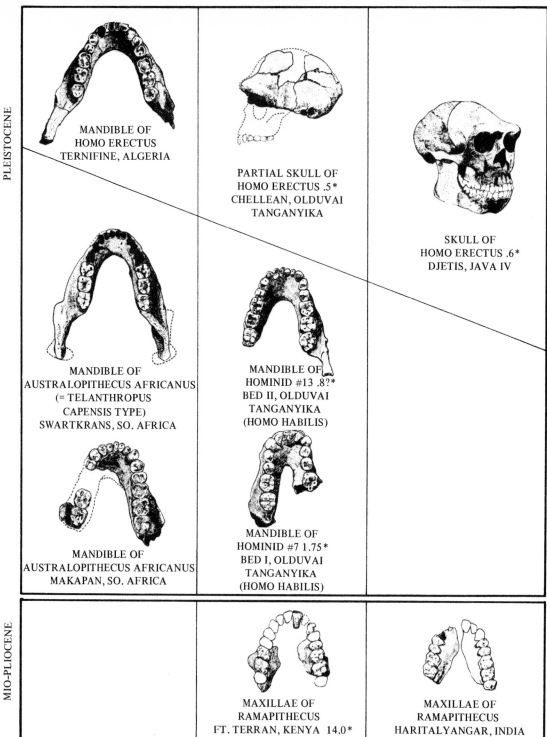

	SOUTH AND NORTH AFRICA	EAST AFRICA	ASIA

PLEISTOCENE

MANDIBLE OF
HOMO ERECTUS
TERNIFINE, ALGERIA

PARTIAL SKULL OF
HOMO ERECTUS .5*
CHELLEAN, OLDUVAI
TANGANYIKA

SKULL OF
HOMO ERECTUS .6*
DJETIS, JAVA IV

MANDIBLE OF
AUSTRALOPITHECUS AFRICANUS
(= TELANTHROPUS
CAPENSIS TYPE)
SWARTKRANS, SO. AFRICA

MANDIBLE OF
HOMINID #13 .8?*
BED II, OLDUVAI
TANGANYIKA
(HOMO HABILIS)

MANDIBLE OF
AUSTRALOPITHECUS AFRICANUS
MAKAPAN, SO. AFRICA

MANDIBLE OF
HOMINID #7 1.75*
BED I, OLDUVAI
TANGANYIKA
(HOMO HABILIS)

MIO-PLIOCENE

MAXILLAE OF
RAMAPITHECUS
FT. TERRAN, KENYA 14.0*

MAXILLAE OF
RAMAPITHECUS
HARITALYANGAR, INDIA

* K/A AGES IN MILLIONS OF YEARS.   The range of error on all dates is of the order of .3 m. yrs. or less.

Figure 1: Mio-Pliocene and Pleistocene hominids from Asia and Africa with potassium/argon dates. Specimens on the left and right are matched with morphologically similar forms from the K/A-dated East African sequence.

thals, for example). On the other hand, this has led to surpise whenever "advanced" characteristics are found in early forms (for example, the modern looking hominid foot from Bed I at Olduvai Gorge, Tanganyika).

Ramapithecus punjabicus (Fig. 1) is known from the Siwalik Hills of North India, from Fort Ternan, Kenya, and possibly from the Swabian Alps in Europe (Simons, 1964), appearing first in the latest Miocene. This species also occurs in sediments of uncertain age in Keiyuan, Yunnan, China (Simons and Pilbeam, 1965). The known morphology of *Ramapithecus* is discussed in Simons (1961, 1964); it is sufficient here to point out that the incisors, canines, and premolars are reduced relative to those of known species of dryopithecines and of present-day apes. In *Ramapithecus*, as in man, internal cingula are absent and molar crowns simple. *Ramapithecus* could have evolved with almost equal probability from a dryopithecine, sometime between early and middle Miocene, or from species more like the Egyptian Oligocene primate *Propliopithecus haeckeli*. Hominoid species evolving respectively in the direction of *Homo* and of *Pan* need not have shared a common ancestor later than early or middle Miocene times.

In our opinion, assignment to Hominidae can reasonably be made for all those species that show evolutionary trends toward modern *Homo*, whenever these trends appear. The evolutionary shift in a major adaptive zone indicated in the case of *Ramapithecus* by its reduced snout and anterior teeth (premolars, canines, and incisors) may well correlate with an increased use of the hands and the incipient development of bipedality, although direct fossil evidence for both these developments is presently lacking. Even if *Ramapithecus* and *Pan* had a more recent common ancestor than either did with the orangutan, the Hominidae are presumably definable in terms of this adaptive shift, as is indicated in Figure 2. Moreover, *Ramapithecus* is presently best re-

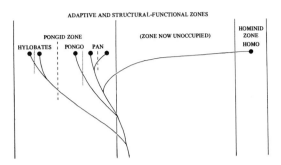

Figure 2: Diagram showing relative closeness of phylogenetic relationships of living hominoids and their radiation into adaptive-structural-functional zones, from Simpson (1963). Reprinted from Sherwood L. Washburn, ed.: *Classification and Human Evolution.* Copyright © 1963 by Wenner-Gren Foundation for Anthropological Research, Inc. First published 1963 by Aldine Publishing Company.

garded as a hominid, not a hominid-like pongid, because it already exhibits the basic dental adaptations of *Homo* and *Australopithecus*. If the other parts of the skeleton, subsequently found, should all be ape-like, this position could require alteration. But why should this be so? Of course, it is quite possible that, if and when cranial and post-cranial remains of *Ramapithecus* are discovered, they will prove to be rather more *Dryopithecus*-like than are those of *Australopithecus*, because *Ramapithecus* lies several million years closer in time to the common ancestor of apes and men. However, the known parts are not ape-like; *Ramapithecus* cannot logically be lumped any longer with the apes.

Fossil ancestors of the living orangutan of Asia are either unknown or unrecognized. Biochemical and serological research underlines the close relationship of modern man to the great apes of Africa. This supports other, mainly paleontological, evidence suggesting that chimpanzee, gorilla, and men are more closely related cladistically, that is, in recency of a common ancestor for all (Harrison and Weiner, 1963), than all three are to the orangutan and the Asiatic gibbon. Even if the orangutan and the African apes are patristically related, that is, if all are more similar in outward (phenotypic or phenetic) morphology than any one of them is to *Homo*, they still could be less similar genetically. However, although the ancestral line leading to the orangutan probably differentiated from an early unknown member of the dryopithecine complex before the hominids did so, the hominids have differentiated more rapidly and now occupy an adaptive niche quite different from that presently filled by the African and Asian apes.

Classification of Hominoidea

In comparison with most other superfamilies, too many distinctions of higher taxa have been drawn among hominoids. This is presumably because much of the taxonomic work on these categories has been done by persons unacquainted with the manner in which higher categories have been, or should be, proposed in the light of the new systematics. Most mammalogists would probably now prefer to use three basic principles in justifying the erection or retention of families and subfamilies. Briefly, these principles are: (1) the group which is thought to deserve such status should have had a considerable time duration as a separate stock, (2) the proposed taxon (a formal unit grouping organisms) should show considerable diversity in terms of contained species and genera, (3) the category should be characterized by a reasonably thorough-going structural distinctiveness shared by its members and not like that of related families or subfamilies. Admittedly, criteria of morphological distinctiveness are subjective, but material on which to base such judgments can be derived from comparative anatomy. For instance, one can make an approximate answer to the question: Do members of the families of man and apes differ *more*, or *less*, in total skeletal and dental morphology than

do species of other related families within one order, such as Canidae and Felidae?

Because classification should also reflect both the past evolution of given taxa and the morphology and adaptation of the present members of such taxa, a compromise must be reached which reflects both cladistic and patristic relationships (Fig. 1). Consequently, it is preferable in a classification of the superfamily Hominoidea to retain a separate family for the genera *Ramapithecus*, *Australopithecus*, and *Homo*, a family sustained primarily by the morphological features which indicate the adaptive shift to hominid feeding patterns and habitual bipedalism.

Species of orangutan, chimpanzee, and gorilla, together with those of *Dryopithecus* and *Gigantopithecus*, should be retained in the Pongidae. Dryopithecinae can be justified as a separate subfamily. Although two further subfamilies, Ponginae and Paninae, could be used, these would contain at the most only one or two genera and species, and the distinction would not, in our opinion, be particularly meaningful. It is even more difficult to justify the division of Hominidae into such subfamilies as Australopithecinae, Homininae, Praehomininae, and the like.

Ecology and Adaptation of Early Hominoids

Modern pongids and hominids are characterized by relative trunk erectness, a feature shared with more "primitive" primate species (Schultz, 1961). For example, many prosimians are vertical tree-clingers, like *Indri*, *Propithecus*, and *Tarsius*, while the New World monkeys *Ateles*, *Lagothrix*, and *Brachyteles* are partial brachiators (Erikson, 1963). Even the more terrestrial Old World monkeys sit erect while feeding, grooming, and resting. Avis (1962) has suggested that the hominoid superfamily differentiated from other primates by becoming arm-swingers confined to a small-branch niche in a forest habitat; in her opinion this differentiation occurred as early as the Eocene. This matter of arm-swinging raises the largely academic question of what is or is not formal "brachiation." (This form of locomotion requires suspension from alternate hands, forward movement being produced by pronation of the arm and trunk around the fixed hand; propulsive force in such locomotion comes entirely from the upper limbs.) *Proconsul africanus,* for instance, is said to have been a "probrachiator" (Napier, 1963), and thus in some ways similar morphologically to modern colobine monkeys. *P. africanus* does not exhibit the extreme forelimb elongation characteristic of modern apes (Napier and Davis, 1959). Does this mean that *P. africanus* could not have "brachiated" in the formal sense? Perhaps so; perhaps not. Several genera of New World monkeys move through the trees in this manner without showing all the anatomical "brachiating" specializations of the Old World pongids.

Whether "brachiators" or "probrachiators," Miocene apes and their Oligocene ancestors probably showed a high degree of trunk erectness and doubtless spent much time walking and running bipedally, either in the trees or on the ground. As Gregory suggested (1928), some brachiation would probably have been essential for the hominids before they could become habitual bipeds. The structure of the human arm, thorax, and abdomen all suggest that, at some stage, our early Tertiary forerunners may have, on occasion, moved by arm-swinging in the trees.

The idea of the "emancipated forelimb" has been greatly overstressed in discussions of hominid tool-using. Hands have been important throughout all of primate evolution; the higher primates, in particular, use their hands in a wide range of activities such as feeding and grooming. The habit of sitting erect, widespread in primates, insures that the hands are free for these activities. However, in nonhominid primates the hands are typically used in locomotion as well; it is in this respect that hominid forelimb "emancipation" becomes important. As Kortlandt (1962) and Schultz (1961) have suggested, stone- and branch-throwing in defense were probably important in early hominid behavior before tool-using became widespread. It is also clear from the dentition of *Ramapithecus* that the early hominids could not have fed by stripping vegetable material with the canines and incisors as do the African apes; such feeding behavior requires relatively large front teeth for nipping, tearing, and shredding. It is possible, as a consequence of both these factors, that hominids were *ad hoc* tool-users at least by the early Pliocene (Napier, 1963). Once hominids became committed to a terrestrial way of life and some degree of habitual bipedal locomotion, the freeing of their forelimbs would have greatly facilitated tool use.

The earliest hominids may, of course, have functioned fairly well bipedally long before noticeable skeletal alterations increasing the efficiency of this maner of locomotion had become genetically fixed. Such an hypothesis gains strength from observation of the crude walking of the living spider monkey (*Ateles*), gibbon (*Hylobates*), and even some lemurs (*Propithecus*). While it can be debated whether this type of progression should formally be called bipedal, it certainly cannot be written off as quadrupedal movement; none of these primates use the hands habitually to support the forebody during locomotion on the ground. Despite such tendencies toward bipedal walking, however, none of these primates show any man-like skeletal adjustments that make upright walking more efficient.

Selection pressures were doubtless strongly in favor of such trends when the hominids were evolving, but the nature of the ecological readjustments involved in the origin of the hominid line is likely to remain a matter of conjecture. A change in diet also occurred during the course of hominid evolution, but, as Schultz (1961) has pointed out, this shift has been overstressed. The modern great apes are often described as vegetarians, but Schultz suggests that, among the primates, perhaps only the colobine monkeys can be termed truly vegetarian. Most of the other primates tend to supplement their diets with animal protein. However, Miocene apes probably ate mostly vegetable material just as modern baboons, chimpanzees and gorillas do, and the earliest hominids presumably had a similar diet. During the Pliocene, the amount of animal protein in the hominid diet surely would have increased as scavenging and hunting, feeding habits evidently well established by the early Pleistocene, became more widespread in hominid populations. As this dietary shift brought with it increased calorific values, less time would have been required for feeding, and the habit of food-sharing could develop.

Bartholomew and Birdsell (1953) have discussed theoretical concepts of early hominid ecology and believe that the early hominids were wide-ranging, food-sharing, weapon-using omnivores. It has been said that "tool-using and tool-making were very probably associated with the tendency for early members of the phyletic line leading to man to take to a certain amount of meat-eating" (Robinson, 1963a, 393). The reduced canines and incisors of *Ramapithecus punjabicus* suggest that tool-using may have been established by the late Miocene, because smaller front teeth require the use of other means to prepare food, either animal or vegetable.[1] Noback and Moskowitz have emphasized that the increasing dexterity of the hand seems to have played a major role in the evolution of the central

nervous system among higher primates, particularly in the case of the Hominidae, and this influence may well have been acting in *Ramapithecus* populations.

Robinson (1962, 1963) has discussed at length the alterations in pelvic anatomy and muscle function consequent to erect bipedalism. Unfortunately, no pelves of Miocene or Pliocene dryopithecines are yet known. It is generally assumed that the pelves of mid-Tertiary higher primates will prove to be similar to those of modern pongids. In this view, the human pelvis is considered to have been derived from an ancestral morphology similar to that of modern apes. It seems more likely, however, that some morphological differentiation has occurred in the pongid as well as the hominid line. Indeed, such pieces of evidence as the hominid-like pelvis of *Oreopithecus* and the broad ilia of New World brachiators, taken together with the considerable probability that early pongids were arboreal arm-swingers with erect trunks, suggest that the immediate ancestors of the hominids were actually pre-adapted as brachiators in terms of behavior, and perhaps to bipedal running and walking in terms of anatomy.

Chimpanzees and gorillas have prognathous, that is, projecting faces; their mid-Tertiary ancestors were evidently more orthognathous (straight-faced), and it seems that facial lengthening occurred, at least in part, as a response to demands of ground living, defensive display and vegetarian diet. Baboons and macaques have prognathous faces also. Large teeth and powerful muscles are required in order to chew tough plant food. Considerable sexual dimorphism in canine size is shown among various species of apes and Old World monkeys and, consequently, it is probable that (among other factors) elongated canines are associated with defensive display behavior. Increased stress on olfaction among mainly ground-feeding species such as baboons probably was important in the development of the snout.

---

[1] It may be argued that all three *Ramapithecus* maxillary specimens are those of small-canined females. This is not too likely, but, even if true, it would not alter the fact that the premolars and incisors are also smaller relative to molar size than is the case in any pongid.

In contrast, colobine monkeys, New World monkeys, and the erect-postured tree-clinging prosimians such as *Indri, Propithecus,* and *Tarsius* all have relatively short faces and show less sexual dimorphism. Among fossil forms the small Miocene species *Proconsul africanus* (Davis and Napier, 1963) was also relatively orthognathous as was *Oreopithecus.* New evidence secured by the recent Yale expeditions (Simons, 1965) indicates that several of the Egyptian Oligocene hominoids were short-faced too.

Trunk erectness and orthognathism are apparently closely linked. Erect posture is associated with changes in orientation of the cranial base, typically exemplified by downward rotation of the facial axis on the basicranial axis (DuBrul, 1950; DuBrul and Laskin, 1961; Biegert, 1963). Mills (1963) has suggested that the assumption of habitual erect posture would cause further flattening of the face. He points out that, in primates with large canines, the lower canines pass behind the upper incisors during chewing. With facial shortening, the canines no longer pass behind, but rather in the plane of, the maxillary incisors. As this happens, selection favors reduction of canine crowns. If tool use (and possible changes in male display behavior as well) had removed the selective advantage of large canines, canine reduction inevitably would have taken place.

Thus, it appears that several anatomical, behavioral, and "cultural" elements—erect posture, orthognathism, changes in diet and display behavior, an increasing use of tools and reduction of the anterior dentition—are here closely linked one to another. Members of the genus *Ramapithecus* have small front teeth and were apparently wide-ranging even in the late Miocene; the dental evidence implies that profound behavioral, dietary, and locomotor changes had already occurred among species of *Ramapithecus* by this time. The commitment to a hominid way of life could conceivably have been made by the late Miocene, and our earliest known probable ancestors, with brains perhaps comparable in size to those of chimpanzees, might have already adopted a way of life distinct from that of their ape contemporaries.

Appearance and Speciation of Man

Near the beginning of the Pleistocene, hominids are represented in the fossil record by two or more species of *Australopithecus,* a small-brained, large-jawed form similar dentally to *Homo.* Postcranially, *Australopithecus* is similar to, although not identical with, later men and evidently was an habitual biped. Early Pleistocene sites at Olduvai in Tanganyika have yielded hominid remains, together with crude stone tools (Leakey, 1959); stone tools of similar type are known from North Africa (Biberson, 1963) and the Jordan valley (Stekelis, 1960), and it seems likely that, at about the same time, bone tools were being made in South Africa (Dart, 1957). Regular tool-making, utilizing bone, stone, wood, and perhaps other material too, possibly began more than two million years ago.

It has been suggested by many authors that the transition from tool-using to regular tool-making was a step of crucial importance in the evolution of man. This may well be true but, like many generalizations in anthropology, this one has been oversimplified. As Napier has pointed out (1963), tool-making may often have been invented and forgotten in the late Tertiary. During Villafranchian time (that is, during earliest Pleistocene time), some hominids were doubtless toolmakers while others were still only tool-users. Differing environmental demands would produce different behavioral responses. However, the advantages of regular tool-making are clear and, once invented, the spread of this skill would probably have been fairly rapid.

Speciation in the Hominidae

Simpson (1961: 90) remarks:

Supposedly intergeneric hybridization, usually with sterile offspring, is possible among animals, for instance, in mammals, the artificial crosses *Bos* × *Bison, Equus* × *Asinus,* and *Ursus* × *Thalarctos.* In my opinion, however, this might better be taken as basis for uniting the nominal genera. I would not now give generic rank to *Bison, Asinus,* or *Thalarctos.*

There is considerable evidence that the African and Arabian baboons, previously thought to belong to several separate genera, can produce viable hybrids, and may, instead, be classified in perhaps as few as two or three species of a single genus. Hybrid studies, by the Russians and others, suggest that species of *Macaca* (the rhesus monkey) and perhaps of *Cercocebus* (the mangabey), too, should be classified as belonging instead to the baboon genus *Papio. Papio* in this sense, can be regarded as a wide-ranging genus with local species populations which show variations in morphology, coloring, and behavior. Freedman's metrical work on cranial variation in *Papio* "species" (1963) lends support to this view. Some of the populations may be sibling species, others may warrant only subspecific rank; only interfertility studies can determine their validity as genetical species. Among members of *Papio,* greater morphological variability is to be seen among samples of adult males than among samples of adult females, particularly in cranial features. This, together with pronounced sexual dimorphism, suggests that differences in mating and display patterns have selected for a great deal of the specific and subspecific morphological differences. The small amount of speciation within the genus is also significant when compared with *Cercopithecus* (guenons) or colobine monkeys, and this is almost certainly a direct reflection of *Papio's* wide-ranging terrestrial way of life. Among

these primates, there is apparently a rough correlation between species range size and the degree of speciation within a genus. Highly arboreal primates, such as species of langurs and gibbons, tend to have more restricted ranges and tend to be less mobile as groups; isolation and speciation become more likely under these circumstances.

The earliest hominids probably were at least as wide-ranging and mobile as the baboons, and presumably would have been much more so by middle and late Pliocene time. As noted already, fossil evidence suggests that *Ramapithecus punjabicus* was already present in East Africa, India, China, and possibly Europe, by the early Pliocene; there is no reason to suppose that hominids have not been widely dispersed since then. Man has capitalized on plasticity rather than becoming restricted to narrow morphological and behavioral adaptations. His mobility, his ability to occupy a highly diversified ecological niche, and his apparently slow development of isolating mechanisms (Mayr, 1963: 644) all tend to reduce speciation. It is a reasonable working hypothesis, therefore, that not more than one genus, and perhaps no more than one or two species of hominid, has existed at any particular time. Like most other mammals, man is polytypic; that is, a number of races are found within the species. We should expect fossil hominid species populations to be polytypic too.

Taxonomy of Australopithecus

Before the student can erect new fossil genera and species he must demonstrate that the new proposed taxon differs significantly from previously described taxa in a number of particular characters. Thus, any diagnosis should take full account of known variability in living related species and genera. Different specific and generic names also imply certain other differences. If two individual fossils or fossil populations have different specific names, this implies that they could not have been members of a single freely interbreeding population; this, in turn, requires a period of reproductive and probably geographic isolation. Different generic names, in their turn, generally imply that the taxa concerned were completely incompatible genetically; to develop such incompatibility would require a long period of isolation. As we have already noted, however, such isolation would probably have been an unusual event during the course of hominid evolution.

Early Pleistocene hominids are known from a number of African localities. The first to be described and discussed was *Australopithecus africanus* from South Africa. It is now fairly generally agreed that two species of this genus are known: *A. africanus* (Fig. 1) from Villafranchian deposits at Taung, Sterkfontein, and Makapansgat, and *A. robustus,* from possibly latest early Pleistocene and middle Pleistocene deposits at Kromdraai and Swartkrans (Robinson, 1963). Another form, *"Telanthropus capensis"* (Fig. 1) has been recovered from Swartkrans; its status is equivocal and will be discussed later.[2] Robinson (1963a) discussed these australopithecine forms at length, pointing out that *A. africanus* is, in his opinion, closer to the ancestry of later men than is *A. robustus.*

Definite or probable australopithecines have been reported also from Java, North Africa, Israel, and East Africa. *Meganthropus palaeojavanicus*—represented by finds from the Djetis beds of Java—is said by Robinson to be closely similar to the African form *A. robustus*. Although Clark (1955, 86) considers the Java specimen's generic separation from another hominid form, *Homo erectus* (Fig. 1), unjustified in view of the fragmentary nature of the material, the fact is that these jaw fragments do not provide enough infor-

mation to allow students to draw species distinctions between the Javan and African material.

Coppens (1962) has reported the recovery of an australopithecine skull from Koro-Toro, near Lake Chad south of the Sahara. The associated fauna suggests an early Villafranchian age. Arambourg (1963: 564) states that this fossil is intermediate in morphology between *A. africanus* and *A. robustus* but with perhaps a greater cranial capacity. Robinson (1963b: 601) considers it closer to *A. robustus*. No pebble tools are associated, although they are present in later Villafranchian deposits of North Africa (Biberson, 1963). *"Meganthropus africanus"* from the Laetolil beds of early Pleistocene age near Lake Eyassi in East Africa has been referred to *Australopithecus* by Robinson (1955). In addition Stekelis (1960) has discovered fragmentary hominid remains of early or middle Pleistocene age associated with a pebble tool culture at Ubeidiya in the Central Jordan valley.

Finally, Leakey has recently described a number of hominid finds in deposits of early and middle Pleistocene age at Olduvai Gorge, Tanganyika (Leakey, 1959, 1961, and Leakey, Tobias, and Napier, 1964). Two distinct species have been recognized and described, *Australopithecus* (= *Zinjanthropus*) *"boisei"* from Bed I at Olduvai and from possibly middle Pleistocene deposits near Lake Natron, Tanganyika, and *"Homo habilis"* (type, hominid #7) from Bed I and other specimens from Bed II at Olduvai. *A. boisei* is bigger and more robust than *H. habilis* (see Fig. 1) and has larger molars and premolars; we believe that it cannot be distinguished at the specific level from *A. robustus*.

The hominid sites from Bed I have been dated by the potassium-argon method (Leakey, Curtis, and Evernden, 1961), the three sites FLK I, FLKNN I, and MK falling between 1.57 and 1.89 million years. The Bed II hominids from FLK II, VEK IV, and MNK II are younger than 1.02 million years, the youngest date for the top of

---

[2] Invalid or doubtful taxonomic terms are indicated here in quotes on initial citation only.

Bed I, and older than 0.49 million years, the date of a post-Chellean II tuff in Bed II (Hay, 1963). The *Homo habilis* material therefore falls into two groups, separated by perhaps as much as one million years. Once again, during the period of deposition of the lower parts of Bed II, two distinct taxa appear to have been present, *H. habilis* at Olduvai and *A. boisei* at Lake Natron.

Altogether, then, some half dozen supposedly distinct taxa (both genera and species) have been proposed for early and early Middle Pleistocene hominids; several of these are based on the most fragmentary and limited material. Schultz has repeatedly stressed the very high level of morphological variability among species of the Hominoidea (see bibliographies in Schultz, 1961 and 1963). Nevertheless, small and taxonomically trivial differences in dental, cranial, and postcranial anatomy have still been used to establish or justify specific or generic distinctions among the earlier Pleistocene hominids. What follows is an attempt to bring some taxonomic order to this situation.

At present, *A. robustus* is known from South Africa (Swartkrans, Kromdraai), Olduvai Bed I, Lake Natron, and possibly Java. The other African forms of roughly equivalent age have been referred to three taxa, *A. africanus, Telanthropus capensis,* and *Homo habilis.* The relative dating of the North, East, and South African sites presents a number of problems. Faunally, there are few mammal species as they are presently defined common to all three sites, and those which are common are often unsuitable for purposes of correlation. Cooke (1963) has discussed this problem at length. He believes that the South African sites which have yielded *A. africanus* are broadly contemporaneous with the later Bed I levels at Olduvai. However, he points out that:

Although ecological differences prevent too close a comparison, the faunas suggest strongly that the sequence in East Africa from the Kaiso and the

Kanam levels through Omo and Laetolil to Bed I corresponds fairly closely in time to the sequence Sterkfontein and Makapansgat to Swartkrans and Kromdraai. Although the evidence is extremely tenuous, the Villafranchian (equivalent) fauna of North Africa could well be contemporary with these East African deposits and the ape-man breccias. The occurrence of pebble tools in similar relationships in all three areas may be significant and if the North African beds are truly pre-Cromerian as has been suggested by several authorities this would provide additional grounds for keeping at least the major part of the ape-man deposits within the Villafranchian. (Cooke, 1964: 104)

Biberson (1963) considers the Koro-Toro site at Lake Chad contemporary with Kaiso and Kanam in East Africa, and, if this is so, the Chad hominid could well be the oldest *Australopithecus* known. *Telanthropus capensis* from Swartkrans is probably the same age as *Homo habilis* from Olduvai Bed II, while *A. africanus* from Taung, Sterkfontein and Makapansgat and Bed I *H. habilis* are possibly of approximately equivalent age.

The New East African Hominids and the South African Australopithecines

Known *Homo habilis* material, as already noted, falls into two main groups separated by perhaps as much as a million years. The type specimen of *H. habilis* consists of a juvenile mandible, two parietal fragments, a hand and an upper molar. A foot and clavicle belonging to an older individual (or individuals—associations of all Olduvai individuals are certainly not clear) have been recovered from the same site (FLKNN I). Two other sites in Bed I have yielded teeth, mandibular and skull fragments, and a tibia and fibula belonging either to *H. habilis* or to *Australopithecus (Zinjanthropus) boisei.* Among remains from Bed II are: a complete mandible (with associated maxillae) together with the occipitals and broken parietals and temporals of possibly the same individual, cranial fragments, isolated teeth, and a damaged palate. Although there is insufficient material from which firm inferences can be drawn, the sequence through Bed I to Bed II suggests that teeth and mandibles became progressively reduced during this time, while there was little alteration in cranial capacity. (This seemingly unchanging brain size may correlate with the presence throughout the section of similar crude pebble tools, or the two faunas may be closer in time than K/A-dated horizons appear to indicate.) The juvenile mandible and teeth from FLKNN I in Bed I are some 10 per cent greater in all measurements than the mandible from MNK II in Bed II. Such a small number of mandibles cannot, of course, be regarded as necessarily typical of the populations from which they come, but it is possible that, during this period, jaws and teeth became reduced while cranial capacity remained fairly constant.

A large number of *A. africanus* specimens have been described. Because this taxon is known so well, some have tended to think typologically in terms of an "australopithecine stage" of human evolution during which all hominids would have been morphologically similar to these South African forms. However, if the hominids evolved in the main as a single, widespread, polytypic species, the Transvaal *A. africanus* more likely represents a sample, drawn from a time segment of unknown length, of a peripheral and perhaps aberrant race of this species (Mayr, 1963: 640). We should not expect contemporaneous or near contemporaneous races within this same species to be morphologically identical with, or even quite similar to, the South African *A. africanus*. A large number of fossil specimens, say, from a restricted geographic area and from a relatively small segment of time, may well resemble each

other more than any one of them resembles a small sample of the same species from a different part of the geographic range and from an earlier or later time. In such a case, however, we must be careful not to regard the large sample as morphologically "typical" of the species. By so doing, we would prevent correct assignment of other specimens of the same taxon. Morphological differences between specimens due to age and sex differences and to geographic and temporal separation, as well as racial variation, must be carefully considered. In erecting new taxa, it is necessary for the discoverer to demonstrate that the new finds are *significantly* different from previously defined taxa.

Thus, when we consider the hominids from Lake Chad and Olduvai Bed I we must ask ourselves, could these represent taxa which are already known? *A. africanus* and *H. habilis* were both habitual bipeds. Unfortunately, we have pelves of the former but not of the latter, whereas we know the foot of the latter but not of the former. It is possible that the *H. habilis* foot from Olduvai Bed I is no more nor less *Homo*-like than is the pelvis of *A. africanus* from S. Africa.

The parietal bones from Olduvai FLKNN I have been reconstructed by Tobias (1964) to indicate a cranial capacity of between 642–724 cc. This volume estimate must be regarded with great caution because of the fragmentary nature of the specimen.[3] Tobias (1963) gives the australopithecine range of cranial capacity as 435–600 cc., this being lower than his estimates for this skull of *Homo habilis*. However, there seems to be no good reason for separating early species of the genera *Australopithecus* and *Homo* on grounds of differences in cranial volume. None of the crania from the Transvaal breccias or from Olduvai Beds I and II indicate volumes outside the range now known among the single species of living gorilla, and all these crania are distinctly smaller than those of *Homo erectus*.

The teeth and mandible of *H. habilis* from

---

[3] The slightest mis-setting of the two bones at the midline, for instance if flared too much laterally, would markedly increase the brain volume estimate for this individual.

Olduvai Bed I FLKNN I do not differ greatly from specimens of *A. africanus* (Fig. 2 and Dart, 1962: 268, Fig. 7) in shape or morphology. The molars are similar in size and shape to those of *A. africanus* from Sterkfontein (Robinson, 1956). The premolars of *H. habilis* are somewhat narrower than those of the South African forms; but shape, as well as size, of teeth is known to vary greatly in all modern primates, including man, and this seems to be a relatively unimportant character on which to base generic and specific separation of the two forms. Unfortunately, some of the Olduvai specimens are crushed and broken and this limits our ability to make comparisons. Collection of further hominids from the Olduvai beds is thus of the greatest importance; recovery of a more adequate sample should enable students to assess the range of variability within the local population represented at Olduvai, and would allow comparisons of this population with others of approximately equivalent age. *H. habilis* and *A. africanus* may represent nothing more than two variant populations within the same widespread species, but this hypothesis can only be verified or rejected when more information becomes available.

The validity of *Homo habilis,* as any new fossil taxon, depends on the reality and the plausibility of its diagnosis. As Campbell states (1964, 451):

It is here that the hypothesis of the new species must stand or fall; . . . The diagnosis must support the hypothesis for the species to stand, not in law, but in reality. . . . (Many examples of this state of affairs could be quoted. The most topical, and one of the most important, concerns the creation of the taxon *Homo habilis*. In their original publication the authors stated that *Telanthropus capensis* "may well prove, on closer comparative investigation, to belong to *Homo habilis*"; thus the effective demonstration of a novel taxon was negated. The name is valid, but the species has not been effectively shown to have existed, as a distinct taxon.)

Telanthropus capensis from Swartkrans is probably broadly contemporaneous with Bed II *Homo habilis*. In spite of its fragmentary nature, some general remarks can be made about *Telanthropus*. The teeth are smaller than those of *A. africanus,* although cusp patterns are similar. The mandible is smaller, too, and is said by Robinson (1961) to be reminiscent of other African and Asian hominids of Middle Pleistocene date. This is to be expected for a form transitional in time between the early Pleistocene hominids and middle Pleistocene *Homo erectus*. It is probable that Bed II *H. habilis* and *Telanthropus capensis* represent two populations of a single species or subspecies, but, once again, further material will be required before firm conclusions can be drawn. Both are similar to the mandible of *H. erectus* from the Djetis beds in Java (so-called "*Pithecanthropus* B").

The primitive stone tools associated with *Homo habilis* throughout Bed I and the lower part of Bed II are evidently of uniform type for what may be a very long period of time; this is perhaps correlated with the equally protracted apparent stability of cranial capacity. Tools of similar type are found in Morocco (Biberson, 1963) and at Ubeidiya (Stekelis, 1961). It should be noted that the early Pleistocene hominid from Chad, found unassociated with tools, has a cranial capacity of the order of that of both *H. habilis* and *A. africanus*. Regular tool-making, as we noted earlier, seems to have been invented during the early Pleistocene, perhaps in Africa at a time when hominids had already become efficient bipeds. Dates from Olduvai suggest the possibility that a full million years passed after the invention and spread of tool-making during which cranial capacity—and presumably manual dexterity, "intelligence," and hunting skill—remained fairly constant. Some time roughly between one million and five hundred thousand years ago, human brain size increased by more than 50 per cent. Also, during this period, the change from simple pebble chopping tools to hand-axes of Chellean type apparently took place. Elaboration of tool types and expansion in brain size were probably interrelated, and both, perhaps, were associated with the final anatomical perfection of hand structure. Napier (1962) has suggested that the hand of *Homo habilis* was not as refined structurally and functionally as that of later men. Undoubtedly, limits of both mental ability and hand anatomy affected the form of tools.

The earliest Pleistocene appearance of tool-making, then, seems to have heralded no immediate anatomical changes in the hominid line. Cranial capacity, in particular, remained constant. Jaws, teeth, and faces became reduced during the era of crude pebble tools, but exactly why this was so remains conjectural. Anthropologists have frequently suggested that the appearance of tool-making was causally related to the expansion of the brain. There was never any fossil evidence to support this view, and now we have some evidence to the contrary. Increase in brain size evidently lagged behind the regular making of tools. This skill had altered the lives of early Pleistocene hominids; apparently it did not immediately alter their morphology.

Taxonomy of Early African Hominids

We have concluded that *A. africanus* and Bed I *Homo habilis* may not be specifically distinct and also that the bulk of Bed II materials and *Telanthropus* may be specifically identical. *Telanthropus* itself is regarded by many students as an invalid genus which should be referred either to *Homo* or to *Australopithecus*. If referred to *Homo* the trivial name *capensis* can no longer be used, since this has already been applied to a Late Paleolithic skull from Boskop (for further discussion of this point see Oakley and Campbell, 1964). If the Olduvai Bed I and Bed II *Homo habilis* material is regarded as belonging to a single taxon, it is not unreasonable also to include therein *A. africanus* and the *Telanthropus* material from South

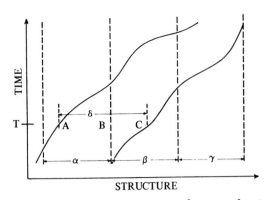

Figure 3: An attempt to represent Pleistocene hominids as a single genetic continuum evolving through time. Modified from Simpson (1963)

Africa. This taxon would extend over a very considerable time period; in fact it would be more than twice as long as the time covered by *H. erectus* and *H. sapiens* combined. Some hominid evolutionary change, particularly trends towards orthognathism and reduced dentition, occurred during this considerable span of time, although the amount of variation within the taxon is probably not greater than that observed in modern mammal species (including man).

If all early Pleistocene hominids ancestral to later men are regarded as members of the genus *Homo*, as the proposal of *H. habilis* by Leakey, Tobias, and Napier suggests, the prior binomial for this taxon would be *Homo africanus*. The evolution of early Pleistocene hominids, first to *Homo erectus*, and finally to *Homo sapiens*, can be shown diagrammatically in Fig. 3 (modified from Simpson 1963, Fig. 3c), which shows a single hominid species evolving through time. A, B, and C are hypothetical contemporaneous individuals, C being more "modern" than B, B more so than A. Simpson (1963: 14) suggests as a possibility that:

. . . there is only one lineage or evolutionary species and only one genetical species at any one time. In that case, the species would have been highly variable, and even more so during much of past time than *Homo sapiens* is at present. At some time around the middle Pleistocene it might have varied all the way from what in purely morphological (or typological) terms could be called marginal australopithecoid through pithecanthropoid to marginal neanderthaloid. Such variation would be improbable within a single deme or local population. It would be less improbable among geographically separate "allopatric" populations or subspecies. Such geographic semi-isolates would of course be variable in themselves, but some might, for instance, vary about a more australopithecoid modal morphology and others about a more neanderthaloid mode. Discovery that fossil hominids fall into such modally distinct, synchronous but allopatric groups would favor this interpretation. Whether current data do or do not tend to follow such a pattern I leave to the specialists in such matters.

We prefer to accept Simpson's model for the moment.

A, B, and C of Figure 3 are contemporaneous at time T and are members of a single species. However, typologically A and B might be placed in one species α while C is referred to species β. The paradox is imagined rather than real, because the taxa α and β, and the taxon δ are of different types. If the hominids have evolved as a single unitary species, δ will represent a sample of the genetical species which existed at time T. α, β, and γ are morphospecies, species "established by morphological similarity regardless of other considerations" (Simpson, 1961, 155). The problem here is largely one of definition and should not be overstressed. Nevertheless, this model will be useful in dealing with problems which will appear should "undoubted" (morphological) *Homo* be found contemporaneous with "undoubted" (morphological) *Australopithecus*.

Both *Australopithecus africanus* and *A. robustus* are bipeds, both have greatly reduced canines and incisors, both almost certainly would have been tool-users, and both probably made tools. If tool-making spread by copying within one species of small-brained hominids, it would

presumably have been copied by any other species of equally small-brained hominids living in the same area.

Australopithecus robustus is said by Robinson (1961) to have been a vegetarian because of its massive premolars and molars. *A. robustus* specimens from Olduvai and Natron exhibit pronounced wear patterns on both upper and lower molars. Such wear patterns are found in certain Australian aboriginal tribes that eat roots and other vegetable material together with large quantities of sand and grit. In contrast, *Homo habilis* has wear patterns similar to those of meat-eating African tribes such as the Masai (Leakey, personal communication). *A. robustus* is said to have been a vegetarian and *A. africanus* (Robinson, 1963) and *H. habilis* more exclusively meat-eaters. Although the *A. robustus* wear patterns suggest that gritty vegetable material constituted a large part of the diet, they do not, however, enable us to state categorically that *A. robustus* did *not* eat meat. Nor are we entitled to assume that *A. robustus* and *A. africanus* were at all times vegetarians or omnivores respectively; diet can vary greatly (within contemporary *Homo sapiens* groups for example), and presumably changes with time too. Hominids were successful because they were behaviorally plastic and adaptable; we must take great care before we place ecological limitations on fossil hominids known only in relatively poor detail.

In summary, *Australopithecus robustus*, like *Ramapithecus punjabicus*, *Homo habilis* and *A. africanus*, has small canines and incisors. This implies that *A. robustus* prepared its food, presumably with tools, and there is no reason to suppose that it could not have eaten prepared animal as well as prepared vegetable food. The diet of modern "primitive" men is varied; could not earlier hominids have been similarly omnivorous? *A. robustus* and *H. habilis* were evidently coexistent in the same general areas for perhaps a million years, if the new dates and stratigraphic-faunal data of Leakey are right. They were, therefore, sympatric species, that is, species occupying the same geographic area. Both were bipeds, both were presumably tool-users and probably tool-makers; their diets might well have been similar at times. As mentioned earlier, there are theoretical difficulties involved in preparing a model of hominid speciation. If we are to distinguish these taxa at a specific level, we need to know far more about geographical barriers during the Pliocene and Pleistocene. Comparative study of closely related pairs of animal species indicates that they must have separate origins in different geographic areas, that is, they must originally be allopatric (Kohn and Orians, 1962). Perhaps one species of hominid evolved in Africa and one in Asia only to mingle at the beginning of the Pleistocene when land connections between Eurasia and Africa presumably became reestablished. The picture as to the number of *Australopithecus* species really indicated by known material is still obscure and the available evidence can be interpreted in a number of ways.

Post-Villafranchian Morphological Changes

The Pliocene was probably a time of great morphological change in hominid evolution. Locomotor adaptations were being improved and, by middle Pleistocene time at least, the skeletons of hominids were essentially like those of modern man even though the skulls were not. Throughout this time, hominids were getting larger; this size increase was probably associated with increased speed and efficiency in running and walking. Brain size increased in consequence. Some relative increase in brain size also occurred during the early Pleistocene, although the time and extent of this expansion is difficult to assess. The changes in cerebrum and cerebellum which must have taken place are still not satisfactorily documented, nor are the selection pressures that

produced them fully understood. These problems are discussed by Garn (1963: 232), who says that:

human brain size did increase, either because brainier *individuals* were at an adaptive advantage, or because *groups* with larger brains survived and groups with smaller brains did not. It gratifies our ego to believe that selection favored intelligence, that our own ancestral lines came to genetic fulfillment because they were so very smart. But it may be that our vaunted intelligence is merely an indirect product of the kind of brain that can discern meaningful signals in a complex social context generating a heavy static of informational or, rather, misinformational noise.

Ryle (1949) has discussed "intelligence" and "intellect" from the philosopher's viewpoint. He states (p. 26) that:

. . . both philosophers and laymen tend to treat intellectual operations as the core of mental conduct; that is to say, they tend to define all other mental-conduct concepts in terms of concepts of cognition. They suppose that the primary exercise of minds consists in finding the answer to questions and that their other occupations are merely applications of considered truths or even regrettable distractions from their consideration . . . (However) there are many activities which directly display qualities of mind, yet are neither themselves intellectual operations nor yet effects of intellectual operations.

Brains expanded as the cultural environment became more and more complex, and larger brains enabled more complex cultures to develop. The actions which we choose, arbitrarily, to term "intelligent," that is those involving theorizing and the manipulation of true propositions or facts, form merely one aspect of our responses to a complex environment.

An increase in adult brain size involves a larger fetal and infantile brain and a prolonged growth period, two of the important trends in higher primate evolution noted by Schultz (1961). Bigger fetal brains require larger maternal pelves, and it is possible that the structural refinements in the hominid pelvis which have evolved since the Villafranchian are, to a large extent, due to the problems posed by the birth of large-brained offspring. During middle Pleistocene times, the brain increased in size with consequent remodeling of the cranial vault (Moss and Young, 1960). The facial skeleton and the teeth became reduced, presumably because of further refinements in food preparation and tool-making (Dahlberg, 1963). Changes in relative size of the brain-case and the jaws and related muscles produced changes in shape and size of the cranium, and in size and form of the supra-orbital ridges. By the late middle Pleistocene, the brain had probably reached approximately its present-day volume, and the morphological evolution of the Hominidae was almost complete.

Conclusions

Earliest hominids known to date are recognizable, in the form of *Ramapithecus punjabicus,* in the late Miocene. This sets back the differentiation of hominids from pongids to the early Miocene or earlier. Circumstantial rather than direct evidence suggests that *R. punjabicus* could have been a tool-using animal and, at least, a partial biped. It was widespread throughout the Old World apparently because of the great mobility in range extension afforded by ground dwelling and/or bipedalism. These factors would have reduced tendencies towards speciation among early Hominidae. Known geographic distribution of *Ramapithecus* (East Africa, India, China) shows that hominids have been wide-ranging, as they are now, at least since late Miocene time.

The early Pleistocene hominids can be classified in *no more than* two species; one of these, *Australopithecus* (or perhaps *Homo*) *africanus,* found in South, East and North Africa, probably inhabited other regions too. The evolution of this species saw the final perfection of the foot and pelvis for habitual bipedal walking, the invention and spread to tool-making and the development of associated refinements in the hand, and finally, late in its history, the rapid expansion of the brain. *Homo erectus,* found throughout the Old World during much of the middle Pleistocene (from 500,000 or 600,000 years ago on), is barely distinguishable taxonomically from *Homo sapiens.*

BIBLIOGRAPHY

ARAMBOURG, C. 1963, in "African Ecology and Human Evolution." Chicago: Aldine, p. 564.

AVIS, V. 1962, Brachiation: the crucial test for man's ancestry. *S. W. Journ. Anthrop., 18,* 119–149.

BARTHOLOMEW, G. A., JR., and BIRDSELL, J. B. 1953, Ecology and the protohominids. *Amer. Anthrop., 55,* 481–498.

BIBERSON, P. 1963, Human Evolution in Morocco, in the framework of the paleoclimatic variations of the Atlantic Pleistocene. In "African Ecology and Human Evolution," Chicago: Aldine, pp. 417–447.

BIEGERT, J. 1963, The evaluation of characteristics of the skull, hands, and feet for primate taxonomy. In "Classification and Human Evolution" (S. L. Washburn, ed.). Chicago: Aldine, pp. 116–145.

CAMPBELL, B. G. 1964, Science and human evolution. *Nature, 203,* 448–451.

CLARK, W. E. LE GROS. 1955, "The Fossil Evidence for Human Evolution." Chicago: Univ. Chicago, pp. 1–181.

COOKE, H. B. S. 1963, Pleistocene mammal faunas of Africa, with particular reference to Southern Africa. In "African Ecology and Human Evolution." Chicago: Aldine, pp. 65–116.

COPPENS, Y. 1962, Découverte d'un Australopithéciné dans le Villafranchien du Tchad in "Problems Actuels de Paléontologie." Paris: Ed. Centre Nat. Rech. Sci., pp. 455–460.

DAHLBERG, A. A. 1963, Dental evolution and culture. *Human Biol., 35,* 237–249.

DART, R. A. 1957, The osteodontokeratic culture of *Australopithecus prometheus. Transvaal Museum Memoir,* No. 10, viii, 105 p., illus.

———. 1962, A cleft adult mandible and the nine

other lower jaw fragments from Makapansgat. *Amer. J. Phys. Anth.*, 20, 267–286.

DAVIS, P. R. and NAPIER, J. R. 1963, A reconstruction of the skull of *Proconsul africanus*. *Folia Primat., 1*, 20–28.

DUBRUL, E. L. 1950, Posture, locomotion and the skull in Lagomorpha. *Amer. J. Anat.*, 87, 277–313.

———, and LASKIN, D. M. 1961, Preadaptive potentialities of the mammalian skull: an experiment in growth and form. *Amer. J. Anat., 109*, 117–132.

ERIKSON, G. E. 1963, Brachiation in the New World Monkeys and in Anthropoid Apes. *Symp. Zool. Soc. Lond.*, no. 10, 135–164.

EVERNDEN, J. F., SAVAGE, D. E., CURTIS, A. E. and JAMES, J. T. 1962, Potassium-Argon dates and the Cenozoic mammalian chronology of North America. *Amer. J. Sci., 262*, 145–198.

FREEDMAN, L. 1963, A biometric study of *Papio cynocephalus* skulls from Northern Rhodesia and Nyasaland. *J. Mammal., 44*, 24–43.

GARN, S. M. 1963, Culture and the direction of human evolution. *Human Biol., 35*, 221–236.

GOODALL, J. M. 1964, Tool-using and aimed throwing in a community of free-living chimpanzees. *Nature, 201*, 1264–1266.

GREGORY, W. K. 1928, Were the ancestors of man primitive brachiators? *Proc. Amer. Phil. Soc., 67*, 129–150.

HARRISON, G. A. and WEINER, J. S. 1963, Some considerations in the formulation of theories of human phylogeny, in "Classification and Human Evolution" (S. L. Washburn, ed.). Chicago: Aldine, pp. 75–84.

HAY, R. L. 1963, Stratigraphy of Beds I through IV, Olduvai Gorge, Tanganyika. *Science, 139*, 829–833.

KOHN, A. J. and ORIANS, G. H. 1962, Ecological data in the classification of closely related species. *Syst. Zool., 11*, 119–126.

KORTLANDT, A. 1962, Chimpanzees in the wild. *Sci. Amer.*, May, 2–10.

LEAKEY, L. S. B. 1959, A new fossil skull from Olduvai. *Nature, 184*, 491–493.

———. 1961, The juvenile mandible from Olduvai. *Nature, 191*, 417–418.

———, EVERNDEN, J. F. and CURTIS, G. H. 1961, Age of Bed I, Olduvai Gorge, Tanganyika. *Nature, 191*, 478–479.

———, TOBIAS, P. V., and NAPIER, J. R. 1964, A new species of the genus *Homo* from Olduvai Gorge. *Nature, 202*, 7–9.

MAYR, E. 1950, Taxonomic categories in fossil hominids. *C. S. H. Symp., 15*, 109–118.

———. 1963, "Animal species and evolution." Harvard Univ. Press, pp. 1–797.

MILLS, J. R. E. 1963, Occlusion and malocclusion in Primates. In "Dental Anthropology" (D. R. Brothwell, ed.). New York: Pergamon, pp. 29–52.

MOSS, M. L. and YOUNG, R. W. 1960, A functional approach to craniology. *Amer. J. Phys. Anth., 18*, 281–292.

NAPIER, J. R. 1962, Fossil hand bones from Olduvai Gorge. *Nature, 196*, 409–411.

———. 1963, The locomotor functions of hominids in "Classification and Human Evolution" (S. L. Washburn, ed.). Chicago: Aldine, pp. 178–189.

NAPIER, J. R. and DAVIS, P. R. 1959, The fore-limb skeleton and associated remains of *Proconsul africanus*. Fossil mammals of Africa, no. 16.

NOBACK, C. R. and MOSKOWITZ, N. 1962, Structural and functional correlates of "encephalization" in the primate brain. *Ann. N.Y. Acad. Sci., 102*, 210–218.

———. 1963, The primate nervous system: functional and structural aspects in phylogeny. In "Evolutionary and Genetic Biology of the Primates" (J. Buettner-Janusch, ed.). New York: Academic Press, pp. 131–178.

OAKLEY, K. P. and CAMPBELL, B. G. 1964, Newly described Olduvai hominid. *Nature, 202*, 732.

PATTERSON, B. 1954, The geologic history of non-hominid primates in the Old World. *Human Biol., 26*, 191–209.

ROBINSON, J. T. 1955, Further remarks on the relationship between *Meganthropus* and australopithecines. *Amer. J. Phys. Anth., 13*, 429–445.

———. 1956, The dentition of the australopithecinae. *Transvaal Mus. Mem.*, no. 9.

———. 1961, The origin and adaptive radiation of the australopithecines. In "Evolution und Hominization" (A. Kurth, ed.). Stuttgart: A. Fischer, pp. 120–140.

———. 1963a, Adaptive radiation in the Australopithecines and the origin of man. In "African Ecology and Human Evolution." Chicago: Aldine, pp. 385–416.

———. 1963b, Australopithecines, culture and phylogeny. *Amer. J. Phys. Anth., 21*, 595–605.

RYLE, G. 1949, The concept of mind. London: Hutchinson, pp. 1–334.

SCHULTZ, A. H. 1961, Some factors influencing the social life of primates in general and of early man in particular. In "Social Life of Early Man" (S. L. Washburn, ed.). Chicago: Aldine, pp. 1–299.

———. 1963, Age changes, sex differences, and variability as factors in the classification of primates. In

"Classification and Human Evolution." Chicago: Aldine, pp. 85–115.

SIMONS, E. L. 1961, The phyletic position of *Ramapithecus. Postilla,* Yale Peabody Museum, no. 57, 1-9.

———. 1963, Some fallacies in the study of hominid phylogeny. *Science, 141,* 879–889.

———. 1964, On the mandible of *Ramapithecus. Proc. Nat. Acad. Sci., 51,* 528–535.

———. 1965, New fossil apes from Egypt and the initial differentiation of Hominoidea. *Nature, 205,* 135–139.

———, and PILBEAM, D. R. 1965, Preliminary revision of the Dryopithecinae (Pongidae, Anthropoidea) *Folia Primatologica,* no. 46, 1–70.

SIMPSON, G. G. 1945, The principles of classification and a classification of mammals. *Bull. Amer. Mus. Nat. Hist., 85,* 1–350.

———. 1961, Principles of Animal Taxonomy. London: Oxford University Press, pp. 1–247.

———. 1963, The meaning of taxonomic statements. In "Classification and Human Evolution" (S. L. Washburn, ed.). Chicago: Aldine, pp. 1–31.

STEKELIS, M., PICARD, L., SCHULMAN, N., and HAAS, G. 1960, Villafranchian deposits near Ubeidiya in the Central Jordan Valley. *Bull Res. Counc. Israel, 9G,* 175–184.

TOBIAS, P. V. 1963, Cranial capacity of *Zinjanthropus* and other australopithecines. *Nature, 197,* 743–746.

———. 1964, The Olduvai Bed I hominine with special reference to its cranial capacity. *Nature, 202,* 3–4.

WASHBURN, S. L. 1963, Behavior and Human Evolution. In "Classification and Human Evolution." Chicago: Aldine, 190–203.

WHITWORTH, T. 1958, Miocene ruminants of East Africa. Fossil Mammals of Africa. 15: Brit. Mus. (N.H.), pp. 1–50.

7 • THE CULTURAL AND PHYLOGENETIC STATUS OF "AUSTRALOPITHECUS BOISEI" AND OF THE AUSTRALOPITHECINES IN GENERAL

P.V.Tobias

In this contribution Tobias attempts to throw some light on the cultural activities and the phylogenetic status of the australopithecines. He begins by accepting the australopithecines' use of bone, teeth, and horn tools, called by Dart their osteodontokeratic culture. Tobias prefers the term "activities" rather than "culture." If, however, the modification of bone, tooth, and horn for use as tools was a part of the way of life of australopithecines, then the term "culture" in refer-ence to that aspect of their behavior can hardly be called inappropriate.

While a number of anthropologists still hold out against admitting even the existence of osteodontokeratic activities on the part of the australopithecines, others are inclined to accept the evidence for it. It will always remain a difficult thing to prove that skeletal parts were in fact modified and used as tools.[1]

In her splendid monograph on excavations in Beds

---

[1] See Robert Ardrey's discussion of this in the first part of his *African Genesis* (New York: Atheneum, 1961), and the claimed existence of a similar osteodontokeratic culture among the paleolithic inhabitants of Pin Hole Cave in Derbyshire by James W. Kitching, *Bone, Tooth & Horn Tools of Palaeolithic Man* (Manchester: Manchester University Press, 1963).

I and II of Olduvai Gorge, Dr. Mary Leakey draws attention to the necessity of distinguishing between tool-using, simple modification of objects by means of the hands and teeth, and *the manufacture of tools by the use of one tool with which to make another*. It is the last achievement which is the functional criterion for distinguishing man from other tool-users.[2] This is a most important distinction, for it is obviously progression from tool-using to tool-making to tool manufacture by means of the use of other tools.

It is not yet clear whether all the australopithecines were tool-makers, although the widespread distribution of pebble tools has suggested to some that they were the makers of these. As can be seen from Tobias' discussion, it is still very much a matter under debate. Both Tobias and the Leakeys consider that the australopithecines were not tool-makers, and that, in fact, *Homo habilis* was the tool-maker, and *Australopithecus boisei* the tool-user or tool-modifier. Tobias believes that the australopithecines did not use tools in the making of other tools, but that they modified natural objects to make tools with their hands and teeth, and that they had become culturally dependent upon them for their continuing survival.

A. Cultural Status

It has long been known that pebble-tools were made in Africa during the period of the australopithecines. But there have been two schools of thought on the relationship between the fossils and the implements. According to one view, *Australopithecus* was the maker of these stone implements. The notion has been forthrightly expressed by J. D. Clark as recently as 1963: 'To take the example of the australopithecines:—Few would now doubt that they were representative of a hominid form responsible for the Pre-Chelles-Acheul Culture' (p. 356). This view has been espoused by Arambourg (1958), by Oakley (1961, 1964) although he earlier (1954, 1956) took the opposing view, by Washburn (1959), Washburn and Howell (1960), Washburn and De Vore (1961), and others.

Exponents of the second view have doubted whether the australopithecines were stone tool-makers (Robinson and Mason, 1957, 1962; Inskeep, 1959; Mason, 1961; von Koenigswald, 1961, etc.).

In favour of the first view are the contemporaneity of the australopithecines and the pebble-tools, and the discovery of a fragmentary, apparently australopithecine maxilla and a few possible pebble-tools in the same layer near the top of the Makapansgat deposit (Brain, Van Riet Lowe and Dart, 1955; Dart, 1955*b*). This discovery Dart (1955*b*) described as 'providing the first concrete evidence that an australopithecine type . . . was contemporaneous with, and may have been responsible for, the concomitant pebble culture found in this sealed Central Transvaal cavern deposit.' The lithicultural evidence from Makapansgat was, however, not convincing—'An artificial origin for the heavily weathered dolomitic specimens from Makapan was not acceptable to most prehistorians attending the Congress [1] owing to the rapid weathering properties of this rock which obscured the nature of the scars' (J. D. Clark, 1962).

More suggestive was the discovery by Brain (1958) of undoubted stone implements in the breccia of the West Pit of the Sterkfontein excavation (an area which has since come to be known, somewhat misleadingly, as the Sterkfontein Extension Site, though it is not a separate

---

SOURCE: P. V. Tobias, *The Cranium of Australopithecus* (*Zinjanthropus*) *Boisei,* vol. 2 (Cambridge: Cambridge University Press, 1967): 236–44.

[2] Mary D. Leakey, *Excavations in Beds I and II, 1960–1963,* Olduvai Gorge, vol. 3 (Cambridge: The University Press, 1971): 278–80.

[1] The Third Pan-African Congress on Prehistory, Livingstone, 1955.

site as some have come to believe). Further implements were recovered by Robinson the following year, along with some hominid fragments identified by him as australopithecine (Robinson and Mason, 1957, 1962). However, Robinson has argued on theoretical grounds against *Australopithecus* having been the author of these Sterkfontein implements, while Tobias (1964b, 1965b) has questioned whether the hominid fragments are all australopithecine and whether two or three of them do not, in fact, represent a more advanced type of hominid such as *Homo habilis*.

What seemed at first to be the most convincing evidence for the association of an australopithecine with early stone tools was provided by the discovery of *Australopithecus boisei* on a living floor along with broken bones and crude artefacts of the Oldowan Culture. *A. boisei* was at once hailed as the maker of the stone implements (Leakey, 1959a, 1960a). This evidence clearly influenced some workers in favour of the australopithecine authorship of the Oldowan Culture. In the rather prophetic words of J. D. Clark, '. . . should no other more advanced form of man be found in this bed (Bed I), there would be strong reason to accept *Zinjanthropus* as the toolmaker' (Clark, 1961, p. 904). Elsewhere, Clark (1962) summed the position up as follows: 'Since no more advanced hominid than *Australopithecus* is known to have been present at this time anywhere in the Old World there would seem to be little room for continued doubt that the Lower Pleistocene Oldowan industries were made by hominids in the australopithecine pattern' (p. 269).

Subsequently, remains of a more advanced hominid were indeed discovered in Bed I (Leakey, 1961a–c). These remains have been recognised as representing a new and lowly species of *Homo*, namely *H. habilis* (Leakey *et al.* 1964; Tobias, 1964a, b, 1965a–d). Furthermore, teeth of *H. habilis* were found on the same living-floor as the type cranium of *A. boisei* and Leakey

(1961c) then stated, 'If I am right in believing that the juvenile from FLK NNI is not an australopithecine, but a very remote and truly primitive ancestor of *Homo,* then it is possible (and I stress the fact here that I only use the word "possible" at this stage of the inquiry) that it was this branch of the Hominidae that also made the Oldowan tools at the site FLK I where *Zinjanthropus boisei* was found' (p. 418).

The fact that Leakey changed his mind about the authorship of the Oldowan tools has been levelled at him as a criticism. Yet, Leakey's second thoughts would seem to be not only legitimate and beyond reproach, but scientifically correct. At the time when *A. boisei* was the most advanced creature known alongside the tools, it was reasonable to suggest an association between them. But once a more advanced hominid was identified, no matter what label we apply to it, it is surely more reasonable to attribute the making of the stone tools to the more advanced hominid. When one takes all the evidence bearing on the association between Australopithecinae and stone tools into account, it becomes not only reasonable, but the hypothesis which meets more of the facts than any alternative.

Elsewhere, I have examined critically the evidence of skeletal and cultural occurrences at Olduvai (three levels in Bed I), Taung, Makapansgat, Sterkfontein (Lower and Middle Breccia), Swartkrans, Kromdraai, Garusi and Peninj (Tobias, 1964b, 1965b, f). Oakley (1956) has rightly warned that 'it is going to be . . . difficult to prove or disprove the theory that australopithecines had advanced to the stage of systematic tool-making. The absence of stone implements from layers containing their remains cannot be held to disprove the theory that they were tool-makers, so long as it is possible that the remains represent the food débris of cave-dwelling carnivores' (p. 6). Mason, too, has warned against speculating on the identity of the toolmaker in terms of negative evidence (Robinson and Mason, 1962). Nevertheless, certain correlations seem worthy of consideration:

1. At every australopithecine site at which stone tools occur in association with hominid remains, there is evidence of the sympatric and synchronic co-existence of a more advanced hominid alongside the australopithecine.
2. At all sites where *Australopithecus* and a more advanced hominid co-exist, there too we find stone tools.
3. At every site where early stone tools are found along with associated hominid remains, the skeletal remains include a more advanced hominid, whether or not australopithecine remains are present in addition.
4. At every early site which has yielded a more advanced hominid, stone tools are present.

Unless we resort to a series of special pleas, it seems that the most reasonable hypothesis to explain these facts is that *Australopithecus* was not the maker of the Oldowan stone implements, but that a more advanced hominid almost certainly was. This hypothesis in no way prejudges the issue of how many kinds of more advanced hominids were involved; present evidence suggests an earlier hominine of the species *H. habilis* and a later hominine of the species *H. erectus*. We are led to conclude that *A. boisei* is unlikely to have been the manufacturer of the Oldowan implements.

This conclusion is not to be construed as denying all implemental activities to *A. boisei*. The australopithecine of Olduvai Bed I may have been a stone tool-maker, as well as *H. habilis*, but the combined presence of the two hominids in the same area and even on the same living-floor makes it almost impossible to decide the question on archaeological grounds. If the stone implements from Olduvai Bed I fell into two distinct groups, clearly distinguishable on typology and technology, and if one assemblage were obviously more rudimentary than the other, it might not be unreasonable tentatively to attribute the more primitive implements to *A. boisei* and the more advanced industry to *H. habilis*. Even if these conditions were fulfilled, such an attribution would have to remain provisional. In any event, there is as yet no evidence for two distinct industries within Bed I.

The fact that Olduvai has not furnished evidence on the implemental activities of *A. boisei* still does not rule out the possibility of a well-developed cultural existence. *A. boisei* is one of the australopithecines and structurally this group is more hominised than the great apes. We have seen that the australopithecines have, on the average, somewhat bigger brains in somewhat smaller bodies, so that their endowment of extra neurones exceeds that of the great apes by about one thousand million on the average. Their front teeth are small and crowded. Furthermore, they possess the general primate structural basis for implemental activities, namely, the ability to *sit upright* (Tobias, 1965f) and to manipulate both powerfully and to an extent precisely (Napier, 1959); in addition, they possess the trait of bipedalism, although, as Chopra (1961, 1962) has shown, they were imperfectly adjusted skeletally to upright stance and bipedal gait. Nevertheless, the greater degree of erectness and bipedalism which the anatomical facts permit us to attribute to *Australopithecus* must have enhanced his implemental potential.

It might reasonably be expected that this structural hominisation which characterises all the australopithecines, albeit to differing degrees, would be paralleled by some hominisation of behaviour over the attainments of apes. When Dart first suggested that the australopithecines were capable of violent manual activities (1926, 1929) and of using and fabricating tools of bone, horn and teeth (1957), relatively little was known of the extent to which other higher Primates were capable of tool-using and even, to a degree, of tool-making. Since that time, more and more information has accumulated and today it is clear that the level of implemental activity which the living great apes can attain, in the wild, in captivity and under experimental conditions, far exceeds what had earlier been thought. Proportionately, the resistance to attributing tool-using and tool-making activities to the australopithecines has lessened, for even if the australopithecines showed no greater degree of implemental activity than living great apes, it is clear that a considerable range of cultural activities would have been within their capacity. Nobody, to my knowledge, has suggested that australopithecines were less capable than apes of implemental activity!

On the contrary, much indirect evidence points to the possibility that the australopithecines were culturally advanced as compared with apes. We have cited the evidence of structural hominisation. To this could be added the evidence of ecology, for the australopithecines lived in a habitat providing little natural protection and they had no natural weapons of offence or defence like large canines.

Thus, the indirect evidence points to the need of implemental activities by australopithecines. Direct evidence of association with stone tools, we have seen, is largely lacking or equivocal. The best direct evidence bearing on the cultural status of *Australopithecus* is provided by the osteodonto-keratic objects from Makapansgat described by Dart (1957 and many articles between 1955 and 1965—*see* review in Tobias, 1965*f*). The facts and Dart's claims are too well known for me to need to review them here; only the following points need be mentioned:

1. The analysis of many thousands of bones from the Makapansgat deposit has shown definite evidence of selection of bones, not only from different parts of the body, but of different parts of the same bone. Thus, the ratio of proximal to distal humeral fragments is 33:336, while the ratio of humeri to femora is 518:100.

2. Tooth-marks of hyaena and porcupine are absent from all but a handful of the many thousands of bones.

3. Eighty per cent of over fifty baboon skulls from Taung (21), Sterkfontein (22) and Makapansgat (15) show signs of damage by localised violence.

4. Large concentrations of ungulate humeri show damage inflicted before fossilisation on the epicondyles, some of which fit the occasional doubly-indented fracture depressions of the baboon crania.

5. Many of the bone flakes show signs of differential wear and tear along one edge or at one end, but not on the other.

6. A number of special cases include horn-cores and smaller long bones rammed and lodged up the marrow cavities of broken larger bones.

7. In several instances, small bones and even stone flakes have been wedged between the condyles of long bones.

8. Many of the long bones show signs of having been broken by a kind of spiral torsional stress.

9. Some fragments suggest that stalactites and/or stalagmites were broken off, presumably for use, and some were further fractured.

10. There is some suggestion of stone-collecting habits: a small number of quartz and quartzite pebbles and fragments have been found in the breccia.

11. So far, the forty-one hominid fragments identified are all of *Australopithecus*. We have no evidence for any other hominid having lived in or near the Makapansgat Limeworks caves during the time that the Limeworks deposit was accumulating.

In sum, Dart's hypothesis on the osteodonto-keratic activities of the Australopithecinae is the most reasonable and plausible explanation of the otherwise almost inexplicable mountains of bones, with their selected, fractured and patterned characteristics at Makapansgat. Furthermore, this kind of activity is entirely within the somatic possibilities which might be inferred from behaviour studies on pongids and from anatomical studies of the degree of hominisation of the australopithecines themselves. To accept this general hypothesis is not necessarily to accept everything that Dart has claimed for the osteodontokeratics; nor am I sure that it is justified to ascribe the epithet Osteodontokeratic *Culture* to the implemental activities of the australopithecines: perhaps the phrase 'osteodontokeratic activities' would be more appropriate.

So far, comparable masses of osteodontokeratic objects have not been reported from other australopithecine sites than Makapansgat. However, at Sterkfontein, not more than a fraction of the breccia has been thoroughly searched for broken bone fragments, other than taxonomically identifiable parts. In the Swartkrans cave, where there are large numbers of australopithecine remains, as well as a few pieces possibly representing *H. erectus* ('Telanthropus'), associated faunal remains are conspicuous by their paucity. This could be understood if the australopithecine in that instance were the hunted rather than the hunter, australopithecine flesh having perhaps provided a major item in the diet of the early Transvaal hominine. Perhaps the same applied in Bed I times at Olduvai, as Howell (1965*b*) has suggested recently.

Hence, the mere absence of hitherto detected osteodontokeratic objects from other australopithecine sites does not weaken Dart's claims based upon Makapansgat. It is suggested that the techniques of *Australopithecus* included tool-making and that osteodontokeratics provided his major cultural outlet. This does not preclude his having tinkered with stone, but we find no convincing evidence that *Australopithecus* was responsible for the first distinctive stone culture, the Oldowan.

Technologically, it has been suggested (Tobias,

1965*f*) that *Australopithecus* had not passed beyond the stage of using natural bodily organs—teeth, hands, feet—or the floor, walls and stalactites of caves for making osteodontokeratic objects. It is suggested that they fell short of one intricate conceptual and technological mechanism: the ability to use a tool to make a tool—that is, 'the highest implemental frontier' of Khroustov (1964).

If it is correct that they could not or did not cross the highest implemental frontier of the apes, it may validly be asked: wherein lies the cultural advance of the australopithecines, including *A. boisei*, over the apes? The answer resides in the *frequency of implemental patterns of behaviour.* In apes, tool-using and tool-making are infrequent, sporadic; it cannot be said that the apes' way of life is built around such implemental activities. Survival does not depend on implemental means, but rather on formidable natural defence mechanisms and on the sheltered forest habitat of the living great apes. The australopithecines, on the other hand, lived in a habitat providing little natural protection and they had poor natural bodily defences. Their implemental activities must have come to loom very largely in their pattern of adjustment. Indeed, it would not be too much to claim that their very survival depended on implemental activities. This, it is suggested, is the great step forward of the australopithecines over the apes. They learned to exploit a mental and manipulative capacity, a cultural potentiality, which even apes possess: and they exploited it so effectively that they became dependent on it for survival. As Bartholomew and Birdsell (1953) put it: 'Rather than to say that man is unique in being the "tool-using" animal, it is more accurate to say that man is the only mammal which is continuously dependent on tools for survival.' In this sense, it is suggested that *Australopithecus* had virtually attained the status of manhood. Cultural capacity was the greatest evolutionary asset of the australopithecines: and it was on this aspect of

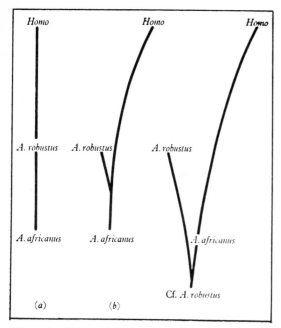

Figure 1: Three earlier interpretations of the relationship between the Lower Pleistocene *A. africanus* and the Middle Pleistocene *A. robustus* (before the description of *A. boisei* and *H. habilis*).

their form and function that selection operated with the greatest vigour.

Robinson (1963) has suggested that cultural capacity was less developed in the robust australopithecines than in the more gracile *A. africanus*. This view seems to be based on the supposed vegetarian habit of *A. robustus* and on the notion that the low brow of the latter betokened a more ape-like brain. Since neither premise is acceptable, it seems that there is no real justification at present for thinking that any of the species of *Australopithecus* was less dependent on cultural activities than any other. The present thesis holds that all of the australopithecines were cultural creatures, all were more proficient than the apes in manipulating and manufacturing, and all had come to depend on their implemental activities, whether with sticks, stones, bones, horns, or stalactites, for survival. It is not impossible that the degree of implemental dependence varied from one australopithecine taxon to another, but the evidence for such variation is as yet lacking.

A. boisei, it is suggested, was subject to the same cultural dependence as the others, even though the concrete evidence may presently be lacking, or may not yet have been recognised as such. If he was the victim of the more skilled hominine hunters of Olduvai, then the presence on the habiline living-floors of his skeletal remains *without bone and horn tools* would be understandable.

B. The Place of *Australopithecus boisei* and the Other Australopithecines In Hominid Phylogeny

Until the discovery of *A. boisei*, the gracile australopithecine, *A. africanus*, was known from earlier sites tentatively identified as Lower Pleistocene, while the robust australopithecine, *A. robustus*, was known only from later sites, probably of the early Middle Pleistocene. It was possible then to see in *A. robustus* a later hominid which either (*a*) represented an intermediate step in the hominisation process between *A. africanus* and *H. erectus*, or (*b*) represented the end-result of cladistic evolution of the australopithecines, a branch which had *specialised* away from the main line of hominisation. A third possible view, espoused by Robinson (1963), was that the Kromdraai-Swartkrans group represented late survivors of a little-changed, little-hominised, ancestral hominid, from which stock *A. africanus* had risen by further hominisation (Fig. 1).

As for the first alternative, Robinson (1963) has adduced strong arguments against the recognition of a phyletic sequence, *A. africanus* → *A. robustus* → *Homo*, and indeed against the idea that *A. robustus* is on the direct human line at all (1965*a*).

If we discount the first alternative, there remain

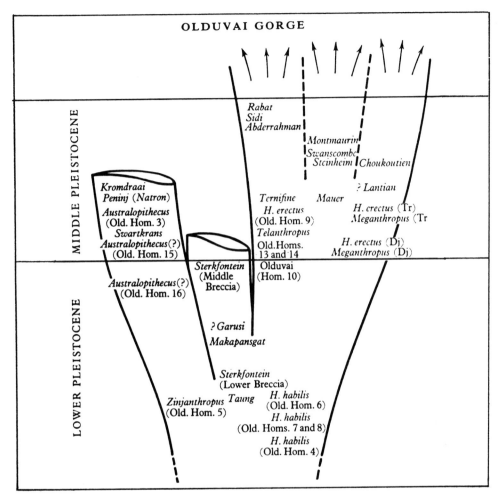

Figure 2: Schema of Lower and Middle Pleistocene hominids, showing the positions in space and time of the most important specimens discovered to date. Tr—Trinil beds; Dj—Djetis Beds; Old. Hom.—Olduvai hominid.

at least two important views, namely, that *A. robustus* is a surviving 'primitive,' or that it has specialised away from the morphology of the presumed ancestral australopithecine (Fig. 1). The discovery of *A. boisei* indicates that already in Lower Pleistocene times at least two different australopithecines were in existence, *A. africanus* and *A. boisei*. In the enlargement of their cheek-teeth, both show a feature which, in any other mammalian line, would tend to be regarded as specialised. The degree of this specialisation differs enormously between the two forms. There seems little doubt that *A. africanus* with its relatively large mandibular canines and moderately enlarged cheek-teeth was the less specialised, and was morphologically closer to the presumed morphology of the ancestral hominines. On the other hand, *A. boisei* with its massive cheek-teeth and supporting structures shows highly specialised features which would tend to place it well off the line of hominisation. Figure 2 attempts to align the known hominids of the Lower and Middle Pleistocene in their position in time and space (after Tobias, 1965c). When the specimens are arranged in this way, it is seen that the large-toothed australopithecines are off the human line, while *A. africanus* is much closer to it. Closer still, it would seem, is the other Lower Pleistocene hominid which has been designated by Leakey *et al.* (1964) *H. habilis.* These remains of which only cursory descriptions have so far been published (Leakey, 1960c, 1961a–c; Leakey and Leakey, 1964; Napier, 1962; Davis, Day and Napier, 1964; Tobias, 1964a, b, 1965a–d) will be described in full in a later volume. . . .

The discovery of *A. boisei* thus demonstrates that the large-toothed specialisation was not a late stage in australopithecine evolution. Already, by the beginning of our Pleistocene fossil record, we have at least three kinds of hominid: the least hominised or most specialised, namely *A. boisei*; a moderately hominised, little specialised *A. africanus;* and the most hominised *H. habilis.* All three are roughly synchronic, but only *A. boisei* and *H. habilis* have been shown to be sympatric.

The question now is: upon what sort of ancestral morphology will the Pleistocene phyletic lines converge, if extended *back* in time? If we use the argument of specialisation, it would seem that the ancestral australopithecine would not have shown the extreme specialisations manifested by *A. boisei* and, later, by *A. robustus.* That is, we might have expected the mandibular canines to be somewhat larger and the cheek-teeth to be smaller: but if we strip an *A. boisei* or *A. robustus* of these features and the concomitant modifications in face, jaw and palate structure, we are left with something very like *A. africanus!* Robinson has recently accepted that the ancestral australopithecine would not have shown the 'exaggerated characters seen in the known specimens of *Paranthropus*' (1963, p. 407). He elaborates this statement as follows: 'The canines, for example, will have been larger and therefore more in proportion to the cheek teeth.

Body size is likely to have been smaller and therefore probably the skull will have been somewhat more gracile. This early *Paranthropus* will therefore have differed less from the known *Australopithecus* material than does the known, later, *Paranthropus* material' (p. 407). This statement clearly indicates that Robinson now accepts that *A. robustus* is a creature of specialisation. However, he goes on immediately to say of the ancestral australopithecine, 'but it will nevertheless have been more nearly *Paranthropus* than *Australopithecus* because of diet, absence of forehead, pongid-like ischium, primitive nasal area, and probably many other things of which we are as yet unaware.'

This study has cast serious doubt on the morphological basis of the dietary inference. Furthermore, until we know more about the causal basis of the low forehead, we certainly cannot assume that the ancestral australopithecine with somewhat bigger mandibular canines and smaller cheek-teeth would have possessed no forehead. The 'pongid-like ischium' cannot be discussed here, as the detailed description of the australopithecine pelves has not yet been published. As to the 'primitive nasal area'—which Robinson describes as 'almost ultra pongid (1963, p. 406)—I have shown above that both in *A. boisei* and *A. robustus*, the shape of the nasal margin and floor, while in general reminiscent of that of the chimpanzee, shows a number of clearly hominine departures, such as the posterior placement of the anterior nasal spine and a tendency for the prenasal fossa to 'drop over' from the floor of the nose to become part of the naso-alveolar clivus as in modern man. These features are shared as well with *A. africanus* and even some modern human crania.

Stripped of the paranthropine specialisations and of most of the features just mentioned, our picture of the ancestral australopithecine is virtually indistinguishable from that of *A. africanus.* By indirect inference from morphology, we are led to see in the ancestral australopithecine a creature akin to *A. africanus* and not to *A. boisei* or *A. robustus.*

If we had an adequate Pliocene fossil record, we should not need to extrapolate from the Pleistocene hominids to their presumed ancestor. However, a large gap in the record leaves the middle and upper Pliocene as one of the most tantalising periods in hominid phylogeny. The lower Pliocene and late Miocene have, however, yielded claimants to australopithecine ancestry. Simons has indicated that *Ramapithecus punjabicus* (to which he assigns as well *Kenyapithecus wickeri* Leakey) has dental and facial characters 'so close to *Australopithecus africanus* as to make difficult the drawing of generic distinctions between the two species on the basis of present material' (Simons, 1964*b*, p. 535). He goes on to say, 'Provisionally the two genera, *Ramapithecus* and *Australopithecus,* are retained as distinct because of their considerable time separation. *Ramapithecus punjabicus* is almost certainly man's forerunner of 15 million years ago.' The important point to note is that it is with *A. africanus,* not *A. robustus* or *A. boisei,* that *Ramapithecus* finds its resemblance.

If Simons is correct, both morphological inferences from the Pleistocene fossils, and the evidence of the Mio–Pliocene fossils themselves, would concur in demonstrating that the ancestral australopithecine resembled *A. africanus,* at least dentally and gnathically.

We should thus arrive at a picture of the ancestral australopithecine as unspecialised and relatively small-toothed. At some time not later than the Upper Pliocene, it must have diversified into several lines. A megadontic line (*A. boisei*) emerged with specialised dentition. Another line remained little changed and unspecialised: presently it dichotomised into a progressively more hominised line represented in Africa by *H. habilis* and later in Asia perhaps by *Meganthropus palaeojavanicus;* and a more conservative residual line (*A. africanus*) which, perhaps because of

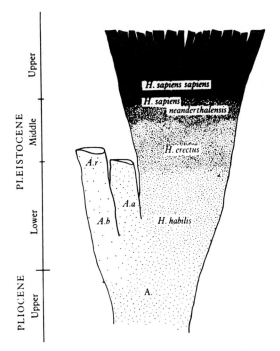

Figure 3: Provisional schema of hominid phylogeny from Upper Pliocene times to the Upper Pleistocene. Progressive degrees of hominisation are represented by progressively darker shading. A—postulated ancestral australopithecine, cf. *A. africanus.* A. *b*–*A. boisei.* A. *a.*–*A. africanus.* A. *r.*–*A. robustus.*

competition, did not long outlast the emergence of this supposed hominine.

The intensive selection pressures which it must be presumed engendered *A. boisei* at the beginning of the Pleistocene must have subsequently relaxed somewhat. Some populations of *A. boisei* then moved forward with a moderate reduction in cheek-tooth size, loss of the cingulum probably as part of the same process, shortening of the face and reduction of the jaws—to become the macrodontic *A. robustus* of the Middle Pleistocene. Figure 3 represents a provisional schema of the interpretation proposed here.

We are thus led to recognise two apparent hominid lineages in the Lower and Middle Pleistocene: one line was seemingly specialising away from the main hominising trend and comprised *A. boisei* → *A. robustus*. The other line comprised *A. africanus* → *H. habilis* → later *Homo*, and seems to have been the main line of structural hominisation and of cultural evolution.

It would be easy, at this stage of our knowledge, to exaggerate the distinctness between the two lineages. One recent work has gone so far as to suggest that the members of each line be regarded as generically distinct from those of the other, the two genera to be *Paranthropus* (*A. boisei* and *A. robustus*) and *Homo* (*A. africanus*, *H. erectus* and *H. sapiens*) (Robinson, 1965a). Such a classification *by clade* would be valid if the fossil record showed unequivocally not only that *A. africanus* evolved into *Homo*, but also that fossils on the *A. boisei–A. robustus* lineage were completely cut off from contributing to the gene-pool of *A. africanus* and its presumed successors. Yet, the overall resemblances between the australopithecines in the two lineages are so great as to suggest that they belonged to the same evolutionary *grade*, not by parallelism but by homology or real genetic relationship. In fact, the evidence seems to indicate that (1) it is unlikely they were genetically isolated from each other throughout the Lower and Middle Pleistocene; and/or (2) they had a not very remote common ancestry.

As to the first suggestion, we cannot exclude the chance of crossing between *A. africanus* and members of the *A. boisei* → *A. robustus* line. It is not outside the bounds of possibility that such crossing may have led to the 'gracilisation' of *A. boisei* into the later and somewhat toned down *A. robustus*. Even among the australopithecine fossils already known, there is a suggestion of intermediates. Thus, the specimens from Makapansgat, although commonly classed with *A. africanus*, show some features more reminiscent of *A. robustus*: these features include very large, buccolingually expanded molars, very robust jaws and the prob-

able presence of a sagittal crest. In these respects, the Makapansgat specimens seem to show a somewhat nearer approach to *A. robustus* than do the Sterkfontein specimens. This reduces the distinctness of the lineages and renders it less likely that they represented two clades, the members of which should be regarded as generically distinct from each other. The discovery of further specimens and new sites will provide better information on variability and may go further towards closing the gap between the two groups of fossils.

The second line of thinking suggests that, when first encountered in the fossil record, the two hominid lineages had not been distinct for very long. It seems reasonable to infer that the common ancestral australopithecines diverged into the two lineages about the Upper Pliocene or, at the latest, the first part of the Lower Pleistocene. Thus, they might not have been isolated long enough to have attained the distinctness of separate clades and separate genera.

At the present state of our knowledge, therefore, it would seem unjustified to classify the robust australopithecines as generically distinct from the gracile ones. The entire australopithecine grade must for the time being be regarded as providing the substrate from which one or more lines of hominisation emerged.

A. boisei represents one part of this substrate, one extreme in the diverse spectrum of hominids which had appeared upon the African scene by the second half of the Lower Pleistocene. It seems to have been the progenitor of an experimental line of dentally modified and perhaps over-specialised creatures, a line which was to prove unequal to the rigorous challenge of highly competitive hunter-hominines. Its robust but ineffectual descendants survived until the Middle Pleistocene, when the experiment seems to have terminated in genocidal extinction.

FIVE • ENVIRONMENTAL CHALLENGES AND THE PROTOHOMINIDS

8 • BRAIN SIZE AND HUNTING ABILITY IN EARLIEST MAN

Grover S. Krantz

The importance of hunting as a factor in differentiating man from the apes seems first to have been worked out and proposed by Charles Morris in his book *Man and His Ancestors* (New York: Macmillan 1900). The book went into a second printing in 1902, and then seems to have been completely forgotten. The hypothesis then independently occurred to Carveth Read and he developed it in brief in 1905, in his book *The Metaphysics of Nature,* and again in 1909 in his *Natural and Social Morals,* both published in London by Adam and Charles Black. He further developed these ideas in his book *The Origin of Man and His Superstitions* (Cambridge: The University Press, 1920). In the second edition, published at Cambridge in 1925, he greatly elaborated his ideas on the hunting origins of man and published them in a separate volume, *The Origin of Man.*

Though writing quite independently of one another, Morris and Read had arrived at virtually identical conclusions concerning the role of hunting in the evolution of man. Their books were read, and shrugged away. General reasoning had fallen into disrepute, as Read mentions in his preface to the 1925 book. He quotes a German reviewer who thought it enough to say of his ideas, "The time when one could have any enthusiasm for such hypotheses in science is definitely over." What a pity!

The fact is that when Read wrote there were few anthropologists, few students of anthropology, and practically no opportunities for fieldwork and experiment. To use an old, and very sad phrase again: Morris and Read were ahead of their time.

It is somewhat astonishing, nevertheless, that it was not until 1965 that hunting was again mentioned as probably the principal factor in bringing about the evolutionary changes which led from ape to man. The first discussion of this in recent times is to be found in Montagu's book *The Human Revolution* ([New York: World Publishing Co., 1965], pp. 92–97; paperback revised edition [New York: Bantam Books, 1967], pp. 60–64). It was there pointed out that from foodgathering early man would have extended his economy by the gathering of small and slow-moving animals, and from that stage would subsequently have moved on to the hunting of larger animals. Hunting places a high premium upon problem-solving ability, the ability to make the most appropriately successful responses—*not* reactions—to the challenges of the situation. This ability is intelligence. Hence, throughout the greater part of man's evolutionary history, during which he was a foodgathering-hunter, intelligence would have been at a high selective advantage. It seems highly probable that hunting was the factor in man's evolution most basically responsible for the evolution of his intelligence, the loss of any dependence upon whatever remnants of instincts he may have started out with, and the concomitant development of an enormous capacity for learning. The need for an appropriately large warehouse in which to store all the necessary information and the mechanisms for retrieving it led naturally to a large brain—a matter with which Krantz deals in this contribution.

Increase in the size of the brain, correlated with the increase in the capacity for learning, storage, and retrieval, resulted in, among other things, a prolonged dependency period lasting years in man, and an acceleration of brain growth during the last month of fetal development rendering necessary the birth of the human infant in a highly immature state of development.

I rather think that the nuclear family, the division of labor between the sexes, food-sharing, mutual aid, kinship relations, and a good many other social as well as physical innovations came about as a direct consequence of the adoption and development of hunting as a way of life.

In the evolutionary step from *Australopithecus africanus* to *Homo erectus,* the most notable anatomical change was a doubling of the brain size. Endocranial capacities increased from about 500 cubic centimetres to around 1,000 (Tobias 1965: 25). Whatever may be said of the reasons for the ultimate development of this human organ, the question remains as to what caused the beginning of the brain's development beyond an ape-like level. It will be shown here how this important step in hominization might be viewed simply as an adaptation to a novel method of hunting which relies heavily on mental time span.

Australopithecus africanus probably occupied an ecological niche much like that of most modern baboons. He lived in regions not heavily forested and subsisted primarily on vegetable foods. Some meat may have been included in his diet, but only that of animals requiring no great hunting skills to obtain. He was primarily a gatherer. The subsequent *Homo erectus* lived in much the same environment and must have depended largely on the same foods gathered in the same manner as his predecessor. There was, however, one important difference in that substantial quantities of meat became a regular part of his diet. *Homo erectus* was a successful big-game hunter as well as a gatherer. It should immediately be suspected that in some manner the enlargement of the brain is related to this extension of ancient man's ecological niche.

SOURCE: *Current Anthropology* vol. 9 (1968), 450–51. Copyright © 1968 by the University of Chicago Press. Reprinted by permission of the University of Chicago Press and the author.

Two other aspects of man's anatomy, the hands and pelvis, appear to have achieved their modern conditions in about this general time range and will be discussed here briefly.

The development of a longer and stronger thumb has been shown to have been a significant factor in providing man with an ability to manipulate tools more effectively than can the great apes. Increases in the motor areas of the brain directly related to these activities may well have added a small amount to the endocranial volume. On the other hand, as Garn (1963:222) has said:

It is no longer enough to attribute even the first increase of hominid brain size to the mere rudiments of technology, and certainly not the second increase that followed *Pithecanthropus.* Surely man did not double and nearly redouble his cerebral volume merely to pick up sticks.

Most of the Lower Paleolithic stone tools are clearly butchering knives and not good weapons. Even the stone balls and the rare wooden spears would not have been effective weapons unless the hunter had some means of trapping or otherwise closely approaching his quarry.

Efficient bipedalism was certainly a requirement for big-game hunting. While *Australopithecus* could probably run at high speed by leaning forward and thus projecting his still ape-like ischia posteriorly to provide leverage for the muscles that extend the thigh, he could do so only at the expense of his view of the quarry. This running position, which would also make the individual less visible in some situations, is better suited to the pursued than to the pursuer. Erect posture, made possible by the broad ilium already present in *Australopithecus* and firmly established by further changes in the pelvis in *Homo erectus,* would provide a good view of the terrain although it also increased the individual's visibility and perhaps decreased his speed in running.

These features, and also the absence of efficient projectile weapons, are consistent with successful big-game hunting of a type I shall call *persistence hunting*. Persistence hunting is a uniquely human technique which is known to have been practiced recently by some primitive peoples but which has been almost universally displaced by the use of projectile weapons and other more sophisticated techniques. An example, occurring among the Tarahumara of Mexico, is the following (Bennett and Zingg 1935:113):

Hunting deer consists of chasing the deer for two days—never less than one day. The Tarahumara keeps the deer constantly on the move. Only occasionally does he get a glimpse of his quarry, but follows it unerringly through his own uncanny ability to read the tracks. The Indian chases the deer until the creature falls from exhaustion, often with its hoofs completely worn away.

Lowie (1924:197) describes the same procedure for the Shoshonean Indians in bringing down antelope, though he does not say just how much time was spent in the pursuit. Passarge (1907:72) describes how the Bushmen would repeatedly trot up to a group of animals, causing them to break and run, and eventually single out one animal for a continuation of this treatment for a day or more until the victim could go no farther and was easily speared. Bjerre (1960:130) describes this hunting tactic as still being practiced by the Bushmen whenever scarcity of vegetative cover makes stealth and concealment difficult and the use of short-ranged poisoned arrows impractical.

In all of these cases of persistence hunting, the game is finally taken primarily because the hunter has been able to persist in the chase for as long as one or two whole days. Brace and Montagu (1965:220–21) have suggested that man's near-hairlessness and wealth of sweat glands may be associated with this hunting technique in that a superior cooling system would enable man to persist in tracking even in the hottest part of the day, when other carnivores are idle and when the quarry may face heat exhaustion. (In the absence of clear evidence of big-game hunting before the

time of *H. erectus,* hairlessness should perhaps be seen not as an attribute of *Australopithecus* but as part of the transition between these two hominid forms.) A more important requirement for persistence hunting, and one which is directly relevant to the development of the brain, is the ability to keep the task constantly in mind for several days and to anticipate the results well into the future.

Rensch (see Rensch and Altevogt 1955:70, and elsewhere) has shown that memory is directly related to brain size. He and his colleagues have tested many pairs of related species of animals of contrasting body (and brain) sizes and compared their learning abilities and memory retentions. In all cases the species with the larger brain proved to have the greater memory. These experiments are summarized in English by Dobzhansky (1962:201), who says:

Rensch concludes that the memory retention is about proportional to the brain size in the animals experimented with by himself and his colleagues.

Judging from Rensch's observations, the increase of some 500 cc. of endocranial volume in *Homo erectus* must certainly represent a tremendous increase in his memory. A brain at least ⅔ the size of modern man's brain should have permitted *H. erectus* to engage in persistence hunting in a manner approaching that observed in recent man.

The idea of persistence hunting permits the following hypothesis as to the selective forces that brought about the transformation from *Australopithecus* to *Homo:* Small steps in the enlargement of the *Australopithecus* brain would have been of selective advantage mainly by increasing the time and distance that the possessor would be able to pursue his mobile food supply. Considering the young, injured, and aged as well as normal adults of all species of potential food available to our ancestors, there was a continuous gradation in pursuit times necessary to bring down game. At first, *Australopithecus* could run down only those animals most quickly exhausted, and must have been in keen competition with many other carnivores. As the reward in food for successful pursuit of game tended, on the average, to go to those individuals with the greater mental time spans, selective pressure would favor larger brains with better memories.

REFERENCES

BENNETT, WENDELL C., and ROBERT M. ZINGG. 1935. *The Tarahumara.* Chicago: University of Chicago Press.

BJERRE, JENS. 1960. *Kalahari.* London: Michael Joseph.

BRACE, C. L., and M. F. ASHLEY MONTAGU. 1965. *Man's evolution.* New York: Macmillan.

DOBZHANSKY, THEODOSIUS. 1962. *Mankind evolving.* New Haven: Yale University Press.

GARN, STANLEY M. 1963. Culture and the direction of human evolution. *Human Biology* 35:221–36.

LOWIE, ROBERT H. 1924. Notes on Shoshonean ethnography. *Anthropological Papers of the American Museum of Natural History* 20(3).

PASSARGE, S. 1907. *Die Buschmanner der Kalahari.* Berlin: Dietrich Reimer.

RENSCH, BERNHARD, and R. ALTEVOGT. 1955. Das Ausmass visueller lernfähigkeit eines Indischen Elefanten. *Zeitschrift für Tierpsychologie* 12(1).

TOBIAS, PHILLIP V. 1965. Early Man in East Africa. *Science* 149:22–33.

9 • HUNTING: AN INTEGRATING BIOBEHAVIOR SYSTEM AND ITS EVOLUTIONARY IMPORTANCE

William S. Laughlin

The many different consequences for the behavioral and genetic evolution of man following upon the adoption of a hunting way of life are dealt with most interestingly in this contribution by Laughlin. It will repay careful critical study, as will the symposium volume from which it is reprinted. The reader will also find much of interest in Carleton S. Coon's, more popular book, *The Hunting Peoples* (Boston: Little, Brown & Co., 1971), and Elman R. Service's *The Hunters* (Englewood Cliffs, N.J.: Prentice-Hall, 1966).

Careful field studies of hunting peoples have overturned some age-old myths about them. The first of these is that hunting is a very difficult and precarious mode of making a living. It is not, as Lee, for example, has shown for the Dobe Bushmen of the Kalahari Desert.[1] In spite of the fact that the Dobe Bushmen are confined to the least productive part of the range in which Bushmen were formerly found, they live quite comfortably on plants and meat. Second, the hunting of males is usually of less importance than the foraging of women in maintaining the economy. The idea that the male has usually or always been the basic food provider is a male prejudice. The evidence seems to me unequivocally to indicate that by far the most important role as food provider has been played by the female, not alone for her offspring and herself, but also for her husband.

The basic foods upon which the foodgathering-hunting group lived, and lives today, are those gathered by the female: plant foods of every kind, insects, small animals, eggs, and the like. Among the

[1] Richard B. Lee, "What Hunters Do For a Living, or, How to Make Out on Scarce Resources," in Richard B. Lee and Irven De Vore, eds., *Man the Hunter* (Chicago: Aldine Publishing Co., 1968), pp. 30–48.

Bushmen, Lee found that 60 percent of the food consumed consisted of plants foraged by the women. By comparison hunting is a more difficult and a less dependable source of food. Hunting a single animal may take several days, and even then is not always successful. This is by no means intended to undervalue the importance of hunting in the evolution of the human species. It was of the first order of importance. Furthermore, it undoubtedly played an important role in producing the increasingly asymmetric development of the roles of the sexes in the course of human evolution. But these facts should not cause us to overlook the important role played by the female as a significant food-provider, a basic food-provider in the evolution of human societies.

Even when food was in short supply the survival of the group often depended upon the ability of the female to breastfeed the infant, and under normal conditions she would breastfeed the child for three or more years. It may be that the form of the human face and the form of the female breast evolved in interactive relation with one another.[2] However that may be, breastfeeding has been a neglected factor in discussions of food-providing, possibly due to the fact that males are usually incapable of this technique.

A third finding is that among hunting peoples "exclusive territoriality with territorial defense by a fixed group of people is rare at best."[3]

There are many cultural traits that foodgathering-hunting peoples have in common—a correlative study of these would be very rewarding.[4]

Introduction

Hunting is the master behavior pattern of the human species. It is the organizing activity which integrated the morphological, physiological, genetic, and intellectual aspects of the individual human organisms and of the population who compose our single species. Hunting is a way of life, not simply a "subsistence technique," which importantly involves commitments, correlates, and consequences spanning the entire biobehavioral continuum of the individual and of the entire species of which he is a member.

That man achieved a worldwide distribution while still a hunter reflects the enormous universality of this kind of behavioral adaptation. The corollary fact that he practiced hunting for 99 per cent of his history indicates the significance of two neglected aspects: (1) hunting is a much more complex organization of behavior than is currently admitted under the traditional "subsistence technique" categorization, and (2) the intellectual and genetic repertoire of the animal developed in this behavioral regime both permitted and enabled the recent acquisition of civilization to be a rapid acquisition and to be developed independently by hunting peoples in different parts of the world.

The total biobehavioral configuration of hunting includes the ethological training of children to be skilled observers of animal behavior, including other humans. The process itself includes five distinguishable components whose combinations and permutations are certainly varied, but with

SOURCE: William S. Laughlin, "Hunting: An Integrating Biobehavior System and Its Evolutionary Importance," R. B. Lee and I. De Vore (eds.) *Man the Hunter* (Chicago: Aldine Publishing Company, 1968), pp. 304–20. Copyright © 1966 by The Wenner-Gren Foundation for Anthropological Research, Inc. Reprinted by permission of the authors and Aldine Publishing Company.
[2] Ashley Montagu, "Natural Selection and the Form of the Breast in the Human Female," *Journal of the American Medical Association,* vol. 180, 1962, pp. 826–827; Ashley Montagu, *The Human Revolution* (New York: Bantam Books, 1967), pp. 91–94.
[3] James N. Anderson, "Analysis of Group Composition," in *Man the Hunter,* p. 154.
[4] For an early general such study see L. T. Hobhouse, G. C. Wheeler, and M. Ginsberg, *The Material Culture and Social Institutions of Simpler Peoples* (London: Chapman & Hall, 1915). Reprinted 1930.

recurrent and widely distributed commonalities.

Hunting is an active process which puts motion and direction into the diagram of man's morphology, technology, social organization, and ecological relations. Hunting involves goals and motivations for which intricate inhibition systems have been developed. Hunting has placed a premium upon inventiveness, upon problem solving, and has imposed a real penalty for failure to solve the problem. Therefore it has contributed as much to advancing the human species as to holding it together within the confines of a single variable species. A study of hunting removes the tedious ambiguity contained in many current discussions of the importance of tools, whether tool use means that tools use humans or that humans use tools.

Hunting as an Integrating Sequence Behavior Pattern

Hunting may profitably be analyzed as a sequence pattern of behavioral complexes. This analysis recognizes the ordered interdependencies of the diverse constituent elements of hunting and it also provides a comparative basis for evaluating the functions and intensities, their similarities and dissimilarities, in radically different cultures. As defined here, hunting consists of five series of patterned activities, beginning early in childhood and extending through the life of the individual engaged in hunting. These five behavior complexes consist of (1) programming the child, (2) scanning or the collection of information, (3) stalking and pursuit of game, (4) immobilization of game, including the killing or capture of game, and (5) retrieval of the game. Although more complexes might be added, such as those concerned with the distribution of game and its various uses, none can be subtracted without impoverishing an appreciation of hunting.

In overall perspective, both for the individual and for the evolution of mankind, this behavior

system has had an integrating function. It has served as an integrating schedule for the nervous system. Hunting is obviously an instrumental system in the real sense that something gets done, several ordered behaviors are performed with a crucial result. The technological aspects, the spears, clubs, handaxes, and all the other objects suitable for museum display, are essentially meaningless apart from the context in which they are used. They do not represent a suitable place to begin analysis because their position in the sequence is remote from the several preceding complexes.

Programming Children

Three indispensable parts of the hunting system are programmed into the child beginning early in life. These are the habit of observation, a systematic knowledge of animal behavior, and the interpretation and appropriate action for living with animals and for utilizing them for food and fabricational purposes. Owing to the fact that in many cultures various animals are endowed with souls, that there are animal beings as well as human beings, the killing and eating of animal beings may be fraught with spiritual hazards (Rasmussen, 1929, p. 56). Appropriate behavior toward animals is prominently based upon familiarity with animal behavior and includes ways of living peacefully with animals, of maintaining a discourse with them, as well as the appropriate behaviors, the highly coordinated movements of the hunter proceeding toward a kill, and appropriate social behavior where other hunters are involved. Within a single community it is possible to arrange the hunters in a rank order in terms of their efficiency or productivity. It is sometimes possible to relate lack of success to inadequate training as well as to the other sources of ineptitude. This is especially apparent where the child has been removed from his village during the crucial years, or where the child has been raised by a grandmother or other nonhunter who was not able to provide the necessary tuition.

A general statement embracing the styles, modes, and mechanisms of neurological patterning in childhood has been provided by Gajdusek:

Phylogeny has already patterned the view of the physical world which a child will receive in the structure of the sense receptors: eyes, ears, nose, taste buds; tactile, temperature, and pain receptors; and proprioceptors. The cultural milieu, however, can determine the schemata of thought and the modes of handling of these sense perceptions as well as it determines the quality and quantity in which they impinge upon the infant and child. There is a vast number of neurological functions of the central nervous system which different cultures have programmed in their own specific ways by the unique environment they provide for the growth and development of their children. These include the style of neuro-muscular coordination in fine and gross movements, even at the level of speech and eye movements; styles of posture, gait, stance, climbing and swimming, etc.; modes of nonverbal communication including gesture and dance; use of language, at times polylinguality; the form of the body image; sense of time, space, rhythm, and tone; color sense and acuity of smell and taste, hearing and vision; conceptions of quantity and number, methods of counting (some nonverbal), and processes of reconning and computation; styles of symbolic representation in play or drawing; patterns of sexual responsiveness and behavior; mnemonic mechanisms; and even methods and mechanisms of imagery and imagination, reverie, trance, and dream (1963, p. 56).

It is useful to realize, as D. A. Hamburg has noted (1961, p. 281) that even the autonomic nervous system is not autonomous but rather that it is substantially under central nervous control. Unfortunately we do not have the full span of physiological and neurological observations on a longitudinal, or cross-sectional, series of children for a single hunting community. However, we do have a body of observations, variously rich or sparse, on comparatively gross activities, and in these we can see the way in which children are progressively trained to become active hunters. We can see the end products, the overt manifestations of deeper and more subtle maturational alterations of the nervous system. Our major problem here is to determine what programming, what childhood instruction, is essential and indispensable to subsequent hunting behaviors.

In any community of hunters it is possible to find general exercises that prepare the child for active hunting but many fewer that involve a specific commitment. Probably all forms of exercise are of some value, but only a few have demonstrable relevance in the sense that they are a necessary and specific prerequisite. Beginning with the different practices for the two sexes which are maximized in hunting groups, a series can be assembled. Thus, those practices leading to use of spear throwers, boomerangs, bows and arrows, lances, boat handling, sledding, harpooning, etc., are ordinarily restricted to males or males are clearly favored in systematic instruction. Nevertheless, there is little data bearing on the question of how much instruction is necessary in childhood. The best preparation for throwing a spear as an adult hunter is probably throwing one at an earlier age, but how early or how many practice hours are required is not amenable to quantified estimate. The bow and arrow is in common use among many hunters—Pygmies, Bushmen, Eskimos, various American Indians, Andamanese, Chukchee, to name only enough to illustrate considerable diversity in the technology and use; however, most observers agree that these hunters are mediocre or indifferent as archers. They hunt effectively with their equipment, but, they compensate for lack of accuracy at appreciable distances, perhaps more than twenty or thirty yards, by spending their time getting closer to the animal. In brief, these hunters clearly spend more time and attention in utilization of their knowledge of animal behavior than in improvement of their equipment or of its use. This generalization, if well founded, probably constitutes an important aspect of primitive hunting and provides a scale for comparisons between groups.

Children were taught to close the distance between themselves and their quarry by sophisticated stalking methods that depended more upon comprehensive observation, detailed ethological knowledge and an equally detailed system of interpretation and action, than upon the improvement of their equipment and the addition of ten or twenty yards to its effective range. In fact, one may pass from this generalization to another and suggest that the very slow improvement in technology, clubs, spears, throwing boards, bows and arrows, as indicated by the archeological record, was contingent upon success in learning animal behavior. It was easier or more effective to instruct children in ethology, to take up the slack by minimizing their distance from the animal prey, than to invest heavily in equipment improvement. The rapid advances in archery of the last fifteen years reflect an application of technological methods to archery equipment that clearly did not arise from a need to depend upon such equipment for any important portion of the annual food supply.

The difference between specifically programmed and generally programmed prerequisite childhood exercises for hunting in adulthood is epitomized in the tendon lengthening exercises for Aleut children, designed for hunting from the kayak, contrasted with their general exercises. These former focused on the shoulder joint of the throwing arm, on the low back, and on the posterior region of the knee joint.

Very early in childhood, apparently as early as beginning to walk, the male child was placed in a sitting position on a flat surface or on a stool with his heels on another stool or box. His preceptor, a father, uncle, or grandfather, stood behind or to the side of him and pulled his throwing arm up and over behind his back. This was done gently and intermittently, often with a little song or rhythmic susurration, so that several excursions were made rather than one prolonged excursion. This exercise created greater mobility at the shoulder joint and specifically enabled the arm to move farther backward and to come directly forward in a flat, vertical plane. As a consequence, the arm functioned as a longer lever than in those persons who cannot rotate their arm backward without moving it progressively to the side of the body at the same time. A spear or harpoon could be thrown farther, more easily, and from a greater variety of positions available to the seated kayak hunter.

The second and related exercise stretched the tendons and ligaments of the low back. The seated child, legs extended in front, was pushed forward by a hand applied to the back. This exercise specifically anticipated the considerable strain placed on the low back while paddling or throwing when seated in a kayak.

The third exercise of this series consisted of depressing the knees of the seated child so that the tendons on the posterior of the leg, especially the semimembranosus and the semitendinosus tendons in particular, were stretched. As a consequence the person was enabled to sit with legs extended for long periods of time and to operate efficiently.

These three specific exercises were reinforced with various games. In one, the child sat on the ground, legs extended, and threw a dart at a small wooden model of a whale suspended from a flexible withe. Two boys played this game, each facing the other and with his own whale target.

An example of a non-specific exercise of general value to a kayak hunter but with no specific relevance to kayak hunting, is that of fingerhanging. The young child was suspended from a ceiling beam of the house by his fingers. His preceptor then withdrew and the child hung until he was forced to drop. He dropped to the floor, an earth floor covered with dried grass. The exercise was intended to strengthen the fingers and to teach the child to fall on his feet with ease and agility.

The peculiar monopoly which the Aleuts and Koniags held on sea-otter hunting and the corollary fact that no European ever became a successful kayak sea-otter hunter, may be traced in part to their childhood training, both the physical and the behavioral aspects. Many Europeans have learned to paddle kayaks, and many have learned to hunt sea mammals, but extremely few, possibly five, ever became kayak hunters. Aleuts and Koniags were transported from their homeland to alien waters off California and Japan by their Russian administrators, because of their non-duplicable skills in sea-otter hunting. The point in citing this well-known history is that it reflects some of the consequences of a complex hunting achievement which is demonstrably and specifically related to childhood training. While kayak hunting represents a rare technological achievement, the use of the throwing board enjoyed a much wider distribution about the world. Certainly one factor in the failure of the throwing board to diffuse from Eskimos to contiguous groups of Indians is that an essential portion of the complex rested in child training practices. It was not a trait, like the axe, the bow and arrow, or the rifle, which could be easily used by adults.

A fear of kayaks, as found among the Eskimos of Wainwright (Nelson, 1969, p. 309), must be distinguished from the relatively localized "kayak fear" found in west Greenland. The possible relationship of the disease, "kayak fear," to inadequate child training has not been explored. The inability of adult hunters to perform normally is a generic category for investigation and might well be especially rewarding in revealing defects in childhood programming.

Scanning

Scanning includes the collection of information on where to hunt, what to hunt, and the scheduling of a hunt. The choice of animals to be hunted and the areas which will be searched reflect sophisticated knowledge concerning the behavior of animals, environmental conditions, and other commitments of the hunter to partners or to the portion of the community which depends upon him. His need for food and fabricational materials may outweigh several other considerations. The independence of scanning and its role may be seen in the common practices conducted prior to the pursuit or stalking of detected animals.

For several days prior to the actual detection and pursuit of an animal or herd the hunter may search an area for signs. Frequently he gets this information from other hunters. He must first find what animals are in the territory and the actual tracks, feces, and browsed plants may provide him with the information he needs. The presence of one animal may signal the presence of another so that the hunter is encouraged to continue with this inspection even if he has not actually sighted the animal he wants. He may sight the animal, or a herd, but wait for it to move into a better position, perhaps closer to camp or in a valley where more can be killed than in the open.

In scanning, the knowledge of tracks and indications of animals generally is the paramount feature and obviously the complex which utilizes previously learned observational information concerning animal behavior. The time invested in this portion of the hunting sequence is usually far greater than for any other portion except for the childhood programming.

The scanning and identification problem is quite different for the marine mammal hunter. He must proceed to the most likely area and then search for the interrupting profile of the mammal when it comes to that horizon (Laughlin, 1967). He may first proceed to a mummy cave and ask for help from the hunters interred there who still maintain an active part in the affairs of living people, and he certainly utilizes the information provided by watchmen, those who sit on vantage points and scan the sea, and upon the weather prognosticators. A man of meteorological sophistication, an "astronome" may even be included in a party of kayak hunters (Heizer, 1960, p. 133).

Choices of hunting routes may involve various sorts of divining, whose effect is to randomize the routes or areas searched. This is based on the fact, well known to the primitive hunter, that animals learn the habits of humans and adjust their behavior accordingly.

The religious elements which pervade the preparation are multitudinous and need only be called to mind here. Cleansing rites and special clothing are ubiquitous. They importantly reflect the reciprocal nature of the interaction between those beings in the animal world and those in the human, or stated less egocentrically, the contingent relations between animal beings and human beings (Marsh, 1954; Hallowell, 1960).

Stalking

Stalking and pursuit of game ordinarily begins once the animal has been sighted. Attention then shifts to getting as close to the animal as necessary for an effective shot. In much of hunting, however, there is no sharp line of demarcation between these two portions of the sequence pattern. The hunter may commit himself to a particular animal or herd without having actually seen it. There may be ample evidence that a particular animal is being followed, and the animal may be aware of the pursuit without an actual visual sighting. The hunter and the hunted may smell each other, they may hear each other, they may see each other's tracks, and the animal may actually be attracted to its human pursuer by his urine. Following a polar bear for one or two days, running down a horse over a three-day period, and certainly some of the desert hunting in Australia and in the Kalahari involves a long pursuit and relatively short period for killing.

The hunter is concerned with the freshness of the track and the direction in which he is moving. He wants all possible information on his quarry's condition; its age, sex, size, rate of travel, and a working estimate of the distance by which the animal leads him. In the final stages, when he is closing with the animal, the hunter employs his knowledge of animal behavior and situational factors relevant to that behavior in a crucial fashion. For all birds, animals, and fish the hunter must estimate flight distance, the point at which they will take flight or run away. Conversely, with animals that are aggressive, he needs to interpret any signs, raising or lowering of tail, flexing of muscles, blowing, or salivation, etc., that indicate an attack rather than a flight. In many cases the animal is intentionally provoked to attack. The variations are innumerable.

One useful generalization of the problem faced by the hunter is that he wants to get as close as possible for the best possible shot but he would rather have a poor shot than none at all. The enormous labor and skill that is expended in approaching the animal, often hours of lying on the ground waiting for a change in direction of wind or in the position of the animal, testifies to the crucial importance of stalking.

The technological equipment of most primitive hunters is such that their quarry is usually shot at relatively short distances, usually less than thirty feet for harpoons, bows and arrows, and spears. Even the one generalization about the minimum distance for the best shot must be qualified because the hunter may want the maximum distance compatible with his weapon, in order to provide time for a second shot. Some animals tend to continue in the direction they were traveling after they are shot. Other animals have a tendency to simply stand and bleed, if not frightened by sight or smell of the hunter. The point here is simply that the enormous range and complexities of animal behavior; the influence of situational factors depending upon time of day, sex, age, nutritional state, degree of excitation, being in the company of a mate, with or without young, etc., these factors must all be read into the decision-making machinery of the hunter.

Hunting with high-powered rifles and telescopic sights, and to a lesser extent with modern archery equipment, is substantially different from the hunting of primitive man. In a general fashion, the better the technological equipment the less intimate knowledge of animal behavior is required. Getting close to an animal represents the major investment of the primitive hunter and explains the extensive attention given to childhood programming and to the location of game.

Immobilization, Killing, and Capture

The vast majority of animals taken by primitive hunters are not killed outright or are not killed upon initial contact. More often they are wounded, stunned, or immobilized to a degree that renders them incapable of rapid or prolonged flight. Even with the use of poisons the larger mammals may live on, traveling slowly, for one or more days. The Pygmy elephant hunter does not expect his quarry to fall over immediately after the first puncture, but he does expect to be able to induce hemorrhaging that will impair the functioning of the elephant and simplify tracking. In other cases the hunter intentionally avoids killing the animal for very practical reasons. An Eskimo may wound a bear and then drive him down to a stream where he can be killed and boated home. If inland on a small island, the Eskimo may wound the bear and walk him over to the edge of the island, then

dispatch him and roll him into the sea where he can be floated and towed away. In many such cases it is practical and highly desirable to save an enormous amount of labor, the backpacking of some 1,200 pounds through difficult country, by wounding the animal and heading him in the preferred direction.

Capture of animals may be an objective and done for many different reasons. One important reason is the need to secure living specimens for study and child instruction, commonly categorized as "pets" in the literature. Live animals may be desired for decoys, and of course live animals may be used for various ritual purposes. Birds may be taken for training in hunting or fishing (cormorants, falcons, etc.), or simply kept as a source of feathers. From the enormous range of methods of taking the quarry it is obvious that immediate and outright killing is only one of many variations. The extensive use of snares, traps, and pitfalls in itself testifies to the concern with capture rather than immediate killing.

Retrieval

Retrieval of game represents the end point of the hunting complex pattern, it is the object of those things which have preceded it. Within the retrieval complex are included the immediate details of retrieving a floating seal or walrus, and of getting it secured to the kayak, or to an umiak, or an ice cake so that it can be cut up. Many items of material culture naturally fall in here and retrieving hooks for securing floating animals before they sink are prominent among them. This complex category broadens out to include the dressing and preparation of the animal for return to the camp or village. Finally, the activities involved in this complex extend ultimately to the distribution and use of the game, and ultimately the return of some of the materials back into earlier portions of the sequence system. A flow chart shows the routes by

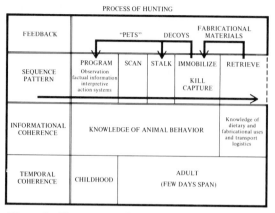

Figure 1: The process of hunting.

which some of the materials return to participate again in the system (Fig. 1). The most obvious is the capture of an animal to be used for instruction of children in animal behavior. Thus, the entire system is activated in proper sequence and reverts to flow again into the system.

The intellectual requirements for appropriate behavior in this portion of the system still depend in part upon those that were prerequisite to the preceding four portions. However, there is a qualitative difference. An animal must be expertly drawn in accordance with the anatomy of the animal, the various fabricational and nutritional uses of the animal, with attention to size requirements that affect carrying it back to the camp, and to social factors such as some desired portions, horns, tail, forward flipper, or fluke meat, for persons of relevant status. Attention shifts over to anatomy rather than behavior, to material characteristics, to the fabricational and dietary qualities of the animal. Some portions may be eaten immediately, and some may be employed in a ritual observance to insure affability of the animal spirit. Hides are carefully removed if they are intended for fabricational use and their cutting is in accord with a particular use. Thus, if a sealskin is to be used for a line, it must be slipped, in tubular fashion, off the carcass so that a continuous, circumferentially spiral line can be cut. But if the seal is to be fed to dogs, or its skin to be used for clothing, or both, it is drawn quite differently. A worldwide survey indicates great differences in the utilization of animal tissues. Some people use the intestines and pericardium, others discard them or feed them to dogs (Table 1). The same animal

Table 1: Multiple Use of Resources

Eumetopia jubata [*Northern or Steller sea lion*]	
PART OF ANIMAL	PARTIAL LIST OF USES
1. Hide	Cover for kayak and umiak; line for harpoon
2. Flesh	Food, for humans
3. Blubber	Food: eaten with meat, rendered for oil
4. Organs (heart, liver, spleen, kidney)	Food
5. Bones	Ribs for root diggers, humerus for club, baculum for flaker
6. Teeth	Decorative pendants
7. Whiskers	Decoration of wood hunting hats and visors
8. Sinew	Back sinews used for sewing, lashing, cordage (less desirable than sinew of whale or caribou)
9. Flippers	Soles used for boot soles; contents gelatinized in flipper and eaten
10. Pericardium	Water bottle, general-purpose container
11. Esophagus	Parka, pants, leggings of boots, pouches
12. Stomach	Storage container (especially for dried salmon)
13. Intestines	Parka, pants, pouches

has different meanings for different peoples and this extends far beyond its rank order in their list of food preferences.

Women and dogs have been the principal beasts of burden since Paleolithic times and these are not universally available for the reason that women are not always at the site of killing and butchering, and many people did not breed dogs suitable for packing. Where long distances and large amounts of meat are involved, a village may move to the animal. Elephants and whales, unless juvenile or easily floated, usually become community projects. It is interesting that, excepting the sled and dog traction, both comparatively recent, the only mechanical advantage accessible to primitive man was water transport. The retrieval flow pattern for the Eskimo or Aleut who harpoons a seal, tows it home behind his kayak, and eats all the meat, contrasted with the sledging Eskimo who harpoons a seal, carries it home on a sled, and then shares it with the dogs, is enormous.

The kayak-hunter can tow much greater weights more easily, than can the sledgers. The kayak-hunter can use the hide of his quarry to make the kayak with which he hunts the beast. Marine hunters use more of the products of the animals they hunt than do terrestrial hunters, and they use them more advantageously. Esophagus, intestines, and pericardia are of little use to most hunting groups as fabricational materials, yet they account for an appreciable part of the clothing of some northern peoples.

The Physical Superiorities of Man

Pound for pound, man is a tough, durable, strong, and versatile animal. To the extent that comparisons between species have validity, he is superior in overall physical performance to all or most other mammals. This physical superiority is intimately related to his hunting habit.

It has become a common routine to observe that man is born helpless and remains dependent upon others for a long period of time, that he is a generalized animal lacking the specializations that characterize other species, and this recitation often leads to the observation that man is physically weak and defenseless because he is dependent upon culture. This in turn provides the argument for the implication that evolution took place in the past and that the rapidity and pervasiveness of cultural evolution has supplanted physical evolution. A more realistic and holistic view is the recognition of the biobehavioral continuum that characterizes the development of each individual (Ginsburg and Laughlin, 1966). The dichotomy between biology and culture, between cultural learning and its neurological base, has been historically conducive to the denigration of man's physical abilities.

In fact, human beings are remarkably versatile, durable, and strong in their physical constitution. As Haldane has observed, only man can swim a mile, walk twenty miles, and then climb a tree (Haldane, 1956, p. 5). The full list of man's physical superiorities, when compared with other mammals, must include his ability to run rapidly and to run long distances. One need only cite the conquest of the four-minute mile and the long-distance running of various Indian tribes. Tarahumara endurance runners have been scientifically studied and the results confirm and extend various anecdotal accounts. Participants in kick-ball races may cover up to 100 miles in 24 hours (Balke and Snow, 1965). That Indians can run down horses and deer is well known, by pacing the animal, keeping him moving, and taking advantage of the tendency of many ungulates to move in an arc by traversing the chord. The Indian hunter who is running down an animal makes use of his own physical superiority and his knowledge of the animal's behavior.

In pulling strength, humans compare favorably with adult chimpanzees. In ability to carry loads, humans regularly display abilities superior to the donkey, and this superiority is demonstrated at high altitudes as well. Loads of sixty pounds are commonly carried and the literature abounds with examples of porters carrying loads in excess of their own body weight.

Functional flexibility permitting a wide range of movements and postures, best seen in young children, acrobats, gymnasts, ballet dancers, wrestlers, swimmers, and divers, is unequivocally superior to other mammals. The closest approach to human flexibility as a whole is probably found in the orangutan and in the spider monkeys, the latter having the advantage of a prehensile tail. However, these contenders are lacking in the fine motor control of the hand and of a specialized foot. Nor can they swivel their heads as far or as easily as humans. They do not have the ability to milk a cow, a manual feat requiring a subtle succession of digital closure, and as runners or weight bearers they cannot even be entered in the lists.

Man's sensory apparatus is excellent. His vision is acute and of course includes color vision. It is exceeded only by that of various birds. His auditory acuity compares well with other animals and is a prime factor in his hunting abilities. His olfactory abilities do appear to be more limited than those of some other species, polar bears for example, but it is adequate to facilitate hunting. The external integument of humans is remarkably tough. Many groups live their entire lives without benefit of clothes and this includes groups living in areas as stressful and divergent as Australia, Tierra del Fuego, the Congo, and the Kalahari Desert. The fallacious idea that man lost his body hair as a consequence of wearing clothes, still recited as a demonstrated fact (Glass, 1965, p. 1254), is easily disposed of by the examples of hirsute and naked hunters, the Australian aborigines, and of glabrous and naked hunters, the Bushmen. Human skin tans well and is far more durable than that of many other mammals. One may speculate on the role hair

has played in human evolution, but a tough skin has been a distinct advantage in a large variety of recurrent situations to the primitive hunter.

Considerable physiological tolerance, an unsurpassed ability to adapt to environmental stresses of which high altitude is most prominent, is surely one of man's major physical superiorities. Few animals, rats and dogs, to cite undomesticated and domesticated examples, compare with humans in this respect. A review of all the areas in which members of our species live serves to indicate our great physiological plasticity. No other single species lives at high and low altitudes, extremely hot and extremely cold climates and in all the combinations of humidity, light and darkness that compose the panel of human habitats.

Among the many other superiorities enjoyed by the human animal is a dental and alimentary system that permits a truly omnivorous diet. Humans can tolerate a large number of plants and animals and can adapt to diets that are composed totally of flesh or of plant foods. Additionally, they can continue work under conditions of deprivation.

When the superior memory and learning abilities of man is included, and the use of tools, language, and other elements of the biobehavioral matrix in which man operates, the remarkable versatility of the human animal becomes even more apparent. However, this should not obscure the basic fact that viewed solely from the standpoint of anatomy, physiology, and neurology man enjoys many superiorities compared with other species. A man can run down a horse in two or three days, and then decide whether to eat it, ride it, pull a load with it, wear it, or worship it.

Simplicity of Basic Technology

The common weapons and related devices used in stalking and in the immobilization of game animals is basically simple and elementary. Over the million or more years in which man has evolved as a hunter, it is probable that the vast majority of mammals, birds, and fish have been killed with clubs, stones, knives, and spears or simply strangled with the hands or in a snare or noose. Examination of the archeological record, even that of Upper Paleolithic big-game hunters, is not impressive except in virtuosity of flaking or in other artistic variations. Diagonal flaking of a spear point has no demonstrable advantage over parallel flaking, and fluting offers no discernible advantage over unfluted points.

As Boas observed, "As soon as a reasonably long shaft allowed an attack from a point beyond the reach of the teeth and paws of the animal, hunting became safer" (Boas, 1938, p. 254). The spear, used as a lance or cast, was certainly a major step forward, and has persisted for some hundreds of thousands of years. Nevertheless, it is basically a simple invention, and the spear-thrower, still in use by some Eskimos and Australian aborigines, is similarly an uncomplicated device. The bows and arrows in use by most primitive hunters were not impressive for their cast, their distance, nor their accuracy. An examination of the variety of arrow releases and their geographical distribution (Wissler, 1926, pp. 30–40) serves to reinforce the idea that cultural styles in the construction and use of various tools and weapons have only limited relevance to the potential efficiency of the weapon. As previously suggested, the enormous variety of harpoon heads that have been used to harpoon the same species of seal, or the variety of fishhooks that are used to catch the same species of fish, illuminates the basic fact that the hunter invests more heavily in knowledge of the behavior of the animals, in methods for approaching them or attracting them close to him, than in increasing the range or firepower of his weapons.

A substantial amount of hunting reveals the way in which animals can be easily approached under suitable conditions, and then dispatched with a club or a spear. Many animals are killed while asleep. Obviously the most ferocious beast in the world is utterly harmless while asleep, or hibernating. Walrus, who are often victors in combat with polar and brown bears, are frequently taken while asleep. Screening noises are prominently utilized in many forms of hunting. During storms, the sea otter hauls up on shore. The Aleuts approached them with ease at this time owing to the animals' inability to hear the approaching hunters, and simply clubbed them (Elliott, 1886, pp. 142–43). To a significant extent, young animals fall in the same accessible category as sleeping animals. The archeological and ethnographic record is unambiguous on the fact that the vast majority of mammals killed are immature or subadult. This reflects the population profile of many species, but it also represents a preference on the part of the hunter. The largest and oldest animals are more difficult to kill or capture, they do not taste as good as younger ones, their hides are often scarred and therefore less desirable for clothing, and they may even be avoided for frankly conservational and for religious considerations.

Driving animals, whether into a net, a pit, over a cliff, or within range of concealed hunters, is again obviously simple so far as the technology is concerned, but considerably more complex with reference to the coordination required of the persons conducting this part of the hunt. The signalling system used by Aleut and Koniag kayak hunters when employing a surround method reflects the solution of a problem in communication where spoken language would frustrate the combined efforts of the hunters. The position of the paddle of the first man to sight the quarry provided ample cues to the other hunters. The many ways in which group hunting provided an effective means of scanning, stalking, and killing, and at the same time placed a premium upon precisely coordinated social organization, simultaneously reveals the importance of alternate forms of communication between the participants. Brief, silent, inconspicuous, and unambiguous cues are absolutely necessary in such operations.

Though the technological sophistication of many poisons is considerably advanced beyond the handax and club, the use of poisons also illustrates the point that much programming must precede the killing complex (Linné, 1957). The development of effective poisons importantly demonstrates the basic inventiveness of primitive hunters.

Among the great inventory of hunting technology is the ancient and widespread bolas. Its principle, common to the bull-roarer sling and centrifuge alike, is simple enough for women and children to manipulate and helps explain some of their substantial contributions to the hunting economy.

The point of drawing attention to the simplicity of the basic technology is of course to draw attention to the sophistication of the complexes preceding the actual use of the weapons. In a very real sense the hunter is taking a final examination with a mortal demerit for failure. It is the preceding period of learning that enables him to perform adequately.

Hunter's Sophisticated Knowledge of Behavior and Anatomy

There is ample documentation, though surprisingly few systematic studies, for the postulate that primitive man is sophisticated in his knowledge of the natural world. This sophistication encompasses the entire macroscopic zoological world of mammals, marsupials, reptiles, birds, fish, insects, and plants. Knowledge of tides, meteorological phenomena generally, astronomy, and other aspects of the natural world are also well developed among some primitive peoples. There are genuinely large variations between groups with reference to the sophistication and extent of their knowledge, and to the areas in which they have concentrated. Empiricism is not

at all uncommon, and inventiveness similarly recurs in widely separated areas with only remote or no discernible historical connections. Having previously discussed these topics (Laughlin, 1961, 1963), I will here only cite the relevance of this sophistication to the hunting behavior system and to its significance for the evolution of man.

Hunters are extremely knowledgeable concerning animal behavior and anatomy for a variety of reasons. Hunting is their profession and this requires such knowledge. They recite events of hunting, they discuss endlessly the weather and its effects on ice conditions, or on the moss on which caribou feed; they make predictions on the numbers of various animals based on weather conditions and its effects on animals and plants that serve as food for carnivores and grazers. Their conversations often sound like a classroom discussion of ecology, of food chains, and trophic levels.

The accuracy of their information is attested by their success in hunting and by comparisons with scientific studies of behavior and anatomy and systematics. In discussing the species concept of the local naturalist, Ernst Mayr includes the opinion of primitive natives:

Some 30 years ago I spent several months with a tribe of superb woodsmen and hunters in the Arfak Mountains of New Guinea. They had 136 different vernacular names for the 137 species of birds that occurred in the area, confusing only two species. It is not, of course, pure coincidence that these primitive woodsmen arrive at the same conclusion as the museum taxonomists, but an indication that both groups of observers deal with the same arbitrary discontinuities of nature (1963, p. 17).

The consultation of native hunters by naturalists extends well back into the nineteenth century. The naturalist Chamisso who visited Unalaska as early as 1817 published a detailed study of whales in which he depended upon the local Aleuts who carved wooden models of each of the whales and provided various information about each of them (Chamisso, 1824).

The ubiquity of sophisticated information among hunters is probably of more importance for interpreting the development and consequences of such information than the unusual and rare achievements that may occasionally be associated with such knowledge. The preparation of mummies and intentional autopsy of the dead to find out why they died are expectable developments where there is the appropriate context and concern.

The Tungus, described in detail by Shirokogorov (1935), compare favorably with Eskimos and even with the Aleuts (Marsh and Laughlin, 1956). They are good gross anatomists, their ideas on physiological functions are based on their observations, they are good naturalists, and they are concerned to acquaint themselves with the behavior and the anatomy of animals or birds not well known to them, capturing live specimens for this specific purpose and for pets for the instruction of children. "He [the Tungu] is interested in the comparative study of bones and soft parts of the body and he comes to form a good idea as to the anatomical similarities and dissimilarities in animals and even man" (Shirokogorov, 1935, p. 73).

As previously indicated, the sources of Aleut anatomical knowledge can be partitioned into five categories: (1) the study of anatomical structures; (2) a rational medicine and physical culture; (3) dissection of human bodies; (4) true comparative anatomy, focused on the sea otter; and (5) the manufacture of dried mummies (Laughlin, 1961, pp. 157–60). The first, second, and fourth categories appear most ubiquitous. The daily butchering and drawing of animals leads to knowledge about them, and to the extent that internal tissues are used for food or fabricational purposes, the knowledge may be considerably detailed. Hunters are well aware of the affinity between man and other animals, and they

all have relevant exercises designed to condition the hunter. A good deal of information inevitably obtains for human biology stemming first from the need for assistance or intervention at birth.

If primitive hunters are compared with ethologists, some common procedures are obvious, and though the goals may rapidly diverge, they are neither antipathetic nor wholly dissimilar. Drawing upon an important position paper of the ethologist, G. P. Baerends, the common element is immediately apparent. "Starting from detailed description of behaviour, ethologists study the factors that underlie their causation, their genetic basis and their ontogeny" (Baerends, 1958, p. 466). The Bushmen, Pygmies, or Aleuts have the detailed description of behavior well in hand, with the emphasis probably on motor systems. Their knowledge of physiology, genetics, and allied disciplines is clearly inadequate to sustain their interests in causation. To my knowledge, no one has inquired into primitive definitions of units of behavior, and how behavior elements enter into their taxonomic groupings. Such studies could only be conducted among hunters who are actively engaged in hunting, not upon reservation natives who have access only to memory.

Genetic Mechanisms in Hunting Societies

The nature of the hunting behavior system early imposed conditions on mating behavior both within and between groups. These conditions have had important influences on genetic mechanisms at any given time, and on trends in human evolution over long periods of time in the history of our species. In succinct form, the most salient generalizations applicable to contemporary or recent hunting societies with a focus on big-game hunting, and which can be extrapolated into earlier times, are these: (1) They are small in numbers, with low effective population size. The nature of a hunting economy does not ordinarily permit the aggregation of large numbers of people in one place at one time. The high population density of marine hunters such as the Eastern Aleuts was achieved by multiplication of the number of demes, less so of the size of demes. Most bands tend to be genetic units, with the obvious exception of Australian bands which tend to be exogamous, in which case the tribal units are the important genetic units. (2) Their populations are isolated and the constituent demes are isolated in varying degree, the ideal condition for maximum evolutionary opportunity as demonstrated by Sewall Wright. (3) The inbreeding effect is usually present and inbreeding is common. This may contribute to rapid action of selection by increasing the number of homozygotes (that would otherwise be undetected). (4) Differential fertility favors headmen, chiefs, or especially successful hunters. They have more wives and more children in proportion to other hunters. Their reproductive success has been a major factor in the evolution of intelligence and will be discussed in more detail. (5) There is a high frequency of accidental deaths. Though the causes of death are poorly known, it does appear that wild animals, disease, and starvation, in various combinations, are prominent among the causes of death of subadults and adults. The category of wild animals may be matched or exceeded by intertribal fights, cannibalism, and related human disaffections. (6) There is a short life span. Although the data are poor and probably over-estimate longevity, twenty years is probably a more accurate estimate for a generation than 25. Outstanding exceptions may be found and the contrast between short-lived Eskimos in the Canadian Arctic and much longer-lived Eastern Aleuts has likely been duplicated in a number of places and times (Laughlin, 1963b, p. 638). (7) There is high infant mortality. This again prominently varies with the richness of the exploitational area and the technological sophistication of the people. Infanticide

plays an extremely important role. When stillbirths and miscarriages are considered, the genetic wastage may be extremely high. (8) There are frequent population bottlenecks. Annual fluctuations in food supply are common, especially for people hunting migratory animals. Related to the annual cycles of the animals are those of environmental conditions. Dramatic annual alterations occur in desert areas where increase or decrease in water supply involves multitudinous correlative changes, and in arctic regions where water is replaced with ice. Meager storage facilities make it impossible to utilize the common superabundance, for example of caribou, much later in the year. Populations appear to adjust to the lower limits of food resources. During periods of privation the practice of abortion, infanticide, exposure of elderly and infirm persons, and "voluntary death" may further reduce the population size. Bottlenecks provide opportunity for inadequate sampling between generations. (9) *Founder's Principle:* New communities or demes are often founded by only a few migrants, and these may be closely related. The genetical importance of such partitioning of the gene pool is recognized in the concept of "founder's principle" (see Mayr, 1963, p. 211). The founders carry a small fraction of the genetical variation of the total population. Some authors identify "founder's principle" with random genetic drift. This kind of migrant sampling has been extremely important in human evolution and may therefore be worth separate itemization. (10) There has been fusion of remnant groups. R. H. Osborne has noted that the fusion of surviving groups following a severe bottleneck has an effect similar to recurrent selection. The resulting recombinations may represent an improvement over either of the parental contributors. (11) Gene flow is predominantly from central to marginal populations. Marginal populations do not ordinarily feed back to central populations.

Two points of special importance to the relationship between the hunting behavior pattern and human evolution are seen in (a) the population characteristics of such hunting groups leading to diversity, and (b) those favoring the evolution of intelligence. The opportunities for random variation and for the development of differences between groups are maximized in these groups. Small, isolated populations, with many subdivisions, frequently strained through genetic bottlenecks, and with migrant sampling ("founder's principle") as a major form of moving into new territories and new continents constitutes the ideal conditions for rapid evolution, when viewed over long time periods, and for the accumulation of many chance differences. In examining the mechanism of human raciation, and especially the role of isolation and migration, G. Lasker provides the relevant comment:

Race formation seems to be a continual process. Although there is no reason to doubt that it has operated on man, natural selection has not been satisfactorily demonstrated as a significant factor in racial differentiation. It is more plausible that small groups would come to differ racially by the purely random process of primarily endogamous mate selection. Subsequent rapid increases in population size based on cultural advantages or historical opportunities could be responsible in the main for the kind of racial pattern manifest today (1960).

High intergroup diversity is a characteristic of the human species which is closely related to the group size, isolation, and generational and migrational sampling inadequacies of hunting groups. To the isolating factors, those of culture as such, of distance and of distributional pattern, the common result of inhibition of gene flow over distance, of dilution of frequencies outward from centers are especially effective. As Shapiro has remarked, "Thus although some cross-cultural miscegenation is an ancient phenomenon and can occur in a variety of ways, the isolating effects of culture are on the whole predominant" (1957, p. 24).

A major function of culture is that of maximizing the welfare of its members and therefore minimizing and screening contacts with non-members. The more cultures there are, the more diffusion barriers there are to gene flow. This is especially important over distance. Contemporary racial diversity has been enhanced by the distributional patterns imposed by the hunting system. In fact, viewing the genetic diversity of our species from the question of why it did not break into separate species, we find that our knowledge of what holds the species together is not well studied. Mayr has remarked, "The essential genetic unity of species cannot be doubted. Yet the mechanisms by which this unity is maintained are still largely unexplored. Gene flow is not nearly strong enough to make these species anywhere nearly panmictic. It is far more likely that all the populations share a limited number of highly successful epigenetic systems and homeostatic devices which place a severe restraint on genetic and phenotypic change" (Mayr, 1963, p. 523). The human species fits this problem and deserves the kind of study necessary to elucidate the ways in which its unity has been maintained.

The rewards accruing to superior hunters within a community throw light on the evolution of intelligence. The headmen, chiefs, or leaders are generally excellent hunters. Their excellence in hunting depends in part on intelligence, which, however defined, is a multigenic trait with moderate to high heritability. The headmen have more wives than other members and consequently more children, and thus contribute differentially to the succeeding generation. This process can be demonstrated for contemporary hunters and its projection into earlier times provides a major insight into the way in which the hunting system has favored the evolution of intelligence.

The Xavante Indians of Brazil illustrate this mechanism. "As befits the chief, he had more wives (five) than any other member of the tribe" (Neel *et al.,* 1964, p. 94). This man had 23 surviving offspring and in descending order of wives, one man had four wives and six off-spring, four men had three wives and thirteen offspring, ten men had two wives and 23 off-spring, and 21 men had one wife and 24 off-spring. Thus, the leader has produced over 25 per cent of the surviving offspring.

The Anaktuvuk Eskimos of Alaska, a small inland group of some 78 caribou hunters, illustrate the disproportionate contributions of a superior hunter. One elderly but able hunter, one of the founders of the isolate, had seven children of whom six had the blood group gene B. Five matings from these children produced ten children of whom eight had at least one gene for blood group B. Thus, he had contributed to some 20 per cent of the total living population (Laughlin, 1957).

It is possible to generalize on headmen from the existing literature. As a rule they appear to be well informed, to have better memories, more equipment or material goods, more wives including access to women who may not formally be their wives, to be above average in physical constitution, and—directly as a consequence of their superior hunting abilities—to have a better food supply than those less well endowed. A multitude of consequences follow. The wife, or wives, of a headman are better fed and more likely to carry a pregnancy to full term, and any infants are likely to be better fed and therefore more likely to survive to reproductive age than those infants that are less well fed.

Crow has suggested that it would be easier, by selection, to change the intellectual or other aptitudes of a population than to change the incidence of disabling diseases or sterility. "This is not to say that there has not been some selection for intelligence in the past, but it has surely been much less intense than that for fertility, for example" (Crow, 1961, p. 429). This is certainly true, but I would suggest that there has been a constant selection for intelligence and that it has been sufficient to prepare the species for a relatively rapid shift over to civilization where assortative mating tracks based on culturally defined interests in very large populations take over the role of selecting for intelligence and aptitudes.

Evolutionary Aspects

Hunting played the dominant role in transforming a bipedal ape into a tool-using and tool-making man who communicated by means of speech and expressed a complex culture in the infinite number of ways now known to us. The evolutionary importance of hunting can be demonstrated by a combination of nutritional, psychological, and anatomical (including neurophysiological) aspects of our contemporary behavior, with the fossil and archeological record, and with primate comparisons.

Three things are essential to this thesis. One, that hunting is a complex sequence behavior pattern beginning in childhood. Two, the nutritional advantages of a carnivorous-omnivorous diet extend into several aspects of life ranging from childhood dependency and longer period for learning over to the increased territorial mobility permitting occupation of any place in the world. Three, hunting behavior is prior, psychologically, to the use and manufacture of tools. In brief, what the tools were used for, how they could be made to serve the objectives of the hunter, what the hunter was doing that he needed tools, and what he was doing that developed the mind that conceived the design of tools, that executed their manufacture, and that employed them and revised them, these are the important considerations. Tools provide a thermometer for measuring intellectual heat generated by the animal, they are not the source of heat. There is of course a constant feedback so that tool use contributes to the patterning of the brain, thus becoming both subject and object in both a neurological and philosophical sense. For these reasons I stress the importance of the behavior first, and the relevance and importance of tools second. Tools did not make the man, man made tools in order to hunt.

The nutritional advantages of a carnivorous-omnivorous diet, its correlates and its consequences are well attested (Oakley, 1961; Spuhler, 1959; Washburn and Avis, 1958). Spuhler has presented the most succinct itemization in a context with six other preconditions for the beginning of culture: accommodative vision, bipedal locomotion, manipulation, carnivorous-omnivorous diet, cortical control of sexual behavior, vocal communication, and expansion of the association areas in the cerebral cortex. A large supply of compact animal proteins, high in caloric values, concentrated and packaged in a container suitable for transport, its own skin, provides a basis for food sharing, for the differentiation of functions in a family unit, for the long dependency of human children, and such a food supply facilitates migration and it provides more time in which to accomplish other things. Plant-eating primates, gorillas for example, must procure a much larger bulk of shoots, leaves, and stems to have an equivalent caloric value, and they must spend a much longer period each day in eating their vegetarian diet (Schaller, 1963, pp. 149–68). They do not share food. One can only remark that if such vegetarians did want to share food they would need baskets or wheelbarrows. The amount of information which must be exchanged between plant eaters is small compared with that needed in group-hunting of large animals, wolves for example. Equally to the point is the lack of challenge or psychological stimulation involved in plant eating. Plants do not run away nor do they turn and attack. They can be approached at any time from any direction, and they do not need to be trapped, speared, clubbed, or pursued on foot until they are exhausted.

The value of plant food in sustaining a hunting population during periods when meat is in short supply, and the value of invertebrates that can be collected by simple methods, for example the crucial use of sea urchins collected in the intertidal zone by Aleuts, cannot be overlooked. It is however the focus on hunting moving game that has organized the structure and functioning of humans, not the casually collected foods.

Washburn has remarked (Washburn and Avis, 1958, p. 433) that hunting has had three important effects on human behavior and nature: psychological, social, and territorial, and he has summarized by indicating that after bipedalism came the use of tools, the hunting habit, increase in intelligence and, finally, the animal we know as man (p. 435). This is a coherent and synoptic view which is well documented. However, the priority of the hunting habit before the use of tools should be considered as a necessary sequence. Bipedalism was a necessary precondition, but at least two apparently well differentiated species, *Australopithecus robustus* and *A. africanus*, and possibly a third, "Homo habilis," to use the names of three groups of uncertain taxonomic status, were bipedal, and only one appears to have continued along the line leading into man. The possibility that desiccation led to a dietary change requiring carnivorism for the Australopithecines is well known, and the possibility that *A. robustus* remained primarily a vegetarian and became extinct is equally well known. The archeological evidence is ambiguous and whether both of these lines used tools and made tools is uncertain. If *A. robustus* was a vegetarian, it is difficult to imagine what he was doing with tools. On the other hand, tools became useful to a bipedal hunter because they do facilitate killing and the reduction of the dead animal for food and fabricational purposes.

Dental morphology is of little help. Gorillas have very large canines and high cusps compared to humans, and they are vegetarian. Humans can and do eat everything from leaves to meat and bones with no detectable correlation between the diet and their dental morphology. In fact, humans the world over promptly remove their cusps and fissural patterns by normal attrition during childhood so that it is difficult to find a readable fissural pattern in an adult male or female primitive. Chipped teeth are found in Eskimos and in Aleuts, in keeping with their extensive chewing on bones and bone splinters, and the use of their teeth for fabricational purposes. Deducing what humans have eaten with their teeth is comparable to deducing what they have held in their prehensile hand.

At what point in the continuous line leading to man we choose to apply the label *human* is subjective in the extreme. Because of the necessity of childhood instruction for hunting, the overall integration of posture, vision, hand, communication, and brain required for hunting behavior, I would suggest that this was the crucial adaptation and therefore provides a meaningful criterion for so labeling the organism who had achieved this level of organization.

Conclusions and Summary

The overall evolutionary efficacy of hunting as a master integrating pattern of our species is illustrated in many ways. Man successfully evolved with a simple technology over hundreds of thousands of years; he migrated into all the continents and climes; he solved all the local problems of adaptation with ingenuity and inventiveness. These feats are climaxed by the relative rapidity with which he developed civilizations and, equally important, that he as a hunter was converted to civilized man independently in different continents. He was obviously preadapted and even predisposed to civilization.

The inherent ingenuity of primitive hunters, of marginal peoples generally, can be attested by citing inventions and by examining the great heterogeneity of marginal peoples (Lowie, 1952). It is commonplace to cite the inventions of various peoples, but I think it more instructive to assemble them within the context of an historical tradition rather than cut across cultures gleaning exotic examples. Two points of interest result: the inventions listed are confined almost entirely to material devices and particular peoples have been more inventive than is generally appreciated. The kayak with three-piece keelson of the Aleuts, the snow dome house of the Arctic Eskimos, the double-purchase pulley, screw-thread, slit goggle, visor, three-legged stool, etc., of the Aleut-Eskimo stock is matched by their development of human anatomical knowledge, their knowledge of natural phenomena, prominently including animal behavior, and by their systems of navigation on sea and land. Goggles and stools are well known, however; the non-material inventions are not. The material things remain clever devices until the intellectual context of their invention and use is comprehended. Where primitive hunters have not invented material devices that capture the attention of observers, they are less often credited with inventiveness and their knowledge in those areas in which they invested their time and interest is underestimated.

The psychological differences between hunters contrasted with farmers and livestock breeders has properly been emphasized (Clark and Piggott, 1965, pp. 157-59). However, it should be noted that primitive hunters domesticated the dog, probably more than once, and this may have provided a model for the domestication of other animals. As I have suggested previously, hunters capture animals for use as pets and a major use is the instruction of children in animal behavior. Domestication of the dog ranks as a great achievement in the investigation of wolf behavior and subsequently in animal breeding.

The theory of cultural advance offered by Ginsburg and Laughlin (1966), suggesting that crossing the biobehavioral threshold leading to civilization depended upon the important ingredient of assortative mating tracks within large populations, is an explanation of how existing variability can be recombined and repackaged without the addition of new genetic materials or of outside intervention.

Man's life as a hunter supplied all the other ingredients for achieving civilization: the genetic variability, the inventiveness, the systems of vocal communication, the coordination of social life. It could not provide the large and dense population size nor the internal genetic restructuring attendant upon the establishment of assortative mating tracks whereby the frequency of matings between persons sharing culturally defined interests and talents could be maximized. The basic anatomical structure, the neurophysiological processes, and the basic patterns of behavior had been so successfully organized and integrated by the attention given to the lifelong study of behavior and anatomy and the other portions of the total sequence pattern that rapid and extensive changes could take place. While learning to learn, man, the hunter, was learning animal behavior and anatomy, including his own. He domesticated himself first and then turned to other animals and to plants. In this sense, hunting was the school of learning that made the human species self-taught.

In the final analysis we return to the informational requirements of the hunting system for the development of the individual. Hunting must be learned by children and the children must learn by observation and by participation the habit of critical observation, the facts concerning animal behavior, and the appropriate responses. It is insufficient to tell children about animal behavior and anatomy; it must be programmed into them in a far more integrated fashion. A corollary point which applies to hunting groups and their history clearly is that a simple technology does not indicate simplemindedness. We know a good deal about the magnitude of the task accomplished with simple tools, the hundreds of thousands of years of successful human evolution. We know therefore that the major information investment went into the nervous system and the non-material aspects of the highly adaptive hunting cultures.

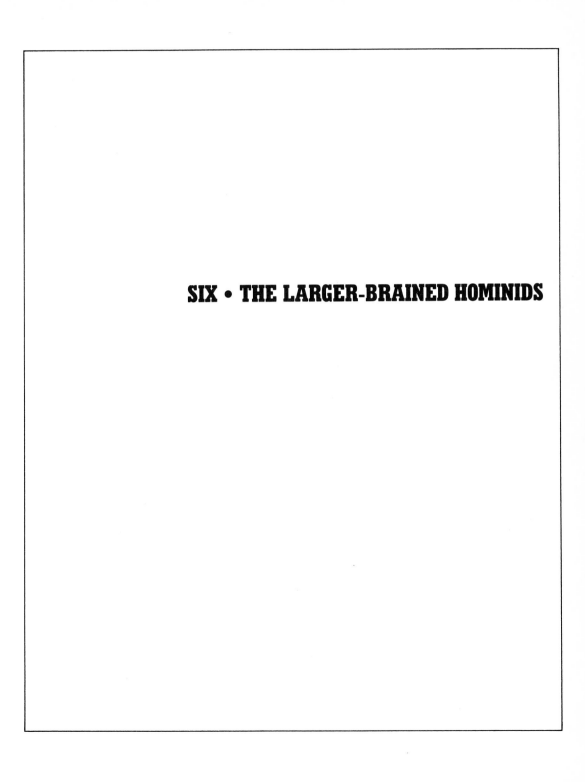

SIX • THE LARGER-BRAINED HOMINIDS

10 • MIDDLE AND LATER PLEISTOCENE HOMINIDS

D. R. Pilbeam

Today we are in possession of a great many more fossil remains of prehistoric man, his artifacts, and knowledge of his chronologic and ecologic horizons, than was the case only a generation ago. This is especially true of Middle and Upper Pleistocene hominids. There is, in fact, a bewildering number of such relics and a great deal of information about them scattered throughout a very large number of different sources. We are, therefore, fortunate to have made available to us a succinct account of these in Dr. Pilbeam's contribution, extracted from his book *The Evolution of Man* (1970).

Rich as this material is it is quite clear that it is not rich enough to enable us to do more than speculate upon the interrelationships which undoubtedly exist between the various forms represented. It is equally evident that many forms are at present unknown and that there is a great need for long extended field trips to promising areas of the world in search of such material.

A large proportion of the finds of prehistoric man were made by happy accident, but there are outstanding examples, from Dubois (1891) and his discovery of *"Pithecanthropus"* (*Homo erectus*) to the Leakeys' discoveries in 1959 and onwards in Olduvai Gorge, which were based on evidence that suggested that if one would seek, one would find. The faith of such seekers has yielded a rich harvest of prehistoric remains, and told us much about our ancestors and their ways of life.[1]

As we see the picture of man's evolutionary relationships in the Middle and Upper Pleistocene, it resembles more than anything else a four-dimensional reticulum with a great many of the threads or struts comprising it altogether missing or else only partly represented. Out of this amalgam of bits and pieces we must make what we can, and to that end Dr. Pilbeam's contribution will be found to be most helpful.

Man's Recent Ancestors

Middle Pleistocene hominids are quite widely distributed throughout the Old World, and are found in Asia as well as Africa. The tools made by middle Pleistocene men broadly resemble those of the early Pleistocene although tool types became more refined and more standardized. In Africa, Europe and western Asia a new type of tool, the hand-axe, appears during this time to join the array of 'pebble-tools.' The appearance of this tool—probably not actually an axe but a digging or scraping tool—may have been due to the invention in certain areas of a particular technique, the ability (according to Glynn Isaac) to strike flakes greater than ten centimeters in length as the raw blanks of future hand-axes. So the presence or absence of hand-axes need not imply anything particularly profound about behavioural changes.

The first middle Pleistocene hominids were recovered by Eugene Dubois in eastern central Java in the late nineteenth century. He named his material *Pithecanthropus erectus* in 1891. Subsequently these hominids have been transferred to

SOURCE: David Pilbeam, *The Evolution of Man* (New York: Funk and Wagnalls, 1970), pp. 169–94. Copyright © 1970 by David Pilbeam. Reprinted by permission of the publisher.

[1] For a good general survey of this material see John E. Pfeiffer, *The Emergence of Man* (New York: Harper & Row, 1972), and Bernard Campbell, *Human Evolution* (Chicago: Aldine, 1966).

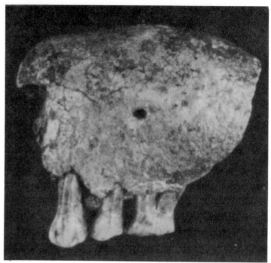

Figure 2: The Meganthropus mandibular fragment found in Java in 1939 by G. H. R. von Koenigswald.

Figure 1: Early Palaeolithic flint hand-axe from the Thames Valley, probably less an axe than a digging and scraping tool. Trustees of the British Museum (Natural History).

our own genus to become *Homo erectus,* although they are still occasionally called 'pithecanthropines,' an unfortunate colloquial term. The fact that this species was first recovered from Asian deposits, and only later from Africa, should not lead to the belief that it was an Asian species which spread to Africa!

Java Man

The Javanese so-called middle Pleistocene sequence consists of two sets of deposits containing similar but distinct faunas. The earlier fauna found in beds on various parts of the island is termed the Djetis; the later, the Trinil. Attempts have been made to correlate these in European terms, but such efforts have been to little avail, since the European earlier middle Pleistocene is so poorly understood. Absolute dates from Java are fairly good; there is a K/A date of 0.5 million years from close to the top of Trinil age beds, and a date

of 0.7 million years for the bottom. The Djetis age beds are probably approaching 1 million years old. In terms of the important East African sequence, the Djetis and Trinil faunas cover approximately the upper parts of Bed II at Olduvai; that is, they may well run back to the end of the early Pleistocene as defined in East Africa.

Rather than discussing finds in the order of their discovery, I prefer to list them stratigraphically from oldest to youngest. A mandible fragment found before the last war by Professor von Koenigswald comes from beds of Djetis age. It was described originally as *Meganthropus palaeojavanicus* because of its massive construction and great size. It has been interpreted variously as a *Paranthropus robustus* (by Robinson), as a large *Homo erectus* (by Le Gros Clark), and it has been compared with Olduvai Bed I hominid 7 (by Tobias and von Koenigswald). These disagreements actually underline the very great dental and mandibular similarities between all these groups. The find could be similar to the Olduvai specimens and still represent a somewhat earlier stage than the first (Trinil) *Homo erectus*. I pre-

Figure 3: The Modjokerto infant skull (*Homo erectus*), found in Java in 1936 in a bed of Pleistocene sands and marine sediments.

fer to classify it with *Homo erectus* for the moment, at least until the skull is known. The skulls which are known from the Djetis levels are clearly *Homo erectus*. A small skull from an individual of less than 5 or 6 years (perhaps as young as 2 or 3 years) already shows the beginnings of brow ridges, marked post-orbital constrictions, and a projecting occipital region. As an adult, its brain volume could hardly have exceeded 800 c.c.

Parts of an adult skull are also known from this level. The back of a skull plus parts of the face and most of the upper teeth have been restored by von Koenigswald using other Javanese material to produce a very reasonable reconstruction. A mandible, although not associated with the skull, comes from the same deposits and is similar enough to be considered as part of the same individual. This composite specimen is the one compared by Tobias and von Koenigswald with hominid 13 from Olduvai. The dentitions are very similar as I have already described, and the gap between them is nicely filled by hominid 16 from Olduvai. The Javanese skull, however, is long and low with large brow ridges. The bones of the braincase are very thick indeed, much thicker than in the earlier East and South African

hominids. There are quite marked contrasts in shape between hominid 13 and the *Homo erectus* skull. The skull volumes are a little different, 620 c.c. for the Olduvai form and 750 c.c. for the Javanese. The Olduvai hominid 16 skull is of 640 c.c. and in shape again fills the gap between the two, although like hominid 13 it is still thin-walled. The principal differences between these *A. africanus* (? *A. habilis*) and *H. erectus* are due to the fact that the *H. erectus* skull is longer and hence (because the brain is still small) lower. It is broader too and so is the palate. Because the skull is long and low the forehead is flatter, the brow ridges more pronounced, and the occipital angulated instead of evenly rounded. All these features may be due to the fact that the *H. erectus* brains grew with the bigger stature of the Javanese men, producing a clear change in skull shape as the relative proportions of the cranium changed. Increases in size generally involve changes in shape and this must not be forgotten (note for example the contrasts between the shape of male and female baboon skulls). Although the exact stature of the earliest Javanese hominids is unknown, they were probably taller than *A. africanus*. So the Olduvai skulls could theoretically represent a state ancestral to *Homo erectus* before these increases in body size. The transition between the stages was nevertheless complex.

The first finds of *Homo erectus* made by Dubois came from the Trinil zone and consisted of a skull cap and a femur. The skull cap is primitive in morphology and barely larger than those from Djetis beds. When first found, it was considered to be an excellent missing link between men and apes. Now, of course, it is known that this individual is millions of years separated from its ape ancestors, and that it really is pointless to talk in those terms. The femur resembles closely that of a modern man of average height. The femur came from an individual 5 foot 7 inches at least, and one perfectly adapted to upright walk-

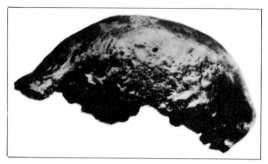

Figure 4: The skull cap found by Eugene Dubois at Trinil, Java, in 1891.

ing. At first there was some argument as to whether this femur represented *Homo sapiens* living alongside *Homo erectus,* or perhaps came from later beds. As with the South African early hominids, there was a great reluctance to associate man-like limbs with primitive skulls. However, chemical tests have shown that the femur and the skull are contemporaneous, and five more femora were found in Dubois' collections showing that the original was no aberration. Without doubt skulls and limbs are associated. Several other skulls from the Trinil levels confirm the general morphology—long, low skulls with big brow ridges and projecting occipital regions. The Trinil skulls vary in volume from 775 to 975 c.c., and appear to be a little larger on average than those from the Djetis. I have already mentioned changes in skull shape from the A. *africanus* stage. Since the brain does not overgrow the orbits—because the whole face is large and projecting—the frontal bone is very flat, and large brow ridges surmount the eyes.

The increase in body size over early Pleistocene hominids is quite marked; from something around 4 feet to 4 feet 6 inches, to an average of more than 5 feet 6 inches (at least for males). As I mentioned, this may account for at least some of the increase in brain size.

All these Javanese specimens are more than 0.5 million years old and may be older than 0.6 or

0.7 million years. A fossil skull and jaw are known from about the same time level in northwest China, from Lantien. The deposits are said to be equivalent to the Djetis levels. The skull is small and primitive like *Homo erectus* from Java; the cranial capacity is only 780 c.c. The mandible is interesting in that there is no evidence at all of the third molar, the first recorded case of a condition which is becoming increasingly frequent in *Homo sapiens.*

Pekin Man

Much more complete and better known fossils come from northeast China, near Pekin, at Choukoutien. From 1921 onwards a large number of fossil skulls were recovered there. These were lost during the war—a terrible tragedy—although fortunately good casts still exist. Remains were recovered of some 16 skulls in varying states of preservation, a dozen or so mandibles, many teeth, and some limb bones. Originally these specimens were described as *Sinanthropus pekinensis.* Later it was realized that they represented a subspecies of the same species as the Javanese forms and so were reclassified as *Pithecanthropus pekinensis.* Finally, when the name *Pithecanthropus* was dispensed with, they became *Homo erectus pekinensis.*

The skulls have large projecting faces and moderate brow ridges. They are long and still rather low, although not so low as the Lantian or Java skulls. The occiput is less sharply angled too. Altogether the skulls are filled out more, because the brain volume was larger than in the skulls we previously discussed. Seven tolerably complete skulls show that the volume ranged from at least 850 to 1300 c.c., and one would expect larger samples to show a larger range. The average is around 1050 c.c. The skeletal material is not particularly extensive but what is known does not differ significantly from modern

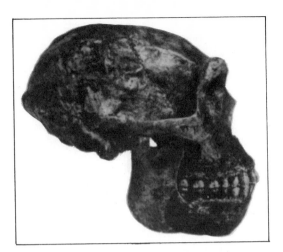

Figure 5: Skull of Java man (*Homo erectus*). This reconstruction by von Koenigswald is based on fossil remains found in the Djetis strata at Sangiran in the 1930's. In most respects except size the teeth resemble those of modern man.

man. Individuals may have been somewhat smaller than the Javanese forms.

Dating Choukoutien is a little difficult. No rocks suitable for absolute dating are known, but if long range correlations are tentatively ac-

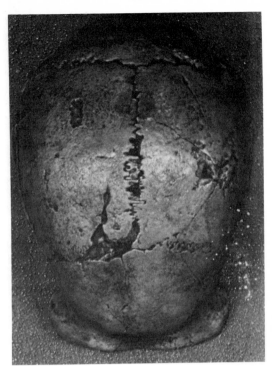

Figure 7: Right: skull cap of Pekin man.

cepted, the deposits appear to fit into the European sequence at approximately the beginning of the Mindel glaciation. Dating this in a European context is difficult, but an age of at least 0.4 to 0.5 million years would not be far off the mark.

A great deal of evidence from Choukoutien shows that *Homo erectus* ate vegetable as well as animal food and was a very successful big-game hunter. From Choukoutien too come signs of the [early] use of fire, used no doubt both for cooking food and for warming bodies. Dr. Edmund Leach has this to say about cooking:

It isn't a biological necessity that you should cook food, it is a custom, a symbolic act, a piece of magic which transforms the substance and removes the contamination of 'otherness.' Raw food is dirty and dangerous; cooked food is clean and safe. So already, even at the very beginning, man somehow saw himself as 'other' than nature. The cooking

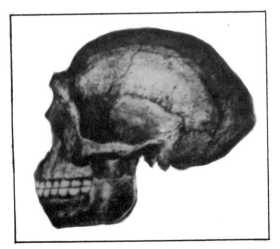

Figure 6: Skull of Pekin man (also *Homo erectus*), as restored by P. Weidenreich—an adult female example. Trustees of the British Museum (Natural History).

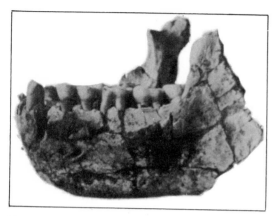

Figure 8: Ternifine I, one of three mandibles found at Ternifine, Algeria, in 1954. Of an adult, probably male, it is nevertheless remarkable for its size and robustness, and bears a strong resemblance to mandibles found at Choukoutien.

of food is both an assertion of this otherness and a means of getting rid of the anxiety which otherness generates.

The *Homo erectus* specimens from Asia cover a fair period of time, from about 1 million years for the Lantien and Djetis level specimens, through 0.7 million for the Trinil, to about 0.5 million for Choukoutien. There appears to have been some evolution during this time, particularly in brain size, the average of which creeps up steadily from 700 or 800 c.c. to over 1000 c.c. These eastern forms are associated with pebble-type tools; hand-axes do not appear in this area or do so only sporadically. The Asian *Homo erectus* fossils are sampled from two closely related subspecies.

At approximately the same time in Africa, similar types of men were living. From Ternifine in Algeria have come three mandibles which resemble those from Choukoutien. A parietal bone is similar too, down to the markings left on the internal side by the arteries supplying the blood to the outside of the brain. These finds are associated with early hand-axes and a fauna like that

Figure 9: Olduvai hominid 9 skull fragment. Despite the very prominent brow ridges, it, also, is basically similar to Asian examples of *Homo erectus*.

of upper Bed II at Olduvai. A cranium of *Homo erectus* (hominid 9) has been found at Olduvai in upper Bed II. The cranial volume is 1000 c.c., like that at Choukoutien. The skull is long and low, with a projecting occipital. Although basically similar to the Asian *Homo erectus*, the African forms do show a few differences. For example, the Olduvai skull has enormous, thick projecting brow ridges, bigger than can be found in men from Choukoutien, and much more similar to some later African hominids.

This emphasizes two points. At this particular time all populations however widely distributed seem to be quite closely connected genetically; they apparently represent subspecies within a single species. But populations also show continuity and connections through time with other populations. Earlier African populations are therefore likely to contribute more genes to later ones than are earlier, or later, Asian populations. Therefore, earlier Africans are likely to resemble later African ones more closely than are early Asians. At any one time level, all hominids within a species are more or less similar to each other, yet there are also lineal similarities within a particular area (as we have already seen at Olduvai, and also in Java). Carleton Coon has called these 'grade' and 'line' similarities respectively.

In the earlier part of the middle Pleistocene,

up to about 0.5 million years ago, primitive members of *Homo* are found in Africa and Asia. They might well have originated in either continent. It would probably be a mistake to think of their origin as occurring in a small restricted area; it would have been considerably more widespread.

What about this origin, presumably from early Pleistocene *A. africanus* stock of South, East and North African deposits? Dr. Leakey believes that the early hominids at Olduvai have nothing at all to do with *H. erectus*, but rather evolved directly into *H. sapiens*, presumably in East Africa. I think it would be a mistake to envisage such highly localized evolution. Unfortunately, we do not have sufficient samples from the various sub-species which must have existed during early and middle Pleistocene time. If we did have more material we could sort out our grade and line relationships, unravel evolution within subspecific lineages, and tie these lineages into the fabric of one species.

Choosing for the moment the simpler hypothesis, let us assume that most early Pleistocene forms had delicate, rounded skulls, large dentitions, and a stature of no more than 4 feet 6 inches or so. Let us also assume that the middle Pleistocene hominids were in general a foot taller; with larger brains; thicker, longer, lower, skulls; and somewhat smaller dentitions. The transition between these two average, or 'polar' types could be tied in with a general increase in body size, for what reason is not known. (There does seem to be a general increase in size of other mammals at this time.) It is obviously necessary to draw a 'species' boundary between the two segments of this single but complex bundle of subspecific lineages. If problems in naming are to be avoided the boundary has to be a 'horizontal'-time boundary. Inevitably, though, the latest *A. africanus* will resemble the earliest *H. erectus* more than either will resemble the 'average' of either 'species' (if indeed these two groups form an ancestor-descendant series).

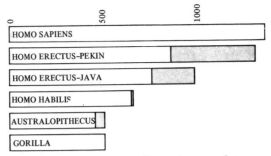

Figure 10: Mean brain volumes (measured in c.c. of the gorilla and modern man compared with estimated brain volumes of some fossil hominids.

The trends within this lineage are interesting. There is the increase in body size and the final adjustments in locomotor behaviour. These changes would have increased greatly the potential mobility of individuals and bands, expanding the area they covered, and extending the range of game they could hunt. The first increases in brain size in *H. erectus* could be correlated with these body-size changes, but later there is clearly change in relative size too, probably due to increased size and complexity of nerve cells as well as to increases in their numbers. Teeth and faces seem to shrink a little during this time. Behavioural changes are also apparent. At least some *H. erectus* populations invented hand-axes, and tools were becoming in general more refined and more standardized. Presumably, social and individual behaviour was developing too; perhaps speech was becoming more important. The invention of fire-use, although useful for providing warmth and protection, indicates too that great conceptual and communicative strides had been made in the recognition for men that man was different and apart from other animals. Some would argue that this would only be possible after the appearance of language.

During the remainder of the Pleistocene hominids ever more similar to ourselves emerge. Modern features seem to appear at different rates at different times in different places. The most gen-

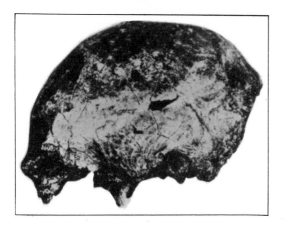

Figure 11: Solo skull (number 6), among Neanderthaloid remains found at Ngandong, central Java, 1931–3.

eral trend is one of increasing brain size, from the later *H. erectus* average of about 1000 c.c. to the modern average of 1300 to 1400 c.c. The jaws and teeth, in general, get smaller still. Now there are two ways of coping with an enlarging brain. You can dispose of it as a long, low, broad package, in which case the surrounding skull will also be long, with brow ridges, sloping frontal and projecting occipital region. Alternatively, the same volume can be squeezed into a higher, shorter, narrower space. In this case the brain comes to overlay the orbits and the skull is shaped then like that of modern man, with vaulted frontals showing small or almost non-existent brow ridges and an evenly curved occipital. Along with this shape goes a chin on the lower jaw, to buttress the tooth row during chewing. These two alternatives represent on the one hand earlier and more primitive subspecies of *H. sapiens,* and on the other, later modern types (known now as *H. sapiens sapiens*).

Carleton Coon claims to be able to recognize the crossing of the *erectus/sapiens* 'boundary' (which is of course entirely arbitrary) by noting certain cranial features; namely, brain size, the shape and relative proportions of various skull

bones, and so on. All these features are, of course, variable within as well as between populations. Theoretically one could find '*erectus*' skulls as defined in this sense alongside '*sapiens*' skulls, although they would belong to one and the same population. Therefore they could only have one name. If hominids during the middle and later parts of the Pleistocene formed a single species, only one name can be used for any one time. If you start with *erectus* and wish to end with *sapiens,* the transition zone has to have a line drawn through it somewhere. I shall discuss the 'somewhere' later on. First, however, I want to discuss later Pleistocene hominids in various parts of the Old World.

Solo Man

An excellent sample of fossil men has been recovered from the Solo River in Java. The beds have a late Pleistocene fauna known as the Ngandong, the absolute age of which is unknown. A fair estimate would place it within the last 250,000 years, possibly around 150,000 years ago, although even this is a guess. The hominid population represented is advanced compared to the earlier *H. erectus* from Java, although its general aspect is primitive. Eleven skulls and two bits of limb bone are known in all. The average brain volume is a little over 1000 c.c. and the face, brow ridges, and occipital region are all still prominent. The Solo population has been described as 'tropical Neanderthalers,' but this is rather like calling living Javanese 'tropical Europeans!' What is really meant is that they have big faces, brow ridges, and so on. The word 'Neanderthaler' is being used here in a descriptive sense. I prefer to use the adjective 'neanderthaloid' to refer to those later Pleistocene post-*erectus* populations that show the characters listed above, other than the Neanderthals proper. These Javanese fossil men were sampled from a population which is broadly contemporary with other similar men from different subspecies in adjacent parts of Asia, Europe and Africa.

Modern-looking *H. s. sapiens* may have appeared in this area as long ago as 40,000 years, at Niah in Borneo; the date, based on a C 14 determination, could be wrong, however. The Niah skull is thought to be from a population related in some way to the now-extinct Tasmanians. It seems rather unlikely that Solo population evolved into Niah types. But Professor MacIntosh of Sydney University who has done much valuable modern work on early Aboriginal skeletons from Australia believes that he can show some continuity from Solo types through to the living Aboriginals. Speculating from quite inadequate data, this looks rather as though we have a combination of local evolution from *erectus* to modern *sapiens,* through a neanderthaloid phase, coupled with migration of modern *sapiens* into the area, and a subsequent fusion with the more archaic indigenous types. Clearly, in this case the modern and archaic populations would have to be classified in the same species, *Homo sapiens sapiens* (modern) and *H. s. soloensis* (archaic). Whence came the migrants is unknown.

In China a continuous sequence from *erectus* to *sapiens* can be traced, but alternatively it could be argued that successively younger and more advanced specimens represent migrants from some other area. The samples are simply too small.

We are better off, however, in North Africa where there is continuity between *H. erectus* and neanderthaloid populations of *H. sapiens.* The material is practically confined to jaws and teeth and the main trends in these portions of the skeleton are towards smaller size and involve subtle changes in morphology.

Rhodesia Man

South of the Sahara is also a story of continuity through to late Pleistocene time. One popula-

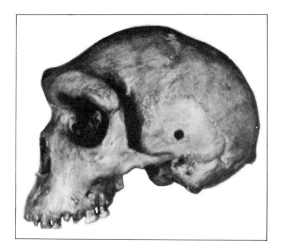

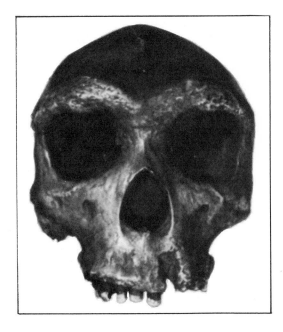

Figure 12: Views of the Neanderthaloid skull of Rhodesian man, found at Broken Hill, Zambia (then Northern Rhodesia), 1921. The brow ridges are more massive than in any other known human skull. Trustees of the British Museum (Natural History).

tion in the southern half of Africa is represented by several skulls; from Saldanha in South Africa and Broken Hill in Zambia (some 40,000 to 50,000 years old), as well as other fragmentary remains. Like the Solo group this sample can be described as neanderthaloid. They have brain volumes well within the modern range (1250 to 1300 c.c. for the fossils), yet the skulls are long, faces are large with inflated nasal regions, and brow ridges are exceptionally thick and projecting. The similarity between the Olduvai Bed II *H. erectus* (hominid 9) and the Broken Hill skull is very obtrusive, and they are almost certainly sampled from a single subspecific lineage which must have evolved slowly in Southern Africa for half a million years or more. The fate of these neanderthaloids (called *H. sapiens rhodesiensis* from the original species name of Broken Hill man) is uncertain. Some workers believe they became extinct without issue; Professor Tobias believes that they may have evolved into Bushmen; while Carleton Coon prefers to connect them with the Negroes. Dr. Don Brothwell thinks of them as a line which became extinct, but not without some hybridizing with intrusive modern populations. This last alternative is perhaps closest to the truth, and resembles the most probable sequence of events in southeast Asia. But we still have to explain the evolution of the invading modern populations, for as Professor Tobias has said of earlier attempts to unravel African evolution, 'It was enough to remove the birth of a race to far-off places—and then it became the responsibility of the unfortunate colleagues in those places to worry about how the race had in fact come into being!' The African evidence does point quite clearly to at least some local evolution, and also to mixing on the sort of scale which implies that subspecies rather than species were involved.

There is also some very tantalizing evidence of modern-looking men from Kanjera in Kenya.

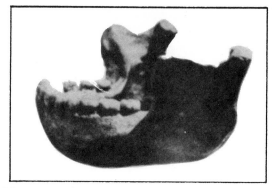

Figure 13: The Heidelberg mandible, found in the Rosch sandpit, near Mauer, 1907.

Fragments of at least three individuals, perhaps more, were found there by Dr. Leakey in 1932. A few pieces were *in situ* but most were on the surface. The age of these finds has been debated vigorously; but if we ignore the many 'ifs' involved, it can be put back to at least 60,000 years ago. Professor Tobias has recently re-examined these specimens and finds them fully modern. They have delicate facial regions and vaulted frontals with no brow ridges. The skulls are longish and lowish, but modern in outline. What can be said about these finds? If only the function of brow ridges and big faces were fully understood it would be possible to say something; but until their reduction can be explained, as well as the apparently associated changes in the braincase, we can only grope in the dark. Are these modern-looking skulls genetically related to much later ones? Or do we have (as seems unlikely) parallel evolution? What relationship does the Kanjera sample have to the archaic *H. s. rhodesiensis*? Was there a great deal of variability in skull form during the latter Pleistocene of Africa, so that the average morphology of certain populations gradually shifted through time from archaic to modern? Until there are better samples we shall not even know how typical these skulls are of the population from which they came.

Neanderthal Man in Europe

At this juncture we might shift our attention to Europe for a brief discussion of the Neanderthal problem—brief because Europe is a relatively small part of the total area in which hominids were living and should therefore not be given undue importance. It is quite possible that the earliest occupancy of Europe was during the Villafranchian, but fossil men are not known before the middle Pleistocene. The earliest human fossil from Europe is the lower jaw from Mauer, near Heidelberg, in Germany, recovered in 1907. The age is either inter-Mindel or just pre-Mindel and the absolute date is probably over 400,000 years. The jaw shows some similarities to Asian *H. erectus* and some to later European hominids, both to be expected.

Of rather more interest is a sealed inter-Mindel site at Vertesszöllös in Hungary. The site contains evidence of hominid living-floors, hearths and Oldowan-type tools. The age is around

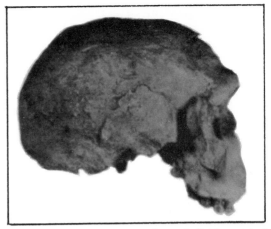

Figure 15: A cast of the Steinheim skull. The original was discovered in the Sigrist gravel pit at Steinheim, near Stuttgart, in 1933.

400,000 years. The hominid fossils include a hominid occipital bone, and a handful of teeth. The teeth show many resemblances to Asian *H. erectus*, while the skull looks more advanced. It comes from a large skull, one with a volume of over 1400 c.c., and is more evenly rounded than *H. erectus* skulls. In this respect it approaches *H. sapiens*. The collection of fossils emphasizes the general similarity of all middle Pleistocene men, but also their variability. In Europe 400,000 years ago, some populations already contained individuals which had big brains and rounded occipitals. These Hungarian specimens are close to any boundary between *erectus* and *sapiens* that could be drawn. The boundary will come therefore around 400,000 years ago. Which side of the boundary they fall does not really matter.

The next hominids from Europe are squarely *H. sapiens*. They come from the Mindel-Riss (or Elster-Saäle) interglacial, and, in all probability, date from about 200,000 years ago. Skulls from Steinheim in Germany and Swanscombe in England are closely similar. They had moderate brain volumes (1200 c.c. or so); skulls were long and low with rounded occipitals. Although claims

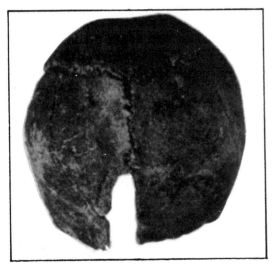

Figure 14: A vertical view of the Swanscombe skull. The first parietal and an occipital were found in the Barnfield gravel pit, at Swanscombe, Kent, in 1936 and 1937; the second parietal was found as recently as 1955. Trustees, British Museum (Natural History).

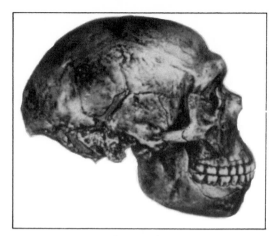

Figure 16: A Neanderthal skull: part of a nearly complete skeleton found in the limestone floor of a cave near the village of La Chapelle-aux-Saints, France.

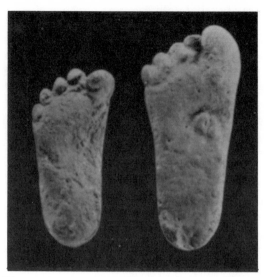

Figure 17: Casts of Neanderthal footprints preserved in the clay of an Italian cave floor.

have been made that they are wholly modern-looking, multivariate analysis has shown that they are relatively primitive and not unlike some later Neanderthalers. The face is known only for the Steinheim skull and is moderately large with quite well developed brow ridges. These men are primitive, or archaic, *Homo sapiens,* though not so primitive as the Solo skulls of the same species, which may be slightly younger than the European finds.

Moving on to the last interglacial, the Eemian, which spans the period between about 70,000 and 100,000 years ago, several fossil men have been found in Europe. The few remains known indicate a fairly homogeneous neanderthaloid population from Italy (Saccopastore) to Germany (Ehringsdorf). In some ways these forms are a little more modern-looking than subsequent European Neanderthals; they have been called the 'early' or 'unspecialized' Neanderthals.

One puzzling set of specimens of this age from Fontéchevade in France has caused a great deal of argument. Parts of a skull cap are primitive and neanderthal; parts of the brow ridge and frontal are advanced and resemble modern man.

Once again we have evidence of great variability —either within or between populations—in late Pleistocene time. The causes and meaning of this variability are unknown. (There is no reason to assume the Fontéchevade and Kanjera material belong to the same population!)

The original (those that were first described) or 'classic' Neanderthalers are known from Western Europe—Spain, France, Germany, Italy and Belgium—and seem to come from a fairly restricted time period, the early part of the last glaciation between 70,000 and about 50,000 years ago. The first adult Neanderthaler was recovered in 1856 from the Neander Valley near Dusseldorf in Germany; this material was known to Darwin. The classic Neanderthals as a group exhibit certain peculiar features. They have large brains (up to 1600 c.c.); large and inflated faces; long, low skulls with projecting occipitals and large brow ridges; long bones with massive joint surfaces; and large, powerful hands. They may be migrants from outside Europe but perhaps more probably they evolved in Europe from a pre-

Würm stock. My own reconstruction of the Ehringsdorf skull (from the Eemian of Germany) makes it appear a great deal less modern and more classic Neanderthal than has been previously thought, and suggests that the Eemian men of Europe were not so very different from classic Neanderthals. Much has been made of the 'ape-like' features of the Neanderthalers. In fact, their ape-like characters are nonexistent. Their supposedly slouching gait was due to the inability of earlier workers to recognize the effects on the skeleton of arthritis! Neanderthal man stood and walked as we do.

In Europe Neanderthals of Eem and Würm age are associated with a complex of industries called the Mousterian. Mousterian industries are found in Eastern Europe, and the contiguous parts of Western Asia, southwestern Asia and North Africa. The Mousterian lasted in Western Europe until around 35,000 to 40,000 years ago, when it was replaced—apparently rather suddenly—by Upper Paleolithic industries. These or related industries are also found outside Western Europe. In the Western regions the transition between Mousterian and Upper Palaeolithic industries is quite abrupt. Fossil men found associated with Upper Palaeolithic industries are similar to modern types. Hence it has been assumed that the break between the industries comes at the same time as a change in human populations, with modern types replacing the Neanderthalers. This traditional view has recently been challenged rather provocatively by Professor C. Loring Brace. As Brace points out, there is no definite evidence that the latest Mousterians in Western Europe were Neanderthals (the youngest of which are around 50,000 years old), nor that the oldest Upper Palaeolithics were *H. s. sapiens* (the oldest known of which in Western Europe being dubiously dated to around 30,000 years). He believes it possible for European Neanderthals to

Figure 18: Site of the discovery of the Tabūn remains on Mount Carmel, Israel. Courtesy of the Israel Department of Antiquities and Museums.

have evolved there into modern types. There probably was some population movement during this time even though the results may not have been quite so drastic as have been imagined. Actually, I think that altogether too much energy has been expended in arguments about Western Europe. Neither the hominids nor the stone tool industries there need necessarily be in any way typical of what was happening in other more important areas.

Mount Carmel Man

Farther east in Europe and the adjacent parts of Asia and Africa, populations similar to the Western Neanderthalers were living during early Würm times. They differ from European men in certain minor ways, and there is some evidence to suggest that local evolution from earlier to modern man did occur in these areas. Perhaps the most interesting area is southwestern Asia and adjacent regions. In the later 1920s and early 1930s a large amount of skeletal material was recovered from Mount Carmel in Israel. The fossil hominids come from two caves and are of two types. The first group comes from Mugharet et Tabūn and is archaic and resembles in some features the Western European Neanderthals—particularly in the post-cranial skeleton. Certain features of skull and teeth also point to ties with Western Europe; however, other characters link these hominids with those living at the same time south of the Sahara in tropical Africa. The Tabūn remains also resemble those from a cave near Shanidar in Iraq. The Israel and Iraq hominids are associated with a variety of the Mousterian industries. I should repeat that they date from the early part of the last glacial (70,000 to 50,000 years ago).

From exactly the same part of the world and, from a similar time, come rather different remains. Hominids with somewhat more modern features are known from Mugharet es-Skūhl on Mount Carmel, and from Djebel Kafzeh in Galilee. Cra-

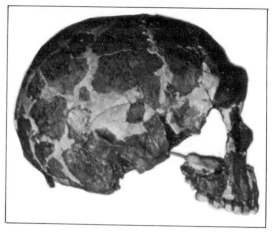

Figure 19: The extensively restored Tabūn skull, that of a Neanderthal woman about 30 years old, unearthed on Mount Carmel in 1931.

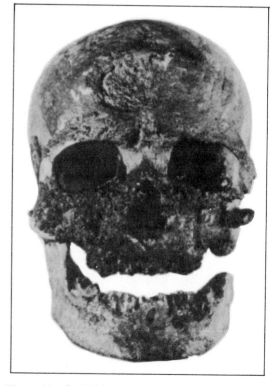

Figure 20: The "Old Man" from Cro-Magnon, France, discovered in 1868. Cro-Magnon man, *Homo sapiens sapiens*, essentially modern man, flourished during the late ice ages.

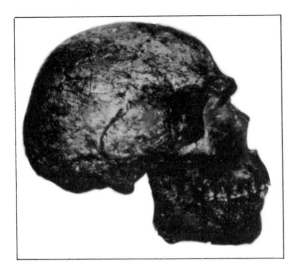

Figure 21: The Skhūl V skull, belonging to one of ten Neanderthal skeletons found buried in the cave Mugharet es-Skhūl on Mount Carmel. Trustees of the British Museum (Natural History).

Figure 22: Early evidence of an elaborate human culture: the ornamented Grimaldi remains, in the Grotte des Enfants, Monaco, probably of a mother and her teen-age son.

nially and post-cranially these men differ from the neanderthaloids of the same area, and they differ in a modern direction. Yet they are clearly related to the Neanderthaloids, and seem to represent at this time no more than different subspecies within a species. This population—or populations—probably represents the ancestors of modern *H. sapiens* in this particular area, as well as in Europe. I suspect that the as yet unknown ancestors of other, non-European, *H. s. sapiens* were living elsewhere in Africa, India and perhaps Asia, at the same time.

Fully modern skull-types first appear spasmodically in the fossil record about 50,000 or more years ago. After this, their frequency increases until whole populations and groups of populations are modern-looking. The reasons for the transformation and for the spread of modern types are as yet largely unknown. Another book would be needed to describe the origin and spread of *H. s. sapiens*, so complex is the story. A few workers, Dr. Leakey among them, believe that *H. erectus* and archaic subspecies of *H. sapiens* are side branches of human evolution and argue that the small, gracile, early Pleistocene hominids evolved directly into modern-looking men without passing through a heavy-skulled, big-browed phase. This argument is a little implausible mainly because of lack of supporting fossil evidence. It also appears unlikely that more than one species of man existed during the middle or late Pleistocene, so extensive would have been the ecological niche occupied by large-brained, cultural, tool-making hominids. Finally, the roundness and gracility of early Pleistocene skulls is probably due to their smallness and delicate construction and need imply no special relationship with *H. s. sapiens*.

Since the middle Pleistocene, the evidence points fairly firmly to the existence at any one time of just one species of hominid within the genus *Homo*. As successively younger fossils are examined, the morphology of hominids is seen to approach ever more closely that of ourselves; their stone tool cultures do likewise. We are dealing, then, with animals which are becoming more and more like us. During this entire time all men were living as hunter-gatherers. Only some 10,000 years ago were certain technological discoveries made which permitted the change to a settled, urban way of life which in turn brought with it great increases in population density, and the subsequent tremendous improvements (mostly in the last 100 years) in our technological prowess. Of course, these changes are all cultural changes, depending upon learned behaviour rather than upon any evolution of the brain. The detectable evolution of the brain and of genetically-determined behaviour, moulded by millions of years of hunting, tool-using behaviour ceased 50,000 or more years ago.

11 • WHERE AND WHEN DID MAN BECOME WISE?

Don R. Brothwell

The question of the origin and antiquity of neanthropic man, that is to say, man of modern type as represented by all the living varieties of mankind, has been answered in one way or another by most authorities: modern man or man of neanthropic type, *Homo sapiens sapiens*, represents the culmination of a more or less straight-line (orthogenetic) development from the well-known fossil forms, either through or bypassing Neanderthal man. Many authorities believe that Neanderthal man was exterminated by neanthropic man. Others believe that Neanderthal man gave rise to neanthropic man, and a few credit the reverse. Some have thought that both types represent separate lineages.[1] Whether one gave rise to the other, or when or where, remains a problem for future solution.

The general opinion on neanthropic man is that he represents the latest, that is, most recent of the forms of man to have evolved. But there have always been a few who have questioned that assumption, and fossil finds made in recent years tend to reinforce their doubts. The brief account and discussion by Brothwell of these finds, and their relevance for a re-evaluation of the antiquity, origin, and relationships of neanthropic man will give the student a much-needed perspective which is not generally offered upon this subject.

The neanderthaloid Tabūn remains and the sapiens remains from Skhūl at Mount Carmel in Jordan have been interpreted by some authorities as representing evidence of admixture between a neanderthaloid and a sapiens type. Brothwell refers to the fact that these finds do not have to be regarded as contemporary since Higgs has shown that they are probably separated from one another by several thousand years.[2] This fact should not make much difference. There can remain very little doubt as to the considerable antiquity of neanthropic man, or of his

---

[1] For a critical discussion of these various viewpoints see C. Loring Brace, "The Fate of the 'Classic' Neanderthals: A Consideration of Hominid Catastrophism." *Current Anthropology,* vol. 5, 1964, pp. 3–43. Ashley Montagu, "Neanderthal and the Modern Type of Man," *American Journal of Physical Anthropology,* vol. 10, 1952, pp. 1–3.

[2] E. S. Higgs, "Some Pleistocene Faunas of the Mediterranean Coastal Areas." *Proceedings of the Prehistoric Society,* XXVII (1961), 144.

rough contemporaneity with Neanderthal man. The possibility of hybridization between neanderthaloid and sapiens ancestors of these later forms still exists.

Niah man, described here by Brothwell, dated some 40,000 years before the present, is in every way a neanthropic type. For an account of Niah man see Tom Harrisson, "The Great Cave of Niah," *Man,* vol. 57, no. 211 (1957); D. R. Brothwell, "Upper Pleistocene Human Skull from Niah Caves, Sarawak," *Sarawak Museum Journal,* IX (1961), 323.

Some biologists and anthropologists have attempted to split man into more than one species. There is, nevertheless, general agreement that all modern varieties should be regarded as one—*Homo sapiens,* or 'man the wise.' This species represents what is as yet the most advanced degree of evolution in terms of brain development—involving the ability to learn and to transmit information, and a capacity for 'original thought.' Moreover the various attempts that have been made to discredit Negroes, Australian aborigines and certain other human groups, alleging that they have an inferior mental capacity, have no sound scientific basis.

It would appear that man's present mental ability was established many thousands of years ago. But when and where did he attain his status as *sapiens* man?

Determining the beginnings of *H. sapiens* is no easy task—it is just as difficult as bridging the evolutionary gap from fossil ape to man. Although it is necessary to think in terms of a definite change from non-sapiens to *sapiens* man, obviously no clear division can be made. As in the majority of evolutionary changes, the time interval before a noticeable change between the

SOURCE: Don R. Brothwell, "Where and When Did Man Become Wise?" *Science Journal* vol. 24 (1963), 10–14. Reprinted with the permission of the author.

ancestral and evolved group can be detected must be thought of in terms of thousands of years at least. At present it is still debatable which 10,000 years or so was particularly significant for the appearance of *H. sapiens.* Differences of opinion place his arrival between upwards of 60,000 years and only 30,000 years ago, but recent views and new discoveries are throwing much more light on this problem.

The Criteria for 'Wisdom'

In reviewing early *sapiens* man, we must rely almost completely upon fragments of skull—but at least these remains are from one of the most significant areas of the body. Within the geologically short period of two million years the primate (hominid) stem leading to modern man has increased its brain size by approximately 1,000 c.c., so that we now have a brain three times as large as that estimated for our unspecialised late Pliocene/early Pleistocene ancestors. The 'cranial capacity' of a fossil skull is certainly of value in differentiating the earlier phases of human evolution. But during the final 100,000 years the very divergent forms in the Upper Pleistocene period, in particular Rhodesian, Neanderthal and 'Cro-Magnon' man, all have brain capacities well within the range for modern man and in some cases the capacities even exceed those generally found today.

Because of the limited information which can be obtained from the external structure of the brain (as revealed by an internal case of the brain box), attention has been directed towards the positioning and general form of the brain, particularly in the frontal region. Also details of skull change, especially at the frontal bone and face, are valuable differentiating features. It is, of course, one matter to see changes taking place in a fossil series, primate or otherwise, but it is far from an easy matter to know which features are the most significant and so deserve more 'taxonomic weight' than others.

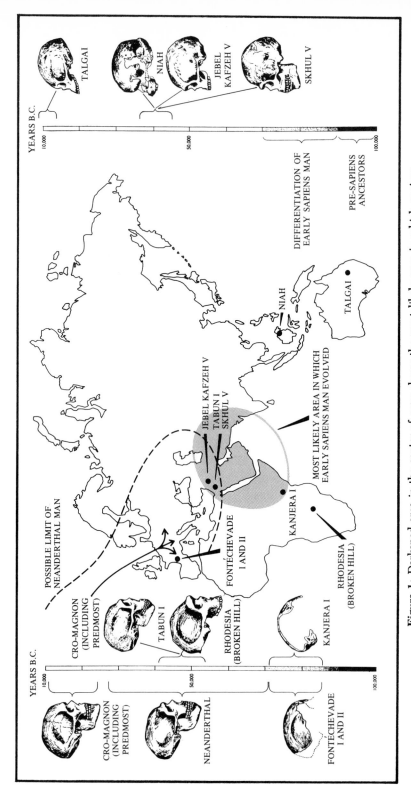

Figure 1: Darkened area in the center of map shows the most likely area in which sapiens man evolved. Time scales on both sides date most of the Upper Pleistocene skulls and place the origin of *Homo sapiens* at about 80,000 B.C.

Bearing this in mind, which fossils may be regarded as contestants for the earliest phases of evolving *Homo sapiens?*

Neanderthal man, the heavy faced, fairly large brained variety of man who spread through Europe, into North Africa, and advanced eastwards at least as far as Uzbekistan in Russia between about 70,000 and 30,000 B.C., was originally considered by some to represent one of modern man's ancestors. But in view of the time period he occupied, and some noticeable skeletal specialisations—such as a very heavy brow ridge—there is increasing opinion that he represents a 'residual,' and to some extent specialised, variety of man, independent for much of his evolution from the developing *H. sapiens* group.

Fontéchevade

The earliest fossil skulls which show a clear division from the Neanderthal form were found at Fontéchevade, Charente, in 1947. The Fontéchevade skull fragments (*see Fig. 1*), recently described in detail by Professor H. V. Vallois of Paris, would appear to date from the Riss-Wurm Interglacial period, and are certainly more than 70,000 years old. The largest skull fragment (No. II) consists of most of the top of the skull vault, but with a little extension down at the brow region. Although the cranial bones were markedly thick, post-mortem pressure had shattered the bones, and accurate restoration has not so far been possible. It would appear, however, from the shape of the frontal area and the positioning of the small area of frontal sinus which remains, that there was a high vault with a fairly vertical forehead. This latter feature is confirmed by the other fragment (No. I) which consists of an area of frontal bone above the nose. If Vallois is correct in saying that this person was a fully adult female, then there can be no doubt that prior to the main spread of Neanderthal man in Europe a group had existed which had the dis-

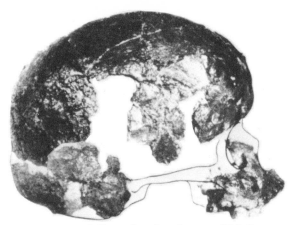

Figure 2: This skull was found in the great Niah Cave in Sarawak and is probably some 40,000 years old. This suggests that modern man had reached southeast Asia at a time when the more robust Neanderthalers still occupied most of Europe.

tinctive features of *sapiens* man—certainly as far as the features of the frontal bone are concerned.

An East African Jigsaw

At the site of Kanjera in Kenya, remains of four skulls were discovered in 1932, and in three of them the absence of heavy brows is noticeable. A new reconstruction by Dr. Bernard Campbell of the most complete specimen is shown in Figure 5—the forehead is clearly vertical but, alas, still looks like an unfinished jigsaw puzzle. There has been much controversy over the date of these fragments, but recent uranium determinations by Dr. Kenneth Oakley support the view that this type of man must have lived in the late Middle or early Upper Pleistocene period. It is thus possible that both in France and East Africa we have *sapiens* man established at least 60 or 70 thousand years ago.

Evidence from Borneo

There now seems little doubt that, by 40,000 years ago, not only had *H. sapiens* become fully differentiated into the varieties we know so well in the Upper Palaeolithic of Europe, but also sufficient time had elapsed for *sapiens* man to have spread into such distant points as south-east Asia. Pioneer work being undertaken in Borneo by Tom Harrisson, Curator of Sarawak Museum, has confirmed this beyond doubt. He has recently undertaken the systematic excavation of the great Niah Cave, Sarawak, resulting in the discovery of numerous skeletons. In February, 1958, at a level which yielded a radio-carbon date for charcoal of 40,000 years, part of a human skull was found. It seems probable that the skull is contemporary with these charcoal remains. This skull, alas somewhat broken and in parts defective, belonged to an ancient Niah individual no more than 17 years of age, as revealed by the degree of dental development and the condition of the 'synchondrosis' at the base of the skull. But the skull shows no close affinities with the Neanderthal group. Moreover, in comparison with the Palaeolithic Talgai skull (*see Fig. 1*) from Australia (which also belonged to a youth of about the same age), it is slenderly built. The Niah skull vault appears smaller, the face less rugged and the jaw and mouth protrude less than those of the Talgai youth. Moreover, the forehead is vertical, whereas the Australian specimen (even allowing for postmortem crushing and deformity) appears to be robust-browed and with a receding forehead. It seems reasonable to assume from the Borneo evidence that true *sapiens* man had migrated well into south-east Asia by 40,000 years ago, and furthermore the slender structure of the Niah skull suggests that these early *sapiens* varieties need not all have been robust forms.

The Caves of Mount Carmel

Until recently, it was generally thought that the human remains from the Mount Carmel (Jordan) sites of Mugharet et Tabūn and Mugharet et Skhūl

were more or less contemporary. But the noticeable differences between these skeletons, in spite of their proximity to one another and apparent contemporaneity, have given rise to much speculation. Do the Mount Carmel people represent the first evidence of a *sapiens* divergence from a Neanderthal-type stock some 45,000 years ago; or do they provide a unique example of intermixing between a Neanderthal and an early Upper Palaeolithic type of man? A recent reconsideration of the faunal remains from these sites, by Eric Higgs of Cambridge, now suggests that the two cave peoples are by no means contemporary, and that the Skhūl people may have been quite a few thousand years more recent.

This re-analysis has helped to emphasise that it is quite unnecessary to speculate on the possibility of hybrids or primitive *sapiens* types diverging from a Palestinian Neanderthaloid stock. It can now be suggested with more confidence that by

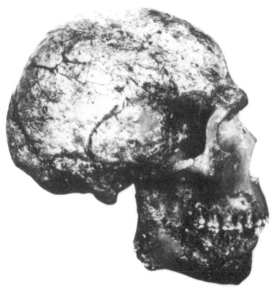

Figure 3: Skhūl V specimen from Mount Carmel in Palestine—as reconstructed by Dr. C. E. Snow—shows that a robust early sapiens variety was present in southwest Asia by about 40,000 B.C. This type continued into Upper Palaeolithic times.

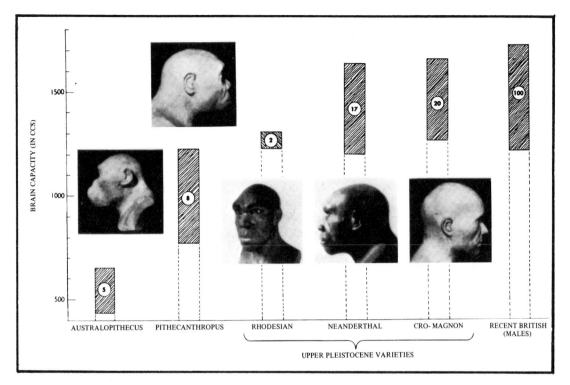

Figure 4: The increase in brain size from the earliest hominids to recent man. Modern range had been attained by Upper Pleistocene times, even though there was considerable physical variation at that time —as shown by reconstructions of the head form of Rhodesian, Neanderthal and Cro-Magnon man. The length of the vertical bars shows variation within the group, and the numbers on the bars show the number of skulls from which the measurements of brain size were made.

about 40,000 years ago, and certainly no more recently than 35,000 years ago, a robust early *sapiens* variety was occupying at least some parts of southwest Asia. (Further supporting evidence is the material from Jebel Kafzeh—still unpublished in detail—and one skull from that site is shown in Figure 1.) The robust skull form of these people certainly continued into later Upper Palaeolithic times, as exemplified by the Aurignacian Predmost III skull (*see Fig. 1*).

Thus we have remains from four widely divergent sites in the Old World to vouch for the considerable antiquity of *sapiens*-type man. Whether we should designate the species 'wise' is a matter for taxonomic hair splitting. I think this must be done on morphological evidence rather than on cultural attainment, and on the former grounds I think 'wise' is right. If the dating is correct for the Kanjera and Fontéchevade fossils, then *sapiens* man had already moved into—but not necessarily stayed in—Europe and Africa by 60,000 B.C., and by 40,000 years ago he had spread right into south-eastern Asia. Considering the apparent rates of evolution seen in earlier hominids and some large mammals, it seems very unlikely that the *sapiens* divergence from a more robust *Homo* species could have occurred in less than 20,000 years. Our own species thus seems likely to be more than 80,000 years old at the very minimum (*see Fig. 1*), though, of course, physical change at least comparable with the extremes of variation

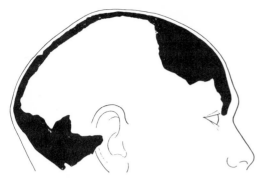

Figure 5: A new reconstruction by Dr. Bernard Campbell of one of the skulls from Kanjera in Kenya. Forehead is clearly "vertical" and there is a notable absence of heavy brow ridges. This is part of the evidence for existence of sapiens man in East Africa (one of his possible places of origin) by at least 70,000 years ago.

to be found in modern races must be expected *within* the species during this long time span.

Pinpointing Man's Origins

Where was the place of origin? This is no easy question to answer in view of the paucity of evidence. Clearly we must look for an area climatically favourable but sufficiently isolated for the 'directives' of evolution to exert an influence upon the potential *sapiens* population. From the occurrence of very robust and morphologically primitive men in the Upper Pleistocene of south-eastern Asia (Java) and the lower part of Africa (Rhodesia and Cape Province), it seems reasonable to eliminate these areas. What Middle Pleistocene fossils are known are very fragmentary and fail to indicate a possible area of initial *sapiens* development. Bearing in mind, however, that the Neanderthal group would appear to have evolved principally in Europe, it seems reasonable to suggest that *sapiens* man diverged either in a part of south-western Asia (Persia, Turkistan, Afghani-

stan, Baluchistan) or somewhere in north-east Africa. This is blatant speculation, but I feel that the evidence so far certainly points in this direction.

To what extent can changes in artifact forms be correlated with the physical evolution of man? This is a controversial topic at present, but there is no doubt in my mind that little if any weight can be given to such correlations, at least in the latter half of the Pleistocene. The differentiation of *sapiens* and Neanderthal lines of man was *not* based on superior or inferior flint technology, but on a mosaic of biological factors (mutation, selective pressures, genetic drift). In other words, the Mousterian industries must not be correlated purely with one physical type, Neanderthal man. Clearly, if we place Fontéchevade, Skhūl, Kanjera and Niah man in the *sapiens* category, even though they represent Stone Age cultures much inferior to the advanced Upper Palaeolithic cultures of Europe, we must concede that artifact change noticeably lagged behind biological change.

Conclusions

Ideas about the evolution of our own form of mankind are changing, and are sure to continue to do so with further discoveries and the increasing application of modern dating techniques. The date of the emergence of *sapiens* man as known today (biologically speaking) seems likely to be much earlier than generally thought. An answer to the tantalising question of *where* cannot be given with any certainty, but the most likely region on the present evidence is as shown in Figure 1. Our species would appear to have had a surprisingly long life, even though for the most part a humble one. Perhaps we might reflect on this before bringing it rapidly to extinction.

SEVEN • ON BEING CAREFUL

12 • THE PILTDOWN HOAX

Ashley Montagu

One of the most curious incidents in the history of science is the story of the Piltdown hoax, or fraud. It is, of course, easy to be wise after the event, and after the technical advances in science as well as the general improvement in our knowledge of the morphological evolution of the Hominoidea would make it virtually impossible for any hoaxer to foist such a chimera as Piltdown man upon the scientific world today.

Harsh words have been uttered about "second-raters" and this "sorry tale of incompetence," on the part of those who should have known better. But then, *that* is the definition of an expert: "one who should have known better." Those who occupy positions of authority are not always authorities on the subjects of their "authoritative" judgments. For an account of these "authoritative" judgments the reader should consult Gerrit S. Miller's paper, "The Controversy Over 'Missing Links,'" *Smithsonian Report for 1928* (Washington, D.C.: Smithsonian Institute, 1929), pp. 413–465.

In the history of science the Piltdown hoax is now of interest mainly insofar as it illustrates the power of a false expectation to create a state of mind on the part of the experts which would prepare them for accepting the frauds of a hoaxer. The belief in "missing links," indeed, in *"the* missing link," made it perfectly possible for the leading anthropologists of the day to accept a human cranium together with an ape-like jaw as belonging to one and the same individual. After all, what *would* the missing link connecting man with his ancestors be expected to look like, if not partly human and partly ape? And so the hoaxer worked with great skill to produce what everyone expected to see. It is a cautionary tale of the willingness to believe catered to by those willing to deceive. As the hoaxer might have said:

> With jawbone of an ass great Samson slew
> A lion; but my deed his feat surpasses
> For forty years, and with a jawbone, too,
> I made our scientific lions asses! [1]

The Piltdown remains are discussed here for several reasons. Firstly, because they have played a leading role for over forty years in discussions concerning the evolution of man, and secondly because they provide something of an illustration of the difficulties besetting the student of the fragmentary remains of hominoids—whether early or late. Finally, the whole story provides something of a cautionary lesson for those engaged in the evaluation of such remains.

"Discovered" between the years 1909–1915, by Mr. Charles Dawson, an amateur English archeologist, at Piltdown, near Lewes, in Sussex, England, Piltdown man's discovery was announced to the world in December 1912, and named the Dawn Man of Dawson, *Eoanthropus dawsoni*. A subsequent series of finds brought the alleged number of the type up to two. The remains consisted of the right half of a lower jaw with two molar teeth *in situ*, the left temporal, parietal, and nasal bones, a turbinate bone, and a good part of the frontal and occipital bones. The second find, stated to have been made at a distance of two miles from the first,

SOURCE: Ashley Montagu, *Introduction to Physical Anthropology*, 3d ed. (Springfield, Ill.: Charles C Thomas, 1960), pp. 220–30. Reprinted by permission of the author.

[1] H. A. C. Evans, *The New Statesman and Nation*, 19 December 1953, p. 805.

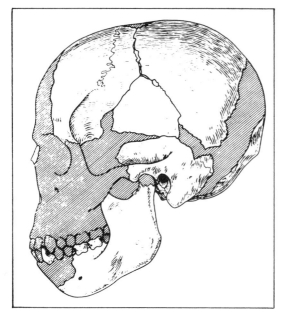

Figure 1: Reconstruction of the spurious Piltdown skull. Only the *right* side of the mandible, the first two molars *in situ* in the orang jaw, and the probable chimpanzee canine are shown in this manufactured specimen. These structures are here drawn as of the left side to match the cranial bones.

consisted of a molar tooth and parts of the frontal and occipital bones. Part of a third skull, found at Barcombe Mills near Piltdown remained undescribed until 1951.[1] The Barcombe Mills skull is in every respect modern, but from the character of its artificial staining it is probable that it was used for experimental purposes in preparing the forger's *chef d'oeuvre*. The Barcombe Mills skull consists of a large part of the frontal bone, a fragment of what may have been part of a right parietal, a pair of zygomatic bones which do not in any way fit the frontal, and a mandibular right second molar tooth.

A canine tooth, allegedly found in 1915 in the same Pleistocene gravels from which the original bones were said to have been removed, is very chimpanzee-like in form.

The Piltdown remains immediately became bones of contention.[2] It was questioned whether the jaw and teeth could possibly belong with the hominid cranial bones. The former were apelike, the latter were unquestionably human. It was asking a great deal of anyone critically considering the evidence to believe that a chimpanzee-like mandible and canine tooth could possibly have belonged to a skull so like that of modern man. Morphologically, the association seemed to be so improbable that most students refused to accept the jaw and canine tooth as belonging to anything but an ape. On the other hand, Broom, who reexamined the Piltdown remains in 1949,[3] had very little doubt that the Piltdown mandible belonged to the same individual as the brain-case. He considered that Piltdown was a big-brained type of man that evolved on a quite different line from true *Homo*. As for the simian shelf (a sort of internal chin) in the Piltdown mandible, that, he reasoned, is probably not an indication of close affinity with the anthropoids, but a specialization due to evolution parallel with that of modern apes, just as the large brain of this type may have been a parallel development to what is found in the line of *Homo*.

There is not the slightest evidence that anthropoid apes ever existed in England. But even if they had it is extremely improbable that an anthropoid ape's mandible would be deposited in the same gravels with a human brain-case. It was pointed out, in opposition to this argument, that when the thigh-bone of *Pithecanthropus erectus* was described many students refused to accept it

[1] Ashley Montagu, "The Barcombe Mills Cranial Remains," *Amer. J. Phys. Anthrop.*, n.s., vol. 9 (1951), pp. 417–426.

[2] For an account of this see Gerrit S. Miller, Jr., "The Controversy Over 'Missing Links,'" *Smithsonian Report for 1928* (Washington, D.C., 1929), pp. 413–465.

[3] Robert Broom, "Summary of a Note on the Piltdown Skulls," *Adv. Sci.*, vol. 6 (1950), p. 344.

as belonging with the skull cap because they felt it was too human-like for so primitive a skull. Today no one hesitates to accept the two bones as having belonged to the same type, if not the same individual. Evolution, insofar as it affects the various parts of the body, has been asymmetrical. The lower extremities attained their manlike form before the skull. Similarly, the skull in its various parts exhibits evidences of asymmetric evolution. In all early forms of man the mandible seems to lag behind the brain-case in its development. The lack of a developed chin in most early forms of man is a good example. In the case of the Piltdown mandible, it was argued, we may be dealing with an example of asymmetric evolution in much the terms suggested by Broom. The simian shelf is not a primitive character in the Anthropomorpha. It is not present in any of the early anthropoid fossil types, but is obviously a late specialization. If it developed in the great apes, why not in an aberrant branch of man as well? Despite these arguments, many students remained unconvinced. The mystery to many scientists will always remain how anyone with the slightest knowledge of osteology, the comparative osteology of the primates, could have failed to recognize that the mandible under no circumstances could be morphologically harmonized with the cranial bones. That it in fact belonged to an anthropoid ape. The great thickness of the cranial bones compared with the slightness of the mandible presents a striking disharmony such as is never seen in any normal skull. The canine tooth perfectly matched the anthropoid character of the jaw, and no known form of man was known to possess such a tooth. The openmindedness of the experts, however, was such that they were willing to grant the possibility that both mandible and canine belonged with the cranial bones.

If there was any doubt about the hominid character of the mandible and canine there was none whatever concerning the brain-case, for in its reconstructed form this revealed an obvious member of the genus *Homo* of an early neanthropic type with skull bones almost twice as thick as those of modern man. The cranial capacity was computed to be between 1,200 and 1,400 cc., McGregor estimating it to be about 1,240 cc.

In association with the Piltdown fragments there was alleged to have been found a number of what appeared to be the simplest type of stone tools, "eoliths," a worked flint, and a large bone implement made from the thigh-bone of an extinct elephant, thought to be *Elephas meridionalis*. Since the latter lived in Europe in the Upper Pliocene and Lower Pleistocene the antiquity of the Piltdown remains was at first referred to the Lower Pleistocene, but it was subsequently shown that animal fossils of later date are found in the same gravels as were the Piltdown remains. A test of the fluorine content of the Piltdown bones showed their fluorine content to be incompatible with an extreme antiquity. The basis of the test is that a form of calcium phosphate, known as hydroxyapatite, is progressively converted to fluorapatite, as fluorine is absorbed from water in the soil. Under the same conditions, and particularly for neighboring fossils, the oldest bones are therefore those with the highest fluorine content. In September 1949, at a meeting of the British Association for the Advancement of Science, Dr. Kenneth Oakley announced the results of the application of the fluorine test on all the available Piltdown materials.[4]

Oakley and Hoskins found that all the animal remains of undoubted Lower Pleistocene age from the Piltdown mélange showed high fluorine content, while all those known to be of later Pleistocene age in the same bed showed a considerably lower fluorine content. All the remains of Piltdown man—and some 20 microsamples were ana-

---

[4] K. P. Oakley and C. R. Hoskins, "New Evidence on the Antiquity of Piltdown Man," *Nature*, 165 (1950), 379.

lysed—showed extremely little fluorine. It was concluded that fluorine had been deficient in the Piltdown groundwater since the gravel was accumulated. Nevertheless the test showed conclusively that none of the bones and teeth attributed to Piltdown man belonged to the Lower Pleistocene. However, the first test failed to be sufficiently discriminating, obtaining a similar fluorine content for both mandible and cranial bones. The mandible and associated brain-case being of the same age, it was argued, it was probable that they dated from the final settling of the gravel, which from the physiographic evidence, the paleontological findings, and the fluorine tests was now revised downwards as being not earlier than the last interglacial.

The position, then, was that it was still open to scientists to argue about the naturalness of the association of an ape-like mandible with a typically human brain-case, but in the light of the revised dating it was suggested that the probabilities were in favor of mandible and cranial bones belonging together.

In 1951, Montagu examined the Piltdown remains and concluded that on morphological grounds the mandible could not possibly belong with the cranial bones.[5] In July 1953, Dr. J. S. Weiner of Oxford University decided that several things were not as they ought to be about the Piltdown remains. The flatness of the occlusal surfaces of the two molar teeth was quite unnatural and un-apelike, the lack of smooth continuity of biting surface from one molar to the other, the unnaturally heavy wear of the immature canine, the whiteness of the dentine beneath the darkly stained surface of the tooth, all suggested that artificial filing and staining had been the methods

by which the superficial appearances had been produced. Proceeding upon this assumption the mandible was subjected to a new fluorine test in which a drilling of deeper substance was analysed. This now yielded a figure of 0.03 per cent, as did the two molar teeth and the canine. The cranial fragments from site I yielded the much higher figure of 0.1 per cent, consistent with the value yielded by specimens of Late Ice Age. The artificial stain which had been used to give the bones an appearance of antiquity had falsified the first fluorine tests. But even before the second test the deeper drilling while in process produced an odor of "burning horn," like that associated with the drilling of fresh bone, an odor which was absent when the cranial bones were drilled. Furthermore, while the drilling of the mandible yielded shavings of bone as fresh bone does, the cranial bones yielded a fine powder as old bones do. It was now reasonably certain that the mandible was recent and did not belong with the older cranial bones.

Following these revealing findings a whole battery of tests were applied to the Piltdown fragments. Meanwhile, Weiner, Oakley, and Le Gros Clark, during the last week of November 1953, published "The Solution of the Piltdown Problem," in which they announced their findings and the conclusion that the Piltdown skull was a fake.[6] In January 1955, "Further Contributions to the Solution of the Piltdown Problem" was published, giving a detailed account of the results of the battery of tests to which the bones had been submitted.[7] This report, the work of a dozen investigators, showed that the mandible, stone artifacts, and the shaped Stegodon (Elephas planifrons) "tool" were all faked. The bone "tool" had been shaped with a steel knife from the long bone of a genuine fossil elephant, and the stone artifacts had been artificially stained and introduced into the Piltdown gravels. Four pieces of broken teeth probably representing two molars "associated" with the Piltdown remains have been identified as belonging to the fossil elephant Elephas planifrons. Since this

---

[5] Ashley Montagu, "The Piltdown Mandible and Cranium," Amer. J. Phys. Anthrop., n.s., IV (1951), 1–7.
[6] Bull. Brit. Mus. (Nat. Hist.), II (1953), 139–146.
[7] Bull. Brit. Mus. (Nat. Hist.), II (1955), 227–287.

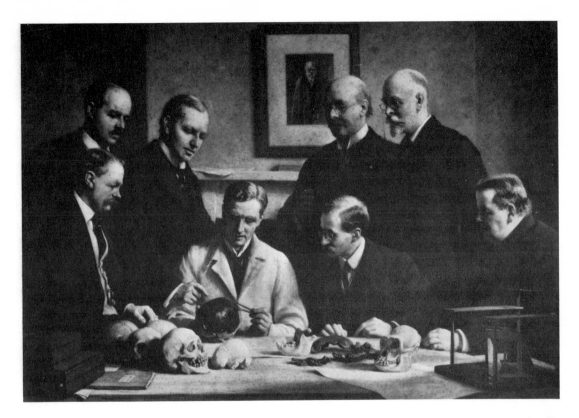

Figure 2: "The Piltdown Committee." Personalities concerned with the Piltdown "discovery." Back Row: Mr. F. O. Barlow, maker of the casts, Prof. G. Elliot Smith, anatomist, Mr. C. Dawson, the "discoverer," and Dr. A. S. Woodward, zoologist. Front Row: Dr. A. S. Underwood, expert on teeth, Prof. Arthur Keith, anatomist, W. P. Pycraft, zoologist and Woodward's assistant, and Sir Ray Lankester, zoologist. (*From the painting by John Cooke, R. A., exhibited at the Royal Academy in 1915.*)

species of elephant does not occur in Western Europe the fragments of teeth must have been imported from some foreign source. A *planifrons* from Ichkeul in Tunisia, where the fossil remains of this species are abundant, yielded a radioactivity count practically identical with the planted Pilt-

down *planifrons* teeth. They were artificially stained to match the color of the other Piltdown plants. *Sic transit Eoanthropus dawsoni.*

In 1959 de Vries and Oakley, by radiocarbon dating, showed that the Piltdown skull was 620 ± 100 years old, and that the orang mandible was 500 ± 100 years old.[8] Oakley points out that it is the custom among Dyaks in Borneo to keep orang skulls as fetishes for many generations, and it was doubtless from such a skull that the mandible was derived.

This is not the place to consider either the possible identity of the forger or his motives. For that story the reader may be referred to Dr. J. S. Weiner's fascinating anthropological "whodunit," *The Piltdown Forgery* (Oxford University Press), 1955, and to Ronald Millar's *The Piltdown Men* (London: Victor Gollancz, 1972).

---

[8] H. de Vries and Kenneth Oakley, "Radiocarbon Dating of the Piltdown Skull and Jaw," *Nature*, 184 (1959), 224–226.

13 • PATHOLOGY AND THE POSTURE OF NEANDERTHAL MAN

William L. Straus, Jr. & A. J. E. Cave

The history of the scientific world's appraisal of Neanderthal man constitutes an illuminating commentary on the nature of "scientific authority," "expertise," and "objectivity." From the discovery of the first remains of Neanderthal man in 1856 to the present day, his "bestial," brutal appearance, stooped-over, shuffling gait, and semi-erect posture have together constituted the generally accepted view of Neanderthal man. In our own time it has become common practice to refer to an unsavory or uncouth person as "Neanderthal." In July, 1941, the *New York Times* published an editorial entitled "The Neanderthal Mind," in which the behavior of the Nazis was likened to that of Neanderthal man. This led me to write a letter to the editor in defense of Neanderthal man, in which I pointed out that he walked perfectly erectly and that on the basis of what we knew about him from his cultural remains he was a highly cooperative, spiritually developed creature of whom we had made a scapegoat.[1] A writer in *The New Yorker,* commenting briefly on the letter, dismissed it with the remark, "Hot, ain't it?" This was clever, no doubt, and perhaps a scientist making a fool of himself by rushing to the defense of a

prehistoric brutish hulk of an extinct man is fair game for such writers. But one point it misses, among others, is that such views of our prehistoric ancestors not only have no basis in fact, but also lead directly to the kind of dehumanized view of human beings that the *New York Times* editorial was attacking.

The prejudices of the nineteenth century allowed everything relating to man's prehistoric ancestors to be seen through the distorting effect of a theory which equated the prehistoric with the "primitive," "undeveloped," and "animalistic."[2] Not only were these traits expected of prehistoric man, but what is worse, they were assumed of living "primitive" peoples. The mandarins of "superior" technological civilizations were able to look down upon the "inferior" undeveloped peoples as "living fossils," "superannuated races," who were being replaced by the "survival of the fittest" in "the struggle for existence."[3]

It is not surprising, therefore, that in such a context of expectation the remains of all prehistoric men tended to be seen as "primitive," "uncouth," and "bestial." In the matter of Neanderthal man, as Wood Jones said of W. P. Pycraft's reconstruction

---

[1] Ashley Montagu, "Unmaking a Scapegoat," *New York Times,* 20 July 1941, p. E7.

[2] See Ashley Montagu, "Some Anthropological Terms: A Study in the Systematics of Confusion," *American Anthropologist,* XLVII (1945), 119–133; Ashley Montagu, ed., *The Concept of the Primitive* (New York: The Free Press, 1968).

[3] Take, for example, Karl Pearson, biometrician and one of the founders of modern statistics and biometry, writing in 1892, "It is not a matter of indifference to other nations that the intellect of any people should lie fallow, or that any folk should not take its part in the labour of research. . . . It is a false view of human solidarity, a weak humani-

tarianism, not a true humanism, which regrets that a capable and stalwart race of white men should replace a dark-skinned tribe which can neither utilize its land for the full benefit of mankind, nor contribute its quota to the common stock of knowledge." And in a footnote to this Pearson adds, "This sentence must not be taken to justify a brutalizing destruction of human life. The anti-social effects of such a mode of accelerating the survival of the fittest may go far to destroy the preponderating fitness of the replacement of the aborigines throughout America and Australia by white races of far higher civilization." *The Grammar of Science,* Everyman Edition (New York: Dutton, 1937).

of Rhodesian Man, "Probably no more sombre practical joke has ever been played upon a human skeleton than that by which Mr. W. P. Pycraft (*British Museum Report on Rhodesian Man and Associated Remains*, 1928; and *Man*, December 1928), for want of a little elementary knowledge of the normal anatomy of the human *os innominatum*, has lately condemned a perfectly upright representative of the genus *Homo* to masquerade as the type of a new genus *Cyanthropus*—since it 'walked with a stoop, with the knees turned outwards.' The study of this latest claim for the shuffling-bent-kneed stage of Early Man confirms the opinion, formed by previous experiences, that the interpretation of the skeletal remains of Early Man is far better left to the professed human anatomist." [4]

Boule, in his reconstruction of Neanderthal man, perpetrated a similar bizarre joke upon a world only too willing to believe in the inferiority of all other kinds of men to ourselves. Straus and Cave, two professional teaching anatomists, thoroughly demolish Boule's sombre joke, and put Neanderthal man together again as he really was, a man who, for all his physical differences, stood and walked as erectly as any one of us, and, as we know from more recent discoveries, was a compassionate and sensitive human being. [5]

Introduction

Neanderthal man is commonly pictured as but incompletely erect; as an almost hunchbacked creature with head thrust forward, knees habitually bent, and flat, inverted feet, moving along with a shuffling, uncertain gait. According to this

SOURCE: William L. Straus, Jr., and A. J. E. Cave, "Pathology and Posture of Neanderthal Man," *Quarterly Review of Biology*, vol. 32 (1957): 348–61. Reprinted by permission of the author and the publisher.

[4] F. Wood Jones, *Man's Place Among the Mammals* (London: Edward Arnold, 1929), p. 363.
[5] Ralph S. Solecki, *Shanidar: The First Flower People* (New York: A. A. Knopf, 1971).

view, he was a thoroughly unattractive fellow who was but imperfectly adapted to the upright, bipedal posture and locomotion characteristic of the modern type of man. This notion of Neanderthal man—and we herein use the term "Neanderthal" in its more restricted and proper sense, i.e., as referring to so-called classic Neanderthal man of the Würm or fourth glacial period—undoubtedly goes back to the discovery of the holotype Neanderthal specimen near Düsseldorf, Germany, just 100 years ago, in 1856. It received impetus from the subsequent discovery of the Spy skeletons (1886) and was finally crystallized by Marcellin Boule's (1911–13) detailed analysis and reconstruction of the skeleton of the man of La Chapelle-aux-Saints found in 1908.

The La Chapelle-aux-Saints skeleton has constituted the type specimen for the assessment of Neanderthal posture; for it is the only Neanderthal skeleton possessing any significant quantity of vertebrae, and vertebrae must needs provide a decisive factor in any attempt at reconstruction of body-posture. Boule (1923), in his book on fossil men, gives a succinct account of his interpretation of Neanderthal man's posture:

. . . the differences between the skeleton of Neanderthal Man and that of modern Man are such that they necessarily imply certain differences in the general bearing and attitude of the body. The great development of the face, the backward position of the *foramen magnum* which must have caused the body to incline forward, the slighter curve of the cervical and lumbar regions of the vertebral column, and the distinctly simian arrangement of the spinous processes of the cervical vertebrae, all testify to this fact. With regard to the lower limb, it is clear that if the formation of the pelvis and the great development of the gluteal muscles indicate that a biped attitude had already been attained, the anatomical characters of femur and tibia, seen in profile in the upright position, show that the leg and thigh, when extended, could not have been in a precisely straight line with each other; that the femur must have sloped downwards and forwards, and that the tibia, sloping in a contrary direction, must have formed a wide angle with the femur. So

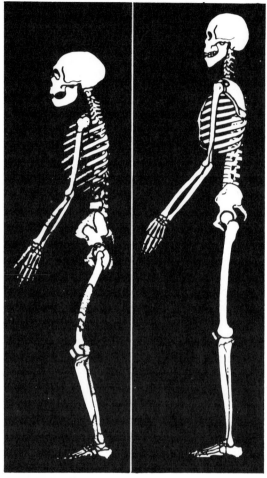

Figure 1: Skeletons of the fossil man of La Chapelle-aux-Saints, reconstructed (left), and an Aboriginal Australian (right). After Boule (1923).

ordinary, normal carriage of Neanderthal Man must then have differed in some degree from our own.

Boule's reconstruction of the La Chapelle-aux-Saints skeleton, with the trunk inclined forward, is shown in Fig. 1, wherein it is contrasted with that of an aboriginal Australian. The contrast is so obvious as to need no elaboration here. This reconstruction has come to be generally, if uncritically, accepted. Over the years it has assumed an almost canonical flavor and has greatly influenced subsequent writers.

Thus, Osborn (1918) pictured Neanderthal man as stooping, with the upper part of his body thrown forward, head and neck "habitually bent forward into the same curvature as the back," and "knees habitually bent forward without the power of straightening the joint or of standing fully erect." His hands lacked "the delicate play between the thumb and fingers characteristic of modern races."

Elliot Smith (1924) displayed an eloquent enthusiasm in describing "uncouth and repellent Neanderthal Man," with body not "truly erect," for which the La Chapelle-aux-Saints skeleton afforded a "clear-cut picture." Thus, wrote Elliot Smith,

His short, thick-set, and coarsely built body was carried in a half-stooping slouch upon short, powerful, and half-flexed legs of peculiarly ungraceful form. His thick neck sloped forward from the broad shoulders to support the massive flattened head, which protruded forward, so as to form an unbroken curve of neck and back, in place of the alternation of curves which is one of the graces of the truly erect *Homo sapiens*. The heavy overhanging eyebrow ridges and retreating forehead, the great coarse face with its large eye-sockets, broad nose, and receding chin, combined to complete the picture of unattractiveness, which it is more probable than not was still further emphasized by a shaggy covering of hair over most of the body. The arms were relatively short, and the exceptionally large hands lacked the delicacy and nicely balanced co-operation of thumb and fingers which is regarded as one of the most distinctive of human characteristics.

that, without being mechanically impossible, the total extension of the knee could not have been normal, and the habitual attitude must have been one of semi-flexion. The fibula, stronger in character, had a most important part to play as a support. The general appearance of the articulations of the foot indicates a greater degree of mobility and freedom. The foot, still only slightly arched, must have rested on the ground on its outer edge, and must have assumed naturally an in-toed position; the wide separation of the great toe shows that it may have played the part of a prehensile organ. In general, the

Writing 20 years later, Howells (1944) was more objective; but he still accepted the Bouleian picture. Thus, Howells' Neanderthal man both stood and walked with rounded back, bent knees, and flattened, inverted foot, and so was less erect than modern man. More recently, Young (1952) has categorically stated that "there is no doubt that Neanderthal man did not walk fully upright," and Coon (1954) has emphasized that "alone of all fossil men so far found, Neanderthal failed to stand completely erect." Additional similar examples from the literature could be given; but those already cited suffice to demonstrate that Boule's reconstruction of the posture of Neanderthal man has persisted to the present day.

Certain authors, nevertheless, have displayed less than a complete confidence in the Bouleian picture of a semi-erect Neanderthalian. Thus, over three decades ago, Schwalbe (1923) contented himself with the conclusion that the structure of femur and tibia indicates that Neanderthal man had an awkward albeit upright gait, with slight knee-flexion and thigh-abduction. Sollas (1924) merely noted that his skeleton exhibits some characters "which suggest that Neanderthal man maintained less habitually a completely erect attitude." Keith (1925), although taking note of Boule's reconstruction, apparently did not accept it fully; for he stated that "all parts of his body are as perfectly adapted to the upright posture as are those of modern man." It is clear that Hooton (1946) also had some doubts. Although he accepted Boule's appraisal of Neanderthal spinal and pedal morphology, and admitted that "the gait may have been a shuffling, bent-knee walk, in which the legs were not completely extended upon the thighs," he noted, on the other hand, that the linea aspera of the femur "is sufficiently marked to indicate an upright carriage," and that the "foot could probably be fitted in a modern shoe shop." Le Gros Clark appears no less undecided than was Hooton; for, after emphasizing that a "limb skeleton adapted for a fully erect posture and gait" is diagnostic of the genus *Homo* (1955), he continues to note that *Homo neanderthalensis* "evidently walked in rather a stooping posture and with a lumbering gait" (1956).

In recent years, however, some students have begun to entertain really serious doubts concerning the validity of the generally accepted concept of Neanderthal posture which stems from Boule's reconstruction of the so-called "Old Man" of La Chapelle-aux-Saints. Thus, Schultz (1942) concluded that the original Gibraltar skull (the first discovered Neanderthal skull, in 1848) must have been balanced on the vertebral column quite as in many modern men. In a later paper, Schultz (1955) definitely rejected the orthodox concept of Neanderthal posture and progression, stating that he "could never understand how any creature can be 'nearly upright' in the manner in which Neanderthal man has sometimes been reconstructed with his trunk leaning forward and taking a long step in order to prevent his falling. Such a posture, in which the center of gravity lies well in front of the center of support, is never maintained by any child learning to walk nor by any ape standing on its hind legs. Even in the beginning stages of upright posture the trunk must have already been held *fully* erect, to be most easily balanced, but this bipedal posture changed only gradually from an occasional attempt to a constant habit." In the same year, Arambourg (1955) came independently to essentially the same conclusion. Like Schultz, he believed that permanent bipedal erectness cannot be other than total. He concluded, therefore, that, contrary to earlier belief, the alignment of the trunk of Neanderthal man, both in habitual posture and in bipedal walking, did not differ appreciably from that of present-day man.

The "Old Man" of La Chapelle-aux-Saints

During July of 1955 the authors attended the Sixth International Anatomical Congress in Paris. A few months earlier, while in Washington, one

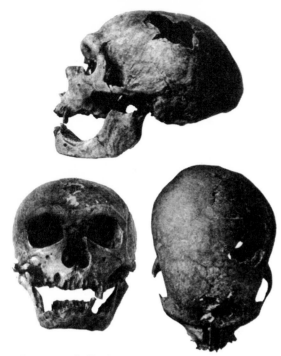

Figure 2: Skull of Man of La Chapelle-aux-Saints. Seen from the side (above), from in front (lower left), and from above (lower right). After Boule (1911).

of us (W.L.S. Jr.) was discussing the problem of Neanderthal man's posture, and particularly Boule's interpretation of the vertebral evidence, with Dr. T. D. Stewart. Largely because of some of Dr. Stewart's catalytic comments, this author was impelled to examine the La Chapelle-aux-Saints skeleton while in Paris. He gratefully acknowledges, therefore, Dr. Stewart's stimulating influence in this connection.

On July 26, 1955, we visited the Musée de l'Homme in Paris. The prime purpose of our visit was, admittedly, an examination of the controversial Fontéchevade skulls. As it turned out, we had access only to casts of these skulls, and we were not allowed to take any measurements. Hence, we soon turned our attention to the skeleton of La Chapelle-aux-Saints and to other original Neanderthal specimens which were housed in the

Museum, which were made available to us for study through the kindness of Mlle. L'Estrange. At that time we were entirely unaware of Arambourg's (1955) study, which came to our attention some months later. Familiar only with the published descriptions and illustrations of the La Chapelle remains and with casts of the skull, we were somewhat unprepared for the fragmentary nature of the skeleton itself and for the consequent extent of restoration required. Nor were we prepared for the severity of the osteoarthritis deformans affecting the vertebral column. It soon became clear why, in his reconstruction of the La Chapelle individual, Boule (1911–13, 1923) had found it necessary to turn to the Spy, La Ferrassie, and other Neanderthal skeletons for aid.

The accepted Bouleian reconstruction of Neanderthal body-posture was based upon an interpretation of the anatomy of skull, spine, pelvis, and lower limb. We therefore gave particular attention to these parts of the skeleton.

It is possible that the La Chapelle-aux-Saints skeleton may not, as commonly believed, be that of an "old man." Its precise age is not easily determined, however, the notoriously unreliable evidence of the cranial sutures being the principal criterion. Boule (1911–13) estimated its age at death as 50–55 years, Keith (1925) as possibly under 40 years, and Vallois (1937) as probably not more than 40 years. Our tentative estimate of age is 40–50 years, the upper limit remaining very uncertain.

As is well known, the nuchal plane of the La Chapelle skull is tilted somewhat upward (Fig. 2), and the curiously elongate foramen magnum and the occipital condyles are situated somewhat more dorsally on the cranial base than they are in modern man—an arrangement which has been an important factor in ascribing a forward tilt to the head of Neanderthal man. Arambourg (1955), however, believes that the base of the La Chapelle skull has undergone deformation in the course of its reconstruction, which, in part at least, accounts for the rather simian position of the foramen magnum. We are disposed to agree to the extent that the cranium has undergone some degree of post mortem deformation and that its reconstruction may not be perfect; but when Arambourg invokes the Saccopastore I, Skhūl V, Solo, and Rhodesian skulls to brand the La Chapelle skull base as anomalous, at best, for Neanderthal man, we are unable to agree with him. For it is questionable whether any of these particular specimens should actually be regarded as genuine Neanderthalians; whatever precisely they may be, they are not Neanderthal *sensu stricto* and therefore cannot be used in determination of the head-posture of classic Neanderthal man of the Würm glaciation.

Vertebral Column

The spine of La Chapelle-aux-Saints is represented by 5 cervical, 11 thoracic, and 4 lumbar vertebrae, most being very imperfect, and a fragment of the sacrum bearing part of the auricular surface (Fig. 3). Boule (1911–13) merely noted that many of these vertebrae exhibit arthritic processes along the margins of their bodies. Vallois (1949), however, stated that the last three cervicals, the first three thoracics, and all of the lumbars were pathologically affected, their bodies being "en diabolo." Yet, Boule's mere passing reference to the spondylitis and the absence of any indication that he regarded it as a factor of any importance in his reconstruction of the spine left us wholly unprepared for the severity and extent of the osteoarthritis deformans in the La Chapelle skeleton.

The atlas, which is incomplete, has been improperly reconstructed, so that its articulation with the equally incomplete axis is unsatisfactory. The restored anterior atlantal arch seems much too small, in consequence of which the articulation of one atlantal lateral mass with the appro-priate superior axial articular process leaves an enormous and unnatural gap contralaterally between the corresponding portions of the two vertebrae. A much broken and decayed odontoid process is abnormally deflected from the median plane. The articular surfaces of both the left and right atlanto-axial joints exhibit a considerable degree of osteoarthritic change. The bodies of the remaining (fifth, sixth, seventh) cervical vertebrae, the corresponding zygapophyses, and the post-zygapophyses of the first thoracic vertebra are all grossly affected by a deforming osteoarthritis. The remaining thoracic and the lumbar vertebrae are so defective that considerable restoration has been necessary; their original portions, however, exhibit evidence of a rather generalized osteoarthritis.

Boule noted that the La Chapelle vertebral bodies were shorter in cranio-caudal dimension than corresponding modern vertebrae, and argued in consequence for a relatively short trunk stature in Neanderthal man. The precise extent to which the La Chapelle vertebrae are reduced in height as a result of both pathological and age change seems not to have received serious consideration hitherto. Yet that such change has occurred is obvious, and a similar change undoubtedly involved at least some of the (lacking) intervertebral disks. The La Chapelle spine therefore does not constitute the most favorable material for an attempted assessment of healthy, normal Neanderthal posture.

In his reconstruction, Boule has pictured the cervical spine as without the lordosis characteristic of modern man, and as flattened (if not actually concave) anteriorly. He likewise assumed the lumbar lordosis to be less than in modern men. Hence the unnaturally straight spine which gives his reconstructed man of La Chapelle an equally unnatural forward tilt and stooping, "top-heavy" posture (see Fig. 1). Some appreciation of spinal osteoarthritis in its several manifestations, and clinical familiarity with its postural consequence,

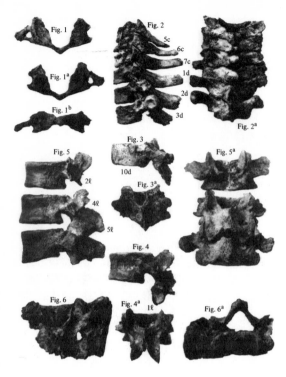

Figure 3: Vertebrae of the man of La Chapelle-aux-Saints. Atlas (1, 1a, 1b); fifth, sixth, and seventh cervical and first, second, and third thoracic vertebrae (2, lateral view; 2a, posterior view); tenth thoracic vertebra (3, lateral view; 3a, posterior view); first lumbar vertebrae 94, lateral view; 4a, posterior view); second, fourth, and fifth lumbar vertebrae (5, lateral view; 5a, posterior view); sacrum (6, superior view; 6a, posterior view). After Boule (1912).

would have prevented so faulty a reconstruction. The fifth, sixth, and seventh cervical vertebrae are crucial to the validity of Boule's argument for his reconstruction of the La Chapelle neck. He noted, correctly, that the spinous processes of these vertebrae are long and but little retroverted (i.e., the long axis of the process forms little or no angle with the ventrodorsal axis of the corresponding vertebral body), an arrangement that contrasts markedly with that occurring in present-day man, whose cervical spinous processes are usually shorter and strongly retroverted. In this "distinctly simian arrangement of the spinous processes of the cervical vertebrae" Boule regarded the La Chapelle skeleton as resembling the anthropoid apes, particularly the chimpanzee (Figs. 3, 4). To this greater length and lack of retroversion of the cervical spinous processes Boule added the tendency towards non-bifidity of their free extremities. On the basis of these characters, plus a diminished obliquity of the cervical zygapophyses, he postulated a reduction or even an absence of the cervical lordosis and included in his skeletal reconstruction a straight cervical spine which gave the La Chapelle head a curious forward thrust.

The La Chapelle cervical spinous processes are certainly longer than their counterparts in modern races of men. In general, such relatively greater length may well be the morphological expression of a relatively less mobile cervical column. Unfortunately, even in modern human racial material, in which spinous-process length varies considerably, there exists as yet no satisfactory method of correlating such length with degree of cervical mobility. The problem therefore awaits further investigation. Long as they are, however, the La Chapelle cervical spinous processes seem to us to be relatively shorter (compared with their vertebral bodies) than in the anthropoid apes. Certainly, moreover, their three-dimensional morphology is very unapelike; they are essentially prismatic or bayonet-shaped, triangular in cross-section, rather than flattened laterally and oar-like as in the apes. This feature, readily noticeable in the actual skeleton, necessarily cannot be seen in drawings or tracings of the bones in normal lateralis.

The supposed significance of the non-retroversion of the La Chapelle cervical spinous processes

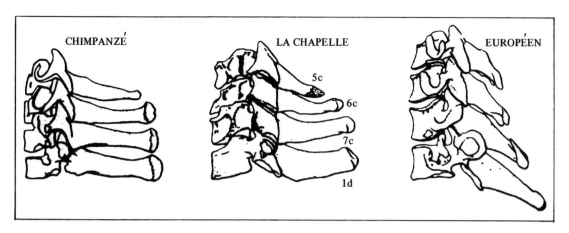

Figure 4: Comparisons of the last Three Cervical and First Thoracic Vertebrae. A chimpanzee (left); the man of La Chapelle-aux-Saints (center); and a modern European (right). After Boule (1912).

disappears in the light of Arambourg's (1955) radiographical findings that elongated, nonretroverted cervical spinous processes occur frequently in modern Europeans with perfectly normal vertebral posture (Fig. 5).

Bifidity (terminal bifurcation) of cervical spinous processes is a notoriously variable feature

Figure 5: Comparisons of the lower cervical and upper thoracic vertebrae. Left, of a modern European (from a radiograph); center, of the man of La Chapelle-aux-Saints (from Boule 1912); right, of a modern European (from Boule 1912). After Arambourg (1955).

of modern vertebral material and, as Le Double (1912) has shown, is devoid of deep significance. In the La Chapelle skeleton the seventh cervical spinous process is typically non-bifid, as in all such hominoid vertebrae, whether human or anthropoid-ape. The sixth cervical spinous process is slightly bifid apically. The tip of the fifth cervical spinous process is lacking, so that its exact condition during life cannot now be determined. Boule obviously regarded the La Chapelle cervical vertebrae as having at least a tendency towards apical non-bifidity and considered non-bifidity itself to represent a simian character; for, in the anthropoid apes, the lower cervical spinous processes usually are non-bifid or, at best, but feebly so. In fact, however, even though all the

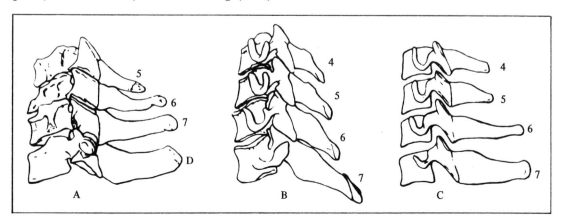

La Chapelle cervical vertebrae had possessed non-bifid spinous processes, such non-bifidity would by no means have constituted a non-human character, since such a condition is not in frequently encountered in present-day human skeletons.

The seventh cervical spinous process is invariably non-bifid in all human spines, of whatever racial group or historic period. The sixth cervical spinous process is remarkably often non-bifid in modern Europeans and is generally so in certain non-European peoples (Le Double, 1912; Terry, 1925). Indeed, all of the infra-axial cervical spinous processes may be non-bifid, as recorded by Le Double (1912) and as observed by one of us (A.J.E.C.). Shore (1931) has shown that, in the cervical vertebrae of both Bushman and Bantu, non-bifidity is the rule and bifidity the exception. Moreover, the accompanying Table 1, summarizing a particular investigation of non-

Table 1: Percentage incidence of non-bifidity of cervical spinous processes in some groups of modern men

RACIAL GROUP	NUMBER OF COL- UMNS	c. 2	c. 3	c. 4	c. 5	c. 6	c. 7
Andamanese	15	?	73.3	73.3	53.3	73.3	100.0
Australians	15	?	73.3	66.7	66.7	80.0	100.0
Ancient Egyptians	40	10.0	47.5	15.0	10.0	42.5	100.0
Europeans	85	15.3	43.5	16.5	16.5	48.2	100.0

bifidity by one of us (A.J.E.C.; see Cave, 1932), reveals this feature to be of much greater frequency than commonly supposed. From these data it is apparent that non-bifidity of cervical spinous processes cannot be interpreted as a "simian" character and that neither bifidity nor non-bifidity affords any diagnostic guide to cervical curvature or to posture of the living neck.

Finally, in considering the neck, there is the matter of the reduced obliquity of the cervical articular processes (zygapophyses) recorded by Boule. But these facets, like their lumbar homologues, exhibit a wide range of variability in both shape and slope in modern men. Although correlated in some degree, perhaps, with body-habitus, it is exceedingly doubtful whether they provide dependable evidence for determination of the precise alignment and carriage of the living neck. Moreover, the La Chapelle facets themselves have been affected by a destructive osteoarthritis and, in consequence, have undergone at least some pathological modification.

Boule seems to have paid scant attention to the role of the intervertebral disks in determining the shapes of the several regions of the vertebral column. Yet it is possible—indeed likely—that the pathological change in the La Chapelle cervical segment was initiated by a shrinkage and diminution of its disks; and it is a commonplace of clinical experience that cervical disk-shrinkage profoundly alters the normal lordosis of the cervical spine.

In view of the foregoing considerations and of the pathological state of the La Chapelle cervical region—which makes any reconstruction largely conjectural—we readily concur with Arambourg that there exists no valid reason for Boule's assumption that the man of La Chapelle-aux-Saints differed fundamentally from modern man in his cervical curvature and the carriage of his head. This conclusion is further supported by the variability of head posture among modern groups of men, as well as by Schultz's (1942) conclusions regarding cranio-vertebral relationships in another classic Neanderthal specimen, the Gibraltar I skull.

We are similarly unconvinced by Boule's assumption that the lumbar curvature (lordosis) in the La Chapelle man was less pronounced than in the majority of modern men. The fragmentary character of his lumbar vertebrae—especially of their bodies—the local osteoarthritis and, above all, ignorance of the inevitably absent intervertebral disks (which have a most important role in determining the shape of the lumbar region), make any truly accurate reconstruction of this portion of the vertebral column impracticable. From our own examination of the La Chapelle spine, we remain unconvinced that, in structure and configuration, the lumbar region lay outside the normal range of variability found in modern man.

Pelvis

The La Chapelle sacral and coxal fragments are morphologically indecisive; they can be readily matched in the pelves of present-day men. There is nothing that is non-human or simian about them. This conclusion is confirmed by the evidence of the more complete os coxae of the Neanderthal specimen from Düsseldorf. An unpublished comparative study of a cast of the latter bone by one of us (W.L.S. Jr.) shows that it is distinctively human in its assemblage of characters and in no sense morphologically intermediate between modern man and other primates (including the anthropoid apes). All of its features fall within the range of variation found in modern man. The ischial tuberosity is quite large (as it also is in the La Chapelle-aux-Saints skeleton), being very broad but not remarkably elongated. Yet, in its general configuration and location it is quite human and not at all like the tuberosities of the anthropoid apes. Klaatsch (1901) thought that both parts of the Düsseldorf sacral surface—iliac tuberosity and auricular (articular) surface—differ from those of modern men, but there is no valid reason for such a conclusion. The iliac tuberosity, although incomplete, was obviously large, both absolutely and relatively, as in living men; whereas in the anthropoid apes it is notably small (Straus, 1929; Schultz, 1930). The auricular surface is definitely human in size and form and falls well within the modern human range of variation, which is very great in respect of exact configuration. Contrari-

wise, it differs from the auricular surfaces of the anthropoid apes (see Straus, 1929). Other characters of the Düsseldorf bone, such as a deep greater sciatic notch and a prominent anterior inferior iliac spine, are peculiarly human and exceedingly unapelike. The iliac tubercle and pillar, structures which are believed to be related to the balance of the body in the fully erect, bipedal posture (Mednick, 1955), are well-developed in the Düsseldorf hip-bone. Moreover, Weidenreich (1913) has stated that the angle between ilium and ischium in the Neanderthal hip-bone is indicative of an erect posture. Thus Boule's attribution of "vestiges of simian structure" (1923) and of approach to the anthropoid apes (1911–13) to the pelvis of Neanderthal man is without basis of anatomical fact. Indeed, if the hip-bones of the Australopithecinae can be regarded—as is the current orthodox view—as indexes of an erect, bipedal posture (whether perfect or imperfect), it is impossible to regard the hip-bones of the Düsseldorf and La Chapelle-aux-Saints skeletons as indicative of anything other than a fully erect posture, in no wise different from that of present-day men.

Limb Bones

The morphology of the bones of the free part of the lower extremity of the skeletons of La Chapelle man and other Neanderthalians has been employed as an argument that Neanderthal man walked with knees habitually bent and upon the outer margins, rather than upon the soles, of his feet. This assumed Neanderthalian habitual genuflexion derives in part from the considerable normal curvature of the femoral shafts and, especially, from the pronounced retroversion of the heads of the tibiae (see Fig. 1). Each of these characters, however, exhibits a very marked degree of individual variability in modern man, as Manouvrier (1893) and others have shown. Indeed, the degree of retroversion present in the Neanderthal tibiae from Spy, La Chapelle-aux-Saints, and La Ferrassie is no greater than that found in many present-day men (see Manouvrier; also Straus, 1927). Marked tibial retroversion is associated with individuals whose habits of life involve frequent bending of the knee, such as mountaineers. It is also found in groups, such as the Panjabi, who consistently adopt the squatting posture (Charles, 1894). Indeed, it seems not unlikely that Neanderthal man was a habitual "squatter." Such a habit would account not only for his considerable tibial retroversion but also for the supernumerary articular facets present on the lower ends of the La Chapelle and La Ferrassie tibiae and upon the corresponding tali. These facets occur in high frequency among modern populations of "squatters," as noted by Charles (1894) and others. Such considerations regarding squatting do not in any way predicate, of course, that Neanderthal man was incapable of extending his knee when standing or when walking on a flat surface. In respect of the significance of Neanderthalian femoral curvature and tibial retroversion, Arambourg (1955) has arrived at a similar conclusion.

Torsion of the tibia apparently varied greatly in Neanderthal man, as it does in modern man (see Straus, 1927). It is significant, however, that the Neanderthalians possessed a "positive" torsion as in modern man, rather than a "negative" torsion as do anthropoid apes (see Boule, 1911–13). His toes must therefore have pointed outward as in modern man, and not inward as in the apes. Boule (1923) therefore erred in assuming a natural "in-toed" position for the foot of Neanderthal man.

The supposed simian characters of the Neanderthal foot, said to indicate its imperfect adaptation for an erect, bipedal posture, have been greatly exaggerated by Boule and others. Indeed, in many details the foot of Neanderthal man can be regarded as "ultrahuman." Weidenreich (1921), in particular, has shown that Boule's reconstruction, which led him to the conclusion that Neanderthal man rested his weight wholly upon the outer border of the foot, is open to serious criticism. Even Morton (1926), who regarded the Neanderthal foot as in some respects intermediate between that of gorilla and that of modern man, did not challenge its fitness for a truly erect posture.

The hand of Neanderthal man merits some attention in view of what Osborn (1918) and Elliot Smith (1924) have said about its assumed incapacity for performing delicate movements, particularly those involving the cooperation of the thumb and other digits. It must first be stated that there is nothing in the morphology of the Neanderthal hand skeleton to support this conjecture. Boule (1923) himself regarded it as "very human in character." The relative proportions of the fingers in the La Chapelle and La Ferrassie skeletons (considering metacarpals as well as phalanges) fall within the ranges of modern human variation and differ markedly from those found in the great apes (Sarasin, 1931). The thumb is not unusually short, as sometimes stated, nor is there any reason to suppose that its power of opposability was less than in present-day men. Boule thought the La Chapelle os capitatum to be remarkably small, and we are able to confirm that impression. Yet, according to the data of Sarasin (1931), when the length of the Neanderthal capitate is compared with that of the third metacarpal, it is found to be quite as large or even larger, relatively, than the capitates of many modern human racial groups. Aside from the concrete evidence provided by his manual skeleton, one cannot ignore the evidence furnished by the worked implements that constitute the Mousterian lithic culture associated with classic Neanderthal man. It is well-nigh impossible to conceive that these could have been manufactured by individuals deficient in manual dexterity.

Elliot Smith (1924) seems to have derived his poor opinion of Neanderthal man's manual skill from a study of his endocranial casts. For he states: "Many recent writers have been puzzled to account for the great size of his brain, seeing that the average capacity of the Neanderthal cranium exceeds that of modern Europeans. But . . . the development of the brain of Neanderthal Man was partial and unequal. That part of the organ which plays the outstanding part in determining mental superiority was not only relatively, but actually, much smaller than it is in *Homo sapiens.* The large size of the Neanderthal brain was due to a great development of that region which was probably concerned primarily with the mere recording of the fruits of experience, *rather than with the acquisition of great skill in the use of the hand and the attainment of the sort of knowledge that comes from manual experiment*" (p. 70; italics ours) . . . "However large the brain may be in *Homo neanderthalensis,* his small pre-frontal region is sufficient evidence of his lowly state of intelligence and reason for his failure in the competition with the rest of mankind" (p. 41). Despite Elliot Smith's eminence as an authority on primate cerebral morphology, we are unable to share his assurance in the interpretation of Neanderthal endocranial casts, or, indeed, of endocranial casts in general. Moreover, it must be recalled that it was Elliot Smith (1913, 1924) who found distinct evidences of primitive characters in the endocranial cast of the notorious Piltdown cranium—a cranium that later proved to be not only human, but of recent origin as well.

In some ways, Elliot Smith's appraisal of Neanderthal mentality is but a modified echo of Boule's earlier estimate derived from endocranial casts and archeological evidence. For Boule (1923), after studying Neanderthalian endocranial casts—in particular that of the La Chapelle-aux-Saints skull—stated that in "the simplicity and coarse appearance of the convolutions . . . the brain of Neanderthal Man more resembles the brains of the great anthropoid apes or of microcephalic man." He also noted that, in respect of "the relative development of his frontal lobe, which is debased and slants backwards," Neanderthal man "may thus be ranked between the anthropoid apes and modern Man, and even nearer to the former than to the latter." He thought, moreover, that both the occipital lobes and the cerebellum, "in the sum of their characters, greatly resemble those of the anthropoid apes." In summary, Boule stated: "It is probable, therefore,

that Neanderthal Man must have possessed only a rudimentary psychic nature, superior certainly to that of the anthropoid apes, but markedly inferior to that of any modern race whatever. He had doubtless only the most rudimentary articulate language. On the whole, the brain of this fossil Man is already a human brain because of the amount of its cerebral matter; but this matter does not yet show the superior organization which characterizes Modern Men" (1923, pp. 232–236). Continuing, Boule stated: "It is important to note that the physical characters of the Neanderthal type are quite in agreement with what archaeology teaches us as to his bodily capacity, his psychology, and his habits. As we have already pointed out, there is hardly a more rudimentary or degraded form of industry than that of our Moustierian Man. His use of one simple material only, stone (apart probably from wood and bone), the uniformity, simplicity, and rudeness of his stone implements, and the probable absence of all traces of any pre-occupation of an aesthetic or of a moral kind, are quite in agreement with the brutish appearance of this energetic and clumsy body, of the heavy-jawed skull, which itself still declares the predominance of functions of a purely vegetative or bestial kind over the functions of the mind" (1923, pp. 237–238; also see 1913, p. 227). "What contrast with the men of the next geological and archeological period, with the men of the Cro-Magnon type, who had a more elegant body, a finer head, an upright and spacious brow, and who have left, in the caves which they inhabited, so much evidence of their manual skill, artistic and religious preoccupations, of their abstract faculties, and who were the first to merit the glorious title of *Homo sapiens!*" (Boule, 1913, p. 227; free translation). It is unnecessary to detail the respective roles of fact, fancy and, perhaps, even emotion, in Boule's estimate. Moreover, other competent students of fossil man have arrived at a far more favorable appraisal of Neanderthal man's intellectual and psychic capacities, as well as of his manual dexterity, after studying the anatomical and cultural evidence.

Conclusions Respecting the Posture of Neanderthal Man

There is thus no valid reason for the assumption that the posture of Neanderthal man of the fourth glacial period differed significantly from that of present-day men. This is not to deny that his limbs, as well as his skull, exhibit distinctive features—features which collectively distinguish him from all groups of modern men. In other words, his "total morphological pattern," in the phraseology of Le Gros Clark (1955), differs from that of "sapiens" man. Yet there is nothing in this total morphological pattern to justify the common assumption that Neanderthal man was other than a fully erect biped when standing and walking. It may well be that the arthritic "old man" of La Chapelle-aux-Saints, the postural prototype of Neanderthal man, did actually stand and walk with something of a pathological kyphosis; but, if so, he has his counterparts in modern men similarly afflicted with spinal osteoarthritis. He cannot, in view of his manifest pathology, be used to provide us with a reliable picture of a healthy, normal Neanderthalian. Notwithstanding, if he could be reincarnated and placed in a New York subway—provided that he were bathed, shaved, and dressed in modern clothing—it is doubtful whether he would attract any more attention than some of its other denizens.

One should not criticize Boule too harshly for his misleading picture of Neanderthal posture. His study must be placed in its proper historical setting. Boule recognized (1913, 1923) that Neanderthal man was no direct, lineal ancestor of modern man, but, rather, the end-product of an evolutionary line collateral to, but independent of, that leading to the modern type of man. For he felt certain that "men of relatively higher organization, direct forebears of various forms of *Homo sapiens,* existed from very early times in Europe simultaneously with the Neanderthal type," which therefore "could not be the ancestor of *Homo sapiens,* since representatives of both species were contemporary." Boule was impressed, however, by the "archaic characteristics" of Neanderthal man, expressed by "the numerous simian traits" which he "retained as so many

relics, still strongly in evidence, of an ancestral state." Thus he believed that this fossil type "represents a degree in the human scale lower, morphologically speaking, than all the stages of modern humanity," and that "the long series of primitive or simian traits which are imprinted on each constituent part of the skeleton, can only be interpreted as the marks of a more backward evolutionary stage than that reached by modern Mankind. . . ." And to give such "simian" morphological characters their appropriate functional expression in skeletal reconstruction was but the logical consequence of this belief. Thus, although an evolutionary side-product, Neanderthal man represented a sort of skeleton in the phylogenetic cupboard, a lingering archaic stage in the evolution of the modern type of man.

Moreover, in the earlier years of this century the concept of a *definite* Neanderthal "phase" or "stage" in the evolution of "sapiens" man was still pretty widely and firmly maintained (despite its rejection by a number of competent students of human evolution). Vigorously expounded by Hrdlička (1927, 1930), this concept has persisted almost to the present day, largely through the influence of Weidenreich (1940, 1943, 1947), who, like Hrdlička, preferred morphological to geological evidence in the dating of fossils. Indeed, there are indications that this concept still lingers in certain quarters, if only in modified form. It is not improbable that Boule's (1913, 1923) appraisal of Neanderthal man was influenced by this hypothesis, despite his clear recognition that actual Neanderthal man could not be a direct ancestor of the modern type of man.

In any event, it is certain that some of Boule's contemporaries regarded Neanderthal man as ancestral to all later hominid forms, and under the influence of the intellectual or philosophical climate in which their studies of human evolution were conducted, it was but natural for them to expect him to be more "simian" and more "imperfect," both cerebrally and posturally, than the

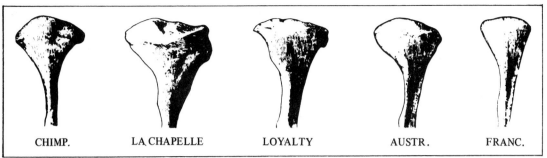

| CHIMP. | LA CHAPELLE | LOYALTY | AUSTR. | FRANC. |

Figure 6: Dorsal Views of Right Mandibular Condyles. From left to right: a chimpanzee, the man of La Chapelle-aux-Saints, a Loyalty Islander, an aboriginal Australian, and a modern Frenchman. After Boule (1912).

later forms of humanity which succeeded and replaced him. This is not an unusual phenomenon. The story of the Piltdown hoax is an even more striking example of the influence of prevailing philosophical climates on scientific thought (Straus, 1954). It seems unlikely, moreover, that we are free from similar influences at the present time. Some of the current appraisals of the Australopithecinae may well prove to be a case in point.

On the Pathology of the La Chapelle-aux-Saints Skeleton

Some further observations on the pathology of the La Chapelle-aux-Saints skeleton may not be out of place. As noted, the spinal column, particularly its cervical component, is severely affected by a deforming arthritis. In addition, there exists a flattening and deformation of the right mandibular condyle (the left is not preserved) attributable to an osteoarthritis of the temporo-mandibular joint. Boule noted a peculiar flattening of this right condyle, but apparently failed to recognize its pathological origin. For he compared the morphology of this condyle to that of a Loyalty Island Melanesian (Fig. 6) which may

well have been deformed by a corresponding pathology. We observed an even more severe condylar flattening and deformation in the La Quina and La Ferrassie mandibles, also obviously the result of temporo-mandibular osteoarthritis. Both condyles in the La Quina skull and the left condyle in one of the La Ferrassie skulls are pathologically distorted; so severe is the extent of the pathological damage in the La Quina specimen that its left condyle is utterly distorted into an appearance of multiple pseudo-exostoses. It would appear that insufficient attention has heretofore been paid to the pathological element involved in the accepted morphology of the mandibular condyle of Neanderthal man. The alveolar borders of the La Chapelle skull underwent extensive resorption during life, so that most of the teeth were lost ante mortem (Fig. 7), a loss clearly recognized by Boule and obviously the result of prolonged and intensive parodontal disease. It is possible that this parodontal disease has a causal association with the pathological deformation of the temporo-mandibular joints and the consequent distortion of the mandibular condyles.

The limb bones of the La Chapelle skeleton show no evidence of osteoarthritis. However, since a number of the articular surfaces are either absent or incomplete, absolute exclusion of arthritis is impossible. Boule recorded the presence of arthritic exostoses along the margin of the acetabulum in both hip-bone (iliac) fragments and noted that the interior of the left acetabular cav-

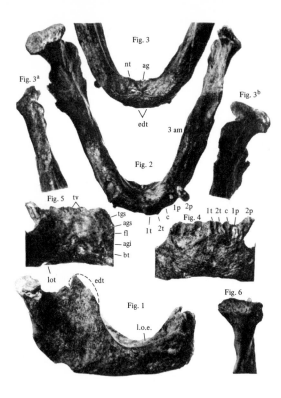

Figure 7: Mandible of man of La Chapelle-aux-Saints. Seen from various aspects. After Boule (1912).

ity is glossy and polished—a condition resembling that found in modern men afflicted with coxal osteoarthritis.

Vallois (1949) has stated that chronic osteoarthritis was a specific malady of paleolithic man. He briefly discussed the spinal and coxal osteoarthritis of the La Chapelle-aux-Saints skeleton and indicated, but without supplying details, that this disease is also present in other Neanderthal specimens. It must be realized that arthritis of some sort is an extremely ancient malady. It goes back at least as far as the Mesozoic era, where it has been found in some of the giant, now extinct, reptiles (Moody, 1923). Essentially a disease of skeletal wear-and-tear, its development in a given skeleton may depend upon a

complex of interrelated factors. In attempted explanations of its incidence, such factors as genetic predisposition to skeletal trauma, climatic conditions, focal sepsis, and metabolic imbalance have all been invoked, without, however, yielding any satisfactory or convincing conclusion. We can only note here that numerous non-human paleolithic mammals were victims of osteoarthritis and that human skeletons of all known periods, both prehistoric and historic, have suffered from it, regardless of climatic, dietary, and other environmental conditions (cf. Vallois, 1949).

Addendum

After this paper was delivered in New York City, on December 27, 1956, at the symposium commemorating the 100th anniversary of the discovery of Neanderthal man, jointly sponsored by the American Institute of Human Paleontology and Section H (Anthropology) of the American Association for the Advancement of Science, and while it was being prepared for publication, the book by Étienne Patte, *Les Néanderthaliens: Anatomie, Physiologie, Comparaisons,* 559 pp. (Masson et Cie., Paris, 1955), came to our attention. Although dated 1955, it obviously was printed and published in 1956, which explains our failure to consider it in this paper—we simply were unaware of its existence.

Patte deals not only with the skeleton of La Chapelle-aux-Saints, which he regards as the "type" specimen, since it is the most completely preserved, but with other Neanderthalians as well. His book is not primarily concerned with the presentation of new or original observations, but is rather a massive detailed compilation and interpretation of the existing literature dealing with Neanderthal man. That some important relevant publications have been overlooked is not surprising in view of the magnitude of the task undertaken. But all students of fossil man will be permanently indebted to the author for this encyclopedic monograph.

It is particularly interesting that Patte should have arrived at the same conclusion as Arambourg (1955) and ourselves respecting Neanderthalian posture. Thus, he does not believe it justifiable to attribute to Neanderthal man a posture different from that of modern man, adding that "il n'avait pas une démarche de Parisien, mais il n'y a pas que des Parisiens sur terre." His treatment is refreshing in that he compares fossil man with all modern racial groups for which pertinent data are available, and not with Europeans alone, as some previous authors have done and which, for obvious reasons, can be misleading.

Patte's conclusions cannot be given in detail here. It is sufficient, for the present purpose, to note that he agrees with Arambourg (1955) and ourselves respecting the postural significance of Neanderthal vertebral morphology (although he does not stress the osteoarthritic distortion), femoral bowing, tibial retroversion and torsion, and pelvic structure. He falls into the same error as Arambourg, however, when he invokes the Saccopastore skull, which is of early third interglacial age (Howell, 1951), to deny a backward displacement of the classic Neanderthal foramen magnum. Notwithstanding, his claim that the disposition of the lateral semicircular canals in the La Chapelle-aux-Saints skull indicates a carriage of the head not sensibly different from that of an Australian aborigine, is interesting and significant.

That three separate studies—those of Arambourg, Patte, and ourselves—all made at or about the same time, should challenge the orthodox concept of Neanderthal posture, is certainly more than mere coincidence. It represents the results of reinvestigation of a limited range of specialized material in the light of experience gained from more extensive special studies in diverse but correlated fields. It also indicates, perhaps, a recent alteration of the philosophical climate that invests the study of fossil man.

REFERENCES

ARAMBOURG, C. 1955. Sur l'attitude, en station verticale, des Néanderthaliens. *C. R. Acad. Sci. Paris,* 240:804–806.

BOULE, M. 1911–13. L'homme fossile de La Chapelle-aux-Saints. *Ann. Paléont.,* 6:109–172; 7:21–56, 85–192; 8:1–67.

———. 1923. *Fossil Men.* Oliver & Boyd, Edinburgh. (English translation of second French edition, 1923.)

CAVE, A. J. E. 1932. The significance of the bifidity of cervical spinous processes. Proc. Anat. Soc., June 1932, *J. Anat., Lond.,* 67:210. (Abstract.)

CHARLES, R. HAVELOCK. 1894. The influence of function, as exemplified in the morphology of the lower extremity of the Panjabi. *J. Anat. Physiol., Lond.,* 28:1–18.

CLARK, W. E. LE GROS. 1955. *The Fossil Evidence for Human Evolution.* Univ. of Chicago Press, Chicago.

———. 1956. *History of the Primates,* 5th ed. British Museum (Nat. Hist.), London.

COON, C. S. 1954. *The Story of Man.* Knopf, New York.

HOOTON, E. A. 1946. *Up From the Ape,* 2nd ed. Macmillan Co., New York.

HOWELL, F. C. 1951. The place of Neanderthal man in human evolution. *Amer. J. phys. Anthrop.,* n.s., 9:379–416.

HOWELLS, W. 1944. *Mankind So Far.* Doubleday & Co., Garden City, N.Y.

HRDLIČKA, A. 1927. The Neanderthal phase of man. *J. R. anthrop. Inst.,* 57:249–274.

———. 1930. The skeletal remains of early man. *Smithson. misc. Coll.,* 83:1–379.

KEITH, A. 1925. *The Antiquity of Man,* 2nd ed. 2 vols. Williams & Norgate, London.

KLAATSCH, H. 1901. Das Gliedmassenskelet des Neanderthalmenschen. *Verh. anat. Ges. Jena,* 15:121–154.

LE DOUBLE, A. F. 1912. *Traité des Variations de la Colonne Vertébrale de l'Homme et de leur Signification au point de Vue de l'Anthropologie Zoologique.* Vigot Frères, Paris.

MANOUVRIER, L. 1893. Étude sur la rétroversion de la tête du tibia et l'attitude humaine a l'epoque quaternaire. *Mém. Soc. Anthrop. Paris,* ser. 2, 4: 219–264.

MEDNICK, L. W. 1955. The evolution of the human ilium. *Amer. J. phys. Anthrop.,* n.s., 13:203–216.

MOODY, R. L. 1923. *Paleopathology.* Univ. Illinois Press, Urbana.

MORTON, D. J. 1926. Significant characteristics of the Neanderthal foot. *Nat. Hist., N.Y.,* 26:310–314.

OSBORN, H. F. 1918. *Men of the Old Stone Age,* 3rd ed. Chas. Scribner's Sons, New York.

PATTE, É. 1955. *Les Néanderthaliens: Anatomie, Physiologie, Comparaisons.* Masson & Cie., Paris.

SARASIN, F. 1931. Die Variationen im Bau des Handskeletts verschiedener Menschenformen. *Z. Morph. Anthr.,* 30:252–316.

SCHULTZ, A. H. 1930. The skeleton of the trunk and limbs of higher primates. *Hum. Biol.,* 2:303–438.

———. 1942. Conditions for balancing the head in primates. *Amer. J. phys. Anthrop.,* 28:483–497.

———. 1955. The position of the occipital condyles and of the face relative to the skull base in primates. *Amer. J. phys. Anthrop.,* n.s., 13:97–120.

SCHWALBE, G. 1923. Die Abstammung des Menschen und die ältesten Menschenformen. *Die Kultur der Gegenwart,* T. 3, Abt. 5 (Anthropologie: G. Schwalbe & E. Fischer, eds.), pp. 223–338. B. G. Teubner, Leipzig & Berlin.

SHORE, L. R. 1931. A report on the spinous processes of the cervical vertebrae in the native races of South Africa. *J. Anat., Lond.,* 65:482–505.

SMITH, G. ELLIOT. 1913. Preliminary report on the cranial cast. *Quart. J. geol. Soc. Lond.,* 69:145–147. (Appendix to: C. Dawson & A. S. Woodward, On the discovery of a palaeolithic skull and mandible in a flint-bearing gravel overlying the Wealden (Hastings Bed) at Piltdown, Fletching (Sussex), *Quart. J. geol. Soc. Lond.,* 69:117–144, 1913.)

———. 1924. *The Evolution of Man.* Oxford Univ. Press, London.

SOLLAS, W. J. 1924. *Ancient Hunters,* 3rd ed. Macmillan Co., New York.

STRAUS, W. L., JR. 1927. Growth of the human foot and its evolutionary significance. *Contr. Embryol. Carneg. Instn.,* 19:93–134.

———. 1929. Studies on primate ilia. *Amer. J. Anat.,* 43:403–460.

———. 1954. The great Piltdown hoax. *Science,* 119: 265–269.

TERRY, R. J. 1925. Osteology. In *Morris' Human Anatomy,* 8th ed. (C. M. Jackson, ed.), pp. 81–253. P. Blakiston's & Sons Co., Philadelphia.

VALLOIS, H. V. 1937. La durée de la vie chez l'homme fossile. *Anthropologie, Paris,* 47:499–532.

———. 1949. Paléopathologie et paléontologie humaine. *Homenaje a Don Luis de Hoyos Sainz,* 1:333–341. Madrid.

WEIDENREICH, F. 1913. Ueber das Huftbein und das Becken der Primaten und ihre Umformung durch den aufrechten Gang. *Anat. Anz.,* 44:497–513.

———. 1921. Der Menschenfuss. *Z. Morph. Anthr.,* 22:51–282.

———. 1940. Some problems dealing with ancient man. *Amer. Anthrop.,* 42:375–383.

———. 1943a. The "Neanderthal Man" and the ancestors of "Homo sapiens." *Amer. Anthrop.,* 45: 39–48.

———. 1943b. The skull of Sinanthropus pekinensis; a comparative study on a primitive hominid skull. *Palaeont. sinica,* n.s. D, 10, 485 pp.

———. 1947a. Facts and speculations concerning the origin of Homo sapiens. *Amer. Anthrop.,* 49: 187–203.

———. 1947b. The trend of human evolution. *Evolution,* 1:221–236.

YOUNG, J. Z. 1952. *The Life of Vertebrates.* Clarendon Press, Oxford.

14 · THE ARGUMENT FROM ANIMALS TO MAN: AN EXAMINATION OF ITS VALIDITY FOR ANTHROPOLOGY

J. B. S. Haldane

Some of the problems that beset those who would argue analogously from findings on animal cultures to those of man are brilliantly set forth in this Huxley Memorial Lecture, delivered by Haldane in November 1956. That genetics had at that time made little contribution to physical anthropology may have been true in a general way in 1956, but it is no longer so today, for if any branch of science is distinguished by the contribution it has made to physical anthropology, it is genetics. Indeed, any physical anthropologist should now have a good basic knowledge of genetics. Haldane also notes Margaret Mead's and Lorenz's description of man as a domestic animal, from which he proceeds to a characteristically incisive criticism of this widespread view among anthropologists, and at the same time to draw attention to the unfortunate political misuse to which this unsound notion was put.[1]

How much time estimates may be changed by more recent work is shown by Haldane's reference to "recent work" on the Pleistocene indicating that it lasted only about 300,000 years, for that estimate is today about 2 million years. It was also only a few years after Haldane made the statement that the australopithecines were not very much, if at all, older than 300,000 years, that their age was more than sextupled, and now has been extended to about 5 million years![2] This protracted period of time requires considerable modification of Haldane's estimate that a genus of Hominidae has a mean life of less than a million years. Evolution has been much less rapid than that in man. Mayr's suggestions toward a revised taxonomy of man have been generally adopted, while Haldane's suggested splitting of the australopithecines into more genera has been abandoned in favor of reducing the number of australopithecine genera.

Haldane's view that the main selective agency acting on mankind during the last few thousand years has been infectious disease has been discussed by him elsewhere.[3] His statement on human behavior, that "environment, and particularly tradition, are more important than innate differences in determining the differences between human cultures," is most impressive, as are his other remarks on this subject, coming as they do from one of the world's greatest geneticists. By "tradition" Haldane, of course, means what the anthropologist calls "culture." His whole discussion of "tradition" is something that has now become a basic interest of ethologists.[4]

Finally, Haldane invites anthropologists to become trespassers, to explore other fields of knowledge, particularly that of animal behavior, for the mutual benefit of communication among the sciences. His call has been heeded.

---

[1] In this connection see also Leon Eisenberg, "The *Human* Nature of Human Nature," *Science,* 176 (1972), 123–126.

[2] David Pilbeam, *The Ascent of Man: An Introduction to Human Evolution* (New York: The Macmillan Co., 1972), p. 150.

[3] J. B. S. Haldane, "Disease and Evolution," *La Ricerca Scientifica* vol. 19 (1949), Supplement: 68–76.

[4] For an early and neglected work on social life as opposed to culture in animals see Carl J. Warden, *The Emergence of Human Culture.* New York: Macmillan, 1936.

In honouring me by associating my name with that of Thomas Henry Huxley, the Royal Anthropological Institute has given me the opportunity to assess the value for anthropology today of the standpoint of this great man. In *Man's Place in Nature* he argued not only for man's close morphological resemblance to other members of the order Primates, but for his descent from members of that order who could reasonably have been described as monkeys. His opponents in his own day of course accused him of degrading men to animals. And in his famous Romanes Lecture he went out of his way (some may think too far) to contrast the ethical process operating in humanity with the cosmic process operating in nature generally.

My theme today will be the legitimacy or otherwise of arguments from what we know of animals to our own species. Such arguments are not, of course, novel. Solomon, Aesop, and the authors of the mediaeval bestiaries, who were undoubtedly influenced by the *Pançatantra*, to mention no more, used them. Above all, Plato argued from dog breeding to the possibility of human eugenics. But with the acceptance of Huxley's thesis that we are descended from non-human animal species such arguments gained in force, and it is desirable to examine them in some detail.

A whole lecture could be devoted to such arguments in the field of anatomy, of physiology, of pharmacology, pathology, or psychology. But I am speaking to anthropologists. And the smattering of anthropology which I have acquired leads me to the conclusion that anthropologists

are mainly interested in the differences between human groups, less so in the differences within groups, and rather little in the characters which are common to all groups, and to almost all members of these groups. This is in no way a reproach. An anthropologist must know some anatomy, physiology, medicine, psychology, statistics, and so on. But he or she is not expected to be an expert in all these fields, even though he may be in one of them. Nor need he be an expert comparative philologist, though again, he may be. I shall therefore devote this lecture mainly to the contributions made by animal studies to physical anthropology and to cultural anthropology.

I hope however that I will be forgiven if I touch very briefly on those human studies which are not the specific business of anthropologists. The gross anatomy of man is better known than that of any other animal. The microscopic and ultramicroscopic anatomy and embryology are not. If for example we want the best possible preparations of the internal ear we must kill animals by special methods and begin to fix the tissues before they are completely dead. If we want to examine nerve cells with an electron microscope we must do much the same. If we want to follow the details of an embryological process we shall be well advised to use mice or rats. In all these cases enough human material is available to justify or to rebut the argument from animal to human structure.

Again, in so far as they can be studied without danger to life, human physiology, pharmacology, and pathology are better known than those of any other animal. Thanks particularly to my late father, we know that human physiology can be extremely accurate: Nevertheless we must often rely on animal experiments. But these seldom give us quantitative information applicable to men. The human heart will probably respond to a drug in the same way as a dog's heart, but it may be a good deal more or less responsive to an equivalent dose in milligrams per kilogram. Still, animal experiments are very helpful in these spheres

SOURCE: J. B. S. Haldane, "The Argument From Animals to Man," *Journal of the Royal Anthropological Institute* vol. 86 (London, 1956): 1–14. Reprinted by permission of the Royal Anthropological Institute.

because in the last ten million years of its evolution the line ancestral to our species has not altered as much in its anatomy, physiology, and so on as some other mammalian lines, except in the physiology of the brain.

The situation in psychology is very different. Human psychology is perhaps as different from that of a chimpanzee as a chimpanzee's is from a bird's. This difference is emphasized by some religions, though Hindus and Buddhists seem to me to evaluate it fairly correctly. Conversely some zoologists class every attempt to argue from human to animal psychology as anthropomorphism. In Huxley's lifetime Darwin and Romanes among others tried to trace the origin of human psychological traits in animals. So, a little later, did Freud, particularly in *Beyond the Pleasure Principle*. A new epoch began with Pavlov, and his approach, based on experiment, has been vigorously followed up, especially in the U.S.S.R. and the U.S.A. From a study of how animals alter their conduct, a process called conditioning, learning, forgetting, and so on, we can, I believe, learn a good deal about how individual human beings alter their conduct, and this has applications to human psychiatry.

Nevertheless, I think that a different approach to the study of animal behaviour may ultimately be at least equally valuable to anthropologists. We are living in a wholly exceptional period, in which human adults have got to continue learning. A failure to learn the meaning of traffic signals is an offence for which the punishment may be death. But in most human cultures of the past, and in a few relict cultures which anthropologists can still study, this was not so. The culture did not change appreciably during a lifetime, and an adult did not have to alter his schedule of conduct in given circumstances. Now it is possible to study the behaviour of animals in an approximately steady state, during which, so far as we can see, they learn nothing and forget nothing. Such a study must however be statistical. Moreau's (1939) observations on the nesting behaviour of birds, and

those of Kinsey, Pomeroy & Martin (1948) on human sexual behaviour fall nearly into this class.[*] Moreau measured the mean times during which swallows stayed on their nests and away from them, and their variation. He found, for example, that the periods of absence were much less variable than those of incubation. Presumably a bird feels the need to return to its eggs even if it has caught few insects, but may not feel the need to leave its eggs. This is an obvious adaptation to the need for keeping the eggs at a fairly constant temperature. A similar study of more or less rhythmical behaviour in human beings in cultures where there is no "clocking in" is much to be desired.

With these prolegomena I pass to my main topics. The differences with which physical anthropologists are concerned are in part genetically determined. How far they are so can only be determined from the results of geographic or social migration. Thus Suski (1933) found that the children of Japanese origin born and bred in California were about as tall, on average, as Californian children of European descent. Mahalanobis, Majumdar & Rao (1949) showed that well-to-do members of other castes resembled Brahmins in many physical characters. When all such allowances have been made it is clear that most of the differences with which physical anthropologists had concerned themselves are mainly determined genetically. A fundamental question is at once posed. Are the principles of human genetics the same as those of animal genetics? And if so was not Plato fully justified in arguing from dog breeding to human breeding? Should not human breeding be controlled scientifically? I have tried to answer some of these questions elsewhere (Haldane 1956b). Perhaps more interesting to anthropologists are such questions as these. Are

---

[*] To quote these authors (p. 446): "Exceedingly few males modify their attitudes on sex or change their patterns of overt behavior in any fundamental way after their middle teens."

the biological differences between human groups comparable with those between groups of domestic animals such as greyhounds and bulldogs, or between related species or subspecies living in different areas or habitats, such as wolves and jackals?

I have no doubt that the fundamental principles of genetics, discovered largely by Mendel, and first applied to men by Bateson and Garrod, are valid for men, as they are for animals and plants. But the applications of these principles to men and the animals so far studied are very different, perhaps as different as the application of the fundamental principles of chemistry to iron and to wood. Let us try to see some reasons why this is so. There are several different reasons. Most work on animal genetics has been done on domesticated animals. Since *Drosophila melanogaster* has 30 or 40 generations a year it has been bred under human control for about as many generations as the cow, and must be regarded as domesticated. Now one of the first things which anthropologists investigate in a culture is its mating system: who has children by whom. The mating system of domestic animals is quite peculiar. In most domestic species there is a number of strictly endogamous breeds. The parents of a member of the breed must be members of the same breed. An Aberdeen Angus can no more become a Jersey on account of her meritorious milk yield than a sudra can become a brahmin by learning or asceticism. We might expect that the Indian castes would differ as much *inter se* as breeds of domestic animals. So perhaps they might but for one fundamental fact. The children of brahmins who could not learn the Vedas were not drowned, castrated, or even demoted to a lower caste. But it is only by such methods as these that the characters of animal breeds are preserved. The same applies to social classes in other societies. Individuals from lower classes may enter a higher one by intelligence, valour, or beauty. But human beings commonly look after the interests of their children, even if

they do not resemble their parents. Hence much of the effort of members of a ruling class is devoted to finding niches within it for those of their children who do not possess the characters needed to enter it from below. Were it not for this fact humanity might by now have divided into several subspecies corresponding to social classes, and aristocracy would be the only possible form of government.

We might however expect that the inheritance of physical characters such as hair and eye colour within a polymorphic race such as Western Europeans would be as simple as it is in mice or poultry. There is a good reason why this is not so. A white hen appears by mutation in a previously black breed. It may be eaten. Or its descendants may be mated together to form a new white breed. It is therefore usually found that the genetical basis of white plumage in all members of a breed is the same. But nothing comparable occurs in our own species. Blue eye colour is, on the whole, recessive to brown. But there are enough well-authenticated cases of brown-eyed children of blue-eyed parents to show that several different gene substitutions may determine the development of blue rather than brown eyes.

However, Spurway (1953b) found that many of the taxonomic differences between geographical subspecies of the newt *Triturus cristatus* were due to single gene differences. We might have hoped that the colour differences between Europeans and West Africans would have been as simply based, though this would seem *a priori* improbable to an anthropologist who considered the almost continuous cline of skin colour found as we travel overland from Ukraine to Nigeria. In fact the colour difference in question has not been analysed genetically. It appears to depend on a number of gene pairs. The analysis will become possible as, on the one hand increasing racial equality makes for unions where paternity is neither doubtful nor likely to be concealed, and on the other, biochemical work such as that of Rothman, Krysa

& Smiljanic (1946) and of Kikkawa, Ogito & Fujito (1955; see also Kikkawa 1956) opens up the possibility of distinguishing, by biochemical methods, between genes with similar effects on pigmentation.

But meanwhile genetics has made little contribution to physical anthropology as our grandparents understood it. The reason is, I believe, simple. Domestic animals are the product of artificial selection, combined with intense inbreeding. The newts in a river basin, as Spurway (1953b) has argued on cytological grounds, may all be descended from the first fertilized female to cross a watershed into it. Perhaps in palaeolithic times human tribes were so endogamous that one could have argued from the genetics of domestic animals, had they existed, to that of men. Today the human mating system is more like that of moderately mobile mammals such as field voles. Since their genetics have not been studied, we cannot argue from it to human genetics.

At this point it may be worth saying a few words on animal mating systems. They may be utterly different in nearly related species. Thus in the mallard duck *Anas platyrhynchos* a brood disperses in its first year, and its members may breed hundreds or thousands of miles apart. This species is not divided into local races or subspecies. But young geese of the genera *Anser* and *Branta* normally migrate with their parents. There are local races with colour differences which have been given sub-specific rank, e.g. *Anser caerulescens caerulescens* and *A. c. hyperboreus*, the blue and lesser snow geese, the latter of which is almost white. Their breeding areas are adjacent but probably do not overlap. Lorenz (1943a) has claimed that wild geese brought up together will not mate, the brother-sister relationship inhibiting sexual attraction. This observation seems to need confirmation. If confirmed it is clearly of great interest for anthropologists.

If genetics has done little for classical anthropology it has revealed a wholly new and unexpected set of anthropological characters, the antigens and haemoglobins of the red corpuscles, whose genetic determination is very simple. As a reader of Mourant's (1954) book can readily verify, their geographical distribution is not. What is worse, no such character sharply differentiates two populations, as skin colour or hair structure may. It is nevertheless true that some antigens, or combinations of antigens, are rare and probably absent in some populations, and very common in others. Thus the Henshaw, Hunter, and Diego antigens have not been found in Europeans, but the first two are common in West Africans, the latter in South American Amerindians. These antigens seem to have very little adaptive value, and just for this reason are particularly valuable as an index of racial origins. Whereas the fact that skin cancer in Bombay is almost confined to Europeans leaves little doubt of the adaptive value of skin pigmentation, and the work of Schreider (1950) is making it more and more probable that many metrical characters are adaptations to climate. Thus we cannot argue that the very dark pigmentations of African negroes and Melanesians indicates common ancestry. However, from the absence of a very dark indigenous race in tropical America we can suggest that the evolution of such a race requires over 10,000 years, and that the ancestors of negroes and Melanesians have mainly lived in the tropics for more than that time.

There is no reason to think that our knowledge of the erythrocyte antigens is anywhere near complete. But if it were so, we know that there are many other antigens found in cells of other types, of which we know nothing in man, except that they differ so much as to render organ grafts impossible. We know a good deal about them and their genetics in mice. It is safe to prophesy that if biology exists fifty years hence they will have provided us with anthropological data of the greatest importance. Recent work (Layrisse & Arends 1956; Lewis, Ayukawa & Chown 1956) which shows that the Diego antigen, commonest in South American Amerindians, is also found in 10 per cent of Chippewas in North America, and of Japanese, and 5 per cent of a smaller sample of south Chinese, fully confirms the usual theory of the derivation of the Amerindians. A search for this antigen among Polynesians and Eskimos will be rewarding. The discovery that the Basques and the Swiss of the Canton of Wallis, with their excess of the d antigen, can be considered as representatives of a proto-European stock, is an example of what we may hope for. I shall speak later of the abnormal haemoglobins.

In recent years Plato's argument from dogs to men has been expanded into the statement, both by zoologists such as Lorenz (1935) and by anthropologists such as Mead (1954), that man, and civilized man in particular, is a domestic animal. From this premise Lorenz (p. 302) proceeded to argue that civilized peoples must inevitably perish "unless selfconscious, scientifically based race politics prevents it" (p. 302). Such politics are based on "the value of racial purity" (p. 311), "the function of the intolerant value-judgment" (p. 308), and other tenets of the *National Sozialistische Arbeiter Partei*. I believe that the statement that man is a domestic animal is almost wholly false. Let us see where it is correct. Civilized men, like domestic animals, are sheltered from the predation of other vertebrate species. They are sheltered from some violent natural forces such as storms and frosts, though more liable than houseless men to be killed by earthquakes. They are, or were till very recently, particularly liable to be killed by infectious diseases promoted by overcrowding. Their food is relatively soft. As against this, domestic animals, with rare exceptions such as reindeers, cats, and bees, are divided into endogamous groups, the differences between which have been produced and are maintained by artificial selection. They have in consequence become highly specialized, and have usually lost many of the characters of their

wild ancestors. From a purely animal point of view, man is unspecialized in many important ways. No other animal can swim a mile, walk twenty miles, and then climb forty feet up a tree. Many civilized men can do this without much difficulty. If so it is rather silly to regard them as physically degenerate. It is characteristic of Lorenz' argument (p. 303) that beside the picture of a wolf he gives that of a bulldog with the caption "Reduction of the locomotory organs in the domestic form." He was not, perhaps, aware of the existence of borzois and Irish wolf-hounds, which run quicker than wolves; nor had it yet been revealed to him that dogs are mainly descended from jackals.

Perhaps the greatest difference between men and domestic animals is a very simple one. The wild ancestors of every domesticated land vertebrate have been at least somewhat social, and their tame descendants exhibit to men some at least of the patterns of behaviour which the wild ancestors exhibited to members of their own species. But as the result of domestication they have ceased to a greater or less extent to communicate with members of their own species (Spurway 1955). In particular, with the abolition of mating choice, sexual communication, including the activities called courtship, has atrophied or been grossly simplified (Lorenz 1940). A few domestic animals, such as sheepdogs, understand some human communications, but even these communicate less with their own species than did their wild ancestors. Whereas man has hypertrophied communication. He speaks, writes, gesticulates, draws, performs rituals, and so forth. The religions of others—not of course our own—can even be described in the language of comparative ethology (Lorenz 1950) as vacuum activities of communication in which human beings communicate with non-existent hearers.

Biologists generally accept Huxley's thesis that man has evolved. But the evolution of our ancestors in the last few million years has been of an unusual kind, involving a considerable increase in the volumes of some parts of the brain. It is difficult to answer the question, "Has man evolved more rapidly or more slowly than the average mammalian species?" Of course this question can only be answered on the morphological level. I shall try to answer it provisionally on this level. At first sight one would undoubtedly answer "Yes." The forms described as *Pithecanthropus, Sinanthropus, Atlanthropus,* and *Meganthropus* probably lived less than a million years ago. Indeed, recent work suggests that the Pleistocene period only lasted for about 300,000 years. The South African Australopithecines are not very much, if at all, older. It is not yet sure that our ancestors belonged to any of these genera, but some cannot be far off our ancestral line. If we accept the validity of the generic distinctions, it would appear that a genus of the Hominidae has a mean life of less than a million years. This would be very rapid evolution. Simpson (1944) finds the mean life of the genus of Carnivora to be about eight million years, and in many other groups it is much longer. But I think the generic distinctions are very doubtful. We have overclassified the Primates. Mayr (1951), who is one of the world's leading taxonomists, may have gone too far in the other direction when he suggested that the genus *Homo* should consist of three species, *sapiens* including the subspecies *neanderthalensis* and *soloensis, erectus* including *Pithecanthropus* and *Sinanthropus,* and *transvaalensis* including the Australopithecines. I should personally incline to put some at least of the latter in separate genera. But if Mayr's view is anywhere near correct, human evolution has not been very rapid on a taxonomic basis.

Some years ago I introduced (Haldane 1949b) a more quantitative measure of evolutionary rate. I defined the unit, a darwin, as the increase or decrease in the mean dimension of a structure by a factor of *e* per million years, or what comes to the same thing, by a factor of 1.001 per 1,000

years. Average rates for tooth evolution in the ancestors of the horse since the Eocene are about 40 millidarwins, and Dinosaur lengths gave similar figures. But if *Sinanthropus* is in any way representative, human skull height has increased at a rate of about one darwin during the Pleistocene. The length and breadth have of course changed very little. But it appears that evolution of height has been abnormally quick. When we have adequate fossil material it will be of the greatest interest to discover whether the human hand evolved as quickly.

I believe, with T. H. Huxley, that the main agent of human evolutionary change has been natural selection. The most varied views have been expressed as to how far, if at all, men are, or have been, exposed to natural selection. I shall not review them, but state my own opinions. Firstly, man, like every other species, is subject to centripetal selection which weeds out extreme variants. These variants are of two kinds genetically. On the one hand there are rare mutants such as haemophilics and microcephalics. The selection approximately balances the mutation rate. On the other hand where the heterozygote for a pair of allelomorphs is fitter in the Darwinian sense than either homozygote, an equilibrium is reached where only a minority of the population is of the most favoured genotype. Penrose (1955b) has developed this notion in some detail. Secondly mankind is subject to natural selection of the type considered by Darwin, producing changes in gene frequencies, with evolutionary consequences. This however is usually a slow process, and much harder to observe, let alone to measure accurately, than centripetal selection. Thirdly, as I have suggested elsewhere (Haldane 1949a) the main selective agency acting on mankind during the last few thousand years has been infectious disease. The inventions of husbandry, of agriculture, and finally of cities, greatly increased the density of populations, and hence the death rate from infectious diseases. Trade led to the exchange of pathogens between different populations.

It is probable that during most of the Pleistocene period mankind was divided into small endogamous tribes. Sewall Wright (1949 and earlier) has produced strong *a priori* arguments that evolution can be very rapid in a population so divided. Keith (1948) later reached the same conclusion independently. We should expect to find very considerable physical diversity between different contemporaneous peoples, and the data assembled by Vallois (1954) support this view; however, the fossil record of the lower and middle palaeolithic is meagre, and the artefacts suggest a considerable uniformity. It is much too early to be dogmatic.

We still know too little of the biochemical basis of resistance to most diseases to say much as to their genetics, except that congenital resistance to disease appears to be specific. A person congenitally resistant to measles is not thereby rendered congenitally resistant to tuberculosis, or conversely. But we are beginning to learn something of the biochemical basis of resistance to malaria, or rather to the various malarias due to different sporozoan species. In the malarious regions of the world large fractions of human populations have red blood corpuscles abnormal in their structure (thalassaemia minor) or in the nature of their haemoglobin (haemoglobin S, C, E, etc.). Beet (1946) was probably the first to suggest that the sickle-cell trait, or in modern terminology, haemoglobin S, conferred resistance to malaria. Allison (1954) showed that the resistance, which is not however so complete as he first believed, is only or at least mainly to *Plasmodium falciparum*. Haldane's (1949c) suggestion that thalassaemia minor has a similar function has not been confirmed or disproved, though the geographical distribution in Italy and Greece supports it. Lehmann (1956) thinks that haemoglobins D and E may give some protection against ankylostomiasis. These abnormal conditions are transmitted as dominants over

the normal state of the erythrocytes, the resistant persons being heterozygous. However, in the case of thalassaemia minor and the sickle-cell trait the progeny of two heterozygotes include one quarter abnormal homozygotes who generally die young of severe anaemia. Homozygotes for C and E haemoglobins are less handicapped. In consequence the frequency of resistant heterozygotes seldom exceeds about 20 per cent, in which case about one per cent of all children die of anaemia.

The gene for thalassaemia appears to be most frequent round the Mediterranean, though it extends at least to Indochina and Indonesia (Brumpt, de Traverse & Coquelet 1956). Haemoglobin S stretched from West Africa to the Nilgiris in Southern India, but is now found wherever African slaves were brought. Haemoglobin C seems to be mainly confined to West Africa, haemoglobin D to North-western India, haemoglobin E to South-eastern Asia and Indonesia. Lehmann (1956) gives the latest data. Once such a gene is present in a population it will spread if the appropriate malarial parasite gives it an advantage, until its further spread is checked by its lethal effect when homozygous. But since haemoglobin C is almost confined to West Africa, though it would be advantageous in East Africa, while haemoglobin E stretches from Indonesia to Ceylon, but has not been found in Africa, and thalassaemia is at least rare south of the Sahara, it is probable that such genes arise very rarely indeed by mutation, less than once in a thousand million gametes, as compared to about once in fifty thousand for the more mutable human loci. If so Lehmann and his colleagues (cf. Lehmann 1953) are justified in drawing conclusions as to racial origins from the presence of haemoglobin S in Southern India and Arabia as well as in Africa.

I shall not develop this topic further, but I think the time has come when a discussion of such matters between anthropological geneticists and animal geneticists like myself who have studied mutation and selection might achieve unanimity on the validity of arguments of this kind.

It is reasonable to hope that within some of our life-times infectious diseases will become sufficiently rare to be unimportant as agents of selection. If so a chapter in human evolution will close. The abnormal haemoglobins will slowly disappear. So probably will a number of other characters which are only advantageous in presence of specific infective agents. As Penrose (1955a) has pointed out, hygiene is more likely to have a eugenic effect than the dysgenic one usually attributed to it. No doubt however it will have a dysgenic effect as regards non-infectious but at least partly hereditary diseases such as diabetes. We do not know what will be the main agents of natural selection among our descendants. In certain circumstances resistance to high-frequency radiation will become as important as was resistance to disease in the past. There is unfortunately no reason to believe that exceptional men, if such there be, who can survive a dose of 1,000 roentgens are any more desirable in other respects than those who recover from plague.

I must now pass to the topic of cultural anthropology. The diversity of human behaviour depends both on innate differences and on differences of culture. There are presumably differences in the median innate capacities of human groups for various forms of achievement. But the differences between members of a group are much greater than the differences between group medians. Hence environment, and particularly tradition, are more important than innate differences in determining the differences between human cultures. The study of animal tradition is therefore important to anthropologists. Unfortunately the statements made about it by some distinguished anthropologists seem to me to be inaccurate.

In my classification of human cultural features I shall use a Hindu classification rather than a modern European or American one for the following reason. Modern cultural anthropology is a

by-product of colonialism. It consists of accounts given by persons almost all of European origin of the behaviour of members of other cultural groups over which they exerted dominance, largely through the greater efficiency of their weapons. Colonialism lasted for about four centuries, and is now drawing to a close. Hindu anthropology is similarly a by-product of the caste system, which is now also drawing to a close, but which lasted for over two thousand years. Soviet anthropology is a by-product of yet a third system. We do not know how long it will last, but it is not yet forty years old, and some of its tenets are taken over from Morgan's study of the Iroquois, which was a by-product of colonialism. I shall therefore employ a terminology of respectable antiquity, in the form given to it by my friend Professor Nirmal Kumar Bose in his *Cultural Anthropology* (reprinted 1953). I shall thus annoy not only British and Soviet anthropologists, but the majority of Indian ones, who may very reasonably object to a terminology associated with ideas which are a hindrance to progress in India. On the other hand I am emboldened to use the terminology of Indian cultural anthropology because some Western anthropologists ignore it completely. Pocock (1956) may be consulted as to the ignoration of recent Indian work.

According to the Hindu classics, human desires can be classified according as they are concerned with *artha*, economic needs, *kama*, reproductive needs, and *moksha*, the need for emancipation from these other needs. Perhaps there is also a *dharma* concerned with beauty, *sundara*. A culture is characterized by various *dharmas* which satisfy these needs to a greater or less extent. Each *dharma* acts through five agencies, *vastu* or material object, *kriya* or habitual action, *samhati* or social grouping, *vicharamalaka tattwa*, namely "knowledge based on experience and subject to criticism," and *viswasamalaka tattwa* or knowledge based on faith. These interact with the *svadharma* of each individual, which, to some extent, corresponds with our notion of genotype. I do not of course suggest that this is the only Hindu classification. Some authors would deny the existence of a *kamadharma*.

Anthropologists study all five of these agencies, and it is clear that the differences between them in different cultures are due mainly to differences of tradition, rather than of biological heredity. A human being brought up in one culture can adopt the traditions of another, though with some difficulty. Perhaps the change is easiest for those who have most nearly achieved *moksha*, to whom the *dharma* of one culture appears as devoid of absolute value as that of another. Such a person is unlikely to wear a *dhoti*, a kilt, or a pair of trousers with full elegance, but may be prepared to wear any of them.

Does tradition exist among animals? Many animal activities are instinctive, by which I mean that many complicated social activities are performed by animals which have been brought up in isolation from members of their own species, and in particular have not perceived other members of it carrying out these activities. Honeybees have a language or set of symbolical movements, first interpreted by von Frisch (1950 and earlier), which enable them to communicate the distance of a food source with considerable accuracy, and its direction rather more accurately than a man can do by such words as "Northeast by east" (Haldane & Spurway 1954). This communication is both made and understood without learning, though Lindauer (1951, 1953) has shown that bees often misinterpret their first instructions for a flight, and usually exaggerate the distance when first reporting a discovery of food. We shall learn little from insects as to the transmission of culture, though we can learn something.

But culture is certainly transmitted in birds and mammals. Von Pernau (1702) and Barrington (1773) founded cultural ornithology, but little further progress was made before the work of the Heinroths (1924–6) and Promptov (e.g. 1949)

in this century. It is now being vigorously prosecuted by Thorpe (1951, 1954) and his colleagues in England. These investigations have mainly been concerned with vocal, or linguistic tradition. In some species, for example the blackbird, *Turdus merula,* there is apparently no tradition. Males brought up by human beings from the egg sing a perfect song. This represents a human aspiration. Several mythical personages were born with a knowledge of the Vedas. But I wish to suggest that it may once have been a human reality. During the lower palaeolithic period, techniques of flint chipping continued with very little change for periods of over 100,000 years. It seems to me possible that they may have been as instinctive as the making of spiders' webs, even if most flint chippers saw other men chipping flints. To assume that these techniques were learned seems to me an anthropomorphic interpretation of beings who were hardly quite human. The contrary assumption is of course equally temerarious. In my opinion we do not know.

Other birds such as the skylark (*Alauda arvensis*) and chaffinch (*Fringilla coelebs*) must learn their song. Reared in isolation the lark's song is said to be unrecognizable, that of the chaffinch very imperfect. Marler (1952) found that within Great Britain he could recognize five local chaffinch dialects, with considerable overlap, and considerable variation within a given area. But the chaffinches of the Azores sing a dialect differing from any of the British dialects far more than they differ from one another.

We can ask what are the conditions for the development of a local dialect given that young songbirds disperse widely during their first year, whereas in later years they generally return to the same area to nest, even if they have migrated southwards in autumn. The answer is not quite obvious. The song must of course be learned. If it were determined genetically local dialects within a country of the size of England would be no more possible than local colour varieties. And the song must not be learned by nestlings from their father, as it is in robins (*Erithacus rubecula*). Such learning has the same observable effects as one type of biological inheritance. The condition for the formation of local dialects is that male birds should learn the song from neighbouring males at the end of their first year, when they are already attached to particular localities.

I have dealt with this case in some detail because the conditions for the development of local cultures differ from one species to another, and a consideration of them may at least give anthropologists a background. In our own species unduly precocious learning is probably inimical to culture. No doubt we learn some very important things from our mothers, but we learn still more important ones from society, and many cultures mark the transition from one type of learning to the other by special rites, which are fortunately not required by chaffinches.

Now let me go back to Bose's classification. Do social animals transmit *vastu* (material objects) from one generation to another? Most certainly. The most striking example is the transmission by females (queens) of the agricultural ant genus *Atta* of pieces of the fungus *Rhozites* which they cultivate. Each piece is carried in a special cavity near the mouth and deposited in the new fungus garden. The analogy with seeds in human cultures is obvious. The immense emotional valence of plant seeds for men is shown by the fact that the word for them in many languages also designates the male reproductive fluid. This is so in a variety of Aryan and Semitic languages, in Magyar (where it is also a reflexive pronoun), and also in Mundari, though Professor Bose tells me that in Mundari the word also means acculturation, a custom being described as "Hindu seed," or "English seed." But as might be expected, this equivalence is absent in Fulani, the language of a pastoral people. Sanskrit has two other official words for the reproductive fluid, and many languages have unofficial words. A world-wide study on this topic would be worth while, unless indeed I am displaying my ignorance and it has already been made.

Do animals use material objects for communication? They do so both to communicate with other members of their species, and with themselves in the future, as men use writing for both purposes. Hediger (1955) in a book which every cultural anthropologist should read, though its title hardly suggests its relevance, gives surprising but probably true answers to two questions: "In what way do men most resemble other mammals psychologically, apart from physiological needs, and in what way do they most differ?" He states (cf. Spurway 1956) that they resemble them most in their sense of property, and differ most in not being chronically afraid. Non-human mammals, particularly males, characteristically mark their property with their individual scent, sometimes, but by no means always, using excretions or glands near the anus for this purpose. You have only to look at a male chamois, black buck, or hynaena to see scent glands on the head. It is even possible to distinguish the marks made by individual hyaenas visually. These odours serve as a warning to other males, and a source of satisfaction to the rightful owners. Other species such as several bears and the domestic dog communicate by depositing odours and scratching objects outside their territories. These odours and marks are material objects whose main function is to arouse certain emotions. Such objects are of course familiar to anthropologists, though in our species they usually act by being seen rather than smelt.

The *kriya* or habitual action is quite often learned. Kuo's (1938) experiments showed that cats would not generally kill mice or rats unless taught to do so by their parents. Chernomordikov (1944) found that young lizards of the genera *Anguis* and *Eumeces* only eat insect larvae if their skin has been broken, and only hunt moving insects if they have previously tasted them. Evans (1955) describes maternal care in *Eumeces*, and it is probable that members of this genus are taught what to eat by their mothers. More remarkably Reyniers (1953) reported that young rats isolated from their parents die from retention of urine unless the external opening of the urethra is mechanically stimulated. After this has been done once or twice they respond to distension of the bladder. Let no psychoanalyst claim that the human species is unique in having psychological difficulties connected with infantile excretion.

Some member of an animal species may invent a new *kriya,* and it can spread, apparently by imitation. A few years ago a Stevin or Watt among great tits (*Parus major*) invented the practice of opening milk bottles left on human doorsteps. This has become common in England (Fisher & Hinde 1949) and has now spread to Holland, whether by cultural diffusion or by independent invention we do not know. Similarly Petterson (1956) reports that greenfinches (*Chloris chloris*) are taking to eating immature seeds of *Daphne mezereum.* This had not been reported till very recently, although the opportunity has probably existed for ten thousand years or so. I need not emphasize the interest of such facts for students of human cultural change.

On the other hand it is more doubtful that *samhati,* or social organization, is traditional in mammals. Vertebrates have to learn their functions in the society into which they are born. And the structure of this society varies with its numbers, its environments, the temperament of dominant individuals, and so on. But there is as yet little evidence that unusual economic circumstances or unusual individuals can induce a change in social structure lasting through many generations, as they can in human societies. The best piece of evidence on this question is Elton's (1933) statement that the muzzling order of 1895 by which dogs were prevented from biting one another for some months has permanently lowered the acerbity of fights between British dogs. It would per-

haps be rash to build too large a theoretical superstructure on this foundation.

The question of a traditional *tattwa,* or knowledge, in animals is difficult, because we can only infer knowledge from habitual actions. But there is an analogy with the two types in Bose's classification. A bird on first leaving the nest where it was hatched already knows that some objects, which it has seen, such as caterpillars or seeds, are edible, while others, such as sticks, are not. This knowledge is however subject to critical revision. De Ruiter (1953) showed that birds can very rapidly learn that stick-like caterpillars are edible, and most vertebrates can be taught (or "conditioned") to avoid food with particular visual or odorous characters. We do not know whether some kinds of infantile learning in vertebrates are as difficultly effaceable as moral and religious notions learned from the mother are in some human beings.

But this seems to be so in insects. Thorpe (1938) made the remarkable discovery of larval conditioning, where there is no question of even such elementary teaching as the offering of a caterpillar to a nestling. Female insects of several species which have spent their larval life eating food with a particular odour will search for food of this odour in which to lay their eggs. It is doubtful whether adult learning can overcome this larval conditioning, which can be compared with *viswasamalaka tattwa.* In such species the choice of food plants and animals is to some extent traditional, and Thorpe was able to alter the tradition. Where such experiments have not been done, egg-laying preference is generally thought to be instinctive, as no doubt it is in some cases.

If we speak of an insect knowing where to lay her eggs as the result of experience, we can also speak of instinctive knowledge, or in deference to philosophers who think that knowledge cannot err, instinctive opinion. Such knowledge or opinion exists in our own species. Every baby "knows" that sweet things are good to eat. This "knowledge" may of course be erroneous, as when a child poisons itself with lead acetate. But the scope of human instinctive knowledge is limited, and we feel the lack of it. Free will is a hard burden to bear. We try to lighten it with knowledge based on faith. We know, according to the culture in which we have been brought up, either that the eating of human flesh is an abomination, or that it is necessary for the acquisition of certain qualities. We also claim to know the truth of some most detailed and complicated assertions about the structure of the universe, its past and its future. It is not known whether human societies can exist without traditional *viswasamalaka tattwa*. They can certainly exist with very different and mutually contradictory ones, and the "knowledge" acquired in this way need not include supernatural elements. It can however be argued that beliefs in the rightness and wrongness of certain actions, held without rational foundations, are essential for the stability of any human society. I shall come back later to the question whether any elements in such beliefs are not of traditional origin.

Returning once more to Bose's classification, a few animals, such as bower birds, show *sundaradharma*, behaviour satisfying aesthetic needs. This is most marked in the bower birds, where Marshall (1954) regards it as a derivative, or displacement activity, of sexual behaviour, as it is in men according to some Freudians. It does not appear to be traditional. Have animals a *mokshadharma?* So far as I know this question has not been asked. It is too seldom asked concerning human cultures. *Moksha* means the state of a human being unaffected by external stimuli such as heat and cold, or internal stimuli (Pavlov 1928) such as those causing hunger and lust. It has a special theological significance for Hinduism, but it can be equated with the ἀταραξία of Epicurus, and the contemplative life of Christian mystics. I do not doubt that some at least of the primitive religions help their adherents towards it, but it is perhaps the hardest function of a religion for field anthropologists to investigate. I think it conceivable that some higher animals can perform *mokshadharma* in their postreproductive period, but there is no evidence for its cultural transmission.

I hope that I have shown that we can legitimately ask the question whether the equivalent of a human social activity is found in a particular animal species, and if so how far it depends on tradition. It always depends on heredity, in the broad sense of that word. Even those songbirds which must learn their song learn the song characteristic of their own species when a choice is offered to them. The examples which I have given are few because zoologists have only recently begun to ask this question systematically, and no comprehensive review of animal tradition exists. I claim that even our very meagre knowledge furnishes a background for cultural anthropology. Perhaps anthropologists may sometimes be able to put a question more clearly if they do so in a form which would be applicable to an animal species, though I trust that they will never imitate some psychologists in thinking that such a form is obligatory.

I also think that the data of animal ethology can throw some light at least on the origins of human behaviour, and above all on its extreme adaptability. Social behaviour in most mammals depends largely on odour signals. That is one reason why we understand their social behaviour less well than that of birds, which, like our own, is mainly based on visual and auditory signals. Odorous signals still have some valence for us men. But when our ancestors took to arboreal life animal odours became less important to them, and plant ones more so. They doubtless developed a set of instincts appropriate to arboreal life. They probably came down from the trees more than a million years ago, and may have gone through a more or less quadrupedal phase before a change in pelvic shape made bipedal running and the emancipation of the hands possible. The great development of the brain probably occurred quite soon after the adoption of the bipedal posture.

Man did not arise with a set of instincts as detailed as those of most other vertebrates, from which he had to emancipate himself. Wordsworth described this human absence of instinct as

> Blank misgivings of a creature
> Moving about in worlds not realised.

Had our ancestors had a few million years in which to develop instincts appropriate to a bipedal mammal I doubt if they could have become men. If our descendants ever achieve a stable and permanent culture lasting with little change over some millions of years, they may develop instincts suited to it, and cease to be men. Our relative lack of instincts has so far enabled us to adapt ourselves to the changes which we have made and are making in our environments. We do however find traces of instinct, by which I mean in this context the release of characteristic emotions and actions by somewhat arbitrary sign-stimuli, in unexpected quarters. I am inclined to accept Jung's conclusion that human beings in different cultures independently produce similar symbols which have for them a high emotional valence and are often incorporated into religions. For reasons given elsewhere (Haldane 1956a) I see no reason to adopt his theory of a collective unconscious. I give just one example, which I believe is novel. Michael Angelo's frescos in the Sistine Chapel are generally regarded as one of the masterpieces of European art. So far as I know my wife was the first to remark that the attitude of Christ in the Last Judgement is that of Siva in one of his destructive aspects. The attitude is certainly rare in Christian art, and it is most unlikely that it was copied from a Hindu original. But it evokes similar emotions in Christians and Hindus.

And here let me return to Hediger's point that man differs from most animals in not being chronically slightly frightened. Our ancestors clearly were so as long as large carnivora were a danger. With their disappearance we have peopled the world with hobgoblins and supernatural beings whose characters inspire fear. They appear to fulfil an emotional need. It is a gross oversimplification to present the needs which are served by mythology in such words as:

> This life cannot be all, they swear
> For how unpleasant if it were.

I suggest that man, or a great many men, demands an object of fear, as some animals appear to do (Spurway 1953a), and that it may be better to believe in Kali, Maryamma or our adversary the Devil than to make foreign governments our principal object of fear. No doubt it would be better still to concentrate on bacteria, but a primitive emotion of this type seems too often to need an object which can be readily imagined. To conclude, I think that the study of animals may tell us a good deal about the human unconscious, and thus about irrational human behaviour.

I must end up by apologizing for my subject matter and my treatment of it. An adequate treatment would have filled several books. I hope that I may stimulate a zoologist to write a book on "Animal Tradition." I have inevitably been both superficial and dogmatic. I have doubtless displayed my ignorance of anthropology. But the sciences are becoming specialized, and it is of immense importance for their healthy development that contact should be preserved between them. The price of such contact is a measure of inaccuracy and superficiality. But the cost of avoiding it is even more serious. Thomas Henry Huxley was primarily an anatomist. But he was not afraid of stating his opinions on physiology, anthropology, theology, and philosophy. I should like to see professional anthropologists trespassing on the fields of other sciences, and particularly, perhaps, on the study of animal behaviour. If I have irritated some of my audience into such a counterattack this lecture will have been justified.

REFERENCES

ALLISON, A. C. 1954   Notes on sickle-cell polymorphism. Ann. Eugen. 19:39–57.

BARRINGTON, D. 1773   Experiments and observations on the singing of birds. Phil. Trans. Roy. Soc. 63:249–91.

BEET, E. A. 1946   Sickle cell disease in the Balovale district of Northern Rhodesia. E. African Med. J. 23:75.

BOSE, N. K. 1953   Cultural Anthropology and Other Essays. Calcutta.

BRUMPT, L., M. DE TRAVERSE, P. M. COQUELET 1956 Interaction entre hémoglobine E et trait thalassémique au Cambodge. C.R. Soc. Biol. 150:147–61.

CHERNOMORDIKOV, V. V. 1944   On inherent and acquired food reactions in reptiles. C. R. (Doklady) Ac. Sci. U.R.S.S. 43:174.

ELTON, C. S. 1933   The Ecology of Animals. London.

EVANS, L. T. 1955   In Group Processes. New York.

FISHER, J., and R. A. HINDE 1949   The opening of milk bottles by birds. British Birds, 42:347.

FRISCH, K. VON. 1950   Bees, Their Vision, Chemical Senses and Language. Ithaca, N.Y.

HALDANE, J. B. S. 1949a   Disease and evolution. La Ric. Sci. Suppl. 19:68–76.

——— 1949b   Suggestions as to the quantitative measurement of rates of evolution. Evolution, 3: 51–6.

——— 1949c   The rate of mutation of human genes. Proc. VIII Int. Congr. Genet. (Hereditas suppl.) 267–73.

——— 1956a   Time in biology. Sci. Progr. 175:385–402.

——— 1956b   The prospects for eugenics. New Biol. 22 (in press), and Proc. Roy. Institution (in press).

HALDANE, J. B. S., and H. SPURWAY 1954   A statistical analysis of communication in Apis mellifera, and a comparison with communication in other animals. Insects sociaux, 1:247–83.

HEDIGER, H. 1955   Studies of the Psychology and Behavior of Captive Animals in Zoos and Circuses. London.

HEINROTH, O., and M. HEINROTH 1924–26   Die Vögel Mitteleuropas. Berlin.

KEITH, A. 1948   A New Theory of Human Evolution. London.

KIKKAWA, H. 1956   Relation between hair color and metals in human hair. Human Biology, 28:59–66.

KIKKAWA, H., Z. OGITO, and S. FUJITO 1955   Nature of pigments derived from tyrosine and tryptophan in animals. Science, 121:43–7.

KINSEY, A. C., W. B. POMEROY, and C. E. MARTIN 1948 Sexual Behavior in the Human Male. Philadelphia and London.

KUO, Z. Y. 1938   Further study on the behavior of the cat towards the rat. J. Comp. Psychol. 25:1–8.

LAYRISSE, M., and T. ARENDS 1956   The Diego blood factor in Chinese and Japanese. Nature, London, 177:1084–7.

LEHMANN, H. 1956   Distribution of abnormal haemoglobins. J. Clin. Path. 9:180–81.

LEWIS, M., H. AYUKAWA, and B. CHOWN 1956   The blood group antigen Diego in North American Indians and Japanese. Nature, London, 177:1087.

LINDAUER, M. 1951   Bienentänze in der Schwarmtraube. Die Naturwissenschaften, 38:509–13.

——— 1953   Bienentänze in der Schwarmtraube. Die Naturwissenschaften, 40:379.

LORENZ, K. Z. 1940   Durch Domestikation verursachte Störungen arteigener Verhalten. Z. angew. Psychol. Characterkunde, 59:1–81.

LORENZ, K. Z. 1935   Der Kumpan in der Umwelt des Vogels. J. Ornith. 83:137–413.

——— 1943b   Die angeborenen Formen möglicher Erfahrung. Z. Tierpsychol. 5:235–409.

——— 1950   The comparative method in studying innate behaviour patterns. Symp. Soc. exp. Biol. 4:221–68.

MAHALANOBIS, P. C., D. N. MAJUMDAR, and C. R. ROA 1949   Anthropometric survey of the United Provinces 1941 A statistical study. Sankhya, 9: 90–324.

MARLER, P. 1952   Variation in the song of the chaffinch Fringilla coelebs. Ibis, 94:458–72.

MARSHALL, A. J. 1954   Bower Birds, their Display and Breeding Cycles. Oxford.

MAYR, E. 1951   Taxonomic categories in fossil hominids. Cold Spring Harbor Symposia on Quantitative Biology, 15:109–28.

MEAD, M. 1954   Some theoretical considerations on the problem of mother-child separation. Am. Jour. Orthopsych. 24:471–83.

MOREAU, R. S. 1939   Numerical data on African birds' behaviour at the nest: Hirundo s. smithii Leach, the Wire-tailed swallow. Proc. Zool. Soc. 109A: 109–25.

MOURANT, A. E. 1954   The Distribution of the Human Blood Groups. Oxford.

PAVLOV, I. P. 1928   Lectures on Conditioned Reflexes, vols. 1 and 2. New York and London.

PENROSE, L. S. 1955a   Genetics and medicine. Adv. Sci. London, 11:387.

———— 1955b Evidence of heterosis in man. Proc. Roy. Soc. B. 144:203–12.

PERNAU, E. A. VON 1702 Unterricht, was mit dem lieblichen Geschoepff denen Voegelen, auch ausser dem Fang, nur durch Ergruendung deren Eigenschaften und Zahmmachung oder anderer Abrichtung man sich vor Lust und Zeitvertrieb machen koenne.

PETTERSON, M. 1956 Diffusion of a new habit among greenfinches. Nature, London, 177:709–10.

POCOCK, D. F. 1956 The social anthropology of India. Man, 1956, 169.

PROMPTOV, A. V. 1949 Vocal imitation in the Passeriformes. C. R. (Doklady) Ac. Sci. U.R.S.S. 45:261.

REYNIERS, J. A. 1953 Germ-free life. (Report of a lecture) Lancet II:933–4.

ROTHMAN, S., A. F. KRYSA, and A. M. SMILJANIC 1946 Inhibitory action of human epidermis on melanin formation. Proc. Soc. exp. Biol. Med. 62:208–9.

RUITER, L. DE 1953 Some experiments on the camouflage of stick caterpillars. Behaviour, 4:222–32.

SCHREIDER, E. 1950 Les variations raciales et sexuelles du tronc humain. L'Anthrop. 54:67–81, 228–61.

SIMPSON, G. G. 1944 Tempo and Mode in Evolution. New York.

SPURWAY, H. 1953a The escape drive in domestic cats and the dog and cat relationship. Behaviour, 5:81–4.

———— 1953b Genetics of specific and subspecific differences in European newts. Symp. Soc. exp. Biol. 7:200–37.

———— 1955 The causes of domestication: an attempt to integrate some ideas of Konrad Lorenz with evolution theory. J. Genet. 53:325–62.

———— 1956 Cultural mammalogy. (Review of Studies of the Psychology and Behavior of Captive Animals in Zoos and Circuses, by H. Hediger, 1956.) New Biol. 20:104–11.

SUSKI, P. M. 1933 The body-build of American-born Japanese children. Biometrika, 25:323–52.

THORPE, W. H. 1938 Further experiments on olfactory conditioning in a parasitic insect. The nature of the conditioning process. Proc. Roy. Soc. B. 126:370–97.

———— 1951 The learning abilities of birds. Ibis, 93:1–42, 252–96.

———— 1954 The process of learning in the chaffinch as studied by means of the sound spectrograph. Nature, London, 173, 465.

VALLOIS, HENRI V. 1954 Neandertals and Praesapiens. Huxley Memorial Lecture 1954 J. R. Anthrop. Inst. 84:111–30.

WRIGHT, S. 1949 Adaptation and selection. In Genetics, Paleontology and Evolution. Princeton.

15 • WOLF CHILDREN

Ashley Montagu

"Wild children" have had a great fascination for their fellow men, and understandably so. "The wild man of the woods" would, so it was believed, resemble our prehistoric ancestors in his behavior. When this notion was finally shed, the appealing idea that soon took its place was if we could study children who had not enjoyed a human socialization process, especially children who had been brought up by wild animals, we should then be able to learn a great deal about the nature of human nature—and indeed we might.

Scarcely a decade passes without the announcement in the press of the discovery of such a child.

There is a momentary flurry of excitement, and then it invariably turns out that the child is shown either to have been recently abandoned or is retarded and has run away from his keepers. Although these children are usually boys, the most famous "feral" children were girls, and they were first elaborately reported in 1942. I was called upon to review the book in which these children were reported, and that review is reprinted here. In spite of the publication of that review more than a generation ago, these "wolf-children" from Midnapore have crept into the literature of sociology on all fours. I have even encountered them as authentic examples of "feral man" in a few anthropological works.

This contribution will have served its purpose if it underscores the principle that it is not the willingness either to believe or to disbelieve that characterizes the scientific method, but rather the desire to discover what the facts are. As the reader will perceive, the "facts" as presented by Singh and Zingg were in many places open to question, and many of them were based on popular beliefs which could have had no basis in reality. Hence, despite all the testimony by scientists and others to the honesty of the Rev. Singh, the verifiable facts against which his "facts" could be measured throw grave doubt upon his story.

Isolated children in civilized societies are not unknown, however, and their study, difficult as it is, has had its rewards.[1]

In 1941 Professor Arnold Gesell of the Clinic of Child Development, Yale University, published a book entitled *Wolf Child and Human Child, Being a Narrative Interpretation of the Life History of Kamala, the Wolf Girl*. A few months later, in 1942, Professor Robert M. Zingg, then of the University of Denver, published a book entitled *Wolf-Children and Feral Man*, his coauthor being the Reverend J. A. L. Singh.

These two books at once brought to the attention of the public the existence of the first "authenticated wolf children," children who had been, so it was claimed, raised by wolves. During the twenty years since the advent of the wolf children was announced to the world, they have steadily crept into the literature on all fours as genuine examples of human beings raised by animals.

The story of Kamala and Amala, the wolf children of "Godamuri" or of Midnapore, constitutes an interesting study in scientific credulity. Very briefly, two children were claimed to have been repeatedly seen by natives and other villagers emerging together with several wolves from the ant-hill den of the said wolves. The Reverend J. A. L. Singh states that, while traveling in the company of two Anglo-Indians who were witnesses to the event, he captured or liberated the two children from the wolves' den at Godamuri on October 17, 1920. At the time of their rescue, or liberation, the younger child was guessed to be about eighteen months old. She was given the name Amala. The older child was estimated to be about eight years of age, and was named Kamala. It is assumed that both children were about six months of age when taken by the wolves, and that they were stolen from different families. Amala died on September 21, 1921, while Kamala died November 14, 1929. Thus Amala was observed for almost a year and Kamala for nine years.

When first observed, Kamala and Amala were unable to stand in the erect position but habitually progressed on all fours. They ate raw meat and entrails in what is alleged to have been wolf fashion, were without sphincter control, howled like wolves, preferred the society of dogs to that of human beings, and exhibited other feral traits. They were entirely without speech and all those other attributes which we have come to regard as specifically human.

In *Wolf-Children and Feral Man* Dr. Robert Zingg makes available an account of the history of these children written by the Reverend J. A. L. Singh based upon the records which the latter kept while the children were under his own and his wife's observation in their orphanage at Midna-

SOURCE: Ashley Montagu, "Wolf Children," *American Anthropologist* vol. 45 (Washington: 1943): 468–72. Reprinted by permission of the author.
[1] The most extended discussion of these is to be found in Ashley Montagu, "Isolation Versus Socialization," in his *The Direction of Human Development*, Rev. ed. (New York: Hawthorn Books, 1970), pp. 267–87.

pore. In the second part of the work Dr. Zingg discusses the subject of feral man in general and records a number of cases of extreme isolation of children in particular, the latter for their own interest and also in order to serve as checks against the description of the behavior of the "wolf children." There are forewords by Professors R. Ruggles Gates, Arnold Gesell, Francis N. Maxfield, and Kingsley Davis, each attesting his belief in the genuineness of the discovery and the account of the children as given by the Reverend Singh. A preface by Bishop H. Pakenham-Walsh, together with an affidavit by the District Judge of Midnapore, E. Waight, to both of whom the Reverend Singh was well known, testifies to his good character and reliability and their belief in the truth of his account of the discovery of the "wolf children."

Let me say that having read the volume very critically I find that despite certain difficulties, the Reverend Singh's account of his discovery and observations has an impressive ring of authenticity about it. The writer impresses me as a naïve but honest person who records his observation frankly, while even those which seem to belong to the realm of folklore, rather than to that of sober fact, read quite as convincingly as those which do not seem to be either a little east or a little west of the truth.

But when all this has been said, it must regretfully be added that this account of the "wolf children" cannot be accepted as true. I say "regretfully" for several reasons. Firstly, because I should very much like to believe the greater part of this story since it appears to fit into the general theory of personal social development fairly well, and we should at long last have at least one authentic case of children reared by animals with which to support our theories. Secondly, because I have a private Franciscan belief in the fellowship of man with all nature which I should like to have seen supported by so striking an instance. But as Mr. Pecksniff would have said, "Facts is facts." And the facts in this book, alas, rest on the completely unsupported testimony of one person, the Reverend Singh. Now, however much and however sympathetically we might be inclined to put our trust in his word, no scientist can accept as true any statement of a fellow scientist or the statement of anyone else until it has been independently confirmed by others. Such confirmation is altogether wanting in the present case, and that being so, with all the good will in the world and in spite of all the prefaces and forewords by learned professors, bishops, and magistrates, we cannot accept as true the story of the discovery of the "wolf children" and their presumed rearing by wolves.

The process of verification and confirmation is a cardinal principle of scientific method, the method of arriving at scientifically supportable results. Whether or not children have been reared by animals can be determined only by observation not necessarily premeditated and carried out under conditions which provide the means of verification. Hundreds of stories and legends say that they have been so reared, and the investigation of these stories constitutes a legitimate and scientific activity. Dr. Zingg has been interested in examining such stories for some time, with not altogether happy results. It seems to me that in the present volume he is not so much concerned with an impartial examination of the evidence as with insisting upon one interpretation of it. I regret to have to say this because I have every sympathy for the enthusiast, and it is quite understandable that once having become enamored of a story one might be carried away by it. But this is just the sort of thing against which even the best of scientists must continually be on his guard. Even scientific structures are sometimes erected on emotional foundations. Emotionally I might favor the Singh-Zingg & Co. story; as a scientist I cannot accept it.

Even if the whole story were better authenticated, here are a few points which would cause me to make some reservations:

Two Anglo-Indians, a Mr. P. Rose and a Mr.

Henry Richards, are said by the Reverend Singh to have witnessed the rescue of the children from the wolves' den, but unfortunately the former is now untraceable and the latter is dead. Why, during all the years the Reverend Singh was studying the children, did he make no attempt to obtain statements from these and other men who were present at the alleged rescue? Neither Mr. Rose nor Mr. Richards ever came forward to avow or disavow the Reverend Singh's story.

Kamala is presumed to have been kept in the wolves' den for about seven and a half years. But wolves do not keep their young for anything like so long a period under normal conditions. Is it likely that they would have departed from the universal practice of wolves in the case of Kamala?

Could a six-month-old child be suckled by a wolf? It is, no doubt, possible, but it is difficult to imagine why a wolf should want to do such a troublesome thing.

Even if the statement were fully corroborated that the children were found together with the wolves in their den, that in itself would not constitute evidence that they were brought there by wolves nor that they had been suckled and reared by them.

The Reverend Singh states that Kamala and Amala used to howl regularly almost every night at about ten o'clock, and at one and three o'clock in the morning. The fact is that the idea that wolves howl at regular hours every night is a widespread folk belief not borne out by the observation of wolves' habits. So that what was obviously intended as an irrefutable indication of the children's lupine nature serves, rather, to arouse further doubts as to the accuracy of the narrative.

The statement that the children were not observed to sweat is yet another example of the obvious influence of folkloristic belief upon the Reverend Singh's narrative. The widespread notion that dogs do not sweat except through the tongue is quite untrue; dogs possess numerous sweat glands on every part of the body. But for the purposes of the Reverend Singh's narrative, since dogs and wolves are closely related—and since the wolf children were alleged to have adopted the habits of wolves—it must follow that the wolf children did not sweat.

The eyes of the children are said to have emitted a blue light at night. "Night glare" is a phenomenon not unknown in human beings, but it is a condition of such great rarity that the chances against its ever occurring in two individuals living together are so astronomically high that we are forced to give up all attempt at normal explanation. The necessary extreme myopia or hypermetropia may have been present, but there is very definitely no evidence of any such condition in the Reverend Singh's account. I have been unable to find any record of children who were brought up in darkness exhibiting a like phenomenon. It is difficult to conceive of the special structure necessary, the tapetum (the iridescent layer of the choroid coat of the eye of certain carnivorous animals), developing as a special adaptation to the conditions of life of Kamala and Amala. But what is even more difficult to conceive is the emission of "a peculiar blue glare, like that of a cat or a dog, in the dark" without the presence, as far as one can gather, of any external source of light. This is, in fact, quite impossible, for the light must always be of external origin and is only reflected back by the eye. It was an old Arab belief that the eye itself emitted light! As for the "blue" glare itself, this would appear to be impossible in the case of human beings for the simple reason that the only possible source of such "glaring" is the fundus (the posterior portion or base of the eye), and this normally reflects either a dark red, or an orange-yellow color. The blue eye glare of cats and dogs, and many other animals, is due to the refraction of particles in the tapetum similar to those which in the human iris produce the appearance of the normal blue eye, but which have no connection in the latter case with "night glare." In the offspring of Malayan-Negro crosses, the fundus, through the ophthalmoscope, may appear somewhat bluish, or even gray, depending upon the presence of certain pigment particles, but it is doubtful whether in such cases one could obtain a bluish or grayish glare from the eyes. It is of significance to note that all the supporting cases cited by Dr. Zingg gave either a dark red or, as in the case referred to by Parsons, "a yellow reflex from the pupil." But the latter case refers specifically to the presence of glioma of the retina.

There are other difficulties which could be similarly discussed. But let us come to the point. The Reverend Singh claimed that Amala and Kamala were reared by wolves. What evidence exists in support of his claim? The answer is *none*. The grounds upon which this answer is based have already been briefly stated.

Were Amala and Kamala abandoned by their parents? No one knows. Were these children congenitally defective in any way? It is impossible to say. If they were not congenitally defective, then it would be a reasonable inference to make that their retardation, or rather nondevelopment as human beings, was due to the fact that during the critical period of their development they were practically entirely isolated from the conditioning influences of human contacts. It is during this conditioning period that it is assumed they spent their lives with wolves, living the life of wolves, so that behaviorally they became what they were assumed to have been exposed to—wolves.

On that point we must suspend judgment, but taking the matter from the general standpoint of the development of behavior one thing is certain: Given all the necessary normal potentialities an individual does not become a functioning human being simply by virtue of being born into the species *Homo sapiens;* indeed, he cannot become a functioning human being until he is exposed to the humanizing influences of other human beings. The attributes of humanity are a function

of human society, of human socializing factors acting upon potentialities capable of being humanized.

Dr. Zingg writes that "radicals" who believe that "environment completely molds the human mind and mentality . . . overlook the fact that mentality is a bioneurological mechanism, and mind, the environmentally conditioned content organized by that mechanism. Though here we see a well-attested case of human beings reduced to wolf-conditioning, the radical case still needs a case of a wolf raised to human behavior."

Dr. Zingg may be allowed a distinction between "mind" and "mentality," though I do not know what that distinction may be, but he certainly entertains some strange notions on the nature of what "radicals" are supposed to believe. Dr. Zingg disagrees with the straw men of his own making that a wolf or other animal could be "educated into the behavior of a man." But surely, whatever Rousseau or the ingenious Monboddo may have thought, no one today, not even the "radicals," believes anything else than that it is utterly impossible to make a human mind out of the cellular characters of the nervous system of any nonhominid animal. The genetics or potentialities of such animals do not possess the necessary qualities.

As for Dr. Zingg's statement that mentality may be regarded as the environmentally conditioned content organized by the bioneurological mechanism, I am not sure that he is not right. But is it not perhaps more in accord with the evidence to say that mind represents the environmental organization—or, better, integration—of the bioneurological mechanism? Does behavior represent the bioneurological organization of environmentally conditioned contents or do the environmentally conditioned contents acting upon a relatively undifferentiated variety of nervous tissues serve to differentiate and organize those tissues into a bioneurological system which then functions as mind? The truth, perhaps, lies somewhere between the two views.

I believe that the work of cultural anthropologists, and of experimental biologists and psychologists, would favor the second view. As Coghill has remarked in the final sentence of that most fundamental of all works on the subject, *Anatomy and the Problem of Behaviour,* "Man is, indeed, a mechanism, but he is a mechanism which, within his limitations of life, sensitivity, and growth, is creating and operating himself."

Since the above was written, Doctors W. F. Ogburn and N. K. Bose have made a thorough on-the-spot investigation of the story of the wolf children. The findings of these investigators indicate that while two children named Amala and Kamala lived for a time in the Singh orphanage, there is no evidence whatever to support the account given of these children's "history" by Singh and Zingg. Even the village, "Godamuri," the alleged site of the wolves' den, does not exist in Midnapore or anywhere else in India.[1]

---

[1] Ogburn, W. F. and Bose, N. K., "On the Trail of the Wolf Children," *Genetic Psychology Monographs,* vol. 60, 1959 (pp. 117–193).

EIGHT • DEVELOPMENT BY JUVENILIZATION

16 • THE MEANING OF NEONATAL AND INFANT IMMATURITY IN MAN

Ashley Montagu

The immaturity of the human neonate and his/her long infancy has been noted by many thinkers, and has very properly been associated with the long learning period which the human child must undergo in order to become an adequately functioning human being. While it is clear that the immaturity of neonate and infant constitute good examples of neoteny—the prolongation of a fetal and early infancy stage of development—the real significance of that immaturity and its consequences for human development have not been understood.

In the following article it is suggested that the gestation period of the human neonate is only half completed when it is born, that it is born when the size of its brain reaches the maximum consonant with its ability to pass through the birth canal, and that its exterogestative period is completed when it begins to crawl around on its own steam.

The evidence marshalled in support of this theory should be critically examined, for its consequences are not merely of theoretical importance, but of considerable practical importance: for example, as regards the tender loving care that the child should be receiving, especially during its neonatal and infancy periods. The mother of the neonate and infant has been beautifully prepared through the whole of her evolutionary history and her own pregnancy to meet all the needs of the infant, but this, in civilized societies with their sophisticated confusions, she is not generally allowed to do.[1]

There is much more to be said on the biological aspects of this subject; for a splendid discussion of it

the reader should consult Kovacs' magnificent study, "Biological Interpretation of the Nine Months Duration of Human Pregnancy," *Acta Biol. Magyar, Tudom. Acad.*, X (1960), 331–361. See also David Jonas and Doris Klein, *Man-Child: A Study of the Infantilization of Man* (New York: McGraw-Hill, 1970).

The immaturity of the human neonate and infant probably led to the establishment of the parental couple—the nuclear family, so vitally necessary for the support, survival, and instruction of the human infant. Among the many other probable social consequences of human neoteny, perhaps the most important was the development of love, the behavior designed to confer survival benefits upon another in a creatively enlarging manner, a profound involvement in the welfare of the other extending over a period of many years.

The social and behavioral consequences of man's prolonged immaturity have only begun to be studied in depth. It remains a fallow field for further investigation.

Why are human beings born in a state so immature that it takes 8 to 10 months before the human infant can even crawl, and another 4 to 6 months before he can walk and talk? That a good many years will elapse before the human child will cease to depend upon others for his very survival constitutes yet further evidence of the

SOURCE: From the *Journal of the American Medical Association*, vol. 178, 1961, pp. 156–157. Reprinted by permission of the publisher.
[1] See Ashley Montagu, "The Young of Human Kind," M. Rasey (editor), *The Nature of Human Nature* (Detroit: Wayne University Press, 1959), pp. 73–92. Ashley Montagu, *Touching: The Human Significance of the Skin* (New York: Columbia University Press, 1971).

fact that man is born and remains more immature for a longer period than any other animal.

The newborn elephant and the fallow deer can run with the herd shortly after they are born. By the age of 6 weeks, the infant seal has been taught by his mother to navigate his watery world for himself. These animals all have long gestation periods, presumably because animals that give birth to small litters, which they are unable to protect as efficiently as predatory animals can, must give birth to young who are in a fairly mature state. A long gestation period serves to allow for such maturation.

The elephant, which has a gestation period of 515 to 670 days, is monotocous, having but one young at a birth. In the polytocous fallow deer, which has 2 or 3 young at a birth, the gestation period is 230 days, and in the seal, which produces only a single pup at a birth, the gestation period varies from 245 to 350 days. Predatory animals, by contrast, are very efficient in protecting their young, and have a short gestation period. Their litters can vary from 3 upwards; the size of the young can be small at birth, and the young can be born in a somewhat immature state. The lion, for example, which generally has a litter of 3 pups, has a gestation period of 105 days. Man has a gestation period of 267 days, which is distinctly in the class of long gestation periods. Since this is so, what can be the reason that man is born in so extremely immature a state? Quite clearly the human infant arrives in the world long before he becomes ready to take it on for himself. How has this come about?

The hypothesis proposed here is that man is born as immaturely as he is because—owing to the great increase in the size of his brain and consequently of his head—if he weren't born when he is, he wouldn't be born at all. As a result of discoveries made during the last 40 years, it now seems probable that during the early evolution of man, several important changes occurred simultaneously. In adaptation to the novel changes presented by the translation from a forest environment to the open plains—associated with the development of a tool-making, hunting economy, and the accompanying high premium placed upon the development of the erect bipedal gait—the brain grew larger while the pelvic outlet grew smaller. At birth the average volume of the brain is 350 cc. Were that volume to increase only slightly, the head could not pass through the birth canal. As it is, in many cases, the size of the baby's head constitutes a hazard to both baby and mother. The rate of growth of the brain is proceeding at such a rate that it cannot continue within the womb and must continue outside the womb. In other words, the survival of the fetus and mother requires the termination of gestation within the womb (uterogestation or interogestation) when the limit of head size compatible with birth has been reached, and long before maturation occurs.

Gestation, then, is not completed by the act of birth but is only translated from gestation within the womb to gestation outside the womb (exterogestation). Professor John Bostock of the University of Queensland, Australia, has suggested that the limit of exterogestation be set at the stage of development of effective locomotion on all fours, a suggestion which has a good deal of merit. According to this hypothesis, man spends the first half of his gestation period within the womb (uterogestation), and the second half of it outside the womb (exterogestation).

It is of interest to note that the average duration of exterogestation—that is, the period from birth to the development of quadrupedal locomotion—lasts exactly the same time, on the average, as the period of uterogestation, namely, 267 days. In connection with this, it is also to be noted that, while the mother nurses her infant, pregnancy will not usually occur for at least 267 days after the birth of the child.

To learn what the child must learn in order to function as an adequate human being, he must have a large brain. It is a striking fact that by the time the human child has attained its third birthday it has also virtually achieved the full adult size of the brain. The brain volume of the human three-year-old is 1,250 cc., while the brain volume of the human adult is 1,400 cc. Significantly, the human brain more than doubles in size during its first year of development, attaining, on the average, a volume of 800 cc. About two-thirds of the total growth of the brain is achieved by the end of the first year, and it will take an additional 2 years to accomplish the same amount of growth, that is, to 1,250 cc. In its first year, the infant's brain does more growing than it will ever do again in any one year.

It is important that most of the brain growth be accomplished during the first year, when the infant has so much to learn and do, for the first year of life requires a great deal of unobtrusive packing for a journey that will last the rest of the traveler's life. To perform this packing successfully, his brain must be much larger than 350 cc, but quite clearly he cannot wait till he has grown a brain of 800 cc before being born. Hence, he must be born with the maximum-sized brain possible, and do the rest of his brain growing after birth. Since the human fetus must be born when its brain has reached the limit of size compatible with its admission through the birth canal, such maturation or further development as other mammals complete before birth the human mammal will have to complete after birth. In other words, the gestation period will have to be extended beyond birth.

If this interpretation of the gestation period is sound, then it would follow that we are not at present meeting the needs of infants in anything approaching an adequate manner. Although it is customary to regard the gestation period as terminated at birth, I suggest that this is quite as erroneous a view as that which regards the life of the individual as beginning at birth. Birth is no more the beginning of the life of the indi-

vidual than it is the end of gestation; it is merely the bridge between gestation within the womb and gestation continued outside the womb. It may be calendrically useful to divide up these periods as we have traditionally done, but it would appear to be quite unbiological to do so. This is unbiological because, by making such arbitrary divisions, we lose sight of the essential fact that the human infant is quite as immature at birth as is the little marsupial immaturely born into its mother's pouch, there to undergo its exterogestation until it is sufficiently matured. The human infant remains immature much longer than the infant kangaroo or opossum, but whereas the marsupial infant enjoys the protection of its mother's pouch during its period of immaturity, the human infant is afforded no such natural advantage. This is all the more reason why the parental generation in such a species must clearly understand what the immaturity of its infants really means: namely, that with all the modifications initiated by the birth process, the baby is still continuing its gestation period, passing by means of birth from uterogestation to postnatal exterogestation. The biological unity, the symbiotic relationship, maintained by mother and conceptus throughout pregnancy does not cease at birth but becomes—indeed, is naturally designed to become—even more intensive and interoperative after birth than during uterogestation. It is not simply the infant who has a great need of continuing support from its mother after birth, but that the mother has, in a complementary manner, an equally great need to continue to support and to give succor to the child. Giving birth to her child, the mother's interest is deepened and reinforced in its welfare. Her whole organism has been readied to minister to its needs, to nurse it at the breast. In nursing, the infant ingests the beneficial colostrum, but nursing also confers benefits upon the mother. The psychophysiological benefits, which in the continuing symbiotic relationship mother and child reciprocally confer upon one another, are vitally important for their future development. The transfer of maternal antibodies to the baby through the milk in breastfeeding during the early exterogestative period, thus conferring immunities upon the infant, underscores both the biological reality and importance of the symbiotic dependence of the infant upon the mother.

These facts are only slowly coming to be recognized in our highly sophisticated, mechanized, Western world, a world in which breastfeeding is considered to be something that (as one expensively educated young woman remarked to me) "only animals do," and in which there are pediatricians who assure mothers that a bottle formula is every bit as good as, and even better than, breastfeeding. We live in the logical denouement of the Machine Age, when not only are things made by machine, but human beings are turned out to be as machine-like as we can make them. We therefore see little wrong in dealing with others in a mechanical manner, since this is an age in which it is considered a mark of progress that whatever was formerly done by human beings is taken out of their hands and done by machine. It is esteemed an advance when a bottle formula can be substituted for the product of the human breast, especially in the United States, and especially in a period when many women misguidedly want to be as much like men as they are capable of becoming.

When mother and child most need each other, they are too often separated from each other, the one isolated in her room, the other banished to a crib in the nursery (so-called, presumably, because nursing is the one thing that is not done there). The separation begins from the moment of birth, so profound has our misunderstanding of the needs of human beings grown.

Perhaps the hypothesis of uterogestation and exterogestation proposed here may cause us to reconsider the meaning of the human infant's immaturity and dependency.

REFERENCES

1. BOSTOCK, J. Exterior Gestation, Primitive Sleep, Enuresis and Asthma: Study in Aetiology, *Med. J. Aust.* 2:149–153 (Aug. 2), 185–188 (Aug. 9) 1958.
2. MONTAGU, A. *Prenatal Influences*, Springfield, Ill.: Charles C. Thomas Publisher, 1962.

NINE • CULTURE AS A FACTOR IN MAN'S PHYSICAL EVOLUTION

17 • IN THE BEGINNING: ASPECTS OF HOMINID BEHAVIORAL EVOLUTION

Robin Fox

In this stimulating paper Fox raises a number of questions which must be considered in evaluating the conditions which have contributed to the development of human behavior. Fox argues that since man's behavior may stem from a nature completely different from that of other primates, we should therefore be wary of drawing conclusions about the evolution of human behavior from the behavior of contemporary non-human primates. But Fox does not believe that this is the case, for his whole discussion is devoted to an examination of which non-human primates present the most likely model for the development of human behavior. He concludes that the savanna baboons most nearly fit the bill.

The tribute to the writings of Freud, Westermarck, and Carveth Read is long overdue, and I would especially urge the student to rush to the nearest library and read a copy of Carveth Read's *The Origin of Man,* 2nd ed. (Cambridge: At the University Press, 1925). Read, who for many years had been Professor of Philosophy at University College, London, published his book originally as a part of an earlier work issued in 1920, *The Origin of Man and His Superstitions* (Cambridge: At the University Press). In this book, he sets forth ideas on the origin and evolution of man which a half century of research has since proved to have been uncannily correct. The importance of Read's book lies in its living demonstration of the great heuristic value of informed speculation. The tragedy is that few anthropologists seem to have read Read's book and followed the paths he so clearly indicated. Freud and especially Westermarck will always remain as brilliant beacons, in the glow of whose writings much that would otherwise

remain obscure may be suddenly illuminated. In reading the works of such seminal thinkers it is always well to remember that it is not so much the truth or falsity by which their theories should be measured, but by their fruitfulness. Theories are or should be heuristic tools; and Fox's contribution represents such a heuristic approach to the examination of some fundamental problems in the physical and cultural evolution of man.

For the further development of Fox's views the reader should consult Lionel Tiger and Robin Fox, *The Imperial Animal* (New York: Holt, Rinehart, and Winston, 1971).

One of the most exciting developments in anthropology over the last decade has been the revival of interest in human social origins. We are once again very much concerned with what happened 'in the beginning . . . ,' but we are approaching this in a very different way from the nineteenth-century anthropologists who asked the same question. They were concerned to project backwards from primitive society to 'the infancy of mankind.' It would be pointless to parade here all the well-known and correct objections to this procedure. But now a combination of new material from several fields has led some anthropologists to try the reverse procedure; that is, to project 'upwards' from the primates. (This method in turn has dangers not unlike those on which evolutionism foundered.) The new material however comes from a more extensive fossil record of primate evolution; an increasing number of excellent field studies of the social behaviour of monkeys and apes; and a realisation

SOURCE: *Man* vol. 2 (London: The Royal Anthropological Institute, 1967): 415–33. Reprinted by permission of the Royal Anthropological Institute.

of the relevance of the work of the ethologists for an understanding of the evolution of behaviour.

All this I am sure would have delighted Malinowski. One half of his tradition—the detailed scrutiny and contextual examination of particular cultures—has survived and flourished among social anthropologists. But the other half—his concern with 'human nature' and the 'biological basis of culture' has languished. It has been argued, perhaps correctly, that he never really made a convincing connexion between the two, but this is primarily because he had no adequate evolutionary framework into which to put them both. The evolutionism of his predecessors he rightly rejected, and the new biology was in its infancy. But he maintained with characteristic forthrightness that 'We have to base our theory of culture on the fact that all human beings belong to an animal species' (1944:75) and he was always willing to explore what he described as 'The no-specialist's land' between the science of man and that of the animal (1927:x). Although the new knowledge of which I have spoken would have led him to rethink and possibly reject many of his views on the nature of culture, I am sure it would have excited his copious imagination, and that he would have seen its relevance at least. Malinowski's importance for me lies in his conviction that the 'biological basis of culture' should be at the forefront of our thinking, and not in his tradition of fieldwork nor in his insistence on contextual interpretation of custom.

It is perhaps a sign of the times that my title was suggested neither by the opening words of the Book of Genesis, nor the Gospel according to St. John, but by the final sentence of Freud's *Totem and taboo* (1952). This in turn was taken from Goethe's *Faust* (Act I), 'Im Anfang war die Tat': 'In the beginning was the Deed.' Freud's attempt in this book to account for the origins of 'human nature' was the subject of a long critique by Malinowski (1927) and rarely has

any theory been so universally condemned. But the fact that so many eminent, learned and authoritative social scientists have condemned the theory suggests to me that there is an even chance of its being right. I want here to argue that there is more than a germ of truth in it, and to show how the Malinowskian questions about human biological propensities can perhaps best be handled in an evolutionary framework of the kind Freud intuitively saw was necessary.

Let me briefly summarise Freud's theory of the 'Deed' or 'primal event.' In the beginning men lived in family hordes in which a single, dominant, aggressive and jealous male monopolised the females and threw out his sons. The ejected sons (the 'brothers' in Freud's terminology) formed themselves into a homosexual band, until the fatal day arrived. 'One day the brothers who had been driven out came together, killed and devoured their father and so made an end of the patriarchal horde.' He continues, 'Some cultural advance, perhaps command over some new weapon, had given them a sense of superior strength' (1952:141). However, although they hated the father, the brothers also envied him and admired him and hence at his death they felt guilty as a result of 'delayed obedience.' Consequently, they invented totemic prohibitions on the one hand and incest taboos on the other. The father was identified with a totem animal which could not be slain except in ritual when the brothers reaffirmed their solidarity, and the incest taboos meant the renunciation of the father's women who were the cause of all the trouble. From these beginnings in ritual and renunciation all that is truly human sprang. And, of course, this was the basis of the Oedipus complex, the fundamental feature of human personality.

Freud was asking a fundamentally important question here: how was the breakthrough from non-human primate to fully-human primate achieved? He saw that the roots of our present social behaviour lay in our primate heritage, and yet there was obviously a great difference. His problem was to account for this difference. It was not enough for him to repeat, in the parrot fashion of anthropologists, that man had culture: of course he had—but why? Or as Konrad Lorenz would put it, the great evolutionary question is 'how come?' What had impelled this evolution towards a radically different mode of adaptation?

For Freud the breakthrough was the result of the imposition of taboos on natural tendencies, this imposition being the beginning of culture. Without accepting his specific proposals most anthropologists have accepted this position. For Lévi-Strauss the rules of incest and exogamy are the first 'intrusion' of culture into nature, and totemic thinking is a basic form of articulate taxonomic thought (1949; 1962). For Malinowski also, the opposition of culture and nature was absolute.

For other writers, for example the unjustly neglected Westermarck, this has not necessarily been the case and instead they have attempted to derive features of human social life from features of primate life. That is, they have looked for an explanation in terms of continuity rather than difference. The human family, for instance, was for Westermarck a natural outcome of primate tendencies (1891). This all depends, of course, on the level at which one is working. Thus, Malinowski stressed the rules and customs of marriage and courtship, lacking in animals and present in man. Of this difference there can be no doubt—animals do not have articulate rules. For Freud, too, the invention of conscious rules and obedience to them was crucial. For Westermarck, however, it was the continuities in the structure of the units that were interesting. The rules of marriage were many and various, but what was interesting was the persistence of the primate familial pattern of mating and socialisation in man.

Thus we are working here at two levels: the structural and the cultural. At the cultural level there are by definition quite pronounced differences, but at the structural level this is not so clear.

This raises another problem. Many of the anthropological arguments concerning the differentiation of man from the non-human primates concentrate almost exclusively on the 'nature-culture' distinction, and the 'substitution' of culture for nature. But man differs from the other primates not only in terms of learned cumulative traditional behaviour (and even this difference is one of degree, not kind); he also differs in genetic endowment—he is a different genus. The hominid line has had a history independent of the other hominoidea for anything up to 30 million years and perhaps more (see, for example, Leakey 1967). Hence many of the differences which we can observe between the most basic behaviours of men on the one hand, and monkeys and apes on the other, may not stem from man's superior cultural achievements but rather from his expression of a completely different biological nature. Moreover this difference need not be a recent one in evolutionary terms but may stem from the remote hominid past. We must not therefore too readily assume that any crucial difference is necessarily the result of cultural adaptations. I will return to this point, which is very relevant to the question of whether or not differences between ourselves and the monkeys and apes are a result of the overthrow of our primate natures, or simply a reflection of the fact that we are a different primate which has evolved a different nature. It should also make us wary, as we shall see, of taking as models for 'pre-human' hominid behaviour, the behaviour of particular contemporary non-human primates.

The whole picture is complicated by the fact that culture did not appear, as Malinowski thought, all of a piece. He never thought to justify this position, and indeed he scarcely needed to do so, as it was subscribed to by most anthropologists as a matter of course. Keith's 'cerebral rubicon' (750 c.c.'s) before which was animal and after which was man, was supplemented by Kroeber's 'critical point' theory, which he likened to the freezing point of water (Keith 1948; Kroeber 1948). These theories were purely deductive rationalisations, and we now know that tools, hunting and probably shelters appeared with the genus *Australopithecus* up to two million years ago, and that the brain size of this little man-ape was no greater than that of the living great apes. The rapid evolution of the brain occurred, in other words, *after* the inception of culture, and the fact that the evolving man-ape became dependent on culture meant that culture itself acted as a selection pressure. In a very real sense then, culture is man's nature (Geertz 1965).

This raises for us the even more difficult problem of where to start looking for human origins. 'In the beginning was . . .' but when was the beginning? We must here take Freud's point, conveniently overlooked by his critics, that in his 'origin myth' he compressed the time-scale of evolution. He insisted in a footnote to which he drew particular attention, that his treatment involved an 'abbreviation of the time factor,' a 'compression of the whole subject matter,' and that 'It would be as foolish to aim at exactitude in such matters as it would be to insist upon certainty' (1952:142–3). We do not need, then, to look for a point in time, but for processes over time. We must examine the social unit among the primates as a clue to the 'raw material of society' (Linton 1936). We must then look at the fossil record to see if this can help us to understand how the raw material became worked into the typically human society of today.

We cannot, as I have said, necessarily accept any particular contemporary primate as the model for the pre-human hominid. What we can do is to narrow down the range of possibilities. We are beginning to know the full range of possible primate behaviours, and we can narrow down our focus to a part of this range that will represent the possibilities open to the pre-human hominid. In this we are going back to the kind of enquiry that Westermarck, Carveth Read, Freud and others were pursuing. They were struggling with an inadequate biology, a poor fossil record, a mistaken geological time-scale, and almost purely anecdotal material on the social life of primates. Rather than jeering at their theories we should marvel that they achieved so much in at least seeing the problems and attempting to solve them. In any case, they were not always as mistaken as is generally assumed.

Both Westermarck and Freud looked to the unfortunate gorilla for evidence, although Westermarck also examined the chimpanzee. Both in fact depended on the work of Savage (1847), but Freud got his material second-hand from Darwin via Atkinson (1903) and Lang (1903). To Westermarck this hearsay evidence (Savage depended on native accounts of gorilla behaviour) suggested that the 'family'—by which he meant the monogamous independent family—was the basis of primate social life, and that the human family was a natural outcome of this. Thus was the hypothesis of 'primitive promiscuity' in early man attacked from the primate angle. Freud also took the gorilla as his model, but came to different conclusions. A single, aggressive, dominant male with a harem of females was seen as the basic group. The 'primal horde' was in fact this cyclopean family.

Derek Freeman (1965) has recently criticised this assumption on the basis of the work of Schaller (1963) on the mountain gorilla. There are several features of gorilla society which do not tally with this picture:

1. There is usually more than one adult male in a group;
2. while there are relations of dominance between the males, there is little aggressiveness and competition;

3. the dominant male is not jealous and allows females to copulate with other males;
4. there is no evidence of young males being driven out, but they may leave and wander for a time and join other bands.

There is no support from the gorilla for Freud's hypothesis, but there is little for Westermarck's either. What of the chimpanzee (Goodall 1965; Reynolds & Reynolds 1965; Reynolds 1965)?

With the chimpanzee we have a somewhat more fluid system in which groups of females seem to be the focus of group cohesion. Within a forest population there will be several such groups with their young, forming the fixed points in a social world of roving male bands. These male bands roam the forest in search of food and when they find it they drum on the trees to attract the females. The males may visit several female groups in turn, spending some time with them. When large parties of chimpanzees gather they indulge in spectacular jamborees. Sexual relations are promiscuous again, with evidence of individual choice and preference being important. Reynolds (1966a) found that some male chimpanzees were more home-loving than others and these tended to hang around the females and children. He refers to them rather charmingly as 'mothers' brothers.'

There is nothing in this behaviour of man's nearest relative to suggest either the bedrock of human familial organisation looked for by Westermarck, or the violent cyclopean family horde that had to be overthrown before a truly human state could be arrived at, sought by Freud. There is no evidence of permanent or even semi-permanent male-female relationships, even less than among the gorilla; and mating, while not totally random, is still promiscuous. The social unit here is either the forest population as a whole, or the groups of males on the one hand, and females on the other; but not the independent family.

However the chimpanzee is still championed by some as the model for proto-human society. Reynolds (1966b) has recently argued that in terms of common descent he is the best candidate and we must therefore take him seriously. His social structure is seen as an excellent pre-adaptation to life on the savannahs. When the early hominids, during the pliocene drought, moved from the forests to the savannahs, Reynolds argues, they took with them a social structure basically like that of the chimpanzee. The female/young group continued to be the basic unit but the wandering groups of males now became foragers and hunters, using their tool-making and carnivorous proclivities more and more efficiently to this end. The mothers' brothers stayed with the females to guard them, and eventually the individual choice/promiscuous mating pattern settled down, with an increasing division of labour, to a more human pattern of assigned mates and families. Thus for Reynolds an evolution of human patterns would be a normal and progressive development from chimpanzee-like patterns, given the historical transition to savannah hunting. The closeness of relationship of the chimpanzee to ourselves, and his obvious likeness in terms of intelligence, tool-making, individuation, curiosity, emotional lability and high sexual drive, reinforce this view.

But the problem of taking the great apes as models lies in the fact of their forest ecologies. Most modern students of primate evolution agree that we should pay close attention to ecology in order to understand the selection pressures at work on the evolving primate lines. This has been shown to be crucial in understanding somatic evolution, and as this is ultimately a result of behavioural adaptations, then it is crucial to behavioural evolution as well.

As we have seen, Reynolds has to project his chimpanzees *forward* on to the savannah; but this, in evolutionary terms, is a move they never made. They stayed on the forest floor and became highly adapted to a life of relative security and plenty in the forest setting. Thus it may be a mistake to project the contemporary chimpanzee, with his long history of forest-floor living, back to the miocene as a model for the evolving hominids, who may have been doing something quite different. In fact it may have been the ancestors of the great apes—at the time a more successful group of animals than the hominids—who denied the shelter of the trees to the ancestors of man.

The only real counter to this argument would be the theory of Kortlandt and Kooij (1963) that the chimpanzees did move out and adapt to savannah living, moving back into the forest later. This would explain why their capacities exceed their achievements. But this theory is not generally accepted.

Here perhaps we should pause to give the gibbon his due (Carpenter 1964). He is a puzzle in that while he is classified with the great apes he has remained in the tree-tops. He is the only permanent brachiator left among the Hominoidea. (The orang certainly brachiates, but we know little about his social habits.) He would have pleased Westermarck in that he is impeccably monogamous and lives in defended territories. The pressures leading to the formation of these territorial families, however, are very different from those which have operated during most of the history of the hominids. Indeed, the gibbon is more like some birds than his primate cousins, and closely resembles many of the prosimians. However, the further back we push hominid ancestry—and it now seems to have crept beyond the early miocene—the more likely it is that rather than hominids being offshoots from a pongid stem (which led to the great apes), they are a relatively independent line (Simons 1964). Gibbons, apes and hominids may have separated early and developed independently (Schultz 1936). It always remains therefore an open question as to whether any of our behavioural heritage has gibbon-like overtones—including the tendencies to pair formation and the territoriality seemingly

absent in the chimpanzee and gorilla. Be that as it may, we must bracket off the gibbon for a moment and return to the ground—and the dry open grassland and desert at that.

Kroeber, when criticising Freud's concept of the primal horde, said, 'It is a mere guess that the earliest organization of man resembled that of the gorilla rather than the trooping monkeys' (1920:44–50). It in fact turns out to be a poor guess, and the overwhelming majority of anthropological opinion now sides with the trooping, ground-dwelling monkeys as the best model for the proto-human horde. It stresses the importance of parallelism and ecology over close genetic relatedness.

Freeman does not pursue this line in his critique, being content with the negative case. What he does is to suggest that the elements of the Oedipus complex, 'the sexual drive, dominance, aggression and fear, are phylogenetically given and basic to the nature of the human animal and to human behaviour in all known forms of family and procreative groups (1965:20).' In other words, these are a part of the primate heritage, and he quotes evidence from pig-tailed monkeys and langurs.

If, then, Freud had looked to the ground-dwelling trooping monkeys, what would he have found? He would have discovered a system in which group size could range from 9 to 200 or more individuals, and in which an organisation of troop defence and even rudimentary predation existed. It is commonly accepted that baboons are the most successful of terrestrial primates after man, and baboons have commonly been taken as the closest guide to the kind of life we might have expected to find in hominid groups, at least in the pre-Australopithecine stage. (By 'baboons' I here mean the ground-dwelling monkeys, including, for example, the macaques.) The problem here is that we have two rather distinct types of baboon society. The original attempts to compare baboons and early man (e.g.

Washburn & Avis 1958; Sahlins 1959; Washburn & De Vore 1962; De Vore & Washburn 1964; De Vore 1965a), were based on the woodland-savannah-dwelling common baboons (chacma, olive, cynocephalus, etc.) and the macaques and rhesus monkeys of Japan and India. I shall call this Baboon 1. This society can be described roughly as a series of concentric circles. In the centre circle are the dominant males, most of the females, and the immature young. In the next circle are the less dominant males, while at the periphery are the sub-adult males and those adults not in the dominance hierarchy. The dominance hierarchy is limited in size; no matter how the group's numbers increase, it never seems to exceed six big males. These males monopolise the females and have choice of females in heat in order of precedence. In a small group the dominant male will do practically all the breeding himself. In larger groups females often form 'consort' relationships with dominant males which last for a few days to a week. As a female comes into oestrus she may be mounted by several sub-dominants, but it is only a dominant who can cover her at peak of ovulation. As dominance is characterised by strength, fighting ability, ability to co-operate and even willingness to baby-sit (which leads to acceptance of leadership by the group of females), such a breeding system has obvious survival value. The group then is structured around this core of dominant males who act as leaders and defenders and even in some cases as predators, although they do not provide for the females and young. (For a general survey of baboons see Hall 1966. For particular studies of this type (1), see Altman 1965; De Vore 1965b.) On the edges of this group are the young adult males. These have a loose dominance order, some bonding processes, and a good deal of homo-erotic behaviour. They may make forays into the group of females and may even be able to mount one who is not in peak oestrus, but they rarely successfully challenge the dominant males who can, and do, combine against them if necessary.

The Japanese macaques certainly have palace revolutions of a sort, and attempts to overthrow dominant males do take place. But usually a male can only get into the hierarchy by patient waiting and by pulling strings. If he has a high ranking mother (for the females have a hierarchy too) then she can keep him close to the centre and he can ingratiate himself with the females and be tolerated by the dominant males. At some point, then, he will get into the court circle. But many of the males must be content with a bachelor existence. Some wander off and become solitaries—the beatniks of the monkey world. Others eventually join other bands where they have more luck. (It is interesting for the theory of exogamy that here it is the females who remain stationary and the males who move between groups. The same is of course true of the chimpanzees. Thelma Rowell (personal communication) informs me that among three groups of baboons in Uganda studied over five years, all the males have changed groups at least once. The idea of these as relatively (or even absolutely) 'closed' breeding groups is thus disproved.)

The full range of complexities and subtleties of social structure among these remarkable terrestrial primates cannot be detailed here, but the overall structure is clear enough. It is not the cyclopean horde with the single jealous male, and indeed such a unit would perhaps not have survived under the conditions we are contemplating; but it does have those elements that Freeman spoke of as basic to the Oedipus complex: the dominance of the adult males, the fear and exclusion of the juveniles, and a whole society held together, in a paradoxical way, by the aggressiveness of the participants.

The other type of baboon social system (which I will call Baboon 2) is quite different, and is only just coming to the forefront of discussion.

This type is common to the hamadryas and gelada baboons, and to some extent to the patas monkey (Kummer & Kurt 1963; Crook 1966; Hall 1966). The first two inhabit harsh arid environments where seasons differ sharply (mostly in Ethiopia). They are found in large herds, possibly as a defence against predators, but the subdivision of the herds and the internal structure of these divisions differ from those of their woodland-savannah cousins. The basic unit is the 'one-male group.' On average there is one adult male to three or four females in each group. These females with their immature young are kept under strict surveillance by their overlord, and reciprocally they are attracted to and follow him. He attacks those who wander too far and accept the approaches of other males (a special 'neck bite' has been developed for this purpose). These one-male groups make up the core of the herd. Again, at the peripheries, there is the group of excluded males. (This superficially represents the organisation of some ungulates, but is different in that the polygynous association of dominant males and females in, for example, the kob, giraffe or red deer, is purely seasonal. With these baboons it is permanent.) The group of excluded males is much more of a unit than in the first type, and in times of food scarcity it wanders off in search of food, much like the roving band of male chimpanzees. At maturity the males are expelled from (or at any event, leave) the family, and after that they can only get back to the breeding system by acquiring a harem of their own. Some older males seem to tolerate 'apprentices' who attach themselves to the harem owner and probably eventually take over some of his surplus females. But we do not yet know enough about 1) what happens in the all-male band and 2) how new harems are formed.

The picture here is much more cyclopean, and several writers have seized on it as the obvious model for proto-human society. There is here the jealous, dominant male, herding his females and defending them, as well as the expelled sons banding together into a fraternal horde. But note that the total unit is still the horde itself. The rejected sons may be excluded from breeding; but they remain a part of the horde structure, and as in the first type of baboon system they act as first line of defence against attack. The big males in both systems act as the ultimate defence against predators. Only in the little patas monkey do we approach the independent family acting as a unit—but here the male interestingly enough acts as a rather gentle watch-dog and not as a dominant jealous husband. Hence some form of co-operative behaviour seems built into baboon social structure, and the excluded juveniles can eventually work their way back to the centre of power and marital bliss if they are tough, patient and intelligent enough. There is no real possibility here of sons ganging up against the 'father,' because there is not a single father but rather a formidable body of big males with established dominance status.

The year-round association of the males and females in the one-male group has led some writers, Westermarck-fashion, to seek in it the origins of the human type of male-female association (Campbell 1966). But there are several difficulties about this to which I must turn later.

To put this account into evolutionary prospective and to lead up to the controversial Australopithecines, let us see how geological and climatic changes have been seen as the rungs of the evolutionary ladder, the essential selection pressures which have moulded the development of structure and function. Napier, primarily interested in bipedal walking and other locomotor functions, has charted the spatio-temporal progress of various primate stocks (Napier 1964). The gibbon stayed in the *forest canopy*, while the other Hominoidea took to the *forest floor*. The chimpanzees and gorillas stayed there, while one of the hominid lines moved out from the *forest edge* to the *tree savannah* as far back as the mid-miocene (20 million years B.C.). Another hominid line stuck to the forest and only moved out much later than its cousin. The first line—the ancestors of *Australopithecus africanus,* and possibly of *Homo erectus* and eventually modern man—broke out into the *open savannah* in the early pleistocene after a long sojourn in the open parklands. The baboons probably followed a line of development through the ecological grades similar to the first hominid line, but stuck to their quadrupedal gait.

The following diagram is an expansion and adaption of one of Napier's diagrams (Napier 1967). It shows the 'distances' that the various genera have travelled through the ecological grades, man having moved out into an enormous variety of biomes. The chimpanzee presents a slight problem in that in fairly recent times it has moved into woodland savannah areas; but it is essentially a forest and forest-fringe animal.

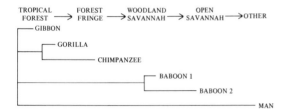

Now we have suggested that ecology and social structure are closely interlinked, and indeed Crook and Gartlan (1966) have classified primates in terms, not of morphology, but of habitat, and have shown that social systems are closely linked to environment. They have distinguished five grades of adaptation, as shown in Table 1, which is a simplified summary of Crook and Gartlan 1966.

We can see that these grades follow the same kind of sequence as that posited by Napier. The striking fact is that no matter how different the animals within each grade are, their social systems broadly correspond, allowing for overlap, marginal and transitional cases, etc.

There are a number of possible criticisms of this scheme, but to spell these out would take too long here, so let us accept it and look at the interesting transition from Grade 4 to Grade 5. This transition, say Crook and Gartlan, is also characteristic of hominid evolution, a position that parallels Napier's on the move from the woodland savannah to the open savannah. 'Paleontological investigations,' they say, 'suggest a radiation of early hominids from dryopithecine stocks in circumstances similar to those controlling the transition from Grade 4 to Grade 5 in the cercopithecids' (1966:1202). This they relate in the hominids to the adaptation of an omnivorous

Table 1: Ecological grades of primate evolution

	GRADE 1	GRADE 2	GRADE 3	GRADE 4	GRADE 5
HABITAT	Forest	Forest	Forest/forest fringe	Forest fringe/ tree savannah	Grassland or arid savannah
SPECIES	Galago (Bush-baby) Dwarf lemur	Indri Lemur Gibbon	Howler monkey Guereza Gorilla	Macaque Common baboon Chimpanzee	Hamadryas baboon Gelada Patas monkey
DIET	Insects	Fruit or leaves	Fruit, leaves, stems	Vegetarian-omnivore	Vegetarian-omnivore
REPRODUCTIVE UNITS	Pairs	'Family parties' (single male)	Multi-male groups	Multi-male groups	One-male groups

NOTE: vernacular names of species have been used, and only a few examples from each grade have been taken.

diet and hence to the development of co-operative hunting and foraging.

Thus it could be argued, as indeed Campbell has done, that we can look for the origins of the human type of reproductive unit in the kind of adaptations that were found necessary for successful breeding in Grade 5. There are, however, certain aspects of baboon 2 behaviour (some of which are shared with baboons generally) that are obviously off on another track from that taken by the hominids, and these animals may therefore not be a good guide to hominid development. For example, females mature at roughly twice the rate of males. Also, the baboon polygynist does not gather as many wives as possible (like the Freudian horde father or some human polygynists) but stops at about four. Both these facts are probably related to ecological adaptation in which a 'one-male group' of this size and composition is the best kind of breeding unit in arid conditions. One large male plus a number of small fast-maturing females is perhaps the most efficient food-utilisation unit in times of maximum aridity. At the limits of their ranges, for example, Japanese macaques are found in small groups of this kind.

Let us look at some factors which have been stressed as particularly 'hominid' characteristics, that is, as end-products of trends in hominid evolution. Such are:

1. year-round breeding and loss of oestrus;
2. growth of co-operation and food-sharing;
3. lack of pronounced sexual dimorphism.

Now if we assume that hominids were moving towards, or alternatively were preserving and developing, these patterns, where does the baboon fit in? The baboon female is still subject to the oestrus cycle, and because of seasonal variations in food supply, breeding in baboon 2 is markedly seasonal. Only 'vigorous seasonal breeding' according to Crook and Gartlan, is compatible with survival in the arid savannahs. As to the second point, Crook and Gartlan argue that under these conditions sexual antagonism *increases* and so does male competition. This also seems to lead to a marked increase in sexual dimorphism.

One feature that does persist even outside the breeding season is the male-female bond. This, as in other primate cases, disproves the theory that only persistent sexual interest of males and females in each other holds the primate group together (Zuckerman 1932). Nor does this sexual interest seem necessary to hold the primate 'family' together, where such a unit occurs. Oestrus and seasonal breeding notwithstanding, the baboon type 2 maintains its family structure. But is this maintained on the same basis as it would have been in the early hominids? All factors seem to indicate that the genetic bases for baboon 'familial' behaviour are very dissimilar from those of man, and that these animals moved in a very different direction of behavioural evolution. The hominids must indeed have brought a different biological equipment to bear, or they must have made a fantastic change in a relatively short period.

Crook and Gartlan seem to realise this and make the suggestion that early hominids 'had initially a social organisation not unlike that of the chimpanzee.' What they did was to 'tighten up' the rather free-and-easy social organisation of the chimpanzee-type and toughen it in the face of arid conditions, seasonal fluctuations in food supply, threats from predators and the demands of a predatory existence. The result was to take the latent dominance pattern and weave it into a baboon-like social structure (type 1 and then type 2). This changed social structure, however, retained the pre-adaptations of the chimpanzee-style, including the all-male bands which became the foragers and hunters. Weapons, they suggest, substituted for gross physical dimorphism, which we know was lacking in the Australopithecines. They are not clear as to exactly how these groups might have been organised, and this, on their theory, might have differed in different habitats. Thus a multi-male dominance hierarchy and its appendages would have characterised the declining number of hominids that remained in the shrinking woodlands, and a one-male-group type of structure those that took to the open grasslands. It is in the latter, where a baboon type 2 structure was grafted onto a chimpanzee-like basis, that we may have the clue to human family origins.

We must pause here to note one or two points. We must remember Kortland's theory that chimpanzees are 'fallen men' and that those chimpanzees able to get to the woodland savannah do indeed tighten up their organisation and display concerted attack on predators, etc. We must also note Rowell's findings that baboons which return to the forests loosen up their social structures and in fact become much more chimpanzee-like with, for example, a much less pronounced dominance hierarchy (Rowell 1966). All these considerations seem to be leading up to a debate on the relative weights to be attached to genetic and ecological determinants of social structure. It does seem, however, that the harem behaviour of the hamadryas baboon, for example, with such specialisations as the neck bite, is genetically determined and hence phylogenetically old (Jay 1965:550).

The theory of Crook and Gartlan inserts a crucial stage into the progression proposed by Reynolds: a stage in which the forest creature developed a baboon-like social structure (type 2) during the pliocene sojourn on the dry savannahs.

If then what I have outlined is the raw material of the primal horde, what of Freud and Westermarck? We have here some of the features of the cyclopean family, as we have seen, but this is not isolated and the total unit is still the horde and not the individual family. In so far as the hominids veered towards a structure of baboon type 1, the family disappeared altogether. There is no question in either case of a 'father versus sons' situation, but there is clearly a 'young expelled males versus older dominant males' situation. In either type of structure the 'fathers' monopolise the 'mothers' and exclude the 'sons.' How far they monopolise the 'daughters' in type 2 is not clear. They probably do, and in type 1 they certainly do. Thus Freud's contention that incest rules were directed primarily towards the maturing male would tally with this situation, and it would tally with the fact that father-daughter incest is by far the commonest type known in man, while mother-son is the least common.

For Westermarck there is a little comfort if type 2 is the model, for here we have a basis for continuity. Even so the basis of hominid polygyny in a one-male group situation must have been different from the baboon basis. This is something we should ponder.

For either hypothesis there are difficulties. Should we try to look for continuities, or should we accept with Freud that something shattering had to happen to jerk the proto-hominid organisation into a human shape? And was that thing the invention of weapons and the killing of the fathers? Did there have to be a period of revolutionary cannibalism acting as a selective process?

Let us look at the kind of creature that our proto-hominid conditions, both ecological and social, were selecting. Here perhaps the work of Michael Chance is the most important (Chance 1962a; 1962b; Chance & Mead 1953). He points out that in a troop structure of baboon type 1 (he worked largely with macaques) several processes are at work. There is 'constant mating provocation' in that the females are receptive for a longer period of the year and for a larger fraction of the oestrus cycle than in any other mammal. This constant provocation leads to constant competition among the males and the establishment of a breeding hierarchy. The survival of the individual male and his chances of success in breeding depend on his capacity to 'equilibrate'—roughly speaking, his capacity to control his sexual and aggressive drives. 'Equilibration demands of the animal an intensification of the control over its emotional responses, both facilitatory and inhibitory' (1962b:125). Because of the number of contrasting stimuli presented and the number of rather close decisions that have to be made, the successful animal has to control its emotional responses rather than simply act them out. Chance then postulates that the enlargement of the neocortex was 'an anatomical adaptation to the circumstances requiring an equilibrational response' (125). The proto-hominids had perhaps gone furthest of all the primates in this development and it was therefore an important pre-adaptation giving them a springboard from which to launch themselves, via tools, hunting and language, into the truly human state.

Clearly I am unable to do justice here to the complexity and detail of Chance's argument. If I had time to elaborate it, I could undoubtedly strengthen my case. It is too simple, for example, just to talk in terms of the 'growth of the neocortex.' For the present however we must be content with this inadequate summary.

Chance can be criticized on several grounds. His theory, as Etkin (1954) points out, would apply only to the male neo-cortex, and much as we may be mystified at the use made of this organ by the female of the species, she undoubtedly possesses it. It does seem to be the case, however, that in primates male cortical control of sexual behaviour is greater than female. Further, Chance was working on the theory that primates lacked a breeding season; but 'vigorous seasonal breeding' characterises many primates including baboons of both types. Provocation to conflict which requires an equilibrational response, however, can surely occur over other things than sex: food, for example, in times of scarcity. I would also like to make the suggestion that dominance itself has provocative qualities; that the young males desire to get into the hierarchy for its own sake. Indeed, sex cannot be the only provocation, for in some baboons the young males do in fact copulate with females at the commencement of oestrus.

The point here is that if Chance is even partly right, then the selective pressures which produced the 'take-off' stage for the 'transition to humanity' involved a social structure with a dominance hierarchy of males in constant and relatively monopolistic association with females, and with a body of excluded males forming a fraternal band. The whole process of enlarging the neo-cortex to take-off point was based on a competition between the dominant and sub-dominant males in which those which survived were those best able to control and inhibit, and hence time, their responses. Here then are the beginnings of deferred gratification, conscience and guilt, spontaneous inhibition of drives, and many other features of a truly human state. The selection pressures we have outlined were well on the way to producing the creature Freud saw as the outcome of the terrible event.

Now what exactly was the outcome? It was a rule-obeying guilt-feeling creature which could live in groups according to a social code of conduct. The primal horde gave way, in Freud's opinion, to 'the most primitive kind of organisation that we actually come across,' and this, 'consists of bands of males' all obeying the same code (1952:141). If however we cease to take the erroneous gorilla evidence then this particular transition is not necessary, for as Chance (1962a) has also pointed out, the basic social bond of gregarious primates is not the male-female bond, but the bond between the males: males of the hierarchy, males of the roving band, and excluded males of the fraternal band. This bond is ambivalent—threat both repels and attracts the sub-dominants—but it is there. Thus in the normal processes of primate evolution we could have had the basis of human society without the necessity of repeated murder.

Must we therefore dismiss the Freudian theory at least on the murderous issue? We do not know for sure, and we cannot aim at certainty, but

Freud himself offers us an alternative. Freeman has contrasted the two solutions as the 'fact and fantasy hypotheses.' Towards the end of his book Freud has second thoughts. Perhaps the transition was not bloody and murderous. He says, 'The mere hostile *impulse* against the father, the mere existence of a wishful *fantasy* of killing and devouring him, would have been enough to produce the moral reaction that created totemism and taboo' (1952:159–60). He continues, 'The alteration might have been effected in a less violent fashion and none the less have been capable of determining the appearance of the moral reaction.' In consequence, 'No damage would then be done to the causal chain stretching from the beginning to the present day, for psychical reality would be strong enough to bear the weight of these consequences' (1952:160).

This seems to me to express beautifully in Freud's own language the point I have been labouring here. If Freud had been equipped with the primatological and other information I have quoted, and had not been misled by the erroneous gorilla evidence, his second hypothesis would have been vindicated. There is moreover no clash here with Westermarck. (It has been my experience that whenever Westermarck and Freud seem to disagree the best thing to do is to assume that they are both right. The hypothesis that can accommodate both of their theories is likely to be a good one.) For Westermarck then there is indeed a continuity here from the bi-sexual groups of the primate to human social organisation—a continuity that need not have been disrupted by murder and cannibalism. Again it is doubtful that this was a straight continuity in form from a primate type of mating and family system to a human, but the human type was nevertheless a direct evolution from the primate type.

Here we must pause and take breath and look once more at the chronology of these events. Chance is dealing essentially with the process of events during the pliocene. The picture he paints of hominid groups here tallies with the theories of Crook, for example, who sees various forms of baboon-like adaptations as being necessary for life in the arid savannahs. However, the known fossil hominids of the late pliocene and early pleistocene (that is, one to two million years ago) are the Australopithecines. These small creatures were bipedal and had a very human dentition, but their average brain-size was only equal to that of the great apes. The rapid expansion of the brain occurred in the pleistocene, and largely during the last million years of hominid existence when brain size increased three times—an almost unprecedented rate of evolution. Chance does not say more than that if such a rapid evolution took place, then it argues for 'some special form of breeding system.' By this he means some system based on dominance, in which the more efficient and intelligent creatures did the breeding.

However, we must add to this two other factors. Not only was this a period of growing sophistication in the use of tools, but this hominid—or at least one branch of the stock—was a hunter. Hence both weapons and the chase must enter our consideration at least one million years ago (Washburn 1959). This has led to a two-pronged attack on the transition problem. Man, it is argued, became a kind of carnivore, and his brain rapidly evolved to cope with the complexities of being a tool-making, symbol-using hunter. Chance does not explore this issue, but even allowing for it his question still stands: whatever the pressures making for a larger brain, by what kind of *breeding system* can such a rapid expansion have occurred? Could a weapon-bearing, flesh-eating hunter have had a social system of a baboon type 1, or 2, or both?

Many authorities doubt this and have argued that the proto-hominids must have lived in territorially independent monogamous nuclear families, thereby taking us back to Westermarck. But these theories were put forward before much of the evidence we have cited was available (Bartholomew & Birdsell 1953; Etkin 1954; Eiseley 1956). Most of their proponents find it necessary to criticise Chance. Etkin goes so far as to say that only as a result of the development of the 'integrated nuclear family' could the brain have evolved at all! Many arguments are used to back up this theory: man's carnivorous tendencies that suggest a wolf-like system; the lack of pronounced sexual dimorphism in man; the helplessness of the human infant; the long period of the child's dependency; the lack of the oestrus cycle in the human female, and year-round breeding; the need for co-operation between males and hence the need to reduce conflict over women; the inability of a male hunter to provide for more than one mate; etc., etc. On careful examination none of these arguments, nor any combination of them, seems adequate to support the conclusion drawn. They are riddled with internal contradictions and their proponents seem uncertain about many features and in particular about the nature of the social unit: was it a single territorially independent nuclear family, or a large hunting band? Etkin, for example, suggests that the individual hominid families may have 'joined up' for hunting. If this is so, then he must agree that the basic unit was still the hunting band. The internal composition of it is a matter of dispute, but as against those who argue for independent nuclear families, Coon (1963) has argued that the polygynous propensity is uppermost in hominid mating patterns and that a dominance structure in which older males took first preference of females would have characterised archaic mating systems. Here we would have had permanent assignment of mates, and not just a monopoly of sexually receptive ones, but the assignment would have been in terms of dominance status. Only strong, successful, intelligent and sociable young males would also have achieved this status. I cannot here rehearse all Coon's arguments, but if he

is right then we would have had a mating structure which would combine developing features of human reproductive physiology (such as the eventual loss of the oestrus phenomenon, the year-round potency of males and the dependence of the human infant) with a type of breeding system compatible with Chance's conditions for rapid cortical development. This breeding system could have evolved from something like either type of baboon structure, which could itself have had its basis in a chimpanzee-like system.

Here I would like to plead for a different approach to this question. It seems to me pointless to try to pin the Australopithecines down to any particular kind of institutional pattern. To wish on to these enterprising creatures a monogamous nuclear-family organisation seems unduly restrictive. The real question should be: what kind of breeding system did there have to be in order for certain crucial developments to take place? Many actual institutional arrangements could have met the criterion of a breeding system that would facilitate and encourage the rapid development of the neo-cortex. The one central fact that we need to grasp is that this system, on Chance's hypothesis, should be based on a dominance hierarchy. As we have seen, there are many variations on this theme, and ecology seems to call the tune.

I can perhaps here suggest one other possibility. The tendency to form pair-bonds for mating purposes seems strong in *Homo sapiens,* yet it is lacking in the great apes and in the baboon 1 types of mating system. (This was pointed out to me by Desmond Morris.) Its appearance in baboon 2 is suggestive but is based on gross dimorphism and other features untypical of hominids. Could it be that a tendency to form such mating bonds is part of an ancient heritage stemming from a gibbon-like period of pair-territory existence in the earliest stages of hominid development? Could this have been a piece of equipment carried over from an ancient past, but masked by the exacting conditions of the pliocene? Or is it something that developed as rapidly as the brain itself during the hunting phase? (Wolves, it could be argued, like many carnivores, form pair-bonds.)

Even if the latter is the case, how old is hunting? Baboons and chimpanzees do hunt, and there is no reason why the hominids of the pliocene and even the Australopithecines should not have resembled a 'hunting baboon.' After all, a prominent victim of the south African ape-man was a species of ancestral baboon. The dentition of the hominids suggests that adaptation to an omnivorous diet may be quite ancient. Thus a sexual division of labour and some form of pair-bonding, even if these are dependent on carnivorous tendencies and hunting, may have developed earlier than the pleistocene. However, this does not necessarily suggest a monogamous, family-loving animal. Indeed, if the little hominids were hunting powerful pack-living baboons, then it is inconceivable that they could have lived in territorially independent nuclear families. (Etkin sees this point.) And insofar as they were living in hunting hordes themselves, the possibility of the sub-units of these being monogamous nuclear families is remote. The pair-bond only means that there should be a relatively permanent assignment of mates. It does not in fact suggest anything about the domestic unit or the minimal unit of socialisation. It is perfectly compatible with an assignment of mates on a dominance basis, and in fact would probably serve to intensify the struggles and problems of the young males and increase even further the pressures to equilibration. The idea that has been advanced that the assignment of mates effectively 'reduces jealous conflict between males' seems somewhat optimistic.

If the hominid band veered towards the baboon-like structure, then the monogamous tendencies of man, such as they are, may simply be an outcome of changed ecological conditions, and a closer correlation of the male and female growth curves. The argument that monogamy occurred because males must provide for relatively immobile females, and that the males could only cope with one female at a time, is not convincing. There is no reason why the males as a whole should not have protected and provisioned the females as a whole, or why female *gathering* of roots, etc., should not have been important. This has nothing necessarily to do with the assignment of mates, and the case of wolves is a poor analogy. (In fact Chance has argued that the pair-bonding tendency of wolves *prevents* brain development!)

Freud notes that the murderous event might have awaited the advent of weapons. The brothers became cannibal savages, he says. Certainly the advent of weapons (or at least tools) and carnivorous tendencies has been held by many to herald a breakthrough in hominid advance, as we have seen. Cannibalism has been postulated for Pekin man. Certainly it would have been difficult for old males to eject permanently and keep at bay well-armed young males. In any case, as Freud sees, a co-operative body of possibly related males was a basic kind of human group. However, this development of weapons did not necessarily lead to murderous clashes, although the deduction that it did is not unreasonable. What it did lead to was elaborate systems of initiation in which the primate urges to dominance in the young males were tamed and reworked. The capacity to equilibrate was the basis from which rule-obedience developed and this was capitalised on in initiation which, after all, is usually ritually phrased in terms of expulsion, exile, and reincorporation (killing, death and rebirth). The impulse to kill the old man is tempered by the impulse to *be* the old man. But as Margaret Mead points out, Freud is wrong to locate this process in the nuclear family alone. That unit is simply one possible focus of it (Mead 1964). It is a tendency directed by the young males as a body against the old males as a body.

Again Freud is to some extent right about the processes (given the fantasy hypothesis), but misled about the focus of them both by his own ethnocentricism and the fictional family life of the gorilla.

We have skirted the other great problem of totemism and the incest taboos. But as we saw earlier, according to Lévi-Strauss, totemism is not so much an institution as a way of thought; a basic form of articulate thought. Now insofar as a critical advance in the growth of the neo-cortex was an essential pre-requisite for such thought, and insofar as this growth was an outcome of the process foreseen by Freud, to describe totemism as a necessary outcome of the great event may not be so far wide of the mark. Of course this is cheating slightly. As to incest, we must leave that to another time, but sufficient has perhaps been said here to make it clear that many ideas about incest, exogamy and culture will have to be revised and can be revised within the framework of analysis we have used (see, for example, Imanishi 1965).

My conclusions have been rather diffuse, and I have only been able to give an outline—even a caricature—of the problems involved. For example, it was clearly not *only* equilibration that led to brain growth, but many other pressures as well. We cannot aim at certainty in this field, but we can by patient sifting of evidence and by avoiding too many slick analogies and imaginative leaps, reduce our area of ignorance, reduce the number of possibilities, until we can perhaps reach a fair approximation of what happened 'In the beginning.' This would itself only be a beginning: a beginning, I would hope, of a revival of the Malinowskian questions about biological needs and cultural behaviour. Once again we may see anthropologists asking the *real* anthropological question: not 'what is social structure,' but 'what is man?'.

REFERENCES

ALTMANN, STUART A. (ed.) 1965. *Japanese monkeys: a collection of translations* selected by Kinji Imanishi. Atlanta: Altmann.

ATKINSON, J. J. see Lang, A. 1903.

BARTHOLOMEW, C. A. & J. B. BIRDSELL 1953. Ecology and the protohominids. *Am. Anthrop.* 55, 481–98.

CAMPBELL, B. G. 1966. *Human evolution: an introduction to man's adaptations.* Chicago: Aldine.

CARPENTER, C. R. 1964. *Naturalistic behavior of nonhuman primates.* Philadelphia: Pennsylvania State Univ. Press.

CHANCE, M. R. A. 1962a. Nature and special features of the instinctive social band of primates. In *Social life of early man* (ed.) S. L. Washburn. London: Methuen.

—— 1962b. Social behaviour and primate evolution. In *Culture and the evolution of man* (ed.) M. F. Ashley Montagu. New York: Oxford Univ. Press.

—— & A. P. MEAD. 1953. Social behaviour and primate evolution. In *Evolution* (Symp. Soc. exp. Biol. 7). New York: Jonathan Cape.

COON, C. S. 1963. *The origin of races.* London: Jonathan Cape.

CROOK, J. H. 1966. Gelada baboon herd structure and movement: a comparative report. *Symp. zool. Soc. Lond.* 18, 237–578.

—— & J. S. GARTLAN. 1966. Evolution of primate societies. *Nature, Lond.* 210:5042, 1200–3.

DE VORE, I. 1965a. The evolution of social life. In *Horizons of anthropology* (ed.) Sol Tax. London: Allen & Unwin.

—— (ed.) 1965b. *Primate behavior: field studies of monkeys and apes.* New York: Holt, Rinehart & Winston.

—— & S. L. WASHBURN. 1964. Baboon ecology and human evolution. In *African ecology and human evolution* (eds.) F. C. Howell & F. Bourlière. London: Methuen.

EISELEY, L. C. 1962. Fossil man and human evolution. In *Culture and the evolution of man* (ed.) M. F. Ashley Montagu. New York: Oxford Univ. Press.

ETKIN, W. 1954. Social behavior and the evolution of man's mental capacities. *Am. Nat.* 88, 129–42.

FREEMAN, D. 1965. *Totem and taboo: a reappraisal.* Mimeo. Canberra: Australian National University.

FREUD, S. 1952. *Totem and taboo* (trans.) J. Strachey. New York: W. W. Norton.

GEERTZ, C. 1965. The transition to humanity. In *Horizons of anthropology* (ed.) Sol Tax. London: Allen & Unwin.

GOODALL, J. 1965. Chimpanzees of the Gombe stream reserve. In *Primate behavior: field studies of monkeys and apes* (ed.) I. DeVore. New York: Holt, Rinehart & Winston.

HALL, K. R. L. 1966. Distribution and adaptations of baboons. *Symp. zool. Soc. Lond.* 17, 49–73.

IMANISHI, K. 1965. The origin of the human family: a primatological approach. In *Japanese monkeys: a collection of translations* (ed.) S. A. Altmann. Atlanta: Altmann.

JAY, PHYLLIS 1965. Field Studies. In *Behaviour of non-human primates* (eds.) A. M. Schrier, H. F. Harlow & F. Stollnitz. New York: Academic Press.

KEITH, A. 1948. *A new theory of human evolution.* London: Watts & Co.

KORTLANDT, A. & M. KOOIJ 1963. Protohominid behaviour in primates. *Symp. zool. Soc. Lond.* 10, 61–88.

KROEBER, A. L. 1920. Totem and taboo: an ethnologic psychoanalysis. *Am. Anthrop.* 22, 48–55.

—— 1948. *Anthropology.* New York: Harcourt, Brace.

KUMMER, H. & F. KURT 1963. Social units of a free-living population of hamadryas baboons. *Folia primat.* 1, 4–19.

LANG, ANDREW & J. J. ATKINSON 1903. *Social origins,* by Andrew Lang; *Primal law,* by J. J. Atkinson. London: Longmans Green.

LEAKEY, L. S. B. 1967. An early miocene member of Hominidae. *Nature. Lond.* 213:5072, 155–63.

LÉVI-STRAUSS, C. 1949. *Les structures élémentaires de la parenté.* Paris: Presses Universitaires de France.

—— 1962. *Le totémisme aujourd'hui.* Paris: Presses Universitaires de France.

LINTON, R. 1936. *The study of man.* New York: D. Appleton-Century Company Inc.

MALINOWSKI, B. 1927. *Sex and repression in savage society.* London: Kegan Paul, Trench, Trubner.

—— 1944. *A scientific theory of culture and other essays.* Chapel Hill: Univ. North Carolina Press.

MEAD, M. 1964. Comment on: The human revolution, by C. F. Hockett & T. Ascher. *Curr. Anthrop.* 5, 160.

NAPIER, J. R. 1964. The evolution of bipedal walking in the hominids. *Arch. Biol.* 75, Suppl., 673–708.

—— 1967. The antiquity of human walking. *Scient. Am.* 216, 56–66.

REYNOLDS, V. 1965. Chimpanzees of the Budongo forest. In *Primate behavior: field studies of monkeys and apes* (ed.) I. DeVore. New York: Holt, Rinehart & Winston.

—— 1966a. Kinship and the family in primates and early man. Mimeo.

—— 1966b. Open groups in hominid evolution. *Man* (N.S.) 1, 441–52.

—— & F. REYNOLDS. *Budongo: a forest and its chimpanzees.* London: Methuen.

ROWELL, T. E. 1966. Forest living baboons in Uganda. *J. Zool. Lond.* 149, 263–76.

SAHLINS, M. D. 1959. The social life of monkeys, apes and primitive man. In *The evolution of man's capacity for culture* (ed.) J. N. Spuhler. Detroit: Wayne State Univ. Press.

SAVAGE, T. S. & J. WYMAN 1847. Notice of the external characters and habits of *Troglodytes gorilla* a new species of orang from the Gaboon river; osteology of the same. *Boston J. nat. Hist.* 5, 417–43.

SCHALLER, G. B. 1963. *The mountain gorilla: ecology and behavior.* Chicago: Univ. Press.

SCHULTZ, A. H. 1936. Characters common to higher primates and characters specific for man. *Quart. Rev. Biol.* 11, 259–83, 425–55.

SIMONS, E. 1964. The early relatives of man. *Scient. Am.* 211, 51–62.

WASHBURN, S. L. 1959. Speculations on the inter-relations of the history of tools and biological evolution. In *The evolution of man's capacity for culture* (ed.) J. N. Spuhler. Detroit: Wayne State Univ. Press.

—— & VIRGINIA AVIS 1958. Evolution and human behavior. In *Behavior and evolution* (eds.) A. Roe & G. G. Simpson. New Haven, London: Yale Univ. Press.

—— & I. DE VORE 1962. Social behavior of baboons and early man. In *Social life of early man* (ed.) S. L. Washburn. London: Methuen.

WESTERMARCK, E. 1891. *The history of human marriage,* Vol. I, London, New York.

ZUCKERMAN, S. 1932. *The social life of monkeys and apes.* London: Routledge & Kegan Paul.

TEN • SOCIAL BEHAVIOR OF NONHUMAN PRIMATES

18 • SOCIAL BEHAVIOR AND ETHOLOGY

John Hurrell Crook

The study of ethology, that is, the characteristic behavior patterns of animals, and especially of non-human primates, can be most helpful to our understanding of the behavior of human beings. This does not mean that the behavior of a bird, a monkey, or an ape necessarily stands in any linear evolutionary relationship to human behavior—or, as Crook points out, not that animal behavior calls for "inferences to man"—but that such studies are useful for comparison of explanatory models. As Tinbergen has said, "What we ethologists do not want, what we consider definitely wrong, is uncritical application of our results to man." [1] But in the same article Tinbergen himself makes a large number of uncritical applications of the findings of ethologists to man.[2] As he says, it is the *methods* of ethology that should be utilized by students of human behavior, *not* its results. It is an injunction apparently more easily issued than followed, but in what Haldane has called "the argument from animals to man" (pp. 233–48 of the present volume) it is extremely important to guard against this new version of the reductionist fallacy.

Crook's discussion of these problems is written with admirable cogency and enviable clarity, sounding the proper cautionary note for all ethologists, and for all those who tend to misapply the findings of ethologists to the behavior of man.

A convergence of interests and methods of ethologists, anthropologists, developmental psychologists, and zoologists in recent years has produced much research of the greatest value.[3] The promise for the future is most encouraging.

Ethological Ideas and Popular Opinion

Social science, even when it concerns animals, is not an activity peculiar to ivory towers and discussed solely over departmental tea tables. The growing interest in the implications of ethology for human biology and behaviour means that ethologists too must take their stand in the market place. Indeed, whether its more reticent practitioners wish it or not, ethological ideas have

SOURCE: John Hurrell Crook, *Social Behavior in Birds and Mammals* (London & New York: Academic Press, 1970), xxi–xxxiii. Reprinted by permission of the author and the publisher.

[1] Niko Tinbergen, "On War and Peace in Animals and Man," *Science*, 160 (1968), 1411–1418.
[2] For a criticism of Tinbergen's view see Ashley Montagu, "Animals and Man: Divergent Behavior," *Science*, 161 (1968), 963.
[3] N. Blurton Jones (editor), *Ethological Studies of Child Behaviour* (Cambridge: At the University Press, 1972); R. A. Hinde, ed., *Non-Verbal Communication* (Cambridge: At the University Press, 1972); Michael Chance and Clifford Jolly, *Social Groups of Monkeys, Apes and Men* (New York: E. P. Dutton & Co., 1970); Hilary Callan, *Ethology and Society: Towards an Anthropological View* (Oxford: The Clarendon Press, 1970); Aristide H. Esser, *Behavior and Environment: The Use of Space by Animals and Men* (New York: Plenum Press, 1971); R. F. Ewer, *Ethology of Mammals* (New York: Plenum Press, 1968); Irenäus Eibl-Eibesfeldt, *Ethology: The Biology of Behavior* (New York: Holt, Rinehart & Winston, 1970); Irenäus Eibl-Eibesfeldt, *Love and Hate: The Natural History of Behavior Patterns* (New York: Holt, Rinehart & Winston, 1972); Lionel Tiger and Robin Fox, *The Imperial Animal* (New York: Holt, Rinehart and Winston, 1971), Desmond Morris, ed., *Primate Ethology* (Chicago: Aldine Publishing Co., 1967); Alison Jolly, *The Evolution of Primate Behavior* (New York: The Macmillan Company, 1972).

become common talking points in any discussion of the nature of man and his problems in the mid-twentieth century. For example, C. L. Sulzburger, political journalist for the *New York Times,* mistaking ethology for anthropology, began his column of 13 October 1968 with the assertion that "modern anthropology teaches that nationalism and imperialism are deeply rooted in animal pasts and, perhaps like our own, the foreign policy of the Kremlin may sometimes derive from remote instincts first noted among wolves, horned owls or lions patrolling their preserves for sustenance." News in the social sciences clearly travels badly and ethological concepts faultily transposed to alien contexts could serve as tools in the presentation of ideological arguments and in the formation of political points of view. Indeed, certain views from classical ethology, although largely anachronistic today, seem to have undergone rebirth in areas far from the quaint preserves in which they were born and with a significance that many would find grievous if not dangerous.

One obvious purpose of this collection of essays [1] is to show that the modern study of animal behaviour, modern ethology, goes far beyond the popularized and naive formulations of outdated hypotheses presented to the general public by some recent authors. Indeed, although the general orientation is similar, the themes . . . that derive exclusively from the classical ethological tradition are quite limited. The range of studies presented reveals, we think, something of the diversity of approaches and techniques current in behaviour research—a diversity of empirical study which lends little support to any oversimplified theory of human behaviour. Our main emphasis lies on the multiplicity of factors that interact to govern the performance of complex social behaviour and on the gradual programming of the development of such behaviour in the individual. Multifactorial

studies of processes definable as systems are thus the prime focus of attention. Such an approach makes clear the complexity, subtlety, evasiveness and beauty of the phenomena with which the ethologist deals.

In any period scientific theories and their translations into general understanding are markedly influenced by the spirit of the times. Conversely, they may themselves play an important role in moulding the values and the supporting rationalizations that people hold. The contemporary ideology of the *status quo* is always to varying degrees confronted with utopian viewpoints demanding social change. Scientific theories are often used to support either a conservative or a progressive ideological theme and fashions in science, especially behavioural sciences, are linked closely with the historical resolution of this process (see Horowitz 1964). The history of animal behaviour study has doubtless been influenced in this way: the fashion for one approach in any period being related to the political and sociological background of that time. For example, the misguided use by philosophers of Darwinian thought in "social Darwinism" was responsible in part for the racial doctrines of German National Socialism in the 1930s. This seems to have provided an academic atmosphere in which the nativistic approach to behavioural determination was more acceptable than that of an environmentalist. The ethological emphasis in the thirties on innate behaviour patterns and releasers could thus be generalized to man without incurring ideological resistance. In America, by contrast, the focus on individualism and enterprise within an ethnically diverse population appears to have encouraged a more environmentalist approach in which modification of behaviour by experience attracted prime attention. It seems that only a puritanical dedication to the laboratory and to behaviourist research techniques prevented more open-ended discussion of animal social organization in that country in the 1930s.

---

[1] See source note.

Why is it that at the present moment there is such an extraordinary public interest in ideas derived from the Lorenzian ethology of the thirties? In part it is a straightforward effect of excellent authorship and simple presentation (Lorenz 1963, Ardrey 1967). A doctrine of the instinctive determination of aggression, for example, is easily understood while a multifactorial view of behavioural determination is difficult to grasp. The contemporary human situation is fraught with political and social instability and danger all magnified by unparalleled means of communication. The breakdown in orthodox religious interpretations of the nature of man together with the popularization of Freudian concepts produces also a crisis in "identity." Purposes, values, self-image—all are in a melting pot. The Lorenzian view of the supposedly instinctive and necessarily repetitive expression of aggression seems for many to provide some relief, some reduction in anxiety, in reading that only the inevitable is happening. Paradoxically, there is a readily acceptable comfort in these pessimistic, faulty and oversimplified doctrines.

The fact that a given viewpoint is academically unsound may not lessen the impact nor prevent it finding expression in the social attitudes and political views of the less disciplined. In particular, views purveyed by Ardrey would suggest that the possible establishment of territorially defended racial enclaves in the United States and in other countries would be a biologically natural event. The casual adoption of such views reduces the likelihood of a more positive search for racial tolerance through mutual understanding and the effective implementation of human rights. The Ardrey argument could quite plausibly be exploited in a right wing ideology sustaining a racist or nationalist *status quo*. Constructive change can only be promoted by a more careful consideration of the facts of the case. The social systems of men and advanced animals are no longer justly interpretable in the terms of the instinct theory of the thirties. The articles in this book can play their part in demonstrating the actual state of contemporary knowledge. The facts stand for themselves—the use put to them remains to be seen.

Ethological and Non-ethological Traditions in the Study of Animal Social Organization

Of considerable interest to our discussion is the finding that the roots of research into the social systems of vertebrate animals date back to largely ignored publications prior to the flowering of classical Lorenzian ethology as we know it and, furthermore, stem from work by sociologists and ecologists rather than from within Darwinian biology. The rekindling within ethology itself of an interest in whole systems is a recent phenomenon foreshadowed to some extent in a number of interdisciplinary conferences since World War II.

1. The Ethological Approach

The traditional subject matter of ethology has been the motivational or physiological causation of behaviour, the ontogeny of behaviour in individual development and the evolution of behaviour (Tinbergen 1951, 1953, Hinde 1966). The comparative approach based primarily on work by Lorenz (1950) and Tinbergen (1951) consisted mainly in studying the fixed action patterns of lower vertebrates which functioned in communication between individuals, for example, in bird courtship. These social "releasers" elicited reciprocal responses in conspecifics in a highly precise way. The species specificity of such patterns supported the proposition that they were innate and genetically inherited; a view that permitted their use as a behavioural supplement to morphology in animal taxonomy. It was suggested that "centers" in the nervous system controlling such action patterns accumulated action-specific energy requiring periodic release which normally occurred on the presentation of a social signal. In the absence of such a signal the behaviour was liable to occur to inappropriate stimulation. This explanatory schema has been adopted by Lorenz for many aspects of behaviour and, as we have seen, even for cases such as aggression where the occurrence of the behaviour does not normally conform even descriptively to the model (Mailer and Hamilton 1966, Hinde 1967, Crook 1968). The motivational approach of Lorenz was first seriously questioned by Lehrman (1953), Kennedy (1954) and Hinde (1959) in the fifties and is not accepted by most ethologists today.

Lorenz's classical studies of behavioural ontogeny gave rise to more productive fruit. His important discovery of "imprinting" led to a large literature on perceptual learning in neonate animals and the basis of early attachments to parental and species-specific companions. His analysis of displays and social signals likewise produced a rich literature on animal communication based on extensive laboratory and field studies of social interactions.

The early ethological approach is well summarized in Tinbergen's useful book of 1953. Social organization is described mainly in terms of the interactions between two individuals in an encounter whether this be in mating, in the family, in fighting, in co-operative behaviour (reciprocal interaction) or in higher-order social units. The social behaviour of an organism thus consists in the response patterns present in encounters involving communication between members of the species. There was, at this date, little discussion of the social structure as an environment within which individuals performed these activities. Questions concerning the division of populations into social units of differing types, concerning contrasts in the composition of social units and the causation of seasonal and progressive change in their structure were not in the forefront of the exposition. Nor was there an explanation as to why some species were more sociable than others.

Working with Tinbergen's group at Oxford Esther Cullen (1957) demonstrated that many behavioural characteristics of a gull species (the Kittiwake) comprised a syndrome of features all co-adapted to a particular set of environmental features. Comparative work with penguins, gulls and terns, finches, weaver birds, estrildine finches, booby birds and also with primates soon showed that behaviour characteristics comprising whole social systems were likewise co-adapted to the complex demands of the environments in which the various species lived. It then became possible to discuss the whole range of avian or primate social structures in terms of adaptive significance (for example see Crook and Gartlan 1966).

Most of these studies had been carried out with birds among which the innate determination of the interaction patterns appeared in large measure demonstrable. The evolution of social structures was thus treated as arising through the processes of neo-Darwinian natural selection. The re-emergence of field studies on primates, initiated by Carpenter (see 1964) before World War II and expanding rapidly after 1955, soon suggested that additional processes might be at work. From this vista much social behaviour in advanced mammals appears to be traditional and maintained from generation to generation through individual and social learning processes. Both the discovery of extensive intra-specific variation in primate social organizations and the work of Harlow and his collaborators on the development of social behaviour in captive monkeys emphasized this viewpoint. The social environment was seen to be of crucial importance in the determination of the social behaviour of young animals maturing within it. In addition, the fact that the demographic structure of populations was in principle directly responsive to environment suggested that much social organization might be attributed directly to environmental determination.

The study of animal society is at present moving towards a consideration of the complex interaction that must occur between the genetic, societal and environmental levels of determination (McBride 1964). Historical change in social organization can no longer be attributed purely to the natural selection of genetic determinants—although their relative roles remain poorly understood other processes are of clear importance. The tendency among more popular writers to attribute group characteristics such as "dominance" or "territory" solely to genetic factors is anachronistic and tends to promote misconceptions regarding the manner in which social processes in higher animals and man develop and are perpetuated through time. One point is clear, ethologists need to pay much greater attention to the social environment within which individual animals behave. This topic indeed requires as much consideration as the traditional areas, physiological causation, development and evolution of behaviour, have already received.

2. Contributions from Outside Classical Ethology

The history of ideas concerning the nature of animal societies and their relation to human ones might have been very different had certain late 19th-century and early 20th-century publications received the attention that they now appear to have merited. In 1878 A. Espinas published "Des Sociétés Animales," a largely ignored classic providing a history of social theory and a documented account of the facts known about animal social life at that time. Much of this relied upon the capacious tomes of Brehm's *Tierleben*. Espinas was a philosopher, economist and historian rather than a naturalist by inclination. His approach blended the positivist sociology of Comte with an evolutionary view of animal societies derived as much from Spencer as from Darwin. This stance was exceptional in his time for he lived and worked in a period dominated by neo-Hegelian ideas.

Espinas observed that animal societies were not random collections of individuals but structures which endured through time, structures that arose through the "habitual reciprocity" of the activities of the individuals that composed them. He noted, moreover, that animal societies were formed primarily by individuals of the same species. Nevertheless, he was perplexed to find that his attempts to classify different types of animal society resulted in no clear correlation with taxonomic classification. Espinas had a clear grasp of the significance of ecology for social structures. He points out, for example, that not only do the territories of carnivorous or piscivorous birds appear better defended than those of other species, but that under conditions of exceptionally rich food supply boundaries are less clearly defined and less well guarded. He also remarks that sea bird colonies can only develop in places where an abundance of local food is available. His arguments not only foreshadow contemporary studies in the evolutionary ecology of birds but leave open the question as to how far ecology, rather than innate species properties, determines the social structures within which animals live.

Espinas focused his attention upon the operation of the social structure as a whole. He was not an interactionist in explanation. He pointed out that societies take their being not from the sum of individuals comprising them but from the relations that rule between the members. Societies could therefore be viewed as analogues of individual organisms. He attempted to account for the integrity, continuity, and durability of societies in a set of principles that have a markedly cybernetic flavour. Societies, he considered, had arisen in evolution in much the same way as species but he was unable to discuss the actual processes responsible for the development through time. Allowing for a certain outdated mentalism in many of his explanations one neverthless finds in Espinas a sure grasp of many problems of behaviour ecology, population dynamics and social organization that are the focus of major research fields today.

In 1905 and 1906 Raphael Petrucci, sociologist at the Institut Solvay in Brussels, published two major works on animal social organization that appear to have been almost totally ignored.[2] The first work (1905) is a major survey of animal property, including territory in animals and in man. Petrucci finds there are three types of "property," individual—determined by individual requirements for protection and self-maintenance, familial—determined by the family (i.e. broadly the reproductive social unit) requirements for sexual and reproductive activity, and collective —determined by the requirements of groups for protection and maintenance. These three types, he maintains, are not reducible one to another nor are collective phenomena necessarily derived from a familial base. Often the formation of couples or families entails the breakdown of a herd or group. There is a balance, says Petrucci, between a social tendency as such and the formation of a family association. Depending on the nature of the balance between these tendencies the family may be integrated with a higher level structure or the latter may become split into family units. The existence of a family is not a prerequisite for the formation of a social structure. The family is a social unit in itself and not necessarily a component of a higher level structure.

---

[2] The writer came across these works by chance while conducting a bibliographic survey in Stanford University library. There appears to be no reference to them in contemporary literature on animal societies. Only W. M. Wheeler, among biologists, in an essay written in 1934 (republished in 1939) makes a clear reference to Petrucci's contribution.

Petrucci notes that there appears to be no correlation between the intelligence of an animal species and the complexity of its social organizations. Animals living in complex communities cannot be considered less intelligent than their close relatives that are relatively solitary. Petrucci argues that therefore it is the adaptations of a species to its environment that are of greater significance for the formation of a given social structure than its psychological qualities. "La courbe de perfectionnement sociologique est loin de suivre la courbe du développement animal: elle lui reste étrangère. La sociologie comporte un domaine d'investigation qui lui est propre; elle a ses lois particulières et ses charactères précis."

This is the starting point for Petrucci's second publication (1906). He is concerned to discover whether it is possible to trace some ascending order of social complexity throughout the animal kingdom upon which inference to human social structures might be based. Like Espinas before him he soon discovered that classifications of social structures do not coincide with phylogenetic taxonomy. Indeed, at each phyletic level he saw a marked tendency for similar social structures to emerge in parallel or convergent adaptation to similar environmental conditions. Social structures may thus be homotypes descriptively but they have arisen polyphyletically and show no evidence of common biological relationship or descent. The only common social element, Petrucci concludes, is the simple tendency to associate in groups. The form of the groups, the spatial dispersion of individuals and the structure of the relationships is however environmentally determined. Social structure is directly a function of the environment. The extrinsic factors which act to constitute groups into patterns are various and include food supply, type and dispersion, effects of predation and requirements concerned with sexual reproduction in particular habitats. There is a limitation on the range of possible social structures because there are only a limited number of permutations of the relevant ecological factors. Petrucci concludes that since societies are determined directly by extrinsic factors they cannot be compared in the way that biologists compare the morphological characteristics of species. It follows that the social evolution of man is not to be explained in Darwinian terms.

Taken together Espinas and Petrucci present a challenging account of the nature and historic "evolution" of animal and human societies—one furthermore in which biological explanation derived from Darwin is relegated to a secondary position. The treatment is whole-heartedly sociological—social processes being interpreted in terms of principles and laws peculiar to them alone. This position however was to remain undebated and indeed almost totally ignored in discussions by biologists of social evolution in the decades that followed.

A major weakness in the approach, particularly of Petrucci, lies in the failure to distinguish between what Baker (1938) was later to call the ultimate and proximate factors in adaptation. Parallel radiation in successive phyla can be examined in terms of convergent processes of natural selection of genetic determinants. Marsupials and Eutherian mammals show many biologically determined morphological and behavioural convergencies that are not explained in terms of direct adaptation to environment. Nevertheless, where adaptation in social structure is concerned Petrucci's thesis is clearly plausible and requires examination. Indeed, as we have already seen, modern study of the social organization of advanced mammals requires close research into the direct effects of habitat and population characteristics in the programming of social behaviour. Petrucci's arguments indeed foreshadow in important respects elements in current hypotheses concerning bird, primate and human social evolution.

Petrucci's papers are of yet further interest because they draw attention to the "school" of sociology at the Instituts Solvay directed by Emile Waxweiler from 1900 until the occupation of Belgium by the Germans in World War I. Waxweiler died in London in 1916 at the age of 49. Undoubtedly, had he lived, he would have contributed greatly to studies of behavioural biology, ethology and sociology. Following the war the Institute he had directed was reorganized within the context of national reconstruction and the project he had initiated was laid aside. That project was nothing less than an intimate synthesis of animal and human social ethology supported by a detailed experimental and theoretical programme of which Petrucci's papers formed a part. The extent to which the work of this school has been ignored is shown by the fact that a thesis reviewing its achievements written in 1934 was finally published only in 1960 (H. H. Frost).

Although dismissed by later sociologists as being too much interested in biology, Waxweiler's approach was in fact broadly based and distinctive. He explicitly rejected the often uncritical search for analogies between the biological and the social "organism." He had little interest in discussing the utility of analogies between processes of biological evolution and the historical course of cultural change in man. Waxweiler was concerned directly with behaviour and the contrasting levels of social complexity shown by animals and man. In his important "Esquisse d'une Sociologie" (1906), Waxweiler traces the origination of the science of Ethology from its common roots with Ecology in the works of Isadore Saint-Hilaire (1805–1861) and Haeckel (1834–1919). His formulation of the subject thus antedates the "classical" synthesis of the subject by Lorenz by some 25 years. Waxweiler considered sociology to be that aspect of ethology pertaining to the special phenomenon arising from the advanced sociability of human beings. In that this was unique in the animal kingdom, he considered the subject basically separable from studies with nonhuman animals. Nevertheless, he was far from concluding that there were not also elements in the social reactivity of man that had a biological foundation and in relation to which research with animals was of the greatest relevance and importance. Waxweiler focused attention on the adaptive reactions of individuals to others in the environment and on the nature of their mutual relationships. This Tardean approach to social study distinguishes Waxweiler markedly from Durkheim and reveals his basic kinship with the later interactionist approach of European ethologists in the thirties. Nevertheless Waxweiler constantly stressed the importance of considering the social "milieu" within which behaviour occurs and to which it ultmately refers.

Another approach that failed to have the impact that might have been expected was pioneered by P. Kropotkin (1902) and discussed in some detail later by Allee (1938). Kropotkin emphasized that mutual assistance between members of a species often seemed as pronounced as the incessant competition between them upon which much of the theory of natural selection rests. Based largely on anecdotal material Kropotkin's point of view has lain fallow for many years. Allee developed the concept of co-operation primarily in relation to environmental conditioning and behavioural mutuality in invertebrates while Kropotkin had been particularly interested in the complex co-operative behaviour of mammals and its significance for man. We now know such behaviour to be especially elaborated in primate groups where it merits a new and more effective analysis in terms of the roles of the performers in their social structure and its relation to social mobility. As Wheeler (1934, see 1939) was aware, the problem of mammalian co-operative behaviour is intimately linked with what he called "the problem of the male," whose aggressive unsociable character compares with the more placid social demeanor of most females. The incorporation of the male into the mother-litter family always seems to have posed problems of social control without which a disorder harmful to procreation and childrearing would prevail. Much complex co-operative behaviour appears to involve the resolution of social tensions so that breakdown is prevented. Co-operation, furthermore, seems often to be a subterfuge whereby an individual is enabled to gain or maintain that degree of social control of others at which his or her own behaviour is relatively unconstrained (see chapter by Crook, p. 103). Ethologists have done little with this material.

We may well enquire why these viewpoints fell upon such stony ground. It is not possible here to attempt a full account of the "sociology of knowledge" in the history of animal behaviour research. A number of points may nevertheless be made. Firstly, neither Espinas nor Petrucci developed their theories further. The former turned to other interests in history and economics while the latter specialized in Far Eastern cultural studies. Kropotkin, not surprisingly perhaps, turned to ethics. These authors worked outside the intellectual environment of a biology in which the prime subject of attention became the nature of the evolutionary process in the context of the Mechanist-Vitalist controversy (for an excellent treatment see Lorenz 1950). Biologists were too concerned, it seems, with their own debates, on instinct for example, to note the arguments of out-group contributors. In addition, the physiological and "behaviourist" approach to behaviour initiated in the work of Pavlov and Watson occupied comparative psychologists almost to the exclusion of any other subject.

In social anthropology the fascination of studying the origins of human society and culture, so apparent in the publications of the late 19th century, had waned rapidly with the realization that cross-cultural transference with concomitant modification of customs and institutions was an important factor in social change. Boas, for example, insisted that discussion of cultural succession from primitive to advanced societies without adequate information from particular societies could no longer be carried on with any confidence. In any case primitive societies leave few records. Attention turned to functional analysis of existing societies rather than their historical origins. In addition a number of influential anthropologists argued persuasively against the inclusion of biological considerations in the analysis of social and cultural behaviour in Man. One important article with this theme, "The Superorganic" published in 1917, was discussed again by its author in 1952. Kroeber wrote then: "In the vista of a third of a century the essay appears like an antireductionist proclamation of independence from the dominance of the biological explanation of socio-cultural phenomena. Yet, as I look back, I cannot recall, in the two decades preceding 1917, any instances of oppression or threatened annexation by biologists. What was hanging over the study of culture . . . was rather a diffused public opinion . . . that left precarious the autonomous recognition of society, and still more that of culture. . . . The biologists, in fact, were generally ignoring society and culture."

Sociologists, impressed by the power of human learning and tradition, were predisposed to consider human social processes as functioning upon a basis quite distinct from the biological—a position sometimes adopted today although without an extended examination such as Waxweiler had forlornly attempted to supply. The opposition to any biological approach, by thinkers such as Durkheim for example, seems in fact to stem, as Kroeber indicates, more from a fear for the autonomy of sociology than from any consideration of the uses to which animal studies could legitimately be put. Unlike Waxweiler, many sociological theorists have nevertheless been influenced, often indirectly, by Spencer's use of the literally ancient analogy between organic and social structure. Parsons invoked the concepts of equilibrium and self-maintenance in explaining social cohesion

and revealed therefore a concern with the early concepts of homeostasis. The emphasis fell on structural entities used as the reference point around which social control was exercised. This essentially static conception of the social process was, however, not likely to concern itself greatly with evolutionary derivation from prehuman systems. Models of society based primarily on the organic and machine analogies tended to be closed and entropic. Social Darwinism at least had the merit of considering possible causes of social change resulting from populations in competition; the model being less concerned with structure and more with processes involved in evolution. Recent theorizing stresses that human social systems are open and may show step-wise changes in levels of organization. Homan's model of society, for example, emphasizes that deviance from social norms is itself part of a system and may contribute to historical change (see discussion of Parsons and Homan in Buckley, 1967). The gradual conversion of sociology to an overt cybernetic "systems-analysis" approach will involve a concern both with stability and change and reveal the utility of "adaptive" cybernetic models and their comparison at both the human and the animal level.

Much early ethology came from studies of captive and hand-reared animals in enclosure conditions provided by private zoological gardens. These workers, together with biologists generally, still seemed to feel that field work was an activity of the unprofessional, the amateur naturalist with time on his hands. One might have expected ethologists working in the years immediately following World War I to have responded more effectively to Espinas's and Petrucci's contribution. Yet, clearly, the study of social structures demanded field work and it was no accident that the prime contributions to social analysis in animals were to come from men like Selous, Howard, Carpenter and Fraser Darling—who rarely set foot within a laboratory. The link between the study of captive animals and research in the field was to come only very slowly.

In any case, ethologists have always been primarily interactionist in their approach to behaviour. The study of the fixed action patterns of courtship and Darwin's discussion of them in his treatment of the heredity of instinctive behaviour was from the beginning a key interest. Julian Huxley was exceptional in carrying out magnificently casual field research as an adjunct to seemingly more serious evolutionary studies. His classic work on grebes greatly extended understanding of the operation of behaviour patterns within the social setting in nature. He was the first to make clear the importance of ecology in the determination of social relationships. Huxley (1923) analysed four contrasting types of avian breeding biology including the courtship systems and showed them to be adapted to differing environmental conditions of food supply and predation. He warned against too exclusive a preoccupation with the epigamic significance of courtship. The courtship system itself, he emphasized, is part of a wider complex of specific social behaviour patterns which, treated as a whole, required examination in relation to the habitat and the annual cycle of the animal. This promising suggestion bore fruit, as we have seen, only much later in Esther Cullen's work on gulls and then by an indirect route.

When field studies came into fashion after World War II, largely through the successes of N. Tinbergen and his colleagues both in Holland and at Oxford, it was natural that the principles first explored should be those of the highly developed Lorenzian position. Only when a firm base had been established upon these grounds did the areas of study open up to include the kind of work Huxley had earlier envisaged. The overall success of these developments, in particular Tinbergen's current experimental demonstrations of the survival value of behavioural attributes in nature, married to the recent field studies of primatologists, have led directly to the promise of the present situation.

Inferences from Animals to Man

The manner in which these studies have relevance to the human condition is a matter for cautious exploration. There are many ways in which a theorist may make inferences from animal behaviour to man. The least reliable consist in a drawing of vague analogies between poorly defined attributes (such as "territory") which animals and men are thought to have in common. The most effective seem to be those cases in which experimentation on homologous or nearly homologous organs such as brains or pituitaries are found to influence behaviour in parallel ways in man and animal. Indeed, medicine and medical psychopharmacology are based on assumptions regarding the reliability of such inference. Arguments from mental states or which use mentalistic terms in comparisons between phyla or between animals and man are very difficult to interpret as are statements about learning abilities at different phyletic levels. Likewise, in cases where social processes or factors (e.g. dominance/submission ranking) appear to be common to animal and human life it is tempting to make inferences from the studies of the one to studies of the other. The value of such inferences is in doubt because the mediating processes of the phenomenon are poorly known in either case, and can usually be expected to be different. Again inferences from social evolution in birds and primates to the likely course of human social evolution may comprise interesting speculation but the hypotheses will be hard or impossible to disprove in the absence of living proto-hominids. Although still atomistic in approach, the direct study of the behavioural significance of some of Man's biological peculiarities such as hairlessness, beards in males, breast shape in women, etc. may provide insight into hidden behavioural functions in our species (i.e. see Freedman 1967).

The importance of ethology to human behaviour study probably lies not in "inferences to man" but rather in the comparison of explanatory models.[3] Each field and sub-field has developed its own theoretical constructs, its own semantics and syntax (e.g. see Bolles 1967, Chapter 1). Suggestive analogies between constructs and experimental designs in different fields set off new patterns of hypothesis making that are then utilized in research within the readers' discipline. Although most of the essays in this book refer indirectly or directly to man, make comparisons between animals and men, or otherwise infer analogies or homologies, their real significance, we think, is in supplying information and ideas that in translation to thought on the human context may correct or promote existing trends in behavioural work. Although the making of inferences is difficult, the relevance of the material can never be in doubt. The vitality of the common biological bases is too strong to be long ignored.

The recent discovery of new and powerful means of analysing complex interaction processes is gradually producing its effect upon all levels of behavioural enquiry. While the articles presented emphasize a multifactorial approach to social phenomena, they do not yet attempt formal interpretations in terms of modern systems theory (Watt 1966, Buckley 1967). In this the authors reflect biological pragmatism rather than sociological theorizing. Nevertheless, the move away from the older interactionist approach to social behaviour in animals to examining the nature of whole socio-demographic systems, their components and the other-level processes that control them clearly reflect cognizance, albeit

sometimes subliminal, of the importance of systems analysis and the new computerized technologies historically based on the General Systems Theory of von Bertalanffy and the cybernetics of Norbert Weiner. A more careful delineation of conceptual models used as bases for research hypotheses is foreshadowed in these new approaches to behaviour.

Themes Presented in This Book

Comparative analysis of the units of any taxonomic level, genera within families or species within genera, commonly reveals an extensive adaptive radiation into a variety of habitats—part of such radiation involving differences in social structure. The birds and mammals discussed in this collection of essays live in organized social structures broadly adapted to the environments in which they occur. Repeatedly, social structures of different taxa living in the same type of habitat show numerous similarities. For example, the grassland sciurid and cricetid rodents living in comparable ecological niches show similar sociable groupings, and relatively unsociable behaviour is common to many marsupial and eutherian carnivores. Ecological influences play major roles as both ultimate and proximate factors in the social structuring of populations. In addition, as studies on rodents have shown very effectively, the structure may vary considerably with population density which in turn is related closely to food supplies. Periodically, some social organizations change in "phase," usually in relation to the altered relations between individuals contingent upon hormonal changes in breeding seasons. The relations between the ecological, the population and the social variables are complex and often interdependent. Indeed, so interrelated are they that any attempt at a clear picture is frustrated unless all are considered, at least at one level of dis-

---

[3] A similar point is made in Tinbergen's wisely worded article published recently in *Science* (1968).

cussion, together. Far from being some form of holistic dream, this approach takes account of the interdependence of controlling variables in a process and, without being antireductionist, maintains an important, and sometimes lacking, realism.

Our topic, then, concerns the species-specific "socio-demographic system" in which environmental attributes, food supply and predation for example, act as extrinsic variables having pronounced effects on variables intrinsic to the system including population size, population dispersion and social organization. These in turn have feed-back effects on the environment. Such a system comprises the socio-demographic environment within which individuals develop and live out their lives. There are thus whole sets of sub-systemic relations within the system as a whole—developmental (parents-young) systems, communication systems (of several functions) between adults, systems of social learning and tradition maintenance, and systems of succession (e.g. in primates) whereby roles are transferred from ageing animals to younger ones. An awareness of the systemic nature—the sociological "wholeness"—of these relations as a subject amenable to empirical investigation is relatively new and the area is wide open for intensive research. Indeed, it seems likely that of all aspects of animal behaviour studied so far this one may ultimately come to have greatest significance for studies of human social life and a direct bearing on problems in social psychology.

An important feature of these major systems is their categorization as open and adaptive rather than closed and entropic (Buckley 1967). Sociodemographic systems, like the systemic relations within the ecology of animal communities, lack a "sollwert" in the sense of a fixed reference point for feed-back processes (Hinde 1966, p. 38). The relative stability of the system is due to the limited range of variation in the determining factors. Changes in extrinsic variables beyond the usual range may in fact impose major shifts throughout the structure including stepwise changes of level affecting all attributes under consideration. Historical change in social systems is thus dependent on alterations in the key constraints governing the process and may be either environmentally or socially driven or both. This aspect indeed seems to distinguish our approach to social organization and its historical origination from that of Wynne-Edwards (1962) which appears to be tied closely to an analogy with homeostatic "closed" systems in physiology.

Conclusion

It is our hope that these studies demonstrate the value of carrying out behaviour research at several levels of analysis within the same institution and of attempting purposefully to show how they may be synthetically related. The interdependence of laboratory and field research has often been stressed by ethologists, especially by Tinbergen, and the importance of this relation will increase as we move into what can only become a systems analysis era.

The study of behaviour has often been bugged by too narrow a viewpoint at one level of analysis or another. Recently the fashion has dictated too exclusive a preoccupation with physiology to the detriment of social studies. We feel a more sensitive balance is required, particularly since the immediacy of human needs for understanding social relations and their control is particularly apparent today. Analysis of systems and the interlocking of subsystems that comprise them is no task for an outdated natural history of yesteryear, nor is it an arena for simple-minded yet trendy speculation by popularizers of the subject. The respectability of the subject can be assured not only through the quality and heuristic value of the work produced by its practitioners but also by the care with which the developing ideas and hypotheses are presented to an eager public.

REFERENCES

ALLEE, W. C. (1938). "Cooperation among Animals." H. Schuman, New York.

ARDREY, R. (1967). "The Territorial Imperative." Collins, London.

BAKER, J. R. (1938). The evolution of breeding seasons. In "Evolution, Essays Presented to E. S. Goodrich" (G. R. de Beer, ed.). Oxford.

BOLLES, R. C. (1967). "Theory of Motivation." Harper, New York.

BUCKLEY, W. (1967). "Sociology and Modern Systems Theory." Prentice-Hall, New York.

CARPENTER, C. R. (1964). "Naturalistic Behaviour of Non-human Primates." Pennsylvania University Press, Pennsylvania.

CROOK, J. H. (1968). The nature and function of territorial aggression. In "Man and Aggression" (M. F. Ashley Montagu, ed.). Oxford University Press, New York.

—— and GARTLAN, J. S. (1966). Evolution of primate societies. Nature, Lond. 210, 1200–1203.

CULLEN, E. (1957). Adaptations in the kittiwake to cliff nesting. Ibis 99, 275–302.

ESPINAS, A. (1878). "Des Sociétés Animales." Bailliere, Paris.

FREEDMAN, D. G. (1967). A biological view of man's social behaviour. In "Social Behaviour from Fish to Man" (W. Etkin, ed.). Phoenix, Chicago.

FROST, H. H. (1960). The functional sociology of Emile Waxweiler and the Institut de Sociologie Solvay. Academie Royale de Belgique. Memoires (Classe de Lettres). T.LIII. Fasc. 5.

HINDE, R. A. (1959). Unitary drives. Anim. Behav. 7, 130–141.

—— (1966). "Animal Behaviour. A Synthesis of Ethology and Comparative Psychology." McGraw-Hill, New York.

—— (1967). The nature of aggression. New Society, 2 March.

HOROWITZ, I. L. (1964). A formalization of the Sociology of Knowledge. Behavioral Science 9, 45–55.

HUXLEY, J. S. (1914). The courtship habits of the Great Crested Grebe (Podiceps cristatus) with an addition to the theory of sexual selection. Proc. Zool. Soc. Lond. 491–562.

—— (1923). Courtship activities in the Red Throated Diver (Colymbus stellatus Pontopp) together with a discussion of the evolution of courtship in birds. J. Linn Soc. 35, 253–292.

KENNEDY, J. S. (1954). Is modern ethology objective? Brit. J. Anim. Behav. 2, 12–19.

KROEBER, A. L. (1952). The superorganic. In "The Nature of Culture" (A. L. Kroeber, ed.). University of Chicago Press, Chicago.

KROPOTKIN, P. (1902). "Mutual Aid—a Factor of Evolution." Heinemann, London.

LEHRMAN, D. (1953). A critique of Konrad Lorenz's theory of instinctive behaviour. Q. Rev. Biol. 28, 337–363.

LORENZ, K. (1950). The comparative method in studying innate behaviour patterns. Symp. Soc. exp. Biol. 4, 221–268.

—— (1963). "Das Sogennante Böse." Dr. G. Borotha-Schoeler Verlag. Vienna.

MARLER, P. R. and HAMILTON, W. J. (1966). "Mechanisms of Animal Behavior." Wiley, New York.

MC BRIDE, G. (1964). A general theory of social organisation and behaviour. Univer. Queensland Papers. Veterinary Science. Vol. I. No. 2, 75–110.

PETRUCCI, R. (1905). Les origines naturelles de la propriété. Instituts Solvay. Travaux de l'Institut de Sociologie. Notes et Memoires. Fasc. 3. Misch et Thon, Bruxelles.

—— (1906). Origine Polyphylétique, Homotypie et Non-comparabilité directe des sociétés animales. Instituts Solvay. Travaux de l'Institut de Sociologie. Notes et Memoires. Fasc. 7. Misch et Thon, Bruxelles.

TINBERGEN, N. (1951). "The Study of Instinct." Oxford University Press, Oxford.

—— (1953). "Social Behaviour in Animals." Methuen, London.

—— (1968). On war and peace in animals and man. Science 160, 1411–1418.

WATT, K. E. F. (ed.) (1966). "Systems Analysis in Ecology." Academic Press, New York.

WAXWEILER, E. (1906). Esquisse d'une Sociologie. Instituts Solvay. Travqux de l'Institut de Sociologie. Notes et Memoires. Fasc. 2. Misch et Thon, Bruxelles.

WHEELER, W. M. (1939). Animal societies. In "Essays in Philosophical Biology." Russell & Russell, New York.

WYNNE-EDWARDS, V. C. (1962). "Animal Dispersion in Relation to Social Behaviour." Oliver and Boyd, Edinburgh.

19 • SOME FACTORS INFLUENCING THE SOCIAL LIFE OF PRIMATES IN GENERAL AND OF EARLY MAN IN PARTICULAR

Adolph H. Schultz

In this contribution the doyen of physical anthropologists draws upon his years of investigation in the laboratory and in the field for a host of ideas on some of the factors influencing social life in the primates and early man. There are enough ideas here to stimulate years of research for scores of workers. Some are intriguing, quite conceivably correct, but difficult to prove, such as the possibility that sexual maturity is achieved in most primates before the eruption of the permanent dentition has been completed, especially the canine teeth, in order to avoid conflict between the young and the older males. Nevertheless, Schultz's reflections do underscore the importance for physical anthropologists to be aware of the role played by cultural-behavioral factors in the development of physical traits. Indeed, it is becoming increasingly evident that the most important factors operative in the production of morphological change in man's evolution in particular have been cultural-behavioral.

Schultz's remarks on the relative unimportance of the sense of smell in the evolution of man are justified, but there has been a tendency to undervalue the olfactory sense in man, and, indeed, frequently to describe it as an atrophied sense. This is far from the case. While it is true that the primates as a whole constitute the group of *microsmatics* (creatures with a poor sense of smell), whereas dogs, bears, deer, and many other animals are *macrosmatics* (creatures with a keen sense of smell), man's nose is nonetheless capable of incredible olfactory feats. For example, a human being can detect the odor of 1/1,000,000 of one milligram of vanillin in one liter of air. The smallest number of molecules of formic acid detectable in 50cc. of air is 1.6×10^{16} (that is, 16 quadrillion); of chloroform 7.6×10^{15} (that is, 7.6 quintillion).[1]

The odor of human sweat is said to be an insect repellent, and it certainly appears to cause most animals to give man a wide berth. As a pheromone it undoubtedly plays a role in stimulating sexual activity as well as producing avoidance behavior. The subject calls for much more investigation than it has yet received.

Schultz's comment on the undependability of canine teeth as weapons is worth reflection, considering that it has been generally believed that the primary function of these teeth was the infliction of injury upon others.

The title of our symposium seems somewhat vague to a physical anthropologist, used to terms that can be defined precisely. Since this is my

---

SOURCE: Sherwood L. Washburn, ed., *Social Life of Early Man* (Chicago: Aldine Publishing Company, 1961). Copyright © by Wenner-Gren Foundation for Anthropological Research, Inc. Reprinted by permission of the author and Aldine-Atherton, Inc.
[1] Wolfgang von Buddenbrock, *The Senses* (Ann Arbor: University of Michigan Press, 1958), p. 115.

See also Frank A. Geldard, *The Human Senses* (New York, John Wiley, 1953), pp. 270–294; Y. Zotterman, ed., *Olfaction and Taste* (New York: Pergamon Press), 1963; Russel C. Erb, *The Common Scents of Smell* (New York: World Publishing Co., 1968). See the long series of studies by Harry Wiener, "External Chemical Messengers," *New York State* first venture into social anthropology, I had to begin by consulting dictionaries for the exact meaning of "social," but found merely that it "appertains to society" and is synonymous with "companionate." These definitions evidently do permit a wide variety of interpretations, since most people still make a distinction between, for example, a *society* wedding and a *companionate* marriage. The words "early man" present similar puzzles. At once I was reminded of the proverbial "early bird that catches the worm," especially with my belief that all "early men" did catch more parasitic worms than were good for them. I am also far from certain in knowing at which stage of his evolution "early man" began to correspond to whatever exact definition may be decided upon for that no longer clear word "man." With these critical remarks I merely wish to explain why at times my discussion may seem to go astray and not bear directly on whatever other specialists expect from the general title of this symposium.

The social life of early man, like that of any other animal, was unquestionably determined and limited by his zoölogical status, that is, his morphological and physiological heritage. Any attempt to visualize the behavior of a species of the past must first of all consider the relevant general conditions of behavior characterizing the entire group of animals, of which the particular species is only one representative, even though possibly a specialized one. Since man is a primate and developed from somewhere among the Old World simian stock, his social behavior, too, must have evolved from within the range of social variations possible to this mammalian group. At all times man's social life had been profoundly

influenced by such typical catarrhine features as the retention of grasping hands, highly developed mimetic musculature; lack of a real breeding season, together with single, slowly maturing offspring; chief reliance on sight and neglect of the sense of smell; prolongation of all periods of life, etc. The basically catarrhine nature of man formed his social behavior as much as it did his bodily construction.

As human anatomy has to rely upon comparative-anatomical studies of nonhuman primates for its full meaning, so the investigation of the evolution of man's behavior is dependent upon our knowledge of the behavior of monkeys and apes. The last few years have produced an exceptional number of highly interesting attempts to trace the emergence of man together with the development of his social behavior, especially in some chapters of *Behavior and Evolution,* edited by Roe and Simpson (1958); some of the contributions to the French colloquium on "Les processus de l'hominisation" in 1958; the American symposium on the evolution of man's capacity for culture, edited by Spuhler (1959); the new German book by Rensch (1959), *Homo sapiens; Vom Tier zum Halbgott,* Heberer's comment on the "Tier-Mensch Übergangsfeld" (1958); and the survey by Count (1958) of the biological basis of human sociality. Never before has there been such intense and widespread interest in the very problems we have chosen as focus of our symposium. Thirty-five years ago the late anthropologist G. Dorsey had published a best-seller entitled *Why We Behave Like Human Beings* (1925); today we should be able to answer this same great question more fully and soundly, if we pool the accumulated experiences of the many different anthropological specialties—what we hope to achieve by this symposium.

When a primate morphologist thinks also of the behavior of primates, he will naturally consider first of all the means by which these animals can perceive and enjoy the world they live in,

Journal of Medicine, LXVI (1966), 3153–3170, et sq. H. M. Bruce, "Pheromones," *British Medical Bulletin,* XXVI (1970), 10–13. G. E. W. Wolstenholme and Julie Knight, eds. *Taste and Smell in Vertebrates* (London: J. & A. Churchill, 1970).

Figure 1: Papuas rubbing noses (*after A. A. Vogel, 1954*).

that is, their *senses*. To all mammals the environment must appear very differently according to their anatomical specializations. Whales, for instance, have practically no sense of smell, very poor eyesight, and extremely limited tactile sense, but their sense of hearing is highly specialized for their exclusively aquatic environment. Among primates the well developed *tactile sense* has gradually become localized. In the mostly nocturnal prosimians we still find many vibrissae distributed on the face and the forearms as essential aids for literal contact with the environment. In the suborder of simian primates the tactile hairs play at best a most insignificant role. The strepsirhine prosimians, distinguished by their common possession of a rhinarium, still rely exten-

sively on this specialized tactile organ, present in many other mammals. Even the Melanesian delight in rubbing noses (Fig. 1) can no longer approach the delicate tactile sensations of a rhinarium. The highly sensitized dermatoglyphic covering of the palms and soles reaches its full development only in simian primates in direct connection with their almost exclusive preference of the hands and feet for tactile exploration. With the great thickening of the soles in bipedal man this function became concentrated in the hands alone.

The *sense of smell* still plays an important role in the life of all those prosimians in which not only is the olfactory apparatus still far better developed than in any simian primates, but there are also various specialized skin glands, secreting odoriferous substances, used for marking territories and pathways. In the suborder Simiae odoriferous glands have been found only among such lower platyrrhines as marmosets and night monkeys, in which they seem not to function before maturity and hence serve most likely as sexual attraction. In view of the fact that in all recent catarrhines the sense of smell is poorly developed, it seems certain that "early man," too, had derived no great benefit from this sense.

To the best of our knowledge all simian primates are distinguished among mammals by having acquired *color vision* in various degrees of perfection, and many prosimian as well as all simian primates can see stereoscopically, an indispensable faculty for arboreal animals, which have to judge distances before jumping. The ability to see in the dark, well developed in the many nocturnal prosimians and in the single night monkey *Aotes*, is lacking in all other primates, which are therefore quite helpless and easily panic-stricken at night. Nocturnal species are in general not social animals but tend to associate only as sexual partners or as parent and young. In significant contrast to this, all diurnal primates live in groups of varying and, for the most part, considerable size. In daylight all diurnal primates rely most of all on their excellent eyesight, which becomes of greatest advantage to a group spread and moving in trees and thereby gaining many different and constantly changing viewpoints, from which any danger is bound to be quickly detected by one or another member of the group. The speed of reactions to visual perceptions appears to be much more rapid in most monkeys and apes than in modern man and may still have been so in early man. The latter also seems to have benefited from a better visual memory than most of us possess today, as proved in later stages of human evolution by the remarkable ability to draw from memory alone.

The *sense of hearing,* especially the capacity to determine the direction of sound, seems to be most highly developed in such nocturnal pro-simians as galago, aye-aye, and tarsier, with their huge and extremely mobile outer ears, which in some forms can also be completely folded over the auditory openings during sleep. Many monkeys still can abduce their outer ears as part of a threatening attitude, but it is very doubtful that these structures are of significant aid in sound-direction finding. Among all higher primates the ear musculature has degenerated so much that the outer ears have become useless decorations, varying between mere vestiges, as in orangs, and huge flaps, as in chimpanzees. While the sense of hearing is of vital importance to all primates, it has not become highly perfected in any simian species but has remained merely adequate for the range of sounds produced by themselves.

It is beyond any doubt that throughout his evolution man never deviated from this order in the relative roles of the main senses, an order that is valid in all catarrhines. The least important role has always been played by the sense of smell and the most important role by that of vision.

The sense of hearing is certainly not of vital help for simian primates in avoiding danger and in escaping predators. Snakes and owls approach noiselessly, and leopards and ocelots stalk their prey at night too silently to wake a monkey out of his notoriously sound sleep. Man-eaters among the large cats invariably get their human victims without having been heard and undoubtedly did so in the days of early man. The great importance of hearing for primates is primarily connected with their *own sounds,* and the simian primates are by far the noisiest of all mammals, at least if judged by the total amount of noise produced throughout the year. From this fact, incidentally, the novice gains the impression that monkeys and apes are the most abundant mammals in the jungles, in which all other mammals are silently hidden except during their rutting seasons. Sounds are the essence of primate life: When a member of a group gets caught by a predator, it usually can still scream for help, with the result that the entire group is alarmed by a pandemonium of sounds. The discovery of a potential danger is immediately broadcast by the entire group with reverberating and persisting noise, as every big-game hunter knows to his own advantage.

Without the hearing of sounds, produced by their own kind, monkeys and apes would never have become the intensely social animals that they are. Sounds of a surprising variety serve continually for the contact between the members of a group, for the orientation of mother and young, for the information of the entire group about possible danger, and, last but not least, for scaring enemies of different or the same species and even for warning rival groups away from territories already occupied. The amount and variety of information that can be exchanged by means of sounds in the highly social catarrhines surpasses that in any other mammals and culminates in human speech. The primatologist regards *language* not as the result of something radically new and exclusively human but rather as a quantitative perfection of the highly specialized development of man's central nervous control of the anatomical speech apparatus in the larynx, tongue, and lips, the latter being as good in an ape as in man. The orgies of noise, indulged in especially by howlers, guerezas, gibbons, sia-mangs, and chimpanzees, seemingly so repetitious and meaningless, are probably at least as informa-tive to the respective species as most after-dinner speaking is to *Homo sapiens.*

The expression of emotions and transmission of information are by no means limited to sounds and the hearing thereof but result, in catarrhines generally, as much from a great variety of postures and gestures. Crouching down, presenting but-tocks, extending hands in pronation, exposing teeth partly or fully, raising eyebrows, protruding lips, shaking branches, pounding chest, dancing in one place, walking backward, etc.—all are actions full of definite meaning. Among catar-rhines the oral and ocular facial muscles have become differentiated with increasing complexity and thereby have provided additional means for the expression of feelings and intentions, readily understood by others (Huber, 1931), especially in combination with sound. The long lists of different postures, gestures, and facial movements characteristic of monkeys and apes have not yet been compiled, but any careful observer realizes that they represent an intricate and voluminous "silent vocabulary" of great aid in social inter-course.

In the perfectly adapted arboreal life of mon-keys and apes, the limited variety of sounds, together with the great variety of meaningful gestures and facial expressions, is fully adequate for all social life within such close contact as permits seeing and hearing these detailed means of communication. As soon as the early hominids had ventured into open spaces, had begun to use and even make tools, and had co-operated in hunting, the total variety of all means of expres-sion needed additions, which could come only from an increase in sounds, since the compara-tively little changed anatomy had already been

fully used for all possible gestures, etc. With the disappearance of an outer tail many eloquent

Figure 2: Orangutan carrying her infant while walk-ing upright (*after H. Wendt, 1954*).

means of intercommunication became lost and could be replaced only by greater reliance on the vocal apparatus. Gestures have always persisted in human evolution, but they have become over-shadowed by an infinitely greater variety of sounds in increasing numbers of combinations.

Bipedal posture and locomotion undoubtedly represented the first and most decisive evolution-ary change of hominids, but it is by no means such a radical innovation as is commonly assumed. Bears, weasels, and many other mammals can and do *stand* erect for raising their level of sight, and so can all monkeys. *Walking* on the hind legs alone, with the trunk naturally held so that the center of gravity is perpendicular above the center of support, is easily possible for at least *Propithecus* among the prosimians, for *Ateles* and *Lagothrix* among the platyrrhines, and for gib-bons, siamangs, chimpanzees, and gorillas. Even the orangutan can readily stand and walk erect on its feet, which are extremely specialized for climbing trees (Fig. 2). Without ever having been trained for it, healthy young gorillas in captivity play by running around upright on their hind legs for minutes at a time, only to drop back on all fours for a quick run, to sit upright for a while, and to resume bipedal locomotion again and again, exactly as a human child who is also as yet incapable of maintaining an upright posture for more than brief spells. Ontogenetically as well as phylogenetically erect bipedal locomotion can develop only from occasional brief to habitual long action, but never through an intermediate half-upright posture. Many different primates *might* have gradually developed bipedalism after their preparation of a pronounced division in function in the upper and the lower limbs. The propelling force in jumping is mostly provided by the hind limbs alone (Fig. 3), most clearly shown by *Tarsius*, which has proportionately longer legs than has man. Only the extreme brachiators, like gibbons or spider monkeys, can

Figure 3: Chimpanzee jumping in upright posture (*after I. T. Sanderson and G. Steinbacher, 1957*).

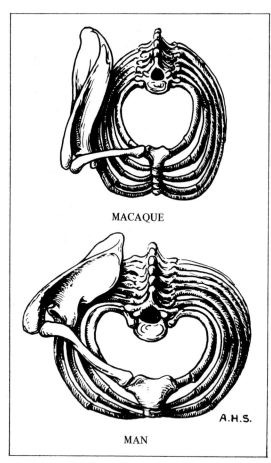

MACAQUE

MAN

A.H.S.

Figure 4: Cephalic view of thorax and right shoulder girdle of adult macaque and man (*after Schultz, 1957*).

throw themselves through space by their arms alone. Man's erect locomotion was prepared for by the shortening and widening of the trunk and the associated shift of the spinal column toward the center of the trunk (Fig. 4), a basic trend common to all higher primates and present already in *Oreopithecus* (Schultz, 1960). In addi-

tion, the iliac blades of man, though broad, as in pongids, remained short, turned from a frontal to a sagittal direction, and the sacrum shifted somewhat ventrally and far caudally (Fig. 5). The useless phalangeal parts of the toes II–V started to become vestigial in hominids as soon as they began their terrestrial career. Quickly they perfected still other typically simian conditions, facilitating erect posture, such as the bending of the spine at the lumbosacral border (Fig. 6) and the ontogenetic retention of the fetal forward position of the occipital condyles.[1] Judging by the australopithecids, the erect posture preceded the acquisition of a well-balanced head, but in the *Pithecanthropus* stage of hominid evolution all significant adaptations for bipedal walk were already fully developed.

Monkeys and apes use their *hands* for catching animals and picking vegetable food, which is conveyed to the mouth with the hands. The nursing young are held with a hand, and food or young is frequently carried in one hand even during locomotion. The hands play a very effective role in fighting and, of course, in grooming, nest-building, and other daily activities. This differential use of the extremities was the long-present inducement for bipedal walk. When the earliest hominids had left the forest, the need for a higher level of vision than that in quadrupedal position led to the upright posture and even to erect walk more and more frequently, and thereby the hands became free for purposes other than locomotion and, we can be sure, were rarely idle. It was no radical innovation for Dawn men to use their hands for picking up rocks or clubs as ready defense to overcome the lack of large teeth. Nearly every captive macaque delights in carrying new objects around its cage, and apes are entertained for hours by a blanket or a bucket, which they will not let out of their hands without a fight.

In all catarrhines the thumb is rotated in prenatal life about 90 degrees and thereby becomes truly opposable even to the index finger. In

---

[1] For a much fuller account of these morphological changes connected with the erect posture of man, the reader is referred to the writer's papers 1950c and 1957.

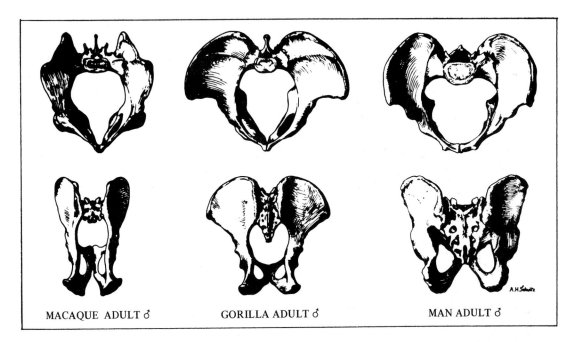

MACAQUE ADULT ♂   GORILLA ADULT ♂   MAN ADULT ♂

Figure 5: Cephalic and dorsal views of pelves of macaque, gorilla, and man.

platyrrhines the thumb has no real opposability but is merely abducable, and the extremely opposable thumbs of some prosimians act against the fourth fingers, while the second are greatly reduced. The hands of man are especially well adapted for holding objects as well as for delicate manipulations because neither have the thumbs been shortened, as in many monkeys, nor have the fingers II–V been lengthened, as in all brachiators. With thumb and index finger any baboon can extract the sting from a scorpion, and every chimpanzee a thorn out of its skin—and this more dextrously than most of us—but their thumbs are of less aid in a powerful grasp than man's, on account of the relatively weaker thumb musculature and the difference in the proportionate lengths of the opposing digits (Fig. 7). There can be no doubt that anatomically our hand itself has undergone no significant change since the days of early man. After our

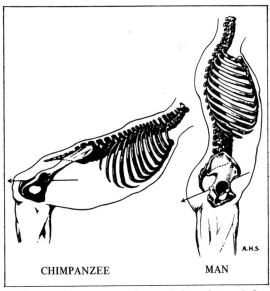

CHIMPANZEE   MAN

Figure 6: The position and size of the pelvis and the curvature of the vertebral column in an ape and in man (*after Schultz, 1957*).

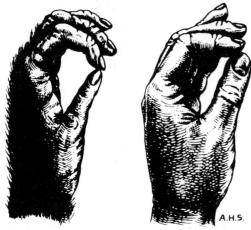

ADULT	Thumb 1. Hand 1.	Thumb 1. Trunk 1.	Hand 1. Trunk 1.	Phalaṇg. III 1. Metacarp. III 1.
CHIMP.	47	23	49	144
MAN	67	25	37	145

Figure 7: The opposability of the thumb in a chimpanzee and in man and averages of some proportions of the hand. The total thumb length is much shorter in relation to the total hand length in the ape than in man, but in relation to the trunk length the thumb has practically the same length in both, while the total hand length has greatly increased in the ape, and this in its phalangeal and metacarpal parts.

typically catarrhine hand had been freed from any routine function of locomotion, it could perform more varied and finally more skilful manipulations exclusively by means of a greatly improved nervous control.

The grasping hands of simian primates, together with their great range in arm movements, can readily be used also for *throwing* objects. In hunting howler and spider monkeys, I frequently had to dodge dead branches and bunches of foliage that, if not thrown, were then certainly dropped deliberately by these monkeys whenever they had been driven into the crown of some high tree from which they could not escape except by coming down toward the hunter. Carpenter (1935) has recorded very similar experi-

ences with platyrrhines, and Hornaday (1922) has given a vivid account of baboons throwing stones. Once I had stalked an orang mother and her half-grown offspring, and, though well hidden, my presence became suspected by the youngster, which had approached very closely. The old ape stood upright on a limb and with both hands broke thick branches and threw them deliberately and with good aim at my hiding place, quite evidently to provoke a movement and exposure of whatever danger she suspected. An old male chimpanzee that had lived in the Washington zoo for twenty-five years was famous for regularly throwing most effectively and accurately potatoes, apples, his drinking cup, and even his feces at any member of the audience who dared to laugh in front of his cage. The psychologist Klüver (1937) experimented with a capuchin monkey that intentionally picked up and threw a mouse, attached to a string, beyond some fruit outside its cage, just to rake in this fruit by means of pulling mouse and fruit within reach. I have seen several other captive apes and one old mandrill throw objects at the public with great force and good aim. I mention these experiences merely in support of my conviction that the earliest men, capable of carrying any odd rocks or clubs in their hands, would have thrown them as defense and fled before risking an enemy's coming close enough to be hit by rock or club.

If early man, before he had fire, really did retire to caves at night, he could drive off a prowling leopard far more effectively by a shower of thrown stones than by waiting until it *might* be hit in the dark by a rock in the hand. Furthermore, the earliest hunters had few chances of overtaking swift prey to hit it to death with a rock in the hand but could stalk unsuspecting, stationary game until it was within reach of thrown stones. It seems most likely that *throwing* objects came sooner and more easily than pounding with objects or using them as "lengthened arms" in the form of clubs or lances. This can hardly be proved directly by archeologists[2] but must remain a matter of relative probability supported by observations on comparative behavior. Soon after these statements had been read at the symposium, I received a copy of the "inaugural lecture" of the animal psychologist Kortlandt (1959) containing many varied and detailed descriptions of *throwing* by monkeys and apes. Among the most significant accounts of this remarkable report are those of a young chimpanzee at the Amsterdam zoo that "attained a hitting accuracy considerably better than that of average children of comparable physical development," of the chimpanzees of the Chester zoo that "often aim in front of a moving target . . . even smashing two windows of the Director's car as he drove past," and of the experiments at the San Diego and Rotterdam zoos, in which captive-born chimpanzees "were suddenly confronted with an aggressively behaving leopard or tiger and in both cases anything at hand was thrown at the large cat . . . as an instinctive reaction resulting from a conflict between fleeing and fighting impulses."

In contrast to most mammals, including the majority of prosimians, there is no real *breeding season* in tarsiers, Cebid monkeys, and all catarrhines, a fact of profound influence for social life, as has already been discussed fully in many recent publications. Some seasonal fluctuations in the relative number of births have been reported for various monkeys and even for man, but generally the two sexes live together all year round, and pregnancies can result at any season. Among the Simiae only the marmosets are exceptional in this, as in many other respects (multiple young and paternal care of infants). According to recent reports, the Japanese macaque also seems to

have a quite restricted breeding season, but most likely on account of the pronounced climatic seasons in the home of this most northern of all macaques. Among apes copulation has been observed as occurring with great regularity not only throughout the oestrous cycle but even well after pregnancy had commenced (Miller, 1931; Schultz and Snyder, 1935). The continual presence of sexually receptive females, together with the helplessness of infants for a relatively long period, necessitated coherence in families and clans with a division of duties. For a relatively very long time the mother will give continual devoted care to her young. This proverbial "monkey-love" is manifested most extremely by the common tendency of females to kidnap infants not their own. In moments of danger it is the mother who flees with her young, while the father covers the retreat with bluff or attack, and this in species with great sex differences in size (baboons, gorillas, etc.) as well as in those in which the males differ comparatively little from the females in strength (many monkeys, gibbons, chimpanzees, and men). Again we find that even in modern man this basic rule is still valid, and in view of the lack of any contrary evidence we are justified in assuming that early man, too, was governed by these same general factors, determining the social life of all simian primates.

Aside from those few mammals that have become specialized for huge bulk, primates are clearly distinguished by their pronounced trend toward *prolonging all periods* of their individual lives (Fig. 8). Prenatal life lasts only about six weeks in *Tupaia*, which still can produce two or more offspring three times a year. Among the highest primates the period of gestation for the normally single young has increased to roughly nine months, and this in the great apes as well as in man. The state of maturity at birth is much more advanced in the lemurs and monkeys than in apes and man (Fig. 9). Measured by the conditions in the former, the average differences in

---

[2] The discovery of the throwing of clay pellets at zoömorphic targets by Neanderthal man, reported by Professor A. C. Blanc in this symposium, is of special interest in this connection.

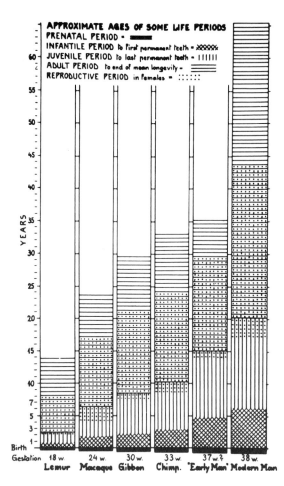

Figure 8: Diagrammatic representation of the approximate average durations of some periods of life among recent primates, based upon data assembled by Schultz (1956*a*), and the most likely corresponding duration in early man.

the great immaturity of the newborn of apes and men are insignificant,[3] in spite of what has been claimed in the literature. There can be no reasonable doubt that early man had just as helpless

---

[3] This has been demonstrated by the writer in a series of reports, referred to in his review of ontogenetic changes in primates (1956*a*), and is supported by recent, new findings.

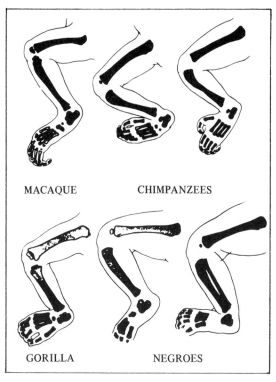

Figure 9: Tracings of X-ray photographs of the lower extremities of some newborn primates. For chimpanzee and man the least and the most ossification in full-term fetuses is shown (*after Schultz, 1957*).

newborns as we produce today and that therefore parental care and group protection was fully as necessary then as now. The clear and general trend toward prolongation of all main periods of *post*natal life has reached its outstanding extreme in modern man, who has to get along with merely his milk teeth for at least his first six years, apes for three years, and most monkeys for only about one year. The diet of apes and primitive man is strictly limited while the food can be bitten off and masticated with only the small and fragile deciduous teeth, hence they rely for much longer periods than do other mammals on the addition of mothers' milk—for over two years in chimpanzees and for three and more years in orangs and in some races of man (Fig. 10). Among Alaskan Eskimos, children formerly often nursed until they were four or even five years old (Spencer, 1959). This is consequential not only for long and close contact between mother and young but also because it greatly prolongs the interval between pregnancies, inasmuch as lactation generally prevents conception.

The onset of sexual maturity also tends to occur steadily later in life among primates (Fig. 8), thereby increasing the minimum interval between generations, which naturally is one of the primary factors determining population growth and evolutionary change within a given unit of time. As far as known, most primates become sexually mature well before they are fully grown and even before their dentition has been completed, though there seem to be some minor specific differences in this respect. In view of the prevailing sexual dominance of the strongest males in most simian groups, the potential male breeders, not yet fully grown and still without fully erupted canines, have little chance for reproduction but are provident, immediate substitutes in case the leading protector is incapacitated through one cause or another. If the gestation period is added to the average age of full sexual maturity, we obtain the shortest possible interval between generations, which equals about five years in Old World monkeys, at least ten years in apes, and eighteen years or more in civilized man. This last extreme has most likely been reached quite recently and had not yet been fully developed in early man. The average duration of life has also become greatly increased in the higher, as compared with the lower, primates and has reached an extreme quite recently in the civilized races of modern man, without, however, having in any way improved the durability of tissues and organs. Among wild monkeys and apes and even in uncivilized man, really senile individuals are comparatively scarce, though occasional specimens are found with clear symptoms of senile degenerations. To insert in

Figure 10: Papua mother nursing her infant and a suckling pig. (*After A. A. Vogel, 1954*).

Figure 8 approximately comparable data for "early man" is not as arbitrary as it may seem in view of the regular, gradual shifting of these data in only one direction, from the lowest to the highest primates. It is justified, furthermore, by some observations regarding relevant racial differences in man, according to which such ontogenetic processes as dental and skeletal maturation still proceed somewhat more rapidly in, for instance, Australians than in whites. It is also permissible to assume that infancy lasted longer in early men than in apes from the finding of a larger percentage of markedly worn milk teeth among the former than among the latter. Such comparative data on the ontogenetic tempos of primates have a direct bearing on social life. The extremely slow maturation of all higher primates, culminating in man, demands unusually prolonged parental care and protection. Even the period of nursing has increased in apes and natural man to a degree unique among all mammals, so that the young are bound to their mothers for years and thereby gain a long period of imitative learning from adults. Any species with such slow rates of reproduction as have apes and men, with their single offspring, would soon become extinct if the young were not protected throughout the long period preceding the age of reproduction. This protection is most effectively provided by the combined alertness and keen vision of an organized social group, especially since primates are not equipped with great weapons,[4] such as horns or claws, or with the outstanding speed of many other mammals.

On my five collecting trips to jungles of America and Asia, I have always found monkeys much more in evidence and apparently more numerous than any other mammals. This impression is due to the fact that monkeys are merely the noisiest and many the gaudiest of all mammals and do not promptly hide quietly or flee upon the approach of man, except when they have been persistently hunted. From my field experience I have become convinced that at least tropical rain forests could easily support far greater monkey populations than actually exist. It is only in areas with marked seasonal changes and possible forest fires at the end of long droughts that the modest density of primate populations seems to be influenced by the fluctuating food supply available throughout the year. The total of all present nonhuman primate populations probably does not surpass the more than two and a half billion human beings of today, though the former are represented by nearly six hundred different spe-

cies, as against the single species of the latter. The causes of this stationary or possibly even diminishing *population* of nonhuman primates consist of geographical factors—such as climate, areas with suitable conditions for mode of locomotion, food, etc.—and, at least as important, of the basic factors of fertility, or rate of reproduction, in relation to mortality.

In regard to the first factors mentioned I have little to contribute except my conviction that many catarrhines are hardy creatures, not closely restricted to tropical or even to temperate zones, but able to survive, if necessary, in seasonally cold climates, as, for example, *Rhinopithecus* in Northern China or *Macaca mulatta* in the thriving outdoor colony of Baltimore, maintained for many years by Dr. C. Hartman. Mountain gorillas, some gibbons, and some *Colobus* monkeys live at altitudes where *Homo sapiens* requires at night the protection of blankets and fires. It is particularly in the peripheral, cooler regions of catarrhine distribution that monkeys invariably spend their chilly nights sitting in mutual close embrace to prevent waste of bodily heat. Whenever the temperature remains at night near that of the body, monkeys and apes prefer to sleep separately and lying down on their sides or prone, that is, in a horizontal position for what amounts to nearly half their lives!

The possible expansion of the home territories of primate species is certainly not limited by water of moderate width or current, since many monkeys are good swimmers (as I have witnessed repeatedly in Central America), as has been reported in the literature (e.g., by Krieg, 1948) and as can be observed in many zoos. Anthropoids, though not in the least afraid of water, usually do not seem to be able to swim without having been trained. Natural barriers to the migration of monkeys and apes are lack of fairly continuous forest and drinking water and lack of shade. As every successful animal dealer has had to learn, most monkeys and apes will not

[4] The long canines of adult male monkeys and apes are not very dependable weapons, since they become broken, abscessed, or even lost, especially after the enamel has partly worn off, far more frequently than they do in carnivores.

stand exposure to tropical midday sunlight for any length of time but have to find shade after a while. Suitable conditions for the night are equally essential. Typical diurnal, arboreal monkeys retire for the night to the comparative safety of carefully selected trees. Once I surprised a group of Panamanian capuchin monkeys at dusk dropping one by one from the lowest branch of a tall tree into the dense crown of a palm with a very thorny stem, which could never have been ascended by a predator and which the monkeys could leave in the morning only by jumping down into lower bushes. Nests of a crude sort are constructed by only a few prosimians and by the three great apes. Rocky clefts and niches with limited and hence readily guarded accessibility are used as refuges for the night by only some species of baboons and macaques, and even these few kinds will never go deep into dark caves under normal conditions. No chimpanzees ever deserved the name "troglodytes," which has been given to them, and none would survive many nights in caves, in which they would be easy prey for leopards and hyenas, especially since many apes snore resoundingly. Incidentally, in many regions of the total range of early man caves were not sufficiently numerous to shelter enough "cavemen" to maintain a viable population. For routine usage and before the added protection of fire, early hominids found greater safety during the night in trees than in caves and, even as bipeds, could climb trees as easily as natural man still can today (Fig. 11).

Population growth depends primarily upon *fertility*. The latter seems to vary extensively among primates according to our few available data. In some monkeys and in gibbons, I found only about 12 per cent of all adult females pregnant, among howler monkeys 20 per cent, in langurs 30 per cent, and in macaques 50 per cent (Schultz, 1944) or even more by other reports. Most nonpregnant females of the same local groups were accompanied by young of widely

Figure 11: Australian boy climbing a tree (*after C. P. Mountford*, 1951).

varying ages, proving the lack of definite breeding seasons and supporting the conclusion that new conceptions do not follow soon upon the termination of pregnancy, provided the offspring lives and is being nursed. Under the most favorable conditions of captivity, macaques can produce during their period of fertility no more than 7 or possibly 8 descendants, if the early loss of some has not shortened a period of sterility due to lactation. We know that in modern mankind a woman *can* have twice as many pregnancies during her greater number of fertile years, but it is exceedingly rare that all her children will survive to puberty. The number of prior pregnancies varies in Pueblo Indian women, over forty years old, between 0 and 14 and averages 9.4, but infant mortality is very high (Aberle, 1931). Rasmussen (1927) encountered an old

Eskimo woman who had had 20 children, of whom 5 grew up, the others having died early. Gusinde (1948) mentions one old Congo pygmy who had lost all her 11 children. Among Melanesians, Powdermaker (1931) reported an average number of children per woman of only 2.9 and found that 12 per cent of all women were sterile and 20 per cent of all children died before marriage. In the Bushmanlike East-African Tindiga, Kohl-Larsen (1958) found 1–10 children per woman, but evidently very few attained their reproductive age, since this hunting tribe is rapidly decreasing in total number. From these and many other relevant reports on "natural man," it appears that fertility in man as well as in monkey always was at least adequate for possible population growth, which, if lacking, must have been prevented by a death rate equal to or surpassing the birth rate. In an excellent book on *Population Problems*, Thompson (1953) has reached practically the same conclusion, stating that "from time immemorial the number of people living in any given area has been determined not so much by the level of the birth rate as by the level of the death rate."

Mortality can be highly selective as to age and sex, and, since the conditions of social life are directly influenced by any changes in the composition of a population according to age and sex, some remarks are inserted here about the all-too-few data which have become available in regard to the age- and sex-ratios among primates in their natural habitat. Most of the voluminous records on primate material in my files are based upon specimens collected in the jungle without any conscious preference for age or sex in order to represent true population samples. Sex, even of the youngest specimens, could always be determined from the corpse, and age from the skeleton. With all my admiration for my old friend Carpenter, with whom I shared many of my field experiences, I doubt that even the most powerful binoculars can determine age and sex of monkeys moving in changing light high in dense forest anywhere nearly as reliably as can direct observations on dead specimens. In attempts to estimate the age or sex of living individuals, the observer is bound to be influenced by behavior and size, though both these factors are variable and that of size is occasionally very misleading. My data on collected population samples are also far from ideal, since differences in behavior might have resulted in unnatural representations of sexes or ages in spite of the best intentions of the collectors. When hunted, adult males do not flee as promptly as do females, but in their escape they are not burdened by infants, since the latter are never hidden and abandoned by their mothers, as in so many other mammals. These facts are mentioned merely as possible explanations for the, at times, considerable discrepancies between the well-known data of Carpenter, Nissen, and other field observers and those based upon my records on dead specimens. According to the latter, immature individuals (= infants + juveniles) constitute from about 20 per cent to a maximum of 40 per cent of the populations of various wild monkeys and apes, percentages that correspond roughly to those in most populations of recent men but do not reach such extremes as the 52 per cent of human beings below twenty years in the population of the United States in 1850 or the percentage nearly as high reported for Greenland Eskimos (Pearl, 1930), or the even 57 per cent of children among North-Canadian Indians, living chiefly by hunting (Wissler, 1942). It is significant also that among the macaques of Santiago Island (Puerto Rico), which were practically free of parasitic and infectious diseases and knew no large predators, Carpenter (1942) found the immature to form about 50 per cent of the population. These data on the surprisingly modest proportionate number of young among many monkeys and apes again support the conclusion that infantile and juvenile mortality must be at least as high in the latter as it is known to be in recent primitive man, who also has mostly stationary or decreasing populations.

The composition of the population by *sex* according to all available data changes with age not only in man but also in apes and monkeys. Among the latter this sex ratio, or the number of males per 100 females, is not culturally altered as it is in some human societies. It is all the more significant, therefore, that the sex ratio decreases with age in nonhuman primates, just as it does in man without artificial interference, such as the custom of killing or exposing unwanted girl babies.[5] Evidently it is a generally valid rule that males have a higher mortality rate than do females, and in some species this sex difference must be very pronounced, indeed, to produce the great preponderance of adult females. For instance, in series of Central American monkeys, totaling nearly a thousand, the sex ratio equals in howler monkeys 67 for the immature, whereas it is only 57 for adults, and in spider monkeys these figures even drop from 118 for the immature to 61 for adults (Schultz, 1959). Among 224 chimpanzees, for which I have exact records, the sex ratio of the young is 91 and that of the adults 75. Even among gibbons, which are distinguished by having practically no morphological secondary sex differences, this ratio decreases with age from 115 to 108 (Schultz, 1944). In South African Negroes the sex ratio of all children under fifteen years is 101, whereas that of adults over fifty years is only 66, and for Switzerland the corresponding figures are 101 and 83. These few examples suffice to show that the stronger sex proves to be universally the weaker one in the course of years or else meets with more accidents while still young.

Even under the best of laboratory conditions many pregnancies of captive primates fail to reach full term, and thereby a considerable part of the reproductive period becomes wasted and the maximum possible number of offspring is reduced. According to Yerkes' (1943) extensive experience with chimpanzees, about one out of every three conceptions ends in death before or at birth, and Hartman (1932) found practically the same proportion in his large colony of macaques in Baltimore, which had been maintained under nearly ideal conditions for many years for the purpose of studying reproduction. This high prenatal death rate in nonhuman primates equals that prevailing in civilized man, according to our best clinical authorities, and there is no justification for doubting that natural man forms no exception in this respect. Though we cannot expect any reliable statistics for the latter, we do have many relevant claims, such as that by Gusinde (1948), who states that among Congo pygmies miscarriages and stillbirths are very common. Since most dead embryos and fetuses are promptly expelled, there seems to be little chance to encounter such cases among wild primates. It is all the more significant, therefore, that we have already found several instances of intra-uterine deaths among wild-shot monkeys of quite a variety of species.

Irregularities in early development, producing congenital malformations of one kind or another, are far from limited to civilized man, as is commonly assumed. I have found such cases, with frequencies unheard of in man, among some populations of wild monkeys and apes. Here I can merely refer to the published instances of polydactyly, syndactyly, and oligodactyly in baboons, gibbons, and chimpanzees (Schultz, 1956b). I might also recall the interesting occurrence of an extremely pronounced oxycephaly combined with the lack of both thumbs and both great toes in a young chimpanzee from Cameroon. This syndrome, well known in man, had so handicapped this ape that he fell out of a tree during the pursuit of his group (Schultz, 1958). Of

---

[5] Among Eskimos, Chinese, and ancient Romans (Russell, 1958), girls have sometimes been permitted to die at birth, causing unnaturally high postnatal sex ratios.

special interest also is an adult wild gibbon we had shot in Siam that had one arm very incompletely formed, containing only a slender proximal part of the humerus (Schultz, 1944). A practically identical profound malformation has just been found in one of the adult Neanderthal skeletons of Shanidar in Iraq, according to my interpretation of the preliminary description of this important find given by Stewart (1959). I am convinced that this case, too, is an incidence of *unilateral peromelia*, well known in recent man and reported for at least three other primates.

The already mentioned modest proportion of young in many primate populations may be partly accounted for by the fact that certain birds of prey, snakes, and the smaller cats will snatch, preferably, such young monkeys as are bound to stray from the protection of the group whenever the notorious curiosity of the young has become stronger than their primary timidity. Such accidents, however, can hardly occur with a frequency sufficient to produce an infant mortality resulting in a more or less stationary population. Far more effective are the minute enemies in the form of the great variety of parasites that have been found in primates (Stiles, Hassall, and Nolan, 1929), of which many are very pathogenic, particularly in the young. Malaria, filariasis, and a great many other parasitic diseases have been reported for monkeys of the Old and the New World, and this often with very high frequencies. In all probability yaws is widespread among African apes and, like malaria, will at least temporarily incapacitate infected individuals so that they cannot keep up with their group and, as single animals, become more exposed to predators. From extensive surveys and tests, the epidemiologist Clark

(1952) reached the conclusion that many wild monkeys must have had yellow fever at one time in their lives and had recovered, while others undoubtedly had succumbed to it. It has also become known that an epidemic of yellow fever wiped out entire populations of howling monkeys in parts of Brazil in 1947 and that in all probability the same disease was responsible for the marked decrease in the number of monkeys on Barro Colorado Island between the census taken by Carpenter (1934) and that taken later by Collias and Southwick (1952). The parasitologist Cameron (1958) has recently stated that man certainly had acquired from his prehuman ancestors his malarial parasites, pinworms, and lice and, most likely, also his taenias, hookworms, ascarids, and filariae.

That arthritis, osteitis deformans, sinus infections, dental diseases, and even arterial lesions have not developed with civilization in recent man, but are at least as prevalent in many kinds of wild monkeys and apes, has already been proved by abundant findings (Figs. 12, 13, and 14).[6] For instance, among 233 wild gibbons, I found marked chronic arthritis in 17 per cent of all skeletons, but this percentage changes markedly with age, being only 2 in juveniles but 55 in the series of the oldest specimens with very worn teeth and closed sutures (Schultz, 1944). Destruction of the dental apparatus also advances rapidly with age in all primates, and apes, at least, frequently outlive the durability of their misnamed "permanent" teeth. For instance, I found alveolar abcesses among 186 adult (but not old) gorillas in 16 per cent of the skulls, whereas among 107 senile gorillas I found them in 60 per cent. Among 110 adult (but not old) chimpanzees, caries existed in 13 per cent, and among 62 senile chimpanzees in 31 per cent (Schultz, 1956b). In the comparatively few and mostly incomplete skeletal remains of early man there have already been encountered several instances of arthritic changes (e.g., Krapina, Shanidar) and of

---

[6] The enormous number and variety of diseases that can occur in nonhuman primates and that are, of course, best known from their occurrence in captive ones have recently been described systematically by Ruch (1959).

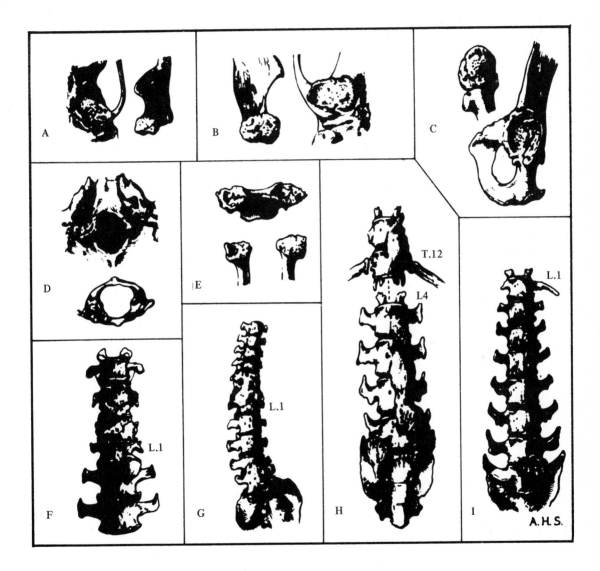

Figure 12: Examples of arthritic changes in skeletal parts of adult wild catarrhine monkeys and apes: A = gibbon; B = orangutan; C = gibbon; D = gibbon; E = same gibbon as A; F = baboon; G = gibbon; H = proboscis monkey; I = macaque (*after Schultz,* 1956b).

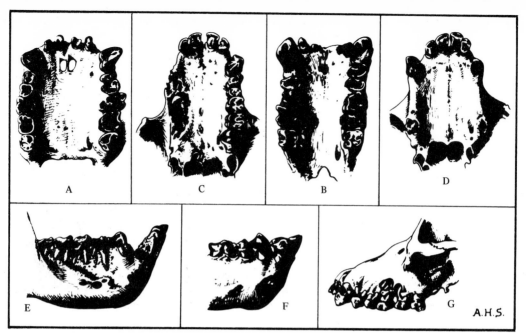

Figure 13: Examples of pathological conditions in the dental apparatus of adult wild apes: A = old gibbon; B = old gorilla; C = chimpanzee (caries on incisors); D = chimpanzee; E = old orangutan; F = same gorilla as B; G = orangutan (*after Schultz, 1956b*).

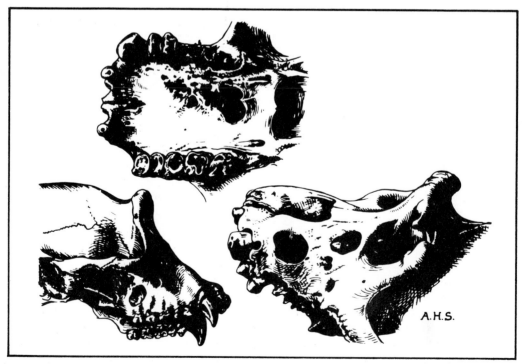

Figure 14: Extensive maxillary sinus infection in a wild chimpanzee and multiple sinus infections and destruction of dentition in a wild gorilla (*after Schultz, 1956b*).

dental decay (e.g., La Chapelle, Rhodesia). Ten out of 28 adult skeletons from the Copper Age of Hungary showed various marked pathological changes, especially arthritic ones (Gáspárdy and Nemeskéri, 1960). It seems certain, therefore, that pain and suffering has existed throughout human evolution, merely varying in prevalence now and then according to racial immunity, environmental conditions, or dietary habits.

That crippling accidents are not at all rare in the life of wild monkeys and apes is proved by the many more or less well-repaired fractures one finds in every large series of skeletons (Fig. 15). The frequency of fractures, as of diseases of bones and teeth, increases markedly with age. Among 233 wild gibbons, I encountered healed fractures in not only some older juveniles, but in 28 per cent of fully grown (but not old) adults and in 50 per cent of the oldest adults, some of which had as many as seven repaired fractures. My survey of 100 skeletons of orangutans shot in the wild lists healed fractures in 12 per cent of juveniles, as against 34 per cent of adults (Schultz, 1941; and a few later cases). Among the less arboreal African apes fractures are not as common as in the Asiatic apes, but they also become much more frequent with age and also are significantly more numerous in males than in females. Some of these fractures have undoubtedly resulted from fights between rivals, as indicated by their greater frequency in males, but this accounts probably only for fractured fingers, toes, or an occasional long bone. Incidentally, intratribal fights also explain the frequently torn ears of adult males. The many cases of severe and even multiple fractures in skulls, hip bones, clavicles, sternums, and ribs that have been recorded in adult wild monkeys and apes (Schultz, 1956b) must have been caused mostly by falls when animals had misjudged the strength of a branch or mismanaged a hurried leap. This seems all the more probable from the fact that fractured bones are decidedly most common in such swift and daring acrobats

as gibbons and some platyrrhine brachiators. Bone-breaking accidents are nowhere nearly as frequent in terrestrial man as in arboreal primates. For instance, Smith and Jones (1910) found healed fractures in only 1 per cent of about three thousand skeletons of ancient Nubians, and corresponding figures for other human populations are rarely much higher. Among the fossil remains of man, repaired fractures have so far been found in only few instances (e.g., ulna from Oberkassal). The striking contrast between arboreal and terrestrial primates in regard to the frequency of fractures implies a corresponding difference in mortality from this cause. It seems incredible that some apes in the jungle can and do survive smashed jaws, cracked skulls, and badly broken thighbones at least long enough for natural repairs. The bodies of those others that succumb to accidents are rarely found on the wet ground of the rain forest, where they disappear in a few days. As soon as the early hominids had become bipeds and had invaded open country, they were favored by much lower rates of incapacitating or fatal accidents than occur in arboreal life. In addition they escaped the prevalent jungle diseases of malaria, yellow fever, etc., which counteract population growth in forest-dwelling primates.

Because early man's attitude toward death represents a prominent "paleopsychological" problem in our symposium, a few remarks may here be inserted concerning the fate of injured, sick, and dying nonhuman primates, especially also since the latter are more frequent than is commonly assumed. Every zoo and primate laboratory has witnessed instances of the pitiful devotion of simian mothers to their sick infants and knows the long struggle needed to take a dead or even decomposed baby away from the mother, who will clutch the corpse to her breast day after day. Sick or wounded juvenile and adult monkeys, incapable of keeping up with the group, search instinctively for a hiding place anywhere in a

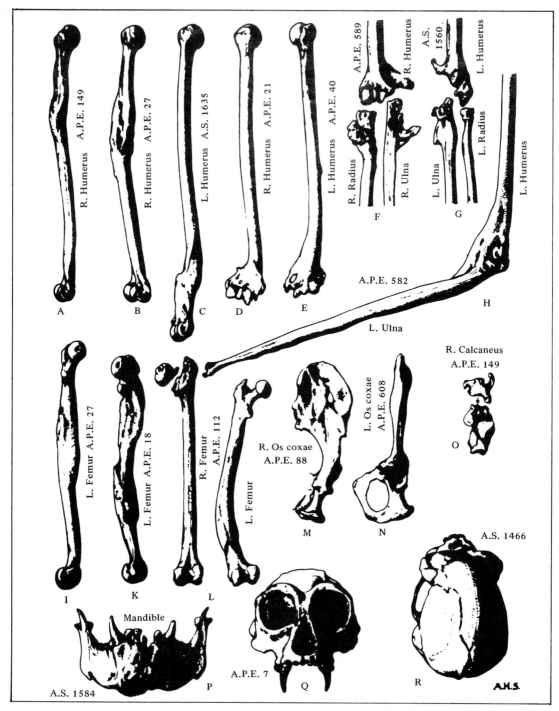

Figure 15: Examples of more-or-less well-repaired fractures in adult wild gibbons. (*after Schultz, 1944*).

cluster of dense foliage, or, if they have fallen to the ground, in the deepest niche among roots or rocks. If any cleft or cave is within reach of their strength, they may soon be found in the remotest and darkest corner thereof; here they quietly remain until recovered or dead, safe from molestation by companions of their own kind and by flies, attracted to their wounds, and hidden from predators stalking by sight or ear. The deeper the cleft in the hillside, the more cooling to fever and the more likely to supply water, the only nourishment they crave while infected teeth or sinuses or broken jaws and limbs preclude any solid food. Zapfe (1954) has recently collected some remarkable evidence showing that many different mammals that do not ordinarily enter dark caves will, under stress, venture far into long cavernous passages, frequently to perish and thus gradually to contribute to the accumulation of the dense masses of bones that have been recovered from many caves and clefts in all parts of the world. Professor von Koenigswald has recently told me of the huge numbers of teeth of pleistocene orangs found in Chinese rock clefts unsuitable for routine occupancy by man or ape. These fossilized teeth of orangs are nearly all from adults. The best explanation for this seemingly quite unnatural occurrence is von Koenigswald's hypothesis that the big pleistocene orangs, when sick or dying of old age, had entered those narrow, dark, and moist fissures, never approached by any healthy orang. Most of our rich Pliopithecus material comes from "Spaltenfüllungen," and the remains of many other fossil primates have been recovered from former rock clefts that would never have been chosen as sleeping quarters by healthy individuals, and into which they had not been dragged by hyenas or washed by floods but had dragged themselves in desperation when death was approaching. There is much in favor of this hypothesis that caves and clefts, wherever they exist in primate territories, have served as last retreats for even monkeys and apes. The early hominids

were no exceptions but also withdrew to the best available hiding places as soon as they became too weak from one cause or another to live with their group. It was not until the later hominids became encouraged by the light and protection of fire that they began to use caves, instead of trees, for the nocturnal retreat of those healthy individuals who could be sheltered therein. The primary role of caves, for primates connected only with illness and death, may very well have influenced the later behavior of "cave men," especially their attitude toward the skeletons found in the innermost darkness.

The *diet* of nonhuman primates does not differ as radically from that of natural man as has been claimed. Most prosimians and some New World monkeys eat more worms, insects, frogs, lizards, and birds' eggs than plant food, and at least some animal food is consumed occasionally by all primates, with the possible exception of the specialized Colobinae. Some marmosets and macaques stalk and consume small fish and other aquatic animals in shallow water; gibbons have been reported to catch birds even in flight; and I have repeatedly seen the chimpanzees I formerly kept kill and eat mice. Stevenson-Hamilton (1912) mentions baboons having killed a small antelope and, with apparently increasing frequency, lambs and ewes. Krumbiegel (1955) reports a remarkable case of two chimpanzees' tearing down a large nest of wild bees and quickly jumping down to escape getting stung while a third chimpanzee was rolling the nest along the ground away from the bees. This, incidentally, is only one of an abundance of examples of co-operation among apes, which is curiously still doubted by some inexperienced authors. The tapeworm *Anoplocephala gorillae* has been found in the intestines of mountain gorillas. It has been found, otherwise, only in small rodents and ungulates of the same region, so it seems highly probable that some of these small animals are occasionally eaten by gorillas (Stiles, Hassall, and Nolan, 1929). A change to a fish or meat diet is frequently followed by new parasites, which may, at least at first, be very pathogenic for their new hosts. For instance, some trematodes occur in human beings only after fishes have been eaten raw or undercooked, and certain nematodes are very commonly acquired by Eskimos from eating walrus and bears (Cameron, 1958). Many more such examples have become known and demonstrate that changes in diet, like changes in environment, can have disadvantageous as well as beneficial consequences that may hinder rather than favor population growth.

It is generally true that the quicker and more radical a change, the greater becomes the potential danger to the health of a population not yet selected for and adapted to the new conditions. It seems very doubtful to me that early hominids had at any time or place changed abruptly from a nearly all-vegetable diet to a mostly meat diet. Like all other primates, early man lived on whatever food nature provided, and, after having left the dense forests and ventured into open country, he found fewer edible plants but more small animals with which to supplement his original menus. The first bipeds in their probably winterless and droughtless homeland were as yet indiscriminate gatherers of food of all kinds, from berries, roots, and insects to small vertebrates. Only after having learned to throw stones and use clubs and spears could they add occasional larger animals whenever their gradually overpopulated and exhausted territory necessitated such effort and risk. This stage of man's dietary evolution has persisted with but little improvement to this day in some remnants of primitive food-gatherers of tropical countries. Only such hardy early men as survived their invasion of subarctic regions had by necessity to rely chiefly on meat for winter food supply and, in addition, on the skins of larger mammals for warmth and thus had acquired an exceptionally

one-sided diet. No matter how quickly and radically the dietary conditions may have become altered, they were certainly not accompanied by corresponding changes in man's masticatory apparatus. Even though many minute distinctions between the dentitions and jaws of early and recent men have been described, there is not one detail which can be proved to be connected with a change in diet. The same human dentition is just as useful for the rice diet of a Malay as for the meat diet of an Eskimo and did not change essentially between whatever raw diet australopithecines had and the cooked diet of modern Europeans. While the diverse preference for and quest of food can influence social life extensively, it seems to have had remarkably little effect on our dental and digestive apparatus.

The *variability* of a species can influence its social behavior to a significant extent. All anthropoid apes and many species of lower primates are surprisingly variable, indeed in many respects more variable than recent man. In general body size, cranial capacity, body proportions, and coloration of skin and hair all apes possess enormous ranges of variations even among individuals from very limited regions (Schultz, 1947). In a large series of spider-monkey skulls from one region, which will soon be published (Schultz, 1959), I found many with remarkably high and bulging foreheads and others, collected from the same camp, with frontal profiles running straight back from the supraorbital ridge. If some of these striking variations had come from widely separated localities, one would have been tempted to regard them as different species. A few decades ago some taxonomists described incredible numbers of subspecies, species, and even genera of orangutans, chimpanzees, and gorillas whenever they had obtained a few skulls from new localities. After having seen a great many large local series of ape skulls, I have become fully convinced that extremely few of all these names for races or species have any justification, and, fortunately, most of them are no longer in use (Figs. 16 and 17).

The classification of fossil men has been even worse than that of the recent apes, but we have come to realize that much of the old nomenclature was not only quite unnecessary but was actually misleading in that it elevated mere individual variations to the rank of racial if not specific characters (Howell, 1957). It seems most likely that hominids were just as variable as are all pongids. There is no need for theories of race mixture or of waves of new immigrants whenever we find an extremely modest random sample of a local population of early man to contain some variations more marked than expected by investigators unfamiliar with the great variability in many nonhuman primates. In view of this variability of all higher primates, the common practice of diagnosing the sex of fossil fragments by size can be quite erroneous. Among adult chimpanzees, for example, one frequently finds some males smaller than some females, and every large series of wild pongids contains in either sex some evident runts as well as exceptional giants. The *average* sex difference in size can be extremely different among primates, and in some species females surpass males even in average body weight, a fact that may quite likely influence their sexual behavior.

As everybody who has worked with living monkeys and apes readily admits, these animals vary in temperament and intellect as widely as they do in size and form. There is no reason, of course, for assuming that early man was exceptional in this respect. Among the five chimpanzees I had kept for many years there was one small female who was far superior to the others in mental alertness, enterprise, and inventiveness, even during her advanced years. In the same way, we can be certain, every group of early man contained occasional individuals surpassing the others in mental faculties and able to create some cultural progress. The latter was desperately needed

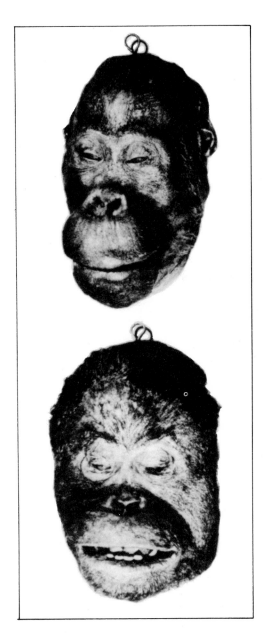

Figure 16: Death masks of two adult female Bornean orangutans showing variations in head formation (*after Schultz,* 1950b).

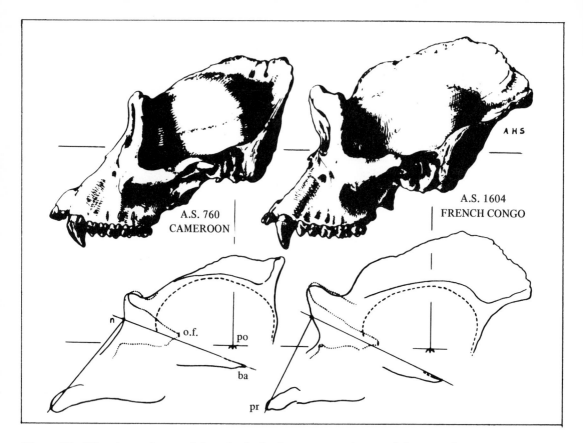

Figure 17: Side views of two adult male lowland gorillas and sections of the same showing frequent variations (*after Schultz*, 1950a).

at the critical time when the first true hominids had for one reason or another abandoned the accustomed protection of the dense forest with but modest size, strength, and speed and without even the large canines of other catarrhines. All they could rely upon at first was the emancipation of their hands, freed for the use of tools, and the old simian endowment of timely discovery of danger by the many quick eyes of closely co-operating social groups, as well as the intensifying trend to prolong the years of dependency of the young on the old, with its corresponding gains from long-continued guidance and imitative learning.

BIBLIOGRAPHY

ABERLE, S. B. D. 1931. "Frequency of Pregnancies and Birth Interval among Pueblo Indians," *Amer. J. Phys. Anthrop.*, 16:63–80.

CAMERON, T. W. M. 1958. "Parasites of Animals and Human Disease," *Ann. New York Acad. Sci.*, 70: 564–73.

CARPENTER, C. R. 1934. *A Field Study of the Behavior and Social Relations of Howling Monkeys.* ("Comp. Psychol. Monogr.," Vol. 10, No. 2.)

—— 1935. "Behavior of Red Spider Monkeys in Panama," *J. Mammal.*, 16:171–80.

—— 1942. "Societies of Monkeys and Apes," *Biol. Symp.*, 8:177–204.

CLARK, H. C. 1952. "Endemic Yellow Fever in Panama

and Neighboring Areas," *Amer. J. Trop. Med. & Hyg.*, 1:78–86.

COLLIAS, N., and C. SOUTHWICK 1952. "A Field Study of Population Density and Social Organization in Howling Monkeys," *Proc. Amer. Phil. Soc.*, 96: 143–56.

COUNT, E. W. 1958. "The Biological Basis of Human Sociality," *Amer. Anthrop.*, 60:1049–85.

DORSEY, G. A. 1925. *Why We Behave like Human Beings.* New York: Harper & Bros.

GÁSPÁRDY, G., and J. NEMESKÉRI 1960. "Paleopathological Studies on Copper Age Skeletons Found at Alsónémedi," *Acta Morphol. Acad. Sc. Hungaricae*, 9:203–19.

GUSINDE, M. 1948. *Urwaldmenschen am Ituri.* Wien: Springer-Verlag.

HARTMAN, C. G. 1932. *Studies in the Reproduction of the Monkey Macacus (Pithecus) rhesus.* (Carnegie Inst. Wash. Publ. 433, "Contrib. to Embryol.," Vol. 23.)

HEBERER, G. 1958. "Das Tier-Mensch-Uebergangsfeld," *Studium Generale*, 11:341–52.

HORNADAY, W. T. 1922. *The Minds and Manners of Wild Animals.* New York: Scribner's.

HOWELL, F. C. 1957. "II. The Evolutionary Significance of Variation and Varieties of 'Neanderthal' Man," *Quart. Rev. Biol.*, 32:330–47.

HUBER, E. 1931. *The Evolution of Facial Musculature and Facial Expression.* Baltimore: Johns Hopkins Press.

KLÜVER, H. 1937. "Re-examination of Implement-using Behavior in a Cebus Monkey after an Interval of Three Years," *Acta Psychol.*, Vol. 2, No. 3.

KOHL-LARSEN, L. 1958. *Wildbeuter in Ostafrika: Die Tindiga, ein Jäger- und Sammlervolk.* Berlin: D. Reimer Verlag.

KORTLANDT, A. 1959. *Tussen mens en dier.* Groningen: Universiteit van Amsterdam.

KRIEG, H. 1948. *Zwischen Anden und Atlantik.* Munich: C. Hauser Verlag.

KRUMBIEGEL, I. 1955. *Biologie der Säugettiere.* 2 Vols. Krefeld: Agis Verlag.

MILLER, G. S., JR. 1931. "The Primate Basis of Human Sexual Behavior," *Quart. Rev. Biol.*, 6:379–410.

MOUNTFORD, C. P. 1951. *Braune Menschen, Roter Sand.* Zurich: Orell Füssli Verlag.

PEARL, R. 1930. "Some Aspects of the Biology of Human Populations." In E. V. Cowdry (ed.), *Human Biology and Racial Welfare*, pp. 515–52. New York: P. Hoeber.

POWDERMAKER, H. 1931. "Vital Statistics of New Ireland as Revealed in Genealogies," *Human Biol.*, 3:351–75.

PROCESSUS DE L'HOMINISATION, LES. 1958. Colloques Internat. Centre National de la Recherche Scientifique, Paris.

RASMUSSEN, K. 1927. *Across Arctic America.* New York: Putnam.

RENSCH, B. 1959. *Homo sapiens: Vom Tier zum Halbgott.* Göttingen Vandenhoeck & Ruprecht.

ROE, A., and G. G. SIMPSON 1958. *Behavior and Evolution.* New Haven: Yale University Press.

RUCH, T. C. 1959. *Diseases of Laboratory Primates.* Philadelphia: Saunders Co.

RUSSELL, J. C. 1958. "Late Ancient and Medieval Population," *Trans.-Amer. Philos. Soc.*, n.s., Vol. 48, Part 3.

SANDERSON, I. T., and G. STEINBACHER 1957. *Knaurs Affenbuch.* Munich: Droemersche Verlagsanstalt.

SCHULTZ, A. H. 1941. *Growth and Development of the Orang-utan.* (Carnegie Inst. Wash. Publ. 525, "Contrib. to Embryol.," 29:57–110.)

—— 1944. "Age Changes in Variability in Gibbons," *Amer. J. Phys. Anthrop.*, n.s., 2:1–129.

—— 1947. "Variability in Man and Other Primates," *Amer. J. Phys. Anthrop.*, n.s., 5:1–14.

—— 1950a. "Morphological Observations on Gorillas." In *The Anatomy of the Gorilla.* (Henry Cushier Raven Mem.) New York: Columbia University Press, 227–54.

—— 1950b. "The Specializations of Man and His Place among the Catarrhine Primates," *Cold Spring Harbor Symp. Quant. Biol.*, 15:37–53.

—— 1950c. "The Physical Distinctions of Man," *Proc. Amer. Phil. Soc.*, 94:428–49.

—— 1956a. "Postembryonic Age Changes." In H. Hofer, A. H. Schultz, and D. Starck (eds.), *Primatologia*, 1:887–964. Basel: Verlag Karger.

—— 1956b. "The Occurrence and Frequency of Pathological and Teratological Conditions and of Twinning among Nonhuman Primates." In H. Hofer, A. H. Schultz, and D. Starck (eds.), *Primatologia*, 1:965–1014. Basel: Verlag Karger.

—— 1957. "Past and Present Views of Man's Specialization," *Irish J. Med. Sci.*, August, 1957, pp. 341–56.

—— 1958. "Acrocephalo-oligodactylism in a Wild Chimpanzee," *J. Anat.*, 92:568–79.

—— 1960. "Age Changes and Variability in the Skulls and Teeth of Central American Monkeys,

Cebus and *Ateles*," *Proc. Zool. Soc. London,* 133: 337–90.

——— 1960. "Einige Beobachtungen und Masse am Skelett von Oreopithecus im Vergleich mit anderen catarrhinen Primaten," *Zs. f. Morphol. u. Anthropol.,* 50:136–49.

———, and F. F. SNYDER 1935. "Observations on Reproduction in the Chimpanzee," *Bull. Johns Hopkins Hosp.,* 57:193–205.

SMITH, G. E., and F. W. JONES 1910. *Report on the Human Remains.* ("Archaeological Survey of Nubia: Report for 1907–1908," Vol. II.) Cairo.

SPENCER, R. F. 1959. *The North Alaskan Eskimo: A Study in Ecology and Society.* (Bur. Amer. Ethnol. Bull. 171.) Washington.

SPUHLER, J. N. 1959. *The Evolution of Man's Capacity for Culture: Six Essays.* Detroit: Wayne State University Press.

STEVENSON, HAMILTON J. 1912. *Animal Life in Africa.* New York: Dutton.

STEWART, T. D. 1959. "Restoration and Study of the Shanidar I Neanderthal Skeleton in Baghdad, Iraq." In *Yearbook 1958,* Amer. Philos. Soc., pp. 274–78.

STILES, C. W., A. HASSALL, and M. O. NOLAN 1929. *Key-Catalogue of Parasites Reported for Primates.* . . . (Hygienic Laboratory Bull. 152, U.S. Treas. Dept. Publ. Health Service.) Washington.

THOMPSON, W. S. 1953. *Population Problems.* 4th ed. New York: McGraw-Hill.

VOGEL, A. A. 1954. *Papuas und Pygmäen.* Zurich: Orell Füssli Verlag.

WENDT, H. 1954. *Ich suchte Adam.* Hamm (Westf.): Grote'sche Verlagsbuchhdl.

WISSLER, C. 1942. "Human Cultural Levels." In E. V. Cowdry (ed.), *Problems of Ageing,* pp. 77–90. Baltimore: Williams & Wilkins.

YERKES, R. M. 1943. *Chimpanzees: A Laboratory Colony.* New Haven: Yale University Press.

ZAPFE, H. 1954. "Beiträge zur Erklärung der Entstehung von Knochenlagerstätten in Karstspalten und Höhlen," *Geologie* (Berlin), No. 12, pp. 1–60.

20 • SOCIAL BEHAVIOR IN JAPANESE MONKEYS "MACACA FUSCATA"

Kinji Imanishi

The Japanese have initiated some highly original ethological studies on monkey populations native to Japan, and have continued to produce a series of important studies in this field. Among the earliest and most significant of these is Kinji Imanishi's study of *Macaca fuscata.*

Among the many valuable contributions made by this study perhaps the most important was its methodology, which has since served as a model for other similar investigations.

The author's account of Itani's recognition of more than 30 kinds of vocalizations and their classification into six distinct types indicates the urgent need for closer study of nonhuman primate vocalizations.[1] It has been customary in the past to dismiss these sounds with such terms as "mood convection," and the like, but clearly they resemble the elements of language much more than anything else.[2] Nevertheless there are considerable differences. The units of animal communication are more like messages of social significance, largely reflecting the physiological state of the animal which sends them out. Clearly,

---

[1] See Stuart A. Altmann, ed., *Social Communication Among Primates* (Chicago: University of Chicago Press, 1967).

[2] Thomas A. Sebeok, ed., *Animal Communication* (Bloomington: Indiana University Press, 1968). Eric H. Lenneberg, *Biological Foundations of Language* (New York: John Wiley, 1967).

also, the syntactic rules of animal language are not amenable to the kinds of rearrangements that characterize human language. And when variations do occur they do not in themselves seem to carry much if any information. It is an inexhaustibly interesting subject.

If the intelligibility of speech is nothing but the unintelligibility of behavior made artificially clear, it will be through studies in the communicative behavior of nonhuman primates that we are most likely to understand how this intelligibility may have evolved.

A correction needs to be made of Imanishi's statement that the habit of washing sweet potatoes before eating them was started by a young three-year-old female. Her age was actually half that—one and a half years! [3]

Imanishi's article was one of the first to throw a clear light on the connection between mother-child interactions and the development of later status relationships. It was also one of the first to draw attention to the manner in which new cultural traits may be acquired in a natural nonhuman primate population.

Among many species of monkeys and apes, there are only six whose social behavior has hitherto been accurately investigated in field studies. Reports on chimpanzees (24) by Nissen and on baboons (27) by Zuckerman are now rather classical. It may be rightly said that primate sociology was advanced markedly by the work of Carpenter. He reported on the behavior and social relations of howlers (2), spider monkeys (3) and gibbons (4). All of these investigations were carried out in [the] natural habitat of the animals. Afterwards Carpenter reported on the sexual behavior of rhesus monkeys (5) which were released in Santiago Island, Puerto Rico, for the purpose of allowing them to establish experimental colonies.

Chance recently reported also on the social structure of a colony of rhesus monkeys (6) on the Monkey Hill at the "Zoological Gardens," Regents Park, London. Collias and Southwick reported on that of howlers (7). So this report will add to already accumulated data those of the seventh species, the Japanese monkey, *Macaca fuscata*.

Japanese monkeys are endemic to Japan. Shimokita Peninsula at the north end of Honshû is the northern limit of their distribution as well as that of all the monkeys and apes in the world. Yakushima, an island south of Kagoshima, is the southern limit. No other wild species of monkeys lives in Japan.

They are found usually in the thick forest of the mountains, where they gather in aggregations and live a social life. Animal sociology has not yet prepared a system of terminology denoting the difference of levels of animal aggregations. Imanishi (8) proposed two terms, "specia" and "oikia," for this purpose. Specia denotes the aggregation of all individuals belonging to the same species which occupies a definite area on the globe. Every species of plants and animals has its own specia. For instance, the specia of Japanese monkeys is confined to Japan excluding Hokkaido. The basic unit of specia, the individual, is called "specion."

In the course of evolution, specia was organized into many part aggregations in the higher vertebrates. This part aggregation is oikia. It is not a chance aggregation, but the aggregation of

SOURCE: *Psychologia: An International Journal of Psychology in the Orient* vol. 1, no. 1 (June 1957): 47–54. Reprinted by permission of the publisher.
[3] Syunzo Kawamura, "The Process of Sub-Culture Propagation Among Japanese Macaques," *Journal of Primatology*, II (1959), 43–60; excerpted and reprinted, as is Imanishi's article, in Charles H. Southwick, ed., *Primate Social Behavior* (Princeton, New Jersey: Van Nostrand, 1963), pp. 82–90.

particular individuals. It is a sociological unit as fundamental and perpetuating as specia is, though the life of each oikia may be shorter than that of specia. Varieties of descriptive terms such as "band," "troop," "group" and even "family" which appeared in the studies of the social life of monkeys and apes, all fall into the same level of aggregation as oikia. The aggregation of Japanese monkeys which forms a concrete unit of their social life is another example of an oikia. The particular individual which is the component of oikia is called "oikion." Then, every individual monkey has double roles. He should be a specion on the one hand and an oikion on the other hand.

In the former days when the population of Japanese monkeys was much greater, oikiae would be also abundant in number and connected with each other through territories or some kind of communication. But as their population gradually decreased under the pressure of exploitation, cultivation and other human interferences, now every remaining oikia is more or less isolated on their last stronghold in the mountains. Only a few places are known where more than two oikiae are closely situated.

It happened in the summer of 1952 that the oikia of Kôshima, an isle on the east coast of Kyûshû, accommodated itself to take provided sweet-potatoes in the presence of man. This phenomenon may be a step towards the domestication, but by no means completes the process. Because provisioning put no restraint upon monkeys, they were free and wild as before, but they were accustomed to appear at the provisioning place and take the provisions. A word "provisionization" will be proposed to denote this incipient stage of domestication. In the winter of 1952–1953 the oikia of Takasakiyama, which had been intensively investigated by J. Itani since 1950 was also "provisionized."

As Takasakiyama was situated in the vicinity of Beppu, the famous recreation center with many hotsprings, provisionized monkeys at once began to attract visitors. To provisionize wild monkeys has three merits. 1) It furnishes a new scientific, educational and recreational resource to the public. 2) It saves farmers of near villages from the crop damage due to the plunder by monkeys. And, finally, 3) It means a profitable business, if the income from entrance-fees will be sufficient. The success of provisionization at Takasakiyama stimulated other localities where wild monkeys were found near at hand. From 1953 onwards at least thirteen oikiae were already provisionized by the same method.

It was pertinent to the occasion that the Japan Monkey Center was established in the autumn of 1956 at Inuyama, near Nagoya. In addition to promoting various investigations about monkeys, it aims also to guide provisionization and to keep the well-being of provisionized oikiae. If an oikia suffers from over-population as an effect of provisionization, it will be ready to remove surplus monkeys and supply them for medical uses.

Because investigations hitherto done on the social life of monkeys and apes were restricted to one or two oikiae as their objects, there is scarcely any comparative study of oikiae belonging to the same specia. But so many oikiae of Japanese monkeys have been provisionized that investigators are now able to compare these oikiae with one another. It is enough to mention here that each oikia is different not only in the population, in the socionomic sex ratio, but also in various aspects of social behavior of its oikions. If every oikion is nothing else but a specion, these behavioral differences which seem to be differences of characteristics of each oikia might not occur. Then how does every oikion acquire these characteristics of an oikia to which it belongs? Here are problems concerning culture and personality, the existence of which in monkeys and apes was already suggested by Imanishi (9).

In the Forest

Before provisionization it was all the investigator could do to trace the swift movement of nomadic oikia in the dense forest covering the steep mountain sides. In this situation discrimination of individual oikions was not yet possible except for the sex and age difference among them. But problems such as patterns of nomadism, vocal communication in the oikia, behavior against the common enemy, etc., were cleared up after extended observation.

Itani and Tokuda (18) reported on the nomadic life in the oikia of Takasakiyama. This oikia has several centers where it rests at night. These centers are usually chosen on ridges commanding a comparatively wide view. Places where it frequents for eating change according as items of available food change from season to season, though a pattern of nomadism is regularly seen so long as the quantity of a certain kind of food is enough to support the total population of the oikia.

Itani (14) reported on items of vegetable food such as buds, shoots, leaves, fruits, barks, etc., which were taken by oikions of Takasakiyama. It covers 119 species of plants. Animal food, for example, spiders, beetles, butterflies, ants, etc., are also eaten. Eggs are eaten by those of Minoo, near Ôsaka. Food preference peculiar to some oikia are not rare. Kawamura (20) suggests that each oikia develops its own food culture.

The area in which an oikia lives a nomadic life may be called its "territory." The extent of territory varies from about 1 square kilo-meter to 8 square kilo-meters according to the size of the population of the oikia and the quantity of available food. Territories of adjacent oikiae sometimes overlap, as in the case of two oikiae of Minoo. But conflict is seldom observed because a dominance-subordination relationship is already fixed between them and the subordinate keeps away from the dominant. It is said that when two adjacent oikiae come close, leaders of each oikia shake trees and utter threatening cries. This seems to be a demonstration to avoid serious conflict. Kawamura and Tokuda (23) did not find any conflict among oikiae which they observed in Takagoyama, near Tokyo.

Vocalization plays an important role in the nomadic life of oikia because there remains only vocal communication in order to bring together individual oikions which in the thick forest scatter in the extent from 100 to 200 square meters. Itani (11) (12) recorded more than 30 kinds of vocalization in the oikia of Takasakiyama, and classified them into six types as follows:

1. calls to one another in calm mood,
2. defensive cries,
3. aggressive cries,
4. warning calls,
5. voices peculiar to babies and infants,
6. voices peculiar to estrous females.

In these six types the important vocalization which is used for ordinary communication in the forest is the first type.

Recently Itani (15) classified between calls and cries more definitely. Cries which are always accompanied by highly emotional expression and directed to a particular individual are useful for short distance communication, while calls which are accompanied by less emotional expression and directed to no particular individual are useful for long distance communication. Two-thirds of more than 30 kinds of vocalization are calls which are utilized as various signals and orders in the nomadic life of oikia. He says calls which are so conspicuous in the vocalization of Japanese monkeys are rather remotely connected with human language because the latter is utilized only for short distance communication as cries are.

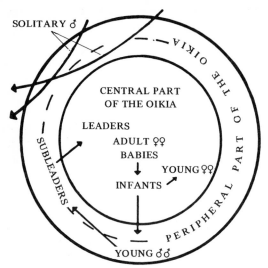

Figure 1: Schematic representation of distribution of oikions in an oikia at the feeding place.

Warning calls "kwan" are usually uttered by one of the males that happen to be there and discover an approaching enemy. These calls have an effect to silence the other oikions and retire them to a safer place. Itani (13) reports that when calls are uttered by a young male, his place is sooner or later taken by a more competent adult male.

Oikia in its nomadic life forms a line when it moves from one place to another. At the head of the procession goes a party of young males. In the middle goes a cluster composed of females, infants, babies and one or several dominant males. The rear part is occupied again by young males. Itani (13) counted the population of oikia of Takasakiyama by observing such a procession from some corners.

After Provisionization

As a result of successful provisionization, an oikia comes out of the forest into the open feeding place where unobstructed observation becomes possible for the first time. At the same time it becomes at last possible for the investigator to discriminate every individual oikion of the oikia. As Itani (13) and Kawamura (21) reported oikiae form in concentric circles at the feeding place. The middle part of the procession is now the central part which occupied the feeding place proper. It is composed of dominant males together with females, infants and babies. The peripheral part which surrounds the central part is composed of younger males. They can enter the feeding place proper only before the central part comes there in the morning or after it has gone away from there in the evening.

Kawamura and Kawai (22) reported that there was once an independent group of six young males in Minoo, a rare case in Japanese monkeys, although Carpenter (3) found a male subgroup in spider monkeys. Judging from the fact that this group is now following one of two oikiae there, it might be the detached form of the peripheral part here mentioned.

Outside of the peripheral part there appear frequently big, solitary males. They enter the feeding place after the oikia has left, otherwise they will be driven off by young males of the peripheral part. The aim of their approach seems to be females and/or provisions. They are either oikions of the oikia or those of different oikiae. Why and how they prefer the solitary life is not certain but it will be not easy for them to be accepted by their approaching oikia. One adult male which was released experimentally at Kô-shima in 1952 even now lives a solitary life in this lonely islet.

In the oikia of Takasakiyama there are six dominant males in the central part. They are bigger and older than any other males of the peripheral part. They are leaders of the oikia and make up a class by themselves. In the peripheral part there are also ten dominant males, a little smaller and younger than the leaders, which make up a class next to the leader class. They may be called subleaders. When leaders go up to the mountain while females, infants and babies still stay at the feeding place, these subleaders enter into the central part and take leader's roles. The number of leaders and subleaders seems to be in proportion to the population of the oikia. But, notwithstanding the increase in population of oikia of Takasakiyama from about 250 in 1953 to about 440 in 1956, the number of leaders and subleaders remains at six and ten respectively. That is contrary to common expectations.

Leaders of the oikia never quarrel in the feeding place but always cooperate with each other to control followers. They look after females and infants, mediate quarrels among them, and guard against the entry of young males into the central part of the oikia. Leaders never quarrel because of the dominance-subordination relationship which is settled among them.

Itani (13) tried a simple test to detect this relation between two individuals. When food, a mandarin orange for instance, is thrown between two individuals, the dominant one behaves as if the food is properly his own, and takes it, while the subordinate averts his eyes from the food and does not try to get it. The test revealed a linear order of dominance rank among six leaders as well as among ten subleaders. But among females and young males it is less definite. Using the similar test, Tokuda (26) clarified the dominance-subordination relationship among eighteen oikions of the oikia of Kôshima.

It is often observed in the feeding place that the dominant male mounts the subordinate one. This means the confirmation of dominance rank between them as Chance (6) remarks about rhesus monkeys. Itani (13) reported that sometimes the dominant one allows the subordinate to mount him in order to let the subordinate groom

him. The change of dominance rank, if it occurs, is also recognized through a corresponding change in these behaviors.

Acculturation

Provisionization is initiated by offering food to which wild monkeys are accustomed. But monkeys gradually come to accept new foods. Oikions of Takasakiyama did not take the peanut at the beginning of provisionization, because they did not know it due to the lack of its cultivation near Takasakiyama. They took it, however, after four months during which it was left everyday at the feeding place.

A new habit is acquired by one oikion through trial and error, and then imitated by other oikions. The habit of eating candies, whose sweetness delighted monkeys once they tried them, is still spreading among oikions of Takasakiyama. Itani (16) tested every oikion six times since July 1954 to determine whether it would eat candies. His conclusion is that adults are very slow in acquiring this new eating habit as compared to infants and babies who acquire the habit rather quickly and easily from their peers. It is also observed that the mother learns to eat candies from her own baby, instead of that the baby learns it from the mother. Regardless of the direction of transmission, a habit is transmitted only through a close relationship between two particular oikions.

The following instance may not be properly called acculturation but be worth while mentioning here. Kawamura (19) reported that there is spreading among oikions of Kôshima a habit to wash sweet-potatoes with water before eating them. This habit was started in 1953 by a young female of three years old. It was then transmitted to her playmates as well as to her mother and during three years it was acquired by eleven oikions including its inventor. To follow its trace consecutively will be desirable for the debated problem of subhuman culture.

Conservation of Oikia

The sexual behavior of Japanese monkeys is another side of their social life that becomes clear after provisionization, The rutting season begins, in most oikiae, at the end of December and lasts till the end of March, though some females are estrous earlier or later than this period. During the period not only the color of faces and sexual skins of both sexes turns bright scarlet, but the sexual skin of young estrous females swells markedly.

Each of the dominant males in the central part follows an estrous female for two or three days and comes into a consort relationship with her. In some oikia the consort relationship is initiated by the male attacking the female, in other oikia this pattern is not found. In the oikia of Takasakiyama where there are so many adult females that many of them are simultaneously in estrus, it is observed that some estrous females escape from the central part and make a secret consort relationship with one of the males of the peripheral part.

The length of pregnancy is about five months and births have been found to occur from the middle of May to the middle of August. Babies become capable of walking in a week or so after their birth, and begin to take solid food in forty days. The close mother-baby relationship which begins with birth lasts for at least ten months. During this period babies seem to learn from their mothers food habits and other fundamental attitudes peculiar to the social life of the oikia.

Itani (13) reported that when the next birth season comes near, most leaders and subleaders of the oikia of Takasakiyama voluntarily take over from the mothers the care of babies. This interesting behavior has not been observed in any oikia except that of Takasakiyama and in no subhuman society except that of Japanese monkeys.

There are two kinds of relationship among oikions. The one is the relationship formed between two oikions heterogeneous with regard to age and sex. The consort relationship between the adult male and the adult female, and the mother-baby or leader-baby relationship here mentioned are examples of heterogeneous relationships. The other is the relationship formed between two oikions homogeneous with regard to age and sex. The first appearance of this homogeneous relationship in the life-history of individual oikion is noticed after eight months from the birth, when babies seek babies and come together to play with each other.

Babies after twelve months old are called infants. They prefer more and more similar sexed playmates to opposite sexed ones, although no preference seems to exist during babyhood. In Takasakiyama, Itani (13) observed that male infants under two years old are still in the central part with their mothers, but they often go out to the peripheral part to associate with young males, and at least leave the central part in order that they themselves become young males.

Female infants, on the contrary, never go out from the central part. They become young females there, mature sexually at three years and a half, and conceive from four years and a half. Males mature sexually at five years.

In due course of time young males of the peripheral part will be raised to the status of subleaders and at last of leaders, then they will return to the central part where they were born. In a large oikia such as that of Takasakiyama, however, there are so many young males that the full careers of only a small part of them can be followed. The life-histories of every oikion which was born after provisionization has been recorded for the last five years. This procedure will ultimately reveal which young males in each oikia become the leaders of the next generation.

Unlike other studies, attention was given to dominance-subordination relationships among females as well as among males. It was observed that in Takasakiyama dominant females are situated near the center of the central part, while subordinate ones [are found] near the margin of the central part. Tokuda (26), reported on a mixed colony of rhesus monkeys and crab-eating monkeys in the Kyoto Zoo, observed that children of the female of higher status show a tendency to be dominant over others. Asakura (1) reported the same phenomenon in a colony of Japanese monkeys in the Ueno Zoo, Tokyo.

Recent field reports mention instances of a young male in the central part of an oikia which is tolerated by leaders and females, or is already appointed to the higher status worthy of staying there. It is probable that he is the son of some dominant female of the oikia. As dominant females are usually on intimate terms with leaders, their babies are the ones most likely to be taken care of by leaders. At any rate it is necessary for males to be accepted by females, especially by dominant females, in order to enter into the central part from outside.

Itani (17) reported that in Takasakiyama since 1955 young males have been leaving the oikia in increasing numbers. He considered the phenomenon as socially pathological if it is caused by the fact that their path to higher status is blocked. However, it may be only a natural remedy for the hypertrophied oikia, containing over 400 oikions, to discharge some excessive oikions in so far as it does not divide itself into two oikiae.

Imanishi (10) considered in introducing the concept of "identification" from psychoanalysis that males which have mothers of higher status are able to identify successfully not only with their mothers but also with their leaders, while those which have mothers of lower status are not able to identify successfully with their leaders in their childhood. If other things are equal, males growing up with successful identification will cooperate with leaders more willingly, be accepted by them as well as by females more easily and finally succeed their leaders, while those with unsuccessful identification will not go on smoothly with the tradition or the culture of the oikia and leave the oikia more unhesitatingly. If the population of the oikia increases under the fixed number of leaders as in the case of the oikia of Takasakiyama, those males with unsuccessful identification will increase and those which desert the oikia will also increase. Thus the oikia itself is conserved.

REFERENCES

1.* ASAKURA, S. Parent-child relationship in a monkey colony. *Iden*, 1957, 11, No. 3, 35–39.
2. CARPENTER, C. R. A field study of the behavior and social relations of the howling monkeys (*Alouatta palliata*). *Comp. Psychol. Monog.*, 1934, 10, No. 2, 1–168.
3. CARPENTER, C. R. Behavior of the red spider monkey (*Ateles geoffroyi*) in Panama. *J. Mammal.*, 1935, 16, 171–180.
4. CARPENTER, C. R. A field study in Siam of the behavior and social relations of the gibbon (*Hylobates lar*). *Comp. Psychol. Monog.*, 1940, 16, No. 5, 1–212.
5. CARPENTER, C. R. Sexual behavior of free ranging rhesus monkeys (*Macaca mulatta*). *J. Comp. Psychol.*, 1942, 33, No. 1, 113–162.
6. CHANCE, M. R. A. Social structure of a colony of *Macaca mulatta*. *Brit. Journ. Animal Behavior*, 1956, 4, No. 1, 1–13.
7. COLLIAS, N., & SOUTHWICK, C. A field study of population density and social organizations in howler monkeys. *Proc. Amer. Phil. Soc.*, 1952, 96, 143.
8.* IMANISHI, K. Social life of semi-wild horses. In *Seibutsu no shûdan to kankyô*, Minka-kagaku-bunkensho, 23. Tokyo: Iwanami, 1950. Pp. 1–9.
9.* IMANISHI, K. Evolution of human characteristics. In K. Imanishi (Ed.), *Ningen* (Mainichi Library). Tokyo: Mainichi Press, 1952. Pp. 36–94.
10.* IMANISHI, K. Problems in the study of Japanese monkeys in print.

11.* ITANI, J. Communication of the wild Japanese monkeys. *Shizen,* 1951, 6, No. 10, 45–49.

12.* ITANI, J. The vocal communication and the social life of the Japanese monkeys. *Gengo-seikatsu,* 1954, No. 44, 44–50.

13. ITANI, J. Japanese monkeys in Takasakiyama. In K. Imanishi (Ed.), *Nihon-dôbutsuki,* Vol. 2. Tokyo: Kôbunsha, 1954. 284 p.

14.* ITANI, J. *Food habits of the wild Japanese monkeys.* I. vegetable food. Publication of Primates Research Group, 1956. 14 p.

15.* ITANI, J. Prehuman language. *Shizen,* 1956, 11, No. 11, 22–27.

16.* ITANI, J. Personality of Japanese monkeys. *Iden,* 1957, 11, No. 1, 29–33.

17.* ITANI, J. The present state of monkeys in Takasakiyama. *Kagaku-yomiuri,* 1957, 9, No. 1, 65–67.

18. * * ITANI, J., & TOKUDA, K. The nomadic life of the wild Japanese monkeys (*Macaca fuscata fuscata*) in Takasakiyama. *Jap. J. Ecol.,* 1954, 4, No. 1, 22–28.

19.* KAWAMURA, S. On a new type of learning habit which developed in a group of wild Japanese monkeys. *Seibutsushinka,* 1954, 2, No. 1, 1–4.

20.* KAWAMURA, S. Prehuman culture. *Shizen,* 1956, 11, No. 11, 28–34.

21. * * KAWAMURA, S. The spatial distribution test of individuals in a natural group of the Japanese Macaque. *Ann. Animal Psychol. (Japan),* 1956, 6, 1–10.

22.* * KAWAMURA, S., & KAWAI, M. Social organization of the natural group of Japanese Macaque. The case of the Minoo-B group. *Jap. J. Ecol.,* 1956, 6, No. 2, 45–50.

23.* * KAWAMURA, S., & TOKUDA, K. Inter-group relationship of the wild Japanese monkeys in Takagoyama, Chiba Prefecture. *Bull. Cultural Assets Chiba Prefecture,* 1955, 1, 8–21.

24. NISSEN, H. W. A field study of the chimpanzee. *Comp. Psychol. Monog.,* 1931, 8, No. 1, 1–122.

25.* TOKUDA, K. Dominance-subordination relationship in the wild Japanese monkeys. *Seibutsu-kagaku,* 1955, 7, 48–53.

26. * TOKUDA, K. Monkeys in the Kyoto Zoo. In K. Imanishi (Ed.), *Nihon-dôbutsuki,* Vol. 4. Tokyo: Kôbunsha, 1957, 163–268.

27. ZUCKERMAN, S. *The social life of monkeys and Apes.* London: Kegan Paul, 1932. Pp. 357.

* Articles written in Japanese.
* * Articles written in Japanese with English summary.

21 • THE SOCIAL DEVELOPMENT OF MONKEYS AND APES

William A. Mason

In this contribution Mason provides a generalized description of the normal socialization process in monkeys and apes, and also shows how early experience may influence their subsequent social growth.[1] His survey makes it clear that, whatever role innate factors may play in the development of primate social behavior, experience is the critically important factor in its normal development. Of course, experience must have social contact to work with, for in the absence of adequate experience socialization either fails to develop altogether or it develops abnormally or inadequately.[2]

---

[1] See also his paper, "Early Social Deprivation in the Nonhuman Primates: Implications for Human Behavior," in David C. Glass, ed., *Biology and Behavior: Environmental Influences.* (New York: Rockefeller University Press, 1968), pp. 70–101.

[2] For further discussions relevant to this subject see Grant Newton and Seymour Levine, *Early Experience and Behavior* (Springfield, Illinois: C. C. Thomas, 1968); Esther Tobach, Lester R. Aronson and Evelyn Shaw, eds., *The Biopsychology of De-*

As a model for possible heuristic observation in the interpretation of human behavior, Mason's account of the sexual inadequacies of the socially deprived male monkey is typical of many observations on nonhuman primates. Indeed, there is a fair amount of evidence now available which strongly indicates that precisely similar mechanisms are operative in human males.[3] The sexual inadequacies of a large number of human males suggests that a great deal more social deprivation is suffered by children in civilized homes than is commonly recognized.[4]

A complex sexual drive is undoubtedly innate, but its normal healthy expression must, apparently, be learned—in man as well as monkey.

Introduction

Until recently information on the social development of nonhuman primates was based on observation of a few individuals, chiefly macaques and chimpanzees, maintained in captivity. The present chapter could not have been written a decade ago—Nissen's excellent review of primate social behavior in 1951 devoted less than three pages to social development—and at the present rate at which new data are appearing, from both naturalistic and experimental investigations, what is written now will probably be out of date within a few years.

There are many sources of interest in the so-cial development of monkeys and apes. It has always been apparent that much is learned during human infancy and childhood that influences adult behavior. The importance of early social experience in the formation of adult personality characteristics was dramatically emphasized by Freud and his followers, and recent years have seen the development of intensive clinical explorations of the impact of adverse conditions during childhood on later psychological development. Studies of the socialization process in nonhuman primates may occasionally aid directly in clarifying problems of human adjustment. The major contribution of these studies, however, will most probably be indirect, by helping to describe trends that have been involved in primate evolution.

One such trend, suggested by studies of physical growth, has important implications for the problem of social development (Schultz 1956: 890): "In regard to all parts of postnatal life one can recognize a clear trend toward prolongation, beginning in monkeys, as compared with lemurs, more pronounced in gibbons, still more in all three great apes and by far the most marked in man." It follows from this that the period of postnatal dependency should change in similar fashion, thereby increasing the opportunity (and probably the necessity) for more intense, elaborate, and enduring social relationships than are found in most mammalian groups. For reasons

SOURCE: William A. Mason, "The Social Development of Monkeys and Apes," 514–43, in *Primate Behavior: Field Studies of Monkeys and Apes,* Irven DeVore, ed. Copyright © 1965 by Holt, Rinehart and Winston, Inc. Reprinted by permission of Holt, Rinehart and Winston, Inc.

velopment* (New York: Academic Press, 1971); Anthony Ambrose, *Stimulation in Early Infancy* (New York: Academic Press, 1969); R. J. Robinson, ed., *Brain and Early Behaviour* (New York: Academic Press, 1969); M. B. Sterman, Dennis J. McGinty, and Anthony M. Adinolfi, eds., *Brain Development and Behavior* (New York: Academic

Press, 1971); Harriet L. Rheingold, ed., *Maternal Behavior in Mammals* (New York: John Wiley, 1963); Allan M. Schrier, Harry F. Harlow, and Fred Stollnitz, ed., *Behavior of Nonhuman Primates.* 2 vols. (New York: Academic Press, 1965).

[3] Frank A. Beach, ed., *Sex and Behavior* (New York: John Wiley, 1965); Ismond Rosen, ed., *The Pathology and Treatment of Sexual Deviation.* (New York: Oxford University Press, 1964); John F. Oliven, *Sexual Hygiene and Pathology.* 2nd ed. (Philadelphia: J. B. Lippincott Co., 1965).

[4] Rose W. Coleman and Sally Provence, "Environmental Retardation (Hospitalism) in Infants Living in Families," *Pediatrics* 19:285–92, 1957.

that are not yet clear, associated with the tendency toward retardation of growth, there is a trend for instinctive behaviors to become more variable and diffuse, and consequently for individual experience to play a more subtle and intricate role in forming these responses into biologically effective patterns.

In man this process has reached a point where it is often difficult, if not impossible, to determine the primitive motivational (*instinctoid*, Maslow) bases of his social behavior, let alone describe the specific manner in which these tendencies interact with experience. Moreover, with the emergence of the human way of life many of these primitive behaviors (for example, clinging, to be discussed more fully below) have lost the obvious adaptive value which they possess for the nonhuman primates, while they may retain some of their original psychological force.

It is still too early, however, to say much about evolutionary trends in primate socialization, and the two main objectives of this chapter are to provide a generalized description of the normal socialization process in monkeys and apes, and to indicate how early experience may influence their psychological growth. Information will be drawn from naturalistic studies, . . . from descriptive studies of the development of captive animals, and from experimental investigations. Documentation, when not indicated in the text, will be found in the references listed below.

Naturalistic studies are the primary source of information on normal aspects of social development. The major focus of naturalistic studies is on the tempo and direction of development within the group, beginning with the infant-mother relationship and terminating when the individual assumes reproductive or other functions characteristic of adult members of the group. The special value of such studies is that the developing individual is viewed as part of an elaborate network of social relations occurring in a complex ecological setting. There are two major benefits resulting from this approach:

1. A clearer and more comprehensive picture of the adaptive value of behavior can be obtained in the field than under artificial conditions. For example, the tendency of young primates to approach another animal who is manipulating or mouthing some object and to engage in similar behavior (social facilitation) is frequently observed in laboratory-reared animals. One might speculate that this tendency is involved in various aspects of adjustment under natural conditions (transition to solid foods, acquisition of new dietary habits, and so on), but its actual role must be established with the aid of studies conducted in the field.

2. A second important benefit of naturalistic investigations is that they are not limited to the analysis of simple dyadic social relationships, as between mother and young or between peers, but may take more complex possibilities into account. Field studies of Japanese monkeys, for example, suggest that the status of the mother within the group may have important consequences for the psychosocial development of her male infant. Low-status mothers are more often found at the periphery of the group than in the central portion with the dominant adult males. Imanishi (1957b) has suggested that the infant male of a low-status female acquires submissive attitudes from its mother and in addition has few opportunities for intimate contact and "identification" with the dominant males. These factors are said to reduce seriously the likelihood that the infant will later achieve high social status.

The naturalistic approach is indispensable in studies of primate socialization, but it is not without limitations. The field worker must take his chances on finding a sufficient number of animals of appropriate age and on being able to observe them long enough and closely enough to secure reliable data. Ordinarily, it is difficult under field conditions to complete a detailed analysis of a restricted phase of development (e. g., the neonatal period) or of a specific aspect of behavior (e. g., postural development, discriminative capacities, learning ability, emotional responsiveness). To obtain such information it is often necessary to observe the same individual repeatedly under relatively constant conditions. Frequently special testing procedures are required, and the animal must be maintained in a situation that permits close contact between the observer and the subject. These conditions, of course, are most readily met by the use of captive specimens.

Studies of captive animals may be principally concerned with describing normal development, that is, development as it occurs under natural conditions; or they may be designed within an experimental framework to investigate the effects of special conditions. Experimental investigations characteristically involve the systematic manipulation of one or more independent variables to study their effects upon some aspect of behavior (dependent variable). Other variables that might affect the behavior being measured are either randomized or controlled. The difference between normative and experimental studies of social development is one of degree only, and the two approaches are basically complementary. To illustrate: Field studies may establish that young primates spend much time playing with each other and that specific play patterns emerge at different stages of development. It might be hypothesized that the experience gained in play contributes to socialization and that the consequences of such experience will depend upon the developmental stage at which it occurs. Whether this is actually so can be completely established only by systematically varying the play opportunities of young animals and determining the effect of such variations on their social development. As experimental investigations proceed new problems emerge or earlier questions are stated more precisely, creating fresh opportunities for normative and experimental research. . . .

Normative Aspects of Social Development

Social Responses of Infancy

NATURE OF INFANTILE RESPONSES

In the beginning the relationship to the mother is, comparatively speaking, quite simple. Like other animals born immature and helpless the monkey or ape is equipped at birth with responses to aid it in adjusting to the mother. However, unlike many other mammals, who are left in a den or nest until they are able to accompany the mother under their own power, the infant monkey or ape must from the very beginning go everywhere with its mother and its survival is dependent upon maintaining the closest possible contact with her. This fact, perhaps more than any other, helps us to understand the behavior and motivations of infant monkeys and apes.

Among the first coordinated behavior patterns to appear postnatally are those that serve to maintain bodily contact with the mother and to make feeding possible. Initially these responses appear reflexlike in form. They are most sensitive to specific forms of stimuli or to stimulation of particular regions of the body, but they are also evoked or augmented by many events that seem to have little more in common than the characteristic of producing a rather abrupt increment in the general level of stimulation. Thus, sucking is elicited most readily by tactile stimulation in or around the mouth, but it may also occur in response to toe-pinching, hair-pulling, or loss of support. In the sections to follow changes induced in this way will be ascribed to an increment in arousal level, following the general approach developed by Bindra (1959), Duffy (1957), Hebb (1955), Malmo (1957), and others. At a minimum, this has the virtue of accommodating events that are physically heterogeneous (for example, loud sounds, pain, loss of support, visual size or complexity, tickling) and diverse behavioral outcomes (for example, withdrawal, aggression, screaming, sucking, clinging, play-fighting) within a single theoretical framework. A more systematic effort to apply this approach to primate social behavior is described elsewhere (Mason in press).

ROOTING, SUCKING, AND CLINGING

Since primate mothers ordinarily do not help the infant to find the breast, it is necessary that the neonate be able to locate the nipple by its own efforts. An important factor in this achievement is the "rooting reflex" or head-turning response. This response has been studied most thoroughly in human infants (Prechtl 1958), but the findings are probably equally applicable to nonhuman primates. The head-turning response is elicited most readily by tactile stimulation around the mouth, but it may occur in hungry infants in the absence of such stimulation. Other factors besides hunger that influence the rooting response are the number, locus, and intensity of preceding stimulations and the degree of wakefulness. Head-turning functions to bring the stimulating object in contact with the lips and this is followed by oral grasping and by sucking movements.

Stimulation in and around the mouth is the most effective stimulus for sucking, although, like head-turning, sucking may occur in the absence of external stimulation. Sucking movements are present at birth in most infants, and their strength and efficiency generally improve with age.

The principal postural adjustment of infancy is grasping or clinging. The infant is generally given some support by its mother, but support is not continuous, and under natural conditions it is necessary that the baby be able to cling independently, particularly in situations that require the mother to run or climb. Systematic studies in this area have focussed mainly on assessing the strength of reflex grasping to stretch stimulation, measured by the length of time that the infant can suspend itself. The grasp reflex is usually present at birth in neonatal humans, chimpanzees, rhesus monkeys, and presumably in all Old- and New-World forms. Intra- and inter-species variations in strength of grasp is large, but the trend is toward decreasing grasp duration from rhesus monkey (recorded maximum, 33 minutes) to chimpanzee (5 minutes) to man (2 minutes) (Richter 1931, 1934; Riesen and Kinder 1952), and there is some suggestion of a complementary trend in the nature and amount of maternal assistance provided. The strength of reflex grasping characteristically reaches a peak several days after birth and then wanes. The grasp reflex is probably only one mechanism involved in the maintenance of contact and support (Halverson 1937; Hines 1942), and Seyffarth and Denny-Brown (1948) have proposed a distinction between the grasp reflex and the instinctive grasp reaction. In contrast to the grasp reflex (which is elicited by deep pressure on the palm and by stretching) the instinctive grasp reaction occurs to light tactile stimulation and is usually accompanied by pursuit movements. Both responses are believed to be present at birth in the human infant.

One aspect of the early grasping activities of monkeys and apes that has obvious adaptive value is a characteristic movement of the arms analogous to the head-turning response. If an infant chimpanzee is placed on its back, this response occurs in the form of a sweeping motion, performed with the hands open. When an object is contacted, it is grasped and drawn toward the belly. In the neonatal monkey reaching and grasping movements give rise to the righting reaction, which is suppressed if an object for clasping is placed on the ventral surface. Reaching and grasping are probably the forerunners of the clinging embrace shown by older infants, in which grasping and ventral contact almost invariably occur together.

FUNCTIONAL RELATIONSHIPS

Although each of these early response patterns may be analyzed individually, they are functionally interrelated not only in infancy but throughout childhood. Thus the coordination of sucking and swallowing reflexes during feeding may be disrupted unless the infant monkey has its hands and feet firmly engaged. Grasping activities are intensified as nursing begins even when the infant is securely supported (Bieber 1940; Halverson 1938). The observation that young monkeys, chimpanzees, and children alternately open and close their hands or engage in various forms of finger play while sucking or drinking from a cup suggests that the association between sucking and grasping may persist in modified form at later stages of development (Foley 1934; Levy 1928), and this is consistent with the finding that infantile forms of sucking and grasping may reappear in human adults suffering neurological damage (Bieber 1940; Seyffarth and Denny-Brown 1948).

The factors that produce momentary increases in sucking and grasping activities have not been fully explored, but the available evidence indicates that there is a broad range of relevant variables, having in common the characteristic of augmenting arousal. Halverson (1938), in one of the few studies of correlated changes in sucking and grasping, found that in human infants the strength of sucking and grasping decreased during nursing and was intensified by thwarting of feeding activities. Jensen (1932) reported that many forms of intense stimulation, including sudden onset of light, loss of support, toe-pinching, and hair-pulling would reinstate sucking in human infants. Although concurrent changes in

grasping were not examined, Halverson's data (1938) suggest that grasping would be similarly affected.

INFANTILE RESPONSES, AROUSAL, AND FILIAL ATTACHMENT

The effect of infantile social responses, especially the clinging reaction, is to insure intimate and continuous contact with the mother, and in the absence of the mother, or a suitable substitute, the infant shows various signs of agitation or distress. One of the earliest accounts of clinging behavior is given by Alfred Russel Wallace. His observations of a baby orang-utan clearly indicate the strength and tenacity of infantile social responses.

For the first few days it clung desperately with all four hands to whatever it could lay hold of, and I had to be careful to keep my beard out of its way, as its fingers clutched hold of hair more tenaciously than anything else, and it was impossible to free myself without assistance. When restless, it would struggle about with its hands up in the air trying to find something to take hold of, and, when it had got a bit of stick or rag in two or three of its hands, seemed quite happy. For want of something else, it would often seize its own feet, and after a time it would constantly cross its arms and grasp with each hand the long hair that grew just below the opposite shoulder. . . . Finding it so fond of hair, I endeavoured to make an artificial mother, by wrapping up a piece of buffalo-skin into a bundle, and suspending it about a foot from the floor. At first this seemed to suit it admirably, as it could sprawl its legs about and always find some hair, which it grasped with the greatest tenacity. I was now in hopes that I had made the little orphan quite happy; and so it seemed for some time, till it began to remember its lost parent, and try to suck. It would pull itself up close to the skin, and try about everywhere for a likely place; but, as it only succeeded in getting mouthfuls of hair and wool, it would be greatly disgusted, and scream violently, and after two or three attempts, let go altogether (Wallace 1869).

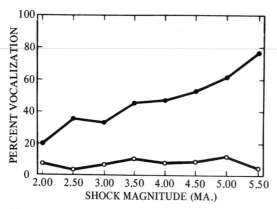

Figure 1: Percentage of shocks producing stress vocalizations (whimpering and screaming) in neonatal chimpanzees while the subjects were held and while they were resting on a bare surface (from Mason and Berkson 1962).

Wallace's description emphasizes two aspects of infantile responsiveness that have been frequently noted by other investigators. First, in the very young primate grasping or clinging is relatively nonspecific in its relation to stimulus conditions and may be evoked by a wide range of materials. McCulloch (1939) believes that the degree to which the material resists grasping determines its effectiveness, and in support of this cites Halverson's (1937) finding that strength of grasping is related to the size (diameter) of the grasped object. Although this may be true for strength of grasping, measured as an isolated response, grasping is but one element in a more complex pattern in which the grasped object is drawn toward the ventral surface. This suggests that the development of preferences for various objects of grasping will be determined not only by their resistance characteristics but also by the nature and amount of cutaneous stimulation the objects provide (Mowbray and Cadell 1962).

A second feature of infant behavior that is clearly indicated in Wallace's account is the extreme agitation produced when clinging [1] is prevented, and, contrariwise, the reduction in distress when a suitable object is attained. The inhibitory effect of clinging on distress reactions has been demonstrated by measuring vocal responses of infant chimpanzees to a painful stimulus (shock) administered when the infants rested on a bare surface and when they were held by the experimenter in a ventro-ventral position characteristic of the normal attitude of the infant on the mother (Mason and Berkson 1962). Figure 1 shows that even at the upper levels of shock crying occurred infrequently when the subject was held. If the shock was administered while the infant rested on a bare surface, however, the frequency of vocalizations increased progressively with increasing shock. Another experiment showed that hunger lowered the threshold for vocalization to shock, but, again, this effect was suppressed if the infant was held during testing (Mason and Berkson 1962). There is some indication that sucking may have inhibitory effects similar to those produced by clinging (Bridger 1962; Kessen and Mandler 1961).

CONTACT-SEEKING AND THE FORMATION OF FILIAL ATTACHMENTS: The strength and persistence of sucking and grasping activities and the distress occasioned when they are prevented have led several writers to conclude that contact-seeking and the seeking of bodily support are the principal drives of the newborn primate (Foley 1934; Tinklepaugh and Hartman 1932). The importance of contact-clinging in the development of filial attachments has been suggested by McCulloch (1939) and by Harlow and Zimmermann

---

[1] In the present discussion we shall refer to grasping accompanied by ventral contact with the object as *clinging*. Although later in development other forms of contact may acquire psychological effects similar to those produced by clinging, the clinging reaction is the modal pattern in the early relationship to the mother and it is the one most frequently observed at much later periods during moments of extreme excitement or distress.

(1958). Harlow (1960), on the basis of data obtained with various types of artificial mothers, concludes that the two dominant systems in the formation of the infant rhesus monkey's tie to the mother are sucking and contact. In an experiment designed to provide a direct comparison of feeding experience and contact stimulation, infant monkeys were separated from their mothers at birth and placed in individual cages with access to a wire mesh cylinder from which they were fed and a cloth-covered cylinder which was the source of contact stimulation. Attachment was formed only to the cloth-covered cylinder. When infant monkeys were given two cloth cylinders identical except for color and were fed from only one of these, the cylinder which provided food was initially preferred, but this preference disappeared at about 100 days of age (Harlow 1962a; Harlow and Zimmermann 1958).

Attachment to an artificial mother develops gradually and may be measured in various ways. The Wisconsin studies have used as primary measures the amount of time spent in contact with the object while it is in the living cage, and its effectiveness in reducing emotional distress. In some tests the object has been used as an incentive for visual exploration, puzzle solution, and detour learning (Harlow and Zimmermann 1958). McCulloch (1939) used claspable objects as incentives for delayed response and discrimination learning by chimpanzees.

As would be expected, age is important in the formation of filial attachments. Rhesus monkeys who were given an artificial mother at 250 days came to spend considerable time on it, but they derived no security from its presence in a strange environment (Harlow 1962a). This effect may not be a general one, however, for rhesus monkeys raised from birth in individual cages show a definite reduction in emotional responses in an unfamiliar situation when another young monkey is present (Mason 1960a), and they remain capable of forming attachments to other monkeys at least through the first year of life. Monkeys paired for the first time at 11 months of age revealed definite preferences for the cagemate in paired-comparison tests and showed a sharp increase in distress vocalizations when the partner was removed from the living cage.

CLINGING AND AROUSAL: It is noteworthy that with the exception of measures obtained in the living cage strength of attachment to objects of clasping has been assessed in situations which seem to produce a high degree of arousal. The importance of such a factor has been emphasized by McCulloch (1939), who noted that claspable objects were maximally effective incentives for young chimpanzees only when the animals were highly excited or disturbed. He proposed that the effectiveness of clasping was dependent upon its inhibitory action:

A common facilitating condition for the . . . [clasping] response in different species and in different levels of development of the same species is a stimulus situation which increases the state of excitement or disturbance. When clasping occurs, it tends to inhibit other responses of the organism. As a consequence of this inhibition, responses that closely precede clasping tend to become established as systematic responses or habits (McCulloch 1939:309).

A number of studies indicate that a high level of arousal increases the likelihood that clinging will occur. Figure 2 shows that contacts with an object of clinging by young chimpanzees increased progressively with conditions designed to produce increasing arousal. The relation of clinging to motivational factors can also be demonstrated by showing changes in the form of responses to the same object presented in different situations. Young chimpanzees given a claspable object (for example, rag mop) in their living cages responded to it playfully; in unfamiliar and presumably disturbing situations, however, play ac-

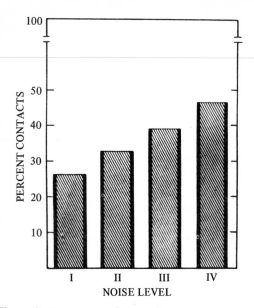

Figure 2: Percentage of time chimpanzees were in contact with a stimulus-person who held them in relation to noise level in the room.

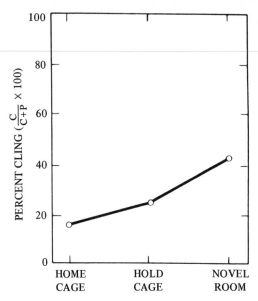

Figure 3: Ratio of clinging (c) to total clinging and play responses (c and p) between pairs of young chimpanzees observed in their living cages (home cage), in an identical cage placed in a different location in the colony room (holding cage), or in a novel room.

tivities diminished and clinging became the dominant response. The same effect has been demonstrated by recording the relative frequency of play and clinging in paired chimpanzees observed in familiar and in strange surroundings (Fig. 3) and by measuring the patterns of interaction between cagemates after they had been separated for intervals of as much as three hours (Fig. 4). Thus evidence consistently shows that a high level of arousal strengthens the tendency to cling. The corollary to this conclusion, namely, that clinging reduces arousal, is less firmly established but is supported by many nonsystematic observations and by some experimental data (Harlow and Zimmermann 1958; Mason and Berkson 1962). It is not yet clear whether reduction in arousal or distress constitutes a major factor in the development of attachments to the mother and to substitute objects, but the evidence now available indicates this is a reasonable conclusion.

The Beginnings of Independence

CHANGES IN MOTHER-INFANT INTERACTIONS

Long before the infant primate is nutritionally or emotionally independent of the mother, the early relationship with her based on the relatively simple clinging-rooting-sucking responses is complicated and enriched by a rapid growth in infant activity and the change this induces in maternal behavior.

Within a few days for monkeys or a few months for chimpanzees and gorillas, the infant forsakes its customary position on the mother's belly and begins to crawl about on her body. Particular interest is shown in her face, probably for the same reasons that the infant is attracted to any bright, distinctive object. Eventually these excursions take the infant short distances into the region surrounding the mother. The factors

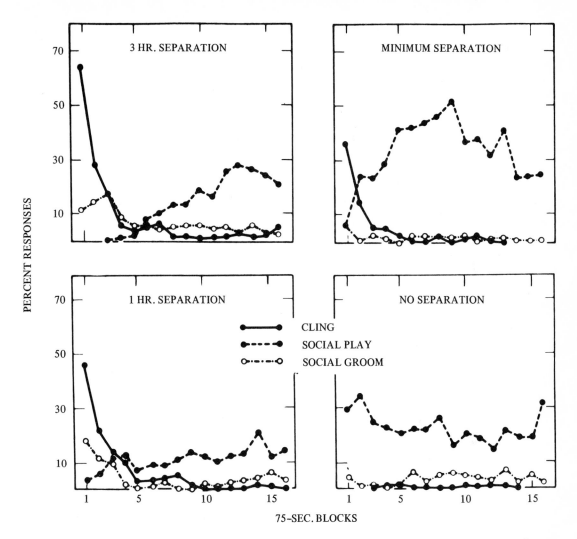

Figure 4: Social behavior of pairs of young chimpanzee cage-mates following four conditions of separation. (No separation consisted of observing interactions in the absence of any experimental manipulation. Minimum separation consisted of separating and immediately reuniting the animals.)

cal restraint. The chimpanzee at one month may be held for half an hour without showing signs of restlessness; at six months it rarely can be kept in the same position for more than a few minutes without a struggle.

The direction and tempo of infant development are largely determined by intrinsic changes, but the specific details in the transition from total dependence to limited independence are influenced by the mother. Mothers vary considerably in diligence and skill. Some, especially the young

involved in this transition probably include, on the positive side, a growth in sensorimotor capabilities and increasing attraction to the relatively novel physical environment and to other animals; and on the negative side, a reaction against physi-

and inexperienced, forcibly reject their infants at birth or appear to be indifferent, or even bewildered or frightened by them (for example, Fox 1929). The importance of experience in the development of adequate patterns of maternal care is shown in recent studies of rhesus monkey mothers raised in the laboratory and deprived of normal socialization experiences (Harlow and Harlow 1962). These animals were deficient in their maternal behavior, showing abnormalities ranging from indifference to active rejection of their young. All mothers failed to nurse effectively and the infants required hand feeding. Such reactions are exceptional under natural conditions, however, and most mothers are strongly attracted to their infants and effectively perform the basic mammalian maternal activities of nursing, grooming, protection, and transportation. Within this framework there are impressive differences in maternal care and temperament, and it has been suggested that these may contribute to broad and persistent differences in infant behavior (Jay 1962; Tinklepaugh and Hartman 1932; Tomilin and Yerkes 1935).

Species differences in maternal behavior are pronounced. For example, baboon and macaque mothers are in continuous contact with their infants for about the first month after birth and vigorously resist any attempts at separation, whereas langur mothers permit other females to hold and carry their infants within hours after birth. The olive colobus monkey is distinguished by the unusual custom of carrying very young infants in the mother's mouth, a phenomenon that has not been observed in the black or red colobus (Booth 1957). Gorillas and chimpanzees show more subtle and varied patterns of maternal care than do monkeys, at least in captivity. Captive chimpanzees actively exercise and play with their babies and the ". . . infant is inhibited, curbed, directed, driven, or encouraged in multitudinous ways by maternal attentions" (Tomilin and Yerkes 1935:335). Similar behavior has not been observed among chimpanzees in the field, and it is possible that some aspects of maternal behavior are exaggerated in captivity. The caged mother is freed from the usual pressures of food-getting and protection, and the infant may provide a potent stimulus for activity in an otherwise monotonous and unstimulating environment.

In all species as the infant grows older there is some relaxation in maternal solicitude and restraint. Control by coercion is gradually supplemented by a more elaborate system of control based on subtle vocal and gestural cues, and the infant must learn to detect slight variations in the mother's posture or facial expressions that signal her mood or intent.

RELATIONS WITH OTHER MEMBERS OF THE GROUP

For most Old- and New-World monkeys and probably for the larger primates as well, the birth of a baby is an event of general interest, particularly for the juvenile and adult females in the group. These may crowd around the mother, inspecting the neonate and seeking to touch it or to hold it. Although the mother is usually reluctant at first to permit such liberties, she becomes increasingly tolerant of the attentions shown her infant by other animals, eventually permitting them to groom it and even to carry it short distances away from her. The peculiar attraction that the infant holds for young and old alike persists for some time after it has taken its first steps away from the mother and it may become the object of attentions that are neither solicited nor welcome. The mother is usually at hand, however, and retrieves her baby at the first signs of distress.

The reaction of adult males to infants is variable, but present evidence indicates that they are more often attentive and protective than hostile. Males have been observed to play with young animals, to retrieve them in emergency situations, and to transport and otherwise assist them during progressions (Bingham 1927; Bolwig 1959a; Carpenter 1934; Collias and Southwick 1952; DeVore 1962; Nissen 1931). Several observers have reported isolated instances of relatively stable associations between an adult male and a younger animal in which the adult served in some ways as mother substitute (Bolwig 1959a; Carpenter 1934; DeVore 1962; Haddow 1952; Imanishi 1957a). The male marmoset is reported to carry the infant at all times except when it is being nursed or cleaned by the mother (Stellar 1960). The most remarkable instance of "paternal" behavior observed thus far in Old-World monkeys occurs in some groups of Japanese macaques (Itani 1959). In three of the 18 groups of Japanese monkeys surveyed it was found that during the birth season adult males of high social rank adopted yearling infants, clutched them, carried them, protected them, and, except for suckling, behaved in general as a mother does toward her offspring.

SOCIAL PLAY

ONSET OF PLAY: Contacts with adults other than the mother probably facilitate socialization and help to integrate the young animal into the group, but for most species such contacts are infrequent compared to activities with other immature animals in juvenile play groups. Laboratory studies indicate that social play is exhibited near the end of the first month by rhesus monkeys and at about six months in chimpanzees. With advancing age play increases in frequency and complexity. With the onset of play the focus of infant behavior shifts progressively away from the mother and toward other young animals, but the infant continues to be emotionally dependent on the mother. Her presence in an unfamiliar situation probably facilitates the emergence of exploratory activities and play, and she continues to be sought when the young animal is frightened or distressed.

FORMS AND CONDITIONS OF PLAY: Rosenblum (1961) has classified the major play activities of rhesus monkeys into three broad categories: (a) rough-and-tumble play, (b) approach-withdrawal play, and (c) activity play. A similar classification would apply to the behavior of many mammals (Groos 1898), and the characteristics differentiating the play of the various genera of primates from each other and from other mammals will be found in comparative analyses of the form, the variety, and the complexity of response sequences and patterns (Welker 1961; Yerkes and Yerkes 1929). Such studies have not been completed and the following discussion is based mainly on observations of rhesus monkeys and chimpanzees.

The most frequent social activity among young chimpanzees and monkeys is play-fighting. Play-fighting in chimpanzees varies in intensity from gentle tapping, pulling, squeezing, tickling, and nudging to vigorous bouts of slapping and wrestling. By comparison the play-fighting of rhesus monkeys seems stereotyped and gross. Mounting occurs frequently in the playful interactions of monkeys and even very young animals may display a nearly perfect replica of the adult mating pattern. Among chimpanzees, gorillas, and gibbons, sex play is relatively less frequent and more loosely organized and diffuse. There have been no detailed studies of the importance of play in the socialization process, but field workers have expressed the conviction that experience gained in play facilitates the development of communicative skills and forms the foundation of adult social relationships. Recent laboratory findings are consistent with this view.

The distinction between social and nonsocial play is not a fundamental one. Characteristics that affect responses to inanimate objects, such as complexity, size, or mobility of the stimulus, also influence reactions to social stimuli. An important variable that is not yet clearly understood is the effect of previous experience. Investigations with young chimpanzees indicate that their initial response to an object of a new "class" is characterized by extreme caution. With successive exposures to comparable objects a generalized adaptation occurs and new objects of the same general type are contacted freely (Menzel 1963; Menzel, Davenport, and Rogers 1961). Moreover, when this point has been reached the moderately novel stimulus generally elicits more contacts than the familiar one (Menzel, Davenport, and Rogers 1961; Welker 1956). The situation seems to be very similar with regard to social stimuli. The home-reared chimpanzee Viki preferred strangers over familiar persons as playmates (Hayes and Hayes 1951). Laboratory chimpanzees of comparable age whose contacts with humans are limited show marked timidity in the presence of strangers, which is only gradually overcome (Hebb and Riesen 1943; Mason, Hollis, and Sharpe 1962). Similarly, young monkeys raised in isolation from adult animals showed a definite increase in affective responses when placed in an unfamiliar situation with a caged adult monkey as compared to their responses when another young monkey was present (Mason 1960a). In general, extreme departures from the familiar tend to depress play, whereas moderate degrees of novelty tend to enhance it. These results may be explained if it is assumed that play is facilitated by moderate levels of arousal and in turn augments existing levels. Thus, in situations in which the level of arousal is low or moderate, young animals are disposed to play (Mason, Hollis, and Sharpe 1962), whereas in situations in which arousal is already high, play is avoided. In view of the earlier discussion of the relationship between clinging and arousal level, it is not surprising that under the latter condition there occurs a pronounced increase in the tendency to cling.

An examination of the patterns of behavior directed toward inanimate objects supports the thesis that social and nonsocial forms of play are not fundamentally different. Threats, wrestling, grooming, and sexual behavior may sometimes occur with objects; some of these responses, for example, wrestling, may even be observed on occasion in the absence of an external stimulus, as a kind of reaction *in vacuo* (Bernstein 1962; Bernstein and Mason 1962; Foley 1934; Menzel 1963; Schiller 1957). Moreover, many activities such as climbing, swinging, and jumping that are often incorporated into social "games" of chasing, dodging, and wrestling are sometimes performed for their own sake, even when playmates are present. Hence, the term *social response* is equivocal unless the nature of the stimulus is specified. We must recognize, of course, that social stimuli possess certain features which distinguish them in degree, if not in kind, from inanimate objects. The appearance of a social stimulus is more variable from moment-to-moment than that of a physical object and such variation probably enhances the attractiveness of social stimuli (Butler 1954). Of greater importance is the fact that social stimuli, in contrast to physical objects, are not passive recipients of contacts, but may reciprocate, repel, or withdraw from the activities of another animal. Such reactions, repeated and modified by experience, provide for the development of subtle and elaborate social cue functions and for the integration of specific responses into broader sequences and patterns.

In spite of the difficulties in arriving at an acceptable and comprehensive definition of play, the fact remains that observers show considerable agreement in judging "playful behavior." Most probably such judgments are based on relatively simple behavioral cues, although knowledge of the situation is certainly a contributing factor. The problem of a comprehensive definition is more serious in theory than in practice. Certainly the responses that are judged "playful" are a normal and conspicuous feature of the heightened responsiveness of youth. This is illustrated by a comparison of the behavior of pairs of young and adult chimpanzees observed in their living cages. The young animals made more than 16 times as many social contacts as the adults, most of them during social play, and their scores for locomotion and contacts with the physical environment were also substantially higher; the only major activities in which the adults surpassed the young animals were self-manipulation and grooming. Field studies are consistent with these findings and indicate that young monkeys may spend as much as four or five hours a day in play groups (Jay 1963a). Playfulness, therefore, is rightly regarded as a useful index of the physical and psychological well-being of the young primate. Its prolonged absence raises the suspicion of retardation, illness, or distress.

Normative Aspects: Overview

INFANTILE RESPONSES

In discussing social development it has been convenient to distinguish the responses present at birth or within a few hours of birth from social responses that appear somewhat later in ontogeny. To the extent that psychological development is a continuous process in which the effects of experience are cumulative, this division is artificial. In defense of this procedure one might argue that in their original form the first social responses should be termed *proto-social*. They are reflexlike in character and their elicitation and development are dependent not so much upon the interaction between two individuals as upon the presence of certain relatively simple physical characteristics—which ordinarily are embodied in the mother. Perhaps the major psychological significance of these neonatal responses is that they are the source of powerful motivations and predispositions which underlie much of the normal social

behavior of infancy. They form the basis of the infantile attachment to the mother, which is probably the most intense social bond in the life of a primate. We are not yet in a position to judge the full significance of this attachment. Among other possibilities, it may provide the infant with the emotional security to venture away from the mother, while predisposing it to remain within the radius of maternal surveillance and protection. Throughout childhood and probably beyond, seeking social contact remains a characteristic reaction to stress, and it is reasonable to suppose that this tendency has its roots in the primitive responses of infancy.

MATERNAL BEHAVIOR

By providing a source of support, nourishment, and protection the mother makes survival possible. Beyond this her interactions with the infant may be presumed to prepare it for later social adjustments. The nature of maternal care depends on the experience of the mother, the characteristics of the immediate situation, and the developmental status of the infant. Generally speaking the relationship between maternal behavior and infant capabilities is complementary. The helpless chimpanzee infant receives more elaborate maternal attentions than the precocious infant macaque. In all species the interactions between mother and young become more subtle and complex as development proceeds, and before the infant has achieved his independence he experiences succor, punishment, rejection, and restraint in a variety of degrees and forms. The endless process of social adjustment begins with the mother, whose behavior is, in many ways, representative of the larger group. From her the infant learns to perceive the meaning of a gesture or a glance, discovers that food may not be taken with impunity from a larger animal, and finds that bites and slaps will be returned in kind.

OTHER SOCIAL CONTACTS

Early in development the young primate's experience is enlarged by opportunities to observe and to participate in social interactions with adults of both sexes and with other young animals whose activities and motivations are congruent with its own. Such experiences presumably carry forward the process of socialization which began with the mother.

Effects of Social Deprivation

Methodological Considerations

Social development within a free-ranging group consists of an orderly progression, through time, from almost complete helplessness and dependence on the mother toward increasing self-sufficiency and orientation toward the group as a whole. In the natural habitat development always occurs in a complex socio-ecological setting in which many factors may contribute to the final behavioral result. Assessing the relative importance of these factors is a difficult and time-consuming task, and it cannot be accomplished without experimental intervention and control.

In the following sections we will consider some of the ways in which development is influenced by variations in conditions of rearing. The broad purpose of research on this question is to establish correlations (functional relationships) between single rearing variables, or combinations of variables, and specific behavioral outcomes. In the early stages of research (as in the present case), the definition of the independent variable is usually provisional and relatively gross, and is then refined as further studies indicate. For example, one might begin an investigation of the effects of maternal care on behavioral development by comparing two groups of animals, resembling each other in all important respects, except that one of them has no experience with a natural mother. If reliable differences between groups are found, one might then ask which of the many variables involved in maternal behavior account for the obtained effects. It would also be important to know whether all the important effects have been detected. The consequences of the rearing variable may be subtle, or they may assume forms that the experimenter does not expect. Isolating the developing organism from normal social contacts may not only prevent or retard the development of some behaviors, it may also create a situation in which other responses, never seen in the natural state, are likely to appear.

Thus far primate research on social deprivation has dealt mainly with gross variations in rearing conditions. Analysis of the consequences of such variations has been completed in considerable detail, however, and information is available on the effects of social deprivation on physical growth and mortality, on the development of infantile social responses (that is, those involved in feeding and the maintenance of contact with the mother), and on the ability to make effective social adjustments in adolescence and maturity.

Growth, Mortality, and Social Stimulation

For some mammals maternal stimulation is required for adequate biological functioning of the neonate. In puppies and kittens elimination is facilitated by maternal stimulation (for example, licking) and such stimulation must be provided artificially to isolation-reared animals if they are to be maintained in good health. It has been suggested that a similar situation exists in respect to the human infant. Ribble (1943), in one of the more radical versions of this thesis, has stated that human infants receiving inadequate maternal stimulation show a syndrome of behavioral and physiological debility (marasmus) which may have fatal consequences. Data on rhesus monkeys and chimpanzees raised in social isolation cast serious doubt on the hypothesis that social stimulation plays a significant part in physical growth and viability in these primates (Davenport, Menzel, and Rogers 1961; Mason 1961c). Davenport *et al.* (1961) compared weight gain and mortality rates between mother-reared chimpanzees and animals removed from the mother at birth and raised in a laboratory nursery. Nursery-reared infants, even those reared in small enclosed cubicles, showed no higher mortality rates than chimpanzees left with their mothers, and they were substantially heavier than the mother-reared animals. Although physical growth in primates is not directly affected by social factors, there is a growing body of evidence that many aspects of psychological development are dependent upon social experience. As would be expected, the consequences of social deprivation vary with the age and developmental status of the organism at the time that deprivation occurs.

Social Deprivation and Responses of Early Infancy

Infantile "contact seeking" behaviors show extraordinary strength and persistence and they may be elicited by a variety of stimulus objects. It would not be surprising, therefore, to find that these behaviors will be expressed in substitute activities when normal outlets are barred.

SUCKING AND SELF-CLASPING

Digit sucking appears to be one such substitute activity; it is seen in a large number of monkeys and chimpanzees raised in the laboratory and is rarely, if ever, observed in wild-born animals (Gillman 1941; Mason and Green 1962; Nissen 1944). Benjamin (1961a) found that nonnutritive sucking appeared within the first ten days of life in infant rhesus monkeys and was more frequent in animals that were bottle-fed than in those receiving their nourishment from a cup. In the latter group, however, nonsucking oral be-

havior (biting, licking) was relatively frequent. Differences between groups reached a maximum at from 40 to 60 days of age and then diminished, owing mainly to the decrease in nonnutritive sucking by bottle-fed monkeys. In both groups sucking persisted at substantial levels until the end of testing at 180 days of age. Another response frequently seen in primates reared apart from the mother that has an obvious parallel in normal filial behavior is self-clasping.

REPETITIVE MOVEMENTS

A conspicuous feature of the behavior of laboratory-reared primates is some form of individually stereotyped repetitive movement, commonly rocking or swaying (Davenport and Menzel 1963; Mason and Green 1962; Nissen 1956). The form of these responses bears no obvious resemblance to normal social responses, and it has been suggested that they should be regarded as an attempt to compensate for low levels of environmental stimulation or for restriction of movement, rather than as a specific reaction to social deprivation (Casler 1961; Levy 1944). Although nonsocial factors may influence the level of repetitive stereotyped movements in animals that habitually display such behaviors (see below), early social experience is rather clearly implicated in the origin of these responses in nonhuman primates. That the general level of environmental stimulation is relatively unimportant in the development of repetitive stereotyped movements is suggested by the finding that animals reared in the laboratory with the mother do not rock or sway (Jensen and Tolman 1962), whereas those reared apart from the mother almost invariably do (Davenport and Menzel 1963; Hines 1942; Foley 1934; Mason and Green 1962; Nissen 1956; Riesen and Kinder 1952). Even the varied stimulation afforded the animal reared in a human household does not prevent the development of repetitive movements (Hayes and Hayes 1951; Jacobsen,

Jacobsen, and Yoshioka 1932). Spatial restriction on movement is also an unlikely primary etiological factor inasmuch as repetitive movements characteristically appear before the animal has attained full locomotor capabilities for the exploitation of the available space; furthermore, it was found that severe restriction of tactual, kinesthetic, and manipulative experience of a chimpanzee during infancy resulted in less, rather than more, stereotyped rocking, as compared to ordinary conditions of laboratory rearing (Nissen, Chow, and Semmes 1951).

ROLE OF MATERNAL FACTORS

The presence of the mother may operate in two ways to prevent the development of stereotyped self-clasping, thumb-sucking, and repetitive movements: First, the hands of the infant are constantly occupied in holding on to the fur and skin of the mother, thus preventing their use in self-clasping and thumb-sucking, and probably this factor also militates against the development of exaggerated repetitive movements. There is some suggestion that for the nursery-reared chimpanzee the onset of swaying in the prone position may be related to initial attempts to crawl. In the mother-reared infant, however, this stage of locomotor development occurs while the infant is still in constant contact with the mother and it is manifested in climbing about on the mother's body. The contours of the mother's physique, the frequent variations in maternal postures and activities, and the requirement that the infant adjust to these while maintaining contact, probably act as deterrents to the development of swaying or rocking as habitual responses. A second way in which the mother may prevent the development of stereotyped activities is by providing adequate outlets for the underlying response tendencies or stimulation needs that such activities presumably reflect.

FUNCTIONAL RELATIONSHIPS

Once stereotyped activities have become established in an animal's repertoire, they show variation in amplitude, frequency, and form as a function of both internal and external factors. A better understanding of the factors producing momentary changes in stereotyped activities can provide important clues to the functions that these behaviors serve for the laboratory-reared primate. Sufficient data exist to suggest that thumb-sucking, self-clasping, and repetitive movements differ in their specific relationship to eliciting conditions (Bernstein and Mason 1962; Smith 1960). Generally speaking, however, these behaviors retain the broad relationship to stimulus conditions that is characteristic of infantile responses. Situations that appear to create high levels of arousal augment substitute behaviors. Among the factors that have been shown to produce an increase in one or more of these responses are hunger (Benjamin and Mason 1963), frustration (Benjamin 1961b; Finch 1942), novel objects or surroundings (Berkson, Mason, and Saxon 1963; Foley 1934; Hines 1942; McCulloch and Haselrud 1939), and intense auditory stimulation (Smith 1960).

It has been suggested that boredom, that is, the absence of varied stimulation, may also influence the level of stereotyped movements once they have become habitual modes of responding (Hayes 1951; Nissen 1944, 1956; Levy 1944). Levy (1944) reports that the incidence of stereotyped movements in institutionalized children was reduced when toys were provided, and Menzel (1963) has shown that repetitive stereotyped movements diminished in chimpanzees in periods of active manipulation of objects and then increased as a reduction in contacts occurred. Possibly, additional work will show that stereotyped activities serve a homeostatic or regulatory function, coming into play whenever the over-all level of stimulation falls above or below a certain critical range.

SIGNIFICANCE OF STEREOTYPED BEHAVIORS

Several considerations suggest that stereotyped behaviors are a potentially significant source of information on the interrelationships among innate tendencies, age, and experience in primate development:

1. There is convincing evidence that the development of these behaviors is related to rearing conditions. Although the specific etiological factors have not yet been demonstrated, the absence of a normal association with the natural mother seems to be an important predisposing condition. The age of onset for these behaviors can be specified and their emergence can probably be related to normal developmental changes.

2. There seems to be a critical period for the development of stereotyped behaviors in the sense that an animal that has passed beyond a certain age without acquiring such responses can be permanently placed in a situation identical to that which produced them in a younger animal and they will not emerge (Davenport and Menzel 1963; Mason and Green 1962). (This is one characteristic by which they may be differentiated from the "cage stereotypes" of pacing and so on, commonly seen in some zoo animals [Hediger 1955; Levy 1944]). Moreover, stereotyped responses show only limited reversibility and may persist indefinitely, although the specific form of the response may change as the animal grows older. Thus, rhesus monkeys frequently begin sucking the true thumb, but most of those that become persistent nonnutritive suckers eventually shift to the big toe. Similarly, repetitive movements may begin in the chimpanzee as head-rolling or swaying in a prone or supine posture; later, similar movements may be made while the animal is sitting or standing bipedally. Some individuals alternate between two patterns, for example, rocking to-and-fro while sitting, and swaying from side-to-side while standing. Although the frequency of stereotyped responses tends to decrease with age, they may be observed on occasion in fully mature animals, particularly during moments of excitement.

3. There is a fundamental similarity in the form of these behaviors as they are seen in the nonhuman primates and in certain human groups, including blind (Keeler 1958) and schizophrenic children (Bender and Freedman 1952) and the severely retarded (Berkson and Davenport 1962; Gesell and Amatruda 1941). As would be expected, phylogenetic differences exist in the number and complexity of these responses and their postural concomitants. Only apes and man sway while standing erect; and even untestable human retardates may display a richness of stereotyped patterns that exceeds the most elaborate behaviors shown by monkeys and chimpanzees.

4. Because stereotyped behaviors become persistent modes of responding, they may substitute for or interfere with the development of responses which are more adaptive or appropriate, thus indirectly retarding psychological growth.

Social Behavior and Social Deprivation

RESPONSIVENESS

A necessary but obviously insufficient condition for effective social interchange is that the organisms involved approach rather than avoid one another. There seems to be a period early in primate infancy when the dominant tendency is approach, but as development proceeds fear responses emerge and with this there occur a differentiation and a refinement of reactions to novel objects (Bernstein and Mason 1962). These changes are determined in part by maturation, but whether a specific social stimulus will elicit approach or avoidance is also dependent upon prior experience (Hebb and Riesen 1943). Animals that have been reared in isolation from their kind but in an otherwise stimulating social environment may show no signs of fear when first confronted with a member of their own species. In fact, there is some indication that such animals are bolder than ordinary laboratory subjects (Foley 1934, 1935; Hayes 1951; Jacobsen, Jacobsen, and Yoshioka 1932; Kellogg and Kellogg 1933). In contrast with these findings, the animal reared in complete social isolation may show a persistent avoidance of social contact. In one experiment (unpublished) two rhesus monkeys were raised in total isolation from birth until they were 18 months of age. They were then placed together in a large observation cage for a total of fifteen 45-minute sessions and during this time were scored with only 25 social approaches, most of which occurred as the animals came into proximity while passing from one end of the cage to the other. Many common rhesus monkey social responses were never observed, and the animals spent much of the time crouched at opposite ends of the cage, clutching themselves and rocking. The reactions of these monkeys to each other and to the test situation suggest the excessive arousal effects shown by visually deprived animals upon being placed in normal visual surroundings (Riesen 1961). A comparison group in this experiment was provided by two monkeys individually housed from birth in wire mesh cages within a room containing other monkeys. In contrast to the isolates, these monkeys made over 500 social approaches and exhibited play, grooming, aggression, and some sexual behavior. Subsequently, the experimental animals were permanently removed from isolation and were paired continuously for successive two-week periods with each other and with the monkeys of the comparison group. Throughout these pairings their behavior showed no important change.

SOCIAL INTERACTION

Although monkeys raised in semi-isolation in the ordinary laboratory environment may be highly responsive to social stimuli, their development is retarded in many respects by the lack of social experience. This has been demonstrated by comparing the behavior of two groups of adolescent rhesus monkeys, one group born and raised in the wild for the first 12 to 18 months, and the other, born in the laboratory and housed from infancy in individual cages (Mason 1960b, 1961a, 1961b). In test situations the laboratory-reared subjects showed less social grooming, as compared to the feral animals, and had more frequent and severe fights. The stability of social relations, determined by competitive tests with food, was much greater in the feral group, and these animals were also more highly motivated to engage in social interaction with other members of their group, as measured by the number of times they released a group member from confinement. Similar tests were conducted in which both feral and socially deprived male monkeys were given an opportunity to interact with feral females. Under these conditions the laboratory-reared subjects showed a definite increase in gregariousness. When the procedure was reversed, however, and the experienced females were permitted to choose between wild-born and laboratory-reared males, their preference for the feral animals was unequivocal.

One of the most striking deficiencies observed in the socially deprived subjects was in sexual relations. Abnormalities in sexual performance were apparent in both sexes, but they were particularly pronounced in males. Socially deprived males were evidently sexually aroused, but their mating attempts were poorly integrated and body orientation toward the partner was frequently inappropriate. These deficiencies were apparent whether the animals were tested with naive or sophisticated females (see Fig. 5). Thus far, all efforts to establish effective sexual performance at maturity in socially deprived male rhesus monkeys have been unsuccessful (Harlow 1962b).

The evidence is conclusive that normal development of primate social behavior is dependent upon experience (Harlow 1962b; Nissen 1953; Yerkes and Elder 1936), but the specific factors involved have not been determined. Male mating behavior probably does not develop as a unitary pattern; rather the various constituents seem to appear at different stages in ontogeny and are differentially related to experience and to eliciting conditions. Penile erection and thrusting are present in infancy in both monkeys and chimpanzees and they occur in many situations in which the general level of excitement is high, for example, upon rejoining a companion after brief separation, at feeding time, when strangers are present, or in response to physical restraint (Bingham 1928; Hamilton 1914). The integration of these responses into the adult mating pattern occurs much earlier in monkeys than in chimpanzees, but it means little to say that experience is more important for one species than for another. If the male monkey is provided adequate social contacts, it develops the sexual pattern characteristic of the adult well in advance of puberty, whereas under similar conditions the chimpanzee apparently does not (Bingham 1928; Nissen 1953; Yerkes and Elder 1936). On the other hand, the male monkey that has not achieved the adult pattern by adolescence is unlikely to do so later, whereas the chimpanzee is capable of such learning. This contrast may be related in part to differences in the sexual patterns of the two groups and in part to differences in behavioral flexibility. Unless the male rhesus monkey succeeds in grasping the female's hind legs during mounting, intromission is impossible, and until this stage has been achieved even a highly experienced female can provide little assistance to the male. The male monkey whose opportunities for social learning have been curtailed until adolescence is probably

Figure 5: Sexual behavior of wild-born and socially deprived rhesus monkeys with socially experienced female partners. (Top right) Rear view of wild-born male in typical copulatory position. (Top left) Side view of wild-born male in typical copulatory position. (Bottom right) Socially deprived male attempting to mount from the side. (Bottom left) Sexual behavior of socially deprived male (from Mason 1960b).

handicapped in his sexual adjustment by the presence of strong playful and aggressive tendencies. In chimpanzee sexual relations the roles are not so sharply differentiated as is the case with monkeys and baboons. The male may approach the female, or he may solicit approach from her by sitting with legs drawn apart, displaying the erect penis (Yerkes and Elder 1936). With some cooperation from the male an experienced female may guide the penis or adjust her posture so as to compensate to some extent for deficiencies in her partner. Thus, there is a strong possibility that early social deprivation may have more severe and lasting consequences for masculine sexual development in the monkey than in the chimpanzee.

A series of experiments summarized by Harlow and Harlow (1962) provides significant information on the relative importance of mother-infant and infant-infant relations in the social development of rhesus monkeys. The results indicate that development is essentially normal if infants are raised by their mothers and given daily opportunities to interact with age-mates. Infants raised apart from the mother and given frequent contact with peers are initially somewhat retarded in their social development, but eventually attain normal social patterns, whereas infants whose only social contacts to the age of seven months were with their mothers are more retarded than either of the other two groups. Although additional data are required before a firm conclusion is warranted, this evidence suggests that the relationship with the mother is not essential to social development, although it may facilitate it, whereas contacts with peers must occur if development is to follow a normal course.

CONTRIBUTION OF EXPERIENCE

A consideration of the consequences of social deprivation offers some suggestion as to the various ways in which experience may contribute to normal social development.

1. RESPONSIVENESS: Perhaps the single most important motivational determinant of primate social responsiveness, particularly in the young, is the general level of behavioral arousal. Level of arousal is dependent upon a complex relationship between experience and the characteristics of the social stimulus and of the physical situation. Generally speaking, the older the animal and the more marked the contrast between the rearing environment and the test situation, the

more extreme and persistent its reaction will be. Precise relationships between level of arousal and behavior have not yet been determined, but sufficient data exist to suggest that higher levels will be associated with withdrawal or aggression, either of which is inimical to effective social adjustment (Mason, in press).

2. RESPONSE INTEGRATION: The importance of response integration is most clearly illustrated by the sexual performance of male rhesus monkeys, but response integration may also be a factor in the formation of other complex social patterns, for example, maternal behavior. Although most of the constituents of male reproductive behavior were present in socially deprived monkeys, these were not combined into an orderly pattern and appropriately applied to social stimuli. Fundamentally this appears to be a form of sensorimotor learning, analogous to that involved in the integration of isolated motor units into the complex patterns and sequences required in effective use of tools (Birch 1945; Schiller 1952). We may expect that for social responses, as for tool-using, significant maturational gradients will be found (Schiller 1952).

3. COMMUNICATION: Communication may involve the discrimination of extremely subtle individualized cues indicating the mood or intent of a particular companion, as well as differential responses to species-characteristic gestures, vocalizations, and postures (Carpenter 1942b). The basic form of many of these responses and their general relations to arousal level or affective state are almost certainly unlearned (Bernstein and Mason 1962; Jacobsen, Jacobsen, and Yoshioka 1932). On the other hand, their connection with specific stimuli and their effectiveness in controlling and coordinating social activity is probably heavily dependent upon the experience of both sender and receiver. Many illustrations could be given of the essential part played by communi-

cative acts in all phases of social intercourse (Hebb and Thompson 1954). We limit ourselves here to a discussion of the contrasts between feral and socially deprived monkeys. Among sophisticated monkeys a dominant male rarely employs force to attain its goals, but instead uses less direct means, such as staring and threat gestures and vocalizations. If the sender's messages are to be effective, they must, of course, be received by one who knows their meaning, that is, responds to them as signals. The orderly progression of social interaction requires this kind of reciprocity between sender and receiver. Thus, when an experienced male rhesus monkey lightly touches a sophisticated female at the waist she responds by rising, bracing herself, and presenting in the typical female posture. If she does not rise, the male ordinarily will not attempt to mount. Among socially deprived monkeys the picture is entirely different. The male does not always touch the female lightly or in a specific region; instead the vigor and locus of his initial responses may vary considerably, leading to a variable outcome, even with experienced partners. And the male may continue his attempts at coition, even when the female does not assume a receptive posture (Fig. 5).

Conclusion

Primate social development passes through various stages or levels that can be loosely characterized in terms of the dominant forms of activity and the social objects toward which these activities are directed. At a descriptive level it is apparent that the normal trend of development is away from the mother and toward more frequent, varied, and prolonged intercourse with other animals and with the physical environment.

The basis for the initial adjustment to the mother is essentially present at birth in monkeys and apes and this is as it must be if the infant is to survive. Infantile responses initially display a reflexlike quality. Many stimuli are adequate to elicit these responses, and stimulus effectiveness seems to be principally determined by physical characteristics. In nature, of course, these characteristics are embodied in the mother, but the evidence shows that inanimate objects may serve as substitute mothers during infancy. The social responses of infancy are highly motivated as evidenced by their persistence and by the various signs of agitation or distress that appear when suitable objects are not available. In the absence of the natural mother or an appropriate substitute the infant often develops self-clasping, thumb-sucking, and repetitive stereotyped movements as habitual modes of responding.

Ordinarily the focus of infant behavior is the mother. She is sought when the infant is hungry, fatigued, or frightened. The quality of maternal care is surprisingly unimportant in giving the mother her status as a refuge and a source of emotional security, and similar functions may be acquired by inanimate objects that are consistently associated with the performance of infantile social responses. When filial responses have become organized around a specific object or class of objects, we may speak of the formation of an attachment.

Experimental investigations using artificial mothers suggest that contact stimulation is more important than feeding experience in the formation of social attachments, but the mechanism involved in the development of attachments is not yet known. We have suggested in this chapter that arousal level may provide a useful conceptual tool for dealing with the problems of social motivation and social rewards, particularly in the young primate. The evidence indicates that many events which seem to have in common the characteristic of raising the level of arousal increase the likelihood that clinging will occur. Clinging appears to raise the threshold of arousal, and it may therefore serve to reinforce the infant's tie to the mother. The adaptive value of the relationship between clinging and arousal level is clear: Any sudden change in the environment (for example, the appearance of a predator) will cause the infant to seek its mother, who affords protection and is far better equipped than he to cope with the threatening situation.

With the formation of an attachment to the mother favorable conditions are created for social learning. The primate's highly developed abilities for discrimination learning and other complex intellectual activities are exercised in social relations as well as in adjustments to the physical environment. The occasions for social learning are multiplied as the growing individual moves away from the mother and encounters other animals. Thus far, experimental investigations have given relatively little attention to the task of specifying the manner in which experience contributes to normal development. It is evident, however, that social learning begins with the mother and we must assume that one of the primary functions of contacts with other animals is to sharpen, strengthen, or generalize learned behaviors that originate in mother-infant interactions.

The task of bringing the behavior of man and the nonhuman primates into meaningful relationship within a comparative-evolutionary framework has scarcely begun. Broadly viewed, the social development of monkey, ape, and child follows the same basic pattern. For each the mother is the primary source of nourishment, protection, and emotional security, but the details of psychological growth and of the relationship between mother and infant vary systematically in primate phylogeny. Consider mother-infant relations during feeding in man, chimpanzee, and macaque. Human babies must be helped to find the nipple and supported while they nurse. The chimpanzee infant makes fewer demands on the mother but seems to require substantially more

help than does the infant macaque, who can nurse virtually unassisted within a few days after birth. A similar pattern can be seen in other aspects of development, suggesting a trend in which the rate of ontogenetic development, the strength and efficiency of infantile responses, and the nature of maternal care change in complementary fashion. As the period of childhood dependency increases, there is a corresponding change in the need for varied forms of maternal care, and in the ability of the mother to provide such care. These changes may originate in common from an evolutionary process that has culminated in the extreme behavioral plasticity so characteristic of man.

REFERENCES

CLARK, W. E. LE GROS. The Antecedents of Man, Edinburgh, Edinburgh Univ. Press, 1959, *also* Chicago, Quadrangle Books, 1960.

DAVENPORT, RICHARD K., JR. and EMIL W. MENZEL, JR. Stereotyped behavior of the infant chimpanzee, *Arch. Gen. Psychiat.*, 1963, Vol. 8, pp. 99–104.

DE BEER, SIR GAVIN. Embryos and Ancestors (3rd edition), London, Oxford Univ. Press, 1958.

HARLOW, HARRY F., ROBERT O. DODSWORTH, and MARGARET K. HARLOW. Total isolation in monkeys, *Proc. Natl. Acad. Sci., U.S.*, 1965, Vol. 54, pp. 90–97.

HARLOW, HARRY F. and MARGARET KUENNE HARLOW. Social deprivation in monkeys, *Sci. Am.*, 1962, Vol. 207, No. 5, pp. 137–146.

HARLOW, HARRY F. and ROBERT R. ZIMMERMANN. The development of affectional responses in infant monkeys. *Proc. Am. Phil. Soc.*, 1958, Vol. 102, pp. 501–509.

HOCKETT, CHARLES F. Animal "languages" and human language, *Human Biol.*, 1959, Vol. 31, pp. 32–39.

JENSEN, GORDON D. and CHARLES W. TOLMAN. Mother-infant relationship in the monkey, *Macaca nemestrina*: the effect of brief separation and mother-infant specificity, *J. Comp. Physiol. Psychol.*, 1962, Vol. 55, pp. 131–136.

KAUFMAN, I. CHARLES and LEONARD A. ROSENBLUM. Depression in infant monkeys separated from their mothers, *Science,* 1967, Vol. 155, pp. 1030–1031.

KUTTNER, ROBERT. An hypothesis on the evolution of intelligence, *Psychol. Rept.* 1960, Vol. 6, pp. 283–289.

MASON, WILLIAM A. The effects of social restriction on the behavior of rhesus monkeys: I. Free social behavior, *J. Comp. Physiol. Psychol.,* 1960, Vol. 53, pp. 582–589.

MASON, WILLIAM A. The effects of social restriction on the behavior of rhesus monkeys: III. Dominance tests, *J. Comp. Physiol. Psychol.,* 1961, Vol. 54, pp. 694–699.

MASON, WILLIAM A. Social development of rhesus monkeys with restricted social experience, *Percept. Motor Skills,* 1963, Vol. 16, pp. 263–270.

MASON, WILLIAM A. Determinants of social behavior in young chimpanzees, *in* Behavior of Nonhuman Primates (Allen M. Schrier, Harry F. Harlow, and Fred Stollnitz, editors), Vol. 2, New York, Academic Press, 1965, pp. 335–364.

MASON, WILLIAM A. The social development of monkeys and apes, *in* Primate Behavior (Irven DeVore, editor), New York, Holt, Rinehart and Winston, 1965, pp. 514–543.

MASON, WILLIAM A. Motivational aspects of social responsiveness in young chimpanzees, *in* Early Behavior: Comparative and Developmental Approaches (Harold W. Stevenson, Eckhard H. Hess, and Harriet L. Rheingold, editors), New York, Wiley, 1967, pp. 103–126.

MASON, WILLIAM A. and PHILLIP C. GREEN. The effects of social restriction on the behavior of rhesus monkeys: IV. Responses to a novel environment and to an alien species, *J. Comp. Physiol. Psychol.,* 1962, Vol. 55, pp. 363–368.

MASON, WILLIAM A. and JOHN H. HOLLIS. Communication between young rhesus monkeys, *Anim. Behav.,* 1962, Vol. 10, pp. 211–221.

MASON, WILLIAM A. and R. R. SPONHOLZ. Behavior of rhesus monkeys raised in isolation, *J. Psychiat. Res.,* 1963, Vol. 1, pp. 299–306.

MEIER, GILBERT W. Other data on the effects of social isolation during rearing upon adult reproductive behaviour in the rhesus monkey (*Macaca mulatta*), *Anim. Behav.,* 1965, Vol. 13, pp. 228–231.

MEIER, GILBERT W. and RALPH J. BERGER. Development of sleep and wakefulness patterns in the infant rhesus monkey, *Exptl. Neurol.,* 1965, Vol. 12, pp. 257–277.

MENZEL, EMIL W., JR. Patterns of responsiveness in chimpanzees reared through infancy under conditions of environmental restriction, *Psychol. Forsch.,* 1964, Vol. 27, pp. 337–365.

MILLER, R. E., W. F. CAUL, and I. A. MIRSKY. The communication of affects between feral and socially-isolated monkeys. *J. Personality Soc. Psychol.,* 1967, Vol. 7, pp. 231–239.

SCHULTZ, ADOLPH H. Postembryonic changes, *in* Primatologia I. (H. Hofer, A. H. Schultz, and D. Starck, editors), Basel, S. Karger, 1956, pp. 887–959.

SEAY, BILL and HARRY F. HARLOW. Maternal separation in the rhesus monkey, *J. Nerv. Ment. Dis.,* 1965, Vol. 140, pp. 434–441.

SIMPSON, GEORGE GAYLORD. The Meaning of Evolution, New York, New American Library, 1951.

THOMPSON, WILLIAM R., RONALD MELZACK, and T. H. SCOTT. "Whirling behavior" in dogs as related to early experience, *Science,* 1956, Vol. 123, p. 939.

WALLACE, ALFRED RUSSEL. *The Malay Archipelago,* London, Macmillan, 1869, also New York, Dover Publications, 1962.

22 · PRIMATE FIELD STUDIES AND HUMAN EVOLUTION

Phyllis Jay

The relation of field studies of non-human primates to the evolution of human behavior is not often given as clear an exposition as in Jay's contribution below. There can be little doubt that primate field studies are capable of throwing considerable light upon the evolution and nature of human behavior, as well as that of human societies. The increasing number of such studies in recent years has been one of the more gratifying developments in anthropology. There are, however, dangers in extrapolations made from such studies and applied to the behavior of men and societies, as has been noted earlier in this volume.

The fact that man is a *human* primate should cause us to ask ourselves what the criteria are by which we define humanity. Are matters of degree or of kind involved in the differences between human and non-human primates? If it is a matter of degree, where, behaviorally, does the non-human primate leave off and the human primate begin? Or has there been a distinct break, a "quantum leap" as it has sometimes been called, in the behavioral continuity of non-human and human primate? Can one maintain the "quantum leap" without denying the continuity, though the leap is so great that it does in a sense resemble a genuine break? Perhaps these are questions that cannot be answered until we acquire a great deal more knowledge about both non-human and human primates. But, unquestionably, they are the questions which will guide much of the future research in primate ethology.

Among Jay's concluding remarks she states that "At earlier stages the individual had relatively few social and emotional bonds in comparison with the extent of commitment to others that society attempts to create in us today." The reader can best evaluate this statement by asking whether field studies on non-human primates and on foodgathering-hunting peoples justify such a conclusion, or offer the slightest support for such a statement. Jay also thinks that lack of concern with other peoples has an evolutionary background, and that this may prove to be a lethal deficiency. The question is, granting that such a lack of concern is widespread, does it really have an evolutionary, a biological origin? Does man really have a biological heritage, as Jay says, that disposes him to be concerned with relatively few people and

to be aggressive? As John Hurrell Crook so wisely points out elsewhere in this volume,[1] ". . . ethological concepts faultily transposed to alien contexts could serve as tools in the presentation of ideological arguments and in the formation of political points of view.[2] . . . The importance of ethology to human behaviour study probably lies not in 'inferences to man' but rather in the comparison of exploratory models."[3]

Introduction

. . . The importance of our practical understanding of the primates and the use of primates in biomedical research is fully documented by the references in *Index Medicus*. Here the concern is with the more philosophical questions of seeking to understand the origins of human nature, of seeing how we differ from nonhuman primates, and of speculating on the causes and history of some of these differences.

This inquiry into human evolution is tentative, and it touches only a very few facets of behavior. In the following pages most of the suggested history of development for specific behavior patterns has to be acknowledged either as only a partial appraisal—a glimpse into what may have occurred—or as reconstructed history that must be stated in terms of probability. Selection is for whole patterns of successful behavior, but, unfortunately for the investigator, many activities vitally important in the way of life of a species are not reflected in the fossils. A great deal can be learned from the bones that comprise our fossil record, but the life of ancestral primates comprised much more than the obvious functions

SOURCE: Phyllis Jay, "Primate Field Studies and Human Evolution," in *Primates: Studies in Adaptation and Variability*, ed. Phyllis C. Jay. Copyright © 1968 by Holt, Rinehart and Winston, Inc. Reprinted by permission of Holt, Rinehart and Winston, Inc.
[1] See p. 284, this volume.
[2] John Hurrell Crook, "Introduction—Social Behaviour and Ethology," in J. H. Crook, ed., *Social Behaviour in Birds and Mammals* (London & New York: Academic Press), 1970, pp. xxi.
[3] *Ibid.*, p. xxxiii.

of these bony parts. For example, a certain kind of roughened surface on a fossilized ischium indicates merely that the primate had ischial callosities. But by looking at how living primates with these callosities behave, it is possible to infer that in all likelihood the ancient animal slept sitting up rather than on its side or in a nest (Washburn 1957). This may seem trivial, but when many such clues to behavior are gathered and collated, the total picture of an animal's way of life fills out to a closer approximation of what it must have been.

Knowledge of the comparative anatomy, physiology, and behavior of living primates, including man, is added to the study of the sequence of fossils and the tools associated with them. Modern human behavior is the result of thousands of generations of change, and today's patterns are the most recent in a long sequence of successful behaviors. Our ancestors were not the same as living primates, but the rich variability of behavior of modern monkeys and apes makes it possible to reconstruct the most probable patterns of behavior of related forms in the past.

The reconstruction of some behavior patterns (aggression, language and the brain) has been discussed elsewhere (see also, Washburn 1963). Here we consider several other complexes of behavior that leave no marks on fossils—the use of space or land by a social group, female sexual receptivity (estrus among monkey and ape females), and primate tool use. Several closely related aspects of behavior that are very important to normal primate life (for example, play) are mentioned briefly.

Difficulties and Potentialities of Reconstructions

Animals' use of space and female sexual receptivity are very different kinds of behaviors, and are examples of widely dissimilar problems in the reconstruction of behavior history. It is not pos-sible to reconstruct behavior in general, but only with respect to very clearly defined specific problems. If a behavior varies greatly among the living monkeys and apes, then reconstructing the ancestral behavior is extremely difficult. Group size is an example of an aspect of life that is exceedingly unamenable to reconstruction for very early stages of human evolution. Information about living nonhuman primates is far more useful in answering questions about the use of land and female sexual receptivity than for supporting speculations about the composition and organization of groups of early man. Evidence from living hunting and gathering societies suggests that the size of early man's groups was small. Because group organization is very different among chimpanzees, gorillas, and gibbons, the problem of relating these patterns to those of early man is correspondingly difficult. The generalization emerges that all monkeys and apes are social, as is man, and this fundamental aspect of human behavior must be deeply rooted in our primate past. (The importance of this has been discussed by Hamburg 1963.)

There are exceptions, then, to the immediate usefulness of reconstructing behavior patterns, but the method is still of great value if it is possible to demonstrate reasons for the exceptions. Consider the question of whether our ancestors slept in trees or on the ground. A great majority of monkeys and apes sleep in trees, and many species spend most of their days in trees. Some gorillas sleep on the ground and can do so with relative impunity because they are tremendously strong and large (Schaller 1963). Whether or not they could continue to sleep on the ground if there were lions in the same area is another question that cannot be answered yet. If our ancestors were larger than gorillas they may have slept on the ground, but this "if" is contraindicated by the fossil record. It is much more probable that until our ancestors were protected by weapons they slept in trees. Some baboons sleep on the ground or on rocks, but only in areas where there are few or no trees. Kummer discusses the adaptation of hamadryas baboons to such desert conditions, but this is a very special case that does not modify speculation about the savanna- and forest-living ancestors of man. The behaviors of the gorilla and the hamadryas baboon have no direct implications for reconstructing conditions of human evolution since there is no evidence that our ancestors were either giants (pace Weidenreich!) or desert adapted.

There is a simple logic for the reconstruction of behavior of our ancestors, and it can be stated briefly. First, there are behavior patterns that distinguish man from the nonhuman primates. Some of these behaviors that are not present in man are universal among the nonhuman primates living in natural conditions, and because of their presence among monkeys and apes there is every reason to suppose that these behaviors were characteristic of our ancestors. Where human behavior patterns differ from those of nonhuman primates, if the reason for changes from the probable ancestral condition can be shown, then this supports the likelihood that the reconstructed condition is accurate. If the condition is variable and is characteristic of only a few kinds of nonhuman primates, the exceptions must be shown to fit into situations that have no place in human evolution. If this is possible, then even these variable behavior patterns may be of use in reconstruction, as contrasts are themselves reconstructable. New data from field studies, more archeological information, additional fossils, and more accurate dates for past events will make it possible to analyze other behavior categories and to reconstruct much more of our ancestors' ways of life. If our purpose is to understand events leading to the differentiation of man and ape, this kind of information is absolutely necessary.

Behavior reconstruction is not limited to probing into man's past. There are studies of the behavior of related macaque species, and it should soon be possible to ask questions about the evo-lution of behavior patterns of some of these closely related species. Eventually this should be possible for species of the genus *Papio*, if it remains a separate genus from *Macaca*, or of still more *Macaca* species if the two genera are combined. However, any analysis of the phylogeny of behavior patterns is not practical until the limits of variability in these patterns, and more of the causes or determinates of variation are known.

Specific Problems in Reconstruction

One of the most important factors in primate life is the relationship of a social group to the area in which it lives. However this area is designated —as territory or as home range—it is correlated with food, water, sleeping locations, and escape routes, all of which are necessary to the daily life and the secure world of the individual. The very nature of this area is a powerful factor in determining group size, frequency of contact among groups, and the relationship of the primate group to other species. The total amount of land one group occupies varies from a few acres as for gibbons and the *Callicebus* monkey to an intermediate few square miles for chimpanzees (Goodall 1965) and gorillas (Schaller 1965), to more than 15 square miles for savanna-living baboons (Hall and DeVore 1965). It is not always quite this simple to generalize for an entire genus, and it may be somewhat misleading in several instances. For example, troops of primarily forest-living baboons occupy smaller areas than do those in the open plains (Rowell 1966). But in general larger areas tend to be characteristic of large ground-living forms, and it appears that the smaller the primate and the more arboreal its way of life, the more likely it is that the area it uses will be correspondingly small. There are exceptions, but in general there is a high positive correlation between spending most of the time on the ground in open areas and having the largest space for group life.

As long as our ancestors were arboreal apes, they probably lived in small ranges, as do all the contemporary arboreal primates. When our ancestors came to the ground their range may have been considerably extended, but perhaps to no larger a space than that used by modern chimpanzees and gorillas. These apes utilize very small areas when compared with human hunters who require something on the order of 100 times the area per individual that is required by an ape. This great difference appears to be purely human, a product of the human way of life, and it is not even suggested in the behaviors of the nonhuman primates.

If Washburn and Lancaster are correct in suggesting that the causes for the change from the "usual" primate pattern to the human pattern of territorial behavior are tool use, carrying, and hunting, then the change can be dated. Men of the Middle Pleistocene time hunted large animals; the tools they used were made from selected kinds of stone that do not occur in all areas. This indicates that social groups of early man must have occupied large areas, since evidence on contemporary hunters and gatherers demonstrates that small areas will not support hunters of large game (Lee 1965). It is a great deal more difficult to reconstruct the behavior of Early Pleistocene *Australopithecus* (*Australopithecus* in a general sense). Some stones found in deposits with these fossils appear to have been brought from considerable distances, but this has not yet been determined exactly (Brain, personal communication). Nor has the controversy been resolved as to whether the *Australopithecus* were responsible for bringing to their living sites the bones that evidence consumption of large animals. Studying the effect of predators on bone remains of their kills and then comparing the results with bones found with early man would make it possible to determine whether it is likely that man at this time hunted large animals for food. If he did, it indicates that, like more recent hunters of large animals, he required large areas where he could hunt freely.

Man's exceptional behavior in his occupation of large areas, this variation from an apparently basic primate way of life, is a pattern of behavior that evolved late in human history. What has been reconstructed has important implications. Monkeys and apes have special senses very similar to those of humans, and this indicates that they are at least able to perceive similar aspects of the environment. Monkeys can easily outrun a man on the ground for short distances, but, nevertheless, nonhuman primate groups limit their activities to highly selected portions within relatively small areas of land. Barring catastrophe or some lesser but still disruptive event, the nonhuman social group lives its entire life in a small area. It is not that they cannot, but that they do not leave the area to investigate the surrounding world. Their world view does not incorporate even the exploration of preferred fruit trees that may be in full view beyond the habitual area of use. There may be reasons for this failure to explore actively; these adjacent areas may be occupied by larger, stronger, or more dominant groups that are hostile to encroachment on their land, but even when no danger appears to threaten, exploratory behavior is strictly limited. The fact remains that living in a small space limits the experience of the environment and the social contacts, and also affects the patterns of interaction among groups. This has substantial effects upon the spread of pathogens, adaptation, and populations genetics, each of which depends upon the numbers of individuals that do change from one group to another.

It is a remarkable aspect of human nature that man's attitude toward his environment is so different from that of his ancestors. The study of contemporary primates makes it possible to see how unique man is, and in turn allows the reconstruction of the most probable ancestral condition.

Estrus

A second example of reconstructing a behavior that cannot be observed directly in the fossil record is female sexual receptivity. Reproductive patterns have not been described for all species of nonhuman primates, but in species observed living under natural conditions the female is sexually receptive only during relatively brief periods of time. In many species (of genera such as *Papio, Macaca, Cercocebus,* and *Pan*), coincident with sexual receptivity, females are subject to physical changes in coloration and/or swelling of the area around the anal and vaginal regions. Other species, such as the Indian langur (*Presbytis entellus*), lack obvious physical signs of receptivity, and the female signals her willingness to copulate by specific gestures or sounds. In most kinds of monkeys adult males seldom, if ever, copulate with a female unless she is in estrus. When additional species are observed some variation from this pattern of clear receptivity or nonreceptivity may be found, especially among the genus *Cercopithecus*. It is also possible that in some species copulations may occur during a longer period of the female's estrous cycle than the few days prior to, during, and immediately after ovulation, or in the first or second month of pregnancy as has been observed for rhesus monkeys in north India (Lindburg, personal communication). Copulations have been observed at different times in a female's cycle in many other-than-normal situations (in cages or colonies), but the references here are only to free-ranging monkeys and apes.

Not all monkey or ape females are sexually receptive for the same amount of time, but when compared with the human, the nonhuman female primate is sexually receptive for a very small part of her adult life, and her periods of receptivity are hormonally rather than directly socially determined. There is undoubtedly a relationship between social stress and the suppression of normal estrous cycles, and it is possible that females may be facilitated in displaying estrous periods when placed with other females in estrus. There are apt to be striking changes in a female's behavior during estrous periods. She is more active and aggressive, and seeks the attentions of adult males, often including the ones she may have avoided when she was not sexually active. Not only are some social relationships at least temporarily altered by the stresses of increased activity, but when many adult females in a group are receptive at the same time there also may be substantial changes in the behavior of the group as a whole (DeVore 1962; Jay 1965a). Some of these changes are alterations in the frequency of grooming, in patterns of foraging, and in intensity as well as frequency of aggressiveness within the group.

The chimpanzee, so like man in many respects, is very dissimilar with regard to female sexual behavior. Goodall (1965) describes as many as twenty males consorting with a single female chimpanzee when she is in estrus. There is no mistaking when a chimpanzee female is sexually receptive because she usually has a swelling, sometimes immense and very bright pink, around the perianal region. Goodall suggests that an obvious function of a large sexual swelling is to signal males, near and far, that the female is in estrus (Van Lawick-Goodall 1966). When a female is in estrus she is surrounded by a much noisier and more boisterous group than when she is not receptive. Males congregate in her vicinity and follow her [more closely] than at any other time, sometimes threatening if she tries to move away without them.

On the basis of our present knowledge of living nonhuman primates it appears that periodic sexual behavior is associated with an estrous cycle, and is characteristic of females living under natural conditions (Lancaster and Lee 1965). Because this cycle is typical of the living non-human primates it is most likely that our female ancestors had a similar sexual pattern, and the intriguing question remains as to why natural selection favored the loss of estrus from our behavior. A great advantage of this loss might have been the furthering of a consistent and orderly social system in which there were no sudden periodic increases in tension and aggressiveness because of sexual activity among group adults. At least, this may have been an advantage as far as human evolution is concerned. Loss of estrus may also have had significant effects on mother-infant relationships; it is possible that with fewer potentially traumatic aggressive interactions when the mother consorted with adult males, the infant experiences a calmer period of early development. The evolution of human society depended on the evolution of a physiology that permitted order (loss of estrus, reduction of rage, and the control of many behaviors) coupled with adaptive social customs that depended on the order. The advantages of controlling rage and sex are apparent when the behavior of the nonhuman primates is observed.

Speculations about the development of the human family all presuppose that estrous behavior disappeared and that females of whatever time level is under consideration had a physiology very similar to that of modern females. This assumption is in spite of general basic similarities of reproductive physiology among primate females. It has been suggested that it would have been difficult for early man to maintain a small family group if the adult female's sexual behavior was based on an estrous cycle. However, the gibbon family or group is composed of an adult male, an adult female, and young, and yet adult female gibbons have estrous cycles. Thus the gibbon might seem an exception that disproves the generalization that estrus is incompatible with the

small group, but there are reasons for the gibbon's ability to live this way. Adult gibbons are very apt to be hostile to each other, especially to others of the same sex, and as the young mature they are gradually forced out of the small social group in which they are born. Sexual behavior is infrequent, and it is certainly possible, even likely, that the sex drive among gibbons is far less strong than among monkeys, and it is definitely much less than among chimpanzees. The gibbon has developed a small-group social organization in which the adult female's sexual behavior is regulated by an estrous cycle of receptivity and nonreceptivity, and the male is probably much less sexually active than most other apes and the monkeys. The complex of gibbon behavior that allows small groups is very unlike man's most probable ancestral behavior.

Field observations indicate that estrous behavior can cause problems even in a group composed of many animals, but these problems are less serious if the intensity of estrous behavior is reduced, or, in addition, if the sexual drive of the males is reduced at least during part of the year. Estrus as a set of behaviors cannot be considered apart from the context that includes the organization of male behavior. There are alternative solutions to the problem of estrus in the small group, but the observation of the apparent exceptional sexual pattern in the gibbon has stimulated investigation that may lead to a better comprehension of the role of estrus in human evolution by a closer look at the possible similarities and differences between the types of small group that characterized both primates.

The female primate and her offspring form an enduring social group (Sade 1965; Goodall 1965) that is important in the daily life of each individual member as reflected by preferred grooming patterns and spatial arrangements. The origin of the human family required only the addition of a male, with cooperation and the division of labor between the male and the female. It appears that the female-young nucleus is far older and more fundamental than what we know as a human family.

Tool Use

Few topics are more interesting to the anthropologist than the evolution of man's uniquely skillful ability to make and to use tools. In his paper, "Tool-using Performances as Indicators of Behavioral Adaptability," Hall effectively interpreted information on use of tools and object manipulation by monkeys and apes to gain insights into the development of human tool-using efficiency. It is a clear statement on an aspect of nonhuman primate behavior that has stimulated a great deal of speculation and generated many theories (Lancaster, in press; Washburn and Jay, in press). Very restricted object use has been described for a variety of animals from insects to mammals, and as one might expect there are some kinds of nonhuman primates in this growing list. Recent observation by the Van Lawicks (1967) of Egyptian vultures' throwing stones to break open ostrich eggs suggests that we still may not have completed the roster of animals capable of manipulating objects, for whatever reason. It is notable, however, that if a species uses tools, it is usually only one kind of tool, such as the cactus spines that a particular kind of finch uses for getting grubs from underneath bark.

Almost all tool use by vertebrates (with the exception of man) has to do with different aspects of either feeding behavior or nest preparation. With rare exceptions, such as elephants' using sticks to rub themselves, the use of sticks, leaves, or other objects in self-grooming is virtually absent in animals (with the exception of the chimpanzee). Aggressive displays during which objects are handled, thrown, or manipulated in some way are observed only among monkeys, apes, and man.

One of Hall's major points is essential to the understanding of tool use by animals: an animal that uses objects as tools is not necessarily especially intelligent. In the example given earlier, a species of finch that uses a cactus spine to spear grubs otherwise out of reach is not necessarily any more intelligent than another kind of finch; it has merely evolved a behavior pattern rather than a morphological structure to increase feeding efficiency and the variety of its foods. This interpretation is of special importance to an understanding of the relationship of tools to intelligence and brain size in man's history.

It is crucial in evaluating an item as a tool to know exactly what the animal does with the object. One stricture Hall followed in his collection of examples of tool-using was to consider as data only those incidents observed under natural conditions. Anyone who has watched a monkey or ape in a zoo or circus knows that it is relatively simple to encourage several species to handle objects, and with training many can be made to perform quite complicated tasks. Equally familiar are the anecdotes and stories of tool use by animals told by travelers and natives which either they or others have observed. The fanciful and fantastic are quickly sorted from the more plausible, but sources must be reliable and the situations in which the actions occurred must be natural if adaptive actions are to be distinguished from activity produced under atypical and unnatural conditions. It is crucial to be able to make these distinctions because monkeys, and apes especially, are capable of many behaviors not representative of their normal patterns of behavior. Learning certain kinds of tasks, such as the use of objects, is easier for some types of monkeys than others, and it is almost inevitable for chimpanzees. A long list of what monkeys and apes do under all conditions shows only that some kinds of nonhuman primates can and do learn manipulative patterns easily. What such a list does not tell us is the relationship of this ability to the biology and survival of the species, except to suggest that it is doubtlessly useful.

According to Hall, observational learning among nonhuman primates is much less common than one would imagine, and, predictably, is highly variable. Whether a monkey or ape does learn by observing others perform depends to a large degree on the particular action or behavior and on the situation in which learning occurs. The normal context for observational learning, the one in which these abilities must have been organized, is the social group. This is the environment of maximum security and close association, in which individuals are surrounded by familiar animals and close emotional ties. Besides differences in habitats and social tradition, other factors are relevant to variation in the ability of primates to learn to use tools. The most important may be a basic biological limitation of the ability to learn, and this probably varies from one species to another, as suggested by the tremendous differences in abilities and tendencies to manipulate objects. As mentioned earlier, part of this variation in ability is probably an artifact of species specializations, rather than a mirror of actual differences in intelligence among different kinds of animals.

The human observer's interest and concern with his own evolution and his awareness of the way in which modern man uses tools has biased descriptions and interpretations of monkey and ape behavior that appears similar to that of man. Of all tool use investigators (for example, Kortlandt 1962; Kortlandt and Kooij 1963), Hall was the first to recognize, on the basis of the evidence available to him, that object manipulation by monkeys was limited to agonistic displays. Such displays are rare in other animals. It was only with more observations, following those that Hall knew, that we discovered additional examples of monkey tool use for getting food.

The most elaborate and frequent use of objects as tools by any nonhuman primate has been reported for the chimpanzee (Goodall 1965; Van Lawick-Goodall, personal communication). Not only do chimpanzees termite [1] with grass stems and twigs, but they also wipe themselves with leaves, chew leaves to use as sponges, pry with sticks, throw stones; and they will undoubtedly be observed to use objects in yet other ways.

It is possible that long-term studies of chimpanzee groups living elsewhere than in the Gombe Reserve will reveal significant variations in the range of chimpanzee tool behavior. Eventually we will understand the ontogeny of these abilities. All chimpanzees may not use the same tools, or even any one type of tool in the same way, since differences in habitat could influence the choice of sticks, grasses, and other objects. Variations in chimpanzee tool-using behavior among different populations, is unknown because Van Lawick-Goodall's analysis is the only long study on habituated animals in which this kind of information could be gathered. Other chimpanzee studies are under way and will surely provide much needed comparative information (particularly the Japan Monkey Centre's research in Tanzania and Uganda; Shigeru and Toyoshima 1961, 1962; and Itani and Kawamura, personal communication).

Of the reliably described displays by chimpanzees (Goodall 1965), by gorillas (Schaller 1963, 1966), and by orangutans (Harrisson 1962), surely the most dramatic and impressive display with the use of objects is that of the chimpanzee. When the animals, especially adult males with fur erect, dash from one place to another, jumping and running, hooting and screaming, flinging branches, and even rolling huge rocks. Only slightly less impressive, at least to the observer, is the gorilla's display when the ape runs, calls, gestures, and, sometimes, pulls grass or other

---

[1] To "termite" is to fish for ants with a twig introduced through a hole in an anthill.—[A. M.]

plants and throws them as he runs (Schaller 1963). Many species of monkeys when excited during agonistic interactions with other monkeys or toward a human will shake branches vigorously by jumping up and down on them (for example, the red spider monkey, Carpenter 1935; baboons, Hall 1962b; Hall and DeVore 1965; rhesus, Hinde and Rowell 1962).

There are some striking features common to these examples. In each, the animal is very effective in making itself appear as large, fierce, and noisy as possible by erecting its hair, gesturing, and calling. When the animal jumps on a branch or throws it (and in rarer instances when a stone is thrown), the display is just that much more effective and impressive to the beholder. This is especially true if the object happens to fall nearby or hits the observer, as when the missile is excrement.

In a recent field study of the South American cebus monkey in Colombia, Thorington (personal communication) watched these animals manipulate twigs by breaking them off and peeling away the bark, and then use them to pick out small insects below the bark of larger trees. Object manipulation is part of their biology and a normal part of their lives in the wild. It is not surprising that these monkeys are well known for their manipulative abilities in captivity, but it is manipulation for obtaining food and not for making or using tools agonistically as in the sense of weapons.

A most important point emerges from Hall's paper, and is touched upon by Washburn and Hamburg. Our confusion of the nonhuman primates' object-in-display type of behavior with man's tool use in the sense of weaponry has impaired our thinking about monkey and ape tool use in general. This had to be made explicit before it was possible to analyze display behaviors and to understand their relevance to the interpretation of the evolution of human tool use.

If using objects in agonistic display is looked

at as a behavioral category we may be closer to answering two questions that have been asked over and over in primate research. First, why didn't efficient and persistent tool use evolve in other primates besides man, and, second, what were the important factors in human evolution that produced man's unique complex use of tools? To humans, tool use has such tremendous advantages in enhancing life that we tend to assume it is so highly adaptive that it would have been selected for whatever and whenever it occurred.

First consider the apparent lack of tool use among living nonhuman primates. Hall recognized that most of the monkey and ape behavior that had been called tool use was either an artifact of captive conditions (where animals lived in greatly impoverished social and physical environments and then were given objects to handle), or an example drawn from natural conditions in which animals were using objects in display. Anyone who has seen a monkey or ape, and particularly a chimpanzee, use a stick or stone in display knows how much more effective the display is than when the animal does not use objects. In most nonhuman primate displays, if the object is thrown rather than merely shaken, it usually does not seem to be accurately aimed. Because the goal does not seem to be to hit the person or animal toward whom the display is directed, this strongly suggests that there has been a lack of natural selection for effective tools and skills; that is, for the ability to choose more suitable branches or for more accurate aiming. There is excellent evidence indicating a high percentage of aimed throwing among chimpanzees (Goodall 1964; Van Lawick-Goodall, personal communication), which is consistent with the chimpanzee's great adeptness in tool using in general in contrast to other nonhuman primates.

Human tools may have developed from several sources, including the use of objects in economic activities and the use of objects in display (Washburn 1965). It is easy to see that the use of objects to increase food-getting efficiency would have been strongly advantageous in the course of human evolution. Similarly, if an opponent or assailant was actually hit with a stone or stick that had been hurtled or swung in display, and this situation occurred many thousands of times over a long period of time, there would have been that many discoveries that actually hitting with an object was much more effective than mere display. It is not difficult to imagine that these might have been the routes via which man evolved efficient tool use for economic purposes and for weaponry.

Additional fossil discoveries (L. S. B. and M. D. Leakey), new methods of dating (Fleischer, Leakey, Price and Walker 1965), and results of primate field studies have changed our thinking on the evolution of man's tool use. New radiogenic dates for the duration of the Pleistocene indicate a long span of time with little change in the biology of the tool-makers. Now the estimate is of approximately two million years of tool use prior to the time when hand-axe cultures developed and *Homo erectus* was present over a large area of the Old World. This means that small-brained man used pebble tools for at least four times as many years as in all the subsequent stages during which culture developed relatively rapidly and man's present biology evolved.

There are still unanswered questions as to why more effective tool use did not develop among some monkeys and apes during the millions of years when man's precursors were developing their skills. At least one aspect of the biological basis for the evolution of skillful object use is apparent among living primates. Species that throw and handle objects in the same way do so because they are similar in the anatomical structure of the arm and trunk (Grand 1964). The actions that are easiest and most natural for men and apes are difficult or impossible for monkeys. To the apes, which walk on their knuckles, underhand grasping and throwing are easy move-

ments—quite similar to those of walking. For a baboon or a macaque, animals that normally walk on all fours, it is very difficult and most inefficient to pick up an object by hand and throw it. To toss or throw, a quadrupedal animal places his hand with the palm down on the object, and then trys to propel it forward with the same motion he uses when he walks. This is awkward and exceedingly inefficient. However, the differences between a chimpanzee and a baboon in manipulating items by hand are functions not only of very different forelimb structure, but also of differences in the brain itself, with consequently dissimilar aptitudes or abilities to learn to manipulate objects in different ways. Some evidence suggests that specific motor patterns important in using objects as tools may be determined by the genetic heredity of a species (Schiller 1957; Chance 1960).

In summary, the outstanding difference between nonhuman and human manufacture and use of tools is *skill* (Oakley 1954), and the biology that makes skill possible. Many primates use tools, usually in the context of feeding, whereas only a few species use tools or objects in agonistic displays and these are limited almost exclusively to apes and men. Tool use per se does not indicate intelligence, as evidenced by man's history when for a long time his ancestors had small brains and yet used tools as part of their way of life. It was not until late in the Pleistocene that there were large-brained hominids and complex tool traditions, and it was at this time that the transition to skillful use of tools occurred.

If Lancaster (1968) and Geschwind (1964) are correct in their estimates of the amount of brain necessary for language, the use of tools long preceded the emergence of human language. Among the other questions that may be raised relating to populations of early Pleistocene hominids (the *Australopithecus*, in a general sense) and the tools that have been found with them is that perhaps not all fossil populations of early man used tools in the same manner or abundance and maybe not all populations had tools. Variability in early hominid patterns of culture has not been determined. Comparative information is lacking, but it is possible that there are substantial differences in the use of tools by modern chimpanzee populations.

The incomplete fossil record has given rise to many controversies as to the taxonomic position and importance of certain isolated fossils from early stages of man's development. The discovery of fragments from the Miocene (Leakey 1967), again emphasizes the question of when tools became associated with man's ancestors. The frustration of having only vague notions of the relationships of different major fossil forms is increased by the dearth of finds in the same locations. Awareness of the dimensions of the range of morphological and behavioral differences among and within species of living primates should help in the assessment of the taxonomic status of certain fossils in the human record. More information on closely related species and subspecies living together in the same or adjacent areas, and on their relationships may suggest adaptations of populations in the past.

Washburn and Hamburg (1968) have discussed some of the implications of tool development on changing selection pressures—for increase in some parts of the brain, decrease in the tooth-fighting complex, and likely new patterns of behavior. With the origin of human language there was probably a reduction in aggressive behavior and displays in general, as complex and especially long-distance signals were developed. After initial behavioral changes, the biological basis and physical structures of early hominids must have changed, or the social and behavioral aspects of these changes would not have continued. Indeed, it is artificial to separate the interaction of structure and behavior through a long and complicated history of development.

In contrast to our interest in tool use, the im-

portance of some other categories of behavior is not always apparent, particularly those activities not considered especially significant in human life. Willingness to recognize important categories of behavior different from those that have concerned traditional anthropology should stimulate innovation in the analysis of human behavior. Appreciating the significance of an activity to monkeys and apes should enable a more accurate assessment of its possible importance to man, and although present ideas of human categories of activity will not be replaced, certain behaviors will be given greater emphasis.

It is not difficult to recognize general categories of behavior for a species of nonhuman primate, even after a relatively short period of observation if the observer is familiar with the behavior of related species. With longer study the list of categories increases in length, and, presumably, in accuracy. The rhesus monkey (*Macaca mulatta*) is one example of a species that has been studied under a variety of conditions, free-ranging and captive, and for which there are relatively complete inventories of behavioral repertoire (Hinde and Rowell 1962; Rowell and Hinde 1962; and Altmann 1962a). The pigtail monkey (*M. nemestrina*) and bonnet macaques (*M. radiata*) have been described by Kaufman and Rosenblum (1966). It is one thing to recognize and describe units of behavior, but quite another to estimate their importance. Until behaviors are observed in a natural situation it is not always clear just what problems most warrant investigation. Field studies offer the great advantages of opportunities to discern relationships of biology to social behavior and to see the meaning of the interrelationship of description and experiment.

Play is one of the most important activities of young primates; it is an activity that is easily recognized, but it has received less than due attention. The significance of play among humans has been overlooked, although it must be a category of overwhelming importance in the behavior of our young. The age-graded behaviors of non-human primates develop in a maturational sequence that appears to be adjusted to the particular species. This sequence of events is an obvious part of the process of acquiring adaptation or organization of behavior in the life span of the individual. The importance to the individual of a peer group continues into adult life when patterns of social dominance established years earlier may influence his eventual status and status changes. Play as motivation for learning has yet to be investigated systematically, but field studies leave no doubt that this will be very fruitful.

The size of play groups varies among species according to total group size. In those species in which the social group consists of only a pair of adults, as among the gibbons and *Callicebus*, the young peer group is almost, if not completely, nonexistent. In contrast, in the macaque group, which is usually much larger, there are at least several young born each year and group play is almost assured for each individual.

The play behavior of chimpanzee and man is remarkably more complex than that of monkey, with man being the most manipulative and object oriented of all primates in his play. Surely it is more than a coincidence that the nonhuman primate taxonomically closest to man according to many investigators (Goodman 1963; Klinger *et al.* 1963; Sarich and Wilson 1966; Simpson 1966) is also the most manipulative, exploratory, and similar to man in play. The range of variation in play form and games among chimpanzees is second only to man.

Diversity of object use by adults could be predicted by watching the play and investigation of young chimpanzees. Object manipulation is an important part of investigating the environment, and sticks and twigs are frequently used to poke and pry, long before any ability to termite appears. That an animal practices in play the skills and activities he needs when grown is of tremen-

dous evolutionary importance. Infant and juvenile stages of development last much longer in the chimpanzee than similar phases do in monkeys, and it is reasonable to suppose that the chimpanzee has correspondingly more to learn. This supposition is supported by the richness of adult chimpanzee social behavior when compared with that of any monkey, and, for that matter, to that of the other apes, although a great deal more is known about several species of monkeys than about any ape other than the chimpanzee.

Comparison of chimpanzee and baboon play would be very revealing, especially comparison of the amount and kinds of attention paid to manipulatable items of the environment. Most, if not all, young primates spend a great deal of time playing, and a comparative study of the patterns and duration of play should be highly correlated with adult behaviors. Infancy is the period during which a young animal can "afford" to make mistakes because he is tolerated to an extent that he never again enjoys. He is protected by his elders and led by the group, and during those early weeks or months his life is sheltered by generally permissive adults. This is a crucial period for the development of social skills, and laboratory experiment has demonstrated that if certain experiences are not part of the animal's early life, the damage may be irreparable or very difficult to correct later in life (Harlow 1962; Harlow and Harlow 1962; Mason 1961*a*, 1961*b*, 1961*c*, 1963; Mason and Green 1962).

When contrasted with chimpanzee play, in which object manipulation is a major feature, monkey play involves predominantly locomotor patterns such as wrestling and chasing with other young. The infant is soon adept at moving quickly and accurately, responding to the cues of adults and especially to those cues that signal threat or danger. Little, if any, attention is directed to play with objects or to manipulation of many items in the environment. Elements of adult gesture and vocalization appear gradually in the repertoire of the infant and juvenile, and with practice they are displayed appropriately and skillfully.

The monkey or ape appears free to experiment and express itself in many ways during play, and, with the exception of preventing the young from disturbing the peace and repose of the adults, and protecting them from harm by predators or other stronger young, the adult nonhuman primate appears to allow the young free rein. Play is of such great importance to the development of monkeys and apes that it is necessary to ask how appropriate it is for us to shape and control the play activities of our young.

Conclusion

The analysis of modern monkey and ape behavior has made it possible to reconstruct some of the early stages of human development. The later phases of man's development may require a different approach. Several authors have assumed that social evolution has progressed too rapidly in recent time for biological evolution to keep pace (Hamburg 1963; Washburn and Hamburg, 1968). If this is true, the phases of man's nature that seem unadaptive today should give us clues to the social systems of times past.

Our ancestors lived in small hunting and gathering societies for many thousands of generations, and the risks and problems of survival must have been quite different from those that confront us today. The life span was much shorter and conditions of survival were more critical and challenging than they are now. It was under those early conditions of life that human nature evolved to meet the rigorous physical demands of daily existence. Patterns of behavior were fitted to these circumstances, and not to the conditions of the crowded, technical society that we live in today.

Man has evolved to think in terms of short intervals of time, short distances, and very small numbers of people. At earlier stages the individual had relatively few social and emotional bonds in comparison with the extent of commitment to others that society attempts to create in us today. It will help if there is an understanding of our apparent lack of concern with the problems of today's world, and our great lack of capacity to be moved by events and conditions that are a long distance away, that happened in the past, or that lie years in the future. This obviously has created and perpetuates problems of relationships in a world where most populations are potentially interacting, in which great distances are traveled quickly and frequently, and in which technology is capable of effecting drastic and irreversible change. The face-to-face group is becoming a large portion of the world as transportation and communication improve, and thus reduce distances. Lack of concern with other peoples may prove to be a lethal deficiency, but to interpret our behavior it is necessary to be aware of its probable evolutionary background. Our deep-rooted preoccupation with the *now* may help us to understand our heedless destruction of natural resources, the pollution of air, and the apparent difficulty of combining ecological and esthetic senses in our pursuit of an expanding technology and ecology. Profound changes in our lives and surroundings have been, for the first time perhaps, rapid enough for one generation to be aware of them. In efforts to increase communication and concern among peoples of widely distant lands, and in attempts to control the potentially destructive tendencies of modern man we must recognize his biological and social heritage that disposes him to be concerned with relatively few people and to be aggressive. With this knowledge we can be more realistic in our efforts to live together in peace.

In summary, the theory of natural selection requires that evolution be understood in terms of successful behaviors. Since behavior does not fossilize, human evolution can best be appreciated through imaginative reconstruction of the long sequence of behavior patterns that separates man from his ape ancestors. To reconstruct patterns of the past requires both a fossil record and field studies of contemporary primates. Since man differs from all living monkeys and apes in many ways, these studies provide the basis not only for reconstructing changes that have taken place in the evolution of modern ways of behavior, but also for an understanding of the apparent exceptions to the general patterns for primates.

This chapter has had to remain tentative and suggestive. It will be some time before we can write with authority on the details of the development of man's behavior, but that time will arrive sooner if we appreciate fully the usefulness of nonhuman primate behavior in gaining insight into our present lives.

REFERENCES

ALTMANN, S. A. 1962. "A Field Study of the Sociobiology of Rhesus Monkeys, *Macaca mulatta*," *Ann. N.Y. Acad. Sci.*, 102 (2):338–435.

CARPENTER, C. R. 1935. "Behavior of Red Spider Monkeys in Panama," *J. Mammal.*, 16:171–180.

CHANCE, M. R. A. 1960. "Köhler's Chimpanzees—How Did They Perform?" *Man*, 60:130–135.

DE VORE, I. 1962. "The Social Behavior and Organization of Baboon Troops," unpublished Ph.D. thesis, University of Chicago.

FLEISCHER, R. L., L. S. B. LEAKEY, P. B. PRICE, and R. M. WALKER. 1965. "Fisson Track Dating of Bed I, Olduvai Gorge," *Science*, 148:72–74.

GOODALL, J. 1964. "Tool-using and Aimed Throwing in a Community of Free-living Chimpanzees," *Nature*, 201:1264–1266.

———. 1965. "Chimpanzees of the Gombe Stream Reserve," *Primate Behavior: Field Studies of Monkeys and Apes*, I. DeVore ed. New York: Holt, Rinehart and Winston Inc., pp. 425–473.

GRAND, T. I. 1964. "The Functional Anatomy of the Shoulder of the Chimpanzee," unpublished Ph.D. thesis, University of California.

GESCHWIND, N. 1964. "The Development of the Brain and the Evolution of Language," *Monogr. Ser. Language and Linguistics*, 17:155–169.

GOODMAN, M. 1963. "Serological Analysis of the Phyletic Relationships of Recent Hominoids," *Human Biology*, 35:377–436.

HALL, K. R. L. 1962. "The Sexual, Agonistic, and Derived Social Behaviour Patterns of the Wild Chacma Baboon, *Papio ursinus*," *Proc. Zool. Soc. London*, 139:283–327.

——— and I. DE VORE. 1965. "Baboon Social Behavior," *Primate Behavior: Field Studies of Monkeys and Apes*, I. DeVore, ed. New York: Holt, Rinehart and Winston, pp. 53–110.

HAMBURG, D. A. 1963. "Emotion in the Perspective of Human Evolution," *Expression of the Emotions in Man*, P. Knapp, ed. New York: International Universities Press, pp. 300–317.

HARLOW, H. F. 1962. "The Development of Affectional Patterns in Infant Monkeys," *Determinants of Infant Behavior*, B. M. Foss, ed. New York: Wiley, pp. 75–97.

——— and M. K. HARLOW. 1962. "Social Deprivation in Monkeys," *Sci. Amer.*, 207:137–146.

HARRISSON, B. 1962. *Orangutan*. London: Collins.

HINDE, R. A., and T. E. ROWELL. 1962. "Communication of Postures and Facial Expressions in the Rhesus Monkey (*Macaca Mulatta*), *Proc. Zool. Soc., London*, 138:1–21.

JAY, P. 1965. "Field Studies," *Behavior of Nonhuman Primates*, A. M. Schrier, H. F. Harlow, and F. Stollnitz, eds. New York: Academic Press, 525–591.

KAUFMAN, I. C., and L. A. ROSENBLUM. 1966. "A Behavioral Taxonomy for *Macaca nemestrina* and *Macaca radiata*: Based on Longitudinal Observation of Family Groups in the Laboratory," *Primates*, 7 (2):205–258.

KAUFMANN, J. H. 1966. "Behavior of Infant Rhesus Monkeys and Their Mothers in a Free-ranging Band," *Zoologica*, 51 (1):17–28.

KLINGER, H. P., J. L. HAMERTON, D. MUTTON, and E. M. LANG. 1963. "The Chromosomes of the Hominoidea," *Classification and Human Evolution*, S. L. Washburn, ed. Viking Fund Publ. in Anthropology No. 37, New York: Wenner-Gren Foundation, pp. 235–242.

KORTLANDT, A. 1962. "Observing Chimpanzees in the Wild," *Sci. Amer.*, 206 (5):128–138.

——— and M. KOOIJ. 1963. "Protohominid Behaviour in Primates," *Symp. Zool Soc. London*, 10:61–88.

KUMMER, H. 1968. *Social Organization of Hamadryas Baboons*. Chicago: University of Chicago Press.

LANCASTER, J. B. (n.d.). "The Evolution of Tool-Using Behavior: Primate Field Studies, Fossil Apes and the Archeological Record."

———— and R. LEE. 1965. "The Annual Reproductive Cycle in Monkeys and Apes," *Primate Behavior: Field Studies of Monkeys and Apes,* I. DeVore, ed., New York: Holt, Rinehart and Winston, Inc., pp. 486–513.

LEAKEY, L. S. B. 1967. "An Early Miocene Member of the Hominidae," *Nature,* 213:155–163.

LEE, R. B. 1965. "Subsistence Ecology of Kung Bushman," unpublished Ph.D. thesis, University of California.

MASON, W. A. 1961a. "The Effects of Social Restriction on the Behavior of Rhesus Monkeys: II. Tests of Gregariousness," *J. Comp. Physiol. Psychol.,* 54: 287–290.

————. 1961b. "Effects of Age and Stimulus Characteristics on Manipulatory Responsiveness of Monkeys Raised in a Restricted Environment," *J. Genet. Psychol.,* 99:301–308.

————. 1961c. "The Effects of Social Restriction on the Behavior of Rhesus Monkeys. III. Dominance Tests." *J. Comp. Physiol. Psychol.,* 54:694–699.

————. 1963. "Social Development of Rhesus Monkeys with Restricted Social Experience," *Percept. Mot. Skills,* 16:263–270.

———— and P. C. GREEN. 1962. "The Effects of Social Restriction on the Behavior of Rhesus Monkeys: IV. Responses to a Novel Experiment and to an Alien Species," *J. Comp. Physiol. Psychol.,* 55: 363–368.

OAKLEY, K. P. 1954. "Skill as a Human Possession," *A History of Technology,* Vol. I, C. Singer, E. J. Holmyard, and A. R. Hall, eds. Oxford: Clarendon Press, pp. 1–37.

ROWELL, T. E. 1962. "Agonistic Noises of the Rhesus Monkey (*Macaca mulatta*)," *Symp. Zool. Soc. London,* 8:91–96.

———— and R. A. HINDE. 1962. "Vocal Communication by the Rhesus Monkey (*Macaca mulatta*)," *Proc. Zool. Soc. London,* 138:279–294.

SADE, D. S. 1965. "Some Aspects of Parent-Offspring and Sibling Relations in a Group of Rhesus Monkeys, with a Discussion of Grooming," *Amer. J. Phys. Anthrop.,* 23:1–17.

SARICH, V. M., and A. C. WILSON. 1967. "Quantitative Immunochemistry and the Evolution of Primate Albumins: Microcomplement Fixation," *Science,* 154:1561–5.

SCHALLER, G. B. 1963. *The Mountain Gorilla: Ecology and Behavior.* Chicago: University of Chicago Press.

————. 1965. "The Behavior of the Mountain Gorilla," *Primate Behavior: Field Studies of Monkeys and Apes,* I. DeVore, ed. New York: Holt, Rinehart and Winston, Inc., pp. 324–367.

SCHILLER, P. H. 1967. "Innate Motor Action as a Basis of Learning," *Instinctive Behavior,* C. H. Schiller, ed. New York: International Universities Press, pp. 264–287.

SHIGERU, A., and A. TOYOSHIMA. 1961–1962. "Progress Report of the Survey of Chimpanzees in Their Natural Habitat, Kabongo Point Area, Tanganyika," *Primates,* 3 (2):61–70.

SIMPSON, G. G. 1966. "The Biological Nature of Man," *Science,* 152:472–478.

VAN LAWICK-GOODALL, J. 1966. *Chimpanzee Social Behavior,* unpublished Ph.D. thesis, University Library, Cambridge, England.

————. 1967. "Mother-Offspring Relationships in Free-ranging Chimpanzees, *Primate Ethology,* Desmond Morris, ed. Chicago: Aldine Publishing Co., pp. 287–346.

WASHBURN, S. L. 1957. "Ischial Callosities as Sleeping Adaptations," *Amer. J. Phys. Anthrop.,* 15 (2):269–276.

————. 1963. "Behavior and Human Evolution," *Classification and Human Evolution,* S. L. Washburn, ed. Viking Fund Publication in Anthropology No. 37, New York: Wenner-Gren Foundation, pp. 190–203.

———— and J. B. LANCASTER. 1965. Field Studies of Old World Monkeys and Apes," *Science,* 150: 1541–1547.

———— and P. JAY. 1965. "The Evolution of Human Nature," unpub. paper presented at the Amer. Anthrop. Assoc. Meeting, Denver, 19 November 1965; and "More on Tool Use in Primates," *Current Anthrop.,* (in press).

———— and D. A. HAMBURG. 1965. "The Implications of Primate Research," *Primate Behavior: Field Studies of Monkeys and Apes,* I. DeVore, ed. New York: Holt, Rinehart and Winston, Inc., pp. 607–622.

ELEVEN • HAIR, SWEAT, TEARS, AND BODY FORM

23 • NATURAL SELECTION AND MAN'S RELATIVE HAIRLESSNESS

Ashley Montagu

Man is the only hairless primate, and it has always been rather puzzling why he is so. The explanation offered in this contribution was earlier made in a brief comment elsewhere,[1] where it elicited criticism in the form of an excellent paper by W. Russell Newman in the contribution which follows this one in this volume.

The subject is certainly one which could be pursued further, and Newman has most interestingly indicated the lines upon which future inquiry might be based. In such matters certainty can only, at best, amount to the highest degree of probability attaching to a judgment based on interpretation of the sufficient and relevant evidence.

Hairlessness is a neotenous trait, preserving the fetal juvenile condition. Where man retains hair, as on the head, on the face in males, on the eyebrows, axillae, pubis and perineum, its function appears to be mainly protective: for the head, eyebrows and face, against injury, light, and the dripping of sweat; in the axillae, pubis and perineum, against chafing. Pubic hair in the female is generally crinkly, in the male lank. The crinkly hair and the pad of fat (mons veneris) beneath serve to protect the female against chafing during intercourse, and since the hairs are, at their bases, associated with highly sensitive sensory nerves, there is an enhancement of sexual excitation.

Still quite puzzling are the forms and colors of head hair in man, ranging all the way from the tightly coiled tufts of the Bushman to the long lank hair of Caucasoids, and from deepest black to almost white, and why, aside altogether from genetic mechanisms, mustache hair, and sometimes beard hair, so frequently differs in color from head hair. These fascinating problems are still largely subjects for speculation, but they also afford grounds for further study.[2]

The order of mammals to which man belongs, the Primates, numbers well over 150 species, all of which are well endowed with body hair. Man's relative hairlessness (glabrousness) stands in marked contrast with the thick pelage which usually covers the bodies of all other primates, especially those of man's nearest relations, the great apes. The reduction of body hair in man almost certainly followed upon adoption of the erect posture and the new way of life which resulted from the increasing desiccation of the hominid homeland—Africa south of the Sahara.

Climatic changes transformed forested woodlands into open plains with low vegetation, savannas. It was not that man's progenitors abandoned the trees, but that the trees abandoned them. Life on the savannas presents very different challenges from those to which forest dwellers are accustomed. Forest dwellers are herbivorous in their diet. The savannas are not sufficiently vegetated

SOURCE: Ashley Montagu, "Natural Selection and Man's Relative Hairlessness," *Journal of the American Medical Association* vol. 187 (February 1, 1964): 356–57. Reprinted by permission of the publisher and the author.
[1] Ashley Montagu, Comment on "The Human Revolution," by C. F. Hockett and R. Ascher, *Current Anthropology*, V (1964), 160–161.
[2] For further discussion of these matters see Ashley Montagu, *The Human Revolution*. (New York: Bantam Books, 1967), pp. 145–148.

to maintain all animals on a vegetarian diet, and all the evidence indicates that man's progenitors were compelled to resort to eating meat in order to supplement their inadequate plant diet. The gathering of the young, immature, the small and slow-moving animals almost certainly preceded the hunting of larger mature animals, but when hunting was initiated, certain accompanying physiological changes favoring the survival and perpetuation of genotypes for reduced hair became operative. It also appears to have been of adaptive advantage for hair to remain, and even to increase in density, on certain parts of the body such as the head, eyebrows, beard, pubic region, face, and axilla. I have dealt with the latter developments in an earlier paper.[1] Here we are concerned with the conditions which probably led to the reduction in general body hair in man.

In the new industrial revolution which hunting represented in the early history of man, running became an activity which was at a high premium. The race was not only to the swift, but also to the most durable, for the chase might last hours and even days. Under the conditions of the hunt, in a torrid environment, the body will become heated. Overheating is not only dangerous but can also be lethal. That man was originally a tropical animal is strongly indicated, among other things, by the fact that his normal body temperature is 98.6 F (37 C). His comfort zone for external temperature is between 65 and 95 F. He tolerates heat better than cold, but by the use of culturally developed devices he is capable of living under all climatic conditions, from the pole of cold to the summers of Philadelphia.

The new way of life which hunting entailed meant that some means of eliminating body heat generated in the hunt was vitally necessary. Indeed, what was even more important was the development of some mechanism by which the body could protect itself against heat accumulation, and not merely as an emergency device for its elimination. Such a mechanism is efficiently provided by sweating.

Animals that customarily live in forest environments do not possess sweat glands; the air with which they are surrounded is heavily saturated with moisture, and this together with their habits of avoiding overheating and prolonged exposure to the sun is more than adequate to protect them against its effects. Our knowledge of the sweat glands in primates is meagre, but all primates thus far investigated possess sweat glands, and the apes appear to possess both eccrine and apocrine sweat glands. Eccrine or exocrine glands excrete fluid without loss of protoplasm; apocrine glands contribute part of their cellular protoplasm to their secretion. Apocrine glands originate from the hair follicles, whereas eccrine glands develop directly from the epidermis and are unconnected in any way with the hair follicles.

The distribution of these two types of glands in the mammals is of great interest. In general apocrine glands are found in areas of skin covered by hair, while eccrine glands occur mostly in the hairless parts of the body. In man the most densely distributed sweat glands over the whole body are the eccrine. In the great apes the distribution of apocrine and eccrine glands over the whole body is roughly equal; the ratio of eccrine to apocrine glands in the lowland gorilla (*Gorilla gorilla gorilla*), excluding hairless surfaces, is approximate—as 7 to 6.[2] Other observations confirm this, so that the apes are "the mixed gland animals," intermediate between other mammals and man.[3] Eccrine glands tend to develop most densely on hairless surfaces, and man, indeed, differs from all other primates in being the most well endowed with eccrine glands. Furthermore, man appears to be the most efficient sweater in the whole animal kingdom. "Man," writes Kuno, "occupies the premier position in the animal kingdom in respect to the development of the sweat apparatus. There are many animals provided with the sweat apparatus, but there is none who shows such a vivid sweat response as does man." [4] On a hot day at the zoo the only animals likely to be seen sweating are the spectators outside the cages and enclosures. There is, however, one exception, the rhinoceros. The rhinoceros, like man, is virtually hairless and has a good layer of fat beneath the skin. When it becomes overheated as a result of unwonted running, it sweats prodigiously. It may be that it is the heat-insulating layer of fat which makes efficient sweating necessary in both the rhinoceros and man. Man sweats from every part of his body surface, having about 750 sweat glands to each square inch of skin.

It is here suggested that it was the hunting way of life which resulted in the development, in man, of the largest number of sweat glands to be found in any mammal. Man's sweat glands are capable of producing amounts of sweat over the body surface up to a maximum of two liters or more than two quarts per hour! This would amount to the removal of 1,200 Calories per hour from the body, and a lowering of the temperature of the body by 20 degrees centigrade. The temperature regulation of the body by sweating, therefore, could hardly be more efficiently performed. The common complaint in hot weather is of too much sweat. The high rate of sweating in man is almost certainly an expression of the physiological necessity of maintaining a constant body temperature under natural conditions in hot weather. This is the kind of habitus to which man has been exposed for the greater part of his history, with only a few exceptions arising during the very recent period. Outdoor life and hunting still remain the principal way of life of the greater number of peoples who have not yet been wholly affected by civilization.

With the adoption of hunting on the savannas massive sweating became the physiologically adaptive mechanism of maintaining the constancy of the body temperature. Massive sweating is incompatible with a dense growth of hair, and because of this incompatibility, natural selection favored genotypes for reduced body hair. In this manner, it is here suggested, man became the only reduced-hair primate, hair of some density being retained only where it served an adaptively useful purpose.

To summarize, then: As a consequence of the adoption of the hunting way of life, entailing much and often prolonged exercise, an extensive development, especially of the eccrine glands, was evolved as a mechanism for reducing the resulting body heat through the evaporation of the excreted sweat which carries off the accumulated heat. A heavy coat of hair would have the precisely opposite effect of conserving the accumulated heat, hence, the selection pressure would be in favor of reduction in both the density and length of the body hair.

The ability to live in torrid zones, and indeed to spread to their farthest reaches, was made possible by the evolution, in man, of the most highly developed system of sweat glands to be found in any animal, and the concomitant reduction of body hair.

REFERENCES

1. MONTAGU, A. Functions of Man's Distribution of Hair, *JAMA* 182:281–282 (Oct. 20), 1962.
2. STRAUS, W. L., JR. "Microscopic Anatomy of Skin of Gorilla," in *Anatomy of Gorilla*, W. K. Gregory, ed., New York: Columbia University Press, 1950, pp. 214–221.
3. SCHIEFFERDECKER, P. Die Hautdrüsen des Menschen und der Säugetiere, ihre biologische und rassenanatomische Bedeutung, sowie die Muscularis sexualis, *Zoologica* (No. 72) 27:154, 1922.
4. KUNO, Y. *Human Perspiration*, Springfield, Ill.: Charles C Thomas, 1956, p. 340.

24 • WHY MAN IS SUCH A SWEATY AND THIRSTY NAKED ANIMAL: A SPECULATIVE REVIEW

Russell W. Newman

In this contribution informed speculation is seen at its best. Newman presents the available relevant facts relating to sweating, thirst, and amount and length of body hair, as known for man and other animals, and from these reconstructs the kind of habitat in which early man probably lived. At the same time he criticizes the view postulated by Montagu and other authors that body hair was lost in man in the course of adaptation to the hunting way of life, in order to avoid overheating by facilitating increased sweating. Another important factor which is involved in the production of sweating is muscular effort in relation to ambient temperature. Man *is* the sweatiest of all animals,[1] and certainly among the thirstiest,[2] as the popularity of soft drinks and the profitability of breweries testify. The reader will have to decide for himself how convincing the criticism is of Montagu's theory of man's hairlessness.

Under high temperatures sweating is much greater than under low temperatures.[3] This rather obvious fact merely contributes support to the tropical origins of man, and the origins of his great capacity for sweating.

Our present view of the earliest differentiation of man's ancestors from the primate stock assumes a gradual shift in habitat from forest to open grasslands in the tropics and sub-tropics of the Old World during the Pliocene epoch. This period encompassed some critical innovations in: morphology (complete upright posture and gait, increased cranial capacity, etc.), economy (increasingly carnivorous), behavior (tool making, speech), and probably others not integrated into the central theory of evolution. This paper presents the argument that this shift from forest to grassland resulted in certain physiological adaptations to environmental heat loads that still characterize our species; Barnicot (1959) suggested just such a relationship a decade ago.

Specifically, the physical avenues of heat exchange between an animal and its environment will be reiterated to establish a common vocabulary; the interplay between these avenues and selected tropical environments will then be examined with reference to human responses to point up the specializations which characterize our species. Water requirements and the associated patterns of thirst and drinking habits are reviewed since they may have influenced the daily regimen. Finally, the experimental data now available on non-human primates under heat stress will be presented to see whether the human response is characteristic of the primate order.

SOURCE: Russell W. Newman, "Why Man Is Such a Sweaty and Thirsty Naked Animal: A Speculative Review," *Human Biology* vol. 42, no. 1 (February 1970): 12–27. Reprinted by permission of the Wayne State University Press and the author.

[1] Yas Kuno, *Human Perspiration* (Springfield, Illinois: C. C Thomas, 1956).
[2] A. V. Wolf, *Thirst* (Springfield, Illinois: C. C Thomas, 1958).
[3] Van Beaumont and Robert W. Bullard, "Sweating: Its Rapid Response to Muscular Work," *Science*, 141 (1963), 643–646. For an ingenious hygrometric method of measuring the excretion of sweat see E. W. Rosenberg, Harvey Blank, and Sorrel Resnik, "Sweating and Water Loss Through the Skin," *Journal of the American Medical Association*, 179 (1962), 809–811.

Avenues of Heat Exchange

There are four channels of energy exchange between the animal and its environment: conduction, convection, radiation, and evaporation. Modern man uses all of them in varying combinations and proportions, as did his ancestors. The first three channels operate toward either a net loss or gain of heat for the organism. The fourth channel, evaporation, is generally considered to result only in heat loss.

Conduction is the flow of heat without displacement of the material and can occur in gases, liquids, or solids. The most familiar example of conduction occurs when touching an object which is either hot or cold; in the first instance we conduct heat towards us, in the second we lose heat. The importance of conduction is tied to the habits of a given species; in man it is not a major source of heat exchange. Conduction is often considered simultaneously with convection as a dual avenue of heat exchange, and this combination will be used here.

Convection is a flow of heat by the physical movement of the gas or liquid in contact. The best example is the increase in cooling (or heating) produced by wind. This convective air current cools by carrying away the heat conducted from the skin and by presenting a steady supply of air which is cooler than the skin surface. Convective exchange thus occurs at the outer boundary of a thin layer of still air which surrounds the body. It acts in the absence of wind because of the air movement produced by the expansion of the warmed air *per se*, but convective exchange increases dramatically with movement of either the air or the body.

Radiation is an exchange of heat from a warmer to a cooler object which is independent of the intervening medium. It includes the direct acquisition of heat from the sun as ultra-violet, visible, and infra-red energy and the more subtle exchanges by which we radiate heat to, or receive it from, our surroundings. This is an exceedingly important channel for heat exchange in man, and some of its complexities will be examined later.

The fourth method, evaporation, results in the loss of "latent" heat required to vaporize water from the skin and from the membranes of the respiratory tract. The total evaporative heat loss, comprised of three parts, includes respiratory loss—which is relatively constant in man since he does not generally pant, diffusional skin loss—which is also rather constant, and sensible perspiration, i.e. active thermal sweating, which supplements the diffusional phase when either the environment imposes a sufficient heat load (at rest at about 30° C) or when exercise increases body heat production.

Environmental Conditions of the Forest and Savanna

Man's ancestors probably did not step from tropical forest to sun-baked grasslands in one short bound. However, these two extremes will be contrasted, with the understanding that there are many intermediate conditions. Except for periods of storms and rain, tropical forests at ground level in the daytime are typified by warm temperatures averaging 28–32° C as the daily maximum, very little air movement, a very high humidity (the air almost saturated with moisture), and little radiant heat from the sun (Richards 1957, Read 1968). This is only marginally stressful to an inactive animal because this combination of an air temperature slightly below skin temperature with a high ambient humidity and low air movement makes it just physically possible for the animal to lose the heat generated by metabolism. An active animal has increased difficulty because it will produce two or three times as much heat and, although the higher skin temperature accompanying the physical activity of an exercising animal increases the heat transferred by radiation slightly, little real increase from convection or evaporation is possible because of the relatively small temperature and vapor pressure differences between the skin and air. We can characterize a forest-dwelling animal as being almost solely dependent on radiational heat loss for thermoregulation with a minor contribution from conductance when lying or sitting on the forest floor.

Open country (savanna or steppe) at comparable latitudes presents a different set of meteorological conditions for mammals. The most obvious difference is that solar radiation becomes an important element since it can impinge directly on the animal and its immediate surroundings. If an animal is not in shade, it will receive radiation directly from the sun; that energy which is not reflected (50–60%) will be absorbed as heat. Even in the shade, air temperatures rises, usually about 5° C, primarily from the heat re-radiated by the ground and all nearby objects which are in sunlight. The radiant heat load absorbed cannot be simply described in terms of surface temperatures since animals have defensive mechanisms which modify this load. Under high radiant heat loads, exposed sand or rock may reach surface temperatures of 60° C, a level painful to touch; the tips of the wool in Merino sheep can reach 85° C in desert sun (MacFarlane 1964), but their skins never reach this level for various reasons. The effect of solar insolation in mammals is best described either in terms of the energy received and absorbed or by some measure of the resulting strain (reaction to the stress). A nude man sitting in the sun in the desert may absorb 200 kcal/m²/hr (Adolph 1947), while Lee (1963) equates desert solar radiation to a rise of 7° C in air temperature. In the tropical savanna, direct radiation is reduced below that in the desert by the increased amount of water vapor in the air which absorbs some of the ultra-violet and visible portions of the light spectrum; a figure of about 100 kcal/m²/hr has been estimated for such an area (Roller and Goldman 1967). This reduces the 7° C equivalent air temperature increase, but nevertheless still represents a stressful condition for a quiet animal. The other two meteorological factors mentioned for the forest environment, air movement and humidity, also change. Air movement increases many-fold outside the forest although it obviously varies from time to time; in fact, the term "windspeed" is only appropriate outside the forest proper. Humidity in the tropics is always higher than that which we associate with higher latitudes, but relative humidities of less than 50% are common outside the forest. These humidities provide much greater potential for evaporative heat loss than the saturated air under the forest canopy.

This "open country" combination of meteorological conditions imposes a higher stress on the animal than did the tropical forest. Both conductive and radiant heat exchanges now flow from the environment to the animal; they have become avenues of heat gain. The only way to re-establish a heat-loss relationship (except by retreating to caves or burrows) is for peripheral vasodilation to raise skin temperature to levels above ambient temperature and, indeed, above the surface temperatures of everything nearby. There are definite limits to this approach since skin temperature must remain below deeper body temperature for metabolic heat to be dissipated from its sites of origin and since the upper tolerable level of skin (as well as deep body) temperature is relatively low. Convective heat loss is now more important, because of increased air movement, but can only assist heat transfer from the skin if the air temperature is lower than skin temperature; if the reverse is true, the warmer air simply increases the heat load as it moves over the skin. Fortunately, the fourth avenue of heat transfer, evaporative heat loss, is much greater in the relatively dry open country than it was under the higher humidities of the forest, if sufficient moisture can be made available at the surface of the animal by panting or sweating or the spreading of saliva or urine on the skin. Finally, it is noteworthy that under conditions where heat storage from radiant insolation is a problem, as in open country, larger body size becomes advantageous since it minimizes the surface area (cm²) per unit of body volume (cm³) and thus spreads the radiant heat load throughout a greater mass, sparing the critical centers.

Adaptations of Heat Stress

Many specific adaptations to environmental stresses have been observed in mammals. Only a few appear relevant to human evolution, and these are observed primarily in ungulates and carnivores. Almost all of these findings are from domestic animals although many of the principles must also apply to related wild species.

Some small animals in hot environments (especially desert forms) have become nocturnal and spend the day underground; this was not man's adaptation. Many of the larger carnivores (especially the cats) kill and feed at intervals of as much as 2–3 days, resting between kills in the shadiest and coolest locations in their territory. On the other hand, man seems to have followed the general primate pattern of frequent feeding, and our ancestors must have spent many of their waking hours in pursuit of food even under conditions of high heat stresses. There may have been some behavioral adaptations in daily activity and feeding habits, but it does not appear that major changes in food acquisition patterns took place specifically to avoid stressful environmental conditions. There is one peculiarity of man that needs to be mentioned although it is not a true heat adaptation. Being erect *per se*, in open grassland, substantially reduces the solar heat load by minimizing the amount of surface area exposed to direct sunlight. For example, a standing man receives only two-thirds as much direct solar radiation as a standing sheep of equivalent size on a daily average and less than one-quarter as much

at the noontime peak loads (Lee 1950). However, the assumption of an upright posture was so fundamental to human evolution that this thermal advantage can only be considered as a minor and fortuitous byproduct.

One of the most important mammalian defenses against radiant heat loads is a dense and highly reflective coat of body hair. This serves multiple purposes: reflecting up to half of the solar energy, absorbing some of the unreflected portion at a distance from the skin for dissipation by convection and re-radiation, and providing an insulative space against the conductance of the absorbed heat toward the skin. A dense coat may be a dual purpose thermal protective system since it is most conspicuous in large desert mammals who face a high radiant heat input during the day and an equally impressive radiant heat loss at night. Man's evolution obviously did not include this specialization; in fact, man has gone in the opposite direction, toward virtual absence of body hair.

Keeping a body surface covered with a film of moisture, thus insuring a relatively high heat loss, is the only alternative to reducing a high radiant heat load by means of insulative fur or wool. Man's most important thermal adaptation is increased evaporative heat loss through thermal sweating. Of course, not all mammals sweat to regulate their body temperature; the dog dissipates body heat by panting. Even well adapted tropical animals such as goats may depend primarily on respiratory heat losses for cooling. However, respiratory heat loss offers much less effective surface area and is not as efficient as sweating. Animals which depend on panting usually show other defensive adaptations and, unlike man, have developed tolerance to hyperventilatory sequelae. Sweat glands have been observed in many animals which do not appear to use this type of evaporative heat loss as their principal defensive mechanism. Man is noted among the mammals not for either the number or size of his sweat glands (Weiner and Hillman 1960), but only for the very high secretory level at which they operate. Man has been observed to sweat at the rate of three liters per hour for short periods of heavy work in high heat (Eichna et al. 1945). Two liters per hour is quite common for the combination of exercise and heat and about the human limit for sustained sweating (Ladell 1964). One liter per hour is a reasonable figure for many hot conditions. No other mammal is known to sweat as much per unit surface area as man. The nearest competitors on a surface area basis are the donkey and the camel (Schmidt-Nielson 1964). Some breeds of cattle are heavy sweat producers but also simultaneously utilize panting (MacFarlane 1968). None of these can produce more than half of the sweat per unit of surface area (500 gm vs. 1000 gm/m²/hr) that can be achieved by man. Sweating and panting are in general complementary, and for a sweating animal such as man panting is a secondary line of defence, used only when sweating is inadequate (Bianca 1968). Panting in man is apt to produce physiological problems of respiratory instead of thermal nature (Goldman et al. 1965).

Since all other primates have considerable hair covering, it has always been accepted that our ancestors must once have had a respectable amount of body hair. The question has been when and why did they lose it. Most of the explanations offered have implied that nakedness was an advantage in hot conditions. For example, Coon (1955) states: ". . . the absence of this covering . . . must be considered adaptive, on the one hand to hot, dry conditions in which the surface of the skin must be free to permit the breezes to evaporate sweat, . . ." La Barre (1964) links nakedness with a need for "diffusion of metabolic heat from the rapid spurts of energy required in hunting"; Montagu (1964) postulates a loss of hair with increased sweating capacity as a mechanism for avoidance of overheating

from a hunting way of life. This concept has been perpetuated in recent textbooks (Campbell 1967) and in a much more qualified format in a recent work for the lay audience (Morris 1967). One of the purposes of this review is to point out that this explanation does not fit the available data from man and other mammals. Unless we postulate an ancestral condition of dense, long fleece such as in wool-bearing sheep or the winter coat of camels, body hair is no bar to convective heat loss and has nothing to do with the radiation of long-wave infra-red heat to cooler objects. There is no evidence that a hair coat interferes with the evaporation of sweat; what can be said is that exposure to the sun after the removal of the body hair increases sweating in cattle (Berman 1957) and panting in sheep (MacFarlane 1968), because the total heat load has been increased. Many men have been studied in heat with a solar load while nude and wearing light clothing which is roughly equivalent to body hair. At rest or light work the clothed man gained about two-thirds as much heat as the nude man and sweated commensurately less, and this is roughly the same savings in heat gain that one gets from going out of the sunshine into shade (Adolph 1947, Lee 1964). It seems obvious that man's present glabrous state is a marked disadvantage under high radiant heat loads rather than the other way around, and that man's specialization for and great dependence on thermal sweating stems from his increased heat load in the sun.

It is much more difficult to evaluate the "metabolic-heat-generated-from-hunting" suggestion with comparative data since there is no other predatory species which seems to have had to lose its hair to be able to catch its prey. This might indicate that our ancestors either pushed their prey to exhaustion in what Krantz (1968) has termed persistence hunting, or that they were woefully inefficient hunters. Sweat rate is not a very good measure of physiological strain under conditions of short and uneven bursts of exercise although it is an excellent indicator for long-term, moderate work in the heat. This is because sweating is a somewhat delayed response, usually requiring at least 20 minutes to reach peak production. There certainly are no data on the energy requirements of our hypothetical early ancestors, but there are well established limits on modern man which place a work limit of approximately 300 kcal/hr of heat production for 8 hours per day if the level is to be maintained day after day without a problem of accumulated fatigue (Passmore and Durnin 1955). This is only about one half the limit of man's capacity for evaporative heat loss by sweating.

Water Requirements and Thirst

Any discussion of evaporative heat losses must include a consideration of the replacement of the lost body fluid. Man is the most dependent on thermal sweating among the mammals thus far investigated and may well be the most dependent on a continuing source of water; his principal competitor would be the horse. The only two aspects of this problem to be considered will be man's drinking requirements and the effects of dehydration.

Every liter of water that an average 70 kg man loses represents nearly a 1½% loss in body weight. Sweating in the heat can reach the level of 2 liters per hour under conditions of sustained work; respiratory water loss in man is small, seldom over 15 grams per hour; and diffusional water loss through the skin probably never exceeds 1½% of weight per day (Ladell 1965). These losses must be replaced to avoid progressive dehydration. A man who has accumulated a 2% weight loss from sweating is thirsty, by 10% he is helpless, and death occurs at 18–20% (Folk 1966). There is much less information on other species, but the cat and dog die at about this same level of dehydration while camels, sheep, and donkeys can survive over a 30% weight loss of water (Whittow 1968). The mechanisms by which species tolerate dehydration vary and lie outside the scope of this survey, but it is interesting that man does not diminish sweating in the heat to fit his state of hydration until he is dangerously dehydrated (Adolph 1947).

Total daily water requirement for an animal in the heat is a complicated problem and many of its facets are not particularly relevant to our consideration of evolutionary forces. Assuming no marked seasonal differences in the water content of the vegetable foods consumed, and that the animal portion of the diet is very constant in water content, then body water losses from increased requirements for evaporative heat loss have to be replaced by additional drinking. In theory, this could be accomplished by either more at one time or by frequent watering. All domestic animals and probably most wild forms increase the frequency of drinking under heat stress provided water is available. Many have a remarkable ability to rehydrate themselves each time they drink. This may involve large quantities in remarkably short periods; camels ingest up to 100 liters within 10 minutes (Schmidt-Nielson et al. 1956), donkeys, 20 liters in 3 minutes (Schmidt-Nielson 1964), guanacos, 9 liters in 8 minutes (Rosemann and Morrison 1963), and sheep, 9 liters in 10 minutes (MacFarlane 1964). Carnivores generally cannot ingest as large a quantity of water as the ruminants for anatomical reasons, although the dog can hold almost 2 liters (Adolph 1947), and the cat has been reported to drink over 7% of its body weight in 10 minutes (Wolf 1958). Except for some small rodents and lagomorphs, man must be the least capable of rapidly ingesting water among all the mammals. Man reaches satiety after rapidly consuming 1 liter of water and cannot imbibe over 2 liters in a 10 minute period (Folk 1966). It is obvious, therefore, that man must resort to frequent rather than copious drinking to prevent even moderate dehydration. It is strange to find, in the same animal, both the least capacity to ingest water and the greatest dependence on thermal sweating. Its occurrence in a species which has in modern times been so successful in the tropics represents a triumph of technology (the ability to carry and store water outside the body) over biological limitations.

Not only is man unable to consume more than a small amount of water at one time, but he does not generally replace his water loss during the heat of the day. This "voluntary dehydration" in man can exceed 2 liters, but such a temporary negative water balance is not unique to man, probably occurring in all species. Presumably, in voluntary dehydration the free circulating water of the gut is being withdrawn and tissue dehydration does not start until the gut water has been largely utilized. This provides an initial buffer against dehydration which may be quite important in ruminants (12–15% of body weight) but of more limited potential in non-ruminants (5% of weight or less) (Chew 1965). The significant point in man is that any voluntary dehydration incurred during the day is routinely replaced at night, with and following his evening meal.

Problems of Changing Patterns of Thirst

Thirst in humans is a personal imperative which is only satisfied by individual drinking. The term "thirst" is difficult to use with the same connotations for other species because our subjective sensations cannot be verified in non-humans. Many gregarious species have group watering periods, widely spaced in time and probably related to both the water content of the diet and the ambient daytime temperature. Individual members of such groups rarely wander off alone in search of a drink. In domestic animals this may be an ancient trait, carried over and perhaps even intensified by breeding selection. In many wild species including the terrestrial primates it must stem from the increased vulnerability of individuals (cf. Washburn and Devore 1961 on baboons). Even the time of day for group drinking is quite consistent. This implies either that the members do not normally develop marked individual differences in thirst or that these are subordinated to the daily regimen of the group. Both alternatives appear to be the antithesis of human thirst behavioral patterns. In our species the young have a propensity for becoming thirsty at inopportune times and are vociferous about satisfying this thirst. In fairness, it must be admitted that daily water requirements for the young are higher than adults per unit of body weight (Wolf 1958), while their capacity per drink is commensurately smaller. A gradual shift from group patterns to individual drinking in accordance with physiological needs would appear first in sub-adults and lactating females, the two most vulnerable portions of a mammalian group. Perhaps this shift could have occurred when, with sufficient economic specialization, part of the group did not wander with the adult male or males but remained relatively sedentary and near the water source. Even adult hominoid males might have been under similar constraints until they developed defensive weaponry to inhibit predators.

Cattle which are normally daytime drinkers increase the frequency and volume of night drinking under hot conditions (Yousef et al. 1968), but cattle are protected domestic animals. It was pointed out earlier that modern man rehydrates by drinking during the evening when evaporative heat loss is minimal. Modern day, terrestrial, non-human primates have not been reported as nocturnal drinkers in the wild. Before water containers were invented this might have posed quite a problem for our ancestors and been just as important as security in dictating the location of campsites.

Heat Responses in Non-human Primates

Human reaction to various levels of heat stress is by far the best known of all animals, but the rest of the primate order are among the least studied. From what little is known, it is obvious that we cannot safely extrapolate what we have learned about man to his primate relatives. Some data are available on the cebus, rhesus, baboon, and chimpanzee. A pertinent question raised by this review is do non-human primates utilize thermal sweating as their important avenue of heat loss under hot conditions? This cannot be answered from the available information; it is not even certain from laboratory experiments whether monkeys can tolerate heat stresses well within the capability of many animals.

A series of cebus monkeys (Hardy 1954) and chimps (Dale et al. 1965) have been measured in calorimeters which distinguish between evaporation, conduction-convection, and radiation as sources of heat loss. Unfortunately for this discussion the chimps were only exposed to one temperature, 24° C. A comparison of these two primates with man is given in Table 1.

Obviously if the percentage for one avenue of heat loss rises the others must decrease. At 24° C, both the cebus and chimp showed greater conductive-convective losses than man, but the cebus were in a metal chair and the chimps in a metal cage; these provided abnormal surface areas for conduction-convection losses. This plus the hair covering on the cebus and chimp and the relatively high evaporative loss explain why the radiant exchange was so much less than that of a naked man. The evaporative heat losses at 24° C were absolutely as well as relatively high in the non-human subjects. This temperature is too low for us to expect thermal sweating in any of the species so the high values must have been caused by higher diffusional skin water losses or increased respiratory exchange. Man and cebus were losing more heat than they were producing at 24° C, but the chimps were very close to thermal balance.

At 34° C, radiation exchange was virtually eliminated since skin and wall temperatures in the calorimeters were practically identical. Evaporative loss increased three-fold in man from sweating. The two-fold increase in evaporative loss in the cebus has been ascribed to sweating because skin temperature remained relatively cool as calorimeter temperature rose, and this requires a moist skin surface. On the other hand the total evaporative cooling in the monkeys was not sufficient to prevent rectal temperature from rising rapidly to 40° C when the experiments were terminated to avoid heat stroke.

Experiments with macaques and baboons in heat present a very confused picture. One young rhesus was exposed to 40° C, 55% RH presumably in a cage and with water (Robinson and Morrison 1957). This monkey's rectal temperature rose very slightly, and the animal showed no evidence of panting. The investigators did not check for sweating but inferred that it must have been present. A group of rhesus were exposed to two temperatures, 29° C and 38° C, with comparable humidity, and two different positions of arm re-

Table 1: Relative mechanisms of heat loss utilized in three primate species

	TEMP.	RADI-ATION	CONDUCTION AND CONVECTION	EVAPO-RATION
Man [1]	24° C	66%	15%	19%
	34° C	0	45%	55%
Cebus [1]	24° C	40%	25%	35%
	34° C	0	35%	65%
Chimp [2]	24° C	30%	35%	35%

[1] From Hardy 1954.
[2] From Dale et al. 1965.

straint while the animals were prone (Frankel et al. 1958). At 29° C, the type of restraint did not make any difference, and the animals maintained a steady, slightly depressed rectal temperature for over 4 hours. At 38° C, those with arms held back along the sides had slightly elevated but steady rectal temperatures while a position with the arms extended resulted in an almost explosive rise in rectal temperature which required premature termination of exposure. As if this were not confusing enough, no evidence of sweat production could be observed on these rhesus during the heat exposures (Folk 1965). Four young male savanna baboons exposed to 45° C, 50% RH (Funkhauser et al. 1967) in a primate restraint chair showed both sweating and panting but with insufficient total evaporative heat loss to prevent a dangerous elevation of body temperature. This combination of heat and humidity was very stressful and would have caused some panting in man (Goldman et al. 1965). The baboons increased their respiratory rate very rapidly, a response expected from a panting species. Unfortunately, these subjects were deprived of water for 24 hours prior to the heat exposure, and most animal species show effect of dehydration in their responses; the oryx, which is primarily a sweating species, shifts entirely to panting for heat loss when dehydrated (Taylor 1969).

Our knowledge of the non-human primates' reaction to heat is obviously fragmentary and contradictory. Whether the contradictions arise from problems in techniques, e.g. the resistance of primates to physical restraint, or for other reasons is as yet unknown.

Conclusions

Man's specialized dependence on thermal sweating appears to be an evolutionary adaptation to the tropics. The marked limitations on the amount of water which man can consume at one time, and the lack of any of the water conserving adaptations observed in desert mammals argues for a well-watered tropical habitat, or, at least certainly not a tropical desert. On the other hand profuse sweating does not in itself provide efficient evaporative heat loss under the high humidity and lack of air movement which characterizes the tropical forest. An environmental niche of tropical parklands and grasslands best corresponds to the observed thermoregulatory responses.

It has been argued here that man's propensity for sweating came about because his nakedness increased the total radiant heat load received and not because loss of hair somehow enhanced the efficiency of sweat evaporation. Therefore, either the two processes developed simultaneously or the decline in body hair preceded the increase in sweating. If nakedness was a disadvantage in a savanna environment which required a compensatory adaptation (sweating), loss of hair must have stemmed from other causes or preceded the occupation of the habitat in question, at least for its inception. Our traditional ideas of what our ancestors looked like have included far more body hair than our own species until forms very similar and closely related to Homo sapiens appear. The illustrations (with one exception) for as recent a work as Howell's "Early Man" (1968) show hirsutism as a rather conservative trait over millions of years. If one had to select times and habitats when progressive denudation was not a distinct environmental disadvantage, the choices would seem to be between a very early period when our ancestors were primarily forest dwellers or a very recent period when primitive clothing could provide the same protection against either solar heat or cold.

The primary difficulty in arguing for the recent loss of body hair is that there seems to be no single and powerful environmental driving force other than recurrent cold that is obvious after the Pliocene epoch. Furthermore, the developing complexity and efficiency of even primitive man's technology would have decreased the probability of a straightforward biological adaptation. Finally, since all modern men lack an effective sunscreen of body hair and all sweat profusely in the heat, this specialization either must have occurred at a time and place when the evolving species was geographically compact, or at least contiguous, or represents a highly improbably parallel evolution in a variety of non-comparable environments.

The obvious time and place where progressive denudation would have been least disadvantageous is the ancient forest habitat. Radiant energy does penetrate the forest canopy in limited amounts, and that portion of the spectrum which is primarily transmitted through vegetation, the near infrared wavelengths of 0.75 to 0.93 microns, is exactly the energy best reflected by human skin (Gates 1968). This may be purely coincidental, but it lends a little support to this suggestion that loss of body hair in man was somehow stimulated much earlier in time than our present estimates.

In conclusion, man suffers from a unique trio of conditions: hypotrichosis corpus, hyperhydrosis, and polydipsia. The appearance and development of this combination must have been the result of some of the habits of our ancestors, or in more popular phraseology, of the ecological niche of the survivors who gave rise to our evolving ancestors. There is little hope that the osseous remains in the fossil record will provide much in the way of clues to the time of initiation and rate of change in these characteristics. There is hope that judicious speculation based on comparative studies which focus on the problems can help us to define the possible limits within which one may safely theorize.

Abstract and Summary

A shift in habitat from forest to tropical grasslands by man's early ancestors in Tertiary times resulted in a rather distinctive reaction to external heat loads. If our ancestors had already lost most of their body hair or were in the process of doing so, the combination of increased solar exposure in open country and greater absorption of solar energy by the naked skin magnified the total heat load. This must have constituted a disadvantage which required some compensation; in man it has taken the form of dependence on thermal sweating for heat dissipation to the point where Homo sapiens has the greatest sweating capacity for a given surface area of any known animal. Heavy sweating without simultaneous drinking inevitably leads to tissue dehydration. Man is very intolerant of dehydration and has limited capacity to rehydrate rapidly. He is dependent on frequent and relatively small drinks of water under hot conditions. This must have influenced species behavior, at least until water containers were invented. Unfortunately, our present knowledge of how our non-human primate relatives react to heat stress is fragmentary and contradictory. We can't be sure that our modern specializations are uniquely human or are part of a general primate pattern.

LITERATURE CITED

ADOLPH, E. F. 1947. Physiology of man in the desert. Interscience, New York.

BARNICOT, N. A. 1959. Climatic factors in the evolution of human populations. Cold Spring Harbor Symposia on Quantitative Biology, 24:115–129.

BERMAN, A. 1957. Influence of some factors on the relative evaporation rate from the skin of cattle. Nature, 179:1256.

BIANCA, W. 1968. Thermoregulation. In Adaptation of

Domestic Animals, ed. by E. S. E. Hafez, pp. 97–118. Lea and Febiger, Philadelphia.

CAMPBELL, B. G. 1967. Human Evolution. An Introduction to Man's Adaptations. Aldine, Chicago.

CHEW, R. M. 1965. Water metabolism of mammals. *In* Physiological Mammalogy, vol. II, Mammalian reactions to stressful environments, ed. by W. V. Mayer and R. G. Van Gelder, pp. 43–148. Academic Press, New York.

COON, C. S. 1955. Some problems of human variability and natural selection in climate and culture. Amer. Naturalist, 89:257–280.

DALE, H. E., M. D. SHANKLINE, H. D. JOHNSON and W. H. BROWN 1965. Energy metabolism of the chimpanzee. A comparison of direct and indirect calorimetry. Tech. Report ARL-TR-65-17, 6571st Aeromed. Res. Lab., Holloman AFB, New Mexico.

EICHNA, L. W., W. F. BEAN, W. B. BEAN and W. B. SHELLEY 1945. The upper limits of heat and humidity tolerated by acclimatized men working in hot environments. J. Indust. Hygiene and Toxicol. 27:59–84.

FOLK, G. E., JR. 1966. Introduction to Environmental Physiology. Lea and Febiger, Philadelphia.

FRANKEL, H. M., G. E. FOLK, JR. and F. N. CRAIG 1958. Effects of type of restraint upon heat tolerance in monkeys. Proc. Exp. Biol. Med., 97:339–341.

FUNKHAUSER, G. E., E. A. HIGGINS, T. ADAMS and C. C. SNOW 1967. The response of the savannah baboon (Papio cynocephalus) to thermal stress. Life Sciences, 6:1615–1620.

GATES, D. M. 1968. Physical environment. *In* Adaptation of Domestic Animals, ed. by E. S. E. Hafez, pp. 46–60. Lea and Febiger, Philadelphia.

GOLDMAN, R. F., E. B. GREEN and P. F. IAMPIETRO 1965. Tolerance of hot, wet environments by resting men. J. Appl. Physiol., 20:271–277.

HARDY, J. D. 1955. Control of heat loss and heat production in physiologic temperature regulation. Harvey Lectures, 49:242–270. Academic Press, New York.

HOWELL, F. C. 1968. Early Man. Time-Life, New York.

KRANTZ, G. 1968. Brain size and hunting ability in earliest man. Current Anthropology, 9:450–451.

LA BARRE, W. 1964. Comments on The Human Revolution by C. F. Hockett and R. Ascher. Current Anthropology, 5:147–150.

LADELL, W. S. S. 1964. Terrestrial animals in humid heat: man. *In* Hdbk. of Physiology, 4, Adaptation

to the Environment, ed. by D. B. Dill, pp. 625–659. Williams and Wilkins, Baltimore.

——— 1965. Water and salt intakes. *In*, The Physiology of Human Survival, ed. by O. G. Edholm and A. L. Bacharach, pp. 235–299. Academic Press, London.

LEE, D. H. K. 1950. Studies of heat regulation in the sheep with special reference to the Merino. Aust. J. Agric. Res., 1:200–216.

——— 1963. Physiology and the arid zone. *In*, Environmental Physiology and Psychology in Arid Conditions, Reviews of Research, 22, pp. 15–36. UNESCO, Paris.

——— 1964. Terrestrial animals in dry heat: man in the desert. *In* Hdbk. of Physiology, 4, Adaptation to the Environment, ed. by D. B. Dill, pp. 551–582. Williams and Wilkins, Baltimore.

MAC FARLANE, W. V. 1964. Terrestrial animals in dry heat: ungulates. *In*, Hdbk. of Physiology, 4, Adaptation to the Environment, ed. by D. B. Dill, pp. 509–539. Williams and Wilkins, Baltimore.

——— 1968. Comparative functions of ruminants in hot environments. *In* Adaptation of Domestic Animals, ed. by E. S. E. Hafez, pp. 264–276. Lea and Febiger, Philadelphia.

MONTAGU, A. 1964. Comments on The Human Revolution by C. F. Hockett and R. Ascher. Current Anthropology, 5:160–161.

MORRIS, D. 1967. The Naked Ape. McGraw-Hill, New York.

PASSMORE, R. and J. V. G. A. DURNIN 1955. Human energy expenditure. Physiol. Rev., 35:801–840.

READ, R. G. 1968. Evaporative power in the tropical forest of the Panama canal zone. J. Appl. Meteor., 7:417–424.

RICHARDS, P. W. 1952. The Tropical Rain Forest, an Ecological Study. Cambridge Univ. Press, London.

ROBINSON, K. W. and P. R. MORRISON 1957. The reactions to hot atmospheres of various species of Australian marsupial and placental animals. J. Cellular Comp. Physiol., 49:455–478.

ROLLER, W. L. and R. F. GOLDMAN 1967. Estimation of solar radiation environment. Int. J. Biometeor., 11:329–336.

ROSENMANN, M. and P. R. MORRISON 1963. The physiological response to heat and dehydration in the guanaco. Physiol. Zool., 36:45–51.

SCHMIDT-NIELSON, K. 1964. Desert Animals. Physiological Problems in Heat and Water. Clarendon Press, Oxford.

SCHMIDT-NIELSON, K., B. SCHMIDT-NIELSON, T. R. HOUPT

and s. a. jarnum 1956. The question of water storage in the stomach of the camel. Mammalia, *20:* 1–15.

taylor, c. r. 1969. The eland and the oryx. Sci. Amer., 220:88–95.

washburn, s. l. and i. devore 1961. Social behavior of baboons and early man. *In* Social Life of Early Man, ed. by S. L. Washburn, pp. 91–105. Aldine, Chicago.

weiner, j. s. and k. hellmann 1960. The sweat glands. Biol. Rev., 25:141–186.

whittow. g. c. 1968. Body fluid regulation. *In* Adaptation of Domestic Animals, ed. by E. S. E. Hafez, pp. 119–126. Lea and Febriger, Philadelphia.

wolf, a. v. 1958. Thirst. Physiology of the Urge to Drink and Problems of Water Lack. C. C. Thomas, Springfield.

yousef, m. k., l. hahn and h. d. johnson 1968. Adaptation of cattle. *In* Adaptation of Domestic Animals, ed. by E. S. E. Hafez, pp. 233–245. Lea and Febiger, Philadelphia.

25 · ON THE RELATION BETWEEN BODY SIZE, WAKING ACTIVITY, AND THE ORIGIN OF SOCIAL LIFE IN THE PRIMATES

Ashley Montagu

Very few correlative studies have been made between physical and functional traits in the primates. The contribution which follows reports a study of the probable evolutionary correlation between two physical and two functional traits, namely: body size, social grouping, eye size, and waking activity. The correlation among these four traits is almost complete, and almost self-explanatory. But this the reader may determine for himself.

What is of great interest, and did not occur to the author when this communication was written, is that nocturnal birds, for example like the owl, have large eyes, and that fishes living in dark waters also tend to have large eyes.[1]

The transition from nocturnal prosimians to diurnal monkeys was a major one adaptively, and the development of gregariousness is surely a fascinating and central factor in primate evolution. This is a line of research which would, we think, be worth further exploration.

During the course of a survey of the morphology and behavior traits of the primates the constancy of the association of certain physical and social traits gradually forced itself upon my attention. Since the association between these traits is virtually complete and invariable, that association would in itself be worth recording, for this has not previously been done. There are, however, additional reasons which, as we shall see, suggest the desirability of recording, and discussing, these particular facts, for it is possible that they may have a very real bearing upon the origin and evolution of social life in the primates.

source: Ashley Montagu, *American Anthropologist,* vol. 46, 1944, pp. 113–7. Reprinted by permission of the publisher.

[1] See Gordon L. Walls, *The Vertebrate Eye.* (Bloomfield Hills, Michigan: Cranbrook Institute of Science, 1942), pp. 208–209, 210–11.

When we examine the living lemurs we find that they fall into two groups; one is practically completely nocturnal in its habits, sleeping by day and spending most of its waking hours during the night, while the other is mainly diurnal, being almost entirely active by day alone. Like most primates all lemurs are arboreal creatures, though the larger lemurs, particularly of the genus *Lemur*, spend a good deal of time among the rocks. It is a striking fact that the lemurs of small body size are all, unexceptionally, the most definitely nocturnal in their habits, while those of larger size are almost entirely diurnal. This in itself is an interesting association. It would also appear that the small nocturnal lemurs have larger eyeballs than the larger diurnal lemurs. Finally, and most interestingly, the small nocturnal lemurs live either in pairs or in single families, while the larger diurnal lemurs tend to live in small groups which contain the members of at least one other family.

Since the lemurs represent the most primitive as well as the oldest type of primates, being, indeed, best regarded as a relict group, it may reasonably be assumed that they preserve the social habits of even earlier ancestral primates. The point is not overly important, but it is worth mention because it is known that the earliest primates were not much larger than small rats, and from this—together with the evidence cited in this communication—it may be inferred that they were probably nocturnal in their habits, and lived in pairs or single families, as do the closely related primatoid menotyphlous insectivores (Tupaiidae, Macroscelidae) to this day.

The evidence provided by the lemurs suggests that small arboreal primates are better able to survive when they are active at night than during the day. Large eyes provide them with the necessary visual power to pursue their nocturnal activities, and these activities can most effectively be pursued in solitude or in pairs, or in small family groups. These seem to be the facts for the lemurs. The reverse conditions seem to be equally closely connected. What are the conditions in the remaining suborders and families of primates? Are these facts or is this association of conditions corroborated by the conditions existing in any other group of primates? It may be said at once that the evidence is strikingly corroborative, and where it is exceptional—exceedingly enlightening.

The tarsiers of the suborder Tarsioidea are very small creatures about the size of a small rat; they are completely nocturnal, and live in pairs or in single families.

The exception to the rule of having all four variables positively correlated is provided by a single family among the Platyrrhini or Old World Monkeys, the Hapalidae, consisting of the marmosets and tamarins. These animals are about the size of a small squirrel, but they all have small or medium-sized eyes, are diurnal in their habits, and are said to live in pairs or single families. The two important correlations here are (1), between body size and the habit of living in pairs or single families, and (2), between diurnal activities and small or medium-sized eyes. I shall return to a discussion of the significance of these facts presently. Meanwhile, we must be grateful for these exceptional cases, for they often serve to throw light on the relative importance of variables which are otherwise too closely correlated to lend themselves to the necessary separation and analysis.

Finally, and most significantly, among the ten genera of the family Cebidae (South American monkeys) embracing some 93 different species, the species of smallest size (embracing ten species) all belong to the same genus *Aotes*, the douroucoulis or night-monkeys. These are the only monkeys, among the Cebidae, that have large eyes, are nocturnal in their habits, and live in pairs or single families. They are about the size of a squirrel.

All other primates of the platyrrhine and catarrhine series are of relatively large body size, with small or medium-sized eyes, are diurnal in their activities, and live in communities or bands.[1]

We have here then, an almost perfect correlation between (1) body size, (2) kind of social life, (3) waking-activity habits, and (4) size of eyes.

Small primates are likely to be nocturnal, to have large eyes, and to live either in solitude, in pairs, or in small single family groups. Large primates are likely to be diurnal, to have small or medium-sized eyes, and to live in bands or communities.

The conditions among the marmosets indicate that when small primates are diurnal their eyes are small or of medium size, and that they retain their habit of living in pairs or in single families.

It need hardly be pointed out here that even a complete positive correlation does not necessarily imply a causal relationship between the variables found in association, their association may be due to still other conditions, and it is a safe general rule to assume that they usually are until every effort has been exhausted to prove

[1] By a community or band I mean a group consisting of the members of two or more families.

them so. In the present case, in virtue of the nature of the data, such attempts to prove the existence of significant additional conditions are not readily feasible. Our task must therefore lie in an attempt to educe the order of most probable relationship existing between the four variables we have noted. In this we are greatly assisted by the apparently aberrant conditions found among the marmosets. From the latter it appears that body size is directly associated with small social groups limited to a single pair or a family, while size of eyes is most directly associated, as would be expected, with type of waking activity.

To conclude then, the evidence renders it highly probable that increase in body size (and, presumably, weight) may have been a potent factor in releasing the early Anthropoidea from their nocturnal or crepuscular habits, by enabling them to hold their own against most aggressors, and that this together with the potentialities released by the assumption of a diurnal life led to the development of more extended social relations with animals of their own species. It is perhaps worth pointing out that this is not a speculation, but an interpretation of facts, to which a high degree of probability attaches.

The Relation Between Body Size, Size of Eyeballs, Waking Activity, and Size of the Social Aggregate in the Primates

PRIMATE	NUMBER OF SPECIES	SIZE	SIZE OF EYEBALLS	WAKING ACTIVITY	SIZE OF SOCIAL AGGREGATE
SUBORDER LEMUROIDEA					
SERIES LEMURIFORMES					
Lemurs of Madagascar and neighboring islands					
I. FAMILY LEMURIDAE					
1. SUBFAMILY LEMURINAE					
True Lemurs (*Lemur*)	14	Large Fox	Medium	Mainly Diurnal	Groups of five to six
Gentle Lemurs (*Hapalemur*)	3	Small Fox	Large	Nocturnal	Pairs
Sportive Lemurs (*Lepidolemur*)	7	Small Fox	Large	Nocturnal	Pairs
The hattock (*Mixocebus*)	1	Small Fox	Large	Nocturnal	Pairs
2. SUBFAMILY CHEIROGALEINAE					
Mouse Lemurs (*Chirogale*)	5	Rat	Large	Nocturnal	Pairs
Dwarf Lemurs (*Microcebus*)	4	Rat	Large	Nocturnal	Pairs
Fat-tailed Lemurs (*Opolemur*)	2	Rat	Large	Nocturnal	Pairs
II. FAMILY INDRISIDAE					
Endrinas (*Indris*)	1	Cat	Medium	Mainly Diurnal	Groups of four or five
Sifakas (*Propithecus*)	3	Cat	Medium	Diurnal	Groups of six to eight
Woolly Avahi (*Lichanotus*)	2	Fox	Medium	Nocturnal	Solitary or pairs
III. FAMILY CHIROMYIDAE					
Aye-Aye (*Chiromys*)	1	Cat	Large	Nocturnal	Pairs
SERIES LORISIFORMES					
Lemurs of Africa and Asia					
I. FAMILY GALAGIDAE					
Bush-Babies (*Galago*)	21	Cat	Large	Nocturnal	Pairs
Lesser Bush-Babies (*Hemigalago*)	3	Rat	Large	Nocturnal	Pairs
II. FAMILY LORISIDAE					
Slender Loris (*Loris*)	2	Rat	Large	Nocturnal	Pairs

The Relation Between Body Size, Size of Eyeballs, Waking Activity, and Size of the Social Aggregate in the Primates (Continued)

PRIMATE	NUMBER OF SPECIES	SIZE	SIZE OF EYEBALLS	WAKING ACTIVITY	SIZE OF SOCIAL AGGREGATE
Slow Loris (*Nycticebus*)	11	Fox	Large	Nocturnal	Pairs
Angwantibo (*Arctocebus*)	2	Fox	Large	Nocturnal	Pairs
Potto (*Perodicticus*)	5	Fox	Large	Nocturnal	Pairs
SUBORDER TARSIOIDEA					
I. FAMILY TARSIOIDEA					
Spectral Tarsier (*Tarsius*)	1	Rat	Enormous	Nocturnal	Pairs
SUBORDER ANTHROPOIDEA					
DIVISION PLATYRRHINI					
I. FAMILY HAPALIDAE					
Marmosets. Genera 5	37	Small Squirrel	Medium	Diurnal	Three or four
II. FAMILY CEBIDAE					
Night Monkeys (*Aotes*)	10	Squirrel	Large	Nocturnal	Pairs
All 9 other genera	83	Dog	Medium	Diurnal	Communities
DIVISION CATARRHINI					
I. FAMILY CERCOPITHECIDAE					
1. SUBFAMILY CERCOPITHECINAE					
8 Genera	137	Dog	Medium	Diurnal	Communities
2. SUBFAMILY SEMNOPITHECINAE					
4 Genera	75	Dog	Medium	Diurnal	Communities
SERIES ANTHROPOMORPHA					
I. FAMILY HYLOBATIDAE					
Common Gibbons (*Hylobates*)	8	2 ft. 6 in.	Medium	Diurnal	Communities
Siamangs (*Symphalangus*)	1	2 ft. 6 in.	Medium	Diurnal	Communities
II. FAMILY PONGIDAE					
Orang-Outang (*Pongo*)	1	5 feet	Medium	Diurnal	Families Communities?
Chimpanzee (*Pan*)	2	5 feet	Medium	Diurnal	Communities
Gorilla (*Gorilla*)	2	5 ft. 6 in.	Medium	Diurnal	Communities
III. FAMILY HOMINIDAE					
Man (*Homo*)	1	5 ft. 6 in.	Medium	Diurnal	Communities

TWELVE • AGGRESSION

26 • THE SOCIO-ECOLOGY OF PRIMATES: GROUP CHARACTERISTICS AND INFERENCE TO MAN

John Hurrell Crook

The following contribution consists of the concluding pages of an excellent survey of "The Socio-Ecology of the Primates." Were it not for the fact that this excerpt runs to more than sixty pages the whole survey would have been reprinted in the present volume. The reader is therefore recommended to read the whole of the original article. In the pages here Crook succinctly presents an evaluation of the writings of authors like Lorenz, Ardrey, Tiger, Fox, and others, who have overemphasized the influence of the genetic element on the behavior of groups. Without in any way meaning to relegate the genetic element to an inconsequential status, Crook's *obiter dictum* that "primate societies, rather than being the product of Darwinian natural selection in any simple sense, in fact seem to determine in an important way the genetical basis of individual social response" (p. 433 this volume), should be hung over the desk of every ethologist engaged in the attempt to argue from animal to human behavior.

Crook has much more to say of great importance on this complex subject, and about the manner in which phenotypic adaptation and collateral genetic adaptation go hand in hand in the development of primate social systems. His emphasis on culture as the major determinant of social change in human societies, and the relative unimportance of ecology, deserves further development and amplification.

Crook's emphasis on the development of compatible field methods in order that the results obtained by different observers may be comparable in terms of the necessary scientific requirements is well placed.

His suggestions for more detailed studies on intraspecific social variation, developmental and longitudinal studies of the social dynamics of well-known populations in the wild, and research into the synecology (that is, the ecological study of different groups) of primates in the more stable environments should encourage responsive interest.

Introduction

Field studies of primate social life, initiated so promisingly by C. R. Carpenter before the last world war, have recently begun to play a major role in the study of mammalian behaviour. The cumulative total of man-months devoted to field studies alone has doubled since 1960 and a comparable increase in laboratory work is evident (Altmann 1967). The establishment of a chain of primate centres in the United States, well endowed with facilities at all research levels and including resources for field study, means that this rate of increase may be maintained, other factors being equal, over a number of years.

An outstanding feature of this movement has been the collaboration between ethologists, psychologists, psychiatrists and social anthropologists in wrestling with the problems presented by the use of primates in research; a collaboration eloquently testifying to the interest of this material to students of human biology.[1] In par-

SOURCE: John Hurrell Crook, *Social Behavior in Birds and Mammals* (London & New York: Academic Press, 1970), pp. 103–66. Reprinted by permission of the author and the publisher.

[1] The new information is available not only in both established and newly created journals but also in recent symposium volumes edited, among others, by

ticular, laboratory workers now show an unaccustomed respect for field study and consider the results of such work significant both in the design of laboratory research and in the making of inferences from animal to human behaviour. Social anthropologists, anxious to underpin theories of human behavioural and social origins with a biological basis, have turned increasingly to ethologists for assistance (e.g. Tiger and Fox 1966, Fox 1967a, b, Reynolds 1968).

To some extent, however, the very abundance of the new information hinders digestion. The use of specialized approaches of differing historical origin limits communication, and a clear picture of the way in which reports on the behaviour of one primate species may be most meaningfully compared with those on another, let alone with the literature on Man, has yet to emerge. There is need for a preliminary synthesis in an attempt to see the extent of contemporary research, the range of current problems, the trends in theory construction, and the problem of choice among lines that may be heuristically developed.

In this chapter some of the current approaches to the study of the relations between primate social organizations and their environments will be described. First, we shall consider the adaptive significance of contrasting primate social structures in relation to their ecology; second, the range of problems posed by intra-specific variation in social systems in primates; third, the socio-ecology of behavioural development and group cohesion; fourth, the manner in which changes in social organization may occur, and finally, the problems involved in inferring from non-human primate behaviour to Man.

Buetner-Janusch (1962), Napier and Barnicot (1963), DeVore (1965), Schrier, Harlow and Stollnitz (1965), Altmann (1967), Morris (1967) and Jay (1968). Still more are on the way.

The Nature of Primate Social Systems

Individual primate species are found in relatively restricted habitats within which they are dispersed in population units or "demes" commonly separated by ecological barriers. Each deme is structured into social units within which the pattern of "face-to-face" relations between individuals known to one another occurs. Rarely does a whole deme appear to be a single social unit; usually, a deme comprises several units each moving within its own home range which may or may not overlap extensively with those of neighbours and which may or may not be defended in characteristic ways as territory. Some social units are restricted to very small territorial areas, while the home ranges of others may be so large that only occasionally do they meet other groups of the species. Some social units wander independently under some conditions, only to congregate into larger units or herds when these conditions are changed. The key social unit of each species is that within which normal social and reproductive activity occurs, and which persists through time showing social cohesion and an integrated pattern of relations between members. It usually consists of females and young with at least one adult male. This is the bisexual reproductive group which Imanishi once termed an "oikia" (1960) and which others have commonly called a "troop" or a "group." In some populations reproductive units contain a number of reproductive adult males (i.e. multimale) but in other populations sub-adult and some adult males are excluded from reproductive units which come to include only one adult male, the "despot," "overlord" or "leader" of earlier writers, with his "harem." Kummer and Kurt (1963) call such groups "one-male groups." In several species reproductive groups are now known to be open to individual movement. Among gorillas, baboons, vervet monkeys and rhesus macaques, males have been seen to move from one group to another and show similar behaviour in each. By contrast females appear to show strong group loyalty to their initial companions and comprise the more stable element of a reproductive unit.

A variety of terms have been used in the literature for different primate groupings. "Troop" usually refers to the reproductive unit comprising several males and females complete with juveniles and infants usually seen in baboons and macaques and some forest primates such as the Howler Monkey. Other primate societies are organized at more than one level; thus "congregations" or "herds" of geladas may comprise both one-male reproductive units and all-male groups, while hamadryas baboons occur in "bands" made up of one-male groups together with peripheral non-reproductive males. These bands sometimes likewise associate together. Solitary individual males have been reported from several social organizations. Careful description of units rather than the use of obsolete and ambiguous terminology has become vital in comparing the work of different writers. The term "party" may usefully refer to a group the composition of which is uncertain or unknown. The term "group" together with appropriate designation may be used to refer to social units the composition of which is known.

Individual primates thus live in populations that comprise "social systems" varying with respect to (i) the numbers of individuals in a given area, (ii) their pattern of spatial dispersion into groups of differing type, (iii) the composition of the groups in terms of age and sex classes, (iv) the sub-structuring of the groups arising out of inter-individual relations, the group composition and the nature and extent of exchange between groups and, lastly, (v) the stability of the group as a social unit, its formation, division or breakdown (Carpenter 1964, Imanishi 1957,

1960, Southwick 1962, Koford 1963, Hall 1965, Crook 1966, Kummer 1968a).

Differences between social systems occur not only with respect to the taxonomic position of the species but also with clear contrasts in ecology. Indeed similar social systems are found in quite unrelated primates living in similar environments. Crook and Gartlan (1966) showed that social systems could be categorized into five "grades" (Huxley 1959), in which close correlations between habitat and diet preferences, diurnal activity rhythms, group size, type of reproductive unit, sex dimorphism and population dispersion patterns indicated co-adaptations of these features to aspects of biome types forming major selection pressures. The five grades represent levels of adaptation to forests, forest fringes, rich savanna, and arid environments and suggest clearly the overall pattern of social evolution in primates. At each major taxonomic level from primitive to higher forms, radiation into some or all of the main available environments has occurred often with strikingly parallel results. The trend lies from primitive forest insectivorous primates, nocturnal and solitary, through more social diurnal fruit- and leaf-eating monkeys in forests, to omnivorous diurnal troop dwellers living in various types of social units in open country.

Interspecific Contrasts in Group Structure

Contrasts in social structure between species are most conveniently studied in the differing monkey and ape societies. Variations are probably best envisaged as continua in relation to gradients in environmental conditions, but for practical purposes we may use a preliminary categorization into five main types.

1. Relatively small groups usually consisting of a single adult male with one or sometimes

more adult females together with juveniles occurring in defended territories (vocalization, visual displays); Forest species—examples: *Colobus guereza* (Marler 1968), *Presbytis cristatus* (Bernstein 1968), *Callecebus moloch* (Mason 1968), *Hylobates* sp. (Carpenter 1940).

2. Larger groups consisting of at least one and sometimes several adult males with adult females and juveniles occurring in territories or home ranges within which group vocal displays are given. Forest and forest fringe—examples: *Allouatta palliata* (Carpenter 1965), *Cercocebus albigena* (Chalmers 1968).

3. Groups containing several adult males and numerically more females with offspring and juveniles in relatively large home ranges in forest fringe, open woodland, and savanna country. Some species show territorial defence but most move in home ranges that overlap extensively. Avoidance rather than overt aggression normally mediates dispersion. Exchange of males between groups has been reported. Examples: *Cercopithecus aethiops* (Gartlan 1966, Struhsaker 1967a, b); *Papio* spp. (not *hamadryas*) (DeVore 1965b, Hall and DeVore 1965); *Macaca mulatta* (Altmann 1962, Southwick 1962, Koford 1963); *Macaca fuscata* (Imanishi 1957).

4. Populations regularly divided into reproductive groups comprising a single adult male with several adult females and young (one-male groups, Kummer and Kurt 1963) and "all-male groups" containing sub-adult and some adult animals. The spatial dispersion of the groups varies in the three species so far known to show these social structures. In *Erythrocebus patas* Hall (1966) reported groups moving separately in large home ranges avoiding contact with one another. In *Papio hamadryas* (Kummer and Kurt 1963, Kummer 1968) one-male groups occur in "bands" that move in large herds. The band's day-ranging is based on sleeping sites that are limited in frequency in the habitat. In *Theropithecus gelada* (Crook 1966) the one-male groups commonly occur in herds but the groups are free to enter or leave at will. These three species live primarily in grassland, arid savanna, and montane grassland respectively and in each case are subjected to long harsh dry seasons.

5. Population demes in forest, forest fringe, and woodland savanna in which little social substructuring is apparent but in which relatively temporary gatherings of various sex and age classes occur at sleeping, feeding and other sites. Individuals drift from one social grouping to another in varying combinations. There is some evidence for links between mothers and grown offspring. Example: *Pan satyrus* (Goodall 1965, Reynolds and Reynolds 1965). Recent work suggests that under certain conditions small chimp groups cohere in larger units (Itani and Suzuki 1967).

The macaques, monkeys and baboons of relatively open country have been studied in most detail. In the humid, relatively food-rich savannas, relationships between numerical density, food availability, seasonal change, and predation appear to produce large groupings (Type 3) in which seasonal reproduction is common. The significance of the different timings of reproductive seasons (Lancaster and Lee 1965) is unclear, and whether advantages are obtained primarily during pregnancy, during lactation, or during the infancy of offspring remains to be ascertained.

1. Terrestrial Savanna Species

An apparent increase in size of terrestrial savanna groups over those of forest dwelling species has been pointed out by DeVore (1963) and Crook and Gartlan (1966). Recent attempts to test this contention by statistical analysis of available reports irrespective of contrasts in observer reliability (Clutton-Brock, personal communication) and from recent counts of forest cercopithecid groups (Struhsaker, in preparation) indicate the need for further study. Clutton-Brock utilized numerical information derived from the whole primate literature to yield joint means for the group size of many species. These he classified according to taxonomic superfamilies and ecology in a comparison between "forest," "woodland" and "savanna." Superficial analysis related the means to ecology, with a trend to increasing size from forest to savanna. An analysis of variance, however, suggested that the only significant degrees of freedom present were those associated with taxonomic contrasts irrespective of ecology. Nevertheless pair-wise comparisons of mean group size between ecologies showed a significantly smaller figure in forest compared with savanna, and savanna means were also larger than those in woodland. Further checks on limited numbers of reports of greater reliability failed to substantiate the position, although in no case was the mean group size of forest species larger than that of savanna. The gross nature of the designated ecologies and the variation in the reliability of reports necessitates further study when better data are available. Struhsaker showed that two mainly ground-dwelling forest species departed markedly from the mean group size of forest *Cercopithecus* species (*circa* eleven). *C. l'hoesti preussi* showed a mean of about half this, while drills (*Mandrillus leucophaeus*) had larger groups comparable with those of open country baboons. Both reports suggest that phylogenetic relations may play a role in the determination of group size. In addition more precise delineation of ecological niches in forests is essential, in particular the maintenance of a distinction between terrestrial and arboreal forest species.

In open environments parties of macaques and baboons cohere remarkably well. Daily routines are strictly followed and individuals do not perform activities such as drinking independently from others. This coherence is doubtless a response to predation, since isolated animals apparently do not survive long. Large coherent groups appear to be permitted ecologically by a dispersion of food items in such manner that the group can move through an area without producing competition between individuals entailing food shortages for some of them (subordinate individuals) to a degree rendering the social structure untenable. An effect of the formation and maintenance of coherent parties is an apparent increase in competition between males for the relatively limited numbers of females in oestrus at any one time. The consequent intra-sexual selection of male characteristics appears primarily responsible for the increased sexual dimorphism so apparent in baboons. Competition also produces the complex male social hierarchies that define in part the roles adopted by individuals in relation to their differential access to females, food, and other commodities in certain well-studied savanna groups. Female baboons and rhesus macaques coming into oestrus are served first by more subordinate or juvenile animals but at the height of oestrus they usually consort sexually with high-ranking individuals. There is thus a constant interchange of mating partners and a form of patterned promiscuity (Hall and DeVore 1965, Altmann 1962, etc.).

In arid African savanna, with its markedly severe seasonal conditions, environmental pressures determining patterns of dispersion appear subtly different from those in more stable environments. Although precise measurement of these differences has yet to be attempted, it seems that there are fewer predators and food availability is more severely diminished in the long arid dry season. The dispersion of food items at such times appears to be such that should there be large coherent troops containing a high proportion of males in relation to females, the latter, being relatively subordinate, would suffer most from food shortage when it occurred—a phenomenon already demonstrated in the dense congregations of an arid country Weaver-bird (Crook and Ward 1968). The division of the population into one-male and all-male groups appears to be the sociological response to these conditions. In the one-male group procreation remains assured while the exploitation of food by adult males relative to females is reduced to a minimum. There is also evidence from field studies of geladas (Crook 1966, 1967b) that all-male groups tend at crucial periods to wander separately from one-male groups and to exploit rather different ground, thus reducing competition further.[2] The incidence of group congregation is low and the size of congregations small, groups travel fast over the unproductive terrain. All-male groups of Patas monkeys likewise move separately from the one-male groups. The population of Hamadryas baboons studied by Kummer and Kurt (1963) comprised one-male groups congregated together with peripheral males into bands within herds. This close association of groups appeared contingent upon the limited number of sleeping sites in the study area. In other areas a greater dispersion of Hamadryas groups may be found. Two very small bands were seen for example in the Semyen Gorges in the Gondar province of Ethiopia in 1965 (J.II.C.).

After the rains and under local conditions of food abundance, one-male and all-male groups of geladas come together into big herds. The canyon cliffs near which geladas live provide a superabundance of sleeping sites and thus play little role in determining dispersion in this species (Crook 1966). Herds of geladas are interestingly structured in ways that recall the distribution of individuals in chacma baboon troops—large subadult males on the outside forming a "protective" screen. In the gelada case sub-adult males from all-male groups, by reason of faster foraging rates and a less nervous disposition, range well "inland" from a gorge edge, while females and juveniles with their male overlords keep closer to the cliff and descend first to safety when danger threatens.

Patas monkeys have only rarely been recorded in herds which appear to form briefly near water holes in the dry season (N. Cameroon) (Sanderson 1957, Struhsaker, personal communication). Members of the small groups scatter at night into the small irregularly distributed trees that form their grassland sleeping sites, a behaviour also reported for vervet monkeys in a comparable habitat (Struhsaker 1967b). Poor food availability throughout the year, high predation risk, and limited sleeping sites appear to account for the highly dispersed character of the patas social system in grassland. These features correlate well with the athletic appearance of these highly mobile animals and their markedly different temperament from baboons (Hall 1966a). In addition their relatively small size, compared to baboons, would presumably lessen the survival value of forming larger social units for improved protection from predators.

The social systems of open country monkeys may be described then as functions of three main extrinsic determinants, the pattern of food availability in terms of food item dispersion and seasonal variations in abundance, the incidence of predation, and the type of sleeping site available in the habitat. Differences in the values of these parameters appear to determine the contrasting grouping characteristics of rich and arid savanna populations and those of grassland. These can be expressed in signal flow diagrams relating the environmental input of information to a social or "socio-demographic" system and the adaptive response of the population in terms of numerical density, population dispersion, and social structure. The formal relations are shown in diagram form in Fig. 1 adapted from Crook and Gartlan (1966).

---

[2] Similar findings are reported from certain African Bovids by Jarman (1968).

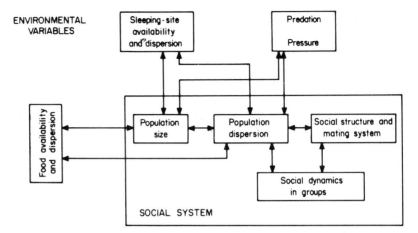

Figure 1: Relations between extrinsic factors and aspects of a primate social system. (*Adapted from Crook and Gartlan 1966.*)

Extrinsic factors affect intrinsic variables primarily through modifying population size and dispersion. Nevertheless, direct environmental pressure, when maintained over long time periods, eventually induces changes in social structure and dynamics. The time scales upon which the different aspects of the social system alter vary with their proximate control—food shortage has an immediate impact upon the population while changes in dispersion affect the traditions of social structuring and the genetics of communication only over longer time periods (see pp. 136–137, 144).

2. Forest Monkeys

Current studies on forest monkeys are revealing a complex diversity of grouping patterns. Not only are there multimale reproductive groups (Howlers, Carpenter 1965; Mangabeys, Chalmers 1968; Spider monkey, Klein, personal communication) but, in addition, a number of species are now known to live in one-male reproductive units (Bernstein 1968, Mason 1968, Marler 1968, Aldrich-Blake, in Crook, *Social Behavior in Birds and Mammals*, Sugiyama 1967, Schenkel and Schenkel-Hulliger 1967). Ecologically, forest monkeys differ from one another in many respects illustrating the diversity of niches they occupy.

Some species feed on leaves, some on ripe fruit. Others feed on unripe fruit, shoots and sometimes bark. Some feed on insects, capturing them from different hiding places in differing ways. One is nocturnal (*Aotus*), most are diurnal but with peak activity at differing times of the day. Some feed and travel at one height in the canopy, others at a different height. Even so several species may exploit the same fruiting tree. Some species associate in mixed bands while others do not. Some show breeding seasons in improbably constant conditions whilst others appear to be breeding in every month of the year. Some species are exclusively arboreal, others partly terrestrial or largely so. A few prefer swamps. None of the relations between such factors and social organizations have yet been worked out in detail for any species.

An explanation of dispersion in one-male groups in terms of habitat seasonality and food shortage seems untenable in the case of forest species living in relatively stable forest ecosystems showing local irregularities in food resources of different kinds, rather than gross overall seasonal fluctuations. It seems probable, nevertheless, that the argument implicating food availability as a prime determinant of the system may still hold in certain of these cases because a relatively poor food availability may be chronic. Ashmole (see Lack

1966) has argued that in bird species living in ecologically stable tropical forests the relatively unchanging environmental conditions imply that the population will oscillate around an asymptote at which numbers are closely regulated by the more or less seasonally constant level of resources. Change in numbers will thus be slight, recruitment balancing mortality, and individuals will have difficulty in rearing young in the absence of seasonal superabundance. Ecologists such as Cody (1966) have pointed out that in relatively stable tropical conditions selection should tend to encourage adaptations permitting increased environmental carrying capacity, rather than a seasonal maximum recruitment common in less stable temperate regions. Selection should favour adaptations reducing intra- and inter-specific competition and increasing means of protection from predation. Even with birds these suggestions await full confirmation but there seems in principle no reason why the argument should not apply to forest primates. Certainly their copulation frequencies and reproductive rates do appear lower than those of open-country animals. Frequencies of child-bearing, durations of lactation, timing of post-partum oestrus and rates of infant development need examining from this perspective.

Arboreal forest monkeys live at higher population densities than their savanna relatives, a condition probably "legislated" (Solomon 1964) by the overall greater productivity of the environment. The groups are in relatively frequent contact with one another, often live in small home ranges and show territorial behaviour or maintain dispersion by vocal displays that appear to function in many ways like bird song. Clearly social forces are present that keep groups apart, for there are no habitat or ecological barriers that would operate to maintain dispersion. In some cases (Rowell 1966a, Gartlan 1966, Sugiyama 1967 etc.) males are known to move from one group to another and to show similar role performances in the adopted group. Females appear

generally to form the more stable membership of a local group. Preliminary data suggest that the size of groups; their composition and the area defended as territory may be related to available food supplies; in particular, for example, the distribution and seasonal availability of fruiting trees. Certainly the seasonal movements of the group within the territory in *Cercocebus albigena* (Chalmers 1967) and *Cercopithecus mitis* (Aldrich-Blake, personal communication) indicate that food is not equally distributed within a forest home range at all seasons. In *C. mitis* the relative crowding or dispersal of group members in a territory varies periodically and appears to coincide with contrasts in food availability. It seems probable that the relation between group size and composition and the size of the defended area is linked to the carrying capacity of the local habitat. In a dense population it would be advantageous for individuals to live in territories in which over-exploitation of resources by numbers in excess of local carrying capacity is prevented, and where the inter-sexual competition for food within groups is reduced by limiting the numbers of adult males in each reproductive unit. We have as yet, however, no clear evidence that supernumerary males are excluded from territories (but see p. 119, Crook, on Langurs). Group size would appear to be a function of the food content of the territory and should in theory vary with the area occupied, other variables being constant.

Research into the ecological reference of social systems in arboreal primates is not easy. In the first place estimates of group size and determination of their structure is a singularly difficult task in many forest species. It is often difficult to know whether apparent group size is little more than a function of the conditions of observation, and a variety of methods of construing the data may be required before a reliable reference to numbers and group constancy can be made (Aldrich-Blake, pp. 79–90, this volume). "Forest," as we have seen, is not a uniform environment and vegetation types show many variations. Monkeys occupy contrasting niches, particularly with regards to different levels in the canopy and differing species diversity in different forests (e.g. Booth 1956, 1958). Each niche condition may contribute to contrasts between species in dispersion and social organization. In some species, furthermore, the Colobus feeding selectively on leaves for example, there is little evidence suggesting any food shortage. Nevertheless, shortage may take the form of deficits in specific nutritional needs rather than in food in bulk, and be more pronounced in certain seasons in correlation with the annual leaf cycle of the trees. Again, if in fact populations are in some state of numerical and social equilibrium in relation to their resources, a demonstration of food control will be difficult without field experimentation. Even so, Aldrich-Blake has reported that in certain months *Cercopithecus mitis* eats leaves rather than the fruits favoured at other times. Some comparable evidence, but involving farm products, has been presented by Chalmers (1967, 1968a). There is also increasing evidence (Gartlan, Aldrich-Blake, Klein, personal communications) for some kind of inter-species sociality among arboreal forest monkeys, suggesting the presence of pressures favouring niche reduction and social adaptations reducing inter-species competition perhaps analogous to those discussed by Moynihan (1963) in regard to neo-tropical forest birds.

An additional complication has been suggested by Chivers (1969) who presents evidence to support the view that the so-called territories of howler monkeys on Barro Colorado island may lack strict topographical reference. The apparent "borders" appear to change with time, suggesting that spacing may be determined more by vocal display and avoidance than by active defence of borders. Aldrich-Blake's observations on *Cercopithecus mitis* and Marler's (1968) on

Colobus guereza suggest that in addition to a topographical confinement of individual ranging and the occurrence of group territorial encounters involving male displays at apparent boundaries, loud vocalization may help to maintain group dispersion through mutual avoidance. A similar situation probably exists in langur populations in forests (Jay 1965).

In a theoretical discussion Chivers (loc. cit.) argues that contrasts in the manner of social control maintaining dispersion in forests may be in part a function of changes in population density in relation to recent ecological history and in part owing to the manner in which inter-group relations develop. He refers to the contrast between *Allouatta* populations at low density in mature forest where they are dispersed in large groups, and those in forest much dissected by agriculture where grouping and behaviour is quite variable, density may be high, group size small, and range very limited. On Barro Colorado the growth of secondary forest since the island was created seems related to shifts in the density of the species population. Comparing *Allouatta* with the strictly territorial *Cebus,* he suggests that in populations where socially unrelated groups are gradually compressed by density changes avoidance is mediated by vocal or visual signals, whereas stricter topographical reference in dispersion is contingent upon a history of group-splitting occasioning frequent contacts between socially related animals. The hypothesis requires further study, and the relations between dispersion behaviour, "solitarization" of males, and male motility (see Crook, pp. 145–52) need examination in the same context.

It seems likely that most leaf-eaters will turn out to live in one-male reproductive units. They share this characteristic, nonetheless, with species of other tastes. Species living in multimale troops are likewise diverse in feeding habits. In mangabeys and forest baboons, common behavioural inheritance (Chalmers 1968b) may contribute to the multimale condition. So, too, however, may the high degree of omnivority in the terrestrial forms and the wide diet tolerance of the mangabey. The baboon is mainly terrestrial and the mangabey arboreal. Howlers and spider monkeys (e.g. *Ateles belzebuth*, L. Klein, personal communication) also move in sizeable multimale groups. In the Columbian flood plain forest the spider monkeys live in widely dispersed multimale groups. Three adult males and some eight adult females were counted in a group of 25. The spider monkey is a ripe-fruit eater (unlike the howler). In addition, it eats leaves at particular times of the year—when fruit is especially mushy, when the leaves perhaps function as roughage, and when fruit is scarce, when leaves are doubtless of real food value. The spider monkey groups were constantly splitting up into smaller units and coming together again at fruit trees. Their social organization may aid in the location of, and rapid assembling at food resources, much in the same way that chimpanzee loose society is said to function (Reynolds 1965).

Diurnal insect eaters such as *Saimiri sciureus* move in much more cohesive multimale groups and sometimes associate with *Cebus apella*—each species exploiting the trees for contrasting insect prey living in different places (L. Klein, personal communication). Nocturnal insectivorous primates are by contrast very unsociable.

The size and composition of forest groups is doubtless programmed by a number of factors not all of which can be sensibly considered with our present knowledge. Dispersion of food items and seasonal variations in the location of abundance may favour the formation of multimale groups of numerous members occupying suitably sized home ranges. The greater the dispersion of food resources in clumped packages (fruit trees) the more likely a "loose" society will emerge. Greater food density and a more even dispersion may favour one-male groups in small territories; seasonal variation in abundance having deter-

mined the nature of the group composition. Little is known of predation in forests, by eagles for example. Possibly the formation of cohesive groups by small-bodied monkeys like *Saimiri* may be influenced by this factor and birth seasonality could likewise be affected. Both are known to be influenced by predation pressure in birds.

Detailed synecological studies would seem to provide a first step to outlining contrasting patterns of dispersion, numerical density, and group motility in species occupying contrasting niches in the same forest environment. Aside from preliminary work by Booth (1956, 1958) and studies by Gautier, Gartlan, Struhsaker and Aldrich-Blake still in progress, this area is wide open for study.

3. Parallel Radiations

Adaptive radiations parallel to that found in the Cercopithecoidea have been described for both Lemuroids and Hominoids. Petter (1962a, b) and Jolly (1966) have described the range of social structures among Madagascan lemurs, and these are closely associated with specific food habits and ecology. Among Pongids the arboreal Gibbons (*Hylobates*) show family structures (Type 1 above) in limited respects not unlike the one-male groups of several forest monkeys. Gorillas, heavily built ground-dwelling animals in tropical and montane tropical forests, live in small parties usually with a large adult male as leader. Avoidance rather than territorial display seems to keep groups apart in large but overlapping ranges (Schaller 1963). By contrast the more arboreal chimpanzees have a very loose social structure (Type 5) and individuals wander over large areas. No territorial behaviour has been detected. Reynolds (1965) considers that the gorilla-chimpanzee contrast is owing to differences in food type and availability. Chimps have to search for locally abundant fruit which is irregularly distributed both in space and time. Their ability to disperse and congregate rapidly again at sources is considered adaptive to the pattern of food dispersion. Preliminary evidence also suggests that in more open woodland savanna chimps are dispersed in a manner somewhat similar to baboons. Gorillas, by contrast, are herbivores rather than basically frugivores and do not appear to suffer from irregularities in food availability. They are nevertheless restricted in geographical distribution to certain tropical forests rich in food resources and lack the adaptability of the chimp, which can live on the forest fringe and survive when forest is destroyed.

The presence of non-reproductive surplus or "insurance" males in many primate populations suggests certain parallels with bird species in which only a proportion of a population successful in competition comprises the effective reproductive group (e.g. Grouse, Jenkins *et al.* 1963; Skylarks, Delius 1965; Kittiwakes, Coulson 1968). In these cases the performance of territorial behavior evidently plays an important role in excluding some individuals from breeding. These diverse avian social structures are functional primarily in relation to the protection and rearing of a clutch or brood and, at least in the two latter cases, the presence of both parents during nesting is essential for a successful outcome. In one-male primate groups only the female is essential for rearing, though the male may have a group protective function as well as mere procreation. An excess of females over males in relation to resources appears adaptive under limiting conditions, and supernumerary males may be excluded. These primate harems are nevertheless unlike avian "lek" or "arena" systems, in which the male's role is exclusively courtship and no bond formation is involved. This latter system is apparently permitted by food superabundance allowing the female birds to rear their young alone (Crook 1965). One-male groups resemble more the harem structures shown by wildebeeste,

deer, and seals; these, however, are in most cases purely seasonal arrangements. As Rowell also thinks (personal communication) the value of a long-term association of primate males with mother-litter families may derive from their utility to the group over many years and in relation to their experience of the habitat. This may apply also to certain Equids and Camilids with comparable group structure.

It seems likely that under certain conditions of population density in relation to resources and predation pressure, similar social systems emerge —not among primates alone but in other mammalian groups also. Indeed recent studies by Peter Jarman (1968) have indicated that correlations between social organization and ecology shown by a wide range of African Bovid species (Antelopes) form a pattern of variation strikingly comparable to that described here for Primates. We seem to be on the threshold of discovering important basic principles of common application to many mammalian groups (Crook, in preparation).

Intraspecific Variation in Social Organization

The relations portrayed in Fig. 1 are systemic in that they reveal feed-back control between environment and numbers and between the distribution of commodities and the dispersion of individuals. The intrinsic features of such a system show considerable stability, apparently as a result of the social selection of individuals best adapted to group norms and to the maintenance of traditions governing relationship through the socialization of young within social structures to which their behaviour eventually conforms. While phylogenetic heritage is doubtless responsible for basic similarities in the social life of related species, evidence is available to show that changes in the values of extrinsic determinants modify the nature of the social system shown by a population and that such differences may arise intraspecifically. In addition we know that experimental modification of the socialization process produces young animals of markedly deviant behaviour (Harlow and Harlow 1962, Mason 1965).

1. Baboons

The baboons included in the *cynocephalus, ursinus, anubis,* and *papio* species of the genus *Papio* are very closely related and, whatever the nomenclature of the moment, are probably best considered as clinal forms of the same species. From these the arid country form, *P. hamadryas,* is clearly distinguished by both morphology and social organization. The species of the main *Papio* taxonomic unit have been studied intensively at several locations situated well apart on the African continent (DeVore and Hall 1965, Hall and DeVore 1965, Hall 1962a, b, 1963, Rowell 1966a, Crook and Aldrich-Blake 1968 etc.). Comparisons between these studies reveal certain notable contrasts in social organization. In the open-country or savanna type environments Hall and DeVore describe the well-known troop structure described as Type 3 (p. 106). Troops may disperse somewhat while foraging over open terrain but a marked cohesiveness of the social unit is normally apparent. By contrast, Rowell (1966a) observed no such closely organized deployment in troops of *Papio anubis* based on the gallery forest at Ishasha in Uganda and she recorded males that moved from membership of one troop to that of another. At the relict montane *Olea* forest at Debra Libanos in Ethiopia, Crook and Aldrich-Blake (1968) observed no coherent troop structure. Instead, small parties of changing composition were found in and near the forest. While these probably formed parts of a "troop" with a core area of activity based on the forest, no clear-cut troop organization was apparent. These differences in social structuring are possibly a consequence of contrasts in inter-individual observability dependent upon differences in the density of vegetation in which the animals live. This view is supported by the author's observation of troops of *P. anubis* baboons in the Ethiopian rift moving in the integrated manner described elsewhere for savanna animals. The contrasts may, however, be additionally related to differences in food availability.

The open-country animals studied by Hall and DeVore (1965) showed a density of ten per square mile and a mean daily range of about three miles. The home ranges of troops studied by DeVore in Kenya were about 15 square miles in extent. Under these conditions the adult sex ratio in the troops averaged one male to 2.7 females and the ratio of adult males to all other individuals was 1:8.1. At Debra Libanos, with the harsh dry season characteristic of Ethiopia, the troop of forest-based animals showed an adult sex ratio of 1:2.1 and a male to all others ratio of 1:7.1, with a troop home range of about three square miles, daily ranging of 0.5–3 miles, and a population density of 30 per square mile. In Uganda near the riverine gallery forest at Ishasha, Rowell reported an adult sex ratio almost at equality (1:1.1) and a male to all other individuals ratio of 1:3.7. Here overlapping home ranges were 1.5–2 square miles in extent, the animals ranged 100 yards to four miles daily, and had a density of 20 baboons per square mile. These figures suggest that under relatively more stable ecological conditions around riverine forests, males are more common in the troops than under more extreme conditions. Similarly the ratio of adults to all juvenile categories at Ishasha was 1:1.25 but 1:1.4 at both Debra Libanos and in Hall and DeVore's account, suggesting rather higher adult mortality under the latter conditions. In addition there were more immature animals relative to adult females under the two forested conditions (Debra Libanos 1:2.48, Ishasha 1:2.5) than in the savanna (1:2), suggesting perhaps a lower infant mortality in the former. Under forested conditions baboons are noticeably arboreal and the young particularly exploit fruit in trees. In savanna there is possibly less difference in the diet of the various age classes. At Debra Libanos 50% of individual animal records were made in forest and at Ishasha 60% of troop time was spent in the forest. Comparable opportunities do not normally exist under savanna conditions.

2. Vervet and Langur Monkeys

Contrasts in group composition and social behaviour comparable to those described for baboons are now known to occur between populations of vervet monkeys, *Cercopithecus aethiops,* in different areas of Africa. These differences likewise involve taxonomic contrasts at what is probably no greater than the sub-species level. The vervet has been studied in Uganda on Lolui Island, Lake Victoria, and at Chobi on the north bank of the Nile near Murchison (32° 10′E) (Gartlan 1966), in Kenya at Amboseli (Struhsaker 1967a, b) and in Rhodesia (Brain, quoted in Gartlan 1966). The contrasts between the populations on Lolui, at Chobi, and at Amboseli are striking. The density on Lolui was high (225 per square mile) and the figures for the Amboseli study areas are about the same (Struhsaker, personal communication). At Chobi, however, there were only 57 animals per square mile. Group size on Lolui was smaller, with a mean of about 12 members. By contrast, in the more arid Amboseli the mean was 24 animals and in the Rhodesias (data quoted by Gartlan 1966 from R. C. Wingfield and C. W. Brain) groups of up to 50 were not uncommon. Groups of between 20 and 50 were reported from Ethiopia (Starck and Frick 1958). Reviewing the admittedly fragmentary evidence, Gartlan (1966) considers that an increased variability in group size occurs in the climatically more varied areas.

The adult sex ratio from 32 groups counted on Lolui was 1:1.37, at Nairobi 1:1.45, at Amboseli 1:1.5 ($n = 10$) and at Chobi 1:1.73 ($n = 3$). In the vervet, therefore, increased variability in group size in less stable environments may be accompanied by a reduction in the numbers of adult males in groups (Gartlan 1966). This may be compared perhaps with the interspecies comparisons (above) revealing the presence of one-male groups to be characteristic of open-country cercopithecoids of arid environments.

On Lolui and at Amboseli, Gartlan (1966), Gartlan and Brain (1968) and Struhsaker (1967a, b) observed territorial defence of circumscribed areas. On Lolui the mean size of territories was 0.06 square miles per group and about 0.12 at Amboseli. The home range of the groups at Chobi appears to have been about 0.9 square miles and here no territorial behaviour was observed, the home ranges overlapping slightly and groups sometimes sitting together and grooming near the edges of their home ranges. Territorial defence included vigorous group displays, adult males facing one another with tails raised. On Lolui, Gartlan describes "scent" marking of boulders and branches near territorial borders, a behaviour pattern not reported by Struhsaker at Amboseli. Gartlan also recorded a number of important behavioural contrasts between the Lolui and Chobi populations. At Chobi the animals dispersed far more when feeding over ground that was poor in food supplies. Related perhaps to this were the more intense mother-infant interactions, the greater frequency of interactions between adult males and infants, and the greater amount of mutual grooming between adult males. In addition a baboon-like greeting between the adult sexes was described and males groomed females in a less perfunctory manner than on Lolui. The frequency of social grooming appeared lower at Chobi. In addition animals when walking in tall grass at Chobi and in Ethiopia (Starck and Frick 1958) raise their tails apparently in indication of a change of position to other group members.

By contrast, raised tails are more commonly associated with aggressive encounters within and between groups on Lolui and at Amboseli. Groups split up for sleeping only rarely on Lolui and show no apparent constancy in their subdivision, whereas at Amboseli Struhsaker (1967b) reports a regular break-up of groups into parties dispersed over a linear distance as great as 750 yards. Preferences for sleeping party companions were demonstrated in the sub-groups so formed, and these appeared to be related to mother-infant and "friendship" relations between individuals. This subdivision of a party at night is considered to facilitate the concealment of the animals from nocturnal predators and resembles the sub-division of patas monkey groups at nightfall reported by Hall (1966).

A major aspect of vervet behaviour on Lolui Island was the interchange of males between groups. This appeared of common occurrence and a male could adopt territorial defence behaviour with respect to a new group and against his previous one without apparent difficulty. Such behaviour was considered unusual at Amboseli. Gartlan (1966, 1968) emphasizes the relatively transitory relationship of adult males within any one group on Lolui and describes inter-individual relations in terms of "roles" rather than in terms of linear dominance hierarchies. By contrast Struhsaker (1967b), emphasizing the relative stability and cohesiveness of his vervet groups, describes the group structure in terms of the dominance relations found within them. His account thus resembles the reports of social structure of savanna baboons (Hall and DeVore 1965) while Gartlan's account resembles more closely the work of Rowell (1966a) on gallery forest baboons.

Recent research on langur populations (*Presbytis entellus*) in India and Ceylon reveal quite dramatic contrasts in different parts of the species range that contradict an earlier contention of widespread similarity in behaviour through-

out the sub-continent. Jay (1965) studied one group intensively at Kaukori near Lucknow in Uttar Pradesh and three forest-based groups near Orcha village, Bastar, Madhya Pradesh. The relatively arid farmland conditions in the Ganges Plain at Kaukori represent an abnormal environment for this forest dweller. Further south at Dharwar in Mysore, Sugiyama (1967) studied a population in deciduous forest, and a further forest population was studied by Ripley (1967) in Ceylon. At Kaukori the very large troop of 54 had an adult sex ratio of 1:3, while at Orcha the mean size of the three troops (10, 18, 28) was 18.6, with an adult sex ratio of 1:1.5. Generally troop sizes in arid central areas were 25–30, but were 18–25 in the Bastar forest area. At Dharwar the mean troop size was 15.1 and, from the socionomic sex ratio given by Sugiyama, it appears that the adult sex ratio in bisexual groups was about 1:4.4. The density of monkeys in this area was considered very high (100 langurs/Km²). Jay found her multimale groups to be relaxed and stable with little male exclusion from membership. Life was peaceful and little aggression or fighting was observed. The most severe fight she observed happened when a non-group male followed a group and was repelled by adult males and one old female member. By contrast Sugiyama's study showed that in most of his reproductive groups (74%, $n=38$) there was only a single adult male and that six of his 44 groups were monosexual male parties. Near Raipur in Central India he still found 50% of his groups to have single males. The all-male groups move over a range that is three to four times larger than that of a bisexual group, entry to which is denied by the usually successful aggression of the single male. Individuals from all-male groups were often seen to attack the reproductive units. In one fight an intruder decamped with all the members of a group except an adult female which remained with the defeated leader. Later, however, three adult females and a juvenile returned to their former leader and remained in their original home range. A group of seven males attacked a large one-male bisexual group repeatedly, so that fighting occurred over ten days until the injured leader and other male juveniles were ousted from their home range. The females remained with the successful intruders. In the following week the six supernumerary males were ejected, leaving a single adult newcomer with the females. He went on to destroy the remaining infants and to mate with their mothers. In another series of incidents a large male group consisting of no less than 50 animals repeatedly attacked four neighbouring bisexual groups and acquired females from each one. Finally they established a new group from which all but one male then departed. In another case, killing of all new infants in a reconstituted group was recorded. Yoshiba (1967) has calculated that ranging is related to food availability and that the high densities at Dharwar may be related to forest felling, reduction of predation, or both. Sugiyama (1967) is inclined also to attribute the interactions at Dharwar to the high population density leading to competition and the exclusion of numerous sexually unsatisfied males from groups. Most of the attacks occurred during the mating period.

In Ceylon, Ripley (1967) recorded aggressive incidents between multimale bisexual groups in forest that may be broadly interpreted as territorial. Here, however, little physical injury resulted. She suggests that conflict occurs when the average range size (maximum three square miles per group with average size of 25 animals) is compressed by high population density to about the size of the average core area of the range. Nevertheless not all the aggressive encounters could be related to changes in home range size.

The closely related *Presbytis cristatus* population studied in city parkland in Malaya by Bernstein (1968) was divided into six troops, each numbering between 20 and 50 animals and all

except one (which contained an additional very old adult male) containing only a single adult male. Only these control males showed consistent hostility to one another when troops met at the genuinely territorial boundaries. A problem posed by this study is the apparent absence of either solitary males or all-male groups which seem necessitated by the group compositions observed. Bernstein remarks that such animals could be living in less favourable mangrove swamps nearby. The one-male group structure could be attributed to similar social and ecological forces as Sugiyama (1967) describes for the *P. entellus* populations he observed. Bernstein reports (without giving the data) that one-male troops were observed in two other *Presbytis* species in Malaya. Clearly until more definitive and more specifically ecological studies on a range of populations of several *Presbytis* species are available general explanations in terms of the factors controlling their grouping patterns cannot be attained.

3. Geladas and Hamadryas

Gelada baboons (*Theropithecus gelada*) have been studied in several localities in the Ethiopian highlands, particularly in the Semyen Mountains (Crook 1966) and at Debra Libanos in Shoa (Crook and Aldrich-Blake 1968). These animals occur in bisexual reproductive units containing single adult males and in monosexual male groups, all of which cohere to form large herds under good feeding conditions. These herds are unlike baboon troops in that the individual groups that comprise them may move quite independently of each other and form herds of varying size and composition at different localities within the area inhabited by the deme. Each deme appears to be restricted to suitable locations containing cliffs, and interchange between such places seems rare. There are considerable differences in pelage colouration between different mountains. Herd sizes were largest in the Semyen Mountains in natural montane grassland. In less stable areas often modified by agriculture, herd sizes were smaller. In both types of environment herd sizes decreased in the dry season when one-male groups (also all-male groups) tended to travel separately. In some areas this increased dispersion appeared more or less permanent, producing a pattern of dispersion not unlike that described for the patas monkey by Hall (1966).

The adult sex ratio was most disparate in areas where shooting was known to occur, and here also sub-adults occasionally led the reproductive units which were generally of larger size. For the Gelada the constraints on social organization include the ecological limitation to gorge flanks or isolated mountains (Ambas), the consequent linear character of the home range, and local contrasts in food dispersion and availability. Natural differences in sex ratios are largely masked by shooting in many areas, which appears to increase adult male mortality.

Kummer (1968) surveyed hamadryas baboons from Alitu near Addis Ababa into Harar province in Ethiopia. He found that in association with an apparent west-to-east gradient in food availability across lowland Ethiopia (more in East) and a coincident decrease in the availability of sleeping sites, the troop size increased and the proportion of adult males in troops increased significantly in relation to the numbers of adult females. Comparable trends for juveniles were not found.

Studies of intraspecific natural contrasts among rhesus monkey populations and Japanese macaques are limited in value by the large extent of agricultural and city habitats utilized by the rhesus in India and by the artificial provisioning techniques often used by the Japanese investigators. Nevertheless clear differences in mean group sizes and the proportion of juveniles in differing Indian environments have been found (Southwick, Beg and Siddiqi 1961a, b). In addi-

tion, Singh (1966) reports contrasts in the behaviour of captive animals obtained respectively from urban and forest habitats. In Japan, group size decreases towards the northern limit of the species range and the counted groups had only one adult male of "leader" status each (Izawa and Nishida 1963).

4. The Problems of Intra-specific Socio-ecology

The significance of comparing sex and age group ratios under differing ecological conditions in these species studies should not be overstressed. Rowell (1966a, 1967a) has pointed out that the composition of a troop can vary through time as a consequence of the random determination of the sex of babies produced in any limited period. In an Ishasha troop the adult sex ratio was equal while all seven juveniles (4–5 years old) were males and the younger immatures comprised two females and two to three males. When the more rapid maturation of females is taken into account it follows that in a few years time the adult sex ratio is likely to be two males to a single female. It is not clear whether troop structure is sufficiently flexible to accommodate such changes in composition or whether extra males may be obliged to move out either as solitaries or to join another troop. It is clear, however, that with increasing numbers, such as Rowell found at Ishasha, changes in troop composition with time are likely to occur. Generalizations from numerical data have yet to take these fluctuations into account and the necessary information is badly needed to support any general comparative account of baboon social structure. In addition the biological basis of contrasts in the sex ratios of baboon and vervet groups that appear in both species to correlate with ecology is far from understood. The differences may be owing to contrasts in the differential mortality of the sexes in different places, to differential rates of sexual maturation in each sex or to a dispersion of solitary males. The latter is known to occur in macaque populations but not certainly in those of baboons. The reduction in male representation in the multimale reproductive units of more arid or cold environments might conceivably illustrate a trend towards the formation of one-male groups. However, one-male groups in open country animals are only found in populations in which excess males occur in all-male units or as peripheral parts of groups, as in the hamadryas bands. In the gelada population studied at Debra Libanos by Crook and Aldrich-Blake (1968) there was virtually no difference in the numbers of the two sexes present when all age classes (except babies) were considered. When the adult sex ratio alone was examined it was found that females outnumbered males approximately six to one in one-male groups and five to one in herds in which at least some all-male groups were also present. In the High Semyen, where the species is not subject to occasional shooting, herds show an adult male-reproductive female ratio of 1:2.1 and when sub-adult males are added the ratio becomes 1:1.7. This contrast seems to reflect the later reproductive maturation of males and perhaps a higher mortality rate for males compared to females (Crook 1966). These points suggest that the distinctions between multimale reproductive units and one-male units may be more dependent upon contrasts in social organization, possibly linked to differential maturation rates of the sexes, than owing to differences in the overall sex ratio of the populations themselves. The occurrence of one-male units in arboreal forest monkeys appears linked with a considerable permeability of groups to male movement from one group to another and perhaps also to the occurrence of solitary males (Japanese macaques) or monosexual male parties (langurs).

The discovery of marked intraspecific variation in primate group composition and social organi-zation demonstrates clearly that descriptions of social structure at limited points in the range of a species do not permit inferences to the social organization of the whole species. Intra-specific variation is indeed likely to be common although its extent may vary from species to species. It may be particularly marked in those adaptable enough to occupy a range of ecologically contrasting habitats. Any explanation of differences in social organization between species must be based upon an adequate understanding of the causation of intraspecific variation. Indeed a satisfactory account at this level would go a long way to explain differences at the species level.

The study of intraspecific socio-ecology is so recent that, apart from Rowell's (1967a) largely cautionary treatment in relation particularly to comparisons between field and captivity studies, there has been no systematic discussion of it. Nevertheless there are major problems of categorization, terminology and methodology that need at least a preliminary analysis at this stage if progress is to be made in any way other than an haphazard one. Some kind of socio-systematics appears necessary to define the problems posed by social lability and to focus attention on key questions. Only in one other branch of biology has intraspecific variation posed problems approaching those with which we are concerned. This is botanical Genecology—a term coined by Turesson in 1923 for the study of intraspecific variation in plants in relation to ecology. The approach here is openly synthetic, involving genetics, ecology and taxonomy and, in as much as differentiation into plant ecotypes is genetically based, the science was founded primarily upon research in genetics. Even so, important work on the direct effects of environment on the phenotype was carried out. The field has been recently reviewed at length by Heslop Harrison (1964). In primate behaviour there is need for a similar synthetic study relating research into the following topics:

i. The intraspecific variance in group composition and social organization shown by different species.

ii. The attributes of social systems found to vary under different environmental conditions and population densities.

iii. The ecological correlates of differences between the values of social parameters.

iv. The manner in which ecologically based social traditions are maintained.

v. The "roles" of age and sex classes in differing social traditions.

vi. Differences in individual mortality within contrasting ecologically based social traditions.

vii. The determinants of differential reproductive success under contrasting social conditions.

viii. The selection pressures, ecological and social (including (vi) and (vii) above), modifying the genetic basis of individual temperament and behaviour within contrasting groups.

ix. The relation between social signalling and the social system in which it occurs.

At the present time a number of correlations between social factors and ecology are apparent in the literature, and these allow the formulation of propositions the validation of which is a key problem for further research. Much of the variation surveyed at the intraspecific level seems to correlate meaningfully with differences in local habitats. The observed variation may express: (i) direct effects of environment on social structure; (ii) long-term processes of acquisition of traditional norms of social organization in a given habitat; (iii) the differentiation between demes of genetically controlled behavioural traits naturally selected for their advantageous effect

within particular social systems; and (iv) combinational effects of all these. Wide-ranging species may thus show a pattern of contrasting "socio-types" particularly apparent wherever a population is dispersed over a mosaic of relatively discrete habitats. Social organization may, however, vary only gradually with relatively subtle changes in ecology along a continuum; in this case the species population may show one or more "socio-clines." In practice the different characteristics that define a social system will not necessarily vary together, for some will be dependent upon aspects of ecology and social environment different from others and some may be resistant to ecologically correlated differentiation. Behavioural attributes may vary in a highly complex way so that correlations with environment may be obscured unless the analysis is sufficiently detailed.

At present the following propositions derived from the literature await elaboration in research:

i. *Ecology and spatial dispersion*

a. The home range size of terrestrial open-country primates is a function of food availability in relation to population density.

b. In arboreal forest primates, spacing behaviour is a function of high density relative to high environmental productivity in more or less stable habitats. It involves the maintenance of group dispersion by social communication patterns with or without the defence of topographically defined territories.

c. In addition to the effects of food availability in relation to density, open country traditions of social structuring are a function of past or present predation upon individuals. Coherent groups with organized deployment occur in areas with greatest predation pressure. The nightly dispersion of groups into sleeping parties arises where protective sleeping sites are limited in frequency and effectiveness. The distribution of secure sleeping sites may therefore also affect density.

d. Populations divided into one-male groups and all-male groups (Type 4) tend to show greater dispersion of social units under conditions of poor food availability and to congregate when food becomes superabundant.

e. The integration of social units, particularly large bisexual troops of Type 3, varies inversely with the density of vegetation and the dispersion of food resources.

ii. *Group size and composition*

a. Group size in open country and forest fringe primates varies with environmental stability, with a trend to larger groups in areas of medium seasonal aridity.

b. Sex ratios in reproductive units show a decrease in male representation under conditions imposing harsh seasonal climates with low food availability, and also under conditions of high density occasioning more or less chronic shortage in relatively stable environments.

c. Populations overcrowded in relation to environmental commodities show an increased male exclusion from reproductive groups, producing a diaspora of solitary males mainly in forest and a high incidence of non-reproductive males or all-male groups in open country. Unless such dispersion patterns are stabilized socially through the formation of traditions, sociosexual frustration may either increase male motility between groups or produce active and disruptive aggression occasioning a rapid turnover in male participation in bisexual group life. These effects may occur seasonally.

iii. *Communication, interactions and ecology*

a. The utilization of expressive gestures in communication may be modified by environmental conditions determining dispersion patterns shown by populations and these, together with social factors, comprise selection pressures modifying the innate basis of signals.

b. Contrasts in the frequency of social interactions such as grooming, friendly relations, dominance relations, play, and other incidents productive of social and observational learning are functions of both inter-individual spacing and the availability of time free from the satisfaction of individual needs—expressed particularly for example in the daily duration of foraging.

iv. *Behaviour and environmental stability*

a. Reproductive seasonality is a function of ecological seasonality.

b. Periodic changes in social structure and spatial dispersion are related to environmental instability as expressed in diurnal and seasonal climatic changes.

In 1961 Anderson attempted to summarize the relationships between habitat, numerical density, social structure, and population regulatory factors in *Mus* populations. Research on mice and other rodents had revealed an association between relatively low numerical densities and the defence of territory of dominance hierarchies, primarily when the possibility of exclusion of individuals low in rank through their emigration was reduced. High densities, especially where emigration is prevented, are also associated with pituitary-adrenocortical hyperfunction indicative of physiological stress (Christian 1963) leading to decreased recruitment and increased susceptibility to disease. Field studies of cercopithecoid populations are as yet insufficiently developed to allow any effective discussion of the natural regulation of their numbers. Nevertheless the suggestions listed above appear to indicate broad correlations between social variables and variables extrinsic to the social system. The present literature on both interspecific and intraspecific variations in social organizations suggests that variance is particularly related to the degree of environmental stability shown by a habitat—particularly with regard to its effects on density through its overall food productivity and the extent of seasonal fluctuations in food abundance. Extremes on the continuum are associated with the social structures described for monkeys living in tropical forests and arid "Sahael" environments. In Fig. 2 these relations are portrayed in a diagram adapted from Anderson and provide a provisional explanatory model of the diversity in cercopithecoid social structures. Because much of the evidence is uncertainly established it would seem inadvisable at the present time to attempt to stretch this model in theoretical speculation. The model may nevertheless stimulate detailed research on particular topics in an attempt to ascertain its credibility.

The current need is clearly for prolonged comparative investigations in carefully selected species groups. A main problem here is to devise common methods of analysis so that reports on different populations by different observers can be more readily compared. At present the comparability of research accounts is often bedevilled by contrasts in methodology and theoretical approach (Plutchik 1964). The following difficulties need particular attention.

i. Different research reports commonly express numerical data, socionomic and sex ratios, etc. in different ways. The reader has to labour to convert these to a common system before any generalization or comparison is

Figure 2: A tentative model showing apparent relationships between aspects of cercopithecoid social systems and environmental variables.

	MORE ← —————— ENVIRONMENTAL STABILITY —————— → LESS		
Variables extrinsic to social system	Reduced seasonal change. Relatively constant food resources. Forests. Supposedly low predation in little cover.	Relatively food-rich areas with some seasonal change. Savanna. Supposedly high predation in thick cover.	Increased seasonal change. Seasonally fluctuating food resources. Open country—arid. Supposedly low predation in little cover.
Variables intrinsic to social system	High numerical density. Small reproductive units with decreased male representation. Some male exclusion. Male motility. Dispersion based on intergroup avoidance or territoriality. Group coherence associated with vocal signalling. Little reproductive seasonality.	Medium numerical density. Large multimale bisexual reproductive social units. Some male motility. Home range with intergroup avoidance. Territories under certain conditions. Group coherence varying with density of vegetation. Reproductive seasonality.	Low numerical density. Small one-male reproductive units with peripheral all-male groups. Herding under food superabundance. Replacement of males with ageing. Home ranges with much overlap and no exclusion allowing herd formation. Group coherence marked in social units—reduced between units under poor conditions. Reproductive seasonality.

possible. The use of the metric system is a first necessity.

ii. Estimates of group composition and ratios, etc. often differ, sometimes necessarily, in their manner of acquisition. For example, counts of relatively coherent baboon and macaque groups are easily made. In the study of geladas this has been impossible owing to the mobility of groups and individuals in the study area. Sample counts have therefore been made over a period of days.

iii. The contrasts in method, and also in the duration of studies, often make it difficult to estimate the reliability of comparison between sets of numerical data. For this reason statistical tests of theoretical propositions against null hypotheses using data accumulated from numerous reports by different authors over the years are of dubious utility.

iv. Discrepancies in the naming of displays and types of social encounter lead to confusion when the work of different authors is considered. This is true even in examining accounts of work on the same species.

v. Assertions regarding territorial and dominance behaviour often depend on the acceptance of differing criteria in different studies. In addition conceptual models relating to these terms differ between authors. The same social phenomena may be described in different ways, depending on the interpretative bias of a writer.

vi. Relationships between individuals are often "explained" without reference to their development. Thus dominance-subordination relations may be a function of differential kinship. This would only be apparent after long-term study.

vii. Random variation in the sex ratio of age sets will produce variations in sex ratio of adults over a long-time course. The degree of oscillation from generation to generation and between groups has in no instance been adequately measured.

viii. Seasonal variation in habitat conditions occur in all environments. Field studies must last a whole year at minimum or sample all seasons.

It would appear that the only effective basis for comparing two studies is that of a system of data collection based on commonly understood categories, parameters, and metric units utilized by both observers. The reports need also to be "comprehensive" (Washburn and Hamburg 1965), with steps taken to promote their continuation over several years as in the case of bird population studies. The only papers at present meeting these criteria comprise the long series on the Japanese macaque and the feral rhesus population on Cayo Santiago. In addition, detailed research on the local environment and the species role in the ecological community is needed. In Table 1, at least some of the parameters requiring attention are set out.

Socialization and the Maintenance of Social Structures

The lability of social structures across a species range, together with their relative local stability, suggests that they are controlled and maintained partly through direct sociological response to environment and partly through social traditions. Primate societies are thus conceived as "protocultural" communities subject to processes of historical change additional to Darwinian selection of inherited individual traits. Social conformity and ecological adaptation are viewed within this context as being largely "shaped" by the environment. The habitat, physical and social, is, as it were, nature's Skinner box providing locally

Table 1: Parameters for comparison in intra-species studies

ECOLOGICAL ASPECTS	SOCIAL ASPECTS
1. Home range in relation to population dispersion, inter-group avoidance, or territory.	1. Composition and size of reproductive and non-reproductive social units (peer groups, infant groups, all-male groups, social isolates, etc.) that comprise a deme under study.
2. Time spent foraging per day in relation to social behaviour.	2. The constancy of these units through time with respect to membership.
3. Times of rising and sleeping, sleeping sites and sleeping parties.	3. The "role" contributions to the social life of a group of differing age and sex classes.
4. Diet, dispersion of food items, size of items, frequency of finding and eating in relation to 2 above.	4. Age and sex ratios of all age classes derived from socionomic ratios of appropriate units.
5. Calculation of daily food intake of individuals and of group requirements in relation to resources.	5. Types of social relations within groups producing dispersion patterns and responsible for inducing social conformity, e.g., male-female bonds, kinship effects, central-peripheral class structure, dominance relations and friendship groupings, monosexual grouping, female solidarity *vis-à-vis* male control, etc.
6. Seasonal change in carrying capacity of environment, i.e., changes in food resources and their nutritional quality.	
7. Seasonal changes in food dispersion affecting density. Differential foraging of different age/sex classes of groups.	6. Phase changes in social dispersion occurring daily and/or seasonally and contingent upon differences in sex or foraging patterns. Seasonality of copulatory behaviour and parturition.
8. Frequency of predation and behaviour in relation to predators.	7. Group structure during deployment in foraging or travel.
9. Incidence of seasonal weight changes, etc.	8. Longitudinal data on effects of individual ageing, with relation to status and the break-up, formation, or reconstitution of reproductive groups.

characteristic types and frequencies of natural learning trials in complex schedules that interrelate to pattern individual behaviour as a whole. Rowell (1966b) has emphasized that contrasting frequencies of naturally occurring learning trials—in relation to food, say—may pattern individual behaviour differentially in different places. Menzel (1966) and Hall (1968) have additionally stressed the acquisition of much primate behaviour through observational learning. An animal learns the consequences of another's behaviour through direct visual experience and adjusts its own behaviour in relation to the other's response. The frequency of events occasioning these types of direct and indirect learning will be much affected by local ecology, in particular the density of vegetation affecting inter-animal observation,

seasonal food shortage occasioning increased rates of travel, increased time in foraging and increased dispersal of individuals or groups, the availability and size of sleeping sites occasioning group splitting or congregation, and population density determining the extent and frequency of both intra- and inter-group interactions. While adult behaviour will itself be moulded by such contingencies through continuous learning, it is clear that the most important behaviour patterns are determined during the socialization of young. Whimbey and Dennenberg (1967) have demonstrated that individual differences in subtle behavioural traits may be programmed experimentally in rats by imposing differential rearing procedures. This was possible in the absence of any contribution from genetic variance.

1. The Socialization Process

Primate social development consists in the passage of the individual through a series of phases the general trend of which is away from the mother and towards a more frequent interaction with peers and adults. Infant monkeys are born showing two basic behaviours involving needs for contact—comfort and suckling with an appropriate mother object (Harlow 1961). The infant's social responses are at first of a reflex nature. In the absence of satisfying stimuli the animal shows marked distress. Infants deprived of mothers or mother substitutes in laboratory experiments develop repetitive and abnormal behavioural stereotypes as habitual modes of response.

The innate neonatal responses of the baby result in the gratification of immediate behavioural needs and form the basis upon which early learning builds. The infant is thereby attached to the mother who provides the basic contact security which later allows the infant to venture forth with assurance in its early contacts with peers. From the mother the infant "learns to perceive the meaning of a gesture or a glance, discovers that food may not be taken with impunity from a larger animal and finds that bites and slaps will be returned in kind" (Mason 1965). Even short periods of maternal deprivation (6 days) have adverse effects on infant behaviour which may persist for some weeks after the mother's return (Hinde, Spencer-Booth and Bruce 1966).

While the form and rate of social development are largely a function of maturational changes, the details are much influenced by maternal attitudes which vary greatly depending on the mother's prior experiences of bearing young. Some young mothers in captivity reject infants at birth or may be indifferent, confused or even frightened by them. Females reared with deprivation of social experience were extremely deficient as mothers and their young had to be hand-raised (Harlow and Harlow 1962). In the field, differences between species in maternal behaviour are known. Baboon and macaque mothers maintain contact with babies for the first month after birth and resist attempts at separation, while langur mothers, at least in Jay's (1965) study area, permit "aunts" to hold and carry infants soon after birth—a behaviour also reported for rhesus macaques in captivity (Rowell et al. 1964). Captive chimpanzees actively exercise and play with their babies in ways not seen in the wild and, as Mason (1965) suggests, mothers freed from the requirements of food-getting and protection may find in the infant a stimulus for activity in a restricting environment.

The extent to which paternal behaviour is shown by males varies greatly interspecifically and intraspecifically. In three of 18 Japanese macaque groups surveyed by Itani (1959) adult males of high social rank adopted yearling infants and behaved towards them exactly as a mother would. Lahiri and Southwick (1966) reported extensive infant care by a captive male Barbary Macaque (*Macaca sylvana*). A continuing field study (Deag and Crook, unpublished) confirms the remarkable degree to which adult males of this species in the Middle Atlas region of Morocco interact with very young babies in prolonged and complex behaviour sequences. A male with a baby may approach or attract other adult and sub-adult males which examine, mouth, handle and groom the baby together with him. Babies move repeatedly from one male to another in the multimale reproductive group before returning to the presumed mother for feeding at the breast. The extent of the behaviour appears to exceed that recorded for any other macaque and probably has major significance for the development of adult social behaviour in this species. In addition there appears to be extensive "aunt" behaviour involving both adult and juvenile females. A frequent grouping pattern involves an adult female and an attendant juvenile, both in close attendance upon a baby.

Social play with peers is doubtless of great importance in facilitating the development of social skills and helps form the foundation upon which adult relations in an enduring group are built. Mason (1965 and quoted) has shown in laboratory studies that for the first 12–18 months the behaviour of rhesus born and raised in the wild differs markedly with respect to the frequency of grooming and agonistic behaviour and the stability of relationships formed, from that of animals raised in individual cages. The feral animals were more active socially, formed stable bonds, groomed more, showed fewer aggressive responses than the others, and did not develop abnormalities in sexual behaviour. Harlow and Harlow (1962) have shown that infant rhesus reared apart from the mother but given frequent contact with peers eventually acquired normal sexual behaviour, whereas infants whose social contacts to the age of seven months were restricted to the mother were more retarded. Peer contacts are thus vital for normal social development.

Communication between primates hinges upon a repertoire of postural and facial expressions (Bolwig 1964, van Hooff 1967, Andrew 1963), the basic form of which and their relation to affective states are almost certainly not learnt (Bernstein and Mason 1962). The employment of and graded responsiveness to these signals does, however, undoubtedly depend upon social learning arising from an increasing familiarity with the group scene. The young animal has to learn to discriminate extremely subtle cues indicating the mood or intent of a companion, and the role of these cues in the group must be accurately comprehended.

As a result of social learning (Hall and Goswell 1964, Hall 1968) the young animal discovers the scope within which it may express its varying motivational states. This is of especial importance when the animal is involved in competitive encounters for food and other commodities. The pattern of rewarded learning and avoidance conditioning that results from such events is doubtless the basis upon which an individual constructs a social role. In multimale groups of baboons and rhesus monkeys latent aggressiveness is high and past experience allows individuals to predict the likely outcome of encounters. Individual roles are distinguished by ranking according to success or influence in competitive situations, and in relation to sexual responsiveness. Relations between adult baboons may, however, be very complex. Seemingly subordinate animals may threaten superiors successfully by positioning themselves near a yet more dominant animal, and by barks and glances they may summon assistance from "friends" in causing the retreat of the opponent (Kummer 1957, Hall and DeVore 1965 etc., Altmann 1962). Adult male baboons may interfere in disputes, and the decision of high-ranking animals as to whom to chase is dependent upon a set of more or less stable relations with others. Similarly complex relations obtain between females but are less easily apparent without very close field observation.

The Japanese macaque (Imanishi 1960) has been observed in the field over many years with techniques involving provisioning at selected sites. Encounters at food stations occur and allow a study to be made of the sub-structuring of the group. High status animals tend to gain prior access to food and their offspring acquire attributes of dominance and assertiveness, indicating that a protected youth in the "establishment" has permanent effects. These groups tend to be divided into high caste and low caste members whose kinship links do not often run beyond the limits of their caste. Koford (1963) and Kaufmann (1967) likewise describe central hierarchies and peripheral animals among the free-ranging rhesus groups on Cayo Santiago Island. There was a positive correlation between aggressivity and social rank.

2. Dominance and Role Development

Although detailed studies remain to be done it is clear that patterns of socialization and role development will be much influenced by the type of social structure within which development occurs. Between groups of patas monkeys, geladas, and hamadryas baboons, contrasts in structure impose types and frequencies of interaction different from those in macaque and baboon groups. The frequencies of agonistic encounters in Jay's (1965) langur groups differed greatly from those in macaque studies even though several males were likewise present in the group. In many of these species, and particularly in Gartlan's vervet monkey groups, descriptions of inter-individual relations in terms of simple dominance have proved very difficult or impossible. Formerly it was accepted that dominance ranking was an ever-present feature of primate relations and the phenomenon was, and sometimes still is, treated as the behavioural basis of group structure. The recent work shows this general approach to be untenable. Indeed the whole concept of dominance has been long in need of conceptual revision and clarification (Gartlan 1964).

Bernstein and Sharpe (1966), Rowell (1966b), and Gartlan (1968), all prefer to treat dominance relations within the wider framework of role development in groups of known structure. When two individuals are caged together for the first time, learning occurs in the establishment of their relationship of which dominance-subordination is but a part. Integration patterns are, however, far from static and, although relationships established in early encounters are important and often enduring, patterns often change with reproductive activity, health and age. Relative rank as measured by various criteria may alter not infrequently (e.g. Koford 1963). Rowell (1966b), working with *Papio anubis*, considers that the expression of hierarchy in social behaviour can best be treated as a continuous learning process in which every interaction between individuals tends to reinforce or extinguish the ranking relations established in earlier encounters. Learnt responses depend primarily upon the number, frequency, and patterning of "trials." However, as Kawamura (1959), Hall and Goswell (1964), Menzel (1966), and Tsumori (1967) have pointed out, social learning through observation is also of importance. Changes in roles may therefore depend additionally on every individual's observation of the ongoing behaviour of each member in relation to others in a group. Rowell (loc. cit.) suggests that shifts in agonistic behaviour might follow changes in affiliative relations between grooming partners; the dominance relation cannot thus be examined without considering other aspects of inter-individual relations. Rowell found in fact that her baboon hierarchy appeared to be maintained chiefly by the responses of low- rather than of high-ranking animals.

3. Socialization Within Different Group Structures

Contrasts between group structures may be expected to affect the socialization processes occurring within them and hence the manner in which behavioural conformity is achieved.

Kummer (1967) describes how *female* hamadryas baboons in tripartite agonistic encounters will position themselves near the male of a one-male group in order to display aggression to an opponent from a protected position ("protected threat"). The females in the group may actively compete for this location, particularly in cases where their relative dominance is about the same. The male usually shows little interest in these encounters but if he attacks it is usually the more distant female that is bitten. Similar events are reported in field studies of chacma and olive baboons (Hall and DeVore 1965) and in rhesus macaques (Chance 1956, Altmann 1962) but in these cases males are primarily involved. The behaviour does not seem to be so consistently a part of the female repertoire as in the hamadryas. Indeed Kummer reports that sub-adult hamadryas *males* do not perform protected threat when encountering adults; instead they may grasp a nearby infant or invite one to jump on their back and then, with behaviour strikingly like that of a mother, move in front of or away from the adult opponent. Circumstantial evidence suggests that this behaviour may reduce the larger animal's tendency to attack.

The marked contrast between young females and males when individuals of either sex are under social stress is closely related to the structure of the hamadryas group. While females form a stable element and may be attacked by their overlord male if they move far away from him, the presence of the sub-adult males is not obligatory in the same way. They may enter or leave the group without restraint and their approach and "presenting" to the male, unlike other *Papio* species, has little appeasing effect. Kummer suggests that both male and female behaviour of this type arises in ontogeny from the infant's relation with the mother. Fearful infants run to their mother's arms for contact comfort and the mother may then threaten the aggressor. Likewise, older infants in play parties flee when frightened to the arms of sub-adult males around which such parties tend to cluster. Although these males do not take part in the play they may threaten the more aggressive player when approached in this way. The male thus acts as a common mother substitute for all the players. The infants soon learn that approach to animals of this status confers protection, from within which they may threaten another. The sub-adult male's role nevertheless may seem ambiguous to a youngster, for it is protected when threatened by a companion, but attacked when it is in turn an aggressor to a peer. As young females become mature their behaviour in such a situation is directed towards the controlling adult male of the one-male group, who then provides the context for "protected

threat" against female competitors. Young males beyond two years of age evidently fail to induce the required response from adult males—and indeed are less associated with them by this time. Again, however, their behaviour relates to the mother-infant situation for, as we have seen, in stress they play the pretended role of mother.

Hall (1966a) and Hall and Mayer (1967) describe the socially withdrawn character of the male patas monkey, a characteristic clearly related to his social role of watchdog and predator detector in the dispersed wild "one-male groups." Among patas it is in fact primarily the activity of group females that determines the pattern of intragroup relations. There is a strongly organized female hierarchy in which a high-ranking female readily threatens the male if her infant should be alarmed by him. Other females may join with her in forcing the male's withdrawal. The females' ranking system appears primarily determined among themselves without reference to the male. Indeed Hall thinks the initiative in keeping a particular male in the group may come from the females. In the Bristol laboratory group the adult male showed intense aggression to a sub-adult male as soon as he matured sexually (blue scrotum), and there was little doubt that in the wild this animal would have left, perhaps to join an all-male party. The socialization of young males within the framework of a marked female hierarchy may lead to the offspring of the highest-ranking female succeeding to the leadership or, should he be driven from the group, this female and her associates may leave the group with him. These ideas require further examination both with enclosed groups and in field research.

The above accounts make clear that contrasting group structures impose differences in the patterns of learning that lead to the formation of individual behaviour and imply that modification of groups, through whatever causes, will alter the socialization process so as to yield individuals with changed behaviour. Gartlan (1968) has pointed out that the incidence of agonistic encounters is commonly greater in captive than in wild groups (Patas monkey, Hall 1965, Hall, Boelkins and Goswell 1965; *Papio ursinus*, Hall 1962; *Papio anubis*, Rowell 1967b; Vervet monkey, Gartlan 1966). Furthermore the frequency with which captive vervets look at other members of their group is much greater in the laboratory. There is also evidence from studies of rhesus monkeys (Mason and Brady 1964) that an increased proximity of individuals elicits physiological changes comparable to those described previously from rodent studies as social stress (Christian 1963, Archer, this volume, p. 169 *et seq.*). The poor health of animals in a number of colonies used in earlier research may indeed be related to overcrowding. Any general statements about species behaviour based solely on laboratory research require caution unless the effect of captivity conditions upon social life and behaviour ontogeny has been properly considered. Nevertheless, monkeys kept carefully in groups that approximate to those in the wild in terms of composition do show behaviour that does not differ greatly from that seen in feral animals (Kummer and Kurt 1965, Hall and Mayer 1967, Rowell 1966b, 1967b). Many problems of socialization, particularly the experimental manipulation of mother-infant relations, depend upon laboratory observation and major insights have resulted from the work of Harlow and Harlow (1962), Mason (1965), and Hinde and Spencer-Booth (1967) in this area. Detailed studies are particularly valuable when workers are familiar with their animals in both the laboratory and the wild.

4. Multi-factorial Programming of Social Development

We may conclude that the behaviour of individual primates is programmed through the interplay of a multiplicity of factors. Clearly simple-minded dichotomies of behaviour elements into the "innate" and the "learnt" or the "bio-social"

and the "psycho-social" are quite inadequate to handle the complexities of the actual process. The social group within which an individual lives is presumably adapted to the environment of the species. We take this to mean that the group structure represents the social organization within which individuals survive and procreate best. Within the group the behaviour of an individual differs according to sex, age, and, in some cases, kinship and is primarily determined by three interacting groups of factors:

i. The species repertoire of biologically programmed neonate reflexes and social signals (postural and facial expressions), together with innate factors affecting temperament and tendencies to learn certain kinds of response more readily than others. This applies also to contrasts between the sexes.
ii. The behaviour of individuals comprising the relevant social milieu, which behaviour controls in part the emergence of individual role playing.
iii. Direct effects of the environment such as the availability of need-reducing commodities and consequent learning of behaviour that exploits the world in the manner ensuring greatest individual survival.

The common behavioural inheritance has been selected, partly through environmental pressures and partly through those operating within the species social system. It seems that learning during socialization and the emergence of a social role has a preponderant effect in shaping the behaviour of an individual. Social conformity and the maintenance of group structure through time results primarily from the adoption of traditional behaviour characteristic of the social system as a whole.

Within a group an individual relates to many animals of differing sex, age, dominance status and kinship. Affiliated animals whose relationship endures through time are said to have established

"bonds." The particular types of bond are closely
related to the characteristic group size, coherence
and group composition of a population—all factors
responsive to ecology. Once a pattern of relationships is established it will tend to become resistant
to change even when environmental shifts impose
alterations in group structure, size and composition together with changes in frequencies of social
events. There will, however, be a limit to which
this resistance is effective; sufficient imposition of
structural alteration to groups will eventually
pattern the relationships of individuals of a new
generation differently. The long-term endurance
of relationship types in given populations must,
nevertheless, encourage natural (social) selection
of those genetic determinants that favour the
emergence of behavioural phenotypes most likely
to take part in the appropriate relationship patterns. A general stabilization of relations and
bonding develops such that they may become
more or less species specific. Social attributes are
thus differentially responsive to the environment;
while spacing and dominance features may alter
quickly in response to ecological change, alterations in relationships and bonds may be expected
to occur more slowly over a time scale of several,
if not many, generations.

The present account has been based in the
main upon laboratory studies of primate socialization supplemented by limited field observations.
Clearly the development of social behaviour in
wild groups under conditions of good observation
must now become a prime object of study. These
must be long-term investigations with data collection covering at least the following types of
information (see also section on Social Dynamics):

i. The extent of mother-exclusive care of young
in comparison to "aunt" behaviour and baby-
care by juvenile and adult males.
ii. The rate of change in maternal attitudes to
infants, producing the separation of child
from parent and the onset of independence.

iii. The extent, manner, and frequency of infant-
infant interactions, particularly in play
groups.
iv. The extent, manner, and frequency of interactions with the opposite sex in infancy.
v. The pattern of interactions between juvenile
males approaching puberty and adult males
and females.
vi. The manner of exclusion of young males
from reproductive units, the extent of exclusion, and the formation of all-male groups
(if present).
vii. The pattern of interactions giving rise to
friendship relations with peers (and adults)
and the formation of role behaviour with respect to defined goals.
viii. The development of male alliances, leadership, and interactive "policing" of troops.
ix. The effects of parental roles and status in
groups on the behaviour of infants and juveniles in relation to their peers and elders.
x. The manner and extent to which kinship ties
are maintained and their significance in stabilizing social relations in groups.

Relatively few species provide in the wild the
conditions of observation upon which the data
collection demanded above depends. Baboons,
vervets, geladas, hamadryas, and macaques living
in open country clearly provide better opportunities than difficult forest animals. Any comprehensive understanding of the factors controlling
and maintaining social structure depends ultimately upon detailed developmental studies utilizing natural groups of wild animals.

Group Division, Reconstitution, and Social Change

A major problem concerns the manner in which
social structure is conserved from one generation
to another and how progressive change from one
type of organization to another may develop.

Within the group develop those social relations that eventually lead to group fission as the unit enlarges as a consequence of reproduction. Multimale groups of provisionized rhesus and Japanese macaques increase considerably in size, with concomitant increases in social tension. Eventually they split into smaller units of similar composition (Koford 1963, Sugiyama 1960, Furuya 1963). The basis for the divisions is related to the substructure of these groups. Not only have central and peripheral "castes" been described but in addition small sub-units of closely affiliated animals, either male or female, are known (Chance 1956, Altmann 1962). Likewise groups of peripheral males occasionally occur in rhesus, apparently separated from troops under stress of aggression from animals within them (Carpenter 1942), and this has also been reported for the Japanese macaque (Itani—quoted in Altmann 1962). The most stable element in the multimale group appears to be the core of mutually affiliated females, for individual males are now known to exchange groups in *P. anubis* (Rowell 1966a), in rhesus (Altmann 1962), and in vervet monkeys (Gartlan 1966). In the Japanese macaque males of high status mothers are observed to affiliate strongly with their leaders, presumably owing to the protective role these adopt when the young perform protected threat. Imanishi (1957) considered that young males born of the peripheral mothers and "identifying" less well with their leaders, and co-operating poorly with the group as a whole, would be the first to form a splinter group when ecological or social conditions contingent upon group growth impose stresses. Presumably they would then depart with low-ranking females to become the core hierarchy of a new but small group. Matrifocal kinship relations correlate intimately with dominance ranking in Japanese macaques and probably in other species as well (Kawai 1965, Kawamura 1965). Males born of high status mothers grew up to occupy high-ranking positions in the group as a whole.

Among rhesus monkeys such precocious young males may outrank older animals (Koford 1963).

1. Japanese and Rhesus Macaques

The long-term study of the Takasakiyama troop of Japanese monkeys (Sugiyama 1960) showed a steady increase from 220 members in 1953 to about 580 in 1958. This rate of increase must be considered in relation to the provisionization procedures adopted by Japanese researchers. So high a rate of increase may not occur in groups not receiving supplementary rations for research purposes. Indeed, disease, starvation and other factors may slow the rate of increase (or even prevent its occurrence) under entirely natural conditions. Rates of group splitting would then be correspondingly affected. Be that as it may, during the five years at Takasakiyama two of the five leading males in the central hierarchy left the troop to become solitary males as also did five of eight senior young males. The alpha male remained in that position throughout the period. No relatively subordinate or "sub-leader" male had moved socially into the central grouping nor did young males "pass the social barrier to reach the sub-leader class." By contrast, a number of females with their young, originally forming part of the central grouping, strayed out to the periphery beyond the direct control of the leaders.

Gradually part of the troop began to forage separately from the main body and to visit the provisioning area later. Eventually the branch troop took to separate ranging and sleeping areas. The leaders of the branch troop were found to have originally ranked second, third, and fifth in the young male class of the main troop. They were 12–13 years old, the remaining remnants of the eight senior young males of 1954, five of which had gone solitary. By 1960 the branch troop had 100 members, most of which were young, highly investigative animals. Most of the females joining the new troop had lived in the periphery of the original troop and about half became regular branch members while others showed some oscillation between the separating lobes of the population. The branch troop became organized in the same manner as the parent unit, with a central part based on the three dominant and three additional males, and a peripheral part. The status hierarchy was not so firmly established as in the main troop. As the groups split, differential affiliation led to reduction in social contact between members of the units and later, after complete spatial separation, antagonism between males of the two units sometimes developed into fighting. Mostly the branch troop quietly avoided or ignored the main one. Those males of the main troop that attacked the branch troop were animals that had been infants when the leaders of the branch troop had belonged to the parent body. Within the parent group social changes continued after separation, and some strong maturing males of the young male class passed above the sub-leader rank to enter the central hierarchy.

In another case study Furuya (1963) found that the leader of a branch troop was a male that had fallen in rank within the central hierarchy of the parent body. He left with some 40 animals. Later more complex changes occurred. Mizuhara (1964) recorded a recently separated group that was taken over by old solitary males which invaded it and became the leaders. These animals were thus by no means the asocial rejects submissive to troop members as had been formerly thought. Mizuhara argues that the blocking of "promotion" in the ranking system of Japanese macaque groups is partly resolved by the "solitarization" of young males as well as by group fission. Before a troop reaches the fission threshold (i.e. it is yet too small or too affiliative) certain males leave rather than emerging as leaders either of the main troop or of its branches. He observed a case in which a very old alpha animal lost the ability to control behavioural interactions going on around him. It was only shortly before this animal's death that other males usurped his

"powers." As Sugiyama (loc. cit.) points out, the details of division are likely to differ between troops.

A long-term study of changes in the social grouping patterns of the provisionized feral rhesus population on Cayo Santiago Island has recently been completed (Wilson 1968). Longitudinal studies of group changes had begun on the island in 1956 (Altmann 1962) when there were two groups present numbering 55 and about 100 animals respectively. The smaller group mainly inhabited the small promontory joined to the main cay by an isthmus. The larger group rarely entered this area. However, all monkeys of both groups could and did wander over the entire island. The smaller of the two groups (A) split to form an offshoot group (J) in 1964, while a chain of splits had led already to the formation of groups C, E, F, H, and I from original group B. Of these A and C contained most animals; the other groups being small by comparison. Of the seven groups, C shows a peculiar dispersion, for it is subdivided into spatially distinct subgroups of about 30–40 animals of both sexes which endure as groups for between a day and several months, in spite of frequent exchanges of membership with other subgroups. Females with relatives commonly move to another subgroup as a unit; some affiliated males may likewise exchange subgroups together. The emergence of these seven distinct groups has been coincidental with about a 16% increase in population per year since 1959 (Koford 1967). Groups C, E, F, H, I, and J are largely confined to the main cay. Group A inhabits the promontory almost exclusively as well as spending much time on the main cay.

Wilson was especially interested in the movement of males from one group to another. In each group the percentage of males in each age class born into their group of membership decreases sharply from around 100% until age three to below 50% after four years. Wilson studied mainly cases of exchange between groups of males of five years or under. The frequency of these changes appears to be increasing possibly in step with the increase in population. Most of the exchanges consisted in movements into one or other of the larger groups A and C, which have large monosexual subgroups of males moving with them. An exchanging male often moves into the peripheral all-male subgroup by acquiring a "sponsor" who defends him against others in agonistic encounters. This sponsorship is apparently set up through the grooming relationship which the exchanging male establishes with him. The sponsor usually turns out to be a relative, commonly a brother, that moved into the non-natal group earlier. Affiliations within all-male subgroups are usually based upon friendships between animals originating from the same natal group. Males of over five years also exchange but few cases have been documented. In one the male established relations directly with females of the non-natal group and did not first enter the monosexual male periphery. Wilson points out that prior affiliation with animals originating in the same natal group might have the effect of reducing aggression between males of differing neighbouring groups.

Captive rhesus monkeys released on small islands off Puerto Rico developed a social structure similar to that of Japanese monkey groups. A basic group of females formed the most stable element, with the presence of a dominant adult male being essential for group maintenance. Extra-troop males lived more or less solitarily or in monosexual groups. Social instability in these monkeys was attributed to the absence of the effect of long-term matrilineal kinship relations among the introduced animals (Vandenbergh 1967).

2. Patas, Geladas, and Hamadryas

Hall (1967) thought that the departure of a maturing male from a one-male patas group may result from the adult male's aggression towards him. Although the young animal's mother and her friends may protect him for a period, an ultimate split in the group seems highly likely. Hall proposed several ways in which this might occur in nature. The sub-adult male may leave with his mother and her affiliated females. Alternatively the adult male may depart, leaving the sub-adult with some or all the females. When several sub-adults are reaching maturity in the same group the splitting process may be complex. When the adult dies one of the sub-adults or an intruding adult may assume his role. Hall had seen only one all-male group in the Murchison Park but Struhsaker (personal communication) and Gartlan (personal communication) have seen several in the Cameroons. Whether these are composed entirely or only partially of sub-adults remains unknown, but their existence suggests that often juvenile males leave their parental groups without females and join the monosexual parties. How some of them then subsequently obtain leadership of groups remains unknown.

Similar processes are likely to occur in gelada groups, but in these the male is a far more assertive "leader" than in the case of the patas. Monosexual groups largely composed of sub-adult males are common. In the one-male reproductive groups a large sub-adult male is often a regular member friendly with but subordinate to the adult male and not apparently ever engaging in copulation. It remains unknown whether such animals eventually succeed the ageing leader. Nor is it known whether they have spent part of their lives in the monosexual groups.

As we have already seen, the exclusion of young males from hamadryas reproductive groups appears to be a consequence of the differential treatment accorded to the juveniles of the two sexes by adult male group leaders. Kummer (1968b) observes that juvenile animals perform "protective threat" in relation to larger males, who become a reference point for their agonistic interaction. The juveniles use the adult or sub-adult animals as substitutes for the mother, who performed this function for them during their infancy. Beyond two years of age young females come to relate to young males whose behaviour is appropriately maternal and around whom the young females' lives become oriented. These groups form the initial basis of new reproductive units. Young males soon cease showing "protected threat" in relation to adult males and associate primarily with males of their own age within the herd or troop. Later they appropriate young females from existing groups.

Kummer's recent paper (1968a) describes how sub-adult males steal very young females from their mothers and attend them with every semblance of solicitous maternal care. The young female is rigorously controlled, and repeated retrieval trains her not to go away. She rapidly complies to the male's requirements and grooms him. The male neck-bite applied to wandering females, a behaviour likewise evidently derived from behaviour whereby a female retrieves her infant, develops later. At this stage there is no sexual behaviour, the female being yet two to three years from child-bearing. Very young males may adopt youngsters of both sexes but soon come to select only females and begin to build up their "harem." Young males may also gain entry to one-male groups remaining, at first, more or less inactive sexually. As these young interlopers mature and the overlord ages, the younger animal starts initiating group movements although the direction of eventual movement is dependent upon the older animal's choice. A highly complex relationship develops between the two animals which, by paying close attention to one another and by reciprocal "notification," co-operate in governing group movement. Old males retain command of group direction but gradually relinquish sexual control over their females to the younger male animal. The older male's role is thus in a very fundamental sense that of a "leader." It seems that eventually old males re-

sign entirely from their original reproductive units but retain great influence within the band as a whole, and young males refer to them continuously, particularly before developing the direction of march.

Kummer considers the fundamental contrast in social organization between hamadryas and other baboons of the genus *Papio* to be owing primarily to the emergence in the former of a means of male control over females, based not merely upon male dominance and periodic development of sexual consort bonds, but rather upon the development of a complex inter-personal bonding based, paradoxically, upon maternal elements probably innately programmed into the male's behavioural repertoire. In addition the relations between males in a group and within the band are controlled by what Chance (1967) has termed the "attention structure," the mutual notification of intention, so that within bands of mutually affiliated animals little or no promiscuity between reproductive groups appears to occur. Only the juvenile males steal matings in secret from females belonging to older animals. In other *Papio* and macaque societies promiscuity within the troop is largely regulated by the hierarchical relations between adult males, and the potentially highly aggressive competition is regulated by the frequent "presenting" of juvenile males to their seniors. As Rowell (1966b) has pointed out, the status hierarchy arises not so much because of the dominant animals' behaviour as of the responsiveness of juvenile and subordinate ones towards their elders. The system, including close notification between affiliated adult males, allows promiscuity; females coming into heat mate first with young or subordinate animals and with the most dominant male only at the height of oestrus. Young females appear less dependent on mothering and young males do not provide it. As a result interpersonal bonding does not develop.

It is not known yet how far the control of one-male units in gelada herds and patas populations parallels that revealed in the hamadryas. Probably all three represent convergence towards a similar sociological arrangement, but the social dynamics whereby the groups are maintained differ considerably. The retention of a troop or "band" structure without a clear-cut independence of one-male and all-male units in hamadryas populations indicates its probable derivation from the normal *Papio* troop. To what extent a greater, more gelada-like, separation of units might occur under harsher conditions than those in Kummer's study area remains to be seen.

3. Historical Change in Social Organization

The actual process of historical change in social organization would seem to depend initially upon shifts in ecological factors affecting individual activities and dispersion. In particular changes in the dispersion, availability, quality, total amount, and seasonal variation of food supplies in an environment would dictate shifts in population dispersion, density, time spent foraging per day, and the daily distance travelled—all factors of importance in determining group size and home range dimensions. Differences in vegetation densities and predation pressures would likewise have effects on grouping and the maintenance of social communication. In turn a gradual shift in grouping tendencies will set up differences in the type and frequency of events occasioning observational learning, and the patterning of learning trials in direct social interaction; these events will affect first those younger animals that are the most likely to set up new groups of their own. In the course of time individuals of a different temperament from that formerly obtaining may gain advantages in terms of reproductive success, so that the environmental change could begin to induce socially mediated selection of innate characteristics. These socially selected animals would be those best able to obtain matings with females and to control groups the size of which and whose orientation to the environment allowed successful child rearing. Changes in traditions governing sexual interaction, status hierarchies, and notification behaviour leading to collaborative performance would be gradual and move in step with changes in the availability of significant environmental commodities. Nevertheless, such is the complexity of several terrestrial primate societies, that a number of alternative sets of role interrelation could conceivably be equally satisfactory within a basic dispersion pattern. Indeed, although geladas and hamadryas have similar social structures, in important respects the social dynamics giving rise to these structures differ. The development of the hamadryas one-male group and the shift towards maternal characteristics in male behaviour appear ultimately a response to ecology; but the nature of the selection, within what environment and within what sort of social structure this occurred, remain questions as yet unanswered.

Any approach to these problems will once more involve difficult long-term and comparative investigations in which gradual changes in environmental and social factors are monitored according to a common system over a period of years. Only for the Japanese macaque and the howler monkey are there records even resembling those that will be needed. Comparisons of demes in areas undergoing natural or controlled environmental changes with those under unchanging conditions would throw light on the manner in which the numerous factors responsible for social organization undergo modification.

Social Dynamics

So far we have been primarily concerned with problems of structure and function and only secondarily with the dynamics of the group processes giving rise to structural forms. We should stress further therefore that while, for example, the social organizations of geladas, hamadryas baboons, and, to a lesser extent perhaps, the patas monkeys appear similar in both structure and function, they are mediated by contrasting social dynamics. The protocultural organization of the face-to-face relations in these and other terrestrial primate societies still needs much further examination. Indeed it is probably at this level that the most remarkable analogies to the human condition will be found, and here that inferences to the social evolution process originally common to both human and non-human primates may be made.

The one-male reproductive units of geladas and hamadryas differ considerably both in their internal relations and in their external relations with other larger social groupings. A comparison of the social dynamics of these species is particularly instructive. Gelada units wander independently from one another in time and space, apparently entering or leaving a feeding congregation (herd) at the will of the adult male (Crook 1966). Within the herds the members of one-male groups may disperse widely, the distances between individuals being as much as several hundred yards. An adult male does not restrict his females' movements greatly, but the latter periodically collect about him even though he has at the time shown no overt behaviour towards them. All members of the one-male unit keep close watch upon the adult male, and when he moves away they all come together from their dispersed positions in the herd and travel out of it together with him. The male periodically surveys the herd, noting the positions of his females and from time to time, if well separated from them, he stands in a particularly impressive posture, tail erect, head high, scanning the assembled company with eyebrows exposed in a "threat face." On sighting a female he runs towards her at great speed and, as he catches up with her, she spins round, faces him and screams up at him

from a crouched position. He does not give the neck bite, this not being part of the species repertoire. Rather he sits down, whereupon she approaches him and grooms him and he commonly gives an enormous yawn exposing his fangs. In this way males maintain their bonds with their females. Female hamadryas in contrast, are hardly ever allowed to stray more than a few metres from their male, upon pain of a neck bite. In disputes between large gelada males, which appear to arise when females inadvertently sit or forage near other harem owners, females may collect near their respective males but never to the extent reported for hamadryas (Kummer 1968a). The male gelada never crouches over his females during aggressive interactions in the herd. In addition sub-adult male geladas have not been seen to form close bonds with infant or juvenile females not yet sexually mature. Instead they appear to remain in quite stable "all-male" groups that may move independently of one another, of one-male groups, and of larger congregations which, however, they may join. A sub-adult male may enter a one-male group and remain there together with the adult harem owner. It is not yet known whether these male-male relations become well established nor how the leadership succession is managed in this species. The younger animal has not been seen to mate with females of the group. This suggests that the process of initial group formation in the two species may differ, although the problem of succession in existing groups may be resolved in similar ways.

In the hamadryas populations one-male units associate into "bands" apparently more closely affiliated together than with members or groups of other bands. These bands also associate together in "troops" at sleeping sites, the numbers and apparent composition of which are not, however, constant (Kummer loc. cit.). These "troops" appear to be the equivalent of gelada "herds," congregating not over limited areas of rich feed-

Figure 3: Gelada baboons assembled near a well on grazed grass near a village of Aostagab, High Semyen, Gondar, Ethiopia. Large male (just off center, right) approaches well (out of view, left) accompanied by some 11 animals together with additional babies on the backs of females or accompanying them. At back, three females feeding on grass with babies typically sitting immediately posteriorly to them. In foreground, adult male rushes off right (perhaps to threaten another male?)—other animals in foreground look at the object of his approach (off right). One black leaps for mother's back in fear of the disturbance. (*Photo J. H. Crook.*)

ing but rather at limited suitable sleeping sites that are regularly used. So far as we know gelada herds are not substructured into bands in the hamadryas manner.

In the gelada there are thus two basic units, one-male and all-male groups which assemble into higher level congregations, the herds, which are of continuously varying composition. In hamadryas the basic unit is a one-male group, the all-male group being less well defined as a unit; sub-adult males form a peripheral element in the band of harems, which is itself of constant composition. The bands associate irregularly into herds or "troops," as Kummer calls them.

As we have seen, adult hamadryas males may form two-male teams in which the younger is the initiator of group movements the direction of which is, however, ultimately decided by the older male. Very old animals are referred to by younger animals by observation prior to band displacements, even when the former have relinquished all their control over females. Old animals thus determine the band movements, and their experience over many years in the habitat

Figure 4: Sub-adult males chase one another vigorously (yelping chase). The two central geladas show "face-lift" expressions—the animal to the right showing this expression in profile. Behind the chase a mother unconcernedly grooms a baby's belly while other animals look on. Such chases are common in all-male groups. They also occur when members of such a group harass the owner of a one male reproductive group in their vicinity. (*Photo J. H. Crook.*)

is apparently made use of by the band as a whole. Their leadership "role" is probably highly functional. We do not know yet whether older gelada males ever play this kind of "higher order" role but it seems doubtful. Old males appear to be members of all-male groups and their influence outside these cannot be great except possibly when a large herd has been formed.

These observations show that in spite of a structural similarity in their social adaptation to similar environmental problems, geladas and hamadryas are yet very different in both their in-

group and out-group relations in herds. This may be partially explicable in terms of differences in taxonomy and phylogenetic history. The animals belong to different genera and it is possible that the gelada originates from a stock that originally dispersed itself in the manner of patas monkeys, the ability of groups to congregate in times of plenty and without reference to home ranges being a secondary feature. If Kummer is correct in deriving the hamadryas organization from that found in other *Papio* populations, the significance of taxonomic relationship in working out the history of particular kinds of social relations gains weight. Additionally, however, it seems probable that contrasting social relations and role categories with distinct functions within social units at different levels may emerge not only between species of otherwise comparable social organizations but also within populations of the same species living in different areas. Such differentiation could moreover conceivably arise as a consequence of group processes largely independent of environmental influence.

Contrasts in the behavioural traits of differing macaque species may be instructive here. Differing degrees of aggressivity or tameness occur between the species of this genus and it has yet to be determined whether these are primarily genetically or socially programmed. A new field study of the Barbary Ape (*Macaca sylvanua*) started in Morocco in the summer of 1968 already reveals differences in the social organization of this species when compared with either rhesus or Japanese macaques (Deag and Crook, unpublished). Not only do the small multimale reproductive groups frequently intermingle near waterholes and when alarmed but also the spatial dispersion of individuals within a group appears unusually large. Adult males interact frequently and for long periods with babies but not apparently with juveniles as reported from Japanese monkeys (Itani 1959). The effects of these situational contrasts on the ontogeny of behaviour in this species remain to be investigated. It is possible that the dominance relations of this species are less related to matrilineal kinship than in other macaques.

The role of the juveniles in promoting shifts in object relations in different groups of Japanese monkeys has been stressed by Kawamura (1959), and Gartlan (1966) has shown that the behaviour of juveniles as a class within the vervet social structure contributes as markedly to group welfare as do the roles of their elders. Menzel (1966) argues that an important effect of juvenile behaviour in the Japanese macaque is the discovery of new food objects. He suggests that the "avoidance gradient" (Miller 1959) is steeper in juvenile animals, permitting them to approach closely to novel stimuli so that habituation and mouthing of objects occur earliest for them. Adults are largely preoccupied with social relations and are commonly indifferent to inoffensive novel stimuli. New food objects are discovered therefore by youngsters and the habit only later passed on to older animals or disseminating as the juveniles become of age. Newly acquired social relations among young animals could, if of differential survival value, also spread through a population in a similar manner, and this may be especially significant when new behaviours are stressed by animals of control and/or leadership role. Conceivably, new ways of exploiting the environment and orienting socially to it may arise without changes in the physical environment, and become part of a gradually evolving social tradition. The relation between such changes and the kinship structure outlined for Japanese monkey groups (Imanishi 1960) will be a major problem in future research.

Bernstein (1966) has pointed out that the performance of a leadership role is not dependent upon the organization of a society into a dominance hierarchy, although it is true that leaders are usually themselves assertive animals. The role of "control animal," writes Bernstein, involves positioning oneself between disturbance and the group, attacking whoever distresses a group member, and approaching and terminating many cases of intra-group disturbance. Group members pay close attention to a control animal, keeping close to him, and enlisting his aid in protection. They may also follow his lead or his notification of preferred direction when on the march. The control animal need not, however, necessarily be the leader during movement. The friendships between control animals and other males provide the teamwork utilized in group policing in baboon groups. The disappearance of a control animal usually results in another adopting the same role. The potentiality for playing the role is therefore present at least in some individuals well in advance of their performance of it. Clearly in such animals a marked ability in observational learning, a capacity to form behaviourally controlled relationships with others, and a high order of social skill (Argyle 1966) are all apparent. In particular the extent to which these terrestrial primate societies are socially controlled by male behaviour and capacity becomes strikingly evident, even though females may provide the main affiliative links between members of social units whatever the type or composition. Even below the hominid level it seems that social psychological ideas concerning role, social skill and kinship are of significance in the analysis of social processes.

Indeed an effective analysis of social processes in primate groups requires some means whereby the allocation of animals to distinctive social positions or "roles" within the group may be effectively described. This would then make possible not only a study of the forces operating in the sorting process of allocation but, in addition, would be a means of studying relationships between role-holders. An understanding of the rules controlling social interaction would then emerge much in the way that observations of position holders (rather than players as such) on a football pitch would disclose the rules of the game.

Gartlan (1968) has shown clearly how attempts to analyse the social dynamics of primate groups in terms of dominance have proven inadequate. Together with Rowell (1966b) and Bernstein and Sharpe (1966) he proposed that attention be turned to analysis in terms of roles. Unfortunately there is a formidable array of types of role theory in sociology and social psychology and the term itself can be used colloquially in a number of different ways. It seems, however, that the most suitable approach is to consider the use of concepts derived from Sarbin (1959) and Nadel (1957). This approach would treat a "role" as a distinct social position within a group structure rather than as that aspect of an individual's behaviour shown in a particular set of circumstances or solely in relation to particular companions. In any given group each individual shows characteristic patterns of response to others—to older animals, dominant animals, to subordinates,

peers, kin, strangers, etc. The sum of behaviours shown to companions comprises that individual's social repertoire—his complete *set of behaviour styles* as shown proportionately in relation to each and every possible companion. The sum of these characteristics defines an individual's *social position* in the group. More generally stated, each individual may be defined socially in terms of its set of proportions of the totals of the various interaction patterns shown in the group. In a number of primate societies, for example hamadryas, geladas, and macaques, social positions differ sufficiently to allow categorization into particular types that recur repeatedly when different groups are compared or when a large group subdivides into branches. Each of these categories may be designated as a "role." The number of distinguishable roles depends on the species concerned and upon the type of social unit described. Not all groups will be describable in terms of the same set of roles. Nevertheless a considerable degree of consistency is expected. In that the description of roles is to be based on statistical studies of behavioural interaction, it will follow that several social positions (of group members) will not be distinguishable from one another. Such members are then considered to show the same "role." In groups with a single large and adult male—only one individual will occupy the role of control animal. The variety of roles possible in any study, of macaques say, is likely to include the *control animal, secondary male role* (animals often supporting the control animal), *peripheral male role, isolate male, control* and *peripheral female* roles including behaviour sets peculiar to oestrus and motherhood.

Now, we call these behaviour styles "roles" because they are *not* fixed and immutable patterns of conditioned behaviour—properties, as it were, of individual animals. Rather they are pigeonholes into which different monkeys may be fitted. A male that falls in social status, becoming peripheral, may opt out of the group and go solitary.

Later on he may enter a small branch group and become the alpha male. Peripheral males that split off from a large group emerge as members of a new central hierarchy. It follows that we are dealing with behaviourally flexible animals whose interactions produce a continuous sorting process by which each is allocated his place in the structure. What is the nature of the sorting machinery?

It is clear that older workers were not entirely misguided in focusing so much attention on the dominance-subordination aspect of group life. It is suggested here that basic to the older findings, and basic too to the sorting process we have described, is the fact that whenever any need-reducing commodity is in short supply (food, water, sleeping place, female, etc.) competition inevitably follows with success going to certain animals and being denied others. As we have described above, the inevitable ranking system produced by competition is stabilized largely by the avoidance behaviour of the subordinates. The behaviour of low-rankers is in almost all social respects constrained and even fearful. Such constraint may place an individual under physiological stress and induce a behavioural depression affecting health, comportment, longevity and chances of reproduction. By contrast, high-rankers move freely about their business unconcerned by either the presence or absence of others. Escape from social positions imposing behavioural constraint appears highly rewarding and means of escape are sought.

There appear to be three avenues of escape. Firstly, there is solitarization, probably followed later by the joining of another group and the occupation of a more advantageous role. Secondly, by affiliating with other individuals and acting in concert individuals can take over roles involving less constraint. Thirdly, individuals may approach and affiliate with infants and babies as a means of entering high status groups and thereby to affiliate with the parents. The first avenue has been amply described by Nishida (1966). The second by many workers on baboons (e.g. Hall and DeVore 1965) and on macaques and the third by Itani (1959) and Crook (in press). In both the second and third avenues a considerable measure of co-operation between individuals may be involved. Co-operation between adults occurs both with respect to gaining social positions and with respect to maintaining them. Co-operation is thus closely related to social competition. Its occurrence as a relationship pattern between certain role-players needs much further examination.

Escape from behavioural constraint is one aspect of the sorting process—certainly perhaps the most important. Ageing is another factor. As males become reproductively mature they are likely to change roles; similarly with ageing animals—as the work on two-male hamadryas teams indicates. In addition as groups increase in size social tensions begin to impose splits in the original structure contributing to a new assumption of roles by the separating individuals.

This outline model of group dynamics in primate groups has been based on existing field data and is discussed further by Crook (in press). Its utility has not yet been tested in an actual analysis of group life. A model of this kind is urgently needed. We have done no more here than take the first steps in the required direction.

Group Characteristics and Inference to Man

In the last few years sociologists and social anthropologists have once more turned attention to the problems of human behavioural origins. This is largely owing to the realization that the rapid increase in our knowledge of mammalian behaviour, combined with the ethologist's approach to behavioural evolution in terms of neo-Darwinian theory, now provides a plausible basis for a biological approach to social origins. Unfortunately the development of an adequate conceptual framework has been marred by a tendency to accept simplicist or unitary explanations of social life, in which the multiplicity of factors involved in behavioural determination and the systemic character of their interplay is inadequately understood.

Part of the problem arises from the publication of certain popular works of a highly controversial and speculative nature in a field that Tajfel (1969) aptly terms the "pseudo-biological." Lorenz (1963) and Ardrey (1966) have both made attempts to generalize from the social behaviour of animals to that of man, adopting one-sided or outdated theoretical approaches supported by a biased selection of supporting "evidence" (Crook 1968). These works not only purport to provide new insights into human nature but also make recommendations as to the correctives sorely needed by a world seemingly falling apart under the rapacity of human instincts. There are in fact grave doubts concerning the inferences made (Hinde 1967), and there is little reason to suppose that Lorenz's view of man is any better founded than earlier views of human behaviour based solely on the laboratory performances of the white rat.

Some authors have discussed the causal mechanisms responsible for evolutionary change in group life leading to the human level (Tiger and Fox 1966, Fox 1967a, b, Reynolds 1966). In general these authors seem to overemphasize the genetic element in the determination of characteristics of groups. Attributes claimed to be universals of human behaviour—such as dominance relations, territorial behaviour, sub-adult male grouping, gregariousness, familial social units, and intra-familial incest taboos—are sometimes treated as if they were the conceptual equivalents of species-specific "fixed action patterns" to which the neo-Darwinian theory of natural selection can be directly applied.

The ethological framework adopted in these studies is fundamentally the classical formulation by Lorenz in the 1930's, an historically important contribution, particularly to our understanding of behavioural evolution in invertebrates and lower vertebrates, but one which has been subjected to considerable conceptual revision (Hinde 1960, 1966). Traditionally, the student of behavioural evolution in animals has been concerned with behavioural traits—such as those involved, for instance, in courtship display in lizards and birds—which are sufficiently stable to be as typical of the species as morphological characters. As Lorenz (1950) has shown, such features, based upon genetic inheritance, are of great value in taxonomic study. Comparative research on living forms allows an understanding of the function of such displays and their probable evolution. The fact that such behavioural characteristics may be typical of a whole species population does not, however, necessarily mean that all species-typical behaviour traits are necessarily under genetic control and their evolution entirely explained by neo-Darwinian selection. Especially is this true when the features concerned refer to group relationships. Many quite stereotyped social behaviours are in fact a consequence of conditions of learning being more or less uniform in a population, and hence a result of common phenotypic adaptation to environment. Williams (1966) among others, has stressed the need for evidence for design, in addition to that for effect, in any discussion of the genetical evolution of behavioural traits. Behaviour that is beneficial to individuals need not be necessarily the product of natural selection over many generations.

Failure to notice these cautions has led certain authors to treat "group characteristics" (Crook 1968) as if they were determined in the same way as species-specific fixed action patterns shown by individuals and presumed to be under direct genetic control. This tendency may lead to a false view of behavioural origins in complex societies. Our discussion has shown that in primate social systems, and indeed presumably in those of other higher mammals, the behaviour of the individual is controlled largely by a continuous process of social learning arising from the pattern of interaction within groups. In addition, any account of the history of behaviour must include consideration of the way in which the environment imposes direct constraints on social organization—itself the milieu within which adaptive learning and genetic selection occurs. L. L. Whyte (1965) discusses the way in which the internal biochemical milieu of each species acts as a filter controlling genetic change. The social milieu imposes comparable effects at a higher level.

The ethologist traditionally treats behaviour as adequately explained when three related viewpoints have been considered—physiological causation, ontogeny, and functional and evolutionary aspects (Hinde 1966). In particular relation to ontogeny, a further dimension needs closer study —the way in which social structure, itself under multifactorial control, constrains individual behaviour development into organized patterns. Here one needs to consider not only the differentiation of behavioural roles but, in addition, the control exerted by social life during socialization on the physiological processes underlying motivation. While the complexities of research will inevitably demand specialist studies in each of these four areas, the theorist should not be blind to the systemic nature of the processes involved. Almost all complex social behaviour in non-human primates is under multifactorial control, cannot be fitted without distortion into any simple unitary explanation, and all hypotheses regarding causation must be taken as tentative at the present time. While the zoological perspective in social science is of major importance (Tiger and Fox 1966), syntheses must await more critical research on the determinants of group characteristics.

Our emphasis on the importance of learning in the control of group behaviour does not mean that the study of primate behavioural genetics is neglected. In primate, and probably most advanced mammalian societies, the social structure acts as an important part of an individual's habitat and, in the same way as the physical environment, imposes selection pressures producing differential reproductive success and perhaps also differential mortality of individuals. Animals, for example, whose behavioural traits do not conform sufficiently to the group norms are less likely to reproduce and may be ejected from the group. Social selection of this kind must have a considerable stabilizing effect upon the genetic basis of temperamental traits and motivational thresholds. Primate societies, rather than being the product of Darwinian natural selection in any simple sense, in fact seem to determine in an important way the genetical basis of individual social response.

Two important questions may be mentioned here. The relative stability of environments is held to affect the relative stereotyping of species characteristics. Klopfer (1962) holds that this should apply to both avian and primate behavioural characteristics, and one would suppose that forest species should show less social variability than open country forms, more behavioural stereotyping, and greater fixity of genetic characters. It will be of interest to examine these points and see whether forest primates have a lower recombination index than do animals beyond the trees. A second problem concerns the effect on genetics of contrasting social organizations—for example, the multimale and the one-male reproductive units. It is not known what differing degrees of heterozygosity may be related to these systems.

We have suggested that historical change in social systems in primates is "driven" primarily by phenotypic adaptation to environment through learning, and that genetic adaptation is collateral. There remains in addition a further possibility. Historical change may become largely independent of ecology and contingent primarily upon social processes. Under ecologically permissive circumstances a variety of contrasting types of sexual bonding, interaction, and display could emerge based entirely upon differential social learning. For example, the adoption of tools in exploitation of foods could lead to major changes in deployment, altering through social learning many basic patterns of response in ape societies. Indeed this is presumed to have happened in protohominid and human society, not only with the discovery of the utility of weapons in hunting but later with such innovations as fire-making, agriculture and animal domestication.

A synopsis of recent views on hominid social evolution would suggest that the loose social groupings of the chimpanzee formed the basis of social life among forest and forest fringe Dryopithecine apes, but when some of these were forced to adapt to savanna conditions as a consequence of climatic change they eventually developed more integrated social structures probably to some extent comparable to those shown today by open-country baboons. The early protohominids probably ranged widely in a number of African habitats, and it seems that in the less stable environments a polygamous and later perhaps a monogamous family pattern developed under ecological and social pressures not unlike those affecting, for example, the Gelada baboon. It may be that we have here some explanation for the origins of the family pattern and male control so characteristic of man. (See Fox 1967a, Crook 1967a, Reynolds 1966, Tobias 1964, Robinson 1964).

Reynolds (1968) has emphasized important similarities between chimpanzee and gorilla societies on the one hand, and those of primitive hunter-gatherers on the other. In both there exists an "open" community wherein non-exclusive groups gather or disperse according to food distribution. There is some limited evidence among the apes for stable matrifocal associations of mother and offspring, and it seems plausible that, as among Japanese macaques, consanguineal kinship ties between females may be important in maintaining social structure. Among hunter-gatherers, Reynolds says, attraction between local families is often matrilineal or bilateral, with recent trends to patrilineality in some societies. In both apes and primitive men there is a tendency for males to join together in "all-male groups" operating independently from other groupings. Reynolds accounts for the incorporation of the male into the matrifocal unit by arguing that a male is essential for group protection in open country and that a mutual exchange of food types (meat and vegetable) between the sexes would be beneficial. The argument neglects the probable significance of both inter- and intra-sexual selection in human societies and the likelihood of male jealousy and acquisitiveness with respect to females. It seems more plausible that the roles played by males in the only other open-country primates (the type 4 animals) have been to some extent paralleled by man as he emerged as a savanna creature. Such a development would explain the assertiveness and leadership roles played by males in most human societies. Reynolds is correct, nevertheless, in arguing that any parallelism with arid-country baboons must have developed upon an older pongid social organization in which patterned kinship and role relations were already established. Such ideas are of broader interest than mere historical speculation. Fox (1967a) and Comfort (1968) have argued that psychoanalytic views concerning the cyclopean family may find a biological basis in primate social psychology and that the insights so obtained may be of value in therapy. Historical explanation in these terms does not, however, yet provide an account of the evolutionary mechanisms involved. Certainly among modern men the dynamics of family life are in large degree a function of the expectations of the society within which they occur, and the development of gender roles is intimately linked with traditions of child-rearing (Sears 1965, Hampson 1965). Tendencies to a psychoanalytic nativism in relation to family relations should therefore be strongly tempered with caution.

We have suggested that in protocultural non-human primate groups some degree of social change may develop autochthonously with little direct reference to ecology. Certainly in studies of very primitive human communities in New Guinea the complex differences in culture and personality between tribes appear to owe relatively little to gross ecological contrasts. It appears therefore that although the role of ecology can never be ignored, at some stage in the emergence of man the major determinants of social change moved to within the sphere of culture. Indeed, once we can envisage clearly the transfer of control over social change from one level of determination to another, it seems that the last barrier to an understanding of human social evolution from the animal level is removed. In a schematic treatment of the interacting factors controlling human societies Talcott Parsons (1966) abstracts four societal systems—the cultural, the social, the personality of the members, and their organismic structure. He argues that these systems differ in their functional contribution to the whole. While organism and personality mediate individual adaptation and the structuring of goal-directed endeavour respectively, the social level consists of factors functioning in the integration of inter-individual interaction. The fourth system, the cultural, is of prime importance in that it is highest in "information" necessary for the regulation of the lower levels within which the actual work that maintains the organization occurs. Parsons argues that the cultural level maintains the pattern of human social life through "legitimation." That is to say, the structural frame of social life resulting from kinship and residence norms, and the activity of individuals within it, only acquires "meaning" to man when it is related to concepts of "ultimate reality" which arise in the rationalization of social norms into ideological or religious values. Individuals are thereby provided with ideas concerning their personal destiny, and these appear of major importance in determining the direction of goal-directed activity. With such ideas people may reduce their situational anxieties. Clearly changes at the cultural level have ramifying effects throughout a system and may operate without reference to ecology. Nevertheless unless some balance with ecology is re-established such changes cannot be stable. Indeed in modern times technological changes have modified ecology to such an extent that the human environment is now primarily of Man's own creation and increasingly out of balance with the natural order. The tragedy that may ensue will affect not only man but all living beings.

Conclusions

This chapter traces a framework for research in primate socio-ecology. In spite of many excellent studies it is clear that methodological and conceptual contrasts between authors reduce the comparability of the research reports available and that generalizations beyond the tentative are still not possible. Not only is there a need for an agreement on comparative methods in field primatology but in addition more attention needs to be focused particularly on intra-specific social variation, developmental and longitudinal studies of the social dynamics of well-known populations in the wild, and research into the synecology of primates in the more stable environments. These approaches would appear to be the most heuristic at the present time, and research would provide the generalizations from which theoretical inferences to man could then be drawn. Much current extrapolation from primates to man is premature, dependent on misleading and anachronistic views and often, in the case of more popular writers, highly uncritical. Nevertheless the outlines are drawn and the way to future research is clear.

Primate social systems may be allocated to "grades" which are defined with reference to ecological parameters. Within the Cercopithecoidea five types of social structure may be distinguished and these again are correlated closely with habitat factors. Studies of intra-specific variation in social organization support comparisons at the specific level, and suggestions relating social systems with their apparent ecological determinants are proposed (Fig. 2).

In addition to factors derived from phylogenetic heritage the social organization of primate species is maintained by behavioural traditions resulting from continuous social and observational learning. Experimental studies have shown how deviations from normal socialization patterns produce asocial individuals incapable of normal group life. Contrasting social structures appear to programme individual behaviour differently, producing different types of social conformity through the operation of contrasting tiers of interdependent natural learning schedules acting upon the given organismic material from birth. With increase in numbers groups are reconstituted or split in patterns that retain the overall social organization. This process differs in different species.

The attributes of primate social structures are "group characteristics" under multifactorial control. Confusion with innate species-specific patterns of behaviour has led to over-simple theorizing concerning their significance to man. Social systems in primates act as environments within which differential social and reproductive success leads to the natural (social) selection of the genetic basis of individual temperament and motivation. The natural selection of the innate basis for primate behaviour is thus subjected to a social "filter" additional to the usual action of pressures from the physical environment. In primates generally, social systems may be determined primarily by ecological factors, but there are suggestions that protocultural processes may yield shifts in social organization independently from environmental pressures. With the emergence of man cultural control of society has come to mould not only social change but, increasingly, human ecology as well.

REFERENCES

ALTMANN, S. A. (1962). A field study of the sociobiology of rhesus monkeys, *Macaca mulatta. Ann N.Y. Acad. Sci.* 102, 2, 338–435.

—— (ed.) (1967). "Social Communication Among Primates." University of Chicago Press, Chicago.

ANDERSON, P. K. (1961). Density, social structure and non-social environment in house mouse populations and the implications for regulation of numbers. *Trans. N.Y. Acad.* Ser. II, 23, 5, 474–451.

ANDREW, R. J. (1963). The origin and evolution of the calls and facial expressions of the primates. *Behaviour* 20, 1–109.

ARDREY, R. (1967). "The Territorial Imperative." Collins, London.

ARGYLE, M. (1966). "The Psychology of Interpersonal Behaviour." Penguin Books, London.

BERNSTEIN, I. S. (1966). Analysis of a key role in a capuchin (*Cebus albifrons*) group. *Tulane Stud. Zool.* 13, 2, 49–54.

—— (1968). The Lutong of Kuala Selangor. *Behaviour* 32, 2–16.

BERNSTEIN, I. S. and MASON, W. A. (1962). The effects of age and stimulus conditions on the emotional responses of rhesus monkeys: responses to complex stimuli. *J. Genet. Psychol.* 101, 279–298.

BERNSTEIN, I. S. and SHARPE, L. G. (1966). Social roles in a rhesus monkey group. *Behaviour* 26, 91–104.

BOLWIG, N. (1964). Facial expression in primates with remarks on a parallel development in certain carnivores. *Behaviour* 22, 3–4, 169–192.

BOOTH, A. H. (1956). The distribution of primates in the Gold Coast. *W. Afr. Sci. Ass.* 2, 2, 122–133.

—— (1958). The zoogeography of West African primates: a review. *Bull. I.F.A.N.* 20, Ser. A, No. 2, 587–622.

BUETTNER-JANUSCH, J. (ed.) (1962). The relatives of Man: modern studies of the relation of the evolution of non-human primates to human evolution. *Ann. N.Y. Acad. Sci.* 102, 2.

CARPENTER, C. R. (1940). A field study in Siam of the behavior and social relations of the gibbon. *Comp. Psychol. Monogr.* 16, 5.

—— (1942). Social behavior in free ranging rhesus monkeys (*Macaca mulatta*). *J. Comp. Psychol.* 33, 113–162.

—— (1964). Social behavior of non-human primates. *In:* "Naturalistic Behavior of Non Human Primates" (C. R. Carpenter, ed.), Pennsylvania State University Press.

—— (1965). The howlers of Barro Colorado Island. *In:* "Primate Behavior" (I. DeVore, ed.), Holt, Rinehart & Winston, N.Y., U.S.A.

CHALMERS, N. (1967). Behaviour of the Black Mangabey. Ph.D. Thesis, Cambridge University Library.

—— (1968a). Group composition, ecology and daily activities of free living Mangabeys in Uganda. *Folia. Primat.* 8, 247–262.

—— (1968b). The social behaviour of free living Mangabeys in Uganda. *Folia. Primat.* 8, 263–281.

CHANCE, M. R. A. (1956). Social structure of a colony of *Macaca mulatta. Brit. J. Anim. Behav.* 4, 1–13.

—— (1967). Attention structure as the basis of primate rank orders. *Man* 2, 4, 503–518.

CHIVERS, D. (In preparation). On the daily behaviour and spacing of free-ranging howling monkey groups.

CHRISTIAN, J. (1963). Endocrine adaptive mechanisms and the physiological regulation of population growth. *In:* "Physiological Mammalogy" (W. V. Mayer and R. G. van Gelder, eds.), Vol. 1. Academic Press, New York.

CODY, M. L. (1966). A general theory of clutch size. *Evolution* 20, 174–184.

COMFORT, A. (1968). Summing up. *J. psychonom. Res.* 12, 117–120.

COULSON, J. C. (1968). Differences in the quality of birds nesting in the centre and on the edges of a colony. *Nature, Lond.* 217, 478–479.

CROOK, J. H. (1965). The adaptive significance of avian social organizations. *Symp. zool. Soc. Lond.* 14, 181–218.

—— (1966). Gelada baboon herd structure and movement: a comparative report. *Symp. zool. Soc. Lond.* 18, 237–258.

—— (1967a). Gesellschaftstrukturen bei Primaten. *Umschau* 15, 488–493.

—— (1967b). Evolutionary change in primate societies. *Science Journal* 3, 6, 66–72.

—— (1968). The nature and function of territorial aggression. *In:* "Man and Aggression" (M. F. Ashley Montagu, ed.), Oxford University Press, New York.

——. Sources of co-operation in animals and man. "Man and Beast. Comparative Social Behaviour." Smithsonian Institution Press, 1971, pp. 235–260.

—— (In preparation). "Social Systems and Evolutionary Ecology." Oliver and Boyd, Edinburgh.

CROOK, J. H. and ALDRICH-BLAKE, P. (1968). Ecological and behavioural contrasts between sympatric ground-dwelling primates in Ethiopia. *Folia Primat.* 8, 192–227.

CROOK, J. H. and GARTLAN, J. S. (1966). Evolution of primate societies. *Nature, Lond.* 210, 1200–1203.

CROOK, J. H. and WARD, P. (1968). The Quelea problem in Africa. *In:* "The Problems of Birds as Pests." R. Murton, E. Wright, eds.). Institute of Biology Symposium. Academic Press, London.

DELIUS, J. D. (1965). A population study of skylarks. *Ibis* 107, 466–492.

DEVORE, I. (1963). A comparison of the ecology and behaviour of monkeys and apes. *In:* "Classification and Human Evolution" (S. L. Washburn, ed.). Aldine, Chicago.

—— (ed.) (1965a). "Primate Behaviour: Field Studies of Monkeys and Apes." Holt, Rinehart and Winston, New York.

—— (1965b). Male dominance and mating behaviour in baboons. *In:* "Sex and Behaviour." (F. A. Beach, ed.). Wiley, New York.

DEVORE, I. and HALL, K. R. L. (1965). Baboon ecology. *In:* "Primate Behavior" (I. DeVore, ed.). Holt, Rinehart and Winston, New York.

FOX, R. (1967a). In the beginning: aspects of hominid behavioural evolution. *Man* 2, 3, 415–433.

—— (1967b). Human mating patterns in ethological perspective. *Animals* 10, 3, 127–133.

FURUYA, Y. (1963). On the Gagyusan troop of Japanese monkeys after the first separation. *Primates* 4, 1, 116–118.

GARTLAN, J. S. (1964). Dominance in East African monkeys. *Proc. E. Afr. Acad.* 2, 75–79.

—— (1966). Ecology and behaviour of the vervet monkey, Lolui Island, Lake Victoria, Uganda, Ph.D. Thesis, Bristol University Library.

—— (1968). Structure and function in primate society. *Folia Primat.* 8, 89–120.

GARTLAN, J. S. and BRAIN, C. K. (1968). Ecology and social variability in *Cercopithecus aethiops* and *C. mitis. In:* "Primates: Studies in Adaptation and

Variability" (P. Jay, ed.). Holt, Rinehart and Winston, New York.

GOODALL, J. (1965). Chimpanzees of the Gombe Stream Reserve. In: "Primate Behavior" (J. DeVore, ed.). Holt, Rinehart & Winston, New York.

HALL, K. R. L. (1962). Numerical data, maintenance activities and locomotion of the wild chacma baboon, *Papio ursinus*. *Proc. zool. Soc. Lond.* 139, 284–327.

—— (1963a). Observational learning in monkeys and apes. *Brit. J. Psychol.* 54, 3, 201–226.

—— (1963b). Variations in the ecology of the chacma baboon, *Papio ursinus*. *Symp. zool. Soc. Lond.* 10, 1–28.

—— (1965). Social organization of the old world monkeys and apes. *Symp. zool. Soc. Lond.* 14, 265–289.

—— (1966a). Behaviour and ecology of the wild Patas monkey *Erythrocebus patas* in Uganda. *J. Zool.* 148, 15–87.

—— (1966b). Distribution and adaptations of baboons. *Symp. zool. Soc. Lond.* 17, 49–73.

—— (1967). Social interaction of the adult male and adult females of a Patas monkey group. In: "Social Communication Among Primates" (S. A. Altmann, ed.). University of Chicago Press, Chicago.

—— (1968). Social learning in monkeys. In: "Primates: Studies in Adaptation and Variability" (P. Jay, ed.). Holt, Rinehart & Winston, New York.

HALL, K. R. L. and DEVORE, I. (1965). Baboon social behavior. In: "Primate Behavior" (I. DeVore, ed.), 53–110. Holt, Rinehart & Winston, New York.

HALL, K. R. L. and GOSWELL, M. J. (1964). Aspects of social learning in captive Patas monkeys. *Primates* 5, 59–70.

HALL, K. R. L., BOELKINS, R. C. and GOSWELL, M. J. (1965). Behaviour of Patas monkeys, *Erythrocebus patas*, in captivity with notes on their natural habitat. *Folia primat.* 3, 22–49.

HALL, K. R. L. and MAYER, B. (1967). Social interactions in a group of captive Patas monkeys (*Erythrocebus patas*). *Folia Primat.* 5, 213–236.

HAMPSON, J. L. (1965). Determinants of psychosexual orientation. In: "Sex and Behavior" (F. A. Beach, ed.). Wiley, New York.

HARLOW, H. F. (1961). The development of affectional patterns in infant monkeys. In: "Determinants of Infant Behaviour" (R. M. Foss, ed.). Methuen, London.

HARLOW, H. F. and HARLOW, M. K. (1962). Social deprivation in monkeys. *Scient. Am.* 207, 5, 137–146.

HESLOP HARRISON, J. (1964). Forty years of genecology. In: "Advances in Ecological Research" (J. B. Crag, ed.), 2, Academic Press, London and New York.

HINDE, R. A. (1960). Energy models of motivation. *Symp. Soc. exp. Biol.* 14, 199–213.

—— (1966). "Animal Behaviour. A Synthesis of Ethology and Comparative Psychology." McGraw-Hill, New York.

—— (1967). The nature of aggression. *New Society,* 2nd March.

HINDE, R. A. and SPENCER-BOOTH, Y. (1967). The behaviour of socially living rhesus monkeys in their first two-and-a-half-years. *Anim. Behav.* 15, 169–196.

HINDE, R. A., SPENCER-BOOTH, Y. and BRUCE, M. (1966). Effects of 6-day maternal deprivation of rhesus monkey infants. *Nature, Lond.* 210, No. 5040, 1021–1023.

HOOFF, VAN J. A. R. A. M. (1967). The facial displays of the Catarrhine monkeys and apes. In: "Primate Ethology" (D. Morris, ed.). Weidenfeld and Nicolson, London.

HUXLEY, J. S. (1959). Clades and grades. *Syst. Ass. Publ.* No. 3, 21–22.

IMANISHI, K. (1957). Social behaviour in Japanese monkeys, *Macaca fuscata. Psychologia* 1, 47–54.

—— (1960). Social organization of sub-human primates in their natural habitats. *Current Anthropology* 1, No. 5–6, 393–407.

ITANI, J. (1959). Paternal care in the wild Japanese monkey, *Macaca f. fuscata. Primates* 2, 61–93.

ITANI, J. and SUZUKI, A. (1967). The social unit of chimpanzees. *Primates* 8, 355–381.

IZAWA, K. and NISHIDA, T. (1963). Monkeys living in the northern limit of their distribution. *Primates* 4, 2, 67–88.

JARMAN, P. (1968). The effect of the creation of Lake Kariba upon the terrestrial ecology of the middle Zambezi valley, with particular reference to the large mammals. Ph.D. Thesis, Manchester University Library.

JAY, P. (1965). The common langur of North India. In: "Primate Behavior" (I. DeVore, ed.). Holt, Rinehart and Winston, New York.

—— (ed.). "Primates, Studies in Adaptation and Variability." Holt, Rinehart and Winston, New York.

JENKINS, D. A., WATSON, A. and MILLER, G. R. (1963). Population studies on red grouse, *Lagopus lagopus scoticus*. *J. Anim. Ecol.* 32, 317–376.

JOLLY, A. (1966). "Lemur Behavior: A Madagascan Field Study." University of Chicago Press, Chicago.

KAUFMANN, J. H. (1967). Social relations of adult males in a free-ranging band of rhesus monkeys. *In:* "Social Communication Among Primates" (S. A. Altmann, ed.), University of Chicago Press, Chicago.

KAWAI, M. (1965). On the system of social ranks in a natural troop of Japanese monkeys. *In:* "Japanese Monkeys. A Collection of Translations" (S. Altmann, ed.). Yerkes Regional Primate Center.

KAWAMURA, S. (1959). The process of sub-culture propagation among Japanese macaques. *Primates* 2, 43–60.

—— (1965). Matriarchal social ranks in the Minoo B group: A study of the rank system of Japanese Monkeys. *In:* "Japanese Monkeys. A Collection of Translations" (S. A. Altmann, ed.). Yerkes Regional Primate Center.

KLOPFER, P. H. (1962). "Behavioural Aspects of Ecology." Prentice-Hall, Inc., Englewood Cliffs, N.J.

KOFORD, C. B. (1963a). Group relations in an island colony of rhesus monkeys. *In:* "Primate Social Behavior." (C. H. Southwick, ed.). Van Nostrand Insight Series, New York.

—— (1963b). Rank of mothers and sons in bands of rhesus monkeys. *Science, N.Y.* 141, 356–357.

—— (1967). Population changes in rhesus monkeys: Cayo Santiago 1960–1964. *Tulane Stud. Zool.* 13, 1–7.

KUMMER, H. (1957). "Soziales Verhalten einer Mantelpavian-Gruppe." Huber, Bern und Stuttgart.

—— (1967). Tripartite relations in Hamadryas baboons. *In:* "Social Communication Among Primates" (S. A. Altmann, ed.). University of Chicago Press, Chicago.

—— (1968a). Social organization of Hamadryas baboons. *Bibliotheca Primatologica* 6, 1–189.

—— (1968b). Two variations in the social organization of baboons. *In:* "Primates: Studies in Adaptation and Variability" (P. Jay, ed.). Holt, Rinehart and Winston, New York.

KUMMER, H. and KURT, F. (1963). Social units of a free-living population of Hamadryas baboons. *Folia Primat.* 1, 4–19.

—— (1965). A comparison of social behavior in captive and wild Hamadryas baboons. *In:* "The Baboon in Medical Research" (H. Vagtborg, ed.). University of Texas Press.

LACK, D. (1966). "Population Studies of Birds." Oxford University Press, Oxford.

LAHIRI, R. K. and SOUTHWICK, C. H. (1966). Parental care in *Macaca sylvana*. *Folia primat.* 4, 257–264.

LANCASTER, J. B. and LEE, R. B. (1965). The annual reproductive cycle in monkeys and apes. *In:* "Primate Behaviour" (I. DeVore, ed.). Holt, Rinehart and Winston, New York.

LORENZ, K. (1950). The comparative method in studying innate behaviour patterns. *Symp. Soc. exp. Biol.* 4, 221–268.

—— (1963). "Das Sogenannte Bose." Schoeler Verlag, Wien.

MARLER, P. (1968). *Colobus guereza:* territoriality and group composition. *Science, N.Y.* 163, 93–95.

MASON, J. W. and BRADY, J. V. (1964). The sensitivity of psychoendocrine systems to social and physical environment. *In:* "Psychobiological Approaches to Social Behaviour" (P. H. Leiderman, and D. Shapiro, eds.). Tavistock, London.

MASON, W. A. (1965). The social development of monkeys and apes. *In:* "Primate Behavior" (I. DeVore, ed.). Holt, Rinehart and Winston, New York.

—— (1968). Use of space by *Callicebus* groups. *In:* "Primates: Studies in Adaptation and Variability" (P. Jay, ed.). Holt, Rinehart and Winston, New York.

MENZEL, E. W. (1966). Responsiveness to objects in free-ranging Japanese monkeys. *Behaviour* 26, 1–2, 130–149.

MILLER, N. E. (1959). Liberalization of basic S-R concepts: extensions to conflict behaviour, motivation and social learning. *In:* "Psychology: A Study of a Science" (S. Koch, ed.), 196–292. McGraw-Hill, New York.

MIZUHARA, H. (1964). Social changes of Japanese monkey troops in the Takasakiyama. *Primates* 5, 27–52.

MORRIS, D. (ed.) (1967). "Primate Ethology." Weidenfeld and Nicolson, London.

MOYNIHAN, M. (1963). Interspecific relations between some Andean birds. *Ibis* 105, 327–339.

NADEL, S. F. (1957). "The Theory of Social Structure." Free Press, Glencoe, Illinois.

NAPIER, J. and BARNICOT, N. A. (eds.) (1963). "The Primates." *Symp. zool. Soc. Lond.* 10.

NISHIDA, T. (1966). A sociological study of solitary male monkeys. *Primates* 7, 141–204.

440   John Hurrell Crook

40

44

PARSONS, T. (1966). "Societies: Evolutionary and Comparative Perspectives." Foundations of Modern Sociology Series. Prentice-Hall, Englewood Cliffs, N.J.

PETTER, J. J. (1962a). Recherches sur l'écologie et l'éthologie des Lémuriens malgaches. *Mém. du Mus. Nat. de l'Hist. Naturelle, Ser. A.* 27, 1–146.

—— (1962b). Ecological and behavioural studies of Madagascar lemurs in the field. *Ann. N.Y. Acad. Sci.* 102, 267–281.

PLUTCHIK, R. (1964). The study of social behaviour in primates. *Folia primat.* 2, 2, 67–92.

REYNOLDS, V. (1965). Some behavioural comparisons between the chimpanzee and the mountain gorilla in the wild. *Am. Anthrop.* 67, 3, 691–706.

—— (1966). Open groups in hominid evolution. *Man* 1, 441–452.

—— (1968). Kinship and the family in monkeys, apes and man. *Man* 3, 209–223.

REYNOLDS, V. and REYNOLDS, F. (1965). Chimpanzees of the Budongo Forest. *In:* "Primate Behaviour" (I. DeVore, ed.). Holt, Rinehart and Winston, New York.

RIPLEY, S. (1967). Intertroop encounters among Ceylon grey langurs (*Presbytis entellus*). *In:* "Social Communication Among Primates" (S. A. Altmann, ed.). University of Chicago Press, Chicago.

ROBINSON, J. T. (1964). Some critical phases in the evolution of Man. *S. Afr. Archaeol. Bull.* 19 (173), 3–12.

ROWELL, T. E. (1966a). Forest-living baboons in Uganda. *J. Zool. Lond.* 149, 344–364.

—— (1966b). Hierarchy in the organization of a captive baboon group. *Anim. Behav.* 14, 4, 420–443.

—— (1967a). Variability in the social organization of primates. *In:* "Primate Ethology" (D. Morris, ed.). Weidenfeld and Nicolson, London.

—— (1967b). A quantitative comparison of the behaviour of a wild and a caged baboon group. *Anim. Behav.* 15, 499–509.

ROWELL, T. E., HINDE, R. A. and SPENCER-BOOTH, Y. (1964). Aunt-infant interaction in captive rhesus groups. *Anim. Behav.* 12, 219–226.

SANDERSON, I. T. (1957). "The Monkey Kingdom." Hamish Hamilton, London.

SARBIN, T. R. (1959). Role theory. *In:* "Handbook of Social Psychology" (G. Lindzey, ed.). Addison-Wesley, Cambridge, Mass.

SCHALLER, C. B. (1963). "The Mountain Gorilla, Ecology and Behavior." University of Chicago Press, Chicago.

SCHENKEL, R. and SCHENKEL-HULLIGER, L. (1967). On the sociology of free-ranging Colobus. *In:* "Progress in Primatology" (D. Starck, R. Schneider, H. J. Kuhn, eds.). Fischer-Verlag, Stuttgart.

SCHRIER, A. M., HARLOW, H. F. and STOLLNITZ, F. (eds.) (1965). "Behavior of Non-human Primates." Academic Press, New York and London.

SEARS, R. R. (1965). Development of gender role. *In:* "Sex and Behavior" (F. A. Beach, ed.). Wiley, New York.

SINGH, S. D. (1966). The effects of human environment on the social behavior of Rhesus monkeys. *Primates* 7, 33–39.

SOLOMON, M. E. (1964). Analysis of processes involved in the natural control of insects. *In:* "Advances in Ecological Research" (J. B. Crag, ed.), 2, Academic Press, London and New York.

SOUTHWICK, C. H. (1962). Patterns of intergroup social behavior in primates with special reference to rhesus and howling monkeys. *Ann. N.Y. Acad. Sci.* 102, 2, 436–454.

SOUTHWICK, C. H., BEG, M. A. and SIDDIQI, M. R. (1961a). A population survey of rhesus monkeys in villages, towns and temples of Northern India. *Ecology* 42, 3, 538–547.

—— (1961b). A population survey of rhesus monkeys in Northern India II. Transportation routes and forest areas. *Ecology* 42, 4, 698–710.

STARCK, D. and FRICK, H. (1958). Beobachtungen an äthiopischen Primaten. *Zool. Jb.* 86, 41–70.

STRUHSAKER, T. T. (1967a). Behavior of vervet monkeys (*Cercopithecus aethiops*). University of California Publications in Zoology 82, 1–64.

—— (1967b). Social structure among vervet monkeys (*Cercopithecus aethipos*). *Behaviour* 29, 2–4, 83–121.

—— (in preparation). Correlates of ecology and social organization among African Cercopithecines. Burg Wartenstein Summer Symposium. "Social Organization and Subsistence in Primate Societies." 1968.

SUGIYAMA, Y. (1960). On the division of a natural troop of Japanese monkeys at Takasakiyama. *Primates* 2, 109–144.

—— (1967). Social organization of hanuman langurs. *In:* "Social Communication Among Primates" (S. A. Altmann, ed.). University of Chicago Press, Chicago.

TAJFEL, H. (1969). The formation of national attitudes:

a social psychological perspective. *In:* "Interdisciplinary Relations in the Social Sciences" (M. and C. W. Sherif, eds.). Aldine, Chicago.

TIGER, L. and FOX, R. (1966). The zoological perspective in social science. *Man* 1, 76–81.

TOBIAS, P. V. (1964). Bushman hunter-gatherers: a study in human ecology. *In:* "Ecological Studies in Southern Africa" (D. H. S. Davis, ed.). *Monographiae Biologicae* XIV. Den Haag.

TSUMORI, A. (1967). Newly acquired behavior and social interactions of Japanese monkeys. *In:* "Social Communication Among Primates" (S. A. Altmann, ed.). University of Chicago Press, Chicago.

VANDENBERGH, J. G. (1967). The development of social structure in free-ranging rhesus monkeys. *Behaviour* 29, 179–194.

WASHBURN, S. L. and HAMBURG, D. A. (1965). The

implications of primate research. *In:* "Primate Behavior" (I. DeVore, ed.). Holt, Rinehart and Winston, New York.

WHIMBEY, A. E. and DENENBERG, V. H. (1967). Experimental programming of life histories: the factor structure underlying experimentally created individual differences. *Behaviour* 29, 296–314.

WHYTE, L. L. (1965). "Internal Factors in Evolution." Tavistock, London.

WILLIAMS, G. C. (1966). "Adaptation and Natural Selection. A Critique of Some Current Evolutionary Thought." Princeton University Press, Princeton.

WILSON, A. P. (1968). Social behaviour of free-ranging rhesus monkeys with an emphasis on aggression. Doctoral thesis. University of California, Berkeley.

YOSHIBA, K. (1967). An ecological study of hanuman langurs. *Primates* 8, 127–154.

27 · INSTINCTS AND CHROMOSOMES: WHAT IS AN "INNATE" ACT?

Peter H. Klopfer

"The biologistic fallacy," as it may be called, holds that in development "heredity" and "environment" can express themselves independently of each other, and that it is therefore possible to measure the effects of one entirely without considering the other. This is simply not true. Whether one can learn to speak French or Kwakiutl may have nothing to do with one's genes; but with very few exceptions, genetic and environmental factors influence reciprocally, and for the most part inextricably, every aspect of development: structural, functional, and behavioral.

The confusion which characterizes this subject is illustrated by the very word "heredity" itself. This is generally taken to mean what the individual is born with, namely, his genetically determined traits and potentialities. This is an utterly erroneous view of the individual's equipment, for by the time the organism is born the expression of its genetic potentialities has already been influenced by its experience

of prenatal life. In brief, "heredity" represents a process of interaction between genes and environments. Neither genes nor environments determine traits; all that each is capable of doing is to influence the expression of traits.

In science and in the cause of clear thinking terminology is very important, ambiguity of language is to be avoided. Toward this end it would be best if the term "heredity" were dropped altogether. But since that seems to be a very unlikely destiny for the word, if it must be used it should always be clearly defined. In that connection Klopfer's contribution is most important in examining the meaning of another frequently used term, namely, "innate."

What is usually meant by the term "innate" is "inborn" or "genetically determined." In genetic terms the inclination has been to think that a specific chromosome or collection of genes is responsible for a certain behavior called an "instinct." The notion of "the-little-homuncular-trait" sitting in a chromosome is to some extent derived from the one-gene-one-enzyme hypothesis. This is now known to be less sound an idea than it was once thought to be.

Klopfer very aptly remarks that we would make more progress with our studies of heritable differences in behavior if we were to cease regarding the gene as a repository of data or a blueprint from which an organism can be constructed, an inchoate homunculus, "but rather as an information device which exploits the predictable and ordered nature of its environment." Taking Hailman's careful study of the feeding behavior of the chicks of the laughing gull as an illustration, Klopfer shows how complex such "instinctive" behavior is, how un-unitary it is, and what opportunities are involved in it for learning. As Klopfer points out, it is nonsense to talk about the inheritance of behavior, however stereotyped it may be. In the human species it is far from stereotyped, and on the continuum from stereotypy to plasticity, man stands as the most plastic of all living creatures.[1]

What is "innate" in man is an unmatched capacity for learning, and except for the instinct-like reactions to sudden withdrawal of support and to a sudden loud noise, he has no instincts. In any case, "the hope of finding an instinct in a chromosome is illusory." As McBride has remarked, "Man is unique in his acquisition of a superb system of cultural genetics, which has almost replaced the genetic system as the mechanism of coding and transmission of behavior." [2]

If chicks of a yellow and of a black variety are reared together and their individual preferences for one or the other variety then determined, of those that do evince a preference, most will select chicks of their own hue as companions. Since the animals have been reared together under identical conditions, we can say that this difference in their preferences is genetically determined (see Kilham, Klopfer, and Oelke 1968). Such a formulation cannot easily be paraphrased without doing violence to its content. It is not identical, for instance, with the statement "preference for own kind is genetically determined." I wish to examine the reason behind this assertion of nonequivalence.

The experiments alluded to above are far from complete. They were originally designed merely to test the validity of conclusions summarized by Howell and Vine (1940) that there are strain differences in the perceptual preferences of chicks; second, they were intended to identify the relevant cues by which chicks make the requisite discriminations and on which their preferences are based; and, finally, they were intended to discover how apparently innate perceptual preferences are programmed by the nervous system. For example, if the discrimination between own strain and alien strain is based on color (but it was not insisted that this is so), we can ask whether this is due to the differential distribution of retinal oil droplets, to sensitivity of the retinal cells, or to central mechanisms. Fortunately, some of the different answers to such questions have been provided in a study by Hailman (1967) which affords an example of what a careful analysis of "innate" behavior may reveal. The stereotyped species-common behavior pattern he examined is the feeding behavior of chicks of the laughing gull, *Larus atricilla*. Typically, gull chicks remain near the nest after hatching and are fed by the parents, which regurgitate semidigested food. Regurgitation by the parent

SOURCE: *The American Naturalist* vol. 103 (1969), 556–60. Copyright © 1969 by the University of Chicago Press. Reprinted by permission of the author and the publisher.
[1] See Chapter 32, pp. 508–14.

[2] Glen McBride, "The Nature-Nurture Problem in Social Evolution," in J. F. Eisenberg and W. S. Dillon, eds., *Man and Beast: Comparative Social Behavior* (Washington: Smithsonian Institution Press, 1971), p. 55.

is apparently stimulated by the chicks pecking at the tip of the parental bill. (The tip is colored and contrasts with the rest of the bill.) Field observations show that as long as the chick pecks at the bill tip, the parent regurgitates the food onto the ground. While the chick continues pecking, the parent takes the food back into its own bill and, after a time, reswallows it. The hungrier the chick is, that is, the longer since its previous feeding, the more intensely it pecks. Thus, this behavior ultimately brings the chick's bill in contact with the food. Once contact is made, the food is quickly swallowed. Thereafter, pecking is preferentially directed to the food. The analysis of movies of this pecking behavior by the chicks shows that the movement itself consists of four discrete, recognizable elements: a forward and upward movement of the head, an opening of the bill, a rotation of the head, and a push with the legs. There seems to be a considerable inter- and intraindividual variation both in the duration of these different components of the total movement as well as in their synchronization. Rearing the chicks under conditions of darkness and force-feeding them, thus denying them many of the usual visual and motor adjustments of normally reared chicks, affected some, but not all of these components. Similarly, the chicks that were kept in the dark until an initial exposure to a variety of simple models that mimicked one or another of the characteristics of the parental head and bill, were shown to respond differently to quite a number of features of the model. The experiments with models show that the important features of the parental head include the figure-ground contrast, the orientation (whether vertical or horizontal), diameter of the simulated bill, its rate of movement, and its color; many of these attributes could be manipulated in a compensatory manner without affecting the overall rate of pecking.

The act of pecking seems as simple and "instinctive" an act as any that has been described.

Indeed, it has long served as a paradigm for ethologists (Tinbergen and Perdeck 1950). But, from the foregoing, we can see that pecking is not a unitary affair. The final outcome, the contact of the chick's bill with bill tip of a parent, may appear to represent a relatively simple and stereotyped behavioral response; but in fact it is a response composed of a multiplicity of movements and choices, many of which can vary without the final result being altered. And the analysis of the pecking could certainly be pushed further along a reductionist path! There is no reason to believe that in the forward movement of the chick's head the same muscle bundles are invariably involved. And, even within one bundle, different fibers doubtless fire at different times. Indeed, the more closely one approaches the molecular level, the more probabilistic and nondeterministic our description must become. Recall how the gas laws of physics permit precise statements regarding pressure-volume-temperature relations while taking for granted indeterminancy in the behavior of the individual gas molecules. The question, then, whether pecking is genetically determined, has to be rephrased; in fact, what is represented on the genome? Surely not the final result of the many motor and perceptual phenomena listed above. A separate gene for each motor element of pecking? And for the color and the speed-of-movement preference, perhaps? Ultimately, must we postulate genes for virtually every nerve or muscle fiber which contributes to a response? The difficulty in relating behavior, however stereotyped it may seem, to genetics actually stems from an obsolete and incorrect notion of gene action. This notion, which, in its essentials, holds the chromosome to be a biochemical homunculus is derived from the one-gene–one-enzyme hypothesis, which is itself an oversimplification.

Consider again the preference of the chick for a particular color. Color preferences in gulls depend, at least partially, on the presence and distribution of oil droplets in the retinal cells. How is their distribution and appearance controlled by the genes? The most reasonable assumption, superficially stated, appears to be that, at a particular locus of a chromosome, a synthetic process is initiated which leads to the formation of certain enzymes which react with substances derived extrachromosomally to produce other substances that lead (eventually) to formation of certain oil soluble pigments. Obviously, this description is but a small distance of the way to a color-coding and perceiving mechanism. But the question of what in fact has been inherited becomes even more difficult to answer when we recognize the complexities of the mechanisms that underlie color preferences.

We might make studies of heritable differences in behavior more intelligible if we view the gene not as a repository of data or a blueprint from which an organism can be constructed, that is, as an inchoate homunculus, but rather as an information-generating device which exploits the predictable and ordered nature of its environment (or in Schroedinger's terms [1951], which feeds on negative entropy). This view accords well with current models of gene action, such as that advanced by Jacob and Monod (1961), among others, or that of Waddington (1966). A segment of the alpha helix specifies a particular species of RNA which ultimately, and in an appropriate environment, leads to the synthesis of a particular enzyme, which in turn may repress or activate further synthetic activity by that portion of the helix, or repress or activate another segment. "Wheels within wheels," and all depends as much on substances external to the helix as on the structure of the helix itself. Hormones, for instance, whose synthesis can be traced ultimately back to the action of particular segments of the alpha helix, are now known to activate genetic transcription at other portions of the helix. The transcription products may further feedback and regulate development (Schneiderman and Gilbert 1964).

It is intriguing to see how Erikson (1968), in his discussion of human development, has perceived parallel situations at the cultural level. He writes: "The human infant is born preadapted to an *average expectable environment* [my emphasis]. Man's ecology demands constant and natural historical and technological readjustment which makes it at once obvious that only a perpetual, if ever so imperceptible, restructuring of tradition can safeguard for each new generation of infants anything approaching an average expectability of environment. . . . In other words the human environment as a whole must permit and safeguard a series of more or less discontinuous and yet culturally and psychologically consistent developments, each extending further along the radius of expanding life tasks."

The implication that human behavior is the outcome of epigenetic processes expressed in the context of a stable environment is profound. For one thing, greater developmental stability is assured than by a homunculus, for the epigenetic system is buffered and self-correcting at many points. At the same time, the system is far more responsive to changes in environmental conditions than a homunculus would be. (Note particularly Waddington's [1966] reference to this labile aspect of epigenetic systems, and his discussion on canalization.)

In short, *behavior* is not a noun, defined and determined by a discrete locus on a DNA molecule. It is a process that derives from a series of interactions, some stochastic, some perhaps deterministic, which at times can achieve a certain level of predictability and stereotypy. At some point this degree of inevitability and sameness become so great that we speak of "an instinct." But let us not neglect that acts, or behavior, are sequences of movements and perceptions and are best described in terms of latencies, frequencies, durations, and intensities. They must be analyzed with a view to unraveling a skein of interactions which tie together particular stimuli and particular responses, for example, in the case of the gull chicks, the sight of the parent, the lunge forward, and the open bill.

A *gene* refers to inheritable differences. But, while it is nonsense to talk about the inheritance of behavior, it is true that behavior may be more or less stereotyped. One can imagine a continuum with acts, perceptions, or responses ranging from highly plastic and variable at one end to highly constrained or stereotyped at the other. Further, it is of interest to ask how behavior falling at either end of this spectrum develops, or to make inquiries about its evolutionary history, the mechanisms which underlie it, or the functions which it serves. The answers to such queries will reveal interesting differences between those kinds of behavior which we know to be highly plastic, falling at one end of the continuum, and those kinds of behavior which we know to be more stable, less flexible, falling at the opposite end. The hope of finding an instinct in a chromosome, in any event, is illusory.

LITERATURE CITED

ERIKSON, E. 1968. Identity: youth and crisis. Norton, New York.

HAILMAN, J. P. 1967. The ontogeny of an instinct. (Behaviour Suppl. 15.) E. J. Brill, Leiden.

HOWELL, T. H., and D. O. VINE. 1940. The innate differential in social learning. J. Abnormal Soc. Psychol. 35:537–548.

JACOB, F., and J. MONOD. 1961. Genetic regulatory mechanisms in the synthesis of proteins. J. Mol. Biol. 3:318.

KILHAM, P., P. KLOPFER, and H. OELKE. 1968. Species identification and color preferences in chicks. Anim. Behav. 16:238–245.

SCHNEIDERMAN, H. A., and L. I. GILBERT. 1964. Control of growth and development in insects. Science 143:325.

SCHROEDINGER, E. 1951. What is life? Cambridge Univ. Press, New York.

TINBERGEN, N., and N. C. PERDECK. 1950. On the stimulus situation releasing the begging response in the newly hatched herring gull chick. Behaviour 3:1–39.

WADDINGTON, C. H. 1966. Principles of development and differentiation. Macmillan, New York.

28 · COMPETITIVE AND AGGRESSIVE BEHAVIOR

Edward O. Wilson

The subject of competitive and aggressive behavior has in recent years received much discussion: a vast literature has grown up, much of it controversial and a good deal based on solid research.[1]

On the other hand, the writings of such authors as Robert Ardrey, Konrad Lorenz, Desmond Morris, and Anthony Storr [2] are tendentious and speculative. Nevertheless, they have been widely read and very

---

[1] For an excellent discussion see Roger Johnson, *Aggression in Man and Animals* (Philadelphia: W. B. Saunders Co., 1972). See also Leonard Berkowitz, *Aggression: A Social Psychological Analysis* (New York: McGraw-Hill Book Co., 1962); John Paul Scott, *Aggression* (Chicago: University of Chicago Press, 1958); J. D. Carthy and F. J. Ebling, eds., *The Natural History of Aggression* (New York: Academic Press, 1964); C. D. Clemente and D. B. Lindsley, eds., *Aggression and Defense*

(Berkeley: University of California Press, 1967); S. Garattini and E. B. Sigg, eds., *Aggressive Behaviour* (New York: John Wiley & Sons Inc., 1969); B. E. Eleftheriou and J. P. Scott, eds., *The Physiology of Aggression and Defeat* (New York: Plenum Press, 1971).

[2] The references to these writings are given in Wilson's paper. They have been critically examined in Ashley Montagu, ed., *Man and Aggression,* 2nd ed. (New York: Oxford University Press, 1973).

influential, for reasons that Wilson sets out at the very beginning of the following contribution.

In the course of his discussion Wilson corrects a number of widespread errors. One of these is that man is the only creature who kills members of his own kind. Ants and other Hymenoptera do, but vertebrates do not. Furthermore, I believe that, as *Pliny* and later Leonardo da Vinci pointed out, man is the only creature who makes organized attacks upon his own kind. I think it necessary to get these matters clear, for if man is the only creature who makes war upon his own kind, it may be that he does so because he is unique in other ways as well as this. He is unique in his culturally learned ways of behaving—far from having it in his genes to make war, genes allegedly inherited from his remote ancestors, it is more likely that such belligerent behavior represents a wholly learned way of life.

If one can argue that it is easy to provoke men to make organized attacks upon others because men are inherently aggressive, one may with equal force argue that it is easy to organize men to cooperate peacefully with other groups of men. This argument does not, of course, constitute a disproof of inherent aggressiveness, nor does it constitute a proof of man's inherent cooperativeness. The two may exist as potentialities side by side, as Eibl-Eibesfeldt has argued.[3] Alternative possibilities are that man is neither innately aggressive nor innately cooperative, but that he learns to be either or both of these things; or alternatively, that he has evolved as a highly cooperative creature who is born with all his drives oriented toward cooperation, and that he becomes aggressive only when those drives are frustrated.[4]

Whatever view one finds most compelling on the basis of the verifiable evidence, the fact of man's

unique educability remains constant. *If* he is endowed with any genetic remnants, as Wilson believes he is, it is certainly clear that to whatever degree he is thus endowed, he can, by the proper training, learn either never to feel its influence, or to control it, or both.

The current popularity of animal behaviorists comes in good part from the comfort and assurance their discoveries offer to humanity. It is, after all, comforting to think that our sins are only animal sins (original sin if you wish) and that we are no more than naked apes momentarily disoriented by our jerry-built civilization. We want to believe that the beastliness in human nature is beastliness in the primordial sense and not some dark angelic flaw, to trust that we have not escaped so far from our ancestral genes as to be due for an early extinction. Perhaps all that is needed, the popular exponents of ethology seem to be saying, is to understand the adaptedness of our behavior and to learn to operate within its constraints. These writers—Robert Ardrey (1961), Konrad Lorenz (1966), Desmond Morris (1967), Anthony Storr (1968), and others —speak of territorial and aggressive instincts which long ago originated as stereotyped, strictly inherited behavioral repertories in our primate ancestors. The instincts are said to survive today in man in slightly abated and more diffuse form, hedged in by social conventions that tend to minimize their overt effects.

Of course nothing so starkly Darwinian could go unchallenged for very long. The contrary view

SOURCE: J. F. Eisenberg and W. S. Dillon, eds., *Man and Beast: Comparative Social Behavior* (Washington: Smithsonian Institution Press, 1971): 183–217. Reprinted by permission of the publisher.
[3] Irenäus Eibl-Eibesfeldt, *Love and Hate: The Natural History of Behavior Patterns* (New York: Holt, Rinehart & Winston, 1972).

[4] For the development of this viewpoint see Ashley Montagu, *The Direction of Human Development*, Rev. ed. (New York: Hawthorn Books: 1970); Ashley Montagu: *On Being Human*, 2nd ed. (New York: Hawthorn Books, 1967); Ashley Montagu, *The Human Revolution* (New York: Bantam Books, 1967).

has been argued by those of liberal humanist persuasion, such as that of Edmund Leach (1968) and Ashley Montagu (1967), and also by animal behaviorists with experience in the raw source material, including S. A. Barnett (1967) and Peter Klopfer (1968). These critics declare that there are no such things as unitary instincts, or drives, that persist through phylogenetic lineages as do vertebrae and eardrums. They point out that territorial behavior and aggression are not universal in lower animals, and that when such traits do occur they are expressed in myriad ways, performing functions that shift subtly from species to species. They condemn as facile and unscientific the analogies between animal and human behavior.

In the midst of these contradictions, what are we to believe?

When I was invited to deal with the subject of competitive behavior, I welcomed it as an opportunity to attempt an objective comparative approach to this most contemporary of subjects. A comparative behaviorist is above all an evolutionist, and he can thus contribute to the discussion of the given problematic species—in this case, man—in at least two ways. First, he can try dispassionately to catalog the phenomenology of the subject. Each species of animal displays a pattern of behavioral phenomena with a texture of emphasis and clarity uniquely its own. What is rudimentary or hidden in one species might be exaggerated and obvious in the next. By considering many species, it is possible to catalog and perceive the significance of a much larger set of phenomena than would be possible from a study of a single example. Each of the behavioral acts in the repertoire of the problematic species, however weakly or deceptively expressed, thus stands a better chance of being recognized and understood. This in essence is the approach to man already taken by ethologists of the Lorenz school.

The second contribution to be desired from the comparative behaviorists is less obvious in nature. It consists of extrapolating trends beyond species already analyzed to encompass the problematic species. The method is not limited simply to fixing the species as a point on a subjective curve. It also evaluates the variability of behavioral characters among species in order to judge the lability of the characters during evolution. For example, if characteristics evolve so quickly as to shift markedly in the course of evolution at the species level, then extrapolation to the genus level or higher in the taxonomic scale is risky and probably worthless. The second approach seems to be the key in evaluating competitive and aggressive behavior in man, yet it has been largely neglected in prior discussions of the subject. I would like to make it the theme of the exposition to follow.

The Occurrence of Competition and Aggression in Animal Species

Competition, as Miller (1967) modified the original Clements and Shelford (1939) definition, is "the active demand by two or more individuals of the same species (intraspecies competition) or members of two or more species at the same trophic level (interspecies competition) for a common resource or requirement that is actually or potentially limiting." This definition is consistent with the assumptions of the Lotka-Volterra equations, which still form the basis of the mathematical theory of competition (Levins 1968). It also matches the intuitive conception held by most modern ecologists concerning the underlying behavioral processes (Miller 1967). Competition arises only when populations become crowded enough for a shortage to develop in one or more resources. When it does come into play, it reduces population growth; and if permitted to increase unimpeded it will eventually reduce the growth rate to zero. When the growth

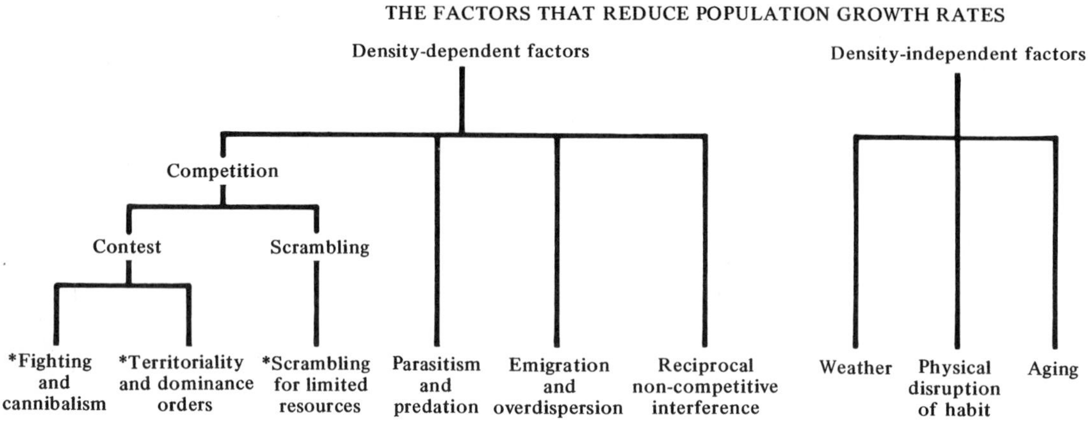

THE FACTORS THAT REDUCE POPULATION GROWTH RATES

Density-dependent factors

Density-independent factors

Competition

Contest   Scrambling

| *Fighting and cannibalism | *Territoriality and dominance orders | *Scrambling for limited resources | Parasitism and predation | Emigration and overdispersion | Reciprocal non-competitive interference | Weather | Physical disruption of habit | Aging |

Figure 1: A simplified classification of the factors that reduce population-growth rates. Those factors grouped under competition are starred to stress that competition comprises but one set of such phenomena and is not a necessary outcome of population growth for all animal species.

rate is zero, competition can no longer increase in intensity. In short, competition is a self-limiting process. It follows that population growth is also a self-limiting process; and we speak of competition as being a *density-dependent factor*—a factor, in other words, whose depressing influence grows as population density increases. But note that competition is not the only density-dependent factor, and furthermore that other *density-independent factors* can play a role in the population regulation of any given species. Figure 1 presents a very simplified classification of both density-dependent and density-independent factors. According to the particular species involved, these can operate singly or in combination to bring the average, long-term growth of a population to zero. The point to bear in mind in looking at this scheme—one which will be documented shortly—is that population growth can be halted before competition occurs. Therefore competition is by no means a necessary consequence of population growth.

Aggression within animal species is almost

always associated with competition. Insofar as aggressive behavior is adaptive, it can usually be regarded as a competitive technique and placed within our scheme as one of the devices of the "contest" form of competition. Since other forms of competition exist, aggressive behavior can be expected to be less common in nature than competitive behavior.

There are probably more than three million species of animals living on the earth today. Our knowledge of the occurrence of competitive and aggressive behavior among them is extremely meager. In Table 1 are tabulated the highly varied forms of population control encountered in eight species of insects. These species were chosen by Clark et al. (1967) solely on the basis of their being among the best-studied cases to date. Aside from the fact that most are also pest species capable of mounting very large populations, there is no reason to suspect that they are atypical in ecology and behavior. It can be seen that although density-dependent controls affect all eight, in only five are the controls known to involve competition; and of the five with competitive controls only two (the codling moth and sheep blowfly) are under the primary influence of competition.

The following generalizations can be made about competition in animals as a whole:

Table 1: The frequency and nature of density-dependent controls in the population growth of eight insect species. (Based on Clark et al. 1967).

SPECIES	OCCURRENCE OF DENSITY-DEPENDENT CONTROLS	NATURE OF THE CONTROLS
Codling moth (*Cydia pomonella*) introduced populations in Australia	Very frequent	Competition for feeding-space among larvae and for cocooning sites among grown larvae.
Grasshopper (*Phaulacridium vittatum*)	Very frequent	Primarily emigration; also (under extreme conditions) competition for food.
Sawfly (*Perga affinus*)	Very frequent; weather also an occasional influence	In some regions, emigration coupled with competition; in other regions, parasitism by other insects.
Cabbage aphid (*Brevicoryne brassicae*)	Very frequent	Primarily emigration (by special alate forms); also reduced fecundity.
Sheep blowfly (*Lucilia cuprina*) in laboratory populations	Very frequent	Competition for food among adults, resulting in reduced fecundity.
Larch budmoth (*Zeiraphera griseana*)	Very frequent	Hymenopterous parasites and granulosis virus, which alternate in prevalence.
European spruce sawfly (*Diprion hercyniae*), introduced populations in Canada	Erratic; weather plays a major role in these unstable populations	Disease and insect parasitism.
Psyllid (*Cardiaspina albitextura*)	Very frequent	At low densities, predation by birds and insect parasites; at high densities, competition for food.

1. The mechanisms of competition between individuals of the same species are qualitatively similar to those between individuals of different species.
2. There is nevertheless a difference in intensity. Where competition occurs at all, it is generally more intense within species than between species.
3. Several theoretical circumstances can be conceived under which competition is perpetually sidestepped (Hutchinson 1948, 1961). Most involve the intervention of other density-dependent factors of the kind just outlined or fluctuations in the environment that regularly halt population growth just prior to saturation.
4. Field studies, although still very fragmentary in nature, have tended to verify the theoretical predictions just mentioned. Competition has been found to be widespread but not universal in animal species. It is more common in vertebrates than in invertebrates, in predators than in herbivores and omnivores, and in species belonging to stable ecosystems than in those belonging to unstable ecosystems. It is often forestalled by the prior operation of other density-dependent controls, the most common of which are emigration, predation, and parasitism.

5. Even where competition occurs, it is frequently suspended for long periods of time by the intervention of density-independent factors, especially unfavorable weather and the frequent availability of newly created empty habitats.

6. Whatever the competitive technique used—whether direct aggression, territoriality, non-aggressive "scrambling," or something else—the ultimate limiting resource is usually food. Although the documentation for this statement (Lack 1966, Schoener 1968) is still thin enough to be authoritatively disputed (Chitty 1967a), there still seem to be enough well-established cases to justify its provisional acceptance as a statistical inference. It is also true, however, that a minority of examples involve other limiting resources: growing space in barnacles and other sessile marine invertebrates (Connell 1961, Paine 1966); nesting sites in the pied flycatcher (Von Haartman 1956) and Scottish ants (Brian 1952a,b); resting places of high moisture in salamanders (Dumas 1956) and of shade in the mourning chat in African deserts (Hartley 1949); nest materials in rooks (C. J. F. Coombs in Crook 1965) and herons (A. J. Meyerriecks, University of South Florida, Tampa, personal communication).

The Mechanisms of Competition

As aggressive behavior is only one form of competitive technique, consider now a series of cases that illustrate the wide variation in this technique actually recorded among animal species. We will start with aggression in its direst and most explicit form and then, by passing from species to species, examine the increasingly more subtle and indirect forms.

Direct Aggression

When the barnacles of the species *Balanus balanoides* invade rock surfaces occupied by the second barnacle species *Chthamalus stellatus,* they eliminate these competitors by direct physical seizure of the attachment sites. In one case studied by Connell (1961) in Scotland, ten percent of the individuals in a colony of *Chthamalus* were overgrown by *Balanus* within a month, and another three percent were undercut and lifted off in the same period. A few others were crushed laterally by the expanding shells of the dominant species. By the end of the second month twenty percent of the *Chthamalus* had been eliminated, and eventually all disappeared. Individuals of *Balanus* also destroy each other but at a slower rate than they do members of the competitor species.

Ant colonies are notoriously aggressive toward each other, and colony "warfare" both within and between species has been witnessed by many entomologists. Pontin (1961, 1963) found that the majority of the queens of *Lasius flavus* and *L. niger* attempting to start new colonies in solitude are destroyed by workers of their own species. Colonies of the common pavement ant *Tetramorium caespitum* defend their territories with pitched battles conducted by large masses of workers (McCook 1909). The adaptive significance of the fighting has been made clear by the recent discovery that the average size of the worker and the production of winged sexual forms at the end of the season, both of which are good indicators of the nutritional status of the colony, increase with an increase in territory size (Brian, Elmes, and Kelley 1967). The following description by Brian (1955) of fighting among workers belonging to different colonies of *Myrmica ruginodis* is typical of a great many territorial ant species. The dispute in this particular case was brought about when workers from one colony approached those of another colony at a sugar bait.

If its approach is incautious, the feeder turns round . . . and grapples, and the pair fall to the ground and break. On the other hand, the incomer may approach slowly, and examine the abdomen of the feeder carefully without disturbing it; then it grips it by the pedicel (with the mandibles) and lifts it up. In this grip the lifted ant invariably remains quiescent, and is carried right back to the nest of the incomer. Sometimes under circumstances when a perfect grip is not obtained, other ants may become involved, and a group of three or four workers, composed of individuals from both nests, may struggle backwards and forwards along a line between the nest and the source (no perceptible track is formed). Mortality does not occur in the field, but those ants that are successfully dragged into the opposing nest will probably be dismembered. Hence the outcome of these struggles should favor the colony that brings the most workers to the site; that is, it will be related to colony size, proximity and recruitment ability.

Direct aggression among colonies of both the same and different ant species is a common occurrence (Talbot 1943, Haskins and Haskins 1965, Yasuno 1965). One of the more dramatic spectacles of insect biology is provided by the large-headed soldiers of certain species belonging to the genus *Pheidole*. These individuals have mandibles shaped approximately like the blades of wire clippers, and their heads are largely filled by massive adductor muscles. When clashes occur between colonies the soldiers rush in, attack blindly, and leave the field littered with the severed antennae, legs, and abdomens of their defeated enemies. Brian (1956) has provided evidence that interference among colonies leads to replacement and "dominance hierarchies" among Scottish ant species that places the winners in the warmest nest sites. He identified the three following competitive techniques: (1) gradual encroachment of the nest; (2) occupation of nest sites abandoned by competitor

colonies following adverse microclimatic change (e.g., the nest chambers becoming temporarily too wet or cold), the occupation being accomplished when conditions improve but before the competitor can return; (3) siege, involving continuous harassment and fighting, until the competitor evacuates the nest site. Interference at the colony level sometimes leads to the total extirpation of one species by another from a local area. This extreme result occurs most frequently in unstable environments, such as agricultural land, or when newly introduced species invade native habitats. An example is given in Figure 2.

There can be no question that fighting and even cannibalism are normal among the members of some insect species. In the life cycle of certain species of parasitic Hymenoptera belonging to the families Ichneumonidae, Trigonalidae, Platygasteridae, Diapriidae, and Serphidae the larvae undergo a temporary transformation into a bizarre fighting form that kills and eats its brothers and sisters occupying the same host insect. This reduces the number of parasites to a number that more easily grow to the adult stage on the limited host tissue available. Two of the cannibalistic species are illustrated in Figure 3.

These facts from the biology of the ants and other Hymenoptera should dispel the impression created by some popular writers that the killing of members of the same species is never a normal event in nature. Lorenz (1966), for example, has stated, "Though occasionally, in territorial or rival fights, by some mishap a horn may penetrate an eye or a tooth an artery, we have never found that the aim of aggression was the extermination of fellow members of the species concerned." This is a purely empirical generalization about vertebrates, one which cannot be extended to the rest of the animal kingdom. I make the point primarily to establish that there are no universal "rules of conduct" in competitive behavior. Species are

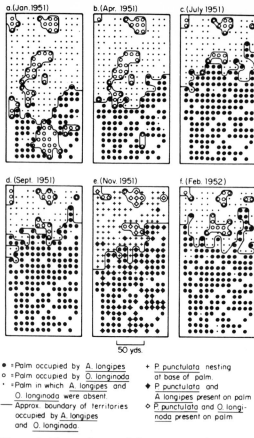

a.(Jan.1951)   b.(Apr. 1951)   c.(July 1951)

d. (Sept. 1951)   e.(Nov. 1951)   f.(Feb. 1952)

50 yds.

● =Palm occupied by A. longipes
○ =Palm occupied by O. longinoda
˙ =Palm in which A. longipes and O. longinoda were absent.
— Approx. boundary of territories occupied by A. longipes and O. longinoda.
+ P. punctulata nesting at base of palm.
◆ P. punctulata and A longipes present on palm
◇ P. punctulata and O. longinoda present on palm

Figure 2: The exclusion of the ant *Oecophylla longinoda* by its competitor *Anoplolepis longipes* in a coconut plantation in Tanzania. The exclusion occurs through fighting at the colony level. In areas of sandy soil with sparse vegetation, *Anoplolepis* replaces *Oecophylla,* but where the vegetation is thicker and the soil less open and sandy, the reverse occurs. A third species, *Pheidole punctulata,* is occasionally abundant but plays a minor role. (*From Way 1953.*)

entirely opportunistic. Their behavior patterns do not conform to any general innate restrictions but are guided, like all other biological traits, solely by what happens to be advantageous over a period of time sufficient for evolution to occur. Thus, if it is of even temporary selective advantage for individuals of a given species to be cannibals, one can expect that the entire species will evolve toward cannibalism.

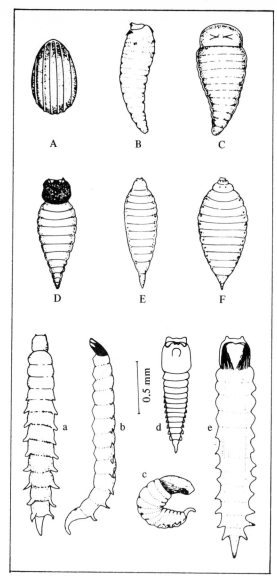

0.5 mm

Figure 3: In certain species of parasitic wasps, the larvae undergo a temporary transformation into a bizarre fighting form, equipped with the sclerotized head and large mandibles. While in this instar the larvae inhabiting a single host insect fight together until only one is left alive. In the upper row are shown the egg and successive larval instars of the trigonalid *Poecilogonalos thwaitesii,* the fighting stage is the fourth instar (D). In the lower row are the first (a, b) and second (c-e) larval instars of the ichneumonid *Collyria calcitrator,* the fighting stage in this case is the second instar. (*From Clausen 1940.*)

Mutual Repulsion

When workers of the ants *Pheidole megacephala* and *Solenopsis globularia* meet at a feeding site, some fighting occurs, but the issue is not settled in this way. Instead, dominance is based on organizational ability. Workers of both species are excitable and run off the odor trails and away from the food site when they encounter an alien. The *Pheidole* calm down, relocate the odor trails, and assemble again at the feeding site more quickly than the *Solenopsis*. Consequently they build up their forces more quickly during the clashes and are usually able to control the feeding sites. *Solenopsis globularia* colonies are nevertheless able to survive by occupying nest sites and foraging areas in more open, sandy habitats not penetrated by *Pheidole megacephala* (E. O. Wilson and R. Levins, unpublished).

Other examples are known in which competition for resources is conducted by indirect forms of repulsion. Females of the tiny wasp *Trichogramma evanescens* parasitize the eggs of a wide variety of insect host species by penetrating the chorion with their ovipositors and inserting their own eggs inside. Other females of the same species are able to distinguish eggs that have already been parasitized, evidently through the detection of some scent left behind in trace amounts by the first female; thus alerted, they invariably move on to search for other eggs of their own (Salt 1936). At high population densities adults of the flour beetle *Tribolium confusum* remain neatly spaced-out because they repel one another by means of two specific quinonic substances secreted by glands in the abdomen and thorax (Loconti and Roth 1953, Naylor 1959).

Chemical aggression and interference can be both insidious and unpredictable in their effects. If a female mouse recently inseminated by one male is placed with a second male belonging to a different genetic strain, she will usually abort and quickly become available for a new insemination. The aborting stimulus is an as yet unidentified pheromone produced in male urine which is smelled by the female and activates the pituitary gland and corpora lutea (Bruce 1966, Bronson 1969). An equally significant effect has recently been demonstrated by Ropartz (1966, 1968). Investigating the causes of reduced fertility in crowded populations, he found that the odor of other mice alone causes the adrenal glands of individual mice to grow heavier and to increase their production of corticosteroids, resulting eventually in a decrease in reproductive capacity and even death of the animal. Here we have part but surely not all of the explanation of the well-known stress syndrome of mammals. Some ecologists have invoked the syndrome as the explanation of population fluctuation, including the occasional "crashes" of overly dense populations.

Territory, Dominance, and Social Distance

Territory was defined by G. K. Noble (1939) and other early students of the subject as any defended area. By this definition the territorial response was understood to consist of an overt action on the part of the territorial animal against intruders of the same species and, in a few cases, intruders belonging to other species as well. In recent years there has been a tendency to employ a broader definition, of the kind suggested by Pitelka (1959) in the following statement: "The fundamental importance of territory lies not in the mechanism (overt defense or any other action) by which the territory becomes identified with its occupant, but the degree to which it in fact is used exclusively by its occupant." We now know that territoriality varies gradually among species from immediate aggressive exclusion of intruders to the subtler use of chemical signposts unaccompanied by threats or attacks.

Maintenance of territories by aggressive behavior has been well documented in a great many different kinds of animals. Dragonflies of the species *Anax imperator,* for example, patrol the ponds in which their eggs are laid and drive out other dragonflies of their species as well as those of the similar appearing *Aeschna juncea* by darting attacks on the wing (Moore 1964). Miller (1967) has described how overt territorial aggression in the red-winged blackbird *Agelaius phoeniceus* and yellow-headed blackbird *Xanthocephalus xanthocephalus* results in the partial exclusion of the former species. The males of both species space themselves by frequent exchanges of vocal and visual displays delivered from perches in the marshy land where they nest. At one study area near Saskatoon, Canada, *Agelaius* males arrived an average of thirteen days earlier than the *Xanthocephalus* and set up their territories throughout the marsh. When the *Xanthocephalus* males appeared they displaced the *Agelaius* from the emergent vegetation in deep water at the center of the marsh. Orians (1961) has found that where the tricolored blackbird *Agelaius tricolor* occurs with *A. phoeniceus* in the western United States, a different kind of interaction occurs. Colonies of the former species do not defend territories and are consequently interspersed in the seemingly less favorable nesting sites not preempted by the aggressive *A. tricolor* males.

Horn (1968) has considered the implications of the variation in social organization among such bird species. He points out that if the food supply is evenly distributed in a stable pattern, it is of advantage for pairs to establish territories over which they have more or less exclusive control. But if the food supply is both concentrated and shifting in location, it is of advantage for pairs to cluster together in a central location—and perhaps go so far as to forage in flocks. Thus it is theoretically possible for a change in a single parameter in the environment of a species to transform its optimal strategy from one employ-

ing open aggression and a tendency toward solitary existence to one of cooperative coexistence. Other aspects that may have equally profound influence on the evolution of aggression include the intensity of predation, the need for cooperative action in flushing and securing prey, the selection of nest sites that may be in short supply, competition for mates, and the degree of danger of a total population crash that results from overpopulating a given habitat (Hinde 1956, Crook 1965).

A somewhat less direct device of territorial maintenance consists of repetitious vocal signaling. Familiar examples include some of the more monotonous songs of crickets and other orthopteran insects (Alexander 1968), frogs (Blair 1968), and birds (Hooker 1968). Such vocalizing is not directed at individual intruders but is broadcast as a territorial advertisement. An even more circumspect form of advertisement is seen in the odor "signposts" laid down at strategic spots within the home range of mammals. Leyhausen (1965) has pointed out that the hunting ranges of individual house cats overlap considerably, and that more than one individual often contributes to the same signpost at different times. By smelling the deposits of previous passersby and judging the duration of the fading odor signals, the foraging cat is able to make a rough estimate of the whereabouts of its rivals. From this information it judges whether to leave the vicinity, to proceed cautiously, or to pass on freely.

We do not have the information needed to decide whether occupied land is generally denied at certain times to other members of the species by means of chemical advertisement. Animal behaviorists have naturally focused their attention on the more spectacular forms of aggressive behavior that arise during confrontations. When such behavior is lacking, one is tempted to postulate that exclusion is achieved by advertisement of one form or other. But such indirect effects have seldom been documented. I suggest that it would be useful to refine our definition of territory in the following way: *Territory is an area occupied more or less exclusively by animals or groups of animals by means of repulsion through overt defense or advertisement.* It remains to be pointed out that the exclusive use of terrain must be owing to: (1) overt defense, (2) repulsion by advertisement, (3) the selection of different kinds of living quarters by different life forms or genetic morphs, (4) the sufficiently diffuse scattering of individuals through random effects of dispersal, or (5) some combination of these effects. Where interaction among animals occurs, specifically in the first two listed conditions, we can say that the occupied area is a territory.

Most of the same considerations apply to those closely related social mechanisms, the social space and the dominance hierarchy. Social space is a kind of floating territory in which the exclusive area is generated simply by the existence of a distance below which an individual animal will not permit another animal to approach it. It produces the sometimes astonishingly regular spacing patterns of roosting birds and swimming schools of fish. Social distance is sometimes maintained by an overt threat. For example, a brooding hen begins to show agitation when another hen comes within twenty feet; if the approach is less than ten feet, she lowers her wings and prepares for attack. In other cases, such as the *Tribolium* flour beetles, it is maintained by chemical repulsion or some other form of indirect exclusion.

Dominance behavior can be conveniently viewed as the analog of territorial behavior in which a group of animals coexist within one territory. The result is that one of them, the equivalent of the territory holder, comes to dominate the others. Below this alpha individual there may be a second, "beta" animal that similarly controls the rest of the underlings, and beneath it a third-ranking individual, and so on.

Dominance hierarchies based on direct interaction are very widespread but not universal among social animals. They have been recorded, for example, in social wasps, bumblebees, hermit crabs, lizards, birds, and mammals. In a few cases they are interchangeable with territories. When territorial iguanid lizards are forced to live together in cages smaller than their natural territories, a single male despot comes to dominate the rest of the group, utilizing the same threat displays employed in natural territorial defense.

The expression of hierarchies may shift with the spatial position of the animals. A group of domestic cats forced to feed together from the same dish form, what Leyhausen has called, an "absolute hierarchy," the rigid ordinal relationship of the classic hen-pecking kind. But when it comes to resting places, the group displays a "relative hierarchy," that is, each individual is dominant in its own chosen spot.

Hierarchies are formed in the course of the initial encounters by means of threats and fighting, but after the issue has been settled, each individual gives way to its superiors with a minimum of hostile exchange. The life of the group may eventually become so peaceable as to hide the existence of such ranking from the observer—until some minor crisis or other happens to force a confrontation. Troops of the baboon *Papio cynocephalus*, for example, often go for hours without enough hostile exchange occurring to reveal the form of the hierarchy; then in a moment of tension—a quarrel over an item of food is sufficient—the ranking is suddenly displayed, like the image on a negative dipped in developer fluid. In its pacific state the hierarchy is often supported by "status" signs. The identity of the leading male in a wolf pack is unmistakable from the way he holds his head, ears, and tail, and the confident, face-forward manner in which he approaches other members of his group. He controls his subordinates in the great majority of encounters without any display of overt hostility (Schenkel 1947). Similarly, the dominant rhesus male maintains an elaborate posture signifying his rank: head and tail up, testicles lowered, body movements slow and deliberate and accompanied by unhesitating but measured scrutiny of other monkeys that cross his field of view (Altmann 1962).

Finally, dominance behavior is mediated not only by visual signals but also by acoustic and chemical signals. Mykytowycz (1962) has found that in male European rabbits (*Oryctolagus cuniculus*) the degree of development of the submandibular gland increases with the rank of the individual. By means of "chinning," in which the lower surface of the head is rubbed against objects on the ground, dominant males mark the territory occupied by the group with their own submandibular gland secretions. Recent studies of similar behavior in flying phalangers and black-tailed deer (reviewed by Wilson 1969) indicate that territorial and other agonistic pheromones (chemical signals) of these species are complex mixtures that vary greatly among members of the same population. As a result individuals are able to distinguish their own scent from that of others.

Scramble Competition

Let us now consider the less direct forms of competitive behavior. So far the account has been deliberately simplified by the adoption of Nicholson's (1955) dichotomy of competitive forms into "contest" versus "scramble" forms, even though more sophisticated (and complicated) classifications can be devised. The following point I wish to make, however, is not compromised by the simplification. It is generally true that the population growth rate of family groups and other genetically allied groups within species, as well as the population growth rate of

other species, can be diminished by mere appropriation of resources in short supply, without any aggression or other kinds of behavior leading to repulsion. Thus scramble competition can be correctly described by the same basic mathematical models used to analyze contest competition. This rather formal way of putting the matter is meant to take care of the celebrated objection by Andrewartha and Birch (1954) to the effect that a mere shortage of resources does not ipso facto provide a density-dependent control of the population.

The curtailment of population growth and even reduction in total population size due to periodic starvation has been well documented in birds (Ashmole 1963, Lack 1966) and mammals (Chitty 1967b). In times of severe food shortage the local effects can be ameliorated by territoriality and emigration, but they cannot be avoided altogether. The effects of capricious climatic change together with a relentless pressure from predators keep most insect species from ever reaching levels that create shortages (Miller 1967). When competition for food does occur—and there are a few species such as the codling moth in which it is a frequent event—its effects are less likely to be buffered by intervening contest competition of the kinds prevailing in the vertebrates. Under uniform conditions the outcomes of scramble competition among differing genetic strains and species can be predicted with reasonable accuracy. The issue is by no means settled simply by who is able to eat or seek shelter the fastest. In his studies of *Drosophila melanogaster*, which like most species of flies exhibits the purest form of scramble competition, K. Bakker (in Miller 1967) detected at least five factors which act together to determine the outcome: (1) rate of feeding, (2) duration of the molting periods, (3) special food requirements, (4) initial larval weight, and (5) resistance to the mechanical and chemical effect of crowding.

The Limits of Aggression

Why is pacifism the rule among animal species? Even if we discount the very large number of species in which density-dependent controls are sufficiently intense to prevent the populations from reaching competitive levels, it still remains to be explained why overt aggression is lacking among most species that do compete. The answer is almost certainly that for each species, depending on the details of its life cycle, its food preferences, and its courtship rituals, there exists some optimal level of aggressiveness above which individual fitness is lowered. For some species this level must be zero, in other words the animals should be wholly nonaggressive. There are in fact at least two kinds of constraints on the evolutionary increase of aggressiveness. First, as Tinbergen (1956) and others have pointed out, an aggressor spends time that could be invested in courtship, nest building, and the feeding and rearing of young. The adverse effects of such "aggressive neglect" on reproduction have been documented in the gannet (*Sula bassana*) by Nelson (1964, 1965) and in sunbirds and honey-eaters by Ripley (1959, 1961). Its theoretical implications have been explored by Hutchinson and MacArthur (1959).

For the aggressor there also exists a danger that its hostility will be directed against unrecognized relatives. If the rates of survival and reproduction among relatives are thereby lowered, then the replacement rate of the genes held in common descent between the aggressor and its relatives will also be lowered. Since these genes will include the ones responsible for aggressive behavior, such a reduction in the "inclusive fitness" (the summed fitness of the aggressor and genes held in common descent) will work against aggressive behavior as well. This process will continue until the difference between the advantage and disadvantage, measured in units of inclusive fitness, is maximized. The theory of the subject has recently been developed mathematically by Hamilton (1964).

The constraints on aggression are such that even when aggression occurs as a genetically determined trait it can be expected to be programed in such a way as to be brought into play only when it gives a momentary advantage. Such episodes in the life of an animal may be few and far between, yet their rarity in a particular case must not mislead us into assuming that the behavior is not "natural," i.e., adaptive and genetically programed. Let me illustrate this point with several examples. Well-fed honeybee colonies are very tolerant of intruding workers from nearby hives, letting them penetrate the nest and even take supplies without opposition. But when the same colonies are allowed to go without food for several days, they attack every intruder at the nest entrance. When snowy owls (*Nyctea scandica*) live at normal population densities, each bird maintains a territory, about 12,000 acres in extent, and it does not engage in territorial defense. But when the owls are crowded together, particularly during the time of lemming highs in the Arctic, they are forced to occupy territories covering as few as 300 acres. Under these conditions, they defend the territories overtly, with characteristic sounds and postures (Pitelka in Schoener 1968). Aggressive encounters among adult hippopotami are rare where population densities are low to moderate. However, when populations in the Upper Semliki near Lake Edward became so dense that there was an average of one animal to every five meters of river bank, males began to fight viciously, sometimes even to the death (Verheyen 1954).

Aggression in primate societies is also strikingly limited in time and space. Hall (1965) describes its occurrence in *Papio cynocephalus* as follows: "Even in baboon groups in the wild, many hours may pass without any signs of aggression, but its readiness to occur is clearly seen when there is competition for an oestrus female, or when tension is experimentally created in a group by presenting it with a disturbing or frustrating situation to which a male may react by directing his aggression onto subordinate males."

This brings us to the subject of the crowding syndrome and social pathology. Leyhausen (1965) has graphically described what happens to the behavior of cats when they are subjected to unnatural crowding: "The more crowded the cage is, the less relative hierarchy there is. Eventually a despot emerges, 'pariahs' appear, driven to frenzy and all kinds of neurotic behaviour by continuous and pitiless attack by all others; the community turns into a spiteful mob. They all seldom relax, they never look at ease, and there is a continuous hissing, growling, and even fighting. Play stops altogether and locomotion and exercise are reduced to a minimum." Still more bizarre effects were observed by Calhoun (1962) in his experimentally overcrowded laboratory populations of white rats. In addition to the hypertensive behavior seen in Leyhausen's cats, some of the rats displayed hypersexuality and homosexuality and engaged in cannibalism. Nest construction was commonly atypical and nonfunctional, and infant mortality among the more disturbed mothers ran as high as 96 percent.

Such behavior is obviously abnormal. It has its close parallels in certain of the more dreadful aspects of human behavior. There are some clear similarities, for example, between the social life of Calhoun's rats and that of people in concentration and prisoner-of-war camps, dramatized so remorselessly, for example, in the novels *Andersonville* and *King Rat*. We must not be misled, however, into thinking that because aggression is twisted into bizarre forms in conditions of abnormally high density, it is therefore nonadaptive. A much more likely circumstance for any given aggressive species, and one which I suspect is true for man, is that the aggressive responses

vary in what can properly be called a genetically programed manner. At low population densities, to take one conceivable example, all aggressive behavior may be suspended. At moderate densities it may take a mild form such as intermittent territorial defense. At high densities territorial defense may be sharp, while joint occupancy of land is also permitted under the regime of dominance hierarchies. Finally, at extremely high densities, the system may break down almost completely, transforming the pattern of aggressive encounters into "social pathology." Whatever the specific program that slides individual responses up and down the aggression scale, however, each of the various degrees of aggressiveness is adaptive at an appropriate level of population density —short of the rarely recurring pathological levels. In sum, it is the total *pattern* of responses that is adaptive and has been selected for in the course of evolution.

The lesson for man is that personal happiness has very little to do with all this. It is possible to be unhappy and very adaptive. If we wish to reduce our own aggressive behavior to levels that make us all happier, we should consider altering our population densities and social systems in such a way as to make aggression nonadaptive.

Is aggression in man *really* adaptive? From the biologist's point of view it certainly seems to be. It is hard to believe that any characteristic so widespread and easily invoked in a species, as aggressive behavior is in man, could be neutral or negative in its effects on individual survival and reproduction. To be sure, overt aggressiveness is not a trait in all or even a majority of human cultures. But in order to be adaptive it is enough that aggressive patterns be evoked only under certain conditions of stress such as those that might arise during food shortages and periodic high population densities. It also does not matter whether the aggression is wholly innate or is acquired part or wholly by learning. We are now sophisticated enough to know that the capacity to learn certain behaviors is itself a genetically controlled and therefore evolved trait.

Such an interpretation, which follows from our information on patterned aggression in other animal species, is at the same time very far removed from the sanguinary view of innate aggressiveness which was expressed by Raymond Dart (1953) and had so much influence on subsequent authors:

The blood-bespattered, slaughter-gutted archives of human history from the earliest Egyptian and Sumerian records to the most recent atrocities of the Second World War accord with early universal cannibalism, with animal and human sacrificial practices or their substitutes in formalized religions and with the worldwide scalping, head-hunting, body-mutilating and necrophiliac practices of mankind in proclaiming this common blood lust differentiator, this mark of Cain that separates man dietetically from his anthropoidal relatives and allies him rather with the deadliest of Carnivora.

This is obviously bad anthropology, bad ethology, and as I shall show shortly even bad genetics. It is equally wrong, however, to accept cheerfully the extreme opposite view, espoused by many psychologists, that aggressiveness is only a neurosis brought out by abnormal circumstances and hence, by implication, nonadaptive for the species. When T. W. Adorno, for example, demonstrated (in *The Authoritarian Personality*) that bullies tend to come from families in which the father was a tyrant and the mother a submerged personality, he identified only one of the environmental factors affecting expression of certain human genes. It says nothing, as Barnett (1967) seems to believe it does, about the adaptiveness of the trait. Bullying behavior, together with other forms of aggressive response to stress and unusual social environments, may well be adaptive—that is, programed to increase the survival and reproductive performance of individuals thrown into stressful situations. A revealing parallel can be seen in the behavior of rhesus monkeys. In-dividuals reared in isolation display uncontrolled aggressiveness leading frequently to injury. Surely this is neurosis and nonadaptive for the individuals whose behavioral development has been thus misdirected. But it does not lessen the importance of the well-known fact that aggression is a way of life and an important stabilizing device in free-ranging rhesus societies.

Does Man Genetically Track His Culture?

It is true that we do not inherit a particular language or a set of customs and attitudes. In the same sense a mammal does not inherit knowledge of its parent's home range. But it does not automatically follow that dominant traits of cultures are never genetically fixed through selection of genotypes conforming to the prevailing culture. The process whereby a trait ("phenotype") is induced first by environmental influences and later fixed by selection of the genes most prone to exhibit the trait is called genetic assimilation. The process has been well demonstrated in laboratory experiments with *Drosophila* (Wallace 1968).

The key to the genetic assimilation of given culture traits, if such is possible, lies in their heritability. In simplest terms, heritability is a precise measure that includes the total amount of variability of a trait in a given population and how much of this variation is due to variation in genes.

Heritability can be defined and measured as follows: The total *phenotypic variance* (V_P) of a trait is the total variation in the population in the outward manifestation of the trait where variation is given precise form as the statistic variance. It is the sum of the *genetic variance* (V_G) and *environmental variance* (V_E). The genetic variance in turn is the variance due to differences among genes affecting the trait, and the environmental variance is the variance due to differing environments as they affect individual development. *Heritability in the broad sense* ($h_B{}^2$) is the proportion that genetic variance contributes to the total variance:

$$h_B{}^2 = \frac{V_G}{V_G + V_E}.$$

In the case of additive inheritance, $V_G = V_A + V_D + V_I$, where V_A = variance due to additive genes, V_D = variance due to dominance deviations, V_I = variance due to epistatic interactions. Ignoring V_D and V_I for the moment as interaction effects chiefly of interest to geneticists, it is possible to separate out a measure of heritability that permits a direct estimate of the rate at which evolution can occur. This *heritability in the narrow sense* ($h_N{}^2$) is defined as follows:

$$h_N{}^2 = \frac{V_A}{V_P}.$$

Further explanations of these measures and the genetic techniques for obtaining them are given in the textbooks by Falconer (1960) and Parsons (1967).

The speed with which a trait is evolving in a population increases as the product of its heritability and the intensity of the selection process. (To be exact, $R = h_N{}^2 S$, where R is the response to selection, $h_N{}^2$ is heritability in the narrow sense as defined in the preceding paragraph, and S is a parameter determined by the proportion of the population included in the selection process and the standard deviation, i.e., amount of variation, of the trait.) In other words the susceptibility of human behavioral characteristics to evolution depends on the amount of genetic material there is to work on in a given population and the intensity with which certain genetic types are favored in the process of differential reproduction. These components can be exactly defined, and the genetic tools exist with which to estimate them.

Hirsch (1967), however, has called attention to a major unsolved problem in the study of human behavioral evolution—how to classify behavioral traits in a way that will permit them to be genetically analyzed as separate entities. Even though this and other technical difficulties stand in the way of any thoroughgoing investigations in the immediate future, there exists abundant evidence that many of the most important measurable behavioral characteristics do possess a moderately high heritability. These include introversion-extroversion measures, personal tempo, psychomotor and sports activities, neuroticism, dominance, depression, and the tendency toward certain forms of mental illness such as schizophrenia (Parsons 1967, Lerner 1968).

It is therefore safe to assume that many important behavioral traits in man can evolve. This leads to the question of the speed with which such evolution occurs. Does it ever move fast enough, say, for human populations to adapt to some of the cultural norms of particular societies? In other words, does behavioral evolution occur faster than some forms of cultural change? At the risk of being dismissed by anthropologists as an ignorant heretic, I would like to present the case for such a possibility in the form of two arguments. First, I will show that strong evolution at the level of single genes can occur under moderate selection pressure in ten generations or less. Such evolution is not only well accommodated by genetic theory but is a commonplace in experimental animal populations. Second, the great variation in social organization among related animal species, especially primates, will be taken as evidence that moderate behavioral evolution can occur at rates at least comparable to the process of ordinary species formation.

Few persons, including even biologists, appreciate the speed with which evolution can proceed at the level of the gene. Consider first the theoretical possibilities. Let the frequency of a given gene in a population be represented by q (so that when $q = 0$ the gene is absent and when

$q = 1$ it is the only gene of its kind at its chromosome locus); and let selection pressure against homozygotes of the gene be represented by s. When $s = 0$, individuals possessing nothing but the gene survive and reproduce as well as individuals with other kinds of genes. When $s = 1$, no such individuals contribute offspring to the next generation. In nature most values of s fall somewhere between 0 and 1. The rate of change in each generation in a large population will be $\dfrac{-sq^2(1-q)}{1-sq^2}$, for which the simpler expression $-sq^2(1-q)$ is a good approximation, since sq^2 is usually a negligible quantity. The rate of change is greatest when $q = 0.67$ but falls off steeply as the gene becomes either rare or very abundant.

Figure 4 illustrates an actual case of microevolution of a character involving behavior in *Drosophila*. Here $s = 0.5$, because the homozygote males (possessing two raspberry genes) are about half as successful in mating as those males which possess one raspberry gene or none at all. The experimental curve of evolutionary change can be seen to be nicely consistent with the theoretical curve. In only ten generations the frequency of the gene declines from 50 percent to approximately 10 percent. Other eye mutants of *Drosophila* often show this degree of reduction in reproductive performance. The exact behavioral basis in the *yellow* mutant of *D. melanogaster* was elucidated by Bastock and Manning (1955) and Bastock (1956). They found that successful courtship by males of the species entails the following rigid sequence of maneuvers: (1) "orientation," in which the male stands close to or follows the female; (2) "vibration," in which he rapidly vibrates his wings close to her head; (3) "licking," wherein the male extends his proboscis and licks the female's ovipositor; and (4) attempted copulation. The *yellow* homozygote males are wholly normal in the movements and sequence of these maneuvers, but they are less

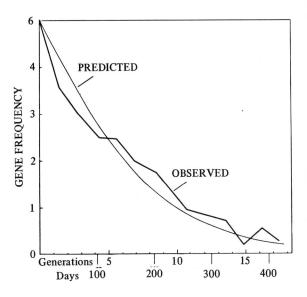

Figure 4: The decline in percentage of a gene in a population when the homozygotes (individuals bearing only that gene at the chromosome locus) reproduce at 50 percent the rate of other kinds of individuals in the population. The smooth curve is the one predicted by theory. The irregular one, which fits the theoretical curve closely, shows the actual decline of the "raspberry" gene, which affects both eye color and behavior, in a laboratory population of the fruit fly *Drosophila melanogaster*. The frequency of the gene declines from 50 to about 10 percent in only ten generations. (*From Falconer 1960; the experimental curve was based on data from Merrell 1953.*)

active at vibrating (movement number 2) and licking (movement number 3). Hence they are less effective in achieving copulation. Such behavioral components are commonplace in the phenotypes of rapidly evolving *Drosophila* populations (Spiess and Langer, 1964a,b).

There exist numerous other examples in which significant evolution in major behavioral characters has been obtained in laboratory populations in ten generations or less—in accordance with the generous limits predicted by theory. Starting with behaviorally neutral stocks, Dobzhansky and Spassky (1962) and Hirsch (1963) have created lines of *Drosophila* whose adult flies orient toward or away from gravity and light. In only ten generations Ayala (1968) was able to achieve a doubling of the equilibrial adult population size within *Drosophila serrata* confined to over-crowded bottles. He then discovered that the result had come about at least in part because of a quick shift to strains in which the adults are quieter in disposition and thus less easily knocked over and trapped in the sticky culture medium (Ayala, personal communication).

Gibson and Thoday (1962), while practicing disruptive selection on a population of *D. melanogaster* in order to create coexisting strains with high and low numbers of thoracic bristles, found that their two lines stopped crossbreeding in only about ten generations. In this brief span of time they had created what were, in effect, two species. The explanation, elucidated in later experiments by Thoday (1964), appears to be that linked genes favoring "homogamy"—the tendency for like to mate with like—were simultaneously and accidentally selected along with bristle number. Evolution leading to rapid species formation can occur even without the application of such intense selection pressure.

In the late 1950s, M. Vetukhiv set up six populations from a single highly heterozygous stock of *Drosophila pseudoobscura* derived from hybrids of populations from widely separate localities. Fifty-three months later the males were observed to prefer females from their own laboratory populations over those originating from the other five (Ehrman 1964). Quite a few cases of rapid microevolution of natural insect populations, some of them entailing behavioral traits,

have been reported by Ford (1964) and his colleagues in England. In these examples selection coefficients (s in our earlier formula) typically exceeded 0.1.

Equally rapid behavioral evolution has been achieved in rodents through artificial selection, although the genetic basis is still unknown due to the greater technical difficulties involved in mammalian genetics. Examples of the traits affected include running behavior in mazes, defecation and urination rates under stress, fighting ability, tendency of rats to kill mice, and tameness toward human observers (Parsons 1967). Behavior can also evolve in laboratory rodent populations in the absence of artificial selection. When Harris (1952) provided laboratory-raised prairie deer mice (*Peromyscus maniculatus bairdii*), a form whose natural habitat is grassland, with both simulated grassland and forested habitats in the laboratory, the mice chose the grassland. This response indicated the presence of a genetic component of habitat choice inherited from their immediate ancestors. Ten years and 12–20 generations later, however, the laboratory descendants of Harris' mice had lost the tendency to choose the habitat (Wecker 1963).[1]

To summarize, there is every justification from both genetic theory and experiments on animal species to suppose that rapid behavioral evolution is at least a possibility in man. By rapid I mean significant alteration in, say, emotional and intellectual traits within no more than ten generations—or about three hundred years. The changes could affect genes shared by a large proportion of the population. Moreover, the

---

[1] *Editor's note:* Although in Wecker's experiments, the prairie deer mouse, *P. maniculatus bairdii* did not retain a preference for the grassland habitat which is its normal habitat type, the captive individuals could, after a brief exposure to grassland habitat, select this habitat preferentially after not being exposed to it again for various periods exceeding a month. The reverse experiment was not true, in that, the same sub-species could not be induced to prefer a woodland habitat based on equivalent early experience. Hence, even though the predisposition to select the appropriate habitat type was no longer present without experience, Wecker's experiments amply demonstrated that this subspecies was still susceptible to a form of early experience predisposing it to choose its ancestral habitat type. (J. F. Eisenberg, *Man and Beast*)

necessary conditions are present for such swift microevolution. I have already mentioned that many measurable behavioral characteristics in man have been demonstrated to have moderate degrees of heritability. There is also overwhelming evidence for the existence of the second prerequisite for continuing evolution, namely varying reproductive performance among different families and family groups within the same society. This is especially characteristic of primitive and impoverished societies (Spuhler 1959, Stern 1960, Dunn 1962, Mayr 1963). Finally, some cultures evolve slowly enough so that their dominant features remain essentially unchanged for hundreds of years, long enough it would seem to permit the occurrence of some amount of genetic assimilation.

Man therefore has the genetic *capacity* to track some of the dominant features of particular cultures. Whether he does so—and to what degree—remains an open question. In order to provide the answer, human geneticists would have to accomplish the following difficult feats: (1) classify behavioral traits in a form amenable to genetic analysis, (2) estimate the heritability of the traits, (3) measure the cross-cultural genetic differences, and (4) estimate intensities of within-culture selection pressures on the heritable traits. I believe it is much too early to attempt to make a judgment on the matter, as Dobzhansky (1963a) has done with the following statement: "Culture is not inherited through genes, it is acquired by learning from other human beings. . . . In a sense, human genes have surrendered their primacy in human evolution to an entirely new, nonbiological or superorganic agent, culture. However, it should not be forgotten that this agent is entirely dependent on the human genotype." Obviously human genes have surrendered a great deal, but perhaps they have kept a little of their old heritability and responsiveness to selection. This amount should be measured, because it is crucial to the planning of future society. Above all, it is not enough to point to the absence of a behavioral trait in one or a few societies as conclusive evidence that the trait is environmentally induced and has no genetic disposition in man. The difference could still be genetic and, in fact, only recently evolved. Meanwhile, the primitiveness of the science of human genetics and its inadequacy to the task at hand cannot be overstressed.

Having completed this excursion into population genetics, let us now return to competition, aggression, and the image of man as the killer primate. Suppose it were true that fifteen million or more years ago our australopithecine ancestors evolved into carnivores who hunted in packs, that these creatures were highly aggressive and territorial, and that their habits persisted to the dawn of agricultural societies around five thousand years B.P. Even if Raymond Dart's most sanguinary imaginings were thus momentarily accepted for the sake of argument, would it follow that australopithecine traits persisted as a genetic legacy into civilized times? The answer is no. If there were selective pressures in other directions, time enough has elapsed since the appearance of the first agricultural and urban societies, and even since the fall of Rome, for evolution of some behavioral traits to have reversed itself many times over. Given even small amounts of heritability and selection pressure, both of which are indicated by our rudimentary understanding of behavioral genetics in man, it seems inevitable that man makes himself genetically as he goes along. If aggressive behavior under stress has a genetic basis, it is likely to be due less to Pleistocene genetic inertia than to the fact that such behavior has continued to be adaptive into modern times.

The conception of great evolutionary plasticity in behavioral and social traits is additionally supported by recent studies of free-ranging primate societies. To the surprise of almost everyone who was ever swayed by the early writings of Sir Solly

Zuckerman, the higher primate species have been found to vary enormously in the most basic properties of individual behavior and social organization. Furthermore, as Hall (1965) has pointed out, the correlations between social behavior and the grosser aspects of ecology are quite weak. The most aggressively organized species, particularly the baboons and rhesus macaques, utilize varied habitats, from trees in gallery forests to clumps of bushes and open ground in savannas. Their versatility fits our intuitive conception of dominant species. But it is also true that the common langur, a monkey with a relatively placid form of social behavior, utilizes an equally wide range of habitats. Even more interesting is the case of the chimpanzee, the most manlike of the great apes. Chimpanzee troops patrol their forest habitats in much the same way as the compact baboon and rhesus groups. Yet they have a remarkably loose and pacific social organization, and they display no trace of the fierce territorial hostility that marks baboon and rhesus behavior. In view of these facts it would be clearly an error to infer anything about the social behavior of man's Pleistocene ancestors from our meager knowledge of their ecology. The science of comparative primate sociology will have to become far more sophisticated before that can be tried again.

This review should make it clear that we are in grave need of a truly scientific and powerful anthropology. Dobzhansky (1963b) put the matter exactly right in the following statement: "The ultimate function of anthropology is no less than to provide the knowledge requisite for the guidance of human evolution. . . . But to fulfill its function, anthropology cannot belong entirely either to biology or to social sciences or to humanities. It must, in the fullness of time, become a synthesis of all three."

From my own point of view as a biologist, the task now before anthropology seems almost overwhelming. Anthropology must encompass human genetics, extending that science to generate a new discipline, anthropological genetics, the study of the heredity of the behavioral traits that affect culture. Only by this means can a measure be taken of heritability and evolutionary potential of the basic personality and cultural traits. Anthropology must continue to promote primate sociology, but in such a way as to translate it into the most advanced theory of population genetics and ecology. Only by this means can an understanding be gained of the adaptive radiation that has occurred in primate social systems. When both of these great tasks are achieved, some of the guesswork can at last go out of comparisons between man and beast.

Conclusions

Competition is widespread but not universal in animal species. Current ecological theory predicts that there are several easily obtained conditions under which competition could be permanently avoided. It is not surprising, therefore, that in numerous instances empirical studies have either failed to uncover evidence of competition or else have revealed it to be of secondary importance.

Aggressive behavior among members of the same species without competition is improbable. Aggression is only one of several competitive techniques that have been documented in animal species. Among the species that engage in competition, the more overt forms of aggression are less common in the vertebrate species than in the invertebrates. A small minority of invertebrate species employ killing and even cannibalism as normal competitive techniques, but the occurrence of such behavior seems to be extremely rare in vertebrates.

Within the species that engage in competition and aggression, these phenomena nevertheless tend to be suspended in periods of low population density and accentuated as population density increases. Aggressiveness is viewed as a pattern of adaptive response—most commonly increasing along the ascending scale of population density—rather than as a "neurotic" response to "abnormal" stresses.

The idea that man's immediate ancestors, the primitive Hominidae, were territorial and very aggressive may be true. But the evidence from comparative studies of primate sociology is wholly inconclusive on this point, and ecological correlation can no longer be invoked with any degree of confidence to argue the matter either way.

Some degree of aggressiveness in man is nevertheless probably adaptive—that is, genetically programed by means of natural selection to contribute to fitness in the narrow reproductive sense. This complex trait cannot be assumed to be due to a useless or harmful genetic residue left over from prehistoric times. It is more plausibly viewed as a trait that has been adaptive within the past few hundreds or, at most, thousands of years. Some of its components might even have *originated* during historical times, since both theoretical considerations and empirical studies on animal populations show that some behavioral traits can evolve significantly within ten generations or less.

Addendum

Robert Ardrey, working from a preprint of this article, has taken issue on several points in his recent book *The Social Contract*.[2] I now have the rare luxury of responding in the very article criticized. Ardrey believes that "competition" occurs everywhere in nature. He asks, "Can one speak of natural selection without it?" The answer is

yes, one can. Ardrey, whose grasp of ecology is somewhat less firm than his grasp of sociobiology, confuses competition between alleles (natural selection itself) with ecological competition. Ecological competition, as biologists define it, is only one of the processes which contribute to the differential reproduction of genotypes and hence the substitution of alleles. Ardrey assails the definition of competition presented as "Triassic" in obsolescence because it was first proposed in 1939. That is irrelevant. What is important is the fact that it is the working definition of most contemporary ecologists. To call it obsolete is equivalent to calling the concept of natural selection obsolete just because it was proposed back in 1858. I can only repeat my generalization: theory predicts that competition is not an essential property of species, and data from empirical studies (for example, see Table 1) show that competition is in fact very far from being universal.

REFERENCES

ALEXANDER, R. D. 1968. "Arthropods." Pages 167–216 in *Animal Communication, Techniques of Study and Results of Research*, T. A. Sebeok, editor. Bloomington: University of Indiana Press.

ALTMANN, S. A. 1962. "A Field Study of the Sociobiology of Rhesus Monkeys, *Macaca mulatta.*" *Annals of the New York Academy of Sciences*, 102:338–435.

ANDREWARTHA, H. G., and L. C. BIRCH. 1954. *The Distribution and Abundance of Animals.* Chicago: University of Chicago Press.

ARDREY, R. 1961. *African Genesis: A Personal Investigation into the Animal Origins and Nature of Man.* New York: Atheneum.

ASHMOLE, N. P. 1963. "The Regulation of Numbers of Tropical Oceanic Birds." *Ibis*, 103b:458–473.

AYALA, F. J. 1968. "Evolution of Fitness, II: Correlated Effects of Natural Selection on the Productivity and Size of Experimental Populations of *Drosophila serrata.*" *Evolution*, 22:55–65.

[2] Robert Ardrey, *The Social Contract: A Personal Inquiry into the Evolutionary Sources of Order and Disorder.* 405 pages. New York: Atheneum, 1970.

BARNETT, S. A. 1967. Review of "On Aggression," by K. Lorenz. *Scientific American,* 216:135–138.

BASTOCK, M. 1956. "A Gene Mutation which Changes a Behavior Pattern." *Evolution,* 10:421–439.

BASTOCK, M., and A. MANNING. 1955. "The Courtship of *Drosophila melanogaster.*" *Behaviour,* 8:85–111.

BLAIR, W. F. 1968. "Amphibians and Reptiles." Pages 289–310 in *Animal Communication, Techniques of Study and Results of Research,* T. A. Sebeok, editor. Bloomington: University of Indiana Press.

BRIAN, M. V. 1952a. "Interaction Between Ant Colonies at an Artificial Nest-site." *Entomologist's Monthly Magazine,* 88:84–88.

——— 1952b. "The Structure of a Natural Dense Ant Population." *Journal of Animal Ecology,* 21:12–24.

——— 1955. "Food Collection by a Scottish Ant Community." *Journal of Animal Ecology,* 24:336–351.

——— 1956. "The Natural Density of *Myrmica rubra* and Associated Ants in West Scotland." *Insectes Sociaux,* 3:473–487.

BRIAN, M. V., G. ELMES, and A. F. KELLEY. 1967. "Populations of the Ant *Tetramorium caespitum* Latreille." *Journal of Animal Ecology,* 36:337–342.

BRONSON, F. H. 1969. "Phenomenal Influences on Mammalian Reproduction." In *Perspectives in Reproduction and Sexual Behavior,* M. Diamond, editor. Bloomington: University of Indiana Press.

BRUCE, H. M. 1966. "Smell as an Exteroceptive Factor." *Journal of Animal Science,* 25 (Supplement): 83–89.

CALHOUN, J. B. 1962. "Population Density and Social Pathology." *Scientific American,* 206 (February): 139–148.

CHITTY, D. 1967a. "What Regulates Bird Populations?" *Ecology,* 48:698–701.

——— 1967b. "The Natural Selection of Self-regulatory Behavior in Animal Populations." *Proceedings of the Ecological Society of Australia,* 2:51–78.

CLARK, L. R., P. W. GEIER, R. D. HUGHES, and R. F. MORRIS. 1967. *The Ecology of Insect Populations in Theory and Practice.* London: Methuen; New York: Barnes and Noble.

CLAUSEN, C. P. 1940. *Entomophagous Insects.* New York: McGraw-Hill.

CLEMENTS, F. E., and V. E. SHELFORD. 1939. *Bio-ecology.* New York: John Wiley and Sons.

CONNELL, J. H. 1961. "The Influence of Interspecific Competition and Other Factors on the Distribution of the Barnacle *Chthamalus stellatus,*" *Ecology,* 42:710–723.

CROOK, J. H. 1965. "The Adaptive Significance of Avian Social Organizations." *Symposia of the Zoological Society of London,* 14:181–218.

DART, R. A. 1953. "The Predatory Transition from Ape to Man." *International Anthropological and Linguistic Review,* 1:201–208.

DOBZHANSKY, T. 1963a. "Genetics of Race Equality." *Eugenics Quarterly,* 10:151–160.

——— 1963b. "Anthropology and the Natural Sciences —The Problem of Human Evolution." *Current Anthropology,* 4:138–148.

DOBZHANSKY, T., and B. SPASSKY. 1962. "Selection for Geotaxis in Monomorphic and Polymorphic Populations of *Drosophila pseudoobscura.*" *Proceedings of the National Academy of Sciences,* 48:1704–1712.

DUMAS, P. C. 1956. "The Ecological Relations of Sympatry in *Plethodon dunni* and *Plethodon vehiculum.*" *Ecology,* 37:484–495.

DUNN, L. C. 1962. *Heredity and Evolution in Human Populations.* Cambridge: Harvard University Press.

EHRMAN, L. 1964. "Genetic Divergence in M. Vetukhiv's Experimental Populations of *Drosophila pseudoobscura,* I: Rudiments of Sexual Isolation." *Genetical Research* (Cambridge), 5:150–157.

FALCONER, D. S. 1960. *Quantitative Genetics.* New York: The Ronald Press Company.

FORD, E. B. 1964. *Ecological Genetics.* London: Methuen.

GIBSON, J. B., and J. M. THODAY. 1962. "Effects of Disruptive Selection, VI: A Second Chromosome Polymorphism." *Heredity,* 17:1–26.

HALL, K. R. L. 1965. "Social Organization of the Old World Monkeys and Apes." *Symposia of the Zoological Society of London,* 14:265–289.

HAMILTON, W. D. 1964. "The Genetical Evolution of Social Behaviour." *Journal of Theoretical Biology,* 7:1–52.

HARRIS, V. T. 1952. "An Experimental Study of Habitat Selection by Prairie and Forest Races of the Deer Mouse, *Peromyscus maniculatus.*" *Contributions of the University of Michigan Laboratory of Vertebrate Biology,* number 56.

HARTLEY, P. H. T. 1949. "The Biology of the Mourning Chat in Winter Quarters." *Ibis,* 9:393–413.

HASKINS, C. P., and E. F. HASKINS. 1965. "*Pheidole megacephala* and *Iridomyrmex humilis* in Bermuda —Equilibrium or Slow Replacement?" *Ecology,* 46:735–740.

HINDE, R. A. 1956. "The Biological Significance of the Territories of Birds." *Ibis,* 98:340–369.

HIRSCH, J. 1963. "Behavior Genetics and Individuality Understood." *Science,* 142:1436–1442.

——— 1967. "Intellectual Functioning and the Dimensions of Human Variation." In *Genetic Diversity and Human Behavior,* J. N. Spuhler, editor. Chicago: Aldine.

HOOKER, B. I. 1968. "Birds." Pages 311–337, in *Animal Communication, Techniques of Study and Results of Research,* T. A. Sebeok, editor. Bloomington: University of Indiana Press.

HORN, H. S. 1968. "The Adaptive Significance of Colonial Nesting in the Brewer's Blackbird (*Euphagus cyanocephalus*)." *Ecology,* 49:682–694.

HUTCHINSON, G. E. 1948. "Circular Causal Systems in Ecology." *Annals of the New York Academy of Sciences,* 50:221–246.

——— 1961. "The Paradox of the Plankton." *American Naturalist,* 95:137–146.

HUTCHINSON, G. E., and R. H. MAC ARTHUR. 1959. "On the Theoretical Significance of Aggressive Neglect in Interspecific Competition." *American Naturalist,* 93:133–134.

KLOPFER, P. H. 1968. "From Ardrey to Altruism: A Discourse on the Biological Basis of Human Behavior." *Behavioral Science,* 13:399–401.

LACK, D. 1966. *Population Studies of Birds.* Oxford: Clarendon Press.

LEACH, E. 1968. "Ignoble Savages." *The New York Review,* 11:24–29.

LERNER, I. M. 1968. *Heredity, Evolution, and Society.* San Francisco: W. H. Freeman and Company.

LEVINS, R. 1968. *Evolution in Changing Environments.* Princeton, New Jersey: Princeton University Press.

LEYHAUSEN, P. 1965. "The Communal Organization of Solitary Mammals." *Symposia of the Zoological Society of London,* 14:249–263.

LOCONTI, J. D., and L. M. ROTH. 1953. "Composition of the Odorous Secretion of *Tribolium castaneum.*" *Annals of the Entomological Society of America,* 46: 281–289.

LORENZ, K. 1966. *On Aggression.* New York: Harcourt, Brace, and World.

MAYR, E. 1963. *Animal Species and Evolution.* Cambridge: Harvard University Press.

MC COOK, H. C. 1909. *Ant Communities and How They Are Governed: A Study in Natural Civics.* New York and London: Harper and Brothers.

MERRELL, D. J. 1953. "Selective Mating as a Cause of Gene Frequency Changes in Laboratory Populations of *Drosophila melanogaster.*" *Evolution,* 7: 287–296.

MILLER, R. S. 1967. "Pattern and Process in Competition." *Advances in Ecological Research,* 4:1–74.

MONTAGU, A. 1967. *The Human Revolution.* New York: Bantam Books.

MOORE, N. W. 1964. "Intra- and Interspecific Competition among Dragonflies (*Odonata*)." *Journal of Animal Ecology,* 33:49–71.

MORRIS, D. 1967. *The Naked Ape: A Zoologist's Study of the Human Animal.* New York: McGraw-Hill.

MYKYTOWYCZ, R. 1962. "Territorial Function of Chin Gland Secretion in the Rabbit, *Oryctolagus cuniculus* (L.)." *Nature,* 193:797.

NAYLOR, A. F. 1959. "An Experimental Analysis of Dispersal in the Flour Beetle *Tribolium confusum.*" *Ecology,* 40:453–465.

NELSON, J. B. 1964. "Factors Influencing Clutch-size and Chick Growth in the North Atlantic Gannet, *Sula bassana.*" *Ibis,* 106:63–77.

——— 1965. "The Behaviour of the Gannet." *British Birds,* 58:233–288.

NICHOLSON, A. J. 1955. "An Outline of the Dynamics of Animal Populations." *Australian Journal of Zoology,* 2:9–65.

NOBLE, G. K. 1939. "The Role of Dominance in the Life of Birds." *Auk,* 56:263–273.

ORIANS, G. H. 1961. "The Ecology of Blackbird (*Agelaius*) Social Systems." *Ecological Monographs,* 31: 285–312.

PAINE, R. T. 1966. "Food Web Complexity and Species Diversity." *American Naturalist,* 100:65–75.

PARSONS, P. A. 1967. *The Genetic Analysis of Behaviour.* London: Methuen.

PITELKA, F. A. 1959 "Numbers, Breeding Schedule, and Territory in Pectoral Sandpipers of Northern Alaska." *Condor,* 61:233–264.

PONTIN, A. J. 1961. "Population Stabilization and Competition Between the Ants *Lasius flavus* (F.) and *L. niger* (L.)." *Journal of Animal Ecology,* 30:47–54.

——— 1963. "Further Considerations of Competition and Ecology of the Ants *Lasius flavus* (F.) and *L. niger* (L.)." *Journal of Animal Ecology,* 32:565–574.

RIPLEY, S. D. 1959. "Competition Between Sunbird and Honeyeater Species in the Moluccan Islands." *American Naturalist,* 93:127–132.

——— 1961. "Aggressive Neglect as a Factor in Interspecific Competition in Birds." *Auk,* 78:366–371.

ROPARTZ, P. 1966. "Contribution à l'étude du déterminisme d'un effet de groupe chez les souris." *Comptes Rendu Academie Science* (Paris), 263: 2070–2072.

——— 1968. "Role des communications olfactives

dans le comportement des souris males." In *L'effet de groupe chez les animaux,* R. Chauvin and C. Noirot, editors. *Colloques Internationaux du Centre National de la Recherche Scientifique,* 173:323–339.

SALT, G. 1936. "Experimental Studies in Insect Parasitism, IV: The Effect of Superparasitism on Populations of *Trichogramma evanescens.*" *Journal of Experimental Biology,* 13:363–375.

SCHENKEL, R. 1937. "Ausdrucksstudien an Wölfen." *Behaviour,* 1:81–130.

SCHOENER, T. W. 1968. "Sizes of Feeding Territories Among Birds." *Ecology,* 49:123–141.

SPIESS, E. B. and B. LANGER, 1964a. "Mating Speed Control by Gene Arrangements in *Drosophila pseudoobscura* Homokaryotypes." *Proceedings of the National Academy of Sciences of the United States of America,* 51:1015–1019.

——— 1964b. "Mating Speed Control by Gene Arrangement Carriers in *Drosophila persimilis.*" *Evolution,* 18:430–444.

SPUHLER, J. N. 1959. "Physical Anthropology and Demography." In *The Study of Population,* P. M. Hauser and O. D. Duncan, editors. Chicago: University of Chicago Press.

STERN, C. 1960. *Principles of Human Genetics.* Second edition. San Francisco: W. H. Freeman & Company.

STORR, A. 1968. *Human Aggression.* New York: Atheneum.

TALBOT, M. 1943. "Population Studies of the Ant, *Prenolepis imparis* Say." *Ecology,* 24:31–44.

THODAY, J. M. 1964. "Genetics and the Integration of Reproductive Systems." *Symposia of the Royal Entomological Society of London,* 2:108–119.

TINBERGEN, N. 1956. "On the Functions of Territory in Gulls." *Ibis,* 98:401–411.

VERHEYEN, R. 1954. *Monographie éthologique de l'hippopotame* (Hippopotamus amphibius *Linne*). Institut des Parcs Nationaux du Congo Belge. Exploration du Parc National Albert. Bruxelles.

VON HAARTMAN, L. 1956. "Territory in the Pied Flycatcher *Muscicapa hypoleuca.*" *Ibis,* 98:460–475.

WALLACE, B. 1968. *Topics in Population Genetics.* New York: Norton.

WAY, M. J. 1953. "The Relationship between Certain Ant Species with Particular Reference to Biological Control of the Coreid, *Theraptus* sp." *Bulletin of Entomological Research,* 44:669–691.

WECKER, S. C. 1963. "The Role of Early Experience in Habitat Selection by the Prairie Deer Mouse, *Peromyscus maniculatus bairdii.*" *Ecological Monographs,* 33:307–325.

WILSON, E. O. 1969. "Chemical Communication within Animal Species." In *Chemical Ecology,* E. Sondheimer and J. B. Simeone, editors. New York: Academic Press.

YASUNO, M. 1965. "Territory of Ants in the Kayano Grassland at Mt. Hakkôda." Scientific Reports of Tôhoku University (Sendai, Japan). Fourth Series. *Biology,* 31:195–206.

THIRTEEN • RACE

29 • THE CONCEPT OF RACE

Lancelot Hogben

When this article was first published in 1931, Lancelot Hogben was Professor of Social Biology, a newly created post, at the London School of Economics. His book, *Genetic Principles in Medicine and Social Science,* from which the present article is taken, still constitutes indispensable reading for every biological and social anthropologist. (Another article from that book, "The Genetic Basis of Social Behaviour," remains a classic. What is too little known about it, among other things, is that in this article Hogben for the first time pointed out the relation between maternal age and mongolism—Down's syndrome—, a discovery usually credited to Penrose.)

Hogben's "The Concept of Race" influenced a great many of those who read it, including this author, to rethink the whole idea of race. It certainly played an important role in the development of my own ideas concerning the deficiencies of the concept of race, and resulted in, among other things, my paper on that subject.[1] This paper was greeted largely with derision, but since then its main ideas have come to be generally accepted among most anthropologists.

Hogben's contribution is reprinted here not only because it drew attention to some fundamental errors which even respected scientists were in the habit of committing whenever they discussed the subject of "race," and especially "race mixture," but also because it is quite as relevant today as when it was published in the many criticisms it makes of the concept of "race."

One thing needs to be added, in justice to the memory of a very noble man, Morris Steggerda. It was Steggerda who carried out the field work on the basis of which C. B. Davenport wrote *Race Crossing in Jamaica* (Carnegie Institution of Washington, D.C., 1929). That is the book containing the ridiculous remarks quoted by Hogben concerning the reason for blacks doing better than whites in simple arithmetic tests. In conversation with me Steggerda strongly dissociated himself from those astonishing words. They nevertheless constitute a deplorable example of the distortions that prejudice can produce in an otherwise able mind. Unfortunately, we still have such scientists on the scene. In this connection the reader is recommended to read another of Hogben's essays, "Race and Prejudice," in his *Dangerous Thoughts* (New York: W. W. Norton, 1940), pp. 44–58, as well as the rest of that splendid volume.

For further criticisms of the concept of race see Ashley Montagu, ed., *The Concept of Race* (New York: The Free Press, 1964). For a discussion of the origin and development of the concept of race see Ashley Montagu, *The Idea of Race* (Lincoln: The University of Nebraska Press, 1965). For the history of the idea of race see Thomas F. Gossett, *Race: The History of an Idea* (Dallas, Texas: Southern Methodist University Press, 1963); George W. Stocking, Jr., *Race, Culture, and Evolution* (New York: Free Press, 1968); John S. Haller, Jr., *Outcasts From Evolution* (Urbana: University of Illinois Press, 1971); George M. Fredrickson, *The Black Image in the White Mind* (New York: Harper & Row, 1971).

---

[1] Delivered at a meeting of the American Association of Physical Anthropologists, at the University of Chicago on 7 April 1941, under the title, "The Meaninglessness of the Anthropological Concept of Race."

The paper was published under the title "The Concept of Race in the Human Species in the Light of Human Genetics," in the *Journal of Heredity,* XXIII (1941), 243–247.

O 1

ne of the first phenomena of hereditary transmission to yield to experimental analysis after the rediscovery of Mendel's Laws and their application to animals was the plumage colour of the Andalusian fowls. The blue Andalusian is a crossbreed between the white and the black Andalusians. The attempt to fix the blue Andalusian is a conceit of the fancier which can never be consummated in practice, because the classifications of the fancier are not founded upon genuine genetic principles. Like the classifications of the fancier, the races into which mankind is divided by the ethnologist are based upon morphological distinctions. Little effort has yet been made to envisage their significance in the light of what has been learned by the pursuit of experimental methods. The particulate theory of hereditary transmission and genetic variation has not yet influenced systematic biology to an appreciable extent. Few zoologists have as yet explored its bearing upon their traditional attitude to the task of classification. Many years will elapse before its influence is evident in the common field of biological science and social philosophy. Lippman once remarked to Poincaré: "Everybody believes in the exponential law of errors, the experimenters because they think it can be proved by mathematics, and the mathematicians because they think it has been established by observation." An analogous statement might be made concerning the race concept. Geneticists believe that anthropologists have decided what a race is. Ethnologists assume that their classifications embody principles which genetic science has proved to be correct. Politicians believe that their prejudices have the sanction of genetic laws and the findings of physical anthropology to sustain them. It is there-

fore of some importance to examine how far the concepts of race employed by the geneticist, the physical anthropologist, and the social philosopher correspond.

Any Linnaean species is characterised by a certain group of physical characteristics which distinguishes it from other related species. The individuality of such a constellation of specific characteristics is preserved by the circumstance that the species is a natural breeding unit. Within the limits of a single Linnaean species there may exist many varieties. Various combinations of characteristics which have arisen as sports may be formed by hybridisation. The fancier, the stock-breeder, and the horticulturalist isolate certain combinations. They select individuals who are genetically pure. They establish what are variously called "breeds," "strains," or "races," whose individuality is ensured by inbreeding. For a period of perhaps twenty thousand years human beings of existing types have multiplied and replenished the earth. All existing types are interfertile and constitute a single Linnaean species. Although, as far as we know, no celestial fancier or cosmic poultryman has undertaken the task of systematically isolating pure stocks of human beings with characteristic combinations of physical peculiarities, natural agencies which tend to ensure a certain measure of inbreeding in human stocks undoubtedly exist. Of these the most obvious and the most effective are geographical. A mountain range like the Himalayas, a desert like the Sahara, vast stretches of water such as those which separate America from the other continents, may be as effective in the long run as a barbed-wire fence, a partition of wire-netting, or other devices employed by the human stock-breeder or human fancier. The concepts of genetics and the methods of physical anthropology can make common cause in exploring the extent to which geographical boundaries, social custom, and other natural agencies have succeeded in accom-

SOURCE: Lancelot Hogben, *Genetic Principles in Medicine and Social Science* (New York: Alfred A. Knopf, Inc., 1932), 123–44.

plishing the task of the fancier and the stock-breeder.

A genetical concept of race thus involves two classes of variables. One is composed of physical differences which depend upon hereditary transmission. The other consists of factors like geographical propinquity tending to stabilise the purity of combinations of particular characteristics. Human beings vary with respect to the texture of the hair, the shape of the head, the breadth of the nose, the colour of the skin, stature, and innumerable less obvious anatomical features. To a very large extent such differences are determined by hereditary constitution. A division of mankind into groups defined in terms of any single criterion of this kind can be correlated with a fairly definite geographical distribution. The geographical distribution of a classification based upon some other characteristic may be just as definite. It does not follow, and it is not a fact, that two such classifications will coincide very closely.

The bulk of mankind can be classified on the basis of two discrete structural characteristics which serve to differentiate three major assemblages concentrated in fairly well-defined geographical regions. These two characters are the texture of the hair and the shape of the nose. To some extent the latter is correlated with the nasal index of the skull. The former, which is the more discontinuous of the two, furnishes no criterion which the palaeontologist can employ. Within these three groups—the Negroids, the Mongoloids, and the Caucasians—great variety of skin colour exists, and both long- and broad-headed skull types are encountered. Consequently, a classification of mankind in geographical units defined by skin, colour, or head form would lead to a very different system from that based on hair texture and nasal index. The Negroid group have woolly hair and broad noses. They include South African Bushmen, the Bantu-speaking peoples of Africa, Negroes, Congo Pygmies, Anda-

manese, and Melanesians. Among these black, brown, and yellow-skinned types, prognathous and orthognathous, long-headed and broad-headed skulls are found, though the most usual type of skull is extremely dolichocephalic. The Caucasian type is characterized by wavy hair and a narrow nose. Here are placed all European and Mediterranean peoples, the peoples of Asia Minor and India, together with the Ainus of Northern Japan. White, light brown, and dark-skinned, long-headed, and broad-headed types are included in the Caucasian group. The Mongoloids, with straight hair and nose of medium thickness, occupy most of Asia east of Persia and north of the Himalayas. They also include the aborigines of America and the Eskimo. The greatest proportion of broad-headed types is found in the Mongoloid group. Brown-, yellow-, and red-skinned peoples are included in it. The Australian aborigines stand outside this scheme, having features in common with both the Caucasian and the Negroid group. The hair texture is of the Caucasian type, but the nose is very broad.

Genetic analysis of human differences which are geographically localised is at present restricted to the blood groups. Ludwig and Hirschfeld carried out more than 8,000 agglutination tests on men of 16 different nationalities and races on the Macedonian front during the European war. In each race group 500 or more individuals were tested. Since that date many independent investigations on restricted areas have been carried out by other observers. Bernstein (1924), who analysed a later selection of data, put forward the hypothesis that there was originally a pure race in which neither A nor B agglutinogen existed. This R-race, according to Bernstein, is not found to-day in a pure form in any part of the world, but the Filipinos and the Amerindians are to be regarded as predominantly composed of unchanged R-stock, which represents a large proportion of the population in all countries. A B-race has arisen from the R-race in the centre of Asia. It corresponds to Group III in Jansky's classification. The maximum number of Group III and Group IV has been found among the Japanese, who are supposed by anthropologists to have arisen from the commingling of a Mongol and a Malay stock. An A-race (Group II) is supposed to have arisen in Europe, and extended into India and Manchuria. On this view Group IV individuals are hybrids of the B and A races.

Bernstein's hypothesis encourages the hope that it may be possible to bring a classification, based on physical resemblance, into closer relationship with genetic principles. The data derived from the study of man's nearest allies do not reinforce the belief that there was ever a homogeneous group corresponding to the R-race of Bernstein. In the Gibbon only the A factor is present. In the Chimpanzee eight individuals have been tested by Landsteiner and Hirschfeld. Only the A factor has been found. In the Orang-Outang both A and B have been identified. From these data it might be plausibly inferred that all four blood groups (O, A, B, and AB) were already present in the human stock when it diverged from the form which gave rise to modern apes. An alternative view will emerge at a later stage.

Young (*Man,* XXVIII, 1928) has applied Pearson's goodness-of-fit formula to a large body of statistics compiled in different countries by different investigators. He classifies them in different samples in pairs to ascertain whether discrepancies in the proportions of individuals of the four types in each group arose from random sampling. He finds that the ratios for 500 Swedes (Lindberger) do not differ significantly from those of 183 Lapps (Schott), 1,391 Italians (Mino), or 502 Alpine Germans from Baden. Similarly, 1,000 Russians (Hirschfeld) do not differ significantly from 500 American Negroes (Snyder), and 500 Spanish Jews do not differ significantly from 1,000 Chinese (Liang). On the other hand, 204 Filipinos (Cabrera and Wade) differ significantly from 183 Filipinos (Pascual);

183 Lapps (Schott) differ from 199 Lapps (Reitz); 933 Arabs (Altounyan) differ significantly from 500 Arabs (Hirschfeld); and 1,000 Chinese (Liu and Wang) differ significantly from 592 Chinese (Bais and Berhoef). On the whole, the B-type is more abundant in the Mongolians, the A-type in the Nordics. In this respect the aboriginals of Australia (Woolard and Cleland) and the Lapps appear to be more Scandinavian than the Scandinavians.

Perhaps the most striking evidence of differences in incidence of the blood groups in communities of different geographical origin is provided by the work of Snyder (1926) on Indians and Americans of European descent, as indicated in Table 1.

Table 1

RACE	NUMBER STUDIED	PER CENT IN GROUP			
		O	A	B	AB
Indians said to be pure	453	91.3	7.7	1.0	0.0
All Indians (mixed and pure)	1,134	79.1	16.4	3.4	0.9
Indians known to be mixed	409	64.8	25.6	7.1	2.4
Americans (white)	1,000	45.0	42.0	10.0	3.0

Woollard and Cleland (1929), in a recent contribution on the blood-grouping of Australian aborigines, have summed up the present status of the problem in the following passage:

Blood-grouping being only a single anthropological character, and therefore in classification not necessarily having any more weight than any other character—such as hair or pigmentation, for instance—has necessarily failed to revolutionise anthropology. Nevertheless, certain facts do stand out. In groups like the inhabitants of Europe the fluctuations of the group percentage do corroborate what is already conceded by everybody, that the inhabitants of Europe are thoroughly mixed. The broad distribution of A and B do suggest what nobody denies, that the ebb and flow of people has been from East to West and West to East. When the analysis is pushed farther great disappointment arises. The percentages fluctuate considerably in groups living in close propinquity and outwardly indistinguishable. For example, Grove, who investigated various Eastern races, found that groups of Ainus differing from one another in no other anthropological feature were characterised by great differences in the percentages of their blood groups. Indeed, Ainus and Koreans showed similar blood groups, though different in every other way. Also there is considerable likeness between Ainus and Malays in their biochemical index—a conclusion at variance with all other anthropological data of these people.

No physical anthropologist would claim that classifications based upon the blood groups, the shape of the head, or the texture of hair and nose breadth, exhibit precisely the same geographical distribution. Consequently, the outcome of anthropometrical studies leads to one of two conclusions. One is that there has been a considerable measure of inter-crossing between the most widely separated groups. The alternative possibility is that the same characters have appeared again and again as sports in different parts of the world, and have established themselves independently in different stocks. In other words, we can speak of a group of individuals distinguished by some single character or by a small group of characters as a relatively pure race in the genetic sense. We have very little justification for assuming a close approximation to genetic purity when we define a group of human beings by a large and heterogeneous assemblage of physical traits. Conversely, the possibility of dividing mankind into discrete groups distinguished by some particular anatomical characteristic for which the peoples inhabiting a restricted geographical area are relatively pure in the genetic sense does not presuppose the probability that the same group will be differentiated from their neighbours by genetic differences affecting other anatomical or social characteristics.

Many, perhaps most, contemporary physical anthropologists would accept these conclusions verbally. Few appear to realise their bearings upon the methods which they employ. In classifying living varieties of men, most anthropologists pay particular attention to discrete structural peculiarities such as hair texture, nose breadth, or the colour of eye and skin. Any information concerning variability in the past history of mankind is based on skeletal characters which can only be expressed as statistical averages. Because they can only be expressed in this way, it is difficult to interpret their correlation with the more definite but perishable structures which serve to define races of living people. To assume that a constellation of characters found among living peoples also existed as a coherent whole in remote antiquity upon the basis of remains found in burial urns finds no sanction in genetic theory. Whether it derives plausibility from some other sources of information need not be discussed in this place.

The standpoint of the geneticist is well stated by East and Jones in their book *Inbreeding and Outbreeding* (p. 249 *et seq.*):

The mission of the ethnologist may be compared to that of the agriculturist who is called upon to produce a usable classification of a variable domesticated species. . . . He does this by taking advantage of isolation; without isolation it is impossible. An appreciation of Mendelian inheritance shows the fallacy involved in making such a system a basis for tracing ethnic relationships. . . . It may serve a purpose to continue to accept certain of these types as implied in the terms white, yellow, and black races. . . . There has been no small amount of inter-breeding even between these main types. . . . Traits originally characteristic of certain peoples because of isolation and the consequent inbreeding have been shifted back and forth, combined and recombined. . . . Even if it were known what the average values of these early strains were, there is very little reason for believing that a present-day individual bearing one or two striking particular traits should be felt to hold any closer relationship to the strain in which these traits are supposed to have arisen than his neighbours had . . .

An extensive refinement of terminology is required if the classifications of physical anthropology are to be brought into harmony with genetic principles, and this will necessitate a more modest estimate of the theoretical conclusions deducible from purely anatomical data. Under the influence of the theory of natural selection, ethnologists accepted the possibility of reconstructing the pedigree of the races of mankind as a matter of course. They shouldered their task with the conviction that their researches would illuminate one of the most controversial issues in social philosophy. This is explicitly stated by Kroeber (*Anthropology,* p. 62) in the following terms:

If one human race shall prove definitely nearer to the apes in its anatomy than the other races, there would be reason to believe that it had lagged in evolution. Also there would be some presumption that its arrears were mental as well as physical.

The generation of Haeckel and Huxley entertained a very generous estimate of the theoretically and socially significant information to be gleaned from a comparative study of human physique. The doctrine of organic evolution had given biological classification a new *raison d'être.* Biological classification arose out of the need to arrange the descriptions of medicinal herbs in a convenient form for reference. The herbals were pharmacopaeias, and the classification of animals received its first impulse from the work of Gesner, Ray, and Linnaeus, the herbalists and the successors of the herbalists. They undertook their task with no theoretical objective other than the manufacture of a serviceable key for the identification of different species. Under the influence of Cuvier in the earlier half of the nineteenth century a new outlook began to dominate a growing body of investigations into the diversity of animal life. The progress of comparative anatomy showed that animals can be grouped in assemblages characterised by large constellations of structural peculiarities independent of habit and climate. The principle of Unity of Type became the basis of new classificatory systems. To the generation of Cuvier, Müller, Owen, and St. Mivart unity of type was something more than mere convenience. It was the manifestation of creative design. The principle of unity of type promoted a new interest in comparative anatomy. The recognition of innumerable transitional forms helped to create an atmosphere in which the evolutionary speculations of Lamarck and St. Hilaire, held in check by Cuvier's influence, revived with reinforced vitality. Unity of descent was accepted as the basis of unity of type. The existence of transitional forms supplied the missing links which Darwin's hypothesis postulated. Fortified by the belief that human fatigue is the only obstacle to the elucidation of pedigrees by the data which anatomy provides, taxonomists now undertook the heraldic task of constructing systems designed to embody the ancestral relationships of animals.

In this faith physical anthropology has been sustained from the publication of *The Descent of Man* to the present day. A less optimistic attitude now prevails in the parent science of comparative anatomy. Zoologists are unanimous in agreeing that the major assemblages of the animal kingdom represent the ultimate twigs of the same tree. The genetic unity of most of the principal classes of vertebrates is vindicated by abundant confirmatory evidence from the record of the rocks. The evidence for this belief has increased enormously since Darwin's time. In deciding how far it is possible to embody the ancestral relationships of animals in the finer ramifications of a classificatory system, there is less justification for confident assertions. At first the progress of palaeontology encouraged zoologists to hope that the pursuit of ancestral relationships might continue to provide unlimited material for the improvement of past systems of classification. Darwinian zoologists believed that the exploration of pedigrees could be extended to the species within a genus and the varieties and races within a species. In recent years there have been indications of a more modest estimate of the scope of taxonomy. Even when he is dealing with the grosser aspects of classification the zoologist has been forced to recognise that the morphology of living forms provides inadequate materials for a system representing pedigrees. Nothing is easier than to draw a sharp line of distinction between living reptiles and living amphibia. The character of the circulation, the developmental history, the skeletal organisation of each group, are highly characteristic. Huxley and Milne Edwards were so impressed with these differences that they divided vertebrates into two main groups, to one of which they attached the reptiles, and to the other the amphibia. On the basis of purely skeletal characters a modern palaeontologist would seek for a common ancestor of the tortoise and the crocodile in a form which would probably be called an amphibian if it were alive to-day. The terms are retained for convenience, but few, if any, contemporary zoologists regard reptiles and amphibia as natural groups in the sense that mammals, birds, and fishes are natural groups. Those who study fossils have provided innumerable examples of similar body modifications which have originated independently in closely allied stocks. The field naturalist is content with a one-toed ancestor for the horse, the donkey, and the zebra. The palaeontologist may yet demand a common ancestor with three toes.

While the study of fossils has exerted a sobering influence upon speculations concerning the ancestry of animal types, recent progress in the study of heredity and variation is even more discouraging to the hopes which a past generation of taxonomists entertained. The ubiquitous occurrence of parallel evolution in the record of the rocks is fully consonant with the findings of experimental genetics, though systematic biology in general and physical anthropology in particular have pursued their course with a serenity unimpaired by the results of experimental investigation. This is perhaps because geneticists have courteously refrained from commenting on the devastating consequences of their discoveries. It has long been known that similar varieties have emerged in closely allied species, but bodily similarities may result from entirely different changes in the hereditary materials. Recent work on the fruit-fly Drosophila has shown that the germinal material of allied species is constantly changing in precisely the same way. In several species of the fruit-fly similar varieties have arisen as sports under experimental conditions. Modern genetical analysis makes it possible to allocate the genes responsible for the production of new varieties or mutants to the chromosomes on which they reside, and to indicate the actual position which they occupy along the length of the chromosomes. Metz and Sturtevant, who have constructed chromosome maps of several different species of the fruit-fly Drosophila, find that a large number of similar varieties have arisen through changes which have occurred at corresponding situations on corresponding chromosomes. They are therefore equivalent in a genetical as well as an anatomical sense. The consequences of this new body of information are immense, and few biologists have as yet realised how far-reaching is its significance. In *Drosophila simulans* Sturtevant has identified some twenty-five mutants bodily, similar to a series of mutants in *D. melanogaster,* with similar serial order on corresponding chromosomes. Thus yellow body, white eye, and rudimentary wing genes occur in the same order in both species on the X chromosome. A black-bodied, vestigial-winged, and a truncated-winged mutant have been found in *Drosophila simulans.* Their genes occur as in *D. melanogaster* on the second chromosome in the same serial relation. There is a sepia-eyed mutant whose gene resides on the third chromosome as in *D. melanogaster*. There is the mutant "minute" with small fine bristles in both species, with its gene located on the fourth chromosome.

To appreciate the importance of Sturtevant's work it will suffice to consider two species, A and B, in each of which has appeared a series of recessive sports, *a, b, c, d, e, f,* and *g*. Their occurrence in nature will be occasional, and may well escape the observation of the field naturalist. The geneticist, who is on the look-out for them, at once isolates each. By simple and direct means he can then build up a stock of A and another stock of B, each characterised by the mutant characters, *a, b, c, d, e, f,* and *g*. Unless previously initiated into the extent of variation exemplified by the parent stock under laboratory conditions, a taxonomist who visited his laboratory and examined these cultures would find himself confronted by two species resembling one another in a series of characteristics and differing from all other species of Drosophila with respect to the same characteristics. Reassured by the convention that these characteristics are not "adaptive," he would infer a common ancestor characterised by the possession of the new constellation of mutant characters. On current assumptions he would be justified in erecting a new subgenus to represent the separation of this common ancestor from the ancestral stock of other species of Drosophila. Metaphorically speaking, it is possible that Nature is continually playing practical jokes of this sort.

It may be confidently predicted that experimental investigations upon interspecific evolution such as the researches of Metz and Sturtevant upon the fruit-fly will continue to progress and provide a basis for a less ambitious attitude to zoological classification. Eventually the principles of genetics will diffuse from the laboratories to the museums, and taxonomists will ask whether

it is possible to draw legitimate inferences concerning family relationships without recourse to abundant fossil remains. We shall be compelled to abandon the hope of embodying the pedigrees of species in the terminal twigs of a classificatory system. A *fortiori* we can entertain no hope of reconstructing racial pedigrees within the limits of a single Linnæan species. In consequence we shall also abandon the hope of determining which of the living races of the ethnologist is more "primitive," and content ourselves with the verdict of Kroeber:

The only way in which a decision could be arrived at along this line of consideration would be to count all features to see whether the Negro or the Caucasian was the most unape-like in the plurality of cases. It is possible that in such a reckoning the Caucasian would emerge with a lead. But it is even more clear, whichever way the majority fell, it would be an evenly divided count. . . .

2

Curiously enough, hardly any satisfactory work has yet been done in connection with the genetic analysis of those characteristics which ethnologists employ to distinguish the races of mankind. Variations of eye colour and hair colour, which would seem to offer especially favourable material for genetical investigation, have hitherto proved too complex for any comprehensive interpretation. If the progress of genetics has tended rather to diminish than to reinforce the hope of discovering which, if any, of the existing races of mankind is to be regarded as the most primitive, neither genetic principles nor ethnological data permit us to decide that culturally primitive races are backward in virtue of their inborn limitations. The development of early civilisations by the coloured races, when the Nordic peoples were still barbarians, does not compel us to believe in the inferiority of the Nordic people. Conversely, the achievements of more backward peoples in the present era do not compel us to assume that they are incapable of assimilating our own type of social organisation. The dissemination of culture is a slow process. The significant factors in cultural evolution are still obscure. If we adopt the view that important contributions are made by comparatively few members of any race, averages have less significance than is sometimes assumed, and the only means of determining the inherent backwardness of the less favoured races of mankind is to extend to them the opportunities which we have enjoyed during a comparatively short period in the history of the human race. The demand for equality of racial opportunity for further social development has largely been justified in the past by mystical beliefs concerning the brotherhood of man. In contradistinction to mystical egalitarianism the exponents of racial supremacy and racial exploitation have affected the sanction of biological realism. A more reasonable position for the biologist to adopt would be an attitude of experimental scepticism. Experiment and experiment alone can decide the limits of development imposed by whatever genetic differences distinguish one racial group considered as a fictitious whole from another racial group considered as a fictitious whole.

It would be possible to derive from the study of physical anthropology conclusions of significance in connection with social organisation, if it were also possible to establish any significant correlation between physical variability and social behaviour in the same social environment. There are, of course, gross physical differences which can be correlated with aberrations of social behaviour. The Mongolian idiot and the microcephalic are examples. Beyond this point attempts to correlate physical structure and intellectual ability have proved fruitless. Such attempts have been very comprehensively reviewed by Karl Pearson in his memoir *On the Present Knowledge of the Relationship of Mind and Body*. Pearson

himself has correlated various anthropometric measurements with "mental grade" as measured by teachers' estimates and examination results. In his own inquiry he assessed the intelligence of 1,011 Cambridge graduates by the tripos lists, and gives correlations with physical characteristics as follows:

Weight	0.046 ± 0.021
Weight per unit stature	0.060 ± 0.021
Stature	-0.006 ± 0.021
Head length	0.111 ± 0.020
Head breadth	0.097 ± 0.021
Cephalic index	-0.061 ± 0.021
Grip strength	-0.024 ± 0.021
Keenness of eyesight	-0.005 ± 0.021

For a group of school children Pearson correlated a series of physical measurements with the teachers' appreciations. The correlation coefficients obtained are given in Table 2.

Table 2

	BOYS	GIRLS
General health	0.099	0.144
Head length	0.139	0.084
Head breadth	0.109	0.113
Auricular height	0.073	0.053
Cephalic index	−0.041	0.067
Eye colour	0.080	0.058
Hair colour	0.090	0.090
Hair form (smooth, wavy, or curly)	0.037	−0.091

Pearson also studied a group of prisoners in Parkhurst prison and gives correlation coefficients for "mentality" and various indices of metabolic activity. He found more definite evidence of correlation between social behaviour and physiological conditions than between social behaviour and anthropometric measurements. The figures he gives for the correlation coefficients are:

Mentality and temperature	-0.229 ± 0.030
Mentality and pulse rate	-0.266 ± 0.030
Mentality and respiration rate	-0.175 ± 0.031
Mentality and general health	-0.085 ± 0.057

Among University College students (250) he found correlation coefficients for:

Mental grade and respiration rate -0.166 ± 0.042
Judgements of spatial relations and
   respiration rate -0.024 ± 0.042

Referring to the work of Wendt, a German anatomist who studied 1,078 brains of individuals of various occupations, including academically trained persons and day-labourers, Pearson states:

Working on his data, I find that the average brain of day-labourers and of the academic class are respectively 1,299 grs. and 1,384 grs. In other words, the professors have about 100 grs. more brain than the day-labourers. This looks very convincing at first sight, but I went a stage further. I examined the body weights of the same individuals, and found that while the day-labourers weighed only 53.9 kgs., the academic class weighed 64.0 kgs., i.e. about 20 per cent. more. Shall we argue that intelligence is connected with the number of stones a man weighs? Further, the professional class were nearly an inch taller and were two and a half years younger. In fact, the day-labourers were an older, shorter, and far less heavy class than the academic class. Hence if the brain weights of the day-labourers were increased in the ratio of the body weights of professors to those of day-labourers, we might anticipate that the day-labourers would have had brain weights of 1,542 grs., as against professors 1,384 grs., and even this correction would not allow for their greater age. Such of course is not a scientific way of computing the matter, but what is quite clear is that we cannot, without correction for age, height, and weight, assume that the day-labourers have less brain weight than the academic class. . . . It is quite true that the heaviest brain recorded by Wendt is that of a professor, but the next eight heaviest brains of persons with known occupations are those of a tailor, a dancing-master, a butcher, two house painters, a day-labourer, a carpenter, and a locksmith. . . .

Pearson sums up the correlation of "mind and body" by saying:

When we come to associate mental and bodily characters we find no correlation whatever of

prognostic value. . . . Vast as the labour spent on this form of inquiry has been, we are yet no nearer than men were fifty years ago to determining mentality from bodily measurements. Our greater knowledge is summed up in the words: We have charted more country, and can say definitely of many routes proposed of old that they do not lead to the desired goal.

Of all physical measurements, brain size and cranial capacity might be expected to show some clear-cut correlation with social behaviour. In a very gross sense this is true, since the microcephalic is one type of primary amentia. On the other hand, there is no significant correlation between cranial capacity or brain size and the stage of civilisation which the different races of the ethnologist have attained. The variations encountered among races and nations are as erratic as the variations encountered among individuals. The cranial capacity of Bismarck was 1,965, and his brain weight was 1,867 grs. The cranial capacity of Leibniz, who discovered the calculus, wrote indifferently on philosophy, and managed the finances of a German state, was 1,422 cc., and his brain weight 1,257 grs. Table 3 (p. 481) gives the mean cranial capacities in cubic centimeters of various samples.

Numerous attempts have been made to assess the mean Intelligence Quotient of groups of children of different racial stocks, especially in America. One of the earliest, that of Brigham, based on the American Army Tests, has been widely quoted as evidence of the superiority of the Nordic. Writing in 1923, Professor East hopefully remarked: "When a complete analysis of the racial data obtained by the Army tests is finally made, it will be sufficiently voluminous to convince the most pronounced sceptic. . . ."[1] Writing with commendable candour in 1930, Brigham himself delivers his final verdict (*Psych. Rev.*, p. 165) thus: "This review has summarised

---

[1] *Mankind at the Crossroads.*

Table 3: Cranial capacities

(1) JAMAICANS (DAVENPORT AND STEGGERDA)

	BLACKS	BROWNS	WHITES
Males	1,403	1,389	1,376
Females	1,235	1,219	1,207

(2) ZÜRICH (ERNST)

Males			1,426
Females			1,326

(3) MARTIN'S DATA (MALES ONLY)

Tirolese	1,359
Netherlands	1,382
South Germans	1,500
Bushmen	1,324
Kaffirs	1,460
Buriats (Mongols)	1,496
Veddas	1,250
Amerindians	1,450
Eskimos	1,563

(4) FROM SOLLAS

Mousterian Man about	1,350
La Chapelle skull	1,620
Australian aborigines	1,250
Homo Rhodesiensis	1,280
Eoanthropus	1,300

some of the most recent test-findings which show that comparative studies of the various national and racial groups may not be made with existing tests, and which show in particular that one of the most pretentious of these comparative racial studies—the writer's own—was without foundation."

In America a great deal of attention has been directed to the detection of differences in the mean scores of negro and white children tested by the Stanford-Binet and analogous methods. The results of such investigations have been summarised recently by Graham (*Journ. Soc. Psychology*, 1930), who draws attention to the enormous disparities of different sets of observations, and expresses the hope that inquiries of the same type will be conducted in Jamaica, where the social environment of the two races is more uniform than in the United States. This has been attempted, in a compendious publication of the Carnegie Institution, by Davenport and Steggerda, who have undertaken an investigation of the white, negro, and hybrid population of Jamaica. The conclusions stated by Davenport and Steggerda have been widely quoted. Less attention has been paid to the actual data which may be elicited by a study of the text. In many of the psychological tests employed by Davenport and Steggerda excellence in early life was found to be correlated negatively with excellence in adult life. From the standpoint of the sociologist it is the adult differences which are specially interesting. The selection of the adult subjects of the investigation therefore calls for close scrutiny. The total number of all three types of adults was 370. This was made up of 105 Blacks, 100 Whites, and 165 Browns. The samples are not so large as to merit neglect of scrupulous care in equalising social environment. It is thus surprising to notice two circumstances disclosed in Table 5 of their monograph. Seventeen Blacks and fourteen Browns were prison inmates committed for "petty larceny or acts of sudden violence." No prisoners are included in the White group. Nineteen black individuals were attending colleges attaining a standard equivalent to the highest forms in an English public school. Only one white student is included in the White group. It would be unchivalrous to suggest that any racial bias entered into this curious selection of the subjects of investigation. On the other hand, it is legitimate to ask whether the choice was wholly felicitous.

It is clearly necessary to proceed with some caution to an interpretation of the differences recorded by Davenport and Steggerda. Of the Seashore musical tests two provide no evidence of significant difference between the Black and White groups. These are the memory and harmony tests. In pitch, intensity, time, and rhythm adult Blacks and Browns score significantly higher marks than Whites. As an initial check to hasty conclusions, one of their tables (224) reveals the circumstance that although Blacks excel Whites in the Intensity Test at ten to thirteen years of age, as well as in the adult groups, Whites excel Blacks in the thirteen to sixteen years of age groups. No exception need be taken to the guarded conclusion that "the African Negro thus appears to have at least ordinarily developed musical senses." For visual discrimination the ability to distinguish faulty and perfect circles, octagons, and triangles was the subject of one series of tests which revealed no significant differences in adults. Whites excelled Blacks and Browns at all ages in drawing tests. A series of tests of the nature of puzzles was performed more rapidly by the White adults than by Blacks and Browns. The authors confine themselves to stating that in the matter of puzzles there is "the possibility of a genetic difference between Negroes and Whites." In repeating seven figures the Whites excelled Blacks to a very small extent. In detecting the absurdity of ridiculous statements the Whites are seen to be "outstandingly superior in their ability." The results obtained with the Army Alpha tests are, for reasons to be stated later, especially interesting. These include one dealing with general information. This is certainly not independent of training, and is most unsuitable for the object of the investigation. Of the remaining seven the Blacks excelled Whites (adults) in four. In three the Whites excelled Blacks. The Blacks excelled in No. I (following complicated directions), No. II (problems in mental arithmetic), No. VI (recognising and continuing numerical series), No. VII (logical relations—analogies). The three tests in which the White adults excelled were verbal ones, namely, No. III (answers to "common-sense" questions), No. IV (meaning of words), No. V (reconstructing pied sentences). None of the differences in the Army Alpha tests imply a high order of statistical significance. Browns excelled Whites in I, II, and VII, but the differences were not certainly significant.

If it is assumed that the psychological tests actually distinguish inborn differences from the effects of training, and if the selection of human material in this investigation is regarded as satisfactory, we should conclude that in some characteristics of a socially desirable nature the average Negro proved to be a little better and in some cases a little worse equipped than the average White included in this investigation. Although Davenport and Steggerda have not set out to minimise the differences, they are not very formidable ones. Certainly the onus of proof lies on the shoulders of any who, on the basis of differences recorded in this investigation, would elaborate legislative policies and reinforce social barriers. Without making assumptions as to the intrinsic value of the tests applied, it is possible to probe more deeply into their genetical significance by a method which is suggested but was not applied by Davenport and Steggerda to their data. The results are sufficiently interesting to call for comment.

If two populations are on the whole genetically different, a crossbred population derived from them and breeding freely *inter se* will generally display greater variability with respect to any measurable characteristics which distinguish the parent populations genetically. On whatever somatic variability exists in virtue of environmental differences beyond the control of the investigator, there will be superimposed genetic variability in virtue of the Principle of Segregation. An inspection of the anthropometrical data in the monograph of Davenport and Steggerda confirms this inference as applied to characters which are of different genetic basis in Negroes and Whites. Table 4 gives the coefficients of variation for Blacks, Browns, and Whites with respect to a group of characters involving undoubted genetic differences between Black and White.

With the exception of the Army Alpha tests (Nos. II–VIII) maximum variability of the crossbed population is seen in none of the psychologi-

Table 4

		BLACK	BROWN	WHITE
Skin Colour	male	11.2	14.4	—
	female	6.8	31.4	—
Hair Colour		16.5	45.8	36.4
Curl Diameter	male	65.1	98.3	53.6
	female	57.7	112.7	45.5
Nasal Breadth	male	7.0	8.2	8.2
	female	6.0	8.1	7.3

cal tests employed by Davenport and Steggerda in this investigation. The coefficients of variation in the Army Alpha tests are given in Table 5.

Table 5

	BLACK	BROWN	WHITE
I (Directions)	69.2	54.7	54.0
II (Mental Arithmetic)	41.5	51.4	35.2
III (Common Sense)	51.8	63.1	29.6
IV (Words)	62.8	82.3	40.5
V (Pied Sentences)	69.4	73.2	58.5
VI (Number Series)	63.8	88.3	54.0
VII (Analogies)	75.8	91.8	79.4
VIII (Information)	54.9	71.6	60.7

The corresponding scores for adults with their probable errors are given in Table 6.

The greater variability of the hybrid population is only indicative of genetic segregation if it is independent of greater variability of social tradition. For that reason it is especially regrettable that the dispersion of the Negro scores is usually higher than that of the Whites. This is not surprising in view of the way in which the subjects were selected.

If any plausibility pertains to the conclusion that scores of Army tests II–VIII represent genetic means, it must be admitted that the differences are small, and opinions will differ in assessing the social importance of these tests in which Whites or Negroes respectively excel. In this connection a rather curious moral is deduced by Davenport and Steggerda. "The Blacks" they state "seem to do better in simple mental arithmetic and with numerical series than the Whites. . . . It seems a plausible hypothesis for which there is a considerable support, that the more complicated a brain, the more numerous its association fibres, the less satisfactorily it performs the simple numerical problems which a calculating machine does so quickly and accurately." Experimental biologists will learn with surprise that the anatomical basis of mathematical operations has been located by the morphologist with such precision. Emergent evolutionists may be dismayed by this tribute to the sagacity of our simian ancestors. The disinterested sociologist may wonder why Davenport and Steggerda did not decide at the outset to take off marks for success in arithmetic. Initially they seem to assume that the customary order of precedence is the correct estimate of "intelligence." It is strange that they only disclose on page 469 [of their paper] their belief that excellence in tests involv-

Table 6

	BLACK	BROWN	WHITE
I (Directions	5.9 ± 0.4	5.1 ± 0.3	4.9 ± 0.4
II (Mental Arithmetic)	10.0 ± 0.5	8.4 ± 0.4	7.5 ± 0.4
III (Common Sense)	5.9 ± 0.4	5.2 ± 0.3	8.5 ± 0.3
IV (Words)	15.8 ± 1.2	12.7 ± 1.1	20.3 ± 1.1
V (Pied Sentences)	8.8 ± 0.7	6.4 ± 0.6	11.4 ± 0.9
VI (Number Series)	7.2 ± 0.5	5.6 ± 0.5	6.7 ± 0.5
VII (Analogies)	13.9 ± 1.3	10.8 ± 1.0	10.2 ± 1.0
VIII (Information)	9.6 ± 0.7	9.4 ± 0.7	12.2 ± 1.0

ing the use of arithmetic betokens a low intellectual level.

3

The investigation of Davenport and Steggerda is the most comprehensive attempt hitherto undertaken with a view to elucidating the significance of intermarriage between two widely separated racial groups. The data which they have amassed provide a very slender justification for the assurance with which many biologists have expressed themselves when discussing the question.

Professor East, whose researches on hybrid vigour entitle his views to special consideration, proclaims the danger of "racial crossing even between widely separated races of equivalent capacity." "The operation of the hereditary mechanism" says Professor East "holds out only a negligible prospect of good results against the high probability of bad results through disturbing the balanced whole of each component." The operation of the hereditary mechanism is subject to publicly demonstrable laws. The terms "good" and "bad" almost invariably imply private values. To ascertain the implications of Professor East's argument, it is necessary to examine the nature of these private values in their proper context. Concerning the purely genetic aspect of the problem the essential considerations are summarised by Professor East in the statement that when two varieties or races are crossed "succeeding generations will tend to combine all the hereditary units by which the original parents differed in every possible recombination." Professor East decides that this is necessarily bad for the following reason: "Though the variability opened up by primary race-crosses is so great that if an all-knowing ruler were permitted to select and mate at will a better type might be evolved, in the slow-going stumbling world of reality in which we will it would be the height of folly to recommend it. The machinery of the

two organisations has been smoothed into an easy running whole by the very fact of survival during the last half-million years. He is a bold tinker who wishes to try his hand at exchanging parts. The stockbreeder will need no argument to support this contention. He would like to produce a better breed of milch cows. He knows what he wants. He can select as stringently as he desires. He realises the possibilities in hybridisation. Nevertheless, he laughs down the man who suggests hybridising the Jersey with the Hereford. . . ."

The justification for employing the words "bold" and "bad" interchangeably resides in the appropriateness of the analogy which Professor East suggests in this citation. The Hereford and the Jersey are highly stable genetic combinations of a large number and variety of mutant characters purified by long generations of a system of close inbreeding. In his capacity as a geneticist Professor East subscribes to a very different view of the purity of anthropological classifications: "Long isolation aided in segregating some well-marked human subspecies. It may serve a purpose to continue to accept certain of these types as implied in the terms, white, yellow, and black races. Yet one must not forget that real isolation belongs to past epochs. There has been no small amount of interbreeding between even the main types. . . ." Elsewhere East and Jones complain that "the data of anthropology are largely those of the historical type in which the control of variables is always uncertain and often impossible. . . . He would be a bold anthropologist who would dogmatise concerning the extent of racial isolation in the past history of mankind" (East and Jones, *Inbreeding and Outbreeding*).

The relevance of the analogy between stockbreeding and miscegenation makes two assumptions. The first is that human races are distinguished by relatively pure and stable constellations of mutant characters. Such a view is at best a very rough approximation to a correct analysis of the race concept. The other assumption is that there is a close analogy between the process of artificial selection and rigorous in-breeding adopted by stock-breeders and the natural agencies which have perpetuated and eliminated the products of genetic variation within geographically isolated groups of human beings. Fifty years ago, when biologists entertained views concerning the nature of artificial selection very different from those which Professor East's researches have elucidated, it was customary to assume that the process of natural selection had a close bearing on the evolution of cultural systems. Unfortunately this assumption has been encouraged by the circumstance that the word evolution is used in several senses. In connection with the problem of race the analogy between artificial and natural selection is imperfect for two reasons. One is that a close system of inbreeding has rarely been practised by human races. The original stock of any race defined in terms of some particular anatomical peculiarity and geographical situation was probably extremely heterogeneous in most other respects at its inception. Under a system of exogamy the initial variability remains stable except in so far as cultural or other influences favour the fertility or viability of particular types. The cultural characteristics which distinguish races at different levels of cultural development at the present moment are comparatively recent. Those who are most vocal in proclaiming a genetic interpretation of the rise and fall of civilisations are most insistent in asserting that civilisation has failed to devise a method of encouraging the fertility of individuals specially adapted to its requirements. We do not know sufficient about the nature of the genetic factors which determine differences of social behaviour in individuals of the same race and different races to justify the confident acceptance of such a view. Conversely, there are not sufficient grounds for denying that there may be an element of truth in it. If it is true, the analogy between the technique of stock-breeding and the regulation of population growth in human communities is grotesquely misleading. That increasing variability will in general accompany the crossing of human races is a legitimate deduction from genetics. With respect to physical race-differences, such as nose breadth, skin colour, and hair form, the data presented in the study of *Race-Crossing in Jamaica* by Davenport and Steggerda show a much greater variability of Browns than of Blacks or Whites. An inspection of their tables shows that the variability of the hybrid population in the majority of the psychological tests they employed was not greater than that of the parent stocks. It thus transpires that Mendelian principles suggest little difference in the level of mental capacity of two widely different races in the only case where Professor East's method of analysis can be applied to recorded data.

Prima facie we cannot be certain that race-crossing is likely to produce what most people would call socially disadvantageous consequences. Statistical studies on the incidence of congenital disabilities and pathological disturbances known to be determined predominantly by hereditary differences in mixed and "pure" races would do much to elucidate the problem. It is clear that so long as social geneticists and biologists persist in discussing this problem with a tacit acknowledgment of their own racial superiority, there will be little hope of treating the problem with the scientific detachment possible in discussing the effect of marriages between cousins.

REFERENCES

BEAN, R. B. (1908–1910): Heredity of Hair Form among Filipinos. Amer. Nat., Vol. XLV. The Racial Anatomy of the Philippine Islanders. Philadelphia, Lippincott, pp. 236, figs. 26.
DAVENPORT, C. B. (1913): Heredity of Skin Colour in

Negro-White Crosses. Carnegie Inst. Wash. Publ. No. 188.

DAVENPORT, G. C. and C. B. (1910): Heredity of Skin Pigment in Man. Amer. Nat., Vol. XLIV, pp. 641–672, 705–731.

DAVENPORT and STEGGERDA (1930): Race-Crossing in Jamaica. Carnegie Institution Publications.

EAST (1924): Mankind at the Crossroads.

GOODENOUGH (1927): Year Book of the National Society for Education.

JORDAN, H. E. (1911): A Comparative Microscopic Study of the Melanin Content of Pigmented Skins,

with Special Reference to the Question of Colour Inheritance among Mulattoes. Amer. Nat.

KROEBER (1923): Anthropology.

MACCAUGHEY, VAUGHAN (1919): Race Mixture in Hawaii. Journ. Hered., Vol. X, 41–47, 90–95.

PEARSON, K. (1909): Notes on the Skin Colour of the Crosses between Negro and White. Biometrika, Vol. VI, pp. 348–353.

——— (1926): On Pure Knowledge of the Relationship of Mind and Body. Ann. Eugen., Vol. I.

SALAMAN, R. N. (1911): Heredity and the Jew. Journ. Genetics. Vol. I., pp. 273–292, pls. 4, figs. 6.

30 • THE CONCEPT OF RACE AND THE TAXONOMY OF MANKIND

Jean Hiernaux

Hiernaux speaks with special authority as an anthropologist who has attempted to discover whether the concept of "race" actually matched anything one could find in natural populations, especially in Africa.[1] He concludes that it is not possible to equate the artificial concept of "race" with the realities one finds when investigating the different populations miscalled "races" living in any sizable geographic area of the world. Insofar as "racial" taxonomies are concerned, he makes it clear that human variability is such that its principal characteristic is its difficulty of classification.[2]

Penrose put the matter very well when he said that he was unable "to see the necessity for the rather apologetic retention of the term 'race,' when what is meant is simply a given population differentiated by some social, geographical or genetical character, or

. . . merely by a gene frequency peculiarity. The use of the almost mystical concept of race makes the presentation of the facts about the geographical and linguistic groups . . . unnecessarily complicated." [3]

The mystique that surrounds the concept of "race" is no longer as strong as it once was, however. It has often been suggested that we would all be better off if the term were entirely dropped from both the lay and the scientific vocabularies. This idea seems to have made some little headway, for one does find journalists and others occasionally speaking of "ethnic groups" where formerly they would have used the word "race."

The trouble with the term "race" is that, on both the layman's and the scientist's level, it has become so embarrassed by false meanings and myths that any

---

[1] Jean Hiernaux, "Analyse de la Variation des Caractères Physiques humains en une Region de l'Afrique Centrale: Ruanda-Urundi et Kivu," *Annales de la Musée Royale, Congo Belge, Science de l'Homme, Anthropologie*, III (1956).

[2] This is a view which has also been ably expressed by Frank B. Livingstone, in "On the Nonexistence of

Human Races," in Ashley Montagu, ed., *The Concept of Race* (New York: The Free Press, 1964), 46–60.

[3] L. S. Penrose, "Review of *Heredity, Race and Society*, by L. C. Dunn and Th. Dobzhansky," *Annals of Eugenics*, XVII (1952), 252.

attempt at redefinition would be virtually impossible. In any event, in man it in fact corresponds to no known demonstrable reality. Hiernaux, at the level of the physical anthropologist working in the field, shows why.

Those who attempt to classify must always be on their guard against forcing the refractory materials of nature into the procrustean beds of their artificial schemes. Custodial taxonomy is not science.

Introduction

R ace has been given numerous definitions. Many of them are similar in meaning, but several modes of thinking about race still persist. Within a single mode, the formulation of the concept may differ, and some vagueness in it is frequent. Moreover, application of the concept of race by an author to a classification of mankind does not always meet the requirements of his own definition.

I do not intend to review the literature on race and human races. Only a few contributions will be cited as examples. I shall attempt, where so many others have failed, to reach the most sensible and useful definition, and this as a development of a previous paper on the subject (Hiernaux 1962) presented at the sixth International Congress of Anthropological and Ethnological Sciences, Paris, 1960. Once this definition is arrived at, I shall endeavor to apply it to current mankind, in other words to apply the concept of race to a classification of mankind into races.

SOURCE: Jean Hiernaux, "The Concept of Race and the Taxonomy of Mankind," in *The Concept of Race,* ed. Ashley Montagu (New York: The Free Press, 1964), 29–45. Copyright © by Ashley Montagu, 1964. Reprinted by permission of the Macmillan Company.

Toward a Definition of Race

1. A Race Is a Grouping of Persons.

There is common agreement on this point: if every individual belonged to a different race, there would be no need for a concept other than that of the individual. The concept of race is obviously a classificatory one: it tends to reduce the immense number of individuals to a more limited number of classes. As in any classification, a hierarchy of groupings may be conceived, for example, one consisting of three grades called grand race, race, and subrace—or similar terms.

2. What in Man Determines Race?

Factors of two orders determine the characters of an individual: heredity and environment. In defining race, do we have to consider the genotype only? Or do we have to consider the phenotype, thus including noninherited characters and the nontransmissible influence of the environment?

All concepts of race are interwoven with that of heredity because all aim to define something that has a tendency, at least, to remain stable from one generation to the next. Suppose two groups of people have identical gene pools, but differ phenotypically because of the imprint of different environments. Would it be useful to call them races A and B, knowing that by reversing the environmental conditions race A would become race B in one generation and vice versa? A negative answer seems evident to me as to many others: in order to be useful, a concept of race must be genetical. When using characters known to be partly sensitive to environmental differences, the concept of race is correctly used only when the genetically induced variability is considered. Coon, Garn, and Birdsell (1950), however, write: "A race is a population which differs phenotypically from all others with which it has been compared." The usefulness of such a concept is much less than that of race as a group of individuals characterized by its gene pool.

3. How to Group Individuals?

Two basic answers have been given to this question. One of them is: let us group together all similar individuals, wherever they live or have lived. Analyzing the various views on race, Vallois (1953) shows how widely this way of grouping has been used until recently: "the notion of race . . . may be understood, first of all, as a combination of characters discernible in individuals." For example, Frankenberg (1956) writes: "Rasse zweierlei bedeutet: 1. Einem komplex erblicher merkmale. . . . 2. Eine gruppe von individuen, die diese merkmale zu besitzen pflegen." ("Race has two meanings: 1. A complex of hereditary characteristics. . . . 2. A group of individuals tending to possess these characteristics.") Though adhered to by a much smaller proportion of anthropologists, this concept of race is still alive today. For example, Wierciński (1962) and Czekanowski (1962) plead in its favour and recent studies on the Swiss (Gloor 1961–62) and on the Basques (Marquer 1963) use it. Arguments against the theoretical bases of such a concept of race have been expressed too often to be listed here again; the discussion in *Current Anthropology* of Wierciński's paper sums up most of them. Only one aspect of this concept will be considered here. We know that mankind has evolved and is still physically evolving. The groups of individuals that constitute our taxonomic units must be such as to allow investigation of those evolutionary processes: Those groups must both show a tendency toward secular stability and reflect evolutionary change. But a race defined as a group of similar individuals is, by definition, incapable of any change. In each generation it will consist of an artificial grouping of people who happen to share a given constellation of characters.

To me, as to many others, it seems that the only useful way of grouping individuals for anthropological analysis is to group together the people participating within the same circle of matings. Such a group shows a genuine tendency toward stability from generation to generation. If it is closed, sufficiently large, and not submitted to selection, the filial generations will have the same gene pool as the parental ones. In contrast, the offspring of a "racial type" may belong to many other types, each member of it having been conceived by two persons who may largely differ, as a result of Mendelian segregation. Evolutionary forces and events will act against the tendency toward stability of the group just defined, and a quantitative study of this process is possible.

To delimit in an absolute way the circle of matings to which an individual belongs is feasible only in the rare case of a strictly closed panmictic community, that is, in an isolate. In all other cases, the delineation is only relative. If two panmictic groups exchange mates but their members marry within their own group with a higher frequency, the partly permeable barrier to gene flow delineates them—be it of geographical, political, social, religious, or linguistic nature. But if both are surrounded by other groups with which they exchange genes at a lower rate, a barrier of a higher order includes them both. If the frequency of matings between different localities is mainly an inverse function of distance, then the only boundaries that can be traced around each locality are delimited in terms of percentage of intragroup matings and the circles overlap. The only way to group individuals in a biological sense thus often requires a probabilistic criterion for its application.

Let us ignore this difficulty and suppose that we could assign each individual to a demarcated circle of matings, for which the term "population" will be used here. Will we equate the concept of race with that of breeding population as just defined? Our grouping of individuals in one population did not take into consideration their characters in any way, it made no use of any taxonomic procedure, it was offered only in order to constitute a biological unit of study. If we want to keep the term "race" for taxonomic purposes, it may not be applied to the population. One word is enough for one thing, and a taxonomic class may not be equated with the units to be classified. Race is a much more useful concept if we consider it as a grouping of populations. Numerous authors however equate race and population. For example, Garn (1961) defines a local race as a breeding population and even uses the term "race-population." Dunn and Dobzhansky (1952) write: "Races can be defined as populations which differ in the frequencies of some gene or genes." Howells (1959) finds Dobzhansky's definition: "Races are populations differing in the incidence of certain genes" the most acceptable. These authors also use, explicitly or not, higher taxonomic classes below the human species, for example, Garn uses "geographical race," and at this level they rejoin the concept of race here proposed: a race is a group of populations.

Application of the Concept of Race to a Classification of Mankind

Let us first approach the problem of a taxonomic subdivision of current mankind without any time depth, from a purely classificatory viewpoint. Several objects are put in front of us, and we are asked to reduce their multiplicity into a lesser number of categories. Why are we asked to do so? First because, if successful, it will provide us with an efficient means of a quicker and easier memorization of the attributes of the individual objects. Instead of having to memorize their characteristics object by object, our mind

has only to apprehend the general qualities of each class, and within the latter framework the peculiarities of each object. Classification is a natural tendency of the mind, a highly satisfying procedure because it saves much time and pain. Another reason is that it makes generalization possible. If we reduced objects numbered one to 100 into ten classes labelled a to j, themselves grouped in three superclasses A, B, and C, we could speak of superclass B or class d in terms of what is common to all objects in these groups.

Classification by itself does not produce any new knowledge concerning individual things: it is only a mental operation performed on existing knowledge. If the things are not such as to allow their grouping into classes, the failure to classify them may be felt as frustrating, but it does not imply any loss of knowledge. For some things are not necessarily of a nature to permit classification.

Suppose we consider things by their qualitative aspects alone. For example, they are white or red, square or round, metal or wood. A classification based on the three properties will be useful only if there are several things in at least one of the eight possible classes. If they only differ quantitatively in a continuous scale, the problem is more complex. If we consider just one quantitative property, classification is possible only if the things cluster into several groups located at different heights along the scale. In order to be useful, one more condition must be satisfied: the range occupied by a cluster on the scale may not exceed the length of the empty spaces between it and adjacent clusters. Suppose, for example, we are trying to classify things by their linear size, and that the total range runs from 10 to 70 cm, with an empty space on the scale from 40 to 45 cm. Two clusters appear, but two objects belonging to different clusters (of 39 and 50 cm for example) may be much more alike than they are to many members of their own cluster. If size is considered a criterion of affinity, what is the validity of generalizing about short and long things?

Cluster analysis still applies to the case of more than one quantitative variable under consideration, but the eventual correlations between them have to be taken into account. For two variables, a graphical representation is still possible; a representation in space can be built for three variables; for a higher number of properties we can no more visualize the situation but we can make use, if a number of assumptions are satisfied, of efficient statistics, like the generalized distance (D^2) of Mahalanobis which still permits cluster analysis. Again a classification is serviceable only if clusters do appear, and if inter-cluster distances are higher than intra-cluster ones.

Turning now to our problem, human taxonomy, what are the things we wish to classify? Human populations, if we accept the proposed definition of race. They are themselves an assemblage of individuals. For no attribute can they be studied qualitatively: owing to human polymorphism, mankind cannot be subdivided in one group with zero per cent and one group with 100 per cent frequencies for any one character. The properties used for a classification will therefore be expressed as frequencies or means. Cluster analysis will be the basic taxonomic procedure.

How many characters shall we use for building a classification? If we use very few characters, human variability is such that markedly different classifications may emerge from different sets of characters. A sufficient number of characters must be considered in order to make it improbable that including an additional one would alter the picture; this can be tested with currently known characters and with new ones when discovered.

All characters are not equally efficient for taxonomic purposes. Their efficiency depends in particular on their world range of variation. The wider their interpopulational variability, the lower will be the number required for a consistent classification. As said before, gene pools are what we really want to classify. Gene frequencies are consequently the ideal materials. Characters for which gene frequencies have been computed on a large scale do not unfortunately constitute that array of highly variable features concerning the most variable aspects of man needed for the attempt to achieve a satisfactory classification: Those traits or characters were imposed on us by the accidents of their discovery. Many important aspects of human variation can be studied today only through metric variables that cannot be translated into gene frequencies. Furthermore, the environment intervenes in influencing the expression of most of them, and even if the environmental factor could be removed or controlled, identical effects could result from different gene pools. On the other hand, a set of metric variables can be chosen in order to represent the main variable traits of human morphology (for example from the results of a factor analysis) which are relatively not very sensitive to environment. If the clusters eventually observed from such a set and from a set of currently computable gene frequencies clearly differ, there is a strong suspicion that one or both of them are inadequate for a comprehensive analysis of overall distances.

The ideal technique of the classifier described in this way, the main question may now be asked: Are human populations such that they form clusters within which the distances are less than the inter-cluster distances? Only regional cluster analysis of human populations has been published so far. I am responsible for one of them (Hiernaux 1956), made on fifteen populations which fill a circumscribed area in central Africa. Mean interpopulational variability in this area is especially high, a fact that increases the chances of successful classification. In fact, one cluster of two closely related populations (the Tutsi of Rwanda and those of Burundi) is clearly apart, but the remaining thirteen populations allow no further clustering, despite their considerable variability. Represented on a two-dimensional plane, their position would clump without any clear internal cleavage, however great the distance between some of the plotted populations (in terms of classical anthropology, the group includes populations so different as to call the one "Hamiticized Bantu" and the other "Pygmoid"). I am now trying to extend the analysis to all Africa south of the Sahara. Only a crude kind of statistics can be applied owing to the nature of most published data. Only very preliminary statements are permissible at the present stage of development. It can, however, be said that an uncleavable clump, showing jagged edges, is the general picture, with maybe a few isolated clusters (the Bushmen, for example). I doubt that any useful classification will emerge beyond the separation of the eventual few clusters.

Such a situation is surely not peculiar to Africa. The total variability of European populations is less. A superficial examination of published data on Asian anthropology does not give the impression that many isolated clusters would emerge. Clustering would undoubtedly be favored in America by the vastly different origins of its current inhabitants, but the races so defined on a continental basis would lose much of their originality when introduced into the world picture.

Following the above procedure would there emerge something resembling the classical subdivision of mankind into three main groups: Whites, Blacks, and Yellows (or whatever more sophisticated terms are used)? I doubt it. We know of so many populations that do not fit into the picture! Adding more "oids" to this threefold primary subdivision would not improve it. The subdivision into nine geographic races (i.e. "the taxonomic unit immediately below the species") proposed by Garn (1961) is no more satisfactory: it only shifts the problems to a lower level. Just as Indians could not be classed

with the Black or White races of the ternary system, numerous populations are unclassifiable in a nine-fold subdivision because they are peripheral to several geographical races. It seems highly probable to me that the more races we create the more unclassifiable populations there would be at fewer and fewer levels of differences, until we should reach a state of subdivision close to an enumeration of all existing populations, i.e., the units to be classified.

Though not based on a systematic testing, my impression is thus that an attempt at a classification of contemporary mankind along the lines here indicated would yield very poor results: an uncleavable mass of populations, however large the constellation they form, and a few isolated clusters, which alone could be called races. This impression was gained from considering monofactorial characters as well as multifactorial ones. Unclassifiability seems to me inherent in the modalities of human variability. What can be built from a detailed knowledge of human variability is a diagnostic key. There are no two identical gene pools nor two phenotypically identical populations. By a system of successive dichotomies any population could be identified, as could also any human being since the probability of finding two identical individuals is exceedingly low (the exception of monozygotic twins is only an apparent one, since genetically they constitute but one individual). But a diagnostic key and an efficient classification are two different devices, though constructed from similar materials.

Many race classifications used to-day did not result from a cluster analysis, but reflect an attempt to extract from the anthropological data the peculiarities common to most populations of vast geographical areas. This is, for example, the case of the classification into thirteen races falling into seven main groups proposed by Boyd (1963), in which the races are defined by characteristic ranges of gene frequencies. Such a splitting of mankind essentially belongs to a diagnostic key. Its equation to a genuine classification is not clear. The conditions necessary for a valid classification will be examined later.

Probably many will find the requirement of a maximal intra-cluster distance lower than the minimal inter-cluster one too exacting. But again what is the usefulness of a classification of races A and B if we know that some populations of race A are nearer to some of race B than to some of their own race?

Though seemingly extreme, the position here expressed concerning the intrinsic resistance of contemporary mankind to any coherent taxonomic subdivision might be partly shared by many who use racial terminology. Dobzhansky (1962), commenting on Livingstone's (1962) paper on the nonexistence of human races (in which arguments similar to mine are set forth), agrees that "if races have to be discrete units, then there are no races," but is satisfied by races as a category of biological classification so vague that ". . . how many [races] should be recognized is a matter of convenience and hence of judgement." Boyd (1950) states: "Whatever races we choose to distinguish will be almost entirely arbitrary, and their distribution will depend on the particular characteristic on which we choose to base them." Washburn (1963) expresses the opinion that "since races are open systems which are intergrading, the number of races will depend on the purpose of the classification." Though defining a local race as a breeding population, Garn (1961) does not apply this concept when listing local races. For example, he considers the Bantu as a local race, while Bantu breeding populations number more than one hundred. In fact, he applies his former concept of a local race (Garn and Coon 1955): "our enumeration [of local races] depends on the minimum size of the population units we wish to consider," thus introducing a highly arbitrary element into his system. There seems to be no basic theoretical

disagreement between these authors' views and those exposed here. The difference lies in the fact that they consider it useful to separate into discrete units, in a somewhat arbitrary manner, the open intergrading systems that they record (there is no escaping it: if you put a label, be it a name, a letter or a number, on something, you make it discrete). What I question is this: If any racial classification is arbitrary, for what purpose can it be of any use? Why spend so much time and effort building a classification, knowing that many others, not any worse, could be opposed to it, and that it runs the risk not only of being useless but also harmful by conveying the erroneous impression that it makes generalization possible?

Washburn's (1963) answer is: "Race is a useful concept only if one is concerned with the kind of anatomical, genetic, and structural differences which were in time past important in the origin of races. . . . If classification is to have a purpose, we may look backward to the explanation of the differences between people—structural, anatomical, physiological differences—and then the concept of race is useful, but it is useful under no other circumstances, as far as I can see." A similar answer is given by Newman (1963): "If indeed the population is the proper unit for biological study—and we have been told this many times in the past 15 years—much of the older racial work that was not so oriented needs to be rescrutinized, screened, and then appraised against the yardstick of modern populational studies. This is laborious work and would be worth it only for the understanding of phylogeny and race process that come from building a taxonomy from the bottom upward."

Human Taxonomy and Phylogeny

These statements lead us to question the possibility and usefulness of human taxonomy in the light of a criterion not yet referred to here: Racial classification is useful if it reflects phylogeny.

Let us first examine the conditions required for making a phylogenetic classification of populations possible. The basic one is this: Evolution must have taken the form of a growing tree. The current populations represent the terminal twigs; the bough common to several twigs may be called a race, the larger limb common to several boughs corresponds to a higher taxonomic unit, and so on until we reach the trunk which represents the human species. Infraspecific evolution takes this form only when the species splits into several groups which are exposed to different evolutionary forces and events under complete or effective genetic isolation, with eventual further splitting under similar conditions of differentiation in isolation. The process of raciation in this mode of evolution is the same as that of speciation, but represents only its initial stage; speciation is attained when and if the accumulated differences have reached the level at which fertile cross-matings no longer occur even when the subgroups come together again. Under such conditions, if we could follow each population back into the past, it would be possible to build an impregnable phylogenetic classification, which would reflect the dynamics of race formation. Would it be possible to derive a phylogenetic tree from data on contemporary populations? Only if great care is taken in the dynamic explanation of differences. The overall distances used for a horizontal classification may be misleading, especially if few characters are considered: each adaptive feature responds to its own specific environmental stimuli, convergence may occur, and the accident of random drift may, in one generation, strongly differentiate two newly separated populations. The difficulty cannot be bypassed by trying to use nonadaptive characters only: even if they could be identified with certainty, the fact remains that their frequencies are especially sensitive to the long-lasting effects of drift, and we should thus reduce the possibilities of classification, since adaptation is an important process of differentiation. By and large, however, if human evolution had been of the type described, a taxonomy built from the current characteristics of human populations would be of great help in the understanding of their phylogeny. Moreover, under such conditions, the chances are large that clear-cut clustering would correspond to characteristic constellations of gene frequencies. The limiting conditions to such a general correspondence between ultimate clusters and characteristic constellations seem to be felt by Boyd (1963) who, while defining races by characteristic constellations, writes: "Racial differentiation is the end result of the action of natural selection on the raw material provided by random mutations in a population sufficiently isolated genetically." But the fact is that no nonarbitrary general classification of mankind is available, and what we know of the migratory habits of man, and of the extent to which population mixture took place, altogether explains why no systematic subdivision of races is possible, and eliminates the hope that a general phylogeny-reflecting classification could be constructed. Human evolution did not take the form of a growing tree, at least, not in recent times. The general picture is not one of isolated groups differentiating in circumscribed areas. Mixture occurred many times in many places between the most various populations brought into contact by human mobility. The tendency toward high adaptive specialization was balanced again and again by migration, and by man's power to transform his environment. Even if we could reconstruct the intricate succession of mixtures that contributed to each living population, the final picture would look like a reticulum more than a tree, and a reticulum defies dichotomizing subdivision.

There have always been forces acting toward raciation, but they conduced to genuine races (in the sense of well-individualized clusters of populations) only here and there. I have already cited the Bushmen as a possible race that could emerge from an analysis of African variability; if this is confirmed, it would mean that this group experienced a differentiating evolution combined with a high degree of isolation. The Bushmen are in the long run facing either extinction or disappearance as a race through mixture, while maybe another race is in process of individualization somewhere else in the world. The few genuine races that could emerge from a cluster analysis of living mankind might not be those of tomorrow, nor those of yesterday.

If the preceding views are correct, the recent biological history of mankind can be visualized as an immense irregular reticulum growing upward; here and there at different time levels a stem grows away from the mass but is later embodied by it. Human populations are such that they defy general classification because of their phylogenetic history. To force them to fit into a classificatory scheme by overlooking a large part of the data can only lead to a grossly distorted idea of their phylogeny.

Conclusion

From whatever viewpoint one approaches the question of the applicability of the concept of race to mankind, the modalities of human variability appear so far from those required for a coherent classification that the concept must be considered as of very limited use. In my opinion, to dismember mankind into races as a convenient approximation requires such a distortion of the facts that any usefulness disappears: on the contrary, only the harm done by such practices remains. They tend to force our minds into erroneous channels of thinking, or, if we manage to retain any lucidity, to enter a maze of distinctions and restrictions.

To give up all general racial classifications would mean for anthropology freeing itself from blinkers it has too long worn, and focusing all its energy on its actual goal: the understanding of human variability, as it really is.

REFERENCES

BOYD, W. C. 1950. *Genetics and the Races of Man.* Boston, D. C. Heath & Co.

BOYD, W. C. 1963. Genetics and the human race. *Science* 140:1057–1064.

COON, C. S., S. M. GARN and J. B. BIRDSELL. 1950. *Races.* Springfield, Thomas.

CZEKANOWSKI, J. 1962. The theoretical assumptions of Polish anthropology and the morphological facts. *Current Anthropology* 3:481–494.

DOBZHANSKY, TH. 1962. Comment on "The nonexistence of human races" by F. B. Livingstone. *Current Anthropology* 3:279–280.

DUNN, L. C. and TH. DOBZHANSKY. 1952. *Heredity, Race and Society.* Rev. ed. New York, New American Library.

FRANKENBERG, G. VON. 1956. *Menschenrassen und Menschentum.* Berlin, Safari-Verlag.

GARN, S. M. and C. S. COON. 1955. On the number of races of mankind. *American Anthropologist* 57:996–1001.

GARN, S. M. 1961. *Human Races.* Springfield, Thomas.

GLOOR, P. A. 1961–62. Premiers résultats d'une enquête sur la structure raciale régionale en Suisse. *Bull, suisse Anthrop. et Ethnol.* 38, pp. 5 et 6.

HIERNAUX, J. 1956. *Analyse de la variation des caractères physiques humains en une région de l'Afrique centrale: Ruanda-Urundi et Kivu.* Ann. Mus. roy. Congo belge, Sci. de l'Homme, Anthrop., 3.

———. 1962. Le concept de race en anthropologie physique. *Actes VIe Congr. int. Sci. anthrop. et ethnol.* (Paris 1960) 1:471–477.

HOWELLS, W. 1959. *Mankind in the Making.* New York, Doubleday.

LIVINGSTONE, F. B. 1962. On the non-existence of human races. *Current Anthropology* 3:279–281.

MARQUER, P. 1963. Contribution à l'étude anthropologique du peuple basque et du problème de ses origines raciales. *Bull. Soc. Anthrop. Paris* 4, XI:1–240.

NEWMAN, M. T. 1963. Geographic and micrographic races. *Current Anthropology* 5:189–207.

VALLOIS, H. V. 1953. "Race" in *Anthropology Today* (edited by Koeber), 145–162. Chicago, University of Chicago Press.

WASHBURN, S. L. 1963. The study of race. *American Anthropologist* 65, 521–531.

WIERCIŃSKI, A. 1962. The racial analysis of human populations in relation to their ethnogenesis. *Current Anthropology* 3:2 and 9–20.

31 · A BIOLOGICAL VIEW OF RACE

Paul R. Ehrlich & Richard W. Holm

In this contribution two biologists consider the problems involved in the taxonomic concept of "subspecies" or "race." Like so many other biologists who have had to deal with this problem in a practical way, they find the concept too artificial and obfuscating for practical use. In addition they underscore the very real social damage that such unsound terms can do. In so sensitive an area as "race" I would especially point out the authors' remarks on the responsibilities of the scientist in immediately disavowing and repudiating any misinterpretation of his work, no matter for what purposes that misinterpretation is made, and their observation that "in the absence of such a disavowal, it may properly be assumed that the scientist supports such use of his work."

The time has passed when, with handwashing indifference to the consequences of his work, the scientist could claim that his responsibility ceased with the publication of his ideas, and that what others chose to do with them was no concern of his. Science may be ethically neutral, but scientists, especially by virtue of the great power they wield, cannot be ethically neutral. Anthropologists in particular stand in a very sensitive relationship to their fellow men, since man is the subject of their interest, and their role should be if anything to serve without false pride as examples to their fellow scientists.

Ehrlich and Holm are supported by many other distinguished biologists in their criticism of the concept of "race" and its equivalent "subspecies." In connection with the use of the term "race," as Simpson has put it: "A word for which everyone has a different definition, usually unstated, ceases to serve the function of communication and its use results in futile arguments about nothing. There is also a sort of Gresham's Law for words; redefine them as we will, their worst or most extreme meaning is almost certain to remain current and to tend to drive out the meaning we might prefer." [1]

The authors' comment on the tendency of physical anthropologists to overemphasize differences in their attempts to classify brings up once more the dangers of concentrating upon differences. The chief danger is, of course, the tendency to become oblivious to the likenesses and to neglect them altogether. A second danger is the tendency to identify difference with inferiority. "Race implies difference, difference implies superiority, and superiority leads to predominance." These words were uttered by Benjamin Disraeli in a speech in the House of Commons on February 1, 1849. They seem to have been uttered in perfect seriousness, and reflect a widespread inclination of human beings to equate difference with inferiority. It is a

[1] George Gaylord Simpson, *The Major Features of Evolution* (New York: Columbia University Press, 1953), p. 268.

tendency which not even anthropologists have altogether managed to avoid.

Let us bear in mind in this discussion of terminology that terms not only serve to describe, but also often create ideas and stereotypes, and that where an idea is particularly fuzzy a word can always be found to take its place.

Most of the problems clouding the study and description of human variation can be traced to the taxonomic premise that *Homo sapiens* is divided into a series of races which are significant biological entities. We shall attempt to deal with this premise in the context of current biological thinking about the taxonomic structure of nature.

The historical development of taxonomy follows closely the changing prejudices and philosophies of other sciences and of the humanities and arts as well. At any period taxonomy more or less reflects the prevailing world view of a somewhat earlier historical period. Thus it is understandable that the first formal taxonomy should have been an outgrowth of herbals and bestiaries. The Linnaean system developed in the 18th century along with the pervasive compulsion to order nature into mechanically logical systems. The taxonomic framework of the recent past is the result of the 19th century's propelling need to think in terms of linear progression. Today, however, in many areas of creative activity, there is a growing interest in problems of portrayal, description, and quantification of complex nonlinear relationships. It is not surprising that the impact of these approaches and of the devices necessary to sustain them is now beginning to be felt in taxonomy.

The New Systematics

In recent years, following the lead of the physical sciences and mathematicians, biologists have begun to examine some of the basic tenets and assumptions of their discipline. Taxonomy, often thought of as the least dynamic of the biological sciences, has assumed a position of leadership in this reevaluation of methods and principles. Taxonomy has experienced what might be regarded as two revolutions (see Kuhn, 1962) in the last 25 years. The first led to the establishment of the "new systematics" and derived primarily from the introduction of ideas from genetics and cytology into a largely museum-oriented field. Awareness of the principles of Mendelian genetics and the analysis of large population samples of organisms resulted in a greater interest in infraspecific categories. Thus the concepts of subspecies and geographic races, championed by Rensch, Mayr, Dobzhansky, and others, increased in importance. The commonly accepted definition of subspecies was well-expressed by Mayr (1942, p. 106):

The subspecies, or geographic race, is a geographically localized subdivision of the species, which differs genetically and taxonomically from other subdivisions of the species.

The new systematics shifted interest away from static species concepts, established by Linnaeus and reinforced, in a sense, by Darwin's emphasis on the term species. Differentiation of populations became the new point of focus and greater understanding was gained of the cytogenetic processes involved. However, the problem of the taxonomic expression of the complex interrelationships discovered was largely ignored or attempts were made to solve the problem with the existing taxonomic framework. The new systematics, in introducing dynamics into taxonomy, laid the groundwork for its own replacement. Extensive investigations of organisms in nature and of forms with widely divergent genetic systems (inbreeding, haplodiploidy, asexual reproduction, etc.), together with studies of multivariate patterns of geographic variation, made it apparent that the classical species-subspecies taxonomic structure (partially retained by the "new systematics") was inadequate for the expression of evolutionary relationships.

Perhaps the first signs of aging of the new systematics came in the early 1950's with the wide realization that the entities placed in the category "subspecies" were not necessarily evolutionary units. The subjective nature of the category had long been recognized (Mayr 1942). The dangers of its use were made clear by the controversy following a paper by Wilson and Brown (1953), who pointed out the arbitrary nature of the category and recommended that it no longer be used.

These problems were not unique to the subspecies category. Intensive studies of species, particularly in plants, have shown that the species itself is not necessarily a self-contained evolutionary unit (Epling and Catlin 1950). Attempts to create a rigorous and objective definition of species based on genetic criteria have failed because it is not possible to make them operational. A return to the original definition of species as "kind" has been recommended (Ehrlich and Holm 1962).

The major triumph of the "new systematics" was to introduce evolutionary thinking into taxonomy, and this led to the inevitable failure of the new systematics at the descriptive level. The inclusion of evolutionary hypothesus and assumptions into the word-symbols of taxonomy greatly reduces their usefulness for objective descriptions of patterns of relationships among organisms. If the process of evolution is to be inferred from the classifications of taxonomists, then the classifications cannot be based upon evolutionary hypotheses.

Numerical Taxonomy

The second post-Linnaean revolution in taxonomy began in the late 1950's and its effects are just beginning to be felt by the practicing taxonomist. The proximal cause of this revolution was the growing access to high-speed data-processing equipment. Although for many years taxonomists had recognized the usefulness of taxonomic systems based on multiple character comparisons (see, for instance, Anderson 1949), systems using large numbers of characters could not easily be analysed without the aid of digital computers. As availability of such equipment increased, people in many parts of the world began investigating phenetic relationships (relationships defined as degree of over-all similarity) among organisms. Developments in this field are largely outside the scope of this discussion; they are discussed concisely by Sneath and Sokal (1962) and in detail by Sokal and Sneath (1963). The broader implications of this approach, which perhaps are more concealed than revealed by the commonly used name, numerical taxonomy, are considered by Ehrlich and Holm (1962).

In brief, numerical taxonomy consists of the quantifying of large numbers of characteristics (usually 75 or more) which vary in the group of organisms to be studied. This is followed by the computation of some kind of coefficient of similarity among the units studied, based upon these characteristics. These coefficients may then be used as the basis for a taxonomic system by clustering the most similar entities. A simplified example is given in Figure 1.

The table (upper left) lists three entities, A, B, C. These entities may be individuals, species, genera, or any other units which are to be compared. In this example, only seven characters are

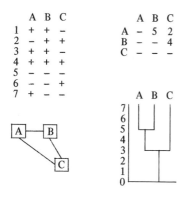

	A	B	C
1	+	+	−
2	−	+	+
3	+	+	−
4	+	+	+
5	−	−	−
6	−	−	+
7	+	−	−

	A	B	C
A	−	5	2
B	−	−	4
C	−	−	−

Figure 1: An Example of numerical taxonomy. (*Explanation in text.*)

evaluated for *A*, *B*, and *C*. A character, in the idiom of the numerical taxonomist, is any characteristic which varies in the group under consideration. In our example, characters which have been coded into two states, plus or minus, have been listed. Certain characters in human beings, such as Rh positive or Rh negative blood types, could easily be coded in this fashion. Coding a character such as height in this manner results in considerable loss of information.

In order to obtain a measure of the degree of resemblance among *A*, *B*, and *C*, a very simple coefficient of association is obtained by counting the number of characters which are the same for each pair of entities. This coefficient may take values from a maximum of 7 (two entities the same in all characters) to a minimum of 0 (two entities different in all characters). Values for all combinations are shown in the table in the upper right. This array of coefficients of similarity among entities is known as a Q-matrix. It can be seen that, with respect to the characters measured, *A* and *B* are more similar than *A* and *C*, *C* is more similar to *B* than to *A*, and *B* is more similar to *A* than to *C*.

Since only three entities are being compared here, it is possible to diagram these relationships

in two dimensions as has been done in the lower left. The higher the coefficient of similarity, the shorter the line connecting any two entities. However, Q-matrices containing coefficients among more than three entities cannot be diagrammed in two dimensions. Nor is it easy by inspection to visualize the multi-dimensional relationships inherent in larger matrices. A matrix showing all of the possible comparisons among, say, 100 species of a genus would contain 4,950 different coefficients regardless of the number of characters employed in the comparisons. In order to obtain some grasp of the relationships in such an array, various methods of searching for and diagramming structure in the matrix have been devised.

The dendrogram (lower right) illustrates one method of structuring applied to our small sample matrix. The ordinate is the scale of values of the similarity coefficient. Since each entity has complete similarity with itself, each is placed at the top of the diagram with a value of 7. The highest coefficient in the Q-matrix is 5, between *A* and *B*, therefore the lines are joined at that level. The *A*–*B* stem is joined to the *C* stem at the average value of the coefficients of *C* with *A* and *C* with *B* (3). The diagram gives a more readily grasped picture of relationships, but only at the cost of the loss of some information present in the Q-matrix. For instance, from looking at the diagram one could not know that *C* is not equally similar to *A* and *B*.

The "taxonomy" of these entities could be viewed as one taxon comprising two entities (or subordinate taxa) and another taxon comprising one. Various methods of applying nomenclature to dendrograms have been employed but their details need not concern us. The decision of how distinctive a group of entities must be before it should be distinguished (with a number or a name) as a "kind" or "species" is a decision which can only be made in the context of a particular investigation. It is important to realize that clusters derived by such analysis are based solely upon resemblances in the characteristics evaluated and are not based upon genetic or phylogenetic hypotheses. They comprise, however, the basic data set upon which such hypotheses may be constructed.

As might have been expected, such procedures have been decried by many taxonomists as being anti-evolutionary or typological. The first criticism is clearly not valid since the system is not concerned with the possible interpretations of the computed similarities. The second is partially true, although, as several authors (Daly 1961, Sokal 1962) have pointed out, there are fewer objectionable typological aspects to numerical taxonomy than there are to so-called phylogenetic taxonomy. A certain amount of the opposition to numerical taxonomy seems to be based on emotional reactions to the growing use of computers. There are dangers from the misuse of computers as with any mechanism extending human capabilities. Such misuse, if it occurs, is the result of a human decision. Emotional reactions to numerical taxonomy can be found even in the anthropological literature. For example (Coon 1962, p. 13):

The determination of species cannot be made by feeding figures into a computer. It is in a sense an art, practiced by men of experience who know, first of all, how species are formed.

It is true that the so-called art or intuition of practicing taxonomists has resulted in classifications of practical and scientific use. These intuitive classifications, however, also have led to some unfortunate misconceptions as will be discussed below. The rigorous and highly specified procedures of numerical taxonomy largely avoid such problems by limiting greatly the opportunity for personal bias to enter undetected at the stage of gathering data and making comparisons. Coon's statement also illustrates the confusion of data with hypotheses mentioned above.

In some instances, the results of numerical

taxonomy have been remarkably congruent with those produced by classical taxonomy. The numerical study retains the advantage, however, of having been done in clearly specified and repeatable steps. The classical taxonomist must depend for the evaluation of a taxonomic work largely upon his personal opinion of its author. Numerical taxonomists may check each other's work by repeating any or all steps. Other advantages of numerical taxonomy, such as precision in estimating relationships and ability to specify questions of character sampling and interrelationships of characters, cannot be discussed here. Most importantly perhaps, numerical taxonomy has retrieved the problem of what is meant by biological relationship from the cloudy realm of art and intuition.

It has long been assumed that satisfactory general classifications of organisms could be based on virtually any sample of the characteristics of individuals. In the past, the majority of these samples consisted of a small number of external characteristics of adult organisms. A few taxonomists have been concerned about the validity of this assumption in holometabolous insects and in plants with alternation of generations. This concern is understandable since larvae and adults or gametophytes and sporophytes may live in quite different environments and may seem strikingly different. Recently, numerical taxonomists have begun to investigate this question. Preliminary results indicate that congruence of taxonomies based on different stages in the life history may not be the rule. For instance, Rohlf (1963) compared the classifications of larval and adult mosquitos using numerical taxonomic techniques. He found significant (but not large) correlations between larval and adult relationships. The sets of relationships were, however, not congruent. He concluded (p. 116):

. . . while there is general agreement between the larval and adult interrelationships, there are also many distinct differences between the classifications. It was recommended that characters should be taken from all life-history stages, if possible, in order to form the most general classification.

Similar difficulties may be found when characteristics of different sexes or different parts of the adult are used in establishing phenetic relationships. Michener and Sokal (1963), for example, have found incomplete congruence in comparing the patterns based on males and females and on head and body characteristics of bees. The taxonomist assumes that the phenotypes he studies are representative of genotypes. The fact that more than one representation of the same genotype may be constructed by studying different stages in the life cycle or different sets of characters from the same stage clearly shows how biased our picture of the genotype may be and how poor is our understanding of the genotype-phenotype relationship.

The magnitude of this problem cannot be judged from the data in hand because so few detailed studies have been made. The data which are available give us little reason to feel sanguine about the precision of inferences about relationships estimated on the basis of small samples of characteristics. When it is remembered that paleontology deals with small samples of characteristics of small samples of organisms, the importance of this problem is easily seen. Little credence can be put in attempts to reconstruct phylogenies at the infraspecific level from paleontological data (as has been attempted by Coon, 1962, in the case of human races). Indeed, the arbitrary subspecific units recognized by Coon almost certainly have no phylogeny to reconstruct. It is difficult enough to trace even major lineages when relatively abundant material is available, as for instance, in the history of horses summarized by Simpson (1951).

A general problem in biology is how to deal with continuous but ever changing phenomena. This problem is especially important for the taxonomist because one of the more unfortunate aspects of the hierarchy inherited from Linnaeus is its requirement for discrete taxa. Therefore continua in space and time must be fragmented by the taxonomist. The patterns created by hybridization, reticulate evolution, apomixis, etc., cannot be adequately expressed by the classical taxonomic structure. Quantified similarities in a Q-matrix are free of this problem, although any *classification* based upon a Q-matrix will inevitably lose some information (but in a predetermined pattern dependent upon the clustering procedure used). Very recently C. D. Michener (1963) has begun to explore ways of making taxonomic classifications more realistic biologically by allowing overlapping taxa. The phylogenetic taxonomist often feels, and always hopes, that his groups represent "real" entities. The numerical taxonomist is always aware of the real source of his groups.

The Subspecies Problem

When one looks at the systems of classification which have been employed by anthropologists, he cannot help but be struck by the diversity of these systems and their tendency to overemphasize differences. Nowhere is this more apparent than in the classification of human subspecies or "races." The ancient observation that men from different areas may differ in superficial characteristics unfortunately has led to the assumption that man could be divided into some number of biological entities known as races. Beginning as a simple folk taxonomy, the idea of distinct or largely distinct races appears throughout the literature of anthropology. As anthropologists became aware of the new systematics, they naturally attempted to interpret their classifications in the genetic and phylogenetic terms appropriate to this approach.

The genetic definition of taxa seemed particularly suitable since modern *Homo sapiens* is perhaps the only widespread species which has been demonstrated to fit the "biological" species definition. In all probability every significant test of interbreeding within the species has been made under natural conditions and there is no known instance of successful interbreeding with a sympatric species. Indeed, the cytogenetic systems and behavioral mechanisms of the hominoids would seem to preclude the latter. Thus it is convenient to describe man in aggregate as the species *Homo sapiens.* Species is here used to connote *kind* and not to imply some sort of biological equivalence with other species of plants, animals, or microorganisms. We can be certain that *Homo sapiens* is quite a different sort of entity from the coast redwood, the common fruit fly, or *Paramecium aurelia.*

While *Homo sapiens* may qualify (perhaps uniquely) as a biological species, treatment of infraspecific variation in man under the rules of the "new systematics" has not proved so simple. As mentioned above, the arbitrary nature of the subspecies has long been recognized. Two general problems have plagued those who wish to circumscribe infraspecific units in plants and animals. The first is the selection of the characters on whose variation the units will be defined. The second is the decision as to the amount of difference which will be recognized as amounting to subspecific differentiation. This decision is a matter of taxonomic judgment and the discussion over percent rules and other guidelines for making decisions need not concern us here.

Concordance and Discordance

The question of character selection is of greater moment. If characters are largely concordant (that is, if they tend to vary together), then the study of the variation in any one character, or a few characters, would reveal the patterns in which population differentiation has occurred. If, on the other hand, variation is mostly discordant (characters are largely independent), then population differentiation must be studied with respect to one variable at a time. With discordance predominating subspecies recognized on the basis of one or a few convenient characters would not be evolutionary units. They would be simply units of convenience for filing specimens. Our zeal for discovering evolutionary units is predicated upon the belief, of course, that such units will have greater information content and hence greater predictive value than units recognized on other bases. Units of convenience for filing would not necessarily have these attributes and are not commonly thought of as useful in this way.

Too few studies have been made to permit a clear statement as to whether concordance or discordance in variation prevails in plants and animals. Subspecies in plants often seem to show concordant variation. In those zoological situations which have been analyzed, however, discordance seems to be the rule. For example, Gillham (1956) has analyzed a series of studies of geographic variation in butterflies in which both continental and insular subspecies have been recognized. His survey revealed widespread discordance, as exemplified by Figure 2. As Gillham puts it (p. 120):

In view of the prevailing discordance of geographical patterns followed by different variates, racial partition of butterfly species is not only arbitrary, but it must also necessarily weight some variates and ignore others, without regard for the biological significance of any of them. The best that can be hoped for now is an analysis of variation by individual characters, avoiding arbitrary subdivision of the species. Such analysis will eventually yield a less distorted picture of species formation than that to which the artificial subspecies now inevitably leads.

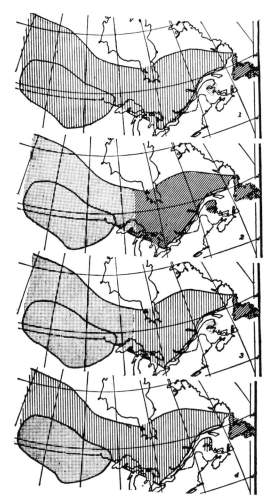

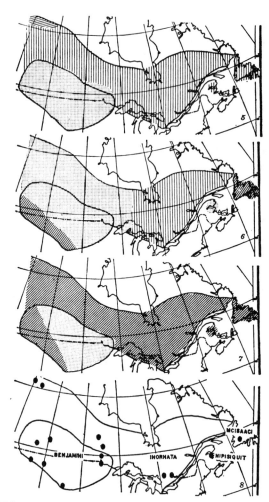

Figure 2: Geographic variation of seven different characters in the butterfly *Coenonympha inornata*. Junctions between different kinds of shading indicate that adjacent populations are significantly different from one another in the particular character mapped. The heavy black lines indicate the approximate ranges of two of the currently recognized continental subspecies, *inornata* and *benjamini*. *Mcisaaci* and *nipisiquit* are disjunct "subspecies." (*After Gillman.*)

It seems fair to state that, as a tool for understanding biological processes, the subspecies has deservedly lost favor. In the past ten years, only a very few papers in the journal *Evolution* have dealt primarily with the subspecies concept.

The Situation in *Homo sapiens*

Is man an exception to this trend of discordance in animals? The problem of taxonomic structure within the species *Homo sapiens* is very complex. Certain statements, however, seem almost beyond dispute:

1. There is geographic variation in numerous human phenotypic traits.

2. This geographic variation has a largely genetic basis.

3. Variation in many instances cuts across cultural lines.

Furthermore, there is reason to believe that differences among populations are largely the result of the action of selective agents. An inspection of a series of maps of the geographic distribution of human traits shows that the observed variation patterns are quite discordant. The problem is not solved even if recent migrations are discounted and only so-called aboriginal populations considered. It is obvious that the choice of a characteristic for the primary division will determine in large measure what races will be recognized. The vast majority of classifications which have been proposed thus far, both folk and scientific, have been based primarily on skin color. Had blood groups, hair type, or body build been the primary standard, the lines would certainly have been drawn differently.

Doubtless there are many internal structural and physiological characteristics which are not immediately obvious, but which show geographic variation. Only a few of these have been studied, especially those relating to metabolism and temperature tolerance. As W. L. Brown has aptly put it (p. 152):

Applied to the wealth of data on the variation of modern *Homo sapiens,* the "no race" idea seems worth considering on this basis [discordance of characters], even though the value of the race concept in studies of man has already been challenged widely on other grounds by anthropologists themselves. In the face of such obvious discordance as, for instance, human skin pigmentation with blood type factors, or hair form with cephalic index (taken on a world basis), the wildly varying opinions of anthropological schools on the racial classification of our species show up as irrelevant and unnecessary.

Psychological characteristics, such as intelligence, drive, and disposition, certainly have a genetic basis (Erlenmeyer-Kimling and Jarvik, 1963). Although there can be no doubt that these psychological attributes are in part determined by the genetic information, the problem of estimating the genetic component of the variation in ability to reason abstractly, for example,

is difficult in the extreme. In other words, the hereditary endowment of an individual and his environment interact to produce the psychological phenotype. It is virtually impossible to separate the two components completely. While most mental characteristics are highly subject to environmental (particularly cultural) modification, it is clear that the range of possible responses is genetically set. One would expect, therefore, the frequency of the genes concerned to vary geographically. Psychological characteristics undoubtedly show basically the same sort of geographical variation as physical characteristics, even though their environmental component may, in many cases, be greater.

It seems very unlikely that satisfactory tests will be devised in the near future which will permit accurate evaluation of the genetic range of psychological characteristics, even within rather close-knit cultural groups, let alone among diverse cultures. One might expect variation in the genetic range of abstract reasoning ability from culture to culture, perhaps based on weak selection for or against individuals showing a high capacity for abstraction. One might hypothesize that, say, a Chinese population would have a slightly higher or lower average genetic ability for abstraction than one from the United States. It is difficult, however, to conceive of any practical way of testing this hypothesis in the face of overriding cultural influences.

It is generally accepted that attributes like intelligence are composite in nature. There would seem to be *a priori* no reason to expect concordant variation in the frequencies of genes controlling these various components (if they could be estimated), any more than in those controlling so-called physical characters. It also seems quite clear that geographic variation in genetic components of intellectual traits must be relatively insignificant in comparison with the variation induced by social and cultural environments.

This does not mean that the differences ob-

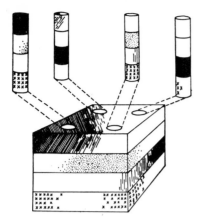

Figure 3: Diagram of discordant variation in four characters. (*Explanation in text.*)

served among men are some sort of mirage. Eskimos and Ubangis are obviously different in many respects. The crucial question is whether or not one can classify human populations into discrete biological units (races or subspecies) one of which contains, say, the Eskimos and the other the Ubangis. This point is clarified in Figure 3. Each layer in the cube represents the geographic variation in a single hypothetical character. For example, if the top layer represented skin color, individuals in the near left-hand corner would have the darkest skin, those in the right-hand half of the cube would have light skin, and so forth. The cores extracted from the cube each represent a sample of individuals taken in that geographic area. Each sample is different; indeed, one might say that each represents a different "race." However, a set of four samples taken at any four places in the "character cube" would also produce four different "races." There is no "natural" racial division because the abundant geographic variation is in discordant characters.

The goal of any system of classification is, or should be, to abstract patterns of variation in such ways that they may be comprehended.

Hiernaux (1963) has clearly expressed the crux of the matter (p. 199):

Classification is not a goal in itself, but a tool, a very useful one indeed when it works. When it does not, discarding it will not withdraw any scrap of knowledge, but on the contrary force us to face the facts as they are, in their full complexity.

Present-day subspecific classifications of man do not satisfactorily abstract the patterns of infraspecific variation apparent in *Homo sapiens.* Numerical taxonomic techniques will permit the evaluation of phenetic relationships among different geographic samples of men. It seems unlikely, however, that such analysis would result in sets of relationships which could reasonably be structured into discrete subspecific entities. It would be interesting to determine if discrete clusters exist at any level and if any indication of hierarchical structure exists.

Thing-Concept Confusion

Why then, in the face of these difficulties, do many biologists still feel that "good species" and "good subspecies" must exist in nature and that, given the time and tools, such entities will be discovered or delimited? The answer may be found in what might be called the "thing-concept confusion." The average biologist, when he says bird, flower, or Negro, feels that he is referring to a real, clearly delimited, biological entity. Although certain items may be referred unambiguously to one or another of these concepts, even a cursory consideration of them reveals that their unity resides primarily in the mind. How are the penguin, the ostrich, and the sparrow related? The systematist would say that they belong to a unit, birds, because of recency of descent from a common ancestor. Unfortunately this answer ignores the question of when, in time, birdlike reptiles became reptilelike birds. The limits of the entity bird become indefinite when the paleontological dimension is considered. The question of how to determine recency of descent is also ignored. One might assert that a penguin's most important biological relationships are with other organisms in their ecological situation such as killer whales, seals, and Antarctic fishes. These relationships at least have the advantage of being amenable to a certain degree of definition. It is only by making value judgments that one can decide which of these sorts of relationship are more important. Many biologists feel that phylogenetic relationship is more important because they can conceive of the transfer of genetic information along lineages back through time. We would not care to make this judgment. The transfer of energy in ecosystems seems equally (or more) significant than transfer of genetic information. In addition little is known about the structure and evolution of ecosystems and the possibilities of exchange of genetic information across what are considered to be phylogenetic lines.

The word flower might be considered to refer unambiguously to a morphological unit. In some plants, however, it is difficult to delimit one flower from another because they are reduced and crowded together in the inflorescence. From the point of view of function, the situation is even more complex. The familiar poinsettia is an example of a group of very specialized flowers arranged in an inflorescence with brightly colored leaves or bracts. Just as most of us think of a daisy as a single flower although it is a cluster of small florets, so could we regard an entire flowering branch of poinsettia as the ecological equivalent of a flower. Nearly all of the grasslike sedges are wind-pollinated and have inconspicuous flowers. The highly modified, small, and clustered flowers of the sedge, *Dichromena*, however, are surrounded by colored leaves and the whole complex resembles a single flower. This genus of sedge is insect-pollinated. As soon as one attempts to make an exclusive definition, he immediately perceives borderline situations which do not clearly fit within the limits he wishes to impose.

The concept Negro has much in common with the concepts bird and flower. Sociologically, Negro is defined differently in the United States and Brazil. In the southern United States anyone who is not "pure white" is a Negro. In Brazil, anyone who is not "pure black" is a caucasian. Biologically the concept Negro has even less unity. Heavy skin pigmentation may be associated with a wide variety of other characteristics.

It is all too easy to decide from one's mental patterns and prejudices or one's distorted percepts from nature that there is an actual structure out there waiting to be found. This is the phenomenon of reification of concepts, well-known to the historian of scientific thought. This concept-thing confusion may seem unimportant when dealing with, say, subspecies of butterflies. With *Homo sapiens* such confusion creates not only social problems in the present, but perhaps evolutionary problems in the future. The evolution of man is an interaction between classical "biological" evolution and psychosocial or cultural evolution (Ehrlich and Holm 1963, Montagu 1962). In the realm of psychosocial evolution, conflicting ideas may be analogous to alleles at a genetic locus, their relative frequency fluctuating through chance effects and what might be termed cultural selection. In this context, one might view the waxing and waning of ideas concerning the significance of races and racism as a problem in population phrenetics.

The Consequences of the Classical Approach

It might be profitable to look more closely at the harm that is done by continuing to use the classical species-subspecies categories and the usual hierarchic structure. Intellectual damage is done at virtually every level of investigation in both theory and practice. It is difficult to specify the extent of "damage" when it involves misfiling of specimens of grosbeak study skins as pointed out by West (1962) or the arbitrary pigeonholing of butterfly populations as was done by Ehrlich (1955). It is even more difficult to determine the extent to which our understanding of the process of evolution has been distorted by the imposition of the rigid set of taxonomic categories. In a recent textbook on evolution, one finds the statement: "The very hierarchy of genera, families, orders, and so forth is in itself evidence for the correctness of the theory of evolution, for that is the pattern that evolution should cause to develop." Since evolutionary theory has almost always been dealt with in terms of this hierarchical structure it is hardly surprising that our present theory may be misconstrued as automatically leading to such a structure. The systems of relationship established by unbiased procedures lend little comfort to the view that the structure of nature is inherently hierarchic.

There is no question, however, about the harm which has resulted from the extension of this taxonomic approach to considerations of the nature of geographic variation in *Homo sapiens*. It has, among other things, led to the mistaken assumption that arbitrary racial subdivisions of *Homo sapiens* can be considered as evolutionary units in space and time. As has been discussed above, there is no basis for assuming, without extensive genetic study, that any population or any taxonomic group is an evolutionary unit. Discussions of the biological origins and characteristics of subjectively determined races (e.g., Coon 1963), based exclusively, as they must be, on evolutionary misconceptions, are useful only for strengthening culturally determined prejudices against groups which have reality only in a social, rather than a biological, sense.

One unfortunate aspect of persisting in considering races to be discrete biological entities

is seen in discussions of the consequences of interbreeding between supposed races of *Homo sapiens*. Many of these discussions do not accurately represent what is known about the genetics of interfertile ("infraspecific") populations in other organisms. For example, much attention has been drawn to the problem of the supposedly deleterious effects of "racial intermixture." Zoologists and some botanists, by their use of a "biological" species concept, are constrained to regard exchange of genetic material between what they call species as somehow detrimental to the continued existence of the species. Such interchange in effect becomes an illicit process and the biologist may unconsciously regard it as "unnatural." In the minds of some, hybridization comes to be thought of as a process deleterious to further evolutionary differentiation and not as a part of the evolutionary repertoire of the populations involved.

Biologists do not take this point of view about genetic interchange among populations of the same species. Indeed, the presumed existence of such interchange of genes is critical to the so-called biological species concept. Anthropologists and others have sometimes proposed that the supposedly harmful effects of gene exchange at the species level in other organisms occur at the racial level in man. The term hybridization with its psychologically based overtones, or the ugly word miscegenation, is then used to describe what is presumed to be happening.

There is evidence that some infraspecific crosses made in the laboratory between geographically distant populations produce offspring which are relatively inviable. This has been found in butterflies, moths, frogs, and some plants. Such evidence seems largely lacking for crosses within *Homo sapiens*, although it is possible to construct models involving such phenomena as Rh incompatibility in which crossing might prove deleterious to a population. However, there is also some reason to believe that progeny of parents drawn from two different human populations would be, on the average, more fit in the sense of the population geneticist than the offspring of individuals from the same population. There would appear to be no genetic support either for the encouragement or the repression of intergroup gene exchange in man. Indeed, the situation of partially differentiated populations with some gene exchange among them has been postulated to be the ideal state for further evolution.

It is not necessary here to dignify the George Report and similar tracts with a point-for-point refutation. The pertinent facts are well known to biologists and anthropologists and are widely available to the interested layman (Commoner et al. 1963). It might be maintained by any scientist that it is his duty to publish facts in his discipline as he sees them. This presumably would include speculations based on these facts. While this is clearly so for the more abstruse ideas of basic science, it does not seem reasonable to absolve the scientist of all social responsibility for his views. The question would rarely arise in the domain of pure science, but it arises frequently wherever *Homo sapiens* is concerned. The situation with race finds an interesting parallel in the discussions of the responsibility of nuclear physicists in designing and building nuclear weapons. Surely no one would wish to prescribe rules of conduct in such matters; one must depend upon the judgment and good faith of the scientist.

It seems little enough to ask, however, that the scientist working in areas where any results are of great social consequence should follow the behavioral pattern of scientists in general. His results should first be published in the scholarly literature. Potential social effects of the results should be considered thoroughly. This would be true whether the scientific results concern nu-

clear fission, cancer-related viruses, extra-sensory perception, organic poisons of potential use as pesticides, or the evolution of *Homo sapiens*. Should the work be misinterpreted or be used to further causes which it does not support, it surely is the responsibility of the scientist immediately to make clear the misinterpretation and to disavow the misuse of his work. In the absence of such a disavowal, it may properly be assumed that the scientist supports such use of his work. Definition of the areas of a scientist's responsibility is an important and vexing question and deserves further discussion. It seems obvious, however, that certain types of behavior are to be avoided. A scientific idea of merit does not become part of the formal structure of science by its acceptance by the public at large. Rather, it must be weighed and reworked by the scientific community. It must not become the basis for social actions until it has passed this important test.

In conclusion it may be said that so-called subspecies or races in man, as in many other organisms, are not evolutionary units. They are arbitrarily created to describe certain variation patterns in one or a few characteristics. They have no common genetic pattern nor may their genetic future be predicted. It is an error to believe that human subspecies or races are *things* that may be discussed and compared or whose separate evolutionary development may be traced. Whereas in other organisms use of the subspecies concept may do only intellectual damage by creating a distorted view of nature, in *Homo sapiens* the results are very different. Promulgation of views of races and their supposed properties may have serious and far-reaching consequences both for man's present behavior and for his future psychosocial evolution. In 1768 the botanist von Haller said:

Natura in reticulum sua genera connexit, non in catenam: homines non possint nisi catenam sequi, cum non plura simul sermone exponere.[1]

---

[1] Nature has linked her kinds into a net, not into a chain; men are incapable of following anything but a chain since they cannot express in words more than one thing at a time. *Historia stirpium indigenarum Helvetiae.*

His words have even greater cogency today when we know so much more about man's evolutionary background, his behavior and culture, and at least some of the possible consequences of his activities.

REFERENCES

ANDERSON, E. 1949. *Introgressive Hybridization.* New York, John Wiley & Sons.

BROWN, W. L., JR. 1958. Some zoological concepts applied to problems in the evolution of the hominid lineage. *American Scientist* 46:151–158.

COMMONER, B., *et al.* 1963. Science and the race problem. *Science* 142:558–561.

COON, C. S. 1962. *The Origin of Races.* New York, Knopf.

DALY, H. V. 1961. Phenetic classification and typology. *Systematic Zoology* 10:176–179.

EHRLICH, P. R. 1955. The distribution and subspeciation of *Erebia epipsodea* Butler (Lepidoptera: Satyridae). *University Kansas Science Bulletin.*

EHRLICH, P. R. and R. W. HOLM. 1962. Patterns and populations. *Science* 137:652–657.

———. 1963. *The Process of Evolution.* New York, McGraw-Hill.

EPLING, C. and W. CATLIN. 1950. The relation of taxonomic method to an explanation of organic evolution. *Heredity* 4:313–325.

ERLENMEYER-KIMLING, L. and L. F. JARVIK. 1963. Genetics and intelligence: a review. *Science* 142: 1477–1479.

GILLHAM, N. W. 1956. Geographic variation and the subspecies concept in butterflies. *Systematic Zoology* 5:110–120.

HIERNAUX, J. 1963. Discussion of *Geographic and microgeographic races* by M. T. Newman. *Current Anthropology* 4:198–199.

KUHN, T. S. 1962. The structure of scientific revolutions. *Foundations of the Unity of Science* 2:1–172.

MAYR, E. 1942. *Systematics and the Origin of Species.* New York, Columbia University Press.

MICHENER, C. D. 1963. Some future developments in taxonomy. *Systematic Zoology* 12:151–172.

MICHENER, C. D. and R. R. SOKAL. 1963. Two tests of the hypothesis of nonspecificity in the *Hoplitis* complex. In preparation. (Cited in Sokal and Sneath, 1963.)

MONTAGU, A. [ed.] 1962. *Culture and the Evolution of Man.* New York, Oxford University Press.

ROHLF, F. J. 1963. Congruence of larval and adult classification in *Aedes* (Diptera: Culicidae). *Systematic Zoology* 12:97–117.

SIMPSON, G. G. 1951. *Horses.* New York, Oxford University Press.

SNEATH, P. H. A. and R. R. SOKAL. 1962. Numerical taxonomy. *Nature* 193:855–858.

SOKAL, R. R. 1962. Typology and empiricism in taxonomy. *Journal of Theoretical Biology* 3:230–267.

SOKAL, R. R. and P. H. A. SNEATH. 1963. *Principles of Numerical Taxonomy.* San Francisco, W. H. Freeman & Co.

WEST, D. A. 1962. Hybridization in grosbeaks (*Pheucticus*) of the Great Plains. *The Auk* 79:399–424.

WILSON, E. O. and W. L. BROWN, JR. 1953. The subspecies concept and its taxonomic application. *Systematic Zoology* 2:97–111.

32 • NATURAL SELECTION AND THE MENTAL CAPACITIES OF MANKIND   Theodosius Dobzhansky & Ashley Montagu

This contribution argues that since man has been a food-gathering hunter for almost the whole of his evolutionary history, and since the pressures of the environments in which he lived have been sufficiently alike, similar behavioral demands were placed upon the individual so that the genetic evolution of behavioral traits in separated human populations must have been much the same. Hence, it is unlikely that there exist any major genetic differences for behavior among the populations of mankind.

In the changing social environments of human populations, especially those living by foodgathering and hunting, fixity of any kind of special traits would have been disadvantageous. Under such conditions natural selection would favor genotypes which permit greater and greater educability and plasticity. Indeed, *educability* is the species characteristic of *Homo sapiens*.

Educability is a general trait. It means that man is the creature who, beyond all others, is capable of learning whatever can be learned—a trait upon which he is dependent for his continued survival. In the course of his evolution the pressures of the environment were not so much upon the development of any special behavioral trait or capacity, but rather upon the capacity to develop *responses* to any and every challenge of the environment. The operative word here is *responses,* not *reactions.* This unique evolutionary history of man constitutes, in addition, one of the reasons for supposing that if he ever had any instincts, he would have lost them, for they would only have detracted from the development of such flexibility of choice.

It should be made quite clear that the authors do not claim that there can be no genetic differences in mental capacities between different populations of mankind. It is quite possible that such differences do exist, but if they do they cannot be very great; and that intragroup differences in mental capacity are undoubtedly greater than intergroup differences. As Muller has put it, "racial genetic differences . . . may well be insignificant in comparison with the individual ones, owing to the lack of any substantial difference in the manner of selection of most of these characters in the major part of the past history of the various human races." [1]

The fundamental mechanisms of the transmission of heredity from parents to offspring are surprisingly uniform in most diverse organisms. Their uniformity is perhaps the most remarkable fact disclosed by genetics. The laws discovered by Mendel apply to human genes just as much as to those of the maize plant, and the processes of cellular division and germ cell maturation in man are not very different from those in a grasshopper. The similarity of the mechanisms of heredity on the individual level is reflected on the population level in a similarity of the basic causative factors of organic evolution throughout the living world. Mutation, selection, and genetic drift are important in the evolution of man as well as in amoebae and in bacteria. Wherever sexuality and cross-fertilization are established as exclusive or predominant methods of reproduction, the field of hereditary variability increases enormously as compared with asexual or self-fertilizing organisms. Isolating mechanisms which prevent inter-breeding and fusion of species of mammals are operative also among insects.

Nevertheless, the universality of basic genetic mechanisms and of evolutionary agents permits a variety of evolutionary patterns to exist not only in different lines of descent but even at different times in the same line of descent. It is evident that the evolutionary pattern in the dog species under domestication is not the same as in the wild ancestors of the domestic dogs or in the now living wild relatives. Widespread occurrence of reduplication of chromosome complements (polyploidy) in the evolution of plants introduces complexities which are not found in the animal kingdom, where polyploidy is infrequent. Evolutionary situations among parasites and among cave

SOURCE: Theodosius Dobzhansky and Ashley Montagu, "Natural Selection and the Mental Capacities of Mankind," *Science*, vol. 105 (June 6, 1947): 587–

90. Reprinted by permission of the publisher.
[1] H. J. Muller, "On the Variability of Mixed Races," *American Naturalist*, LXX (1936), 409–442.

inhabitants are clearly different from those in free-living forms. Detection and analysis of differences in the evolutionary patterns in different organisms is one of the important tasks of modern evolutionists.

It can scarcely be doubted that man's biological heredity is transmitted by mechanisms similar to those encountered in other animals and in plants. Likewise, there is no reason to believe that the evolutionary development of man has involved causative factors other than those operative in the evolution of other organisms. The evolutionary changes that occurred before the pre-human could become human, as well as those which supervened since the attainment of the human estate, can be described causally only in terms of mutation, selection, genetic drift, and hybridization—familiar processes throughout the living world. This reasoning, indisputable in the purely biological context, becomes a fallacy, however, when used, as it often has been, to justify narrow biologism in dealing with human material.

The specific human features of the evolutionary pattern of man cannot be ignored. Man is a unique product of evolution in that he, far more than any other creature, has escaped from the bondage of the physical and the biological into the multiform social environment. This remarkable development introduces a third dimension in addition to those of the external and internal environments—a dimension which many biologists, in considering the evolution of man, tend to neglect. The most important setting of human evolution is the human social environment. As stated above, this can influence evolutionary changes only through the media of mutation, selection, genetic drift, and hybridization. Nevertheless, there can be no genuine clarity in our understanding of man's biological nature until the role of the social factor in the development of the human species is understood. A biologist approaching the problems of human evolution

must never lose sight of the truth stated more than 2,000 years ago by Aristotle: "Man is by nature a political animal."

In the words of Fisher, "For rational systems of evolution, that is, for theories which make at least the most familiar facts intelligible to the reason, we must turn to those that make progressive adaptation the driving force of the process." It is evident that man by means of his reasoning abilities, by becoming a "political animal," has achieved a mastery of the world's varying environments quite unprecedented in the history of organic evolution. The system of genes which has permitted the development of the specifically human mental capacities has thus become the foundation and the paramount influence in all subsequent evolution of the human stock. An animal becomes adapted to its environment by evolving certain genetically determined physical and behavioral traits; the adaptation of man consists chiefly in developing his inventiveness, a quality to which his physical heredity predisposes him and which his social heredity provides him with the means of realizing. To the degree to which this is so, man is unique. As far as his physical responses to the world are concerned, he is almost wholly emancipated from dependence upon inherited biological dispositions, uniquely improving upon the latter by the process of learning that which his social heredity (culture) makes available to him. Man possesses much more efficient means of achieving immediate or long-term adaptation than any other biological species: namely, through learned responses or novel inventions and improvisations.

In general, two types of biological adaptation in evolution can be distinguished. One is genetic specialization and genetically controlled fixity of traits. The second consists in the ability to respond to a given range of environmental situations by evolving traits favorable in these particular situations; this presupposes genetically controlled plasticity of traits. It is known, for example, that the composition of the blood which is most favorable for life at high altitudes is somewhat different from that which suffices at sea level. A species which ranges from sea level to high altitudes on a mountain range may become differentiated into several altitudinal races, each having a fixed blood composition favored by natural selection at the particular altitude at which it lives; or a genotype may be selected which permits an individual to respond to changes in the atmospheric pressure by definite alterations in the composition of the blood. It is well known that heredity determines in its possessor not the presence or absence of certain traits but, rather, the responses of the organism to its environments. The responses may be more or less rigidly fixed, so that approximately the same traits develop in all environments in which life is possible. On the other hand, the responses may differ in different environments. Fixity or plasticity of a trait is, therefore, genetically controlled.

Whether the evolutionary adaptation in a given phyletic line will occur chiefly by way of genetic fixity or by way of genetically controlled plasticity of traits will depend on circumstances. In the first place, evolutionary changes are compounded of mutational steps, and consequently the kind of change that takes place is always determined by the composition of the store of mutational variability which happens to be available in the species populations. Secondly, fixity or plasticity of traits is controlled by natural selection. Having a trait fixed by heredity and hence appearing in the development of an individual regardless of environmental variations is, in general, of benefit to organisms whose milieu remains uniform and static except for rare and freakish deviations. Conversely, organisms which inhabit changeable environments are benefited by having their traits plastic and modified by each recurrent configuration of environmental agents in a way most favorable for the survival of the carrier of the trait in question.

Comparative anatomy and embryology show that a fairly general trend in organic evolution seems to be from environmental dependence toward fixation of the basic features of the bodily structure and function. The appearance of these structural features in the embryonic development of higher organisms is, in general, more nearly autonomous and independent of the environment than in lower forms. The development becomes "buffered" against environmental and genetic shocks. If, however, the mode of life of a species happens to be such that it is, of necessity, exposed to a wide range of environments, it becomes desirable to vary some structures and functions in accordance with the circumstances that confront an individual or a strain at a given time and place. Genetic structures which permit adaptive plasticity of traits become, then, obviously advantageous for survival and so are fostered by natural selection.

The social environments that human beings have created everywhere are notable not only for their extreme complexity but also for the rapid changes to which immediate adjustment is demanded. Adjustment occurs chiefly in the psychical realm and has little or nothing to do with physical traits. In view of the fact that from the very beginning of human evolution the changes in the human environment have been not only rapid but diverse and manifold, genetic fixation of behavioral traits in man would have been decidedly unfavorable for survival of individuals as well as of the species as a whole. Success of the individual in most human societies has depended and continues to depend upon his ability rapidly to evolve behavior patterns which fit him to the kaleidoscope of the conditions he encounters. He is best off if he submits to some, compromises with some, rebels against others, and escapes from still other situations. Individuals who display a relatively greater fixity of response than their fellows suffer under most forms of human society and tend to fall by the way. Suppleness, plasticity, and, most important of all, ability to profit by experience and education are required. No other species is comparable to man in its capacity to acquire new behavior patterns and discard old ones in consequence of training. Considered socially as well as biologically, man's outstanding capacity is his educability. The survival value of this capacity is manifest, and therefore the possibility of its development through natural selection is evident.

It should be made clear at this point that the replacement of fixity of behavior by genetically controlled plasticity is not a necessary consequence of all forms of social organization. The quaint attempts to glorify insect societies as examples deserving emulation on the part of man ignore the fact that the behavior of an individual among social insects is remarkable precisely because of the rigidity of its genetic fixation. The perfection of the organized societies of ants, termites, bees, and other insects is indeed wonderful, and the activities of their members may strike an observer very forcibly by their objective purposefulness. This purposefulness is retained, however, only in environments in which the species normally lives. The ability of an ant to adjust its activities to situations not encountered in the normal habitats of its species is very limited. On the other hand, social organizations on the human level are built on the principle that an individual is able to alter his behavior to fit any situation, whether previously experienced or new.

This difference between human and insect societies is, of course, not surprising. Adaptive plasticity of behavior can develop only on the basis of a vastly more complex nervous system than is sufficient for adaptive fixity. The genetic differences between human and insect societies furnish a striking illustration of the two types of evolutionary adaptations—those achieved through genetically controlled plasticity of behavioral traits and those attained through genetic specialization and fixation of behavior.

The genetically controlled plasticity of mental traits is, biologically speaking, the most typical and uniquely human characteristic. It is very probable that the survival value of this characteristic in human evolution has been considerable for a long time, as measured in terms of human historical scales. Just when this characteristic first appeared is, of course, conjectural. Here it is of interest to note that the most marked phylogenetic trend in the evolution of man has been the special development of the brain, and that the characteristic human plasticity of mental traits seems to be associated with the exceptionally large brain size. The brain of, for example, the Lower or Middle Pleistocene fossil forms of man was, grossly at least, scarcely distinguishable from that of modern man. The average Neanderthaloid brain was somewhat larger than that of modern man, though slightly different in shape. More important than the evidence derived from brain size is the testimony of cultural development. The Middle Acheulean handiwork of Swanscombe man of several hundred thousand years ago and the beautiful Mousterian cultural artifacts associated with Neanderthal man indicate the existence of minds of a high order of development.

The cultural evidence thus suggests that the essentially human organization of the mental capacities emerged quite early in the evolution of man. However that may be, the possession of the gene system, which conditions educability rather than behavioral fixity, is a common property of all living mankind. In other words, educability is truly a species character of man, *Homo sapiens*. This does not mean, of course, that the evolutionary process has run its course and that natural selection has introduced no changes in the genetic structure of the human species since the attainment of the human status. Nor do we wish to imply that no genetic variations in mental equipment exist at our time level. On the contrary, it seems likely that with the attainment of human status that part of man's genetic system which is related to mental potentialities did not cease to be labile and subject to change.

This brings us face to face with the old problem of the likelihood that significant genetic differences in the mental capacities of the various ethnic groups of mankind exist. The physical and, even more, the social environments of men who live in different countries are quite diversified. Therefore, it has often been argued, natural selection would be expected to differentiate the human species into local races differing in psychic traits. Populations of different countries may differ in skin color, head shape, and other somatic characters. Why, then, should they be alike in mental traits?

It will be through investigation rather than speculation that the problem of the possible existence of average differences in the mental make-up of human populations of different geographical origins will eventually be settled. Arguments based on analogies are precarious, especially where evolutionary patterns are concerned. If human races differ in structural traits, it does not necessarily follow that they must also differ in mental ones. Race differences arise chiefly because of the differential action of natural selection on geographically separated populations. In the case of man, however, the structural and mental traits are quite likely to be influenced by selection in different ways.

The very complex problem of the origin of racial differentiations in structural traits does not directly concern us here. Suffice it to say that racial differences in traits such as the blood groups may conceivably have been brought about by genetic drift in populations of limited effective size. Other racial traits are genetically too complex and too consistently present in populations of some large territories and absent in other territories to be accounted for by genetic drift alone.

Differences in skin color, hair form, nose shape, etc. are almost certainly products of natural selection. The lack of reliable knowledge of the adaptive significance of these traits is perhaps the greatest gap in our understanding of the evolutionary biology of man. Nevertheless, it is at least a plausible working hypothesis that these and similar traits have, or at any rate had in the past, differential survival values in the environments of different parts of the world.

By contrast, the survival value of a higher development of mental capacities in man is obvious. Furthermore, natural selection seemingly favors such a development everywhere. In the ordinary course of events in almost all societies those persons are likely to be favored who show wisdom, maturity of judgment, and ability to get along with people—qualities which may assume different forms in different cultures. Those are the qualities of the plastic personality, not a single trait but a general condition, and this is the condition which appears to have been at a premium in practically all human societies.

In human societies conditions have been neither rigid nor stable enough to permit the selective breeding of genetic types adapted to different statuses or forms of social organization. Such rigidity and stability do not obtain in any society. On the other hand, the outstanding fact about human societies is that they do change and do so more or less rapidly. The rate of change was possibly comparatively slow in earlier societies, as the rate of change in present-day nonliterate societies may be, when compared to the rate characterizing occidental societies. In any event, rapid changes in behavior are demanded of the person at all levels of social organization even when the society is at its most stable. Life at any level of social development in human societies is a pretty complex business, and it is met and handled most efficiently by those who exhibit the greatest capacity for adaptability, plasticity.

It is this very plasticity of his mental traits which confers upon man the unique position which he occupies in the animal kingdom. Its acquisition freed him from the constraint of a limited range of biologically predetermined responses. He became capable of acting in a more or less regulative manner upon his physical environment instead of being largely regulated by it. The processes of natural selection in all climes and at all times have favored genotypes which permit greater and greater educability and plasticity of mental traits under the influence of the uniquely social environments to which man has been continuously exposed.

The effect of natural selection in man has probably been to render genotypic differences in personality traits, as between individuals and particularly as between races, relatively unimportant compared to their phenotypic plasticity. Instead of having his responses genetically fixed as in other animal species, man is a species that invents its own responses, and it is out of this unique ability to invent, to improvise, his responses that his cultures are born.

33 • RACE AND IQ: THE GENETIC BACKGROUND

W. F. Bodmer

Questions relating to genetics, IQ, and race constitute a staple of the racist's armamentarium. The argument that physical, mental and cultural traits constitute a genetic triad, each of them indissolubly linked with the others, represent the doctrine of racism.

There can, in fact, be no doubt whatever that there is not the slightest linkage between genes for physical, mental, and cultural traits. Certainly there are genes which influence the development of physical and mental traits; but these are quite independent of each other. There is something on the order of between 5 million and 10 million genes in the genome of each individual, and each of these, in any event, undergoes independent assortment. As Kirtley Mather has said, "Many non-European peoples, especially savages, have been regarded as genetically inferior because their level of social development was below that of the European, and this view has drawn strength from these people's obvious genetical departure from the European in colour and physical characteristics. The existence of one genetical difference makes it easier to impute another. The falsity of such an argument is self-evident. Since genes can recombine, their effects can be reassociated, so that differences in the genetic determinants of one character do not imply differences in the determinants of another." [1]

The important thing about human diversity is that it is composed of individuals who vary, and it is individuals who matter. Hence, it is difficult to see what practical use could be made of any knowledge of a supposed genetical basis for racial differences in IQ. But as Bodmer notes, perhaps the only practical use such knowledge could have would be to answer the question raised by the racists.

Intrinsically interesting as the subject of individual differences may be, it is my own view that the value of the results obtainable from such inquiries hardly merits the amount of time, energy, and money that would have to be devoted to it. It is quite impossible to separate genetic from social influences in the development of whatever capacity it is that IQ tests

---

[1] Kirtley Mather, *Human Diversity* (New York: Free Press, 1965), p. 114.

measure. But even if this were possible, I cannot see what the practical value of such measurements would be. We have long known that variability in the capacities of the members of any population is considerable; that, indeed, this variability constitutes the genetic as well as the potential social wealth of human populations. It should, therefore, be evident that what is required are social environments which will afford the individual optimal opportunities for the development of his potentialities. It is not further scientific investigations of so-called "racial" differences that we, as human beings, stand in need of, but more humane approaches to the solution of our pressing social divisiveness.

As a geneticist, in throwing light upon the genetic problems involved, Bodmer makes the social nature of the problem very clear.[2]

This chapter is a review of the meanings of race and IQ, and the approaches for determining the extent to which IQ is inherited. The first question to consider is 'What is race?' and then one must demonstrate how one can study the biological inheritance of mental ability as measured by IQ tests. These two aspects of genetics form the main underlying theme for this chapter.

What Is Race?

In almost all the psychological studies carried out on racial groups, race is defined sociologically or culturally and not biologically. However, biological race boundaries often coincide with those that are culturally evident, though not always. An example of a sociological or cultural definition of race that is not strictly valid biologically is that of children of black–white marriages in the USA who are still regarded as black.

To a biologist a race is just a group of individuals or populations which form a recognizable sub-division of the species. The group is identified by the fact that the individuals within it share characteristics which distinguish them from other sub-groups of the species. The species itself is most simply defined as that set of individuals which includes all those who could produce fertile offspring if they mated with each other. This means, of course, that matings between members of different races are just as fertile as matings within races. The members of a race or a sub-group are however most likely to find their mates within their own group. This results in the groups becoming separated from one another as far as reproduction is concerned. Because such groups mate among themselves rather than with other groups, they tend, as we shall see, to become more and more different. The more different they become and the more they are separated from each other, the less likely it becomes that individuals marry outside their own group. This tends to make the groups become more and more distinguishable from each other.

The sorts of things that keep groups physically apart are, for example, mountain ranges, wide rivers, seas and deserts, and just distance alone. It took many thousands of years before Europeans crossed the Atlantic in significant numbers and came into contact with the American Indians. And even then, they hardly intermarried—it was mainly germs causing diseases like measles, which

---

SOURCE: Walter F. Bodmer, "Race and I.Q.: The Genetic Background," in *Race, Culture and Intelligence*, eds. Ken Richardson and David Spears (with Martin Richards) (Baltimore, Md.: Penguin Books, 1972), 83–113. Copyright © 1972 by Martin Richards, Ken Richardson, and David Spears. Reprinted by permission of the publisher.

[2] See also W. F. Bodmer and L. L. Cavalli-Sforza, "Intelligence and Race," *Scientific American*, 223 (1970), 19–29. L. L. Cavalli-Sforza and W. F. Bodmer, *The Genetics of Human Populations* (San Francisco: Freeman, 1971).

crossed the racial barriers. But even in a comparatively small country like England, distances are such that at least until quite recently, it was not very likely if you came from the north you would marry someone from the south. In fact, you would be most likely to marry someone from your own parish, or at least one quite nearby. Modern transport, of course, has scaled down the significance of distance as an isolating factor. Partly as a result of this, many of the differences that have accumulated in past years, even between neighbouring towns, are now rapidly disappearing. But most of the sub-divisions of man which are nowadays called races, originated long before the Industrial Revolution and modern transport. Greater mobility, as well as affecting local marriage patterns, certainly has an enormous impact on the larger sub-divisions of the human species by bringing together groups of people who had previously lived more or less in isolation from each other. This happened when slaves were taken over to the Americas from Africa and more recently when American blacks moved into the northern states and their cities, from the southern states.

Major migrations have led also in the past, often in the form of invasions, to new marriage patterns and the emergence of new population groups. The bringing together of different peoples should eventually bring about a blending of the differences between them, but at the same time it can be a cause of many of the racial tensions that we see in the world today.

Groups of people who are geographically and reproductively isolated from one another, tend to become different for a number of reasons, all of which may interact with each other. The environment itself may have a direct effect, for example, a diet deficient in iodine leads to high frequencies of goitres, and sunlight makes the skin darker. Environment factors may lead to different patterns of living, adapted to differences in the climate for example, and these in turn may lead to cultural differences. Differences in the ways of living and in language can also, however, arise simply by chance and historical accident. Cultures change continuously at varying rates, and it is not necessary to suppose that all the changes are adaptations to the prevailing environment or way of life. Exactly the same is true of inherited or genetic differences. In any population there are, as we shall see later, very many genetic differences between individuals. People may differ genetically, in such outwardly obvious features as their hair colour or their eye colour, or in unseen 'constitutional' characters, such as their blood types. Geneticists call the makeup of an individual his genotype. Thus people with blue eyes have a different genotype from those with brown or green eyes, at least as far as those genes determining eye colour are concerned. The frequencies of the various genotypes may be quite different in different populations. Thus the frequency of the blue-eyed genotype is, for example, much higher in Caucasian populations of European origin than in any other type of population. Genotype frequencies may change simply by chance, just like cultural differences, but such chance variations tend to be more important for small than for large populations.

Many, if not most, genetic changes are adaptive. By adaptive I mean that some one or more of those genotypes which are better suited to the environment leave more offspring or survive better, and so contribute relatively more to the next generation of individuals. This is the process of natural selection. Natural selection is the major agent of evolution because it is a major cause of changes in the genetic constitution of a population.

There are two major differences between cultural and inherited characteristics of populations. First, cultural characteristics tend to apply to all individuals of a population, whereas inherited differences are mostly measured by the frequency with which they occur in the population. Thus, while all members of a population will, for example, speak the same language and wear similar types of clothing, an inherited variation, such as blue versus green or brown eyes, may be found in a number of different populations, but it may occur with different frequencies in each of them. This means that a population is mostly characterized, not by being altogether of one or another genotype, but by the frequency with which the genotype is found in it. Blue eyes, for example, are certainly more common in northern than in southern Europe. But by no means are all northerners blue-eyed, and some blue eyes will be found in the south. The second major difference between cultural and inherited characteristics, is in the way that they are transmitted from individual to individual. Inherited traits are passed on from parents to offspring in accordance with Mendel's laws of genetics. Changes in the frequency of inherited traits depend on differences in the rate at which people of the various genotypes reproduce relative to one another. Genetic changes like these always take many generations, even when fairly strong natural selection is involved. Cultural characteristics, on the other hand, are not only passed from parents to offspring, but may be passed on from any one individual to another by word of mouth or by writing. So some cultural changes may be adopted quite quickly by a whole population. Transmission of culture is rather like transmission of an infection. Flu and cold epidemics spread very quickly, especially with the large amount of contact that people of all countries of the world now have with each other. In the same way cultural habits such as pop music preferences and clothing fashions may spread very quickly nowadays especially through the media of radio and television. However, other deep-rooted cultural characteristics of races and racial subgroups are much more difficult to change. These are the cultural patterns that are so resistant to alteration that they have the appearance of being innate; indeed, the difficulties in changing attitudes to school performance and in changing IQ in deprived populations, reflect in part, the difficulty in changing a cultural pattern.

Genetic Polymorphism

Traditionally people have thought of human races in terms of outwardly obvious features such as skin colour, hair colour and texture, facial and other physical characteristics, whose inheritance cannot yet be explained in terms of simple gene differences whose pattern of occurrence in families follows Mendel's laws. Many common genetic differences are, however, known which are simply inherited but are not outwardly obvious and have no untoward effects. Most geneticists now would say that the only biologically valid approach to defining races is in terms of such simply inherited differences.

These simply inherited differences are mostly identified by laboratory tests on blood cells or serum. Perhaps the best known example of such differences, are the ABO blood types. Blood donors always have to have their blood ABO typed for transfusion, so as to match their potential recipients. There are four common ABO types, A, B, AB and O which are genetically determined. An individual's type is determined by which versions of the gene responsible for making A, B or O substances he carries. Thus one form of the gene makes A, another B, and the third form neither. For example, individuals both of whose ABO genes are of the third form, are type O, while those with one A and one B gene, are type AB. (Remember that genes occur in pairs, one from each parent.) Geneticists call different versions of a gene, like those for the A or B substances, alleles.

Apart from identical twins, all people look different. The outward physical features by which we distinguish people are paralleled by simple inherited differences such as the ABO blood types. Such genetic traits are called polymorphisms, when the alternative versions of the genes that determine them, or the alleles as the geneticist calls them, each occur within a population with a substantial frequency. In the case of the ABO blood types, the allele A occurs in Cauca-

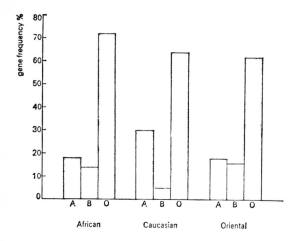

Figure 1: Frequencies of polymorphic genes among Africans, Caucasians and Orientals provide a means of differentiating these three races biologically. The columns represent the frequencies with which the genes of the ABO blood group system occurs in these races.

sian populations with a frequency of 28 per cent, the B allele in 6 per cent and the O allele in 66 per cent. Over thirty such polymorphic genetic systems, including the blood groups, in which alternative genetic forms of a trait occur are already known and new ones are being discovered all the time. These thirty polymorphisms alone are enough to identify almost everyone as unique.

What proportion of genes occurring with a substantial frequency are polymorphic? The answer seems to be at least 30 per cent and could be even more.

So, the thirty or so polymorphisms we now know are a minute fraction of the total of more than 300,000 that must exist, taking into account the total number of genes in the human genome. The potential for genetic differences between individuals is truly staggering. The numbers of genetically different types of sperm or eggs which any one single individual could in principle produce, is many millionfold more than the number of humans that have ever lived. The polymor-

phisms so far discovered concern mainly chemical substances in the blood. Among those still to be discovered must surely be many which affect the chemical substances of the brain and involve behavioural differences. It is clear that the extraordinary genetic uniqueness of human individuals applies not just to the blood but to all physical, physiological and mental attributes. This enormous genetic variety within a population seems to be a property of almost all species.

Variation in Gene Frequencies Between Races

If we look at the blood types and other polymorphisms in races we find that the frequencies of polymorphic genes vary widely. Geneticists use these frequencies to define races. In Oriental populations, for instance, the frequency of the gene for the blood type B is 17 per cent while it is only 6 per cent in Caucasians (see Figure 1). This means that type B individuals are generally three times as common in most of Asia than they are in Europe. All the known polymorphisms differ at least to some extent in their frequencies between different populations, though some are much more variable than others. One of the major tools in helping to work out the relationships between populations or races has been the analysis of the frequencies of genetic polymorphisms. In simple terms, the more similar are the polymorphic frequencies, the more closely related are the populations. A comparison of polymorphic frequencies in different races shows three very important features of the nature of genetic variation within and among them. Perhaps most important, the extent of variation *within* any population is usually far greater than the average difference *between* populations; in other words there is a great deal of overlap (for IQ see, for example, Figure 5). Then, differences between populations and races are mostly measured by differences in the frequencies of the various genetic polymorphisms. They are not measured by whether or not a given gene is present. Any particular genetic combination may be found in almost any race, but the *frequency* with which it is found will vary from one race to another. Some genetic differences may simply be present or absent and so are, to some extent, characteristic of a race. Genes like this are clearly very useful in helping to delineate the human races, but they are very much the exception rather than the rule. Most genetic differences between populations can only be measured on average. It is this fact which underlies the need to distinguish differences among *individuals* from differences among *populations*. The final point about the study of polymorphic frequencies is that the distinction between races is often quite blurred. This is mainly the result of interbreeding between races at their boundaries, and of the mixing effect of large migrations. Even in the United States, where marriage between American blacks and whites is still quite rare, it is estimated that up to 30 per cent of the genes of the average black American from the northern states can be traced to white ancestry. This, of course, represents the cumulative effect of a number of generations during each of which a small amount of interbreeding took place. The American blacks are now clearly a new population genetically, which has been formed from a mixture of black Africans and white Americans. The Jews provide another example of the blending of racial distinctions. They are all presumably derived from one population, or at most a few closely related populations, of biblical times. Gene frequency studies, however, show that now Jewish populations in different parts of the world tend to resemble their surrounding populations at least as much, if not more, than they do each other. Such genetic studies, when combined with historical information, and sociological ideas of race and culture, can be very useful in understanding the origin of modern populations. Still remembering that most of the psychological and sociological studies of race are based on cultural determination of the boundaries, the definition of race in terms of differences in the frequencies of genetic polymorphisms is fairly arbitrary. How much difference does there have to be between populations before we call them different races? After all, even the people of, say, Lancashire and Yorkshire are likely to differ significantly in the frequency of at least some polymorphisms, but we should hardly refer to them as different races. On the other hand, most people would agree that the differences between the indigenous peoples of the major continents, such as the differences between Africans, Orientals and Caucasians, are obvious enough to merit the label race. Between these two extremes, however, lie a multitude of possibilities and it is largely a matter of taste as to whether one is a splitter or a lumper of population groups into races.

Inheritance of Complex or Quantitative Characters

Heredity refers to the transmission of characteristics from parent to offspring. The primary biological functional unit of heredity is the gene, and the human genome—the complete set of genes which characterizes the biological inheritance of an individual—may consist of as many as five to ten million genes. Some of these genes can be individually identified by their patterns of inheritance in families, and the expression of many of these analysed at the biochemical level. The inheritance of differences between individuals which are known to be determined by one or a few genes can thus be reliably predicted and, in some cases, the biochemical or physiological basis for the inherited differences clearly established. Intelligence is, however, a composite and complex character, the expression of which must be dependent on a combination of the effects of environmental factors and the products of many different genes, each gene probably only having a small effect on measured IQ. The tools for dealing with the inheritance of such complex characters are necessarily complicated and still relatively ineffective.

As we have noted, intelligence must be a complex characteristic under the control of many genes. However, extreme deviations from normal levels, as in the cases of severe mental retardation, can sometimes be attributed to single gene differences. Such deviations can serve to illustrate important ways in which genetic factors can affect behaviour. Consider the disease phenylketonuria (PKU). Individuals with this receive from both of their parents a mutated version of the gene controlling the enzyme that converts one amino acid, phenylalanine, into another, tyrosine. The mutated gene allows phenylalanine to accumulate in the blood and in the brain, causing mental retardation. The accumulation can, to some extent, be checked early in life by a diet deficient in phenylalanine.

The difference between the amounts of phenylalanine in the blood of people with PKU and that in the blood of normal people, which is closely related to the primary activity of the gene causing PKU, clearly creates two genetic classes of individuals. When such differences are compared with differences in IQ, there is a slight overlap, but individuals afflicted with PKU can be distinguished clearly from normal individuals. It is, indeed, routine today to test all babies for the tell-tale presence of ketone bodies with a nappy or urine test that reveals the phenylketonuric genotype, that is, the genetic constitution that leads to PKU which is associated with extreme mental retardation. If differences in head size and hair colour in phenylketonuric individuals and normal individuals are compared, however, they show a considerable overlap. Although it can be said that the phenylketonuric genotype has a statistically significant effect on both head

size and hair colour, it is not, given the large variations of head size and hair colour among PKU individuals, an effect large enough to distinguish the phenylketonuric genotype from the normal one (see Figures 2a and 2b). Thus the genetic difference between phenylketonuric and normal individuals contributes in a major way to the variation in blood phenylalanine levels but has only a minor, although significant effect on head size and hair colour.

The phenylketonuric genotype is very rare, occurring with a frequency of only about one individual in 10,000. It therefore has little effect on the overall distribution of IQ in the population. However, among all the genes which are polymorphic must be included many whose effect on IQ is comparable to the effect of the phenylketonuric genotype on head size or hair colour. These genotype differences cannot be individually identified, but their total effect on the variation of IQ may be considerable.

The nature of PKU demonstrates another important point: the expression of a gene is profoundly influenced by environment. Phenylketonuric individuals show appreciable variation. This indicates that the genetic difference involved in PKU is by no means the only factor, or even the major factor, affecting the level of phenylalanine in the blood. It is obvious that dietary differences have a large effect, since a phenylalanine-deficient diet brings the level of this amino acid in the blood of a phenylketonuric individual almost down to normal. If an individual receives the phenylketonuric gene from only one parent, his mental development is not likely to be clinically affected. Nevertheless, he will tend to have higher than normal levels of phenylalanine in his blood. The overall variation in phenylalanine level is therefore the result of a combination of genetic factors and environmental factors. Measuring the relative contribution of genetic factors to the overall variation is thus equivalent to measuring the relative importance of genetic differences in

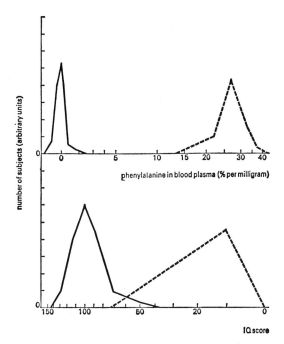

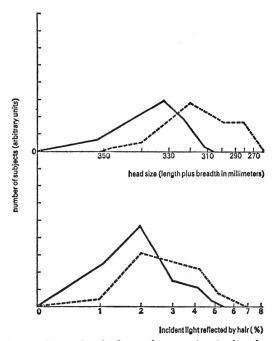

Figure 2a: Phenylalanine levels in blood plasma in first set of curves (top) distinguish those who carry a double dose of the defective gene that causes high phenylalanine levels (broken curve), a condition called phenylketonuria from those normal phenylalaline levels (solid curve). Second set of curves (bottom) show that this genotype has a direct effect on intelligence: phenylketonurics (broken curve) have low IQs because accumulation of phenylalanine and its by-products in blood are nerve tissue damages to the brain. Individuals with functioning gene (solid curve) have normal IQs.

Figure 2b: In the third set of curves (top) phenylalanine levels are related to head size (displayed as the sum of the head length and breadth), and in the fourth set (bottom) phenylalanine levels are related to hair colour (displayed as percentage of light with the wavelength of 700 millimicrons reflected by the hair). In both cases it is obvious that the phenylketonuris genotype has a significant effect on each of these characteristics: the reflectance is greater and the head size is smaller (broken curves) among phenylketonurics than they are among normal individuals (solid curves). Yet the distribution of these characteristics is such that they cannot be used to distinguish those afflicted with phenylketonuria from those who are not.

determining this type of quantitative variation.

Characters determined by the joint action of many genes, like height and IQ, are often called quantitative characters because they are measured on a continuous scale. They are much more susceptible to environmental influences than are polymorphisms such as the blood groups which seem to be pretty well independent of all environmental factors. Because the contribution of individual genes to such characters cannot easily be recognized, one has to resort to complex statistical analyses to sort out the relative contribu-

tions of heredity and environment. These analyses try to assess the extent to which relatives tend to be more like each other than they are to unrelated or to more distantly related people.

The occurrence of identical and non-identical twins is a sort of natural experiment that illustrates very simply the way in which environmental and genetic factors can be separated. Identical (or monozygotic = MZ) twins are derived from a single fertilized egg and so are identical genetically. Any differences between them must, therefore, be due to the environment. Non-identical (or dizygotic = DZ) twins come from two eggs fertilized at the same time by different sperm and so are as different, or alike, genetically as any brothers or sisters. Both types of twins are usually brought up within a family and so, on average, are subject to more or less the same types of environmental variation. The extent to which non-identical twins differ more than identical twins is thus an indication of the importance of genetic factors in differentiating the non-identical twins. Differences in IQ among non-identical pairs show a greater spread than those among identical pairs, indicating that the genetic diversity among the non-identical pairs adds to the purely environmental differences which differentiate the identical pairs of twins. A comparison of the average difference between members of individual identical pairs and the average difference between members of non-identical pairs, could in principle be taken as a measure of the relative importance of genetic and environmental factors. (For statistical reasons, it is usually better to consider not the mean differences but their squares. These are directly related to the *variance*, which is a well-known statistical measure of the spread of a distribution.)

There are two major contrasting reasons why such a simple measure is not entirely satisfactory. First, the difference between members of a dizygous pair represents only a fraction of the genetic differences that can exist between two individuals. Dizygous twins are related to each other as two siblings are; therefore they are more closely related than two individuals taken at random from a population. This implies a substantial reduction (roughly by a factor of two) in the average genetic difference between dizygous twins compared with that between two randomly chosen individuals. Secondly the environmental difference between members of a pair of twins encom-

passes only a fraction of the total environmental difference that can exist between two individuals, namely the difference between individuals belonging to the same family. This does not take into account differences among families, which are likely to be large. Within the family the environmental differences between twins are limited. For instance, the effect of birth order is not taken into account. Differences between ordinary siblings might therefore tend to be slightly greater than those between dizygous twins. It also seems possible that the environmental differences between monozygous twins, who tend to establish special relations with each other, are not exactly comparable to those between dizygous twins. In short, whereas the contrast between monozygous and dizygous twin pairs minimizes genetic differences, it also tends to minimize environmental differences.

In order to take account of such difficulties one must try to use all available comparisons between relatives of various types and degrees, of which twin data are only a selected case. For technical reasons one often measures similarities rather than differences between two sets of values such as parent IQs and offspring IQs. Such a measure of similarity is called the correlation coefficient. It is equal to 1 when the pairs of values in the two sets are identical or, more generally, when one value is expressible as a linear function of the other. The correlation coefficient is 0 when the pairs of measurements are completely independent, and it is intermediate if there is a relation between the two sets such that one tends to increase when the other increases.

The mean observed values of the correlation coefficient between parent and child IQs and between the IQs of pairs of siblings, are close to 0.5. This is the value one would expect on the basis of the simplest genetic model in which the effects of any number of genes determine IQ and there are no environmental influences or complications of any kind. It seems probable, however, that the observed correlation of 0.5 is coincidental. Complicating factors such as different modes of gene action, tendencies for like to mate with like and environmental correlations among members of the same family must just happen to balance one another almost exactly to give a result that agrees with the simplest theoretical expectation. If we ignored these complications, we might conclude naively (and in contradiction to other evidence, such as the observations on twins) that biological inheritance of the simplest kind entirely determines IQ.

Heritability of IQ

We need a means of determining the relative importance of environmental factors and genetic factors, taking account of several of the complications. In theory this measurement can be made by computing the quotients known as heritability estimates. To understand what such quotients are intended to measure, consider a simplified situation. Imagine that the genotype of each individual with respect to genes affecting IQ can be identified. Individuals with the same genotype can then be grouped together. The differences among them would be the result of environmental factors, and the spread of the distribution of such differences could then be measured. Assume for the sake of simplicity that the spread of IQ due to environmental differences is the same for each genotype. If we take the IQs of all the individuals in the population, we obtain a distribution that yields the total variation of IQ. The variation within each genotype is the environmental component. The difference between the total variation and the environmental component of variation leaves a component of the total variation that must be accounted for by genetic differences. This component, when expressed as a fraction of the total variance, is one possible measure of heritability.

In practice, however, the estimation of the component of the total variation that can be accounted for by genetic differences (from data on correlations between relatives) always depends on the construction of specific genetic models, and is therefore subject to the limitations of the models. One problem lies in the fact that there are a number of alternative definitions of heritability depending on the genetic model chosen, because the genetic variation may have many components that can have quite different meanings. A definition that includes only those parts of the genetic variation generally considered to be most relevant in animal and plant breeding is often used. This is called heritability in the narrow sense. If all genetic sources of variation are included, then the heritability estimate increases and is referred to as heritability in the broad sense.

The differences between these estimates of heritability can be defined quite precisely in terms of specific genetic models. The resulting estimates of heritability, however, can vary considerably. Typical heritability estimates for IQ (derived from the London population in the early 1950s, with data obtained by Sir Cyril Burt) give values of 45 to 60 per cent for heritability in the narrow sense and 80 to 85 per cent for heritability in the broad sense.

A further major complication for such heritability estimates has the technical name 'genotype–environment interaction.' The difficulty is that the realized IQ of given genotypes in different environments cannot be predicted in a simple way. A given genotype may develop better in one environment than in another. In man there is no way of controlling the environment. Even if all environmental influences relevant to behavioural development were known, their statistical control by appropriate measurements and subsequent statistical analysis of the data would still be extremely difficult. It should therefore be emphasized that, because estimates of heritability depend on the extent of environmental and genetic

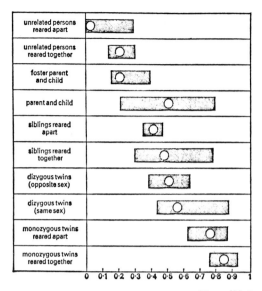

correlation coefficient

Figure 3: Correlation coefficients are representative of similarities and differences. A coefficient of 1 indicates that the two classes compared are identical. 0 indicates independence of one value from the other. The horizontal bars represent the range differences in coefficients found in the relationships shown. The mean of the range is represented by the circle in each bar. A mean coefficient of 0.50 is that which would be expected if there were no environmental effects in IQ. As other evidence indicates that environment exerts a significant effect, these calculations must be further refined. These data are extracted from the work of Erienmeyer-Kimling and Jarvik.

variation that prevails in the population examined at the time of analysis, they are not valid for other populations or for the same population at a different time.

The investigation of the same genotype or similar genotypes in different environments can provide valuable controls over environmental effects. In man this can be done only through the study of adopted children. A particularly interesting type of 'adoption' is that in which monozygous twins are separated and reared in different families from birth or soon afterwards. The outcome is in general a relatively minor average

decrease in similarity. Following the same line of reasoning, the similarity between foster parents and adopted children can be measured and contrasted with that between biological parents and their children (see Figure 3). The results show that, though the correlation between foster parents and their children is significantly greater than 0, it is undoubtedly less than that between biological parents and their offspring. However, a complete analysis of such data is difficult because children are not adopted at random and so even adoption does not provide a convincing control over the environment. Nevertheless, on the basis of all the available data and allowing for the limitations to its interpretations, the heritability of IQ is still fairly high. It must be emphasized however, that the environmental effects in essentially all the studies done so far are limited to the differences among and within families of fairly homogeneous sections of the British or United States populations. The results cannot therefore be extrapolated to the prediction of the effects of greater differences in environment or to other types of differences.

IQ and Social Class

There are significant differences in mean IQ among the various social classes. One of the most comprehensive and widely quoted studies of such differences and the reasons for their apparent stability over the years was published by Burt in 1961 (see Figure 4). His data come from schoolchildren and their parents in a typical London borough. Socio-economic level was classified, on the basis of type of occupation, into six classes. These range from Class 1, including 'university teachers, those of similar standing in law, medicine, education or the Church and the top people in commerce, industry or civil service,' to Class 6, including 'unskilled labourers and those employed in coarse manual work.' There are four main features of these data:

1. Parental mean IQ and occupational class are closely related. The mean difference between the highest and the lowest class is over 50. Although occupational class is determined mostly by the father, the relatively high correlation between the IQs of husband and wife (about 0.4) contributes to the differentiation among the classes with respect to IQ.
2. In spite of the significant variation between the parental mean IQs, the residual variation in IQ among parents within each class is still remarkably large. The mean standard deviation of the parental IQs for the different classes is 8.6, almost three-fifths of the standard deviation for the entire group. That standard deviation is contrived in test construction to be about 15.
3. The mean IQ of the offspring for each class lies almost exactly between the parental mean IQs and the overall population mean IQ of 100. This is expected because it is only another way of looking at the correlation for IQ between parent and child, which as we have already seen tends to be about 0.5 in any given population.[1]
4. The last important feature of the data is that the standard deviations of the IQ of the offspring, which average 13.2, are almost the same as the standard deviation of the general population, namely 15. This is another indi-

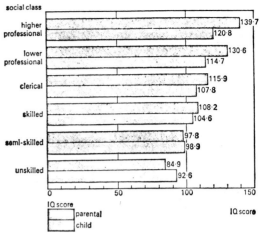

Figure 4: An English study by Burt indicates that intelligence and social class are closely related. The darker bars represent parental IQs for the social classes while the lighter bar indicates the IQ of their children. The phenomenon of children of above average parents having lower IQ scores is known as regression to the mean, and children of low-IQ parents exhibit an upward trend towards the population mean.

cation of the existence of considerable variability of IQ within social classes. Such variability is almost as much as that in the entire population.

The most straightforward interpretation of these data is that IQ is itself a major determinant of occupational class and that it is to an appreciable extent inherited (although the data cannot be used to distinguish cultural inheritance from biological). Burt pointed out that, because of

---

[1] We must note an important fallacy in Eysenck's (and others') argument that 'regression presents strong evidence for genetic determination of IQ differences.' In any multi-causal system, such as that involved in the determination of IQ, there will be many factors which will tend to increase performance, and others that work to decrease it. In the average situation these will balance and give the mean IQ of 100. Less commonly they will not balance and we will get extreme IQs, well above or below the mean. These extreme cases arise from relatively rare interactions of genes and environment where (at least statisti-

cally) most of the causal factors are pushing in one direction. It is extremely unlikely that this situation will hold for children of very high or very low IQ parents. Things will tend to be more equal and causal factors more nearly balance, so the children's IQ will regress to the mean and the largest regression will be seen in the children of extreme IQ parents. All the presence of regression tells us is that the system is multi-causal. It says nothing about the origin of these causes. Indeed, it is theoretically possible to have regression to the mean in an entirely environmentally controlled system. [Eds.]

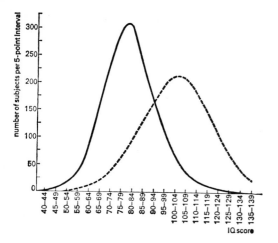

ever since Francis Galton pointed out this correlation for the British ruling class in the second half of the nineteenth century. If there were such a persistent association, if IQ were at least in part genetically determined and if there were no counteracting environmental effects, such a decline in IQ could be expected. The fact is that no significant decline has been detected so far. The existing data, although they are admittedly limited, do not support the idea of a persistent negative correlation between IQ and overall reproductivity.

Figure 5: IQ difference between blacks and whites in the USA emerges from a comparison of the IQ distribution in a representative sample of whites (broken curve) with the IQ distribution among 1800 black children in the schools of Alabama, Florida, Georgia, Tennessee and South Carolina (black curve). Wallace A. Kennedy of Florida State University who surveyed the students' IQ found that the mean IQ of this group was 80.7. The mean IQ of the whites is 101.3, a difference of 21.1 points. The two samples overlap distinctly but there is also a sizable difference between the two means. Other studies show a difference of 10 to 20 points, making Kennedy's results one of the most extreme reported.

IQ–Race Differences

The average frequency of marriages between blacks and whites throughout the U.S. is still only about 2 per cent of the frequency that would be expected if marriages occurred at random with respect to race. This reflects the persistent high level of reproductive isolation between the races, in spite of the movement in recent years towards a strong legal stance in favour of desegregation. Hawaii is a notable exception to this separation of the races, although even there the observed frequency of mixed marriages is still only 45 to 50 per cent of what would be expected if matings occurred at random.

Many studies have shown the existence of substantial differences in the distribution of IQ in U.S. blacks and whites. Such data were obtained in an extensive study published by Wallace A. Kennedy of Florida State University and his co-workers in 1963, based on IQ tests given to 1800 black children in elementary school in five south-eastern states (Florida, Georgia, Alabama, Tennessee and South Carolina) (see Figure 5). When the distribution these workers found is compared with a 1960 sample of the U.S. white population, striking differences emerge. The mean difference in IQ between blacks and whites is 21.1, whereas the standard

the wide distribution of IQ within each class among the offspring and the regression of the offspring to the population mean, appreciable mobility among classes is needed in each generation to maintain the class differences with respect to IQ. He estimated that to maintain a stable distribution of IQ differences among classes, at least 22 per cent of the offspring would have to change class, mainly as a function of IQ, in each generation. This figure is well below the observed intergenerational social mobility in Britain, which is about 30 per cent.

Fears that there may be a gradual decline in IQ because of an apparent negative correlation between IQ and fertility have been expressed deviation of the distribution among blacks is some 25 per cent less than that of the distribution among whites (12.4 v. 16.4). As one would expect there is considerable overlap between the two distributions, because the variability for IQ within any population is (like the variability for most characteristics) substantially greater than the variability between any two populations. Nevertheless, 95.5 per cent of the blacks have an IQ below the white mean of 101.8 and 18.4 per cent have an IQ of less than 70. Only 2 per cent of the whites have IQs in the latter range.

Reported differences between the mean IQs of blacks and whites generally lie between 10 and 20, so that the value found by Kennedy and his colleagues is one of the most extreme reported. The difference is usually less for blacks from the northern states than it is for those from the southern states, and clearly it depends heavily on the particular populations tested. One well-known study of army 'alpha' intelligence-test results, for example, showed that blacks from some northern states achieved higher average scores than whites from some southern states, although whites always scored higher than blacks from the same state. There are many uncertainties and variables that influence the outcome of IQ tests, but the observed mean differences between U.S. blacks and whites are undoubtedly more or less reproducible and are quite striking.

There are two main features that clearly distinguish IQ differences among social classes described above from those between blacks and whites. First, the IQ differences among social classes relate to the environmental variation within the relatively homogeneous British population. It cannot be assumed that this range of environmental variation is comparable with the average environmental difference between black and white Americans. Secondly, and more important, these differences are maintained by the mobility among occupational classes that is based to a significant extent on selection for higher IQ

in the higher occupational classes. There is clearly no counterpart of this mobility with respect to the differences between U.S. blacks and whites; skin colour effectively bars mobility between the races.

The arguments for a substantial genetic component in the IQ difference between the races assume that existing heritability estimates for IQ can reasonably be applied to the racial difference. These estimates, however, are based on observations within the white population. We have emphasized that heritability estimates apply only to the population studied and to its particular environment. Thus the extrapolation of existing heritability estimates to the racial differences assumes that the environmental differences between the races are comparable to the environmental variation within them. Let us consider a simple model example which shows that there is no logical connection between heritability as determined within races and the genetic differences between them. Suppose we take a bag of seed collected from a field of wheat and sow one handful on barren, stony ground and another one on rich, fertile ground. The seeds sown on fertile ground will clearly grow more vigorously and give a much higher yield per plant than that sown on barren ground. If we were to study the extent to which individual differences in yield between the plants grown on the fertile ground were genetically determined, we should expect to find comparable genetic differences to those which existed between the plants grown in the original wheat field from which our bag of seed was collected. The same would be true for the differences between the individual plants growing on the barren ground. The fact that there are genetic differences between these plants both on the fertile and on the barren ground clearly does not have anything to do with the overall differences between the two sets of plants grown in these two very different environments. This we know must be due to the differences in the soil.

The genetic stock from which all the plants were derived was, after all, the same. It was the original one bag of seed. The same logic must apply to the human situation. How can we be sure that the different environments of U.S. blacks and whites are not comparable to the barren and fertile soils? Our original bag of human genes may not be as uniform as the wheat field, but why should the differences between the original human samples, the Africans and the Caucasians, have anything to do with conventional IQ measurements? Whether or not the variation in IQ within either race is entirely genetic or entirely environmental has no bearing on the question of the relative contribution of genetic factors and environmental factors to the differences between the races.

IQ and Environment

A major argument given by Jensen, Eysenck and others in favour of a substantial genetic component to the IQ difference is that it persists even when comparisons are made between U.S. blacks and whites of the same socio-economic status. This status is defined in terms of schooling, occupation and income, and so it is necessarily a measure of at least a part of the environmental variation, comparable to the class differences we have discussed here.

Taken on face value—that is, on the assumption that status is truly a measure of the total environment—these data would indicate that the IQ difference is genetically determined. It is difficult to see, however, how the status of blacks and whites can be compared. The very existence of a racial stratification correlated with a relative socio-economic deprivation makes this comparison suspect. Black schools are well known to be generally less adequate than white schools, so that equal numbers of years of schooling certainly do not mean equal educational attainment.

Wide variation in the level of occupation must exist within each occupational class. Thus one would certainly expect, even for equivalent occupational classes, that the black level is on the average lower than the white. No amount of money can buy a black person's way into a privileged, upper-class, white community, or buy off more than two hundred years of accumulated racial prejudice on the part of the whites, or reconstitute the disrupted black family, in part culturally inherited from the days of slavery. It is impossible to accept the idea that matching for status provides an adequate, or even a substantial, control over the most important environmental differences between blacks and whites.

Let us consider just two examples of environmental effects on IQ which show both how complicated is the environment and how large can be the effects of environmental differences. The first concerns a comparison of the IQs of twins and triplets as compared to single births. A number of studies have shown that twins have an IQ that is systematically about 5 points lower than non-twins. This reduction seems to be independent of socio-economic variables and of such other factors as parental age, birth order, overall family size, gestation time and birth weight as has been shown particularly convincingly by a recent study carried out in Birmingham, England, by Record, McKeown and Edwards. These authors based their study on the results of verbal reasoning tests given in the 11+ examinations during the period from 1950 to 1954. The average scores for 48,913 single births and 2164 twin births were 100.1 and 95.7 respectively. Furthermore the average score for 33 triplets was 91.6, another 4 points lower, while the average score for 148 twins, whose co-twins were stillborn or died within four weeks after birth was 98.8. This, they point out, is only very little lower than the score of 99.5, which is obtained by standardizing the data to the maternal ages and birth ranks observed for these 148 twins. The environmental factor involved in this remarkable effect on IQ must be post-natal and may well have something to do with the reduced attention parents are able to give each of two very young children born at the same time. This one subtle factor in the familial environment, which clearly is not reflected in standard measurements of socio-economic status, has an effect on IQ which is about one-third of the overall average difference between U.S. blacks and whites. Measuring the environment only by standard socio-economic parameters, is a little bit like trying to assess the character of an individual by his height, weight and eye colour.

The second example of a major environmental effect comes from a well known study of adopted children. Skodac and Skeels studied the IQs of a series of white children placed into adopted homes through Orphans' Home Institutions in Iowa, mostly before the infants were six months old, and compared these IQs with the IQs of their foster parents and of their biological parents. As in other similar studies they found a higher correlation between the IQs of the adopted children and their biological parents than with their foster parents. Most strikingly, however, they found that while the mean IQ of the 63 adopted children who had been followed through until they were about thirteen to fourteen years old was 106, the mean IQ of the biological mothers of these 63 children was only 85.5, a difference of fully 20 points! Even if one assumes that the biological mothers came from a low socio-economic group and that their husbands had the population average IQ of 100 and that IQ is completely genetically determined, the expected average IQ of the children would be only one half $(100 + 85.5) = 92.75$. The difference between expected and observed is still $106 - 92.75 = 13.25$ points, which is just about the same as the average U.S. black–white IQ difference. The adoptive homes were strongly biased towards the upper socio-economic strata. This study thus shows what a striking effect an improved home background can have on IQ. In Skodak and Skeels's own words, 'the implications for placing agencies justify a policy of early placement in adoptive homes offering emotional warmth and security in an above average educational and social setting.'

Why Should There Be a Genetic Component to the Race–IQ Difference?

Jensen has stated that because the gene pools of whites and blacks are known to differ and 'these genetic differences are manifested in virtually every anatomical, physiological and biochemical comparison one can make between representative samples of identifiable racial groups . . . there is no reason to suppose that the brain should be exempt from this generalization.' But there is no *a priori* reason why genes affecting IQ, which differ in the gene pools of blacks and whites, should be such that on the average whites have significantly more genes increasing IQ than blacks do. On the contrary, one should expect, assuming no tendency for high IQ genes to accumulate by selection in one race or the other, that the more polymorphic genes there are that affect IQ and that differ in frequency in blacks and whites, the less likely it is that there is an average genetic difference in IQ between the races. The same argument applies to the differences between any two racial groups.

Since natural selection is the principal agent of genetic change, is it possible that this force has produced a significant IQ difference between American blacks and whites? Using the simple theory with which plant and animal breeders predict responses to artificial selection, one can make a rough guess at the amount of selection that would have been needed to result in a difference of about 15 IQ points, such as exists between blacks and whites. The calculation is based on three assumptions: that there was no initial difference in IQ between Africans and Caucasians, that the heritability of IQ in the narrow sense is about 50 per cent and that the divergence of black Americans from Africans started with slavery about two hundred years, or seven generations, ago. This implies a mean change in IQ of about 2 points per generation. The predictions of the theory are that this rate of change could be achieved by the complete elimination from reproduction of about 15 per cent of the most intelligent individuals in each generation. There is certainly no good basis for assuming such a level of selection against IQ during the period of slavery.

Eysenck has actually suggested as one basis for genetic differences that significant selection might have taken place during the procurement of slaves in Africa. He proposes, for example, that the more intelligent were less likely to be caught or that the less intelligent were the ones that were sold off by their tribal chiefs. If one makes the extreme assumption that this initial selection is the sole cause of a 15 point IQ difference between U.S. blacks and whites, then following the same lines of analysis that were used above, the slaves that were caught or sold must have been in the bottom 5 per cent as far as IQ is concerned. This would seem to indicate that the tribal chiefs knew how to administer and interpret IQ tests almost as well as we do today! It is clearly very difficult, if not impossible, to assess the role that natural selection might have played in accentuating IQ differences between the races. Certainly any hypothesis one chooses to put forward is in the realm of unsubstantiated speculation and cannot be claimed as even suggestive evidence for a substantial genetic component to the race–IQ difference.

One approach to studying this question that has been suggested by Shockley, Eysenck and others is to correlate IQ measurements with an assessment of the proportion of Caucasian genes in different samples of U.S. blacks. The proportion of Caucasian genes in a sample of U.S. blacks can be estimated from a comparison of the frequencies of polymorphic genes in Caucasians, African blacks and U.S. blacks. This approach would mean that groups with different degrees of admixture of 'white' and 'black' genes would have to be studied for their IQ. It is known, however, that the degree of admixture varies from less than 10 per cent in some southern states to more than 30 per cent in some northern states. For this knowledge to be useful, one has to assume that the environment is the same for all these populations and that there is no correlation between differences in the environment and the extent of the black–white admixture. One example of data that shows quite clearly that this is not true has been analysed by Spuhler and Lindzey. They pointed out that for both blacks and whites, the mean values per state of U.S. army alpha intelligence-test scores obtained during the First World War correlated precisely with the *per capita* state expenditure, at that time, on education. The states with a mean expenditure of less than $5 per head (Arkansas, Florida, Georgia, Kentucky, Louisiana, Mississippi, North and South Carolina, Tennessee, Texas and Virginia—*all* southern states) gave overall mean alpha scores of 50.2 for whites and 24.9 for blacks. The states with a mean expenditure of more than $10 (Illinois, Indiana, Kansas, New Jersey, New York, Ohio and Pennsylvania) gave mean alpha scores of 65.3 for whites and 44.9 for blacks. Southern whites hardly scored better than northern blacks, as pointed out long ago by J. B. S. Haldane. Any hope of using such data for genetic studies is clearly out of the question.

The only approach applicable to the study of the IQ difference between the races is that of working with black children adopted into white homes and vice versa. The adoptions would, of course, have to be at an early age to be sure of taking into account any possible effects of the early home environment. The IQs of black children adopted into white homes would also have to be compared with those of white children adopted into comparable white homes. To our knowledge no scientifically adequate studies of this nature have ever been undertaken. It is questionable whether or not such studies could be done in a reasonably controlled way at the present time. Even if they could, they would not remove the effects of prejudice directed against black people in most white communities. It therefore seems that the question of a possible genetic basis for the race–IQ difference will be almost impossible to answer satisfactorily before the environmental differences between U.S. blacks and whites have been substantially reduced.

Jensen has stated on the basis of his assessment of the data (and Eysenck quotes him):

so all we are left with are various lines of evidence no one of which is definitive alone, but which, viewed all together, make it a not unreasonable hypothesis that genetic factors are strongly implicated in the average Negro–white intelligence difference. The preponderance of evidence is, in my opinion, less consistent with a strictly environmental hypothesis than with a genetic hypothesis, which of course does not exclude the influence of environment or its interaction with genetic factors.

My assessment of the evidence made together with my colleague Professor Cavalli-Sforza and published in an article in the *Scientific American* —and this is an assessment that we share with many of our geneticist colleagues—is that we simply do not have enough evidence at present to resolve the question. It seems to us that differences in IQ, for instance, between American blacks and whites, could be explained by environmental factors, many of which we still know nothing about. This does not mean that we exclude the possibility that there might be a genetic component to such a mean IQ differ-ence. We simply maintain that currently available data are inadequate to resolve this question in either direction and that we cannot see how the question could be satisfactorily answered using presently available techniques.

What Use Can Be Made of Knowledge Concerning Genetic Components to Race–IQ Differences?

The Nobel prize-winning U.S. physicist, William Shockley, has repeatedly asked for a major expenditure of funds directed specifically at finding the answer to the question of a genetic component to the race–IQ difference and other similar questions, because of their practical importance. He has in fact said in this context:

I believe that a nation that achieved its ten-year objective of putting a man on the moon can wisely and humanely solve its human quality problems once the objective is stated and relevant facts courageously sought.

No one surely should argue against the need for a better scientific understanding of the basis of intellectual ability and the benefits to society that might accrue from such an understanding. But why concentrate this effort on the genetic basis for the race–IQ difference? Apart from the intrinsic, almost insurmountable difficulties in answering this question at the present time, it is not in any way clear what practical use could be made of the answers. Perhaps the only practical argument is that, since the question that the difference is genetic has been raised, an attempt should be made to answer it. Otherwise those who now believe that the difference is genetic will be left to continue their campaigns for an adjustment of our educational and economic systems to take account of 'innate' racial differences.

A demonstration that the difference is not primarily genetic could counter such campaigns. On the other hand, an answer in the opposite direction should not, in a genuinely democratic society free of race prejudice, make any difference. Our society professes to believe there should be no discrimination against an individual on the basis of race, religion or other *a priori* categorizations, including sex. Our accepted ethic holds that each individual should be given equal and maximum opportunity, according to his or her needs, to develop to his or her fullest potential. Surely innate differences in ability and other individual variations should be taken into account by our educational system. These differences must, however, be judged on the basis of the individual and not on the basis of race. To maintain otherwise indicates an inability to distinguish differences among individuals from differences among populations.

FURTHER READING

L. L. CAVALLI-SFORZA and W. F. BODMER, *The Genetics of Human Population*, Freeman, 1971.

T. DOBZHANSKY, *Mankind Evolving*, Yale University Press, 1962.

I. M. LERNER, *Heredity, Evolution and Society*, Freeman, 1968. This book is particularly suitable for the non-biologist.

J. MAYNARD-SMITH, *The Theory of Evolution*, Penguin, 1966.

Myths in Human Biology, BBC Publications, 1972. A collection of transcripts from recent radio talks.

34 • BRAIN SIZE, GREY MATTER AND RACE— FACT OR FICTION?

Phillip V. Tobias

It was, I believe, Havelock Ellis who once remarked, in connection with a discussion of the relation of intelligence to the characters of the brain and "race," that many a scientific reputation has been lost in the sinuous convolutions of that organ. Number, character, and depth of convolutions or gyri, thickness of the gray matter, form, weight, and volume of the brain, have all been cited by various writers as traits not only helpful in distinguishing one "race" from another, but also as supporting the view that some "races" are intellectually inferior to others. There is, in fact, an enormous literature on the subject, and the best book-length discussion of it I know is Donald G. Paterson, *Physique and Intellect* (New York: The Century Co., 1930), even though, paradoxically enough, it does not deal with the brain or central nervous system as such, but rather with measurements of the size and volume of the brain. It is a book too little known, out of print, and difficult to come by, but very much worth seeking out.

In the following contribution Tobias restricts himself to an examination of the claims that White or Caucasoid and Negro brains differ significantly in brain size and other cerebral traits. What he says in this contribution can be extended to the supposed differences alleged to exist between any populations and the relevance of those differences to any understanding of differences in achievement.

In most discussions in which such "differences" have been brought in to bolster the argument for "racial" superiority or inferiority, it is worth remarking that never to my knowledge have any of the proponents of these views pointed out that Mongoloid peoples have, on the average, larger brains than Caucasoid peoples by more than 100 cubic centimeters by volume, and that they should therefore be considered superior to all other peoples. There has, of course, been far too much prejudice and too little science in the discussion of these matters. Tobias' thoughtful contribution is therefore all the more welcome, since it presents without prejudice the facts as they are known to science.

Among the important facts established by Tobias is that brain size correlates more significantly with stature than it does with body weight; that much error has been committed in expressing brain size in relation to body weight instead of to stature; indeed, that all such body-weight–brain-weight comparisons are invalid.

Tobias also draws attention to the relation between brain size and nutritional experience. The evidence is today beyond dispute that poor nutrition of the mother during pregnancy may be severely damaging to the development of the brain, just as poor nutrition is damaging postnatally. Tobias cites some of the studies on which these conclusions are based.[1]

It is becoming increasingly clear that impoverished social conditions, even in the presence of adequate physical nutrition, may be just as damaging to the brain as poor physical malnutrition. For a discussion of this see Ashley Montagu, "Sociogenic Brain Damage," *American Anthropologist,* vol. 74, 1972, pp. 1045–61. Such considerations render worthless almost all conclusions about intellectual functions drawn from intergroup comparisons of the brain.

Tobias has a whole section on the meaninglessness of most studies on brain weight. The largest brain on record, weighing 2850 grams, belonged to an epileptoid idiot.[2] His position with respect to brain weight, brain size, or any of the other characteristics of the brain that have been cited in the literature as marks of difference between "the races" is that they simply cannot be used as such. That is the long and the short of it.

In this age of cellular and molecular biology, ever more refined techniques are being focussed on the central nervous system. Brains are being studied by electron microscopy, autoradiography, ultraviolet absorption spectromicrophotometry, biochemical analyses, cybernetic models, tissue culture and a host of other methods. In the light of these developments, it is almost inconceivable that anything remains to be said at all about so gross and crude a measure as the overall size of the brain. Yet, it is an astonishing fact that a great deal remains to be said and, I am afraid, much of it negative—for most that has already been asserted does not stand up to the cold light of scientific scrutiny.

The theme of this paper—"Brain-size, Grey Matter and Race—Fact or Fiction?"—is based upon the oft-repeated claims that the races of man have been shown to differ in quantity of brain substance and, especially, of grey matter in the cerebral cortex. More specifically, it is based upon the claims that Negroes have smaller brains than White or Caucasoid peoples and upon the frequently drawn inference that an apparently lesser intellectual performance by Negroes is based upon such supposed differences of brain size.

It will be my aim to examine the evidence for such claims; to try to dissect apart the facts from supposed facts. We shall find that the evidence is inadequate or, in some respects, totally lacking.

source: Phillip V. Tobias, "Brain Size, Grey Matter and Race—Fact or Fiction?" *American Journal of Physical Anthropology* vol. 32 (1970): 3–26. Reprinted by permission of the publisher.
[1] Several others may be listed here: P. György and O. L. Kline, eds., *Malnutrition Is a Problem of Ecology* (Basel and New York: Karger, 1970); Herbert G. Birch and Joan Dye Gussow, *Disadvantaged Children* (New York: Harcourt, Brace, and World, 1970); Rodger Hurley, *Poverty and Mental Retardation* (New York: Random House, 1969).
[2] G. C. van Walsem, "Über das Gewicht des schwersten bis jetzt beschriebenen Gehirns," *Neurologisches Centralblatt,* vol. 13, July 1, 1899, pp. 578–80.

Further, I shall try to examine the meaning of brain-size differences in the light of recent neuro-histological and neurophysiological researches, as well as from an evolutionary standpoint. We shall find that, even were differences in brain size validly demonstrated among different populations, they would be unable to explain adequately variations in cerebral function and achievement among living human beings. Furthermore, we shall find that such variations, if they do exist, are apparently not of much importance in modern man. We shall see that in this expanding universe, ours is a world of contracting brains. Finally, we shall be led to regard somewhat more critically the claims made about grey matter in the men of today.

Some Claims About Race and Brain Power

It has often been claimed that races differ in intellectual capacity. For example, in 1961 and again in 1962, in a report on "The Biology of the Race Problem," prepared by commission of the Governor of Alabama, George quotes I.Q. test performances, crime statistics, behaviour and temperament traits, for all of which differences are claimed to exist between Whites and Negroes. These statements by George have been quoted by Hofmeyr ('61), Swan ('64), Putnam ('63, '67) and others. Not being a psychologist, a criminologist or a sociologist, I do not feel competent to offer any authoritative comment on the statistics, the objectivity with which they were obtained, the degree to which such factors as economic and educational background were considered in the study of the crime statistics, nor the validity of claims that the alleged differences are based upon racial factors, i.e., inherent or genetic differences.

However, I do feel better able to express an opinion when George ('62), Swan ('64), Putnam ('63, '67) and others attribute these differences to inherent *anatomical* causes. The most impor-

tant features cited by these writers are the size of the brain, the fissuration of the cortex and the thickness of the supragranular layer of the cortical grey matter. For example, we find Putnam ('67) stating:

We have enough studies of the Negro brain, under varied enough circumstances, to speak with assurance of its relative weight. When this factor is combined with studies of its other features, such as sulcification of the cortex and thickness of the supragranular layer, we can also speak with assurance of its relative evolutionary status. (Op. cit., p. 103.)

These writers claim that this group of supposed facts points to the Negro's brain being of lower evolutionary status, which, in turn, implies a lesser capacity to learn (e.g., Putnam, '67, p. 106).

Similarly, after detailing crime statistics among Negro and White communities, George ('62, p. 25) turns to consider the brains of Negroes and Whites with the words, "We must now turn to a consideration of the degree to which these differences may be attributable to inherent morphological rather than to environmental causes." He goes on to add:

"Are there hereditary structural and other biological differences between individuals and races that might serve to explain the observed differences in intelligence and in behaviour in those areas of activity that make western civilization? The presence of such differences is not only a reasonable expectation but is supported by evidence." (Op. cit., p. 25.)

The validity of the argument hinges on two sets of premises: (i) the correctness of the statements about the differences in the anatomy of the brains; and (ii) the validity of the inference that these anatomical variations, if present, connote functional differences relevant to social behaviour, learning ability, "behaviour in those areas of activity that make western civilization," and so on.

Perhaps the most important claimed anatomical difference relates to brain size. Thus, Swan ('64,

p. 33) states: "Despite sampling difficulties and variations in methods, enough comparative racial studies of brain weight have been completed to warrant a quantitative description of the racial differences. The average cranial capacity of European Whites is from 100 to 175 cm³ greater than that of African Negroes, and their average brain weight is some 8 to 12% greater" (op. cit., p. 33).

What facts do we have about brain size? First, what measure of brain size should we use? If the actual brain is available, we may weigh it or, less satisfactorily, determine its volume. If the brain itself is not available, we can still derive an approximation to brain size by determining the capacity of the cranium or brain-case. However, the brain-case accommodates a great deal more than simply brain. Thus, when we say that a skull has an endocranial capacity of 1400 cm³, this includes not only brain-tissue, but the roots and intracranial trunks of no fewer than 24 cranial nerves, the thick outer brain covering or dura mater, the two thinner, inner coverings, the arachnoid and pia mater, the subarachnoid space and its enlargements called cisterns containing fluid, numerous blood-vessels including special enlarged venous channels called cranial venous sinuses, blood, cerebrospinal fluid.

Thus, only a proportion of the cranial capacity is made up of brain-tissue: estimates of this proportion vary from 10% (Brandes, '27) to 33.33% (Mettler, '55). Furthermore, the ratio is not a constant figure within the adult lifetime of any one individual, for the brain shrinks with age, in certain illnesses and under some other conditions, though the brain-case itself has not been shown to diminish. Hence, as the quality of life changes, the amount of non-neural cranial capacity increases and one's head may become progressively filled more and more with emptiness.

For these reasons, cranial capacity is a less reliable indicator of brain size than brain weight itself. When dealing with fossil man, we are perforce obliged to consider cranial capacity, as our sole guide to brain size. But when speaking of living man, we are able to determine brain size itself and thus eliminate at least some unnecessary sources of error. In this discussion on the brain size of living man, attention will be confined largely to the actual brain weight. We shall see that even this measure of brain size is not as easy to determine as it may sound and that, even though we avoid certain errors by not relying on cranial capacity, we nevertheless remain with a large number of possible sources of variance.

Some Facts About Brain Weight

For over 130 years, data have been accumulating on the weight and/or volume of the human brain, or the cranial capacity, in samples drawn from different racial groups. As long ago as 1849, S. G. Morton published observations on the cranial capacity of skulls drawn from different populations: the mean capacity of a small sample of Negro skulls was 91.3% of the mean for a very small sample of Caucasoid skulls, the values being 1360.1 cm³ and 1489.6 cm³ (converted to metric units by Pearl, '34). Other early studies on cranial capacity gave similar results (Peacock, 1865—88.4% on 9 Negro skulls and 16 "European" skulls; Duckworth, '04—92.5%).

As far as can be traced, the earliest references to the brain weight of the Negro were those of Soemmering (1788) who weighed two brains, Tiedemann (1836) who weighed one and Sir Astley Cooper one (cited by Peacock, 1865). In 1865, Peacock weighed another five brains of Negroes; according to Pearl ('34), Peacock copied an additional two brain weights from tables compiled by John Reid. Five of the seven individuals represented were males, and three of them are reported to have died of phthisis in a greatly emaciated state. The mean weight for these five was computed by Pearl ('34) as 1256.8 gm. By 1885, Topinard could cull data for 29 male Negro brains from diverse sources in the literature: the mean was 1234 gm.

In 1894, Waldeyer recorded a mean brain-weight of as low as 1148 gm for 12 male African Negro brains, 11 of which were weighed fresh. But, as Pearl pointed out ('34, p. 432), two of these belonged to 15-year-olds, while several had died of wasting diseases and were severely emaciated. In 1909, Mall made the forthright statement that the average brain weight of the Negro is about 100 gm less than that of Whites. Bean, too, found a lower brain weight in Negro males than in White males ('17).

Perhaps the most frequently quoted study is that of Vint ('34) who found an average brain weight of 1276 gm in 389 adult male Kenya Africans. This is the longest Negro series on record. Pearl ('34) analysed brain weights collected by Surgeon Ira Russell of the Eleventh Massachusetts Volunteers during the American Civil War and published by S. B. Hunt in London in 1869. The sample of brains of enlisted soldiers had been broken down a century ago into White, varying grades of "mixtures," and Black. It seems that the various mixtures were determined by the simple, though grossly misleading expedient, of examining skin colour. Pearl found that the mean for 139 brains of Negroes was 1354.8 gm, that is, 92.1% of the mean for 24 brains of Whites (1470.6 gm). Strangely enough, the mean for 240 brains of people believed to be mixtures was 1333.6 gm i.e., lower than both the White and Negro means! (Table 1).

Table 1: Pearl's ('34) Analysis of Brain Weights of American Civil War Dead. Measurements made originally by uncertain technique by Surgeon Ira Russell of the Eleventh Massachusetts Volunteers.

CLASSIFICATION	NUMBER	AVERAGE BRAIN WEIGHT
		gm
White	24	1470.6
Mixtures	240	1333.6
Black	139	1354.8

As I have recited them, these figures look consistent and convincing. Indeed, they have been immediately and uncritically accepted as indicating a lower average level of intelligence of the Negro. As Putnam has put it:

"The evidence is simply that, as a racial average, the Negro brain is lighter than the White and that this, in turn, indicates a lower average level of intelligence." ('63, p. 10)

We shall return later to the claim that less brain weight means less intelligence. For the moment, let us examine the figures on brain size more closely.

It is true that the studies just cited have demonstrated a lower average brain weight, or smaller average capacity of the brain-case, in Negroes than in Whites. The biggest series of White or Caucasoid brains to have been weighed was 2752 Americans: their average weight was 1301 gm, or, if 672 diseased brains are excluded, the average for the remaining 2080 brains was 1305 gm (Appel and Appel, '42). This is only 29 gm heavier than the average for the sample of Kenya African brains. On the other hand, Davis (1868) recorded capacities from which Pakkenberg and Voigt ('64) computed a mean brain weight in "Africans" of 1293 gm, whilst the average for 139 American Negro brains was 1355 gm (Pearl, '34) —just 50 gm heavier than the mean of the most comprehensive White series. Other Caucasoid series range up to means of 1440 gm for 724 adult male Danes (Pakkenberg and Voigt, '64), 1450 gm for 581 brains weighed at the Institute for Forensic Medicine in Prague (Matiegka, '02) and 1455 for 372 brains of Bohemians (Pearl, '05).

That is, the means for three fairly long Negro series range from 1276–1355 gm, while the means for some 11 White or Caucasoid series range from 1301–1455 gm. It must be stressed that these are ranges *of averages;* ranges of individual values are much wider and overlap to a greater extent.

For comparison, means for three Mongoloid series range from 1360–1375 gm (Kusumoto, '34; Shibata, '36—cited by Bailey and von Bonin, '51 and by Pakkenberg and Voigt, '64). Bailey and von Bonin ('51) have given an overall average (weighted mean) of 1344 gm for many modern human series irrespective of race, i.e., for the living species *Homo sapiens* at large (Table 2).

Table 2: Average Brain Weight

	gm	
Kenya Africans (389)	1276	Vint ('34)
Africans	1293	Davis (1868)
American Negroes (139)	1355	Pearl ('34)
American Whites (2752)	1301	Appel and
11 White (Caucasoid) Series	1301–1455	Appel ('42)
3 Mongoloid Series	1360–1375	Kusumoto ('34) Shibata ('36)
Modern *Homo sapiens* (weighted mean)	1344	Bailey and von Bonin ('51)

Negro populations sampled have averages above and below the overall modern human average. None the less, the overall Negro average would seem to be somewhat lower than the overall European average in absolute terms, that is, when uncorrected for general bodily size and other related variables. However, a mere comparison of average figures may be misleading unless allowance is made for these other variables: we shall consider first the simple notion that one might expect people with bigger body sizes to have bigger brain sizes.

Brain Size and Body Size

The size of the brain in relation to body size has been employed chiefly in comparisons between species, in an effort to show how predominant the brain has become in man. It was Cuvier who first introduced the concept of relative brain-weight, that is, the weight of the brain expressed as a fraction of the weight of the body (Krompecher and Lipak, '66). A picture given by Cobb of a small Asian woman standing alongside a rhinoceros shows graphically the difference in relative sizes of brains. The woman may have a brain weight of 1200 gm in a body weighing, say, 45 kg, whereas the rhinoceros has a brain which may weigh 600 gm in a body of about 2000 kg (Cobb, '65). The brain:body ratio in the rhinoceros is 1:3,000 in such a case, that of the woman 1:38. Even more revealing is a glance at the *Brontosaurus*, one of the great dinosaurian ruling reptiles, perhaps 65 feet long, that lived in the Jurassic period: its brain constituted a mere 1/100,000 of its 35-ton bulk. A whale has a brain/body weight ratio of 1:10,000; an elephant 1:600; a gorilla 1:200 and a man about 1:45.

But it is sobering to see that while Man's exalted brain constitutes just over 2% of his body weight, this percentage is surpassed by the lowly house mouse (2.50% or 1:40), the porpoise with 1:38, the marmoset with 1:19, and the attractive little squirrel monkey of tropical America whose brain occupies 1/12 or 8.50% of its body weight (Cobb, '56)! Because Man, the sapient, did not come out at the top, it is not surprising that Man, the vainglorious and the arrogant, has been searching ever since for an index which would place him unequivocally and unassailably on the highest branch of the tree of life. For example, when the length of the hypothalamus is expressed as a fraction of the brain weight, Man has the fraction and so comes out on top (Kummer, '61); when the weight of the spinal cord is expressed as a fraction of the brain-weight, Man has the lowest fraction and so comes out on top (Latimer, '50; Krompecher and Lipak, '66); when the cranial capacity is related to the area of the foramen magnum, Man has the highest value and still ends up on top (Radinsky, '67)!

All the indices I have cited have a certain

though limited usefulness when comparisons are made between one species and another. However, few studies have seriously addressed themselves to the problem within the species of man.

Matiegka ('02) and Pearl ('05) claimed that, in Man, brain weight varies with body weight and with body height. That is to say, they claimed to find that taller people and heavier people have larger brains. However, more recent workers have questioned the correlation claimed to exist between brain weight and body weight within the human species.

Pakkenberg and Voigt ('64) have made a more refined statistical analysis on the brains of European subjects. They showed that the increasing brain weight with increasing body weight found by the earlier workers is really owing to the fact that people with higher body weight are usually taller than average (Chart 1). The earlier workers had failed to correct for body height when evaluating the relation between brain weight and body weight. When this correction was made (Chart 2), it was found that *brain weight depends significantly on body height but not on body weight* (Pakkenberg and Voigt, '64, p. 303).

Chart 1

Taller people tend to have bigger brains

Heavier people tend to be taller

∴ Heavier people APPEAR to have bigger brains

Chart 2

Heavier people, adjusted for height, do NOT have bigger brains

Taller people have bigger brains irrespective of weight

∴ Brain-weight is positively correlated with body height, but not with body-weight

Exactly similar results were obtained by Spann and Dustmann ('65) in a study of 1229 male and 632 female brains in the medico-legal insti-

tute at the University of Munich: brain weight rose with increasing stature (Chart 3), but no association could be determined between brain weight and body weight. In 1966, Schreider reanalysed some old brain and body measurements made in Paris in 1865–1870 by Paul Broca, one of the great anatomists of the last century. Schreider found that between brain weight and body height there was a positive correlation coefficient of 0.26 for 224 males and 0.31 for 111 females.

Chart 3

Adult men have on the average 8.3 gm of brain for every centimetre of body height

Adult women have on the average 8.0 gm of brain for every centimetre of body height

SPANN AND DUSTMANN ('65)

Clearly, if one does not allow for the varying average body sizes of different populations, one may be misled into making false statements about the existence of real differences in average brain size among the populations compared.

With this in mind, one has re-examined the main original sources on Negro brain weight in comparison with White brain weight. Neither Davis (1868) nor Vint ('34), nor Pearl ('34), the three main students of Negro brain weight, have taken body height into account, nor made any allowance for it. Yet, when it is pointed out that many Negro groups have a lower average body size than many White groups, Putnam's reply is that such variables are eliminated in the initial hypothesis, which reads as follows:

"There is, I suppose, no dispute about the fact that, *other things being equal* (such as sex, body size, proportion of parts and sulcification), the weight of the brain correlates with intelligence." (Putnam, '63, p. 10.)

Elsewhere, too, Putnam ('67, p. 53) states ". . . constant efforts like Simmons' occurred to confuse the issue by injecting variables which properly were eliminated in the initial hypothesis." Putnam's reference to his "initial hypothesis" in this context is both seriously misleading and an error of logic. The wording may eliminate such sources of variance as different mean body weights from the hypothesis, but this by no means eliminates these sources of variance from the facts to which Putnam tries to apply the hypothesis. By citing the "initial hypothesis" as eliminating body weight and other variables, Putnam creates the impression that the value he quotes of 8–12% lower brain weight in the Negro *has* been corrected for body size. He states explicitly in another place ('67, p. 43), "Brain weight or size comparisons were never attempted without first allowing for sex and body size, and when these adjustments were made the averages were both consistent and clear." But no height measurements were recorded for Vint's Kenya Africans nor for Pearl's Civil War Negroes, the two longest series of Negro data on record, nor for any of the earlier cited studies. Where and by whom were the claimed adjustments made? Putnam's statement is totally erroneous: in none of the studies cited, nor in Putnam's own writings, has a correction been made for the varying heights of the subjects concerned, nor are corrected or adjusted figures recorded. The figures of 8–12% shortfall cited by him are absolute figures as measured, not as corrected for body height differences.

In comparisons between different animals, Lashley ('49) suggested that the total amount of brain material, expressed as a fraction of total body size, *"seems to represent the amount of brain tissue in excess of that required for transmitting impulses to and from the integrative centres"* (op. cit., p. 33). Following up this notion, Jerison ('63) has demonstrated that brain size may be considered as two separate components: one is directly related to the size of the body, and it is bigger in Primates with bigger body size, and vice versa. The other component seems to vary independently of body size; it comprises the "surplus" nerve-cells which are present over and above those required for the satisfaction of immediate bodily needs. These "surplus" nerve-cells, Jerison suggests, are available for response to the challenge of the environment through a wider range of brain-behaviour mechanisms; that is, for intelligent adjustment.

On the basis of cell-counts in a variety of Primates and, given certain assumptions, Jerison claims that it is possible to estimate the number of cortical nerve-cells, not only in the brain as a whole, but in each of the two components. He has developed a series of equations for the calculation of these neuronal values, given the size of the brain and the size of the body. By applying these formulae, he has been able to compute the number of 'extra' neurones regarded as being available for brain:behaviour adaptive mechanisms. With this second parameter, the number of "excess neurones," he has found it possible to distinguish the Primates and, especially, the family of Man, on the basis of the relative development of the extra neurones. Modern man has far more excess neurones than, say, the chimpanzee and gorilla. While the African great apes can be shown by Jerison's equations to possess 2.4–3.6 billion excess neurones, modern man has over eight billion.

The method involves many assumptions. It does not adequately take into account regional variations in the density of neurones, in the ratio between neuroglia and neurones, in the size of nerve-cell bodies, in the length and complexity of the dendritic processes of the neurones. None the less, it provides a novel, approximate gauge of cortical development. Above all, the method has been developed for comparisons between species. However, as an exercise, I have tentatively assumed that similar patterns of variation may occur between populations within a species, like *Homo sapiens,* to those which occur between species. Purely to emphasize the need for body size to be taken into account in discussions on human brain sizes, I have made some calculations, using Jerison's formulae, of the number of such "surplus" nerve-cells in various races, for which large samples of data on male brain size and body size are available. The results are given in Table 3.

Table 3: Excess Neurones in Populations of Modern Man (Estimated by the Method of Jerison, '63)

POPULATION	N	AVERAGE BRAIN WEIGHT	MILLIONS OF EXCESS NERVE-CELLS
		gm	
Kenya Negro	389	1276	8,400
American White	2080	1305	8,500
French	292	1325	8,600
English	457	1333	8,600
American Negro	139	1355	8,700
Japanese	342	1360	8,900
Korean	136	1370	8,900
Swedish	416	1400	8,900

These results suggest that the differences among various racial or population groups are negligible, *once allowance has been made for body size.* Further, it should be noted that the figures quoted are *averages* for each group: but individuals *within* each group vary above and below the average, so that considerable overlap occurs.

It is stressed that this is only an exercise: it has yet to be shown whether Jerison's method of analysis is valid in general, and, more particularly, whether it can validly be applied in this manner *within* a species.

We may conclude this section by stating that no comparisons between the mean brain size of different populations or races permit valid statements to be made on interracial differences, unless corrections have been made for differences in body height. On this basis alone, all comparisons between Negro and White brain sizes to date are invalid.

Brain Size and Age

It has long been known that the average weight of the human brain decreases with advancing years (e.g. Pearl, '05; Appel and Appel, '42; Tiakahasi and Suzuki, '61; Pakkenberg and Voigt, '64; Spann and Dustmann, '65; Schneider, '66), and that the decline may begin as early as the twentieth year. The drop in average brain weight from young adulthood to about 80 years of age varies from 95 gm in Swedes (Pearl, '05, after Retzius, 1900) to 170 gm in Danes (Pakkenberg and Voigt, '64). Among the Danes, the drop from the age of 25 years to the age of 70 years is approximately 100 gm. These figures suggest a drop in the average of 7 to 11% of the maximum brain size (chart 4). Schneider ('66) showed negative correlation coefficients between brain weight and age as high as -0.39 in males and -0.46 in females.

Chart 4

Average brain weight : Decline with years	
Young adulthood ⟶ ± 80 years	
Drop of 95 gm	Swedes
Drop of 170 gm	Danes
Drop in average	7%–11%

The cause of the fall with age need not concern us here, but the relevance of this finding is that if one series of brains includes a large proportion from old people, the overall average would tend to be lower than that of another series which includes more young adult brains, even though both series may stem from the same population. For many European series the ages at death are known (e.g. Schneider, '66, on Broca's material), but this is not true for Negroid series, such as that of Vint ('34) on Kenya African brains. We simply do not know the ages of his Negroid subjects and cannot therefore decide to what extent his relatively small average figure of 1276 gm is attributable to age, and how much to stature and to other variables in that population. A valid comparison between two series of brains drawn from different racial groups should take the age composition of the sample into account. It cannot be claimed that this has been done for comparisons between the brain sizes of Caucasoids and Negroids.

Brain Size and Nutritional State

Evidence has accumulated, especially in recent years, that undernutrition at critical stages during ontogeny of experimental animals may lead to permanent impairment of the brain, including diminution of brain size. This effect occurs provided the period of undernutrition begins before the cerebral cortex has reached its adult state, or, at least, during the period of maximum vulnerability of the brain to stress. If the nutritional insults are administered within this critical postnatal period, or even if it is the pregnant mother which is undernourished, the impairment to the size, structure and chemistry of the brain is not reversed by subsequent restoration of normal nutrition. These results have been obtained on pigs, rats and mice (Jackson and Stewart, '20; Dobbing and Widdowson, '65; Davidson and Dobbing, '65; Dickerson and Dobbing, '67; Dickerson and McCance, '67; Dickerson and Walmsley, '67; Guthrie and Brown, '68; Zamenhof, van Marthens and Margolis, '68; Chase, Lindsley and O'Brien, '69).

Is there any evidence for impaired brain growth in *man* under conditions of malnutrition? The studies of Engel ('56), Nelson ('59, '63), Stoche and Smythe ('63, '67), Cravioto and Robles ('65), Brown ('66), Eichenwald and Fry ('69) and Baraitser and Evans ('69) have all noted functional impairments of the human brain

following early undernutrition. These workers have studied electro-encephalographic readings, psychometric testing, rate of psychomotor development, and head circumference, to demonstrate abnormalities. It is still too early to say whether the changes demonstrated are permanent; the analogy of animal experiments would suggest a permanent effect, while the recent study of Baraitser and Evans ('69) in the Department of Neurology at the Groote Schuur Hospital, Cape Town, would tend to support the notion that the E.E.G. changes outlast the acute stage of the nutritional insult.

In their recent review, *Nutrition and Learning*, Eichenwald and Fry ('69) summarise as follows:

"Observations on animals and human infants suggest that malnutrition during a critical period of early life results in short stature and may, in addition, permanently and profoundly affect the future intellectual and emotional development of the individual. In humans, it is not known whether these results may be caused by malnutrition alone or whether such intimately related factors as infection and an inadequate social and emotional environment contribute significantly to the problem. Field studies to test these hypotheses are, at best, difficult to design and to carry out; it seems likely that it will prove impossible to separate clearly the individual effects of malnutrition, infection and social environment."

In a subsequent editorial in *Science*, Abelson ('69) summarised the results of their study and of an International Conference on Malnutrition, Learning, and Behaviour (Scrimshaw and Gordon, eds., '68) as follows:

"Children reared in poverty tend to do poorly on tests of intelligence. In part this is due to psychological and cultural factors. To an important extent it is a result of malnutrition early in childhood . . . It seems likely that millions of young children in developing countries are experiencing some degree of retardation in learning because of inadequate nutrition, and that this phenomenon may also occur in the United States . . . animal experiments suggest that (in the human infant) good nutrition during the first three years of life is particularly important . . ."

Further follow-ups are obviously necessary to confirm the hypothesis that malnutrition at a critical age results in permanent brain damage, with permanent impairment of intellect and emotions, and of brain rhythms.

The substantial body of evidence for such impairment leaves undecided the question of whether changes have occurred in the brain size and structure. What *direct* evidence do we have for *such* changes following early undernutrition? Several students have demonstrated that a smaller brain weight in man may result from early undernutrition. Kerpel-Fronius ('61) found a reduction of 10–20% in brain weight of the malnourished human infant. Brown ('66), working on Uganda African children at Mulago Hospital, Kampala, found a significant reduction in the brain weight of malnourished children compared with other Ugandan children. Even among his control "nonmalnourished children," Brown stressed, many, if not most, showed suboptimal nutrition, though not rating the autopsy diagnosis of kwashiorkor, marasmus or general undernourishment.

Recently, belated after-effects of starvation and other forms of maltreatment of Second World War prisoners held in concentration camps have been investigated in Norway (Strøm, '68). Nearly 20 years later, a number of survivors showed a reduction in the size of the brain, accompanied by signs of intellectual deterioration. Further, an article by W. Osler entitled "Belated scars of war prison," which appeared originally in the London "Sunday Times" and was quoted by the Johannesburg "Star" on November 11, 1968, stated, "Research in Japanese camps had shown that starvation causes the brain to swell, and it is thought that on return to normal conditions the brain then shrinks to less than its original size."

On the structural side, Eayrs and Horn ('55)

showed histologically that undernutrition impairs the elaboration of nerve-cell processes: this may be one of the mechanisms behind both the reduced brain size and impaired brain function. Fishman, Prensky and Dodge ('69) have recently shown changes in the brain lipids of starved (or chronically malnourished) human beings, resembling those found in experimental animals. Not only is the total lipid reduced, but most severely affected are those classes of lipids of which myelin is composed. Here, too, we may have a clue as to the mechanism, or one of the mechanisms, responsible for the lower brain weight and the impaired function in undernourished subjects.

One interesting point that emerges from the studies on both men and experimental animals is that the brain weight reduction, though definite and significant, is not as marked in degree as that of the body as a whole, or as those of other organs, such as muscles, spleen and liver (Platt et al., '65; Brown, '66; Guthrie and Brown, '68; Chase et al., '69; etc.). In the study of Kerpel-Fronius ('61), while the infant's body weight was 50% below the expected value, the brain weight was only 10–20% reduced. Thus, although the absolute brain weight was depressed, the brain/body weight ratio is elevated in such cases—which perhaps provides one further indication of the relative meaninglessness of the brain/body weight ratio! It seems that some protective mechanism may be operating which gives the brain priority in access to nutrients during periods of undernutrition (Hammond, '44; Kerpel-Fronius, '61).

Nevertheless, enough has been said to show that in any population widely exposed to varying degrees of undernutrition, it would be reasonable to expect that heads and brains would be significantly smaller, on the average, than those of a population on a good average level of nutrition. The widespread incidence of varying degrees of suboptimal nutrition in the African population is well-known (cf. Gillman and Gillman, '51; Tobias, '58; Brown, '66; Smit, '69). I am referring here not merely to an extreme form, such as kwashiorkor, but to lesser and subtler grades of undernutrition, such as have been uncovered by the multidisciplinary study of Pretoria school-children of African, Asian, Coloured and European origin, by the National Nutrition Research Institute of South Africa (Smit, '69). The relevance of these malnutritional effects for the interpretation of the mean brain weight of the Negro, and of other poorly-nourished and emergent peoples, is obvious: if lower mean brain weights can be validly demonstrated (and they have not yet been validated), the degree to which undernourishment is responsible for the shortfall would have to be considered, before such differences are lightly ascribed to racial or genetic differences.

Brain Size and the Influence of the (Non-nutritional) Environment

Is there a relationship between brain size and structure on one hand, and the degree of challenge, of enrichment, or of impoverishment of the environment on the other? Although there is little direct evidence for man, indirect evidence of several kinds is available.

Marian Diamond and her co-workers at Berkeley ('64, '66) have studied the brains of rats reared in an enriched, stimulating environment and of their littermates reared in an impoverished and isolated environment. Definite structural differences have been demonstrated between the brains of the two groups. Those from the enriched milieu showed a significantly deeper visual cortex and a higher glia-neuron ratio than those from the isolated environment. Unfortunately, I have not been able to trace any refer-

ence to brain size measurements made in such experiments. At any rate, one can say clearly that the "educational environment" of a growing rat influences the fine internal structure of the cerebral cortex.

A second line of evidence is the demonstration that closely related animals may differ in brain size, according to the amount of activity and the challenges, or protective influences, emanating from their environments. Thus, Poliakova ('60) has shown that the agile, climbing, red field-mouse possesses a larger brain weight than the relatively sluggish, grey field mouse, although both are classified as belonging to the same species. Another series of studies on dogs, pigs, rabbits, rats, guinea-pigs, cats and ducks showed that domestication causes a decrease of about 20%, in some cases as high as 30%, in brain weight (Herre, '58). Klatt (quoted by Herre, '58) showed that when wild animals are kept in captivity from an early age, their brain weight decreases markedly. Conversely, asses which have been allowed to run wild on the pampas of Argentina and Peru show an increase in brain size of about 15%. A similar figure obtains for cats which have been allowed to run wild (Klatt). It would seem that the docile life, in which animals are fully protected from their enemies, provides a similar absence of environmental stimulation to the developing brain of young animals, as obtains with Marian Diamond's isolated rats reared in an impoverished environment.

One cannot help thinking of the enriched environment in which the "haves" are reared and the deprived and neglected upbringing of the "have-nots." There is a distinct possibility that such differences in the early home-upbringing and nursery school facilities between members of different populations may contribute towards structural and even size differences in their brains. Here is one factor, which, as far as I can determine, has not been examined in studies on human brain size structure.

Brain Size and the Source of the Sample

Yet another variable which may influence the average brain weight is the source from which the brains were obtained. As Pakkenberg and Voigt ('64) have recently pointed out, most of the series published have been from hospitals, including mental hospitals (as is the case with the largest series, that of Appel and Appel ('42)). This implies that, with relatively few exceptions, the brain weight of the normal or healthy human being is not known! The only real exceptions are brains which have been obtained through institutes of forensic medicine, i.e., *following sudden death without prior disease.* Only three such series have been traced in the literature, namely those of Matiegka ('02) from the Forensic Institute in Prague, of Pakkenberg and Voigt ('64) from the Neuropathological Laboratory of the Kommunehospitalet and the University Institute of Forensic Medicine in Copenhagen, and of Spann and Dustmann ('65) from the Institut für Gerichtliche Medizin and Versicherungsmedizin at the University in Munich. No Negro series from such a source has been published: we do not know the brain weight of the normal, healthy Negro! Vint ('34), whose low average for the Negro brain (1276 gm) has been most often quoted, obtained his material from hospitals in Nairobi, excluding the Mental Hospital. His series therefore did not fulfill the ideal requirement of sudden death without prior disease.

Although many hospital patients may suffer and die from diseases which probably do not affect brain weight (and even on this point we lack precise information), hospital populations as such are often not a good cross-section of all levels of society. They tend to reflect the lower social strata, while the upper strata tend to go to private nursing homes or to receive medical care at home. Vint even says of his Kenya African series, "These 100 brains represent the average native population, but do not include any of the so-called educated class" ('34, p. 216).

Even bodies which are studied and dissected in Medical Schools are a far from random sample. The law caters for two main groups of subjects: those who die as paupers in State Institutions—in South Africa these tend to be largely Africans; and those who bequeath their bodies to the Medical Schools—and these people are commonly better educated and often of the higher social strata. As Burial Societies come more and more within the reach of the poorest sections of the community, fewer and fewer people die as unclaimed paupers: and so gradually the face of the dissecting room population itself changes. This phenomenon is particularly vividly to be seen at present in the Anatomy School of the Witwatersrand University.

T. Wingate Todd ('27) has recounted how dramatic an effect an economic depression had on the dissection room population; all sorts of people took to dying as unclaimed paupers who had previously been numbered among the university's financial benefactors. The average brain size of the cadaver population increased. Todd entitled his address, "A liter and a half of brains!"

We may conclude that no series of brain-weights is available for healthy, normal Negroes who have died a sudden death; no Negro series can therefore be compared validly with the best available European series from Forensic Medical Institutes.

Brain Size and Occupational Groups

Closely related to the source from which the brain was obtained is the question of the occupational groups represented in the sample (Chart 5). Matiegka ('02) showed an association between brain weight and occupation in his studies at the Forensic Medical Institute in Prague. Results obtained in the recent study of Spann and Dustmann ('65) tally remarkably closely with those of Matiegka. Thus, in both studies, unskilled workmen had a mean brain-size of just over 1400 gm, and the academic, the professional and the senior official group of just on 1500 gm. Spann and Dustmann found some correlation among women: three groups of skilled and unskilled workers, handworkers, and lesser officials all had mean brain weights between 1300 and 1315 gm, while six female academics had the absurdly high mean value of 1422 gm (just within the lower end of the range of occupational means among males!).

Chart 5: Brain Size and occupation. Matiegka-Prague, '02; Spann and Dustmann, Munich, '65

OCCUPATION	AVER-AGE BRAIN SIZE
	gm
Unskilled workmen	1400
Academics, professional men and senior officials	1500
Paul Broca, Paris, 1865–70	
Unskilled labourers	1365
Semi-skilled and skilled workers	1420

But the latter were taller than the former!

Question: Has there been a *secular trend* towards increased brain size, in parallel with the secular trend towards increased stature?

The tendency is apparently not a new one: Broca's results from the late 1860's yielded a mean brain weight of 1365 gm for 51 unskilled labourers and of 1420 gm for 24 semi-skilled and skilled workers: the difference is almost significant at the 5% level (Schreider, '66). Schreider comments, however, that the differences in brain weight between the occupational groups are probably related to differences in body height, for the skilled and semi-skilled group were on the average 1.34 cm taller than the unskilled group.[1]

The degree to which any sample of brains represents, or departs from, a cross-section of occupations may thus affect the validity of any comparisons between such a sample and any other.

Brain Size and Cause of Death

In a large hospital population, Appel and Appel ('42) found that the mean weight of the brain was highest (1374 gm) in cases of violent and accidental deaths. On the other hand, patients who died of arteriosclerosis and cancer had average brain weights of 100 gm less (1273 and 1275 gm respectively). For other categories of causes of death, the average weights lay between these two extremes. Of the various disease groups, tuberculotics showed the highest mean weight (1328), that is, 55 gm above the mean for arteriosclerotics and 46 gm below the mean for victims of accidental and violent deaths (Chart 6).

In the large Copenhagen medico-legal series of Pakkenberg and Voigt ('64), the highest mean brain weights were found among those who had died from hanging, poisoning (mainly by carbon monoxide or barbiturates) and shock: similar results were observed in the Munich series of Spann and Dustmann. Low values, on the other hand, were encountered in those who had died following brain diseases, general pathology, head

---

[1] It is doubtful however whether this relatively small difference in stature is adequate to explain all the difference in brain weight between the two groups. On Spann and Dustmann's figure of 8.3 gm of brain for every centimeter of body height in men, the difference of 1.34 cm might account for some 11.0 gm of brain weight difference: this would reduce the discrepancy to non-significant levels (with these small samples), but there remains a shortfall of 44 gm between the two groups.

Chart 6: Brain Size and cause of death. St. Elizabeth's Hospital, Washington, D.C. (Male white data—after Appel and Appel '42)

CAUSE OF DEATH	NUMBER	AVERAGE BRAIN WEIGHT
		gm
Violence/accidents	54	1374
Tuberculosis	533	1328
Urogenital diseases	200	1315
Digestive diseases	284	1307
Respiratory diseases	1023	1300
Circulatory disease (incl. Arteriosclerosis)	955	1295
Nervous diseases	430	1285
Cancer	112	1275
Arteriosclerosis	358	1273

trauma, drowning, asphyxiation, electrocution and protracted haemorrhage.

Again, in his study of Broca's century-old data, Schreider ('66) showed that those who died from accidents had a mean brain weight 60 gm greater than those who had died of infectious diseases. It seems that even 100 years ago, accidents were common in the streets of Paris—though they were seemingly often owing to horse kicks.

Thus, whether death is lingering or sudden, disease processes themselves may influence brain weight at death and, indirectly, the rate of increase in brain weight with each passing hour after death. It is well known that the patterns of fatal diseases differ appreciably among different populations, especially where one group lacks adequate medical and hospital facilities (as is the case with many African Negro populations). Thus, two groups may show differences in average brain weight simply because of a different pattern and incidence of fatal diseases in the two groups. Such a factor may account for some of the discrepancy between, for instance, two Negro series, one in Africa with an average brain weight of 1276 gm and one in America with an

average of 1355 gm. Similarly, some of the differences found in interracial comparisons may be accounted for by such differential disease-patterns.

Brain Size and the Lapse of Time After Death

Another source of variation in the average brain size is the time that elapses between death and the removal of the brain (Chart 7). Chemical

Chart 7: Time after death

	BRAIN WEIGHT
	gm
24 hours	+40
48 hours	+75
Maximum change	+90
	(+9%)

changes go on in the brain for several days after death, tending towards an equilibrium that is appreciably heavier than the original weight (Appel and Appel, '42). Thus, if left for 24 hours after death, the brain weight is no less than 40 gm heavier than if removed within a few hours of death; 48 hours after death, it weighs on the average 75 gm more. The average maximum increase in weight is 90 gm, whilst the increase from the lowest mean weight to the highest is no less than 117 gm, or 9% of the average weight for the total array. Statistically and biologically, this is a significant and appreciable increment. It is almost as great as the decrease with age (11%) and it is greater than most of the recorded differences between the averages for various racial groups, including Negroes and Whites.

Then, too, the temperature at which the cadavers are kept between death and removal of the brains may affect the rate of chemical change and, so, the increase in weight after death.

Brain Size and the Treatment of the Brain After Death

"To weigh the human brain is not as easy as it sounds" (Bailey and von Bonin, '51). Thus, the measured weight will depend upon where exactly one severs the brain from the spinal cord. It is an agreed definition that everything cranial to the pyramidal decussation is "brain"; but the decussation is not a point: it extends for some little distance down the central nervous system. Different workers may sever the brain from the cord at a systematically higher or lower level (Bailey and von Bonin, '51).

Other technical points on which no standardization has been achieved include whether and how one drains the cerebrospinal fluid from the brain; Brandes ('27) stated that the complete drainage of the cerebrospinal fluid from the fresh brain may change its weight by as much as 50 gm. Again, there is the question: which of the covering membranes (or meninges) one removes from the surface of the brain and which of them one includes; Brandes ('27) determined the weight of the outer, thick covering, the dura mater, as no less than 50–60 gm. Should one strip the blood-vessels from the brain surface? Inconsistency between workers in every one of these points may import additional variance in the results obtained by different workers on different races or populations. Some studies in the literature (e.g., Pakkenberg and Voigt, '64; Spann and Dustmann, '65) carefully define their methods; in others, it is stated simply that the brains were weighed.

As in other branches of science, standardization of technique and precise description of the methodology followed in each study must obviously precede any meaningful comparisons between any two sets of data.

On the Meaninglessness of Most Studies on Brain Weight

For all these reasons, it is not surprising that contradictory results appear in the scientific literature for the brain sizes of Negroes and Whites. We have seen that brain size may vary according to body size, the age at death, the cause of death, the selection of the sample, the sex, the early environment, especially nutritional, the lapse of time after death, the level at which the brain is severed from the spinal cord, the mode of drainage of the cerebrospinal fluid and the treatment of the covering membranes and blood-vessels; other factors may intrude as well, such as the temperature at which the body is kept between the time of death and the removal of the brain (Chart 8). These factors may cause fluctuations in the measured brain size up to 9% too high if the brains are left for several days after death, or 11% too low if the sample of brains comes from elderly subjects. This order

Chart 8

MEASURED BRAIN SIZE VARIES WITH: —

1. Sex
2. Body size
3. Age at death
4. Nutritional state in early life
5. Non-nutritional environment in early life (?)
6. Source of sample
7. Occupational group
8. Cause of death
9. Lapse of time after death
10. Temperature after death
11. Anatomical level of severance
12. Presence or absence of C.S.F.
13. Presence or absence of meninges
14. Presence or absence of blood-vessels

of variability, stemming from only one or two of these possible variables, is greater than most of the supposed interracial differences which have appeared in the literature. The ideal sample is from subjects who have died suddenly *without prior disease,* as from violence and accidents. No such study has been recorded for Negro subjects.

It must be concluded that among the widely varying estimates for Negro brain size, none reflects the normal brain size of a healthy Negro group. *We do not know the brain size of healthy Negroes who have died suddenly without prior disease.* Few of the published studies on *any racial group* have been corrected for body size, age at death and the lapse of time after death; it is clearly difficult, if not impossible, to correct for all the other factors enumerated.

These considerations largely invalidate most interracial comparisons so far published. Certainly, it is invalid at this stage in our knowledge to claim, as Swan ('64) and Putnam ('63) have done, that the average brain weight of European Whites is some 8–12% greater than that of African Negroes. Equally misleading is the bald statement of Gates ('46) that "Comparative weights are given as 1380 gm for Caucasoids, 1300 gm for Mongoloids, 1280 gm for East Africans, 1240 gm for Negroes, and 1180 gm for Australian Aborigines." These figures are meaningless without any attempt to consider the body size of the various groups, let alone all the other variables.

A fortiori, it is totally invalid at this stage of our knowledge to cite the alleged smaller brain weight of Negroes as the physical basis for differences in intelligence and behaviour tests.

What Do Differences in Brain Size Mean?

It has been known for long that in living men, enormous variations in brain size may occur within the limits of normal healthy functioning.

Chart 9: Brain size and achievement. A pot-pourri of big and small brains

BRAIN WEIGHT	
gm	
1000–1100	Anatole France
	Franz Joseph Gall
	Leon Gambetta
1282	Walt Whitman
± 1900	Daniel Webster
	Ivan Turgenev
	Dean Swift
	Otto Von Bismarck
2230	Oliver Cromwell
	George Gordon,
	Lord Byron

Even well-known men of high achievement may vary considerably (Chart 9). Thus, the great French writer, Anatole France, is reported to have possessed a brain weight of as little as 1017 gm (or an endocranial capacity of about 1100 cm³); similar in size were the brains of Franz Joseph Gall, the German anatomist, physiologist and founder of the pseudo-science of phrenology; and of the French statesman, Léon Gambetta (Dart, '56); while only slightly larger was the brain of the great American poet, Walt Whitman (1282 gm) (Cobb, '65).

At the other extreme, George Gordon, Lord Byron, is said to have had a brain weight of 2238 gm and Oliver Cromwell of 2231 gm (Keith, '12, cited by Dart, '56). Brain weights of about 1900 gm were possessed by Daniel Webster, the American lawyer, statesman and orator; by Ivan Turgenev, the Russian novelist; by Dean Swift, the English satirist, and by Bismarck, the Prussian statesman and creator of the German Reich (Dart, '56).

Thus, considerable human achievement is possible at very nearly both ends of the scale of modern human brain size. Further, as Dart ('56) has pointed out, apparently normal human beings have existed with brain sizes in the 700's and 800's. Schlaginhaufen ('50–'51) reported the skull of a Melanesian woman from one of the Feni Islands in the Bismarck Archipelago with an endocranial capacity of only 790 cm³. As far as Dart ('56) could trace in the literature, this is the smallest capacity yet attested for a normal human skull—for it was not the skull of a pathological microcephalic! This capacity was found not in an ape-man or a pre-man, but in an individual classifiable as a member of our living species, *Homo sapiens* (Dart, '56); yet her capacity was a mere 38 cm³ greater than the maximum capacity recorded for an anthropoid ape, namely a gorilla with a cranial capacity of 752 cm³ (Schultz, '62).

Thus, normal human beings exist with brain sizes three times that of other human beings. So fantastic a range would single out brain size as one of the most highly variable parameters in modern man. Perhaps only body weight exceeds brain size in the discrepancy between the top and bottom of the range in normal healthy human beings.

What then do the different brain sizes in normal men signify? Do people with bigger brains have more nerve-cells, or bigger nerve-cells, or more neuroglia (the non-neural elements which lie between the neurons), or more nerve-processes, or longer nerve-processes, or thicker nerve-processes, or more highly-branched nerve-processes? Or are larger brains larger through a combination of any two or more of these seven possible variables?

We simply do not know the answers to these questions for modern human brains within the range of normality. We shall see in a moment that we have a little more information when it comes to comparisons between different animals of different average brain sizes. But within our species, we do not know what the microscopic or cellular basis is of varying brain sizes. If we do not know that simple *physico-physical correla-*

tion, how can we hope to make meaningful statements about the correlation between gross brain size and cellular structure on one hand, and about psychical and behavioural attributes on the other? For the *physico-physical* correlation is basic to the *physico-psychical* association. We do not have the requisite information at either level.

No wonder that a leading neurologist, Gerhardt von Bonin ('50), was led to remark, "The correlation between brain size and mental capacity is insignificant" and, again, "Brain size as such is none too meaningful." Similarly, Holloway ('68), moving outside the human species, has concluded that "Gross size of the brain alone does not explain differences of behaviour within the primate order." He is at pains to point out that "such correlations (as between brain size and specific behavioural traits like memory, insight, forethought, symbolization) are not *causal* analyses, and that a parameter such as brain weight in grams, or volume in milliliters, or area in square millimeters, cannot *explain* the differences in behaviour which are observed" (op. cit., p. 125) (italics mine). A more encompassing theory, Holloway states, should entail not merely the changes in brain weight which have occurred in evolution, but the internal reorganization of the cellular material of the brain. It is precisely at this level that we are most ignorant.

If we compare different species of mammals, many studies have demonstrated that bigger brains are correlated with clearly defined cellular and chemical features. For instance, the bigger the brain, the lower is the density of nerve-cells in that brain (Nissl, 1898; von Bonin, '48; Tower and Elliott, '52; Shariff, '53; Tower, '54). Further, it has been claimed that neurones are bigger and nerve-cell processes longer and more complex in bigger brains. The glia-neurone ratio is likewise higher. The claims and their validity have been well summarised by Holloway ('68). As he points out, an increase in dendritic branching means more synapses, more connectivity, and with this goes more complex behaviour.

On this kind of analysis of different species, increase in brain size is coming to be meaningfully analysed in terms of its structural units and these, in turn, may provide a more rational basis for understanding increasingly complex behaviour. But all this has been shown to apply in an assumed evolutionary progression from one form to another as one passes up the scale. To a lesser extent, similar changes have been shown to apply to the ontogenetic development of individuals within a species. At the adult level, however, I reiterate the view expressed earlier: we do not have any clear picture of the histological and chemical differences between big and small brains among members of the same species. Therefore, we cannot pinpoint any cellular and chemical differences between big and small brains which would indicate a basis for different behaviour. *Are* there differences in behaviour between individuals with big brains and with small brains? Evidence for such differences does not seem to exist.

We are back at square one.

We must confess our ignorance of the functional meaning and value of different sized brains in modern human individuals.

Will a long-term evolutionary look at the problem throw any light on it?

Brain Size, Evolution and Survival

We showed above that, when allowance is made for body size, the differences in the computed numbers of "excess" nerve-cells in the cerebral cortex of various racial or population groups are negligible—despite variations in the source, composition and treatment of the brains. Even if further studies did demonstrate that one group had fewer surplus nerve-cells on the average than another, how valid would it be to jump to

the conclusion that fewer surplus nerve-cells automatically connote lesser cerebral development (cf. Vint) or lesser evolutionary advancement (cf. Gates)? Putnam ('63) assumes that there is no dispute on this question, but his assumption is far from justified.

When one takes a long-term evolutionary look at this problem, it seems clear that increasing brain size (and the organization, fine structure and chemistry that went with it) may once have been vitally important in aiding survival—for instance in a world of wild animals and ape-men, bereft of fire. It seems, too, that the further development of man has placed less and less of a premium on the size of brain, the numbers of nerve-cells and other internal organizational details. For during his evolution, culture and the benevolence of social life have taken the place of nimble wits as an insurance policy against extinction. Beyond a certain stage in the increase of brain size, we have no evidence that further increase in any way improved man's adaptive abilities. For aught we know, the slight preponderance of brain size which is claimed for Caucasoid or White men of today may, if it exists as a genetic feature at all, be a somewhat superfluous and gratuitous heritage from Stone Age ancestors, like Cro-Magnon and Neanderthal men. For these ancestral men had bigger brains on the average than their present-day European descendants.

In fact, there is some evidence to suggest that the trend towards increased brain size, which marked the first two million years of human evolution, has spent itself; the wave of brain expansion has passed its peak. This is true, as I have just said, of early and modern Europeans; to a certain extent, it may be true of Africa as well. Some of our Stone Age men had carried the twin processes of reduction of teeth and jaws, on the one hand, and expansion of brain, on the other, so far that they seem to represent an ancient foreshadowing of the popular idea of the man of the future. At any rate, that is the view of them adopted by Professor Loren Eiseley of Philadelphia, in his delightful and penetrating book of essays called "The Immense Journey" ('58). Listen to the way in which he describes the man of the future:—

"I have stared so much at death that I can recognize the lingering personalities in the faces of skulls and feel accompanying affinities and repulsions . . .

"One such skull lies in the lockers of a great metropolitan museum. It is labelled simply: Strandloper, South Africa. I have never looked longer into any human face than I have upon the features of that skull. I come there often, drawn in spite of myself. It is a face that would lend reality to the fantastic tales of our childhood. There is a hint of Wells's Time Machine folk in it—those pathetic, childlike people whom Wells pictures as haunting earth's autumnal cities in the far future of the dying planet.

"Yet this skull has not been spirited back to us through future eras by a Time Machine. It is a thing, instead, of the millennial past. It is a caricature of modern man, not by reason of its primitiveness but, startlingly, because of a modernity outreaching his own. It constitutes, in fact, a mysterious prophecy and warning. For at the very moment in which students of humanity have been sketching their concept of the man of the future, that being has already come, and lived, and passed away." (Op. cit., pp. 127–128.)

When Eiseley shows his students in Philadelphia a picture of what the man of the future may be expected to look like, they say, "It's O.K. Somebody's keeping an eye on things. Our heads are getting bigger and our teeth are getting smaller. Look!"

"Their voices," says Eiseley, "ring with youthful confidence, the confidence engendered by my persuasive colleagues and myself. At times I glow a little with their reflected enthusiasm.

"I should like to regain that confidence, that warmth. I should like to but . . .

"There's just one thing we haven't quite dared to mention. It's this, and you won't believe it.

It's all happened already. Back there in the past, ten thousand years ago. The man of the future, with the big brain, the small teeth.

"Where did it get him? Nowhere. *Maybe there isn't any future.* Or, if there is, maybe it's only what you find in a little heap of bones on a certain South African beach.

"Many of you who read this belong to the White race. We like to think about this man of the future as being White. It flatters our ego. But the man of the future in the past I'm talking about was not White. He lived in Africa. His brain was bigger than your brain. His face was straight and small, almost a child's face. He was the end evolutionary product in a direction quite similar to the one anthropologists tell us is the road down which we are travelling." (Op. cit., pp. 129–130.)

In Africa, no less than in Europe, it seems a corner has been turned, a peak has been surmounted and something of a downslope presents itself. Perhaps, we can put it this way: the selective pressures which once placed a considerable premium on big brains have been somewhat relaxed. Perhaps, we have reached a stage in human evolution, and I am convinced we reached it thousands of years ago, where 100 people with smaller brains stand just as good a chance of surviving to childbearing age as 100 with bigger brains, and are likely to leave no fewer children than the others. Brain-size is no longer a yardstick to survival as it may once have been. We have used these very brains to develop new mechanisms of adaptation, tools, shelters, clothing, fire, social institutions—and central heating, air-conditioning, refrigeration, disinfection, mink coats and sun shades. You can have these things with a size 5.50 hat or with a size 8.50, just as it makes no difference what size shoe you take.

Brain-size seems to make no difference to your ability to avail yourself of the joys of modern living. So, too, it seems that brain size does not limit your ability to contribute to society, culture, science. Some gifted people have had very small brains. Others, also gifted, have had large brains.

And some very ordinary persons had equally large brains. Small wonder that Gerhardt von Bonin could say in 1963,

"Certainly, the weight of the brain is a very poor indicator of its functional value" and, again, "Brain size as such is a very poor indicator of mental ability."

A century earlier, James Hunt (1863) had stood before the Anthropological Society of London and declared,

". . . we know that it is necessary to be most cautious in accepting the capacity of the cranium as any absolute test of the intellectual power of any race" (p. 13).

In the face of these individual variations of brain size and achievement within a single race, in the face of a decline in average brain size over the last tens of thousands of years, in the face of our knowledge that a large part of man's adaptability to new environments and to new ways of life is culturally determined, who would confidently assert that slightly smaller brains could be any deterrent whatever to achievement, or set any brake upon mental capacity?

The Amount of Grey Matter

Thirty-five years ago, Vint ('34) examined the grey matter of the cerebral cortex of Kenya Africans under the microscope and claimed that it was narrower on the average than that of the European. This work has often been quoted in publications distributed by the Putnam Letters Committee: e.g., by George ('62), by his reviewer, Sanborn (n.d.), by Swan ('64) and by Putnam ('63, '67), as well as by Hofmeyr ('61). More particularly, this group of writers has drawn attention to the supragranular layer of nerve-cells in the cortex, which they claim Vint found to be 14% (Sanborn, n.d.), more than 14%

(Putnam, '63, p. 9), about 15% (Putnam, '67, p. 51), about 14% (George, '62, p. 33) and 16% (Swan, '64, p. 28) smaller than that of Europeans. This layer is held by some to be the "most advanced" layer in the cortex; and that is presumably why its supposed shortfall is stressed in all the publications mentioned, although the shortfall claimed by Vint for one other layer of the cortex, the internal granular layer, is greater.

Yet, when one goes back to the original sources, one is left with serious doubts about the validity of the data on which the comparison was based. First, let us look at what Vint actually reported: he claimed that the average total reduction of the whole cortex, as compared with that of the European, is 14.8% in the cortical areas examined. His figures for the Negro were based on one single study of Negro brains, which, he states, did not include any of the "so-called educated class." He did not study any European brains himself, although at least two of the references quoted give the impression that Vint studied European brains directly. Thus, Swan ('64) speaks of "Dr. F. W. Vint's careful comparative studies of the cortical histology of the brains of European Whites and African Negroes" (p. 27). Similarly, and equally erroneously, Putnam ('67) states, "In 1934 F. W. Vint of the Medical Research Laboratory, Kenya, Africa, published the results of a *comparative study of Negro and European brains* in which he found that the supragranular layer of the Negro cortex was about 15 per cent thinner than the Whites" (p. 51) (italics mine). In both quotations, the wording conveys the impression that Vint had himself made a careful study of the cortex of European brains, as well as of Negro brains, whereas he had in fact studied only Negro cortices and compared his results with those obtained in one other study, by a different worker, namely von Economo ('29) in Europe.

In eight different regions of the cortex, he measured the total cortical thickness and the thickness of each of four layers comprising the total cortex, namely the lamina zonalis, the supragranular zone, the internal granular zone and the infragranular zone. Each of the five measurements in seven out of eight regions was then compared with a corresponding measurement as given in von Economo's ('29) book, and a percentage increase or decrease recorded, as compared with "the European brain."

There are many possible sources of error in these comparisons. First, Vint himself points out that there is even some doubt among different workers as to where exactly to cut the little section of tissue to measure the thickness of the layers—whether from the tops of the convolutions of grey matter, or from their sides, or from the depths of the fissures between them. Vint states that Bolton ('03, '14) had recorded measurements which were the average in each case between thickness readings (i) on the flat external surface of the convolution; (ii) at the lip of the adjacent sulcus or fissure; (iii) on the side of the fissure; and (iv) at the bottom of the fissure.

Von Economo ('29) pointed out that the thickness of the cortex on the summits of the convolutions was twice as great as in the floor of the fissures, but unfortunately he did not make clear whether he had followed Bolton's averaging method or some other approach. Thus, Vint makes clear that he is not exactly certain whether von Economo's measurements on European brains were made in the same area as were his (Vint's) measurements on Negro brains, namely only on the summit or crown of the convolutions.

Secondly, the actual measuring of the layers of the cortex is not as easy as it may sound. Although the various layers are fairly readily identified, the boundaries between them are not. The boundaries are frequently wavy and exactly where to set the termini for a particular measurement may vary from worker to worker, even in the same laboratory. It would be easy for one worker consistently to measure from a different part of such a wavy boundary, compared with another, and so to introduce a systematic error into his results. Vint had received no specific training under von Economo, as far as we know, and there is no reason to believe that his technique of making measurements would have been precisely the same as that of von Economo. Furthermore, Vint nowhere states how his measurements were made, nor are the boundaries of the layers marked in on his photographs, in contrast, say, with the illustrations on the human cortex by Bailey and von Bonin ('51).

A third most serious difficulty is the technical procedures employed. To prepare a brain for microscopical study requires a number of chemical and staining procedures, a variety of which is available to workers in most laboratories. Different chemical treatments are known to produce different degrees of shrinkage or swelling. These influences readily affect measurements, especially when one is dealing with a total cortical thickness as small as 1.886 to 3.006 mm (the range of average cortical thicknesses found by Vint in 8 different areas of the brain).

As an illustration, Diamond et al. ('64, '66) measured the thickness of the rat's visual cortex by two different techniques: frozen sections stained by thionin and celloidin sections stained by Windle's modified Nissl stain. The thickness measurements by the second method were only 60.5% of those by the former.

Even within one laboratory, with the use of only a single technique over and over again, most variable results may be obtained in the state of preservation (*fixation*) and staining of brains. As Carothers ('53, p. 82) has pointed out, "Comparative assessments of cerebral histology are notoriously difficult and require special knowledge of this type of work . . ." Here, then, we have the unsatisfactory position of a series of fine measurements made on brains treated in one laboratory by one worker and derived from

Negroes, being compared with the results of another series of fine measurements made by another worker on European brains prepared in a different laboratory, possibly under very different conditions. And Vint's are the only data on record for Negro cortical thickness! If we left the matter there, anyone with a logical mind would realise that no conclusions could validly be drawn about alleged differences between races culled from such unsatisfactory material. To quote Carothers again, "Comparative assessments of cerebral histology . . . are of little value unless the preparation of material and the techniques that are used are virtually identical for the two groups. These requirements were not convincingly fulfilled (in Vint's comparisons)" (op. cit., p. 82).

Vint himself points out a further serious shortcoming. He states specifically, "Owing to climatic and other conditions, it was impossible to fix the brain by injection of the carotid arteries."

If all these sources of variation apply to the thickness of the entire cortex, how much more strongly do they apply to the supragranular layer alone, which Vint found to vary in average thickness from 0.338 to 0.922 of a *millimetre* in six different parts of the cortex! (Chart 10).

It is clear that Vint's study, which has been so widely quoted, permits only one definite conclusion about cortical thicknesses, namely that there is a need for more carefully controlled studies. Yet, we find the alleged 15% difference in total cortical thickness and the supposed 16% shortfall in the supragranular layer being quoted and re-quoted as established facts, as further

Chart 10: Range of thickness measurements (Vint, '34)

	CORTEX		
1.886	—	3.006	millimetres
	SUPRAGRANULAR LAYER		
0.338	—	0.922	millimetres

evidence of the supposed inferiority of the Negro's brain. What is more, the inferences drawn from these so-called facts are used to create the impression that the Negro is a less highly-evolved being—as for instance when Putnam ('63, p. 9) states, "The thickness of the supragranular layer of the cortex, which is found to increase as we move up the scale from animal to man, may thus be said to be another measure of evolutionary development."

We are led to conclude that there is no scientifically acceptable proof that the cerebral cortex of Negroes is thinner in whole, or in any layer, than that of Europeans.

Concluding Thoughts on Brains and Races

I have singled out only two of the so-called well-established differences between the brains of Negroes and of Whites, namely brain size and the thickness of the cortex, and shown that they provide highly unsatisfactory evidence of structural differences in the Negro's brain, and of differences in intellectual capacity. Other claims have been made, such as one about the size of the frontal lobe and the degree to which it is broken into convolutions, claims which have been denied equally strenuously by many other workers. From my little venture into the study of the brain, I have emerged with the conviction that vast claims have been based on insubstantial evidence. I conclude that there is no acceptable evidence for such structural differences in the brains of these two racial groups; and certainly nothing which provides a satisfactory anatomical basis for explaining any difference in I.Q. or in other mental and performance tests, in temperament or in behaviour.

The exploding of the myth about brain size and grey matter differences leads to the realisation that, in science, the truth does not gain acceptance by mere repetition of a set of facts. Hypotheses are not confirmed by statement and re-statement of the hypotheses. Science requires rather the patient testing of the facts, the repeating of early studies by more modern, better controlled and better standardized methods, the constant re-examination and critical re-appraisal of premises and assumptions, the elasticity of mind which permits, nay demands, old hypotheses to be modified when new facts emerge which cannot be adequately explained by them, resistance to the tendency to develop a vested interest in a particular viewpoint, avoidance of ascribing motives to scientists of opposite viewpoint, in favour of the unbiassed examination of the evidence they may advance, the eschewing of premature hypotheses based on over-tenuous evidence. It is to these stern and rigorous demands of scientific method and to one who proved himself a trenchant devotee of this philosophy that my address is dedicated.

LITERATURE CITED

ABELSON, P. H. 1969 Malnutrition, learning and behavior. Science, 164:17.

APPEL, F. W., and E. M. APPEL 1942 Intracranial variation in the weight of the human brain. Human Biology, 14:48–68 and 235–250.

BAILEY, P., and G. VON BONIN 1951 The Isocortex of Man. Urbana: University of Illinois Press, pp. 1–301.

BARAITSER, M., and D. E. EVANS 1969 The effect of undernutrition on brain-rhythm development. S. Afr. Med. J., 43:56–58.

BEAN, R. B. 1917 The weights of the organs in relation to type, race, sex, stature and age. Anat. Rec., 11:326–328.

BOLTON, J. S. 1903 The histological basis of amentia and dementia. Archiv. Neurol., 2:424–620.

———— 1914 The Brain in Health and Disease. London: Arnold.

BRANDES, K. 1927 Liquorverhältnisse an der Leiche und Hirnschwellung. Frankfurt. Ztschr. f. Path., 35:274–301.

BROWN, R. E. 1966 Organ weight in malnutrition

with special reference to brain weight. Develop. Med. Child. Neurol., 8:512–522.

CAROTHERS, J. C. 1953 The African Mind in Health and Disease. World Health Organization Monograph Series, No. 17.

CHASE, H. P., W. F. B. LINDSLEY and D. O'BRIEN 1969 Undernutrition and cerebellar development. Nature, 221:554–555.

CRAVIOTO, J., and B. ROBLES 1965 Evolution of adaptive and motor behaviour during rehabilitation from kwashiorkor. Amer. J. Orthopsychiat., 35:449–464.

COBB, S. 1965 Brain size. Arch. Neurol. (Chicago), 12:555–561.

DART, R. A. 1956 The relationships of brain size and brain pattern to human status. S. Afr. J. Med. Sci., 21 (1 and 2):23–45.

DAVIS, J. B. 1868 Contributions towards determining the weight of the brain in different races of man. Philos. Trans., 158:505–527. (Cited by Pakkenberg and Voigt, '64.)

DAVISON, A. N., and J. DOBBING 1965 Myelination as a vulnerable period in brain development. Brit. Med. Bull., 22:40–44.

DIAMOND, M. C., D. KRECH and M. R. ROSENZWEIG 1964 The effects of an enriched environment on the histology of the rat cerebral cortex. J. Comp. Neur., 123:111–119.

DIAMOND, M. C., F. LAW, H. RHODES, B. LINDNER, M. R. ROSENZWEIG, D. KRECH and L. BENNETT 1966 Increases in cortical depth and glia numbers in rats subjected to enriched environment. J. Comp. Neur., 128:117–125.

DICKERSON, J. W. T., and J. DOBBING 1967 Prenatal and postnatal growth and development of the central nervous system of the pig. Proc. roy. Soc., B, 166:384–395.

DICKERSON, J. W. T., and R. A. MC CANCE 1967 Effect of undernutrition on the postnatal development of the brain and cord in pigs. Proc. roy. Soc., B, 166:396–407.

DICKERSON, J. W. T., and A. L. WALMSLEY 1967 The effect of undernutrition and subsequent rehabilitation on the growth and composition of the central nervous system of the rat. Brain, 90:897–906.

DOBBING, J., and E. M. WIDDOWSON 1965 The effect of undernutrition and subsequent rehabilitation on myelination of rat brain as measured by its composition. Brain, 88:357–366.

DUCKWORTH, W. L. H. 1904 Morphology and Anthropology. Cambridge University Press, xxviii + 564 pp.

EAYRS, J. T., and G. HORN 1955 Development of cerebral cortex in hypothyroid and starved rats. Anat. Rec., *121*:53–61.

EICHENWALD, H. F., and P. C. FRY 1969 Nutrition and learning. Science, *163*:644–648.

EISELEY, L. 1958 The Immense Journey. London: Victor Gollancz.

ENGEL, R. 1956 Abnormal brain-wave patterns in kwashiorkor. Electroenceph. and Clin. Neurophysiol., *8*:489–500.

FISHMAN, M. A., A. L. PRENSKY and P. R. DODGE 1969 Low content of cerebral lipids in infants suffering from malnutrition. Nature, *221*:552–553.

GATES, R. R. 1946 Human Genetics. New York: Macmillan.

GEORGE, W. C. 1961 Race, Heredity and Civilization. (Cited by Hofmeyr, '61.)

——— 1962 The Biology of the Race Problem. Report commissioned by the Governor of Alabama, 1–87.

GILLMAN, J., and T. GILLMAN 1951 Perspectives in Malnutrition. New York: Grune and Stratton, pp. 1–584.

GUTHRIE, H. A., and M. L. BROWN 1968 Effect of severe undernutrition in early life on growth, brain-size and composition in adult rats. J. Nutrition, *94*:419–426.

HAMMOND, J. 1944 Physiological factors affecting birth weight. Proc. nutr. Soc., *2*:8–12.

HERRE, W. 1958 The influence of the environment on the brain of the mammals. Dtsch. Med. Wschr., *83*:86.

HOFMEYR, J. D. J. 1961 Gedifferensiëerde ontwikkeling: 'n genetiese standpunt. Pretoria, University of Pretoria Branch of Afrikaanse Studentebond, pp. 8–15.

HOLLOWAY, R. L. 1968 The evolution of the primate brain: some aspects of quantitative relations. Brain Research, *7*:121–172.

HUNT, J. 1863 On the Negro's place in Nature. Anthrop. Soc. Lond., viii + 60 pp.

HUNT, S. B. 1869 Journ. Anthrop. Soc. Lond., *7*: 40–54. (Cited by Pearl, '34.)

JACKSON, C. M., and C. A. STEWART 1920 The effects of inanition in the young upon the ultimate size of the body and the various organs in the albino rat. J. Exp. Zool., *30*:8.

JERISON, H. J. 1963 Interpreting the evolution of the brain. Human Biol., *35* (3):263–291.

KERPEL-FRONIUS, E. 1961 Somatic stability in the newly born. Ciba Foundation Symposium.

KROMPECHER, ST., and J. LIPÁK 1966 A simple method for determining cerebralization. Brain weight and intelligence. J. Comp. Neurol., *127*: 113–120.

KUMMER, H. 1961 Beitrag zur quantitativen Bestimmung der Entwicklungshöhe des Säugetiergehirnes. Psychiat. Neurol., Basel, *142*:352–375.

KUSUMOTO, M. 1936 On the biometrical constants of the Japanese brainweight. Jap. J. Med. Sci., *6*(91) (abstract) (cited by Bailey and von Bonin, '51).

LASHLEY, K. S. 1949 Persistent problems in the evolution of mind. Quart. Rev. Biol., *24*:28–42.

LATIMER, H. B. 1950 The weights of the brain and its parts and the weight and length of the spinal cord in the adult male guinea pig. J. Comp. Neur., *93*:37–51.

MALL, F. P. 1909 On several anatomical characters of the human brain said to vary according to race and sex, with special reference to the frontal lobes. Am. J. Anat., *9*:1–32.

MATIEGKA, H. 1902 Über das Hirngewicht, die Schädelkapazität und die Kopfform, Sowie deren Beziehungen zur psychischen Thätigkeit des Menschen. S.B. kgl. böhmischen Ges. Wiss. Prag. mathnat. Cl., No. 20, 1–75.

METTLER, F. A. 1955 Culture and the structural evolution of the neural system. James Arthur Lecture on the Evolution of the Human Brain. New York: American Museum of Natural History.

MORTON, S. G. 1849 Proc. Nat. Acad. Sci. Philadelphia, *4*:221–224. (Cited by Pearl, '34.)

NELSON, G. K. 1959 The electroencephalogram in kwashiorkor. Electroenceph. Clin. Neurophysiol., *11*:73–84.

——— 1963 Electroencephalographic studies in sequelae of kwashiorkor and other diseases in Africans, 777–787. Proceedings of the Central African Scientific and Medical Congress, August 1963. In: Science and Medicine in Central Africa. George J. Snowball, ed. Pergamon Press.

NISSL, F. 1898 Nervenzellen und graue Substanz. Munch. med. Wschr., *45*:988.

OSLER, W. 1968 Belated scars of war prisons. The Star, Johannesburg, 11 November 1968.

PAKKENBERG, H., and J. VOIGT 1964 Brain weight of the Danes. Acta Anat., *56*:297–307.

PEACOCK, T. B. 1865 Mem. Anthrop. Soc. Lond., *1*, 65–71 and 520–524. (Cited by Pearl, '34.)

PEARL, R. 1905 Biometrical studies in man. I. Varia-

tion and correlation in brain weight. Biometrika, 4:13–104.
—— 1934 The weight of the Negro brain. Science, 80:431–434.
PLATT, B. S., G. PAMPLIGLIONE and R. J. C. STEWART 1965 Experimental protein-calorie deficiency. Develop. Med. Child Neurol., 7:9.
POLIAKOVA, R. S. 1960 Interspecial differences in brain size. Arkh. Anat. Gistol. i. Embriol., 39:58–64. (Read in abstract.)
PUTNAM, C. 1963 Three new letters on science and race. New York: National Putnam Letters Committee, 3–23.
—— 1967 Race and Reality: A Search for Solutions. Washington, Public Affairs Press, 1–192.
RADINSKY, L. 1967 Relative brain size: a new measure. Science, 155:836–838.
SANBORN, H. C. n.d. DR. W. C. GEORGE's "The Biology of the Race Problem": a review. New York, National Putnam Letters Committee, 1–8.
SCHLAGINHAUFEN, O. 1950–51 Ein Melanesierschädel von ungewöhnlich kleiner Kapazität. Bull. Schweiz. Ges. Anthrop. u. Ethnol., 27:26–37.
SCHREIDER, E. 1966 Brain weight correlations calculated from Original results of Paul Broca. Am. J. Phys. Anthrop., 25:153–158.
SCHULTZ, A. H. 1962 Die Schädelkapazität männlicher Gorillas und ihr Höchstwert. Anthrop. Anz., 25:197–203.
SCRIMSHAW, N. S., and E. GORDON (eds.) 1968 Malnutrition, Learning and Behaviour. Cambridge, MIT Press.
SHARIFF, G. A. 1953 Cell counts in the primate cerebral cortex. J. Comp. Neur., 98:381–400.
SHIBATA, I. 1936 Brain weight of the Korean. Am. J. Phys. Anthrop., 22:27–35.
SMIT, P. J. 1969 Anthropometric, motor performance and physiological studies on South African children involved in a nutritional status survey. Thesis accepted for the degree of Ph.D., Anatomy Dept., University of the Witwatersrand.
SOEMMERING, S. T. 1788 Vom Hirn und Rückenmark. Mainz: P. A. Winkpp. 115 pp. (Cited by Bailey and von Bonin, '51.)
SPANN, W., and H. O. DUSTMANN 1965 Das menschliche Hirngewichte und seine Abhängigkeit von Lebensalter, Körperlänge, Todesursache und Beruf. Deutsche Zeitschrift für gerichtliche Medizin, 56:299–317.
STOCH, M. B., and P. M. SMYTHE 1963 Does undernutrition during infancy inhibit brain growth and subsequent intellectual development? Arch. Dis. Childh., 38:546–552.
—— 1967 The effect of undernutrition during infancy on subsequent brain growth and intellectual development. S. Afr. Med. J., 41:1027–1031.
STRØM, A. (ed.) 1968 Norwegian Concentration Camp Survivors. Oslo: Universitetsforlaget, pp. 9–186.
SWAN, D. A. 1964 Juan Comas on "'Scientific' racism again?": A scientific analysis. Mankind Quarterly, 2 (4): Reprinted in Mankind Monographs VI (3), 24–36.
TIAKAHASI, K., and I. SUZUKI 1961 The brain weight of Japanese. Sapporo Med. J., 20:179–184.
TIEDEMANN, F. 1836 On the brain of the Negro, compared with that of the European and the orangoutang. Phil. Trans. Roy. Soc. Lond., 126:497–527.
TOBIAS, P. V. 1958 Some aspects of the biology of the Bantu-speaking African. Leech, 28:3–12.
TODD, T. W. 1927 A liter and a half of brains. Science, 66:122–125.
TOPINARD, P. 1885 Elements d'Anthropologie Générale. xv, 1157 pp. Paris, A. Delahaye and E. Lecrosnier.
TOWER, D. B. 1954 Structural and functional organization of mammalian cerebral cortex: the correlation of neurone density with brain size. J. Comp. Neur., 101:19–53.
TOWER, D. B., and K. A. C. ELLIOTT 1952 Activity of the acetylcholine system in the cerebral cortex of various unanaesthetized mammals. Am. J. Physiol., 168:747–759.
VINT, F. W. 1934 The brain of the Kenya native. J. Anat. Lond., 68:216–223.
VON BONIN, G. 1948 The frontal lobe of the primates, cytoarchitectural studies. Res. Publ. Assoc. nerv. ment. Dis., 27:67–83.
—— 1950 Essay on the Cerebral Cortex. Charles C Thomas, Springfield, Illinois.
—— 1963 The Evolution of the Human Brain. Chicago: University Press, xiv + 92 pp.
VON ECONOMO, C. 1929 The Cyto-architectonics of the Human Cerebral Cortex. Oxford University Press.
WALDEYER, W. 1894 Sitzungber. d.k. Preuss. Akad. d. Wiss. Berlin, pp. 1213–1221 (cited by Pearl, '34).
ZAMENHOF, S., E. VAN MARTHENS and F. L. MARGOLIS 1968 DNA (cell number) and protein in neonatal brain: alteration by maternal dietary protein restriction. Science, 160:322–323.

35 • AFRICAN ANCESTRY OF THE WHITE AMERICAN POPULATION

Robert P. Stuckert

Ever since the first blacks were landed on the shores of North America in 1619, admixture between whites and blacks has proceeded apace. That admixture has resulted largely from matings between white men and black women. The convention of respectable white society has been to evade any recognition of this fact and its consequences. Where references have been made to the subject, they have traditionally been pejorative. Such unions have been declared abhorrent and even illegal. Until 1967, when the United States Supreme Court ruled unanimously that states cannot outlaw marriages between whites and blacks, at least 19 states had such laws on their books.

Where such attitudes prevailed, a negative sanction existed on any studies inquiring into the quantitative aspects of what has been called "miscegenation." [1] In recent years, however, with the breakdown in many traditional walls of prejudice, several excellent studies have appeared on the quantitative and genetic aspects of black-white admixture. Among the most important of these is Stuckert's contribution, reprinted here. It is far too little known, and I have seldom seen a reference to it.

It is usually assumed that the passage of genes is largely one way, from white to black, and that the offspring of such unions usually return to the black population. The larger number may, in fact, do so, but what contribution their genes may continue to make to the white population is quite another matter. That contribution is greater than is customarily supposed. Here Stuckert considers the flow of genes from the black to the white American population. His figures may startle some readers, but if they err, they probably do so on the conservative side.

There can be very little doubt that from the biological standpoint such admixture has benefited both groups.

Defining a racial group generally poses a problem to social scientists. A definition of a race has yet to be proposed that is satisfactory for all purposes. This is particularly true when the racial group has minority group status as does the Negro group in the United States. To many persons, however, the matter of race definition is no problem. They view humanity as being divided into completely separate racial compartments. A Negro is commonly defined as a person having *any known trace* of Negro ancestry or "blood" regardless of how far back one must go to find it. A concomitant belief is that all whites are free of the presumed taint of Negro ancestry or "blood."

The purpose of this research was to determine the validity of this belief in the non-Negro ancestry of persons classified as white. Current definitions of Negro may have serious limitations when used as bases for classifying persons according to ancestry (Berry, 1951). The terms *African*

SOURCE: *Ohio Journal of Science* vol. 58 (1959): 155–60. Reprinted by permission of the author and the publisher.
[1] For the origin and discussion of this unfortunate word see Ashley Montagu, "The Term 'Miscegenation,'" in his book, *Man's Most Dangerous Myth; The Fallacy of Race*, 4th ed. (New York: World Publishing Co., 1964), pp. 400–401.

and *non-African* will be used rather than *Negro* and *white* when discussing the ancestry of an individual. Each of the former pair of terms has a more specific referent which is the geographic point of origin of an individual. At the same time, the two pairs of terms are closely related. Hence, this paper is the report of an attempt to estimate the percentage of persons classified as white that have African ancestry or genes received from an African ancestor.

This raises a question concerning the relationship between having an African ancestor and receiving one or more genes from this ancestor. Since one-half of an individual's genetic inheritance is received from each parent, the probability of a person with one African ancestor within the previous eight generations receiving *any single gene* from this ancestor is equal to or greater than $(0.5)^8$ or 3.9063×10^{-3}. It has been estimated that there are approximately 48,000 gene loci on 24 chromosome pairs (Stern, 1950). The probability that an individual with one African ancestor has *one or more* genes derived from this ancestor is equal to $1 - (1 - 3.9063 \times 10^{-3})^{24,000}$ or greater than 0.9998. Having more than one African ancestor increases this probability. One final remark needs to be made. Some degree of African ancestry is not necessarily related to the physical appearance of the individual. Many of the genes possessed by virtue of descent from an African do not distinguish the bearer from persons of non-African ancestry. They are the genes or potentials for traits which characterize the human race. Nevertheless, these genes represent an element in the biological constitution of the individual inherited from an African.

Research Methodology

The research methodology of this study involved constructing a *genetic probability table*. The primary function of this type of table is to ascertain the distribution within a known population of a variable that cannot be observed directly. It is frequently used to estimate the changes that occur in the genetic composition of a population over a period of time. There are three basic steps in the computation of a genetic probability table.

1. A series of assumptions which serve as a basis for the table is made. These assumptions may refer to the initial distribution of the variable within the population, the effect of biological and non-biological factors on the distribution, or the interrelationships of these factors. In some cases, these assumptions may be derived from available empirical data.

2. On the basis of these assumptions, the probability distributions of the variable within the population for successive time intervals are computed. This is done by applying the rules of probability relevant to the principles of biological inheritance to the changes that are known to have occurred in the observable characteristics of the population.

3. The validity of the probability table is determined by comparing the probability values included in the table to probability values obtained from empirical studies based on other research methods. The extent to which these values correspond is a measure of the validity of the table.

Sources of Data

The best data available for use in estimating the biological background of Americans are those dealing with the population of this country. Official records have been kept of the white and Negro population since 1790 by the Bureau of the Census and of the influx of foreign population to this country since 1820 by the Immigration and Naturalization Service. Numerous estimates of population and immigration figures have been made for the period 1660 to 1820. There is general agreement among historians, statisticians, and population analysts on the relative reliability of the data for the years since 1750 only (Carey, 1853; Bromwell, 1856; Bancroft, 1891; Greene, 1932; U.S. National Resources Committee, 1938). Estimates have been made of the volume of illegal smuggling of slaves into this country between 1808 and 1860 (U.S. Bureau of the Census, 1909; Dublin 1928). Thus, it was possible to obtain usable data for each decennial period since 1750.

Assumptions and Estimating Equations

In this study, all persons were classified into four racial-ancestral categories: white persons with no African ancestry (wna), white persons with some degree of African ancestry (wa), Negroes with some degree of non-African ancestry (nna), and Negroes with African ancestry only (na). The following assumptions were used as bases for statistically estimating the probability of African and non-African ancestry.

1. The white population of the American colonies in 1750 contained no persons of African ancestry. Any African element introduced into the background of supposedly white persons prior to 1750 was regarded as unimportant since the probability of possessing genes from any given ancestor decreases rapidly after ten generations from the introduction of these genes.

2. All individuals classified as Negro have some degree of African ancestry.

3. The probability of a male member of any of the four racial-ancestral categories being a partner in a fecund mating during a given period of time is equal to the proportion of the total population in the category at the beginning of the time period. In other words, if one-tenth of the total population are white persons of non-African ancestry, one-tenth of all fecund sexual contacts involve white males of non-African ancestry. The same is assumed for females.

4. The probability of persons classified as white mating with persons classified as Negro is one-twentieth of what would be expected if mating were random. To illustrate, if 90 percent of the population were white and 10 percent were Negro and *mating were random*, 18 percent of all fecund matings would involve a white and a Negro. According to this assumption of *selective mating*, the percentage of fecund matings involving members of different racial categories would be nine-tenths of one percent in this case. It should also be remembered that virtually all of the offspring of these mixed matings would be classified as Negro.

5. The proportion of the increase in population due to causes other than immigration from Africa and Europe during a given period that can be assigned to a racial-ancestral category is equal to the probability of a live birth being a member of that category. These causes include natural increase, emigration, and immigration from racially mixed areas (West Indies, Mexico, Central and South America). If one-third of the live births during a given period are white persons of non-African ancestry, one-third of the increase due to these causes is comprised of white persons of non-African ancestry.

6. All persons immigrating to the United States from Europe are of non-African ancestry only. Due to the small number of African Negroes in Europe, the incidence of African ancestry among Europeans is relatively small.

7. All persons immigrating to the United States from areas in Africa are of African ancestry and one-tenth of them have some degree of non-African ancestry.

Several equations were used in computing the probability of an individual drawn at random from the population being a member of each of the four racial-ancestral categories. The first was used to estimate the number of white persons with only non-African ancestry. The crucial problem was estimating the portion of the population increase due to causes other than immigration from Europe and Africa during a censual period that had no African ancestry. The symbol P(wna) was used to represent the proportion of the population that was both white and of non-African ancestry only in a given censual year. Under the third and fifth assumptions, the proportion of the population increase mentioned above during the subsequent period assigned to this racial-ancestral category equalled $P(wna)^2$. The assumption of selective mating (assumption 4) required an additional increment. $P(w)$ and $P(n)$ represented the proportions of the population that were classified as white and Negro, respectively. The proportion of the increase falling in the mixed parentage category during the following ten-year period was calculated to be $P(w)P(n)$. Although 95 percent of this group was assigned to the white category under the .05 selective mating factor of the fourth assumption, only a proportion equal to

$$.95 \frac{P(wna)^2}{P(w)^2}$$

was assigned to the category of white with no African ancestry. This limitation was imposed by assumption 3. Hence, the proportion of the increase classified as white with no African ancestry equalled

$$P(wna)^2 + .95 \frac{P(wna)^2 P(n)}{P(w)}$$

The absolute number in this category was obtained by multiplying by the magnitude of this population increase.

According to the sixth assumption, immigration from Europe during a censual period included no persons of African ancestry. The number of whites with no African ancestry at the end of a censual period was obtained by adding these two figures to the number in this category at the beginning of the period. The final form of the equation was

$$N(wna) = Y + (wna)^2 Z$$
$$+ .95 \frac{P(wna)^2 P(n)}{P(w)} Z + I_E$$

where Y = estimated number of whites having no African ancestry in the preceding censual year

$P(wna)$ = Probability of a person being classified as white with no African ancestry in the preceding censual year

$P(n)$ = probability of a person being classified as Negro in the preceding censual year

$P(w)$ = probability of a person being classified as white in the preceding censual year

Z = increase due to causes other than immigration from Europe and Africa during preceding decade

I_E = immigration from Europe during preceding decade

The estimated number of whites having some degree of African ancestry was obtained by subtracting the estimated number of whites having no African ancestry from the total number of persons classified as white.

A similar procedure was followed for the Negro ancestral categories. To estimate the number of individuals that are Negro and have only African ancestry for a given censual year, another equation was used.

$$N(na) = X + P(na)^2 Z$$
$$+ .95 \frac{P(na)^2 P(w)}{P(n)} Z + .90 I_A$$

where X = estimated number of Negroes having only African ancestry in the preceding censual year

$P(na)$ = probability of a person being classified as Negro with African ancestry only in the preceding censual year

$P(n)$ = probability of a person being classified as Negro in the preceding censual year

$P(w)$ = probability of a person being classified as white in the preceding censual year

Z = increase due to causes other than immigration from Europe and Africa during preceding decade

I_A = immigration from Africa during preceding decade

The estimated number of Negroes having some degree of non-African ancestry was obtained by subtracting the number of Negroes with only African ancestry from the total number of Negroes in the population. The probability values for a given censual year needed to complete the genetic probability table were obtained by dividing these four sets of numerical estimates by the total white and Negro population at that time.

Criteria of Validity

Three types of empirical studies were used in determining the validity of the genetic probability table based upon the above assumptions. These included studies of the mixed ancestry of Negro groups, the frequency of children born of mixed parentage, and the frequency of passing.

Research Results

A genetic probability table was constructed on the basis of the above data and assumptions. This table included the probabilities of an individual drawn at random from the population of the United States being a member of the four racial-ancestral categories. These probabilities were computed for every tenth year from 1750 through 1780 and each censual year since 1790. In order to highlight the relative size of the two groups with mixed ancestry, the probability values in this table were converted to absolute numbers. Table 1 includes these data for successive cen-

Table 1: Total white and Negro population, white population with African ancestry and Negro population with non-African ancestry, United States, 1790–1950

| | WHITE POPULATION | | | NEGRO POPULATION | | |
| | Total (000's) | African ancestry | | Total (000's) | Non-African ancestry | |
Year		Number (000's)	%		Number (000's)	%
1790	3,172	62	2.0	757	144	19.0
1800	4,306	164	3.8	1,002	209	20.9
1810	5,862	303	5.2	1,378	450	32.7
1820	7,887	623	7.9	1,772	620	35.0
1830	10,537	1,134	10.8	2,329	842	36.2
1840	14,196	1,939	13.7	2,874	1,041	36.2
1850	19,553	2,975	15.2	3,639	1,389	38.2
1860	26,923	4,508	16.7	4,442	1,738	39.1
1870	33,589	6,035	18.0	4,880	1,935	39.7
1880	43,403	7,961	18.3	6,581	3,248	49.4
1890	55,101	10,383	18.8	7,489	3,902	52.1
1900	66,809	13,020	19.5	8,834	5,002	56.6
1910	81,364	14,150	17.4	9,828	6,050	61.6
1920	94,120	16,703	17.7	10,463	6,780	64.8
1930	108,861	20,120	18.5	11,891	8,086	68.0
1940	118,215	23,035	19.5	12,866	8,993	69.9
1950	134,942	28,366	21.0	15,042	10,980	73.0

sual years. The percentages of the two racial categories that have both African and non-African ancestry are also included.

The data in table 1 indicate that approximately 21 percent of the persons classified as white in 1950 have an African element in their inherited biological background. The percentage of persons classified as white having some degree of African ancestry was extremely small in 1790. The percentage figures for successive censual years increased most rapidly between 1790 and 1850. Although this is partly a function of the computational methods used, it is characteristic of interbreeding populations. The figures for the period 1850 to 1890 were comparatively stable. Between 1900 and 1930, the percentage declined slightly. These two shifts were primarily the result of large-scale immigration from Europe. With the curtailing of this immigration, the percentage values began increasing again in 1930.

One final question pertains to the validity of these data. As mentioned above, three criteria were used to ascertain the validity of the probability values used in deriving Table 1. Two of the criteria involved the incidence of mixed ancestry among persons classified as Negro. First, the percentage of Negroes that had some degree of non-African ancestry was computed for each censual year. Table 1 shows that from 64.8 to 73.0 percent of Negroes had some degree of non-African ancestry in the last four censual years. These figures correspond closely to those included in studies of Negro groups made by Hrdlicka (1928), Herskovits (1930), and Hooton (1939). Second, estimates of the percentage of Negroes born of mixed parentage were made on the basis of the probability values included in the genetic probability table. The percentage born of mixed parentage varied between 7.9 percent in 1850 and 8.4 percent in 1920. These computed values do not conflict with any of the data cited by Herskovits (1928), Day (1932), and Frazier (1939). Furthermore, these values

are almost the exact values needed to account for the rates of gene transfer computed by Glass and Li (1953).

The third criterion centered around the phenomena of passing. The increase in the number of persons classified as white having some degree of African ancestry given in Table 1 could have occurred only if there were a continuing influx of persons into the white group from the Negro group. The magnitude and rate of passing needed to account for the indicated increase were computed for the period 1860 to 1950. These data are given in Table 2. They fall well within the

Table 2: Estimated extent and rate of passing, United States, 1861–1950

PERIOD	ESTIMATED NUMBER OF PERSONS PASSING	ANNUAL MEAN	ANNUAL RATE [*]
1861–1890	90,900	3,030	0.68
1891–1910	101,300	5,065	0.68
1911–1930	183,200	9,160	0.93
1931–1940	42,700	4,270	0.36
1941–1950	155,500	15,550	1.21

[*] Rate per 1,000 Negro population per year.

range of frequency of passing as empirically estimated by Hart (1921), Burma (1946), and Eckard (1947). The data in Table 2 also indicate that the rate of passing is increasing.

Conclusions

The data presented in this study indicate that the popular belief in the non-African background of white persons is invalid. Over twenty-eight million white persons are descendants of persons of African origin. Furthermore, the majority of the persons with African ancestry are classified as white. Finally, if the volume of immigration remains at the present relatively low level, the percentage of persons having mixed ancestry will increase in the future. One conclusion stands out from these data. The belief in the racial uniformity of an individual's ancestors may be the basic myth of the white man's past.

LITERATURE CITED

BANCROFT, G. 1891. History of the United States. Vol. 2. D. Appleton and Co., New York. 565 pp.

BERRY, B. 1951. Race Relations. Houghton Mifflin Co., Boston. 487 pp.

BROMWELL, W. 1856. History of Immigration to the United States. Redfield, New York. 225 pp.

BURMA, J. H. 1946. The measurement of Negro "passing." Amer. Jour. Sociol. 52:18–22.

CAREY, H. C. 1853. The Slave Trade. A. Hart, Philadelphia. 426 pp.

DAY, C. B. 1932. A Study of Some Negro-white Families in the United States. Harvard African Studies. Vol. 10. Harvard University, Cambridge. 126 pp.

DUBLIN, L. J. 1928. Health and Wealth. Harper and Brothers, New York. 361 pp.

ECKARD, E. W. 1947. How many Negroes "pass"? Amer. Jour. Sociol. 52:498–500.

FRAZIER, E. F. 1939. The Negro Family in the United States. The University of Chicago Press, Chicago. 686 pp.

GLASS, B. and C. C. LI. 1953. The dynamics of racial intermixture—an analysis based on the American Negro. Amer. Jour. Human Genet. 5:1–20.

GREENE, E. B. 1932. American Population Before the Federal Census of 1790. Columbia University Press, New York. 228 pp.

HART, H. 1921. Selective Migration as a Factor in Child Welfare in the United States, with Special Reference to Iowa. University of Iowa, Iowa City. 137 pp.

HERSKOVITS, M. J. 1928. The American Negro: A Study in Racial Crossing. Alfred A. Knopf, New York. 92 pp.

———. 1930. The Anthropometry of the American Negro. Columbia University Press, New York. 283 pp.

HOOTON, E. A. 1939. Crime and the Man. Harvard University, Cambridge. 403 pp.

HRDLICKA, A. 1928. The full-blood American Negro. Amer. Jour. Phys. Anthrop. 12:15–33.

STERN, C. 1950. Principles of Human Genetics. W. H. Freeman and Co., San Francisco. 617 pp.

U.S. BUREAU OF THE CENSUS. 1909. A Century of Population Growth from the First Census of the United States to the Twelfth, 1790–1900. Government Printing Office, Washington. 303 pp.

U.S. NATIONAL RESOURCES COMMITTEE. 1938. The Problems of a Changing Population. Government Printing Office, Washington. 28 pp.

36 • CAUCASIAN GENES IN AMERICAN NEGROES

T. Edward Reed

Methods for estimating the genetic contribution of whites to the black gene pool have been devised by several workers. In this contribution Reed subjects these methods to a critical examination, and finds most of them wanting on the grounds of either deficiencies in gene-frequencies reported, or statistical inaccuracies, or both. Reed's approach overcomes these difficulties, and provides a model for the analysis of gene contributions from one population to another, as well as for the detection of the action of natural selection for certain traits. The low frequency of phenylketonuria in blacks, for example, and its much higher frequency in the white American population suggests the white population as an origin of the disorder [1] for American blacks. It would be possible to trace similar relationships for other genetic conditions transmitted from one population to another by using Reed's methods.

While it may be true that between 2 and 50 percent of the genes of blacks are derived from white ancestors, it is not at present possible to give even a remotely accurate account of those genes. But with methods such as those which Reed presents here, and the necessary research, that may be achievable in the future.

I t is very difficult to describe the genetic history of a large, defined human population in a meaningful way. As a result there have been few opportunities, at the population level, to study the consequences of known genetic events in the recent past of modern populations. The Negro population of the United States, however, is one of the exceptions to these generalizations. The American individual to whom the term *Negro* is applied is almost always a biracial hybrid. Usually between 2 and 50 percent of his genes are derived from Caucasian ancestors, and these genes were very probably received after 1700. While it is obviously of social and cultural importance to understand Negro hybridity, it is less obvious that there are several pertinent genetic reasons for wishing to know about the magnitude and nature of Caucasian ancestry in Negroes. Recent data, both genetic and historical, now make possible a better understanding of American Negro genetic history than has been possible heretofore. Here I review and criticize the published data on this subject, present new data, and interpret the genetic significance of the evidence.

In order to put the genetic data in proper context, I must first give a little of the history of American slavery. The first slaves were brought to what is now the United States in 1619. Importation of slaves before 1700 was negligible, however, but after that date it proceeded at a high rate for most of the 18th century. Importation became illegal after 1808 but in fact continued at a low rate for several more decades (1, 2). The total number of slaves brought into the United States was probably somewhat less than 400,000 (3). Charleston, South Carolina, was the most important port of entry, receiving 30 to 40 percent of the total number (4). More than 98 percent of the slaves came from a very extensive area of West Africa and west-central Africa—from Senegal to Angola—and, in these areas, from both coastal and inland regions. Shipping lists of ships that brought slaves to the United States—and to the West Indies, often to be sent later to the United States—provide a fairly detailed picture of the geographic origins of the slaves and a less complete picture of their ethnic origins. Table 1 gives the approximate proportions of American slaves brought from the eight major slaving areas of Africa. The contribution from East Africa is seen to be negligible, whereas the area from Senegal to western Nigeria contributed about half the total and the region from eastern Nigeria to Angola contributed the other half. An earlier tabulation for entry at Charleston alone (5) is quite similar, except that the con-

SOURCE: *Science* vol. 165 (1969), 762–8. Reprinted by permission of the publisher.
[1] Reed refers to it as "disease." But phenylketonuria is not a disease, it is a genetic disorder resulting from an enzymatic deficiency. For a discussion of the difference between "disease" and "disorder," see Ashley Montagu, "On the Distinction Between Disease and Disorder," *Journal of the American Medical Association*, 179 (1962), 826; also vol. 181, p. 151.

Table 1: African origins of slaves imported into the North American mainland [date of Curtin (37)]. Distribution by areas is approximate and is an average of data for Virginia (1710–1769), for South Carolina (1773–1807), and for the British slave trade (1690–1807).

COASTAL REGION OF ORIGIN	APPROXIMATE PRESENT AREA	PEOPLES	APPROXIMATE PROPORTION FROM REGION
Senegambia	Senegal and Gambia	Mainly Bambara and Malinke (from interior)	0.133
Sierra Leone	Sierra Leone	Sierra Leone, Guinea, Portuguese Guinea peoples, plus Bambara and Malinke	.055
Windward Coast	Ivory Coast, Liberia	Various peoples of area	.114
Gold Coast	Ghana	About ¾ Akan people from southern part, the rest from northern part	.159
Bight of Benin	Togo, Dahomey, Nigeria west of Benin river	Peoples of Togo, southern Dahomey, and western Nigeria	.043
Bight of Biafra	Nigeria (east of Benin river) to 1° S (Gabon)	About ¾ Ibo, the rest Ibibio and people from Cameroon	.233
"Angola"	1° S to southwest Africa (Gabon, Congo, Angola)	Many peoples of the area, from the coast to far inland	.245
Mozambique and Madagascar			.016
Region unknown			.002

tribution from the Bight of Biafra is much less (0.021 as compared to 0.233) and that from "Angola" is appreciably greater (0.396 as compared to 0.245).

At some early point in American slavery, matings between slaves and Caucasians began to occur. Quantitative data are lacking, and we can say only that most of these matings occurred after 1700. Our concern here is the genetic consequences of the matings—the introduction of Caucasian genes into the genome (or total complement of genetic material) of the American Negro. We could, in theory, estimate the Caucasian contribution to American Negro ancestry in a very simple way *if* certain strict criteria were met. In practice it is not possible to show that all these criteria are met, but this fact has not stopped geneticists, including myself, from making estimates.

The usual estimation procedure is simple and direct. Consider some gene—say the allele A of the ABO blood group locus, whose frequency was q_a in the African ancestors of American Negroes and q_c in the Caucasian ancestors, while in modern American Negroes the frequency is q_n. If M is the present proportion of genes at this genetic locus (and, ideally, at every other locus too) which are derived from Caucasians, and if race mixture is the only process affecting q_n, then, by definition,

$$q_n = Mq_c + (1 - M)q_a \qquad (1)$$

and therefore

$$M = (q_n - q_a)/(q_c - q_a) \qquad (2)$$

This formula for M, or an algebraic equivalent, was used for all estimates of M given in Table 2 except one. [This one differed only in that three alleles were used simultaneously at one locus to obtain a maximum likelihood estimate for M; for each allele an equation of the type of Eq. 1 could be written, and used to eliminate M (6).] We see that if we know q_a, q_c, and q_n (for a defined area) without error and if there were no factors affecting q_n other than race crossing, estimation of M would be simple. Unfortunately, such is not the case.

Criteria for Critical Estimation of M

Critical evaluation of estimates of M requires complete specification of the needed criteria and judgment on the degree to which these criteria are met. These criteria are simple and obvious, but the demands they make have not always been appreciated. They are as follows.

1. The exact ethnic compositions of the two ancestral populations, African Negro and Caucasian, are known.
2. No change in gene frequency (for the gene in question) between ancestral and modern populations either of African Negroes or of American Caucasians has occurred.
3. Interbreeding of the two ancestral populations is the only factor affecting gene frequency in U.S. Negroes—that is, there has been no selection, mutation, or genetic drift.
4. Adequate samples (that is, samples that are unbiased, from correct populations, with small standard error) of the modern descendants of the ancestral African Negroes and U.S. Caucasians, and of modern U.S. Negroes, are available.

It should be said immediately that none of these criteria has been shown to be fully met in any study. In particular, point 1 is not met,

because the detailed ethnic origins of slaves from the various slaving areas are unknown (4). Point 2 can never be met because ancestral gene frequencies are unknown and point 3, at best, can only be inferred from indirect evidence. Point 4 cannot be fully met for African Negroes, since the proportions of various ethnic contributions are only roughly known. The problem is simpler for U.S. Negroes and Caucasians, although marked heterogeneity in values of M between different Negro populations is now known to complicate the matter.

Somewhat more affirmative views on these criteria can also be given, however. *If* it can be shown that gene frequencies in neighboring modern tribes and in populations of adjacent former slaving areas do not differ appreciably, point 1 becomes less important. For example, this appears to be the situation for the ABO blood groups, the best-known genetic system throughout the slaving area. With regard to point 2, since the populations concerned usually were, and are, large, it is probable that this criterion is quite well satisfied. If point 1 is satisfied in the way suggested, point 4 may be met by using large, carefully collected samples. Unfortunately, it is less easy to overcome the problem posed by point 3. This is discussed below.

Review of Published Estimates of M

Table 2 is a tabulation of published estimates of M for American Negroes, beginning with the well-known estimate of 0.31 for Baltimore Negroes given by Glass and Li in 1953 (7). The estimates are grouped according to the authors' statements as to their validity or lack of validity (due to selection) as estimates of M. They are further classified as "southern" (estimates for Georgia, South Carolina, and Tennessee) or "nonsouthern." As has been noted elsewhere (6, 8, 9), among the presumed valid estimates, all "non-

Table 2: Published estimates of the proportion (M), **in American Negroes, of genes that are of Caucasian origin.** All estimates except those based on genes Fy^a, Gm^1, $Gm^{1,2}$, or Gm^5 (and perhaps AK^2) require an estimate of African gene frequency appreciably different from zero. Within regions, localities are listed in chronological order of the estimates. Standard errors for M were not given (except for reference 6).

REGION [*] AND LOCALITY	GENE(S) [†]	SAMPLE SIZE		M	REFERENCE
		NEGRO	CAUCASIAN		
Estimates for M presumed by their authors to be valid					
Non-southern					
Baltimore	R^0	907	7,317	0.306	(7)
Baltimore	R^0	907	7,317	.216	(15)
Five areas	R^0, R^1, Jk^b, T, S	96 to 3,156	189 to 7,317	~.20	(16)
Cleveland and Baltimore	Gm^1, Gm^5	623	249	.310	(11)
Various	R^0, R^1, R^2, r, M, S, Jk^b, k, Fy^b			.232–.261	(17)
Chicago	AK^2 [‡]	1,063	1,315	.13	(14)
Washington, D.C., Baltimore, New York City	R^0, R^1, Fy^a			.20–.24	(8)
Oakland, Calif.	Gm^1, $Gm^{1,2}$, Gm^5	260	478	.273 ± .037	(6)
Southern					
Evans and Bullock counties, Ga.	R^0, R^1	340	331	.104	(9)
Evans and Bullock counties, Ga.	Gm^1, $Gm^{1,5}$	189	295	.073	(12)
	Gc^1	231	292	~.10	
Charleston, S.C.	R^0, R^1, Fy^a	515		.04–.08	(8)
James Island, S.C., and Evans and Bullock counties, Ga.	R^0, R^1, Fy^a	394		.09–.12	(8)
Estimates of M presumed by their authors to indicate selection					
Non-southern [§]					
Four areas, mainly Seattle	Hp^1	936	865(?)	~.40	(21)
Seattle	Hp^1	1,657	?	.478	(8)
Seattle	Gd^{A-}	658 ♂ ♂		.490	(8)
Southern					
Evans and Bullock counties, Ga.	T	285	314	.466	(9)
	Hp^1 ‖	167	145	.42–.70	
	Gd^{A-}	76 ♂ ♂		.34–.44	
	Hb^S	247		.46–.69	
	Tf^{D1} ‖	133	107	.495	
Memphis	Gd^{A-}	97 ♂ ♂		.175	(8)

[*] An estimate of 0.34, from Hb^S data on 10,858 Negroes, is based on 11 sources in both the North and the South (38). It is therefore not placed in a regional category.

[†] Locus and alleles used are as follows. Blood groups: Rh (R^0, R^1, R^2, r), Kidd (Jk^b), M-N-S-s (M, S), Kell (k), Duffy (Fy^a, Fy^b); serum protein genes: Gm (Gm^1, $Gm^{1,2}$, Gm^5), haptoglobin (Hp^1), Gc (Gc^1), transferrin (Tf^{D1}); hemoglobin: HbS (Hb^S); red cell enzymes: adenylate kinase (AK^2),

glucose-6-phosphate dehydrogenase deficiency (Gd^{A-}); phenylthiocarbamide tasting (T).

[‡] Newly investigated gene. The African frequency of AK^2 is poorly known, but it is assumed to be zero. The 95-percent confidence interval for M is 0.03–0.23, according to my calculation.

[§] Seven non-southern estimates ranging from 0.270 to 0.685, obtained by Workman (8) (using Hp^1 or Gd^{A-}) on small samples (79 to 238 Negroes) are omitted here.

‖ "Possibly" reflecting selection.

southern" estimates are greater than "southern" estimates. Also, the estimates presumed to indicate selection are usually appreciably higher than the estimates presumed to be valid. Among the "valid" estimates of M, that of Glass and Li (7) is by far the best known, and is often quoted as "the" estimate for the amount of Caucasian ancestry in "the" American Negro (see, for example, notes 10–14). A revision of this estimate from 0.31 to 0.216 (15) appears to have escaped general notice.

The estimates of Table 2 must be considered in the light of the four criteria given above. As already noted, criterion 1 cannot be strictly satisfied for any estimate because the detailed ethnic origins of the slaves are unknown. The estimates for M in Table 2, however, do not even roughly meet criterion 1, since none of them is based on quantitative information on distribution of origins, such as is given in Table 1. Typically, data from only one or two regions of West Africa are taken to represent the whole slaving area. Ironically, for the best-known estimate, that of Glass and Li (7), Rh blood group data from East and South Africa, as well as from Ghana, were used to represent ancestral Rh blood group frequencies because better data were not then available. Glass, for his revised estimate (15), used only Rh data from Nigeria and Ghana. Of the 540 individuals from Nigeria studied (15), 105 were Ibos, who may be representative of ancestral inhabitants of the Bight of Biafra region, the area of origin of about 23 percent of American slaves (Table 1); the remaining 435 individuals from Nigeria may be representative of the slaves (4 percent) who came from the Bight of Benin. The 274 individuals from Ghana studied (15) may be representative of the slaves (16 percent) from that region. The slaves (57 percent) from areas other than Nigeria and Ghana are unrepresented in Glass's revised estimate. These same Rh blood group data were used by later investigators in arriving at their own estimates (8, 9, 16, 17).

These critical comments on the best-known estimate are made to illustrate the nature of the problem; similar comments could be made about each of the other estimates of Table 2.

With regard to criterion 4 (adequacy of samples), one can distinguish between (i) adequate representation (by the mean gene frequency used) of the entire slaving area and (ii) adequate sample size (as shown by a small standard error for M). If the gene used has a uniform frequency over the entire slaving area, any large sample from one part of the area could adequately represent the whole. The problem, of course, is to demonstrate uniformity. If, as one would expect, gene frequencies vary from region to region of the slaving area, appropriate samples over the whole area are needed if one is to obtain a properly weighted mean frequency. Neither of these approaches has been used in making any of the estimates. [I made an attempt to confirm the belief that the frequency of certain Gm alleles is near zero in African populations (6) but found that not enough surveys had been made.]

To make the problem more concrete, let us consider Glass's estimate of M (15) in the light of more recent Rh data. For the R^0 allele of the Rh locus, he used 0.5512 for the frequency in West Africa (on the basis of the data from Nigeria and Ghana). The frequencies in present-day U.S. Negroes and Caucasians were found to be 0.4381 and 0.0279, respectively, so that, from Eq. 2, we estimate M to be $(0.5512 - 0.4381)/(0.5512 - 0.0279)$, or 0.216. However, the frequency of R^0 in Liberia is 0.60 (18), and in Bantu of the Congo (Leopoldville) it is also about 0.60 (19). If the true overall value for the slaving area were 0.60, the estimate for M would be 0.283.

With regard to the purely statistical accuracy of the estimates of M, as shown by standard errors, calculation of the standard errors for several pertinent estimates indicates that they may be much larger than the authors may have suspected (*20*). The standard error for Glass's estimate (*15*), for example, is 0.042, giving a 95-percent confidence interval of 0.133 to 0.299. The estimate in Table 2, of 0.13 for M for gene AK^2 (the lowest estimate for the non-southern region) has a standard error of 0.053, producing a 95-percent confidence interval of 0.025–0.234, overlapping Glass's estimate. This large error seems particularly surprising at first, in view of the large sample sizes, but it is explained by the very low AK^2 gene frequencies (<5 percent). The standard errors of the other estimates appear to be of comparable size or larger (due to smaller sample sizes).

I have said enough to show the deficiencies of most of the estimates of Table 2 with regard to both African gene frequency and statistical accuracy. I should also comment on the classification of M estimates as "valid" (not affected by selection) or as indicating the effects of selection. Classification of an estimate in this way requires a "standard" M that is thought to be free from the effects of selection. Such a "standard" can then be used to determine whether an M estimated for some other gene demonstrates selection. The M estimates from Rh genes R^0 and R^1 have been assigned this role of "standard" by various investigators [Parker *et al.* (*21*) chose R^0 alone; Workman and his associates (*8, 9*) chose R^0 and R^1 in combination]. In addition, M estimates from frequencies of the Fy^a allele of the Duffy blood group locus (*8*) and the Gm^1 and Gm^5 alleles of the Gm serum group locus (*21*) have been considered as possible standards. Yet, as discussed above, it is not possible to prove directly that selection has not affected a particular gene frequency in American Negroes, and no evidence in support of the belief that it has not has been offered. We can only draw inferences of varying degrees of rigor as suitable data become available. I attempt in the remainder of this article to draw and apply such inferences.

An Approach to a More Critical Estimate of M

To constitute a critical estimate in the light of the four criteria listed above, an estimate of M should substantially meet three of them—1, 3, and 4 (2 is, of course, untestable). This means that we should (i) have good survey data on gene frequency from most or all of the seven West African and west-central African slaving areas of Table 1; (ii) be able to calculate a mean African gene frequency properly weighted according to the origins shown in Table 1; (iii) have adequate data on Caucasians and U.S. Negroes; (iv) have samples large enough to give an acceptably small standard error for M; and, very importantly, (v) have some evidence that in U.S. Negroes the gene in question is not subject to strong selection. With regard to points (i) and (ii), an ideal situation is to have a gene which can be shown to be absent or rare in all parts of the slaving area but common in Caucasians. The problem of finding "the" African-ancestor gene frequency is then eliminated, and M is simply q_n/q_c. The Caucasian gene contribution is then directly determinable. It has been claimed that Gm alleles Gm^1, $Gm^{1,5}$, and Gm^5 are of this type (*22*); it is quite likely that they are, but not enough of the slaving area has been surveyed for Gm alleles for us to be sure (*6*).

The Fy^a gene may be almost an ideal "Caucasian gene" for estimating M. Available survey data for regions from Liberia to the Congo (Leopoldville), presented in Table 3, show that in this region (from which about 56 percent of the ancestral slaves came) the mean frequency of Fy^a is probably not over about 0.02. The mean frequency for all Africans of the slave area is probably less than 0.03. The frequency for U.S. Caucasians is about 0.43 (Table 4). Moreover, recent extensive studies in a population of California Negroes revealed no evidence for natural selection (evidence pertaining to fetal and infant

Table 3: Frequences of Duffy blood group Fy (a+) in West African and Congo (Leopoldville) populations.

REGION	SAMPLE SIZE (N)	PROPORTION OF Fy (a+)[*]	REFERENCE
Liberia (many tribes)	661	0.00	(18)
Ivory Coast	163	.043 †	(18)
Upper Volta	75	.00	(18)
Dahomey	20	.00	(18)
Ghana (Accra) and Nigeria (Lagos)	37	.00	(39)
Congo (Bantu)	501	.078 ‡	(40)

[*] Reacting positively with anti-Fy^a, indicating a genotype of Fy^aFy (most likely), or Fy^aFy^b, or Fy^aFy^a (rare) (39).
† The true proportion is probably zero because the Ivory Coast positive reactions with anti-Fy^a are believed to be incorrect.
‡ The gene frequency for Fy^a is 0.040.

growth and viability and to adult growth and fertility) associated with Duffy blood group phenotypes (23). Strong selection due to this locus seems excluded, so there is some protection against bias in the estimation of M. Table 4 presents available Fy^a frequency data for U.S. Negroes and for some U.S. Caucasians, and the resulting M estimates. The M estimates for the three non-southern regions studied do not differ significantly, so the estimate 0.2195 ± 0.0093 for California Negroes—the largest of the three samples—may tentatively be used as the best estimate of M for a non-southern area. The very small standard error of this estimate reflects both the discrimination power of this "Caucasian gene" and the large sample sizes for the Negro and Caucasian populations. The two estimates from the "Deep South" do differ significantly and should be kept separate. The smaller one, 0.0366 ± 0.0091 from Charleston, appears to justify the statement that these Gullah Negroes have an unusually small amount of Caucasian ancestry (5). It is clear that the data of Table 4 are especially useful in comparing M for different U.S. Negro populations, because the same gene, Fy^a, is used as the basis for all estimates. Any bias due to selection should operate quite similarly in the different Negro populations. The dif-

Table 4: Estimates of M derived from Fy^a gene frequencies for American Negroes from various areas. The frequency of this gene in the African ancestors of American Negroes is assumed here to be zero; if it is not zero, these are *maximum* estimates. N = number in sample, $q = Fy^a$ gene frequency, S.E. = standard error of q (all estimates by T. E. Reed).

REGION AND LOCALITY	NEGROES N	$q \pm$ S.E.	CAUCASIANS N	$q \pm$ S.E.	$M \pm$ S.E. [*]	REFERENCE
Non-southern						
New York City	179	0.0809 ± 0.0147			0.189 ± 0.034	(39) †
Detroit	404	$.1114 \pm .0114$			$.260 \pm .027$	(41)
Oakland, Calif.	3146	$.0941 \pm .0038$	5046	0.4286 ± 0.0058	$.2195 \pm .0093$ ‡	(25)
Southern						
Charleston, S.C.	515	$.0157 \pm .0039$			$.0366 \pm .0091$	(5)
Evans and Bullock counties, Ga.	304	$.0454 \pm .0086$	322	$.422 \pm .0224$	$.106 \pm .020$	(9)

[*] The q for Oakland Caucasians (who are of West European ancestry) was used in all estimates. $M = q_n/q_c$.
† Two other New York City studies (42) are omitted because they involved selection for dark skin color. The data used here were grouped with both anti-Fy^a and anti-Fy^b. The observed distribution of four Duffy phenotypes differs from the Hardy-Weinberg expectation at the 0.025 level of significance.
‡ If the frequency of Fy^a in the African ancestors were 0.02, this estimate would be 0.181.

ference between "southern" and "non-southern" M values evident in Table 2 is also marked in Table 4 and must be regarded as real.

Thus Fy^a, for the reasons given, may be the best gene presently available for estimating M. When more African survey data are available, the "Caucasian" alleles Gm^1, $Gm^{1,5}$, and Gm^5 of the Gm locus, used jointly, may be as good. The AK^2 gene (Table 2) may be of some use if further African data establish a general zero frequency, but the low frequency, 0.047, of the AK^2 gene in Caucasians considerably reduces its discrimination power. The K gene of the Kell blood group system is sometimes thought of as a "Caucasian gene," but this is not strictly the case. This gene was present in 8 of 1202 Africans from the Liberia-Dahomey (18) and western Nigeria (24) region, at a mean frequency of 0.0033. The California Negroes of Table 4 (N = 3146) have a K gene frequency of about 0.0083, and the California Caucasians, a K gene frequency of about 0.046 (25). If we consider q_a to be zero, we obtain an estimate of 0.181 $\pm$ 0.026 for M for this population—clearly a maximum estimate and not reliable. This maximum does not differ significantly from the Fy^a estimate for this same population. The relatively large standard error here again reflects the low Caucasian gene frequency.

Although a zero q_a is generally preferable, there is one situation where a q_a value appreciably different from zero might yield a useful estimate of M. This could occur when there are sufficiently extensive and detailed data on African gene frequency to make it possible to calculate a mean African gene frequency, with weighting of regional gene frequencies according to the proportions of Table 1. At present, the ABO blood groups provide the only such usable genetic marker [the gene for hemoglobin S is known to be affected by selection, and much less information is available for other loci (26); for selection data on hemoglobin S, see (27)]. Table 5 gives the gene frequencies for genes A and B of the ABO system from relevant surveys in the seven major slaving areas of Table 1.

These extensive surveys reveal an overall uniformity in gene frequency, with the one exception of a somewhat low B frequency for the Bight of Biafra (Ibos). From these mean values for African frequencies of genes A and B and from extensive data on ABO-system distribution in California Negroes and Caucasians (25), a maximum likelihood estimate for M of 0.200 $\pm$ 0.044 was obtained (28). This estimate is not greatly affected by the accuracy of the proportions given in Table 1 or by the exactness of the values for individual regional gene frequencies (29). A good fit of the observed number of individuals in each of the eight race and blood-group classes with the corresponding number expected from the estimated parameters (gene frequencies and M values) tested by the chi-square method, indicates both that the estimation is reasonable and that there are no large selective differences between genes A and B in U.S. Negroes (28). This procedure therefore seems justified for the case of ABO blood groups. Practically, however, the large standard error for M indicates that, in spite of large samples, the estimate for this locus is too imprecise to be very useful.

Since there are now three different estimates of M, and since extensive data on other aspects of the problem, including selection, are available for this one large California population of Negroes, these estimates are presented in a single table, Table 6. We note that they do not differ significantly from each other; this is due at least in part to the relatively large standard errors for the Gm and ABO estimates. The marked superiority, for estimating M, of Fy^a over A and B for samples of equal size is evident (30), whereas, if the sample sizes were the same for Fy^a and the three Gm alleles, it would be found that these are equally efficient for estimating M. An extensive search for evidence of natural selec-

Table 5: Frequencies of genes A and B of the ABO blood-group system in surveys in the major slaving areas of Africa (see Table 1); p = frequency of A gene, q = frequency of B gene.

REGION	PEOPLES OR POPULATION	SAMPLE SIZE (N)	$p \pm$ S.E.[*]	$q \pm$ S.E.[*]	REFERENCE
Senegambia	Bambara, Malinke	2,120	0.159 ± .006	0.174 ± .006	(43)
Sierra Leone	Gbah-Mende	1,015	.159 ± .009	.151 ± .008	(44)
Liberia	>18 tribes [†]	2,337	.143 ± .005	.148 ± .006	(18)
Gold Coast	Unspecified, from Accra	1,540	.130 ± .006	.122 ± .006	(45)
Bight of Benin	Yoruba of Lagos, Ibadan	1,003	.130 ± .008	.141 ± .008	(46)
Bight of Biafra	Ibo ("Eastern")	572	.161 ± .011	.089 ± .009	(47)
"Angola"	"Bantu"–8000 (mainly Bakongo) near Leopold-ville and 8000 from Angola	16,000	.152 ± .002	.138 ± .002	(48)
Mean frequencies [‡] over the entire slaving area			.150	.131	

[*] Maximum-likelihood estimate (49).
[†] Exclusive of Americo-Liberians.
[‡] Calculated from values for p and q given in the body of the table, weighted by the proportions of Table 1 (after the removal of values for Mozambique, Madagascar, and "region unknown").

tion due to the presence of ABO blood groups in these Negroes, similar to the search reported above for the Duffy blood group, also failed to reveal any consistent selective effect (23). This finding, plus the good chi-square fit in the estimation of M, which implies that the A and B genes are not very different with respect to their selective values in U.S. Negroes, gives some assurance that the ABO estimate is not greatly disturbed by selection (28). No selection studies for Gm were made on these California Negroes, but extensive studies on a Brazilian population which was about 30 percent Negro, 11 percent Indian, and 59 percent Caucasian (13) revealed no evidence of selective effect (31). Further evidence is provided by the good chi-square fit in the multi-allelic estimation obtained with the three Gm alleles (6). It seems reasonable to conclude that strong selective effects on these three estimates of M may be excluded. The existence of weaker effects, however, still sufficient to bias these estimates appreciably, cannot be ruled out. As more independent estimates on these and other genes become available, each having regard to the criteria listed above and including some safeguard against a strong bias due to

Table 6: Estimates of M calculated from data on Gm serum groups, Duffy blood group, and ABO blood group from Negroes and Caucasians of the Oakland, California, area. [Data of the Child Health and Development Studies (6, 25).]

LOCUS	ALLELES USED	SAMPLE SIZE (N) NEGROES	SAMPLE SIZE (N) CAUCASIANS	M
Gm	Gm^1, $Gm^{1,5}$, Gm^5	260	478	0.273 ± 0.037 [*]
Duffy	Fy^a	3146	5046	.220 ± .009 [†]
ABO	A, B	3146	5046	.200 ± .044 [†]

[*] See (6).   [†] See text.

selection and having a relatively small standard error (say, less than 0.02), it should become possible to obtain a "consensus" on the true value of M (for specified Negroes). Estimates biased upward or downward by selection will be separated from those little affected by selection, and so, in time, the former can be identified and rejected.

Use of M To Detect Selection

Several investigators (8, 9, 21, 32) have argued that selection for or against a gene may be clearly inferred from the M value that the gene produces. From the foregoing section it is clear that if (i) the true (unbiased) value of M (say, M_0) is known, (ii) the estimate in question (M_e) is calculated with regard to the criteria given above, and (iii) M_e differs significantly from M_0, then we may reasonably suspect that selection has caused the observed deviation. These conditions have not been met. In particular, we have no M_0. The M estimates obtained with R_0 (8, 9, 21), R^1 (8, 9), and Fy^a (8) were considered to be valid estimates unbiased by selection, but no objective evidence was offered to support these views. With one or more of these M estimates used as reference standards, it has been claimed that the deviant M estimates of the following genes demonstrate selection on these genes in U.S. Negroes: Hp^1, T, Gd^{A-}, Hb^S, and Tf^{D1} (see Table 2). These results can, at present, be considered only suggestive, but it must be admitted that the usually high M estimates obtained with Hp^1 and Gd^{A-} argue for an effect of selection (27).

A different approach was used to show that M estimates obtained with r, R^0, and R^1 alleles of the Rh locus ranked in this (decreasing) order of size for a Georgia population and also for two Brazilian populations (32). Accepted at face value, this is evidence of differences between M values from different Rh alleles. The investigators attribute these differences to selection. This same approach in these populations also indicates that M for the B allele is greater than $1.5M$ for the A allele (32). African Rh and ABO gene frequencies, weighted by slaving-area origins, were not used, however, although the African areas of origin of Brazilian Negroes are known (2). Again, these findings are interesting and suggestive but far from conclusive.

Workman (8), from inspection of A_1, A_2, and B allele frequencies in various West African, U.S. Negro, and U.S. Caucasian populations, concludes that there has been strong selection in U.S. Negroes against A_1 and for A_2. He identifies the various African data only as "West Africa," and does not use significance tests. Since Workman and also Hertzog and Johnson claim to find selection in the ABO system, it is pertinent here to recall that the M estimate obtained from ABO-system distributions that is discussed earlier in this article (an estimate based on *large* populations and good estimates for African gene frequency) did not suggest selective differences between the A and B alleles.

This critical review of claims for selection would be incomplete if I did not mention that there *is* an important theoretical reason to look for selection in hybrid populations such as the American Negro. As has been previously recognized (6, 8, 32), selection in U.S. Negroes over several generations can produce a cumulative effect in present-day individuals appreciably greater than the effect of a single generation of selection—the type of data usually available. There is thus a possibility of detecting, in hybrids, selection due to common polymorphisms which is too small [usually less than 5 to 10 percent of the mean (23)] to be detectable by ordinary one-generation studies. This possibility, together with the probability that some of the genes are selective [because it is most unlikely that a new genotype (the hybrid) in a new environment would be exactly neutral in selective value], makes the search for selection here especially worthwhile. Some of these selective genes may already have been identified.

Other Uses of M Estimates

In addition to the definite likelihood of their yielding valuable information on the action of natural selection in human populations, good estimates of the amount of Caucasian ancestry in U.S. Negro populations have at least two other "uses."

1. They provide objective information about the genetic heterogeneity among various populations of U.S. Negroes. Evidence of marked differences between southern and non-southern Negroes with respect to the amount of Caucasian ancestry, as shown in Tables 2 and 4, is the first clear result from this use of M estimates. As more good estimates from defined U.S. Negro populations become available, we may expect further heterogeneity to be revealed.

2. They provide an understanding of the distribution in American Negroes of those genetic traits, including diseases, that are due primarily to genes of Caucasian origin. There are few examples of such genes at present, but, aside from common genetic polymorphisms, like blood groups, few genes have been sufficiently studied to permit possible identification of racial differences in gene frequency. One probable example of such a genetic trait is phenylketonuria—a condition resulting from homozygosity for a rare autosomal recessive gene, producing a deficiency of phenylalanine hydroxylase and resulting (if untreated) in severe mental defect. This occurs in about 1 in 10,000 births of persons of North European ancestry (33) but appears to be much rarer in U.S. Negroes (34). This rarity is understandable if the gene frequency in African Negroes is much lower than that in Caucasians (about 0.01). For example, if U.S. Negroes have,

on the average, 20-percent Caucasian ancestry, the frequency of occurrence of phenylketonuria at birth in U.S. Negroes would be only 1/25th that in Caucasians, or roughly 1 in 250,000—rare indeed.

An example of a disease which is not simply inherited but which may show a similar racial distribution is cirrhosis of the liver. A study in Baltimore Negro cirrhotics revealed, relative to Negro controls, a significant increase in Fy (a + b +) Duffy blood group phenotype and a decrease in Fy (a − b −) phenotype, whereas Caucasian cirrhotics showed no such difference from Caucasian controls (35). The simplest interpretation is that the disease is more frequent in Caucasians, and that Negroes with some degree of Caucasian ancestry, as shown by their Duffy blood group, are more likely to develop the disease than those lacking such ancestry (35). Other examples of traits whose frequency of occurrence in U.S. Negroes is affected by the amount of their Caucasian ancestry will surely be reported (36). Accurate information on M will be clinically useful here.

Summary

Published estimates of the proportion, in American Negroes, of genes which are of Caucasian origin are critically reviewed. The criteria for estimating this proportion (M) are discussed, and it is argued that all estimates published to date have either deficiencies pertaining to the African-gene-frequency data used or statistical inaccuracies, or both. Other sources of error may also exist.

Evidence is presented that the Fy^a gene of the Duffy blood group system may be the best gene now available for estimating M. Estimates based on Fy^a frequencies have been obtained for Negroes in three non-southern and two southern areas. The value of M is found to be appreciably greater in non-southern areas, the best estimate being 0.2195 ± 0.0093 (Oakland, California). This estimate is still subject to some uncertainty. The value of M in the South is appreciably less.

Natural selection can introduce a bias in the estimate of M. Claims that selection acting on certain genes in American Negroes have been demonstrated are reviewed, and it is concluded that they are not yet proved. The approach discussed here may be valuable in the future as a sensitive method for detecting the action of natural selection. In addition, knowledge of the amount of Caucasian ancestry may be of medical value in explaining the frequencies of occurrence of certain hereditary diseases in Negroes.

REFERENCES AND NOTES

1. J. H. FRANKLIN and T. MARSHALL, in *World Book Encyclopedia* (Field Enterprises Educational Corporation, Chicago, 1966), vol. 14, p. 106.
2. P. D. CURTIN, personal communication (1969).
3. J. POTTER, in *Population in History: Essays in Historical Demography*, D. V. Glass and D. E. Eversley, Eds. (Univ. of Chicago Press, Chicago, 1965), p. 641.
4. P. D. CURTIN, personal communication (1968).
5. W. S. POLLITZER, *Amer. J. Phys. Anthropol.* 16, 241 (1958).
6. T. E. REED, *Amer. J. Hum. Genet.* 21, 71 (1969).
7. B. GLASS and C. C. LI, *ibid.* 5, 1 (1953).
8. P. L. WORKMAN, *Hum. Biol.* 40, 260 (1968).
9. ——, B. S. BLUMBERG, A. J. COOPER, *Amer. J. Hum. Genet.* 15, 429 (1963).
10. C. STERN, *Principles of Human Genetics* (Freeman, San Francisco, ed. 2, 1960), p. 356.
11. A. G. STEINBERG, R. STAUFFER, S. H. BOYER, *Nature* 188, 169 (1960).
12. B. S. BLUMBERG, P. L. WORKMAN, J. HIRSCHFELD, *ibid.* 202, 561 (1964).
13. H. KRIEGER, N. E. MORTON, M. P. MI, E. AZEVÊDO, A. FREIRE-MAIA, N. YASUDA, *Ann. Hum. Genet.* 29, 113 1965).
14. J. E. BOWMAN, H. FRISCHER, F. AJMAR, P. E. CARSON, M. K. GOWER, *Nature* 214, 1156 (1967).
15. B. GLASS, *Amer. J. Hum. Genet.* 7, 368 (1955) (non-D^u-tested data for Africans, Negroes, and Caucasians; use of D^u-tested data for Africans and non-D^u-tested data for others gives $M = 0.281$).
16. D. F. ROBERTS, *ibid.*, p. 361. The estimate is "provisional"; 66 separate estimates were made, ranging from 0.0404 to 0.3341.
17. —— and R. W. HIORNS, *ibid.* 14, 261 (1962). No sample sizes are specified.
18. F. B. LIVINGSTONE, H. GERSHOWITZ, J. V. NEEL, W. W. ZEULZER, M. D. SOLOMON, *Amer. J. Phys. Anthropol.* 18, 161 (1960).
19. P. V. TOBIAS, in *The Biology of Human Adaptability*, P. T. Baker and J. S. Weiner, Eds. (Clarendon Press, Oxford, 1966), p. 161.
20. The following formula for the standard error (S.E.) of a ratio $R = y/x$ was used:

$$\text{S.E. } R = R \left[\frac{V_y}{y^2} + \frac{V_x}{x^2} - \frac{2C_{xy}}{xy} \right]^{1/2}$$

where the variance of y is V_y, that of x is V_x and the covariance between x and y is C_{xy} [see, for example, L. Kish, *Survey Sampling* (Wiley, New York, 1965), p. 207]. This formula is adequate for large or moderate-sized samples when it is unlikely that x is near zero. In terms of Eq. 2 for M,

$$\text{S.E. } M = M \left[\frac{V(q_a - q_n)}{(q_a - q_n)^2} + \frac{V(q_a - q_c)}{(q_a - q_c)^2} - \frac{2V(q_a)}{(q_a - q_n)(q_a - q_c)} \right]^{1/2}$$

where V represents the variance of the adjoining quantity in parantheses. The covariance between numerator and denominator of Eq. 2, due to the presence of q_a in both, is allowed for in this standard error.
21. W. C. PARKER and A. G. BEARN, *Ann. Hum. Genet. London* 25, 227 (1961). The total number of American, Canadian, and British individuals tested in the study reported is 865. A weighted estimate for the frequency of gene Hp^1 in U.S. Negroes, based on the data of Parker and Bearn, is 0.55; this value gives an M of 0.53.
22. A. G. STEINBERG, in *Symposium on Immunogenetics*, T. J. Greenwalt, Ed. (Lippincott, Philadelphia, 1967), pp. 75–98.
23. T. E. REED, *Amer. J. Hum. Genet.* 19, 732 (1967); *ibid.* 20, 119 (1968); *ibid.*, p. 129.

24. B. S. BLUMBERG, E. W. IKIN, A. E. MOURANT, *Amer. J. Phys. Anthropol.* 19, 195 (1961).

25. T. E. REED, *Amer. J. Hum. Genet.* 20, 142 (1968).

26. For gene distributions, see J. Hiernaux, *La Diversité Humaine en Afrique Subsaharienne* (Institut de Sociologie, Université Libre de Bruxelles, Brussels, 1968), figs. 2, 3, 7, 8, 12, 14.

27. There are good a priori reasons, entirely separate from M values, for expecting, in U.S. Negroes, a decrease in the frequency of the genes for sickle-cell hemoglobin, Hb^S, and for glucose-6-phosphate dehydrogenase deficiency, Gd^{A-}. (i) There is good evidence that in Africa the high frequency of the Hb^S gene is due to a selective advantage of heterozygotes for Hb^S in regions where malaria is endemic [see, for example, F. B. Livingstone, *Abnormal Hemoglobins in Human Populations* (Aldine, Chicago, 1967), pp. 105–107; A. C. Allison, in *Abnormal Haemoglobins in Africa,* J. H. P. Jonxis, Ed. (Davis, Philadelphia, 1965), pp. 369–371; D. L. Rucknagel and J. V. Neel, in *Progress in Medical Genetics,* A. G. Steinberg, Ed. (Grune & Stratton, New York, 1961), vol. 1, pp. 158–260]. There is strongly suggestive evidence that the Gd^{A-} gene in Africa is similarly kept at high frequencies due to selective advantage in malarious areas [see F. B. Livingstone, *Abnormal Hemoglobins in Human Populations* (Aldine, Chicago, 1967); A. G. Motulsky, in *Abnormal Haemoglobins in Africa,* J. H. P. Jonxis, Ed. (Davis, Philadelphia, 1965), pp. 181–185)]. (ii) Both genes are known to have selective disadvantages which can explain their rarity in nonmalarious areas. It is therefore to be expected that Negroes moved from their highly malarious homelands to the less malarious, and now nonmalarious, regions of North America would have lower frequencies of these two genes. This selective decrease would raise M estimates above the true value.

28. The computer program [see T. E. Reed and W. J. Schull, *Amer. J. Hum. Genet.* 20, 579 (1968)] estimated M and Caucasian A and B gene frequencies, given the two African mean frequencies as constants and the two California populations determined by the gene frequencies to be estimated, subject to the constraints that, for both A and B, $q_n = Mq_c + (1 - M)q_a$. This equation is Eq. 1 applied to both alleles and is true when there is simple gene mixture without selection (see 6). Comparison of the observed numbers of the eight race and blood-group classes (2 races

× 4 groups) with the corresponding numbers expected on the basis of parameter estimates gives a chi-square value of 5.910 for 3 d.f., $P > .10$.

29. When the negligible contribution from Mozambique, Madagascar, and "Unknown" is excluded, the proportions of Table 1, column 4, become (in order): 0.135, 0.056, 0.116, 0.162, 0.044, 0.237, and 0.249. The corresponding proportions for South Carolina (1773–1807) are 0.197, 0.068, 0.164, 0.134, 0.016, 0.021, and 0.399 [data of Curtin (4)], yielding overall African mean values of 0.149 and 0.144 for p and q. These two series differ appreciably with respect to the final two values yet when the South Carolina series is used, the estimate of M is 0.256 ± 0.042, a difference of just over one standard error. Also, q for the Bight of Biafra is the only markedly variant gene frequency among the frequencies for the seven regions, but replacing the p and q for this region by the p and q for the Bight of Benin or for "Angola" does not significantly change M (0.281 ± 0.040 or 0.251 ± 0.042, respectively, when corrected proportions of Table 1 are used).

30. The Fy^a estimate is based on $(0.044)^2/(0.0093)^2$, or 22 times as much statistical information as the ABO estimate.

31. N. E. MORTON, H. KRIEGER, M. P. MI, *Amer. J. Hum. Genet.* 18, 153 (1966).

32. K. P. HERTZOG and F. E. JOHNSTON, *Hum. Biol.* 40, 86 (1968).

33. V. A. MC KUSICK, *Mendelian Inheritance in Man* (Johns Hopkins Press, Baltimore, ed. 2, 1968), p. 346.

34. For example, H. P. Katz and J. H. Menkes [*J. Pediat.* 65, 71 (1964)] report the first definite case of phenylketonuria in a U.S. Negro. R. G. Graw and R. Koch [*Amer. J. Dis. Child.* 114, 412 (1967)] report two "pale skinned" Negro brothers with phenylketonuria, bringing the total for U.S. Negroes at that time to five.

35. N. C. R. W. REID, P. W. BRUNT, W. B. BIAS, W. C. MADDREY, B. A. ALONSO, F. L. IBER, *Brit. Med. J.* 2, 463 (1968).

36. Differences between Caucasians and Japanese with respect to gene frequency are instructive here. Phenylketonuria appears to be much rarer (perhaps a tenth as frequent) among Japanese than among Caucasians [K. Tanaka, E. Matsunaga, Y. Hanada, T. Murata, K. Takehara, *Jap. J. Hum. Genet.* 6, 65 (1961)]. Another single-gene trait, Huntington's chorea, also appears to be

about ten times as frequent in Caucasians as in Japanese, according to T. E. Reed and J. H. Chandler, *Amer. J. Hum. Genet.* 10, 201 (1958). Examples of congenital abnormalities which are commoner in Caucasians than in Japanese, and vice versa, are given by J. V. Neel, *Amer. J. Hum. Genet.* 10, 398 (1958).

37. P. D. CURTIN, *The Atlantic Slave Trade: A Census* (Univ. of Wisconsin Press, Madison, in press).

38. J. V. NEEL and W. J. SCHULL, *Human Heredity* (Univ. of Chicago Press, Chicago, 1954), p. 255; J. V. Neel, personal communication (1969). The estimate refers to "non-Negro" ancestry.

39. R. R. RACE and R. SANGER, *Blood Groups in Man* (Blackwell, Oxford, ed. 5, 1968).

40. M. SHAPIRO and J. M. VANDEPITTE, *Int. Congr. Blood Transfusion, 5th, Paris* (1955), p. 243; M. Shapiro, personal communication (1969).

41. H. GERSHOWITZ, unpublished data.

42. E. B. MILLER, R. E. ROSENFIELD, P. VOGEL, *Amer. J. Phys. Anthropol.* 9, 115 (1951); R. Sanger, R. R. Race, J. Jack, *Brit. J. Haematol.* 1, 370 (1955).

43. R. KOERBER, *C. R. Seances Soc. Biol.* 141, 1013 (1947); R. Koerber and J. Linhard, *Bull. Soc. Anthropol. Paris* 2, 158 (1951). The frequencies for Bambara and Malinke do not differ significantly.

44. P. JULIEN, *Z. Rassenphysiol.* 9, 146 (1937).

45. G. M. EDINGTON, *West Afr. Med. J.* 5, 71 (1956).

46. H. R. MULLER, *Proc. Soc. Exp. Biol.* 24, 437 (1927); J. P. Garlick, quoted in A. E. Mourant, A. C. Kopeć, K. Domaniewska-Sobczak, *The ABO Blood Groups* (Blackwell, Oxford, 1958), p. 173; J. P. Garlick and N. A. Barnicot, *Ann. Hum. Genet.* 21, 420 (1957). The frequencies in these three surveys do not differ significantly from each other.

47. J. HARDY, *Roy. Anthropol. Inst.* 92, 223 (1962). I have not used Hardy's data on "Onitsha Ibo" (sample size, 228) because I consider the subjects to be probably not of Ibo origin. I have not used data of J. N. M. Chalmers, E. W. Ikin, and A. E. Mourant [*Ann. Eugenics* 17, 168 (1953)] on "southeastern" Nigeria (105 Ibo and 1 Tiv) because information on the type of Ibo was not given. Table 1 describes this region as "about ¾ Ibo," and I could find no suitable data for the remaining quarter.

48. G. VAN ROS and R. JOURDAIN, *Ann. Soc. Belge Med. Trop.* 36, 307 (1956); L. Mayor, *Bull. Clin. Statistics* 7, No. 3, suppl. 126 (1954). The first study (for the Congo) gave values of 0.1556 ± 0.0030 for p and 0.1244 ± 0.0027 for q. The second (for Angola gave values of 0.1486 ± 0.0029 and 0.1514 ± 0.0030, respectively. An unweighted average of these values was used. The values for Angola do not differ significantly from the mean p and q values for seven central-coastal named tribes in Angola (total population, 1285) tabulated by Hiernaux (see 26).

49. T. E. REED and W. J. SCHULL, *Amer. J. Hum. Genet.* 20, 579 (1968).

50. Preparation of this article was begun while I was engaged in work for the Child Health and Development Studies (Division of Biostatistics, School of Public Health, University of California, Berkeley, and the Kaiser Foundation Research Institute, Oakland, California), on leave from the University of Toronto, and was supported there by U.S. Public Health Service research grants HD 00718 and HD 00720 from the National Institutes of Health. The analysis was supported in part by a grant from the Medical Research Council of Canada. I thank Professor Philip D. Curtin for making unpublished data available and for commenting on the manuscript, Dr. Arthur E. Mourant and Mrs. K. Domaniewska-Sobczak for recent references to African blood group distributions, and Professors Curt Stern, Donald Rucknagel, and Peter Carstens for their comments. Dr. H. Gershowitz and Dr. M. Shapiro made available unpublished data on Duffy blood groups in Negroes.

37 · EVIDENCE OF HETEROSIS IN MAN

L. S. Penrose

The existence of hybrid vigor in man is a subject still very much under debate. Among the studies published on the subject Penrose's contribution is outstanding—it is also too little known. It has been argued that the gene differences between different populations are too insignificant to make any contribution to hybrid vigor, except in populations in which high frequencies of a deleterious gene might be reduced by the introduction of a significant number of its normal alleles. This "heterozygote advantage" might certainly benefit such a population. In Tierra del Fuego, for example, it was the unmixed natives who succumbed to measles, whereas the hybrids were able to resist the disease.[1] Another example of such heterozygote advantage is sickle-cell anemia, in which the heterozygotes have a strong natural immunity to the disorder. There are many kinds of immunities that have probably been transmitted in the course of man's evolution in the same way.

Heterosis is defined as the superiority of heterozygous genotypes with respect to one or more characters in comparison with the corresponding homozygotes. If it is the result of gene interaction between heterozygotes, then there is a high probability that it is a phenomenon which really exists in man on both the interpopulational level and the individual level of hybridization. Hybridization is understood to mean any cross-mating of two genetically different individuals or populations leading to hybrid progeny.

Hybrid vigor may not always be easily measurable in metrical traits. Nevertheless such heterotic changes in metrical traits have been recorded in man. Hulse has observed such changes in a Swiss population in which there were significant increases in height, sitting height, chest depth, head breadth, and prolongation of growth period.[2] Increase in stature is believed to be the result of admixture between Africans and Europeans in the population of Martinique.[3] Weight increase during the growth period in the offspring of Franco-Vietnamese children is also believed to be due to heterosis.[4] There is a good deal of other evidence, but much of it impresses most scientists as of an equivocal nature.[5]

In animal species the principle of balanced polymorphism due to heterosis has been accepted for many years, but the serious application of the same idea to man has been slow. Human experimental breeding is not possible, and effects,

SOURCE: L. S. Penrose, "Evidence of Heterosis in Man," *Proceedings of the Royal Society of Medicine,* vol. 144 (1955): 203–13. Reprinted by permission of The Royal Society of Medicine and the author.

[1] E. Lucas Bridges, *Uttermost Part of the Earth* (London: Hodder and Stoughton, 1948).

[2] F. S. Hulse, "Exogamie et Hétérosis," *Archives Suisse d'Anthropologie Générale,* XXII (1957), 103–125. Engl. trans. "Exogamy and Heterosis," *Yearbook of Physical Anthropology,* IX (1964), 241–257.

[3] Jean Benoist, "Les Martiniquais. Anthropologie d'Une Population Metisée. *Bulletins et Mémoires de la Société Anthropologique de Paris,* vol. 11, 1963, pp. 241–432.

[4] J. Hilenaud and N. Heintz, "Croissance Biometrique des Franco-Vietnamiens," *Bulletins et Memoires de la Société d'Anthropologie de Paris,* vol. 1, XIIe Série, 1967, pp. 55–89.

[5] See Ashley Montagu, "The Creative Power of 'Race' Mixture," in his book *Man's Most Dangerous Myth: The Fallacy of Race.* 4th ed. (New York: World Publishing Co., 1964), pp. 185–223.

demonstrable in laboratory animals, may be concealed in a randomly breeding population. On the other hand, populations under natural selection may be suitable for certain kinds of studies not possible in experimental work.

Evidence for the existence of some kind of hybrid vigour in man comes from both direct and indirect measurement. Most of the evidence is indirect, but the few examples of direct measurements on known or supposed heterozygotes may be considered initially.

It is natural to inquire into the effects of crossing previously isolated population on the principle that stocks which are inbred tend towards homozygosity. Both the physique and the fertility of the offspring of such unions can be examined for evidence of increased vigour. Relevant measurements are scarce, particularly on the results of the first cross. Trevor (1953) surveyed the data on physical traits in populations derived from geographically distinct parental groups. With regard to almost all characters studied, the mean measurement of the hybrid population was found to be intermediate between those of the two parent populations, often close to their arithmetical average. The work of Davenport & Steggerda (1929) on the mental traits of hybrids in Jamaica led to similar conclusions.

These results are in agreement with what might be expected in view of observations on the genetics of metrical traits, both physical and mental, made on more homogeneous populations, dating from the original observations of Galton on stature and Pearson's extensive studies on several physical measurements. The accumulated information concerning intelligence test measurements on parents and children, since Burt & Moore's (1911) pioneer investigation, agrees roughly with the results on physical measurements. The evidence in both cases favours the assumption of additive, or at least intermediate, types of inheritance. Thus, the apparent absence of hybrid vigour in population crosses may simply be due to the fact that metrical

traits in man do not show over-dominance. It might also be due to insufficient homozygosity in the parent populations.

In a natural population, heterosis must primarily be concerned with fitness, as determined ultimately by the number of offspring who reach reproductive age, or the natural logarithm of this number as recommended by Fisher (1930). The survival of the individual is a necessary but not a sufficient condition for biological fitness in this sense. Nevertheless, genes which reduce viability must very often also reduce fertility. Thus, fitness can be more directly studied by examining reaction to disease than by taking measurements of characters whose relationship to health and fertility is not known.

Direct evidence on hybrid vigour would be found by counting the number of offspring of unions between members of formerly geographically isolated populations. An interesting example is quoted by Boas (1948) in which females of mixed European and American Indian ancestry were shown to be exceptionally fertile as compared with the original populations from which they were derived.

Another kind of direct inquiry is to count the offspring of known heterozygous carriers of known traits due to single genes. A good example of this is the comparative fertility of parents in different blood-group types. This could be easily studied in transfusion centres or maternity hospitals, but little work of this kind has yet been done. Among very few published figures are those of Bryce, Jakobowicz, McArthur & Penrose (1950), in which a small advantage in fertility was shown by *AB* mothers, but it was not significant statistically. The task of measuring true family size and comparing it with accurately chosen controls is not easy, particularly because large families attract special attention. It is a common finding that large families exist in which disabilities of many kinds occur, some of which are attributed to heredity, and they also show a high infant mortality rate. For example, this was so in the data of the Merseyside survey, collected by Jones (1934). This author was careful to note that, after allowing for the statistical effects of ascertainment, the increased mean family size would be much less noticeable. Using standard methods to allow for selection, Delbue (1950) found a slightly increased family size, as compared with control estimates, in the data collected by Mollenbach (1947) on hereditary coloboma (a dominant defect). There was also some evidence of increased family size in sibships containing cases of phenylketonuria (a recessive defect); otherwise the results of the inquiry were negative.

Large-scale direct counting of the offspring of heterozygous microcythaemics in the Ferrara district, by Montalenti, Silvestroni & Bianco (1953), failed to indicate any significant increase in fertility as compared with the homozygous normals in the same population. A slight decrease in fertility among female heterozygous carriers of haemophilia genes, which produce serious disease in hemizygous form, can be inferred from Andreassen's (1934) survey.

There is, however, a recent example which suggests other possibilities. The sickle-cell gene, common among Africans, causes the production of an abnormal haemoglobin, identified by Pauling, Itano, Singer & Wells (1949). In the homozygous form there is no normal haemoglobin and severe anaemia results, which is often fatal. Metrically, the heterozygotes are intermediate between the normal and abnormal homozygotes and they possess, on the average, about 40% abnormal haemoglobin. On purely metrical grounds, they might be expected to have fitness somewhat below the average. Recently, Allison (1954) has demonstrated experimentally that heterozygotes have strong natural immunity to subtertian malaria. Even so, it is difficult to demonstrate any marked difference between normals and heterozygotes with respect to infection rate in an exposed population (Raper 1954). Nor has there

been, as yet, any census of family size in relation to parental phenotypes. In the absence of subtertian malaria the heterozygous advantage is removed and the gene should become less frequent. This seems to have happened among Indians in the United States. Genes responsible for immunity to infection may have played a large part in human evolution (Haldane 1949). If they are dominant or intermediate, the hybrid will have considerable advantages. When two isolated groups mix, hybrids should be immune to infectious diseases which have previously been selective factors in the parent populations. Such a phenomenon is suggested by the survival of hybrid Fuegans when the pure-bred natives perished from measles (Bridges 1948).

The results of direct inquiry, although very scanty at present, point consistently to the conclusion that heterosis in man is shown, if at all, not by metrical overdominance of the heterozygote but by changes in fertility connected with subtle mechanisms such as potential resistance to disease.

This assumption can be used as a starting point for other kinds of less direct investigations. It is often found that extreme types, as judged by any measurement, are somewhat less fit than the average. Information on this point can be obtained either by measuring viability or fertility of different phenotypes or by comparing the distribution of offspring with that of parents. For example, differential viability at extremes is clearly shown by the metrical character, weight at birth. The parental population must be recruited mainly from the middle region of the distribution because there is a high mortality for infants who are very heavy or very light at birth (Karn & Penrose 1951). Since only about one-fifth of the variance of birth weight can be attributed to the foetal genotype and another like portion to maternal genotype, selection against the genes responsible for extreme variations is not as strong as it appears to be at first glance, but it is still considerable (Haldane 1953). For stature in adults there is probably a similar effect, though not so obvious. Pearson & Lee (1896) found stature less variable in parents than in their offspring. With regard to cephalic index, a measurement of shape, the data of Pearson & Fawcett (1898) and of Frets, summarized by Penrose (1950a), both show the same phenomenon.

In stature, as with birth weight, the disadvantage is most marked at the lower end of the scale. If the character studied is intelligence, measured by a standardized test, there is decreased fertility at both the high and the low levels, but especially among the low-grade mentally defective. There are some peculiar features in the relationship of intelligence to fertility, but, in principle, the pattern agrees with that for stature.

On the assumption that the genic background of all these metrical traits is mainly additive, the extreme values must be markedly homozygous as compared with those in the centre. It follows that breeding must take place predominantly from heterozygotes. It should be noted, however, that the assumption is implied that the variance of the population with respect to the measurement is not diminishing. This assumption of constant variance from generation to generation, together with the complementary assumption of constant mean, make it possible to investigate heterosis in man indirectly.

Many controversial questions arise at this point. The first concerns rate of gene mutation, and it can be conveniently introduced by an example. Haldane (1939) suggested that the heterozygous carriers of juvenile amaurotic idiocy might have a slightly increased fertility. Such a possibility, in relation to this and other rare recessive sublethal diseases, makes estimates of fresh mutation rate unreliable. In a randomly mating population, the amount of extra fertility needed in the heterozygote, to maintain a lethal recessive gene in stable equilibrium, is very slight. The heterozygote must have a proportional excess fitness above the average level about equal to the gene frequency of the lethal trait itself. Thus, juvenile amaurotic idiocy in Sweden, which has a case frequency of about 10^{-4} and a corresponding gene frequency of 10^{-2}, need only have its unaffected heterozygotes 1% more fit than the general population in order to be maintained in equilibrium at the observed frequency. Such a small effect would be very difficult to identify in practice, and this knowledge might reasonably discourage investigators from making direct observations by counting offspring. For some other genes, which are seriously disadvantageous in homozygous form and which are more frequent, the difficulty of accounting for their persistence in the population solely by fresh mutation leads to the supposition of rates, per gene per generation, rather too high to be credible. Examples are 5×10^{-3} for a recessive type of mental illness (Böök 1953), 1×10^{-3} for the sickle-cell trait (Neel 1953) and 1×10^{-3} for fibrocystic disease of the pancreas (Goodman & Reed 1952).

An alternative is to postulate a degree of increased fitness in the heterozygote sufficient to maintain equilibrium at the existing frequency level. The same argument can apply when a defect is only known in the heterozygote and recognized as a dominant disability. In Huntington's chorea, for example, which has a mean age of onset at about 35 years, a slightly increased fertility before that age could more than compensate for the deficiency at later ages and render frequent mutation an unnecessary assumption.

The genetical stability of the human population with respect to rare abnormalities, whether due to mutation or to heterosis, is accepted very generally as a fact. Similarly, the existence of stable polymorphism with respect to common traits, regarded as part of the normal constitution, like hair colour, taste sensitivity and blood groups, is not considered improbable. Changes may be occurring all the time in response to natural selection, but they must be almost imperceptibly slow. With respect to one special trait, namely, measured intelligence or I.Q., the situation is believed to be far from stable, although there is no evidence of any detectable changes, and it is interesting to examine the evidence for this belief.

The relation between intelligence and fertility has been studied mainly in sibships taken by themselves, though sometimes parents have been included or paternal occupation recorded instead of test score. In all cases, ascertainment is through the existence of at least one child in the family, and no information is obtained about non-fertile members of the population. At the lower end of the distribution this leads to conflicting observations. Social workers can identify exceptionally large sibships with parents of defective intellectual capacity (Brock Report 1934). At the same time, direct counting of all the children occurring in representative samples of known cases of similar mental grade leads to the conclusion that the mean fertility of the whole defective group is much below the population average.

The fertility of the phenotype at any given mental level cannot therefore be directly inferred from the number of sibs. Nevertheless, the sib number tells something important about fertility, and the results of inquiries in this field are so consistent that they have to be taken seriously. The observed correlation coefficients between family size and intelligence of the propositus are shown in Table 1. The data which these figures summarize have been almost always assumed to indicate that the mean level of intelligence is falling. The family size, conveniently, though not quite accurately, estimated by sib number, rises approximately 20% for each unit fall of intelligence measured in terms of its standard deviation. If the regression of fertility·on intelligence in the general population were of this negative magnitude, and if the different levels were determined by neutral additive genes, then an extremely rapid decline would be expected. If the variation were due to additive genes which were in equilibrium on account of heterosis, the

Table 1: Correlation between family size (sib number) and metrical traits

TRAIT	SOURCE	DATE	NUMBER OF SUBJECTS	r
intelligence	Chapman & Wiggins	(1925)	632	−0.33
	Bradford	(1925)	393	−0.25
	Sutherland & Thomson	(1926)	1924	−0.22
	Lentz	(1927)	4330	−0.30
	Dawson	(1932)	1239	−0.19
	Roberts, Norman & Griffiths	(1938)	1271	−0.22
	O'Hanlon	(1940)	293	−0.21
	Thomson	(1949)	1110	−0.32
	Thomson	(1949)	70200	−0.28
stature	Boas	(1910)	15008	−0.09
	Maxwell	(1953)	6921	−0.20
weight	Maxwell	(1953)	6894	−0.14

negative sib number differential would still persist. However, in this case, the correlation for intelligence and fertility in the general population, before selection acts, would be zero. These points are shown in Tables 2 and 3. The mean sib number continues to move up in its initial direction, although the fitness is at a maximum for the metrically intermediate heterozygote. The reason for this is that an uncommon but very disadvantageous homozygote usually has the fittest kind of parents. The maximum correlation of sib number and intelligence, −0.070, occurs if the gene in stable equilibrium is rare and is lethal in homozygous form.

If the logarithm of the sib number is used as the standard measurement certain calculations are simplified. It can be demonstrated that the correlation of sib-number logarithm with quantitative effect is unaltered if the phenotype is determined by a number of additive gene pairs with the same properties, provided that fitness is always combined by multiplication. Two or more loci each may be supposed to contribute similar amounts to the measurement under consideration. The

Table 2: Relationship between fitness and sib number: A single gene pair in stable equilibrium

| GENOTYPE | QUANTI-TATIVE EFFECT (d) | FRE-QUENCY | FITNESS | | MEAN SIB NUMBER (S) |
			IN GENERAL	AT STABLE EQUILIB-RIUM *	
AA	2	p^2	f	$1 - k/p^2$	$(1 + k^2/p^3q)^2$
Aa	1	$2pq$	g	$1 + k/pq$	$(1 + k^2/p^3q)$ $(1 + k^2/pq^3)$
aa	0	q^2	h	$1 - k/q^2$	$(1 + k^2/pq^3)^2$
total	—	1	—	—	—
mean	$2p$	—	$p^2f + 2pqg + q^2h$	1	$(1 + k^2/p^2q^2)^2$

* k/pq is equivalent to the measures of intensity of selection, used by Fisher and Haldane.

number of gene pairs supposed to be acting in any given case depends upon certain limiting factors. One of these is the regression of the sib number on the quantitative effect which is being studied. The rise of 20% per sigma unit, observed for intelligence, is close to the maximum possible value for an effect due to a single gene pair in a system of random mating. The combination of several gene pairs, however, produces a greater effect than one pair because more gene units are then included in each sigma unit. Table 4 shows, for different frequencies, the number of lethal additive genes required to produce a rise in sib number of 20% per sigma unit.

Another most important limiting factor is the total quantity of lethality and in fertility in the initial general population of zygotes. According to Yerushalmy (1945), 15% of human pregnancies

Table 3: Data for estimation of theoretical sib number

| PARENTS | | RELATIVE FITNESS (SIB NUM-BER, S) | NUMBER OF OFFSPRING, n | | | |
| RING TYPE | FRE-QUENCY | | GENOTYPE | | | TOTAL |
			AA	Aa	aa	
AA × AA	p^4	f^2	p^4f^2	—	—	p^4f^2
AA × Aa	$1p^3q$	fg	$2p^3qfg$	$2p^3qfg$	—	$4p^3qfg$
AA × aa	$2p^2q^2$	fh	—	$2p^2q^2fh$	—	$2p^2q^2fh$
Aa × Aa	$4p^2q^2$	g^2	—	$2p^2q^2g^2$	$p^2q^2g^2$	$4p^2q^2g^2$
Aa × aa	$4pq^3$	gh	$p^2q^2g^2$	$2pq^3gh$	$2pq^3gh$	$4pq^3gh$
aa × aa	q^4	h^2	—	—	q^4h^2	q^4h^2
sum $[n]$			$p^2(pf + qg)^2$	$2pg(pf + qg)$ $\times(pg + qh)$	$q^2(pg + qh)^2$	$(p^2f + 2pqg + q^2h)$
sum $[n \times S]$			$p^2(pf^2 + qg^2)^2$	$2pq(pf^2 + qg^2)$ $\times(pg^2 + qh^2)$	$q^2(pg^2 + qh^2)^2$	$(p^2f^2 + 2pqg^2$ $+ q^2h^2)^2$

mean sib number = sum $[n \times S]$ sum $[n]$.

N.B. $r_{\text{in } S.d} = -k(p - q)/(p^2q^2 + 4kpq - k - k^2)^{1/2}p^{1/2}q^{1/2}$, when k/p^2q^2 is small or when k approaches q^2.

Table 4: Combination of additive lethal genes, $h = 0$

GENE FREQUENCY q	CORRELATION OF SIB NUMBER, S, AND I.Q. MEASUREMENT, d $r_{\text{in } s.d.}$ *	PROPORTIONAL CHANGE IN S PER SIGMA UNIT CHANGE IN d b †	APPROXIMATE NUMBER OF LOCI NEEDED TO PRODUCE THE EFFECT $b = -0.2$ N
0.50	−0.000	−0.0000	∞
0.45	−0.302	−0.1140	3
0.40	−0.408	−0.1891	1
0.35	−0.480	−0.2001	1
0.30	−0.534	−0.1912	1
0.25	−0.577	−0.1635	2
0.20	−0.612	−0.1244	3
0.15	−0.640	−0.0836	6
0.10	−0.667	−0.0463	19
0.05	−0.688	−0.0163	150
0.01	−0.704	−0.0014	20,000
0.00	−0.707	−0.0000	∞

* $r_{\text{in } s.d.} = -(1 - 2q)^{½}(2 - 2q)^{-½}.$

† $b = (2Nq^3)^{½}(2q - 1)(1 - q)^{-½}(1 - 2q + 2q^2)^{-1}.$

terminate in miscarriages or abortions. Stillbirths account for another 3% and there are 2% neonatal deaths. According to the observations of Sutter & Tabah (1952), many of these losses are caused by lethal recessive genes. Early mortality, after the first month, amounts to 3%. Beyond this, 20% do not marry and 10% of those who marry are believed to be infertile. It is clear that a very large part of the population of human zygotes, 40%, do not actually reproduce. This proportion represents only an upper extreme limit of genetical loss due to infertility of homozygotes.

A further point to be considered is the effect of assortative mating. For a trait due to a single gene, if the correlation for assortation were strongly positive, the effect on equilibrium would be marked (Penrose 1950b). In man, a high degree of assortation with respect to intelligence is usual, producing a correlation between parents of the order of +0.5. However, spread over ten or more gene pairs at different loci, the effect would probably be negligible.

In Table 5 (a) and (b) are shown the calculated combined effects of ten pairs of hypothetical additive genes. Each locus has a frequency 4:1 for two alleles, **A** and **a**. The fitness of the homozygote **aa** is made equal to 0.3, and those of the other genotypes are arranged so as to produce stable equilibrium at this frequency. The genes are of the same order of frequency as the sickle-cell trait but rather less unfavourable. Comparison with observed mean sib number is shown in Figure 1 (see Table 6). The calculated correlation between sib number and intelligence is close to − 0.3 here; the angle of the regression line is made to agree with observation on the assumption that the standard deviation of intelligence quotient is 16% (Terman & Merrill 1937). The agreement is good between the limits of +2 sigma and −2 sigma, but thereafter the assumption of multiplicative combination fitness implies a continuous rise in mean sib number to a very high level, while the observed sib number actually tends to fall. The crude hypothesis, indeed,

Table 5: Theoretical distributions derived from 10 pairs of autosomal additive genes with equal effects and equal frequencies

(a) Data for a single gene pair

GENOTYPE	QUANTITATIVE EFFECT	FREQUENCY	RELATIVE FITNESS	RELATIVE MEAN SIB NUMBER
AA	2.0	0.64	0.9562	0.9559
Aa	1.0	0.32	1.1750	1.0645
aa	0.0	0.04	0.3000	1.1863
total	—	1.00	—	—
mean	1.6	—	1.0000	1.0000

(b) Effects of combining ten such gene pairs, multiplying fitness throughout

QUANTITATIVE EFFECT	STANDARD σ UNITS	I.Q. EQUIVALENT, σ = 16	FREQUENCY	RELATIVE MEAN FITNESS	RELATIVE MEAN SIB NUMBER
20.0	2.24	136	1.15	0.64	0.64
19.0	1.68	127	5.76	0.79	0.71
18.0	1.12	118	13.69	0.93	0.79
17.0	0.56	109	20.54	1.04	0.88
16.0	0.00	100	21.82	1.10	0.98
15.0	−0.56	91	17.46	1.10	1.09
14.0	−1.12	82	10.91	1.01	1.22
13.0	−1.68	73	5.45	0.86	1.35
12.0	−2.24	64	2.22	0.66	1.51
11.0	−2.80	55	0.74	0.45	1.68
10.0	−3.35	46	0.20	0.27	1.88
9.0–0.0	—	—	0.06	—	—
total	—	—	100.00	—	—
mean	0.00	100	—	1.00	1.00

leads to absurdly high values for the fitness of some very rare multiple heterozygotes, rising theoretically to five times the average level. Absence of excessively large families, expected theoretically at this I.Q. level, probably does not imply instability leading to an increase in intelligence level. True, the data from the Scottish survey (Thomson 1949) have recently suggested that this can actually happen. Stability could, however, be obtained if a small amount of extra fertility were distributed among heterozygotes with measurements nearer the centre of the dis-

tribution. The maximum amount of heterozygosity in this model would be tenfold. This would occur phenotypically at an I.Q. level of 46, which is, in fact, associated with very low fertility, a consequence which agrees with Haldane's (1955) conjecture that very high degrees of heterozygosity are unfavourable.

There is, of course, plenty of evidence that a large proportion of the variance in sib number and in intelligence measurement is environmentally determined. Family size depends upon occupation, income, religion, education and so on.

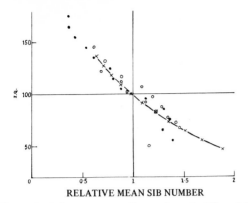

Figure 1: Relative mean sib number at different IQ levels. Comparison of observed data with combined effects of ten additive gene pairs. · observed (Thomson 1949), o observed (Roberts *et al.* 1938), x – – x calculated.

Table 6: Observed relative mean numbers of sibs for subjects classified by Stanford-Binet I.Q. (see figure 1)

ROBERTS ET AL. (1938)[*]		THOMSON (1949)[†]	
I.Q. INTERVAL	MEAN NUMBER OF SIBS	I.Q. INTERVAL	MEAN NUMBER OF SIBS
135–154	0.61	170–179	0.37
130–134	0.62	160–169	0.37
125–129	0.52	150–159	0.43
120–124	0.68	140–149	0.54
115–119	0.88	130–139	0.61
110–114	0.88	120–129	0.77
105–109	1.08	110–119	0.80
100–104	0.94	100–109	0.88
95–99	1.19	90–99	1.12
90–94	1.12	80–89	1.30
85–89	1.28	70–79	1.35
80–84	1.22	60–69	1.29
75–79	1.34	50–59	1.39
70–74	1.42	–	–
65–69	1.45	–	–
35–64	1.15	–	–
all	1.00	all	1.00

[*] 1271 subjects.   [†] 1110 subjects.

There is also evidence that part of the negative covariance between I.Q. and sib number is environmental because large family size itself seems to cause low scoring on intelligence tests (Nisbet 1953). The situation perhaps resembles some cases studied by Waddington (1953) in which heredity and environment have a synergic effect.

I have dealt with the intelligence problem in detail because it shows many interesting new possibilities in the interpretation of human metrical genetical data. Analyses on comparable lines can be made for stature, weight and other characters which show the same kind of fertility differentials. The conclusion I wish to draw is that, since there is no evidence of decline in the mean levels of stature or of intelligence, it is probable that these fertility differentials are due, in part at least, to heterosis. If so, they provide some of the best evidence of hybrid vigour in man. The slight heterosis effects of many individual genes here combine to produce significant fertility differentials.

REFERENCES

ALLISON, A. C. 1954 *Brit. Med. J.* 1, 290.
ANDREASSEN, M. 1943 *Haemofili i Danmark.* København: Ejnar Munksgaard.
BOAS, F. 1910 *Changes in bodily form of descendants of immigrants.* Washington: Government Printing Office.
BOAS, F. 1948 *Race, languages and culture* (collected papers), 2nd ed. New York: Macmillan.
BÖÖK, J. A. 1953 *Acta genet.* 4, 1, 133 and 345.
BRADFORD, E. J. G. 1925 *Forum of Education,* 3, 186.
BRIDGES, E. L. 1948 *Uttermost part of the earth.* London: Hodder and Stoughton.
BRYCE, L. M., JAKOBOWICZ, R., MC ARTHUR, N. & PENROSE, L. S. 1950 *Ann Eugen., Lond.,* 15, 271
BURT, C. & MOORE, R. C. 1911 *J. Exp. Ped.* 1, 93.
CHAPMAN, J. C. & WIGGINS, D. M. 1925 *Pedagogical Seminary,* 32, 414.
DAVENPORT, C. B. & STEGGERDA, M. 1929 *Race cross-*

ing in Jamaica. Washington: Carnegie Institute Publication.

DAWSON, S. 1932 *Brit. J. Psychol.* 23, 42.

DELBUE, S. M. 1950 *Ann. Eugen., Lond.,* 15, 184.

FISHER, R. A. 1930 *The genetical theory of natural selection.* Oxford: Clarendon Press.

GOODMAN, H. O. & REED, S. C. 1952 *Amer. J. Hum. Genet.* 4, 59.

HALDANE, J. B. S. 1939 *Ann. Eugen., Lond.,* 9, 232.

HALDANE, J. B. S. 1949 *Ric. Sci.* 19 (Suppl.), 2.

HALDANE, J. B. S. 1953 *Proc. IXth Int. Congr. Genet.*

HALDANE, J. B. S. 1955 Personal communication.

JONES, D. C. 1934 *Social survey of Merseyside,* 3. London: Hodder and Stoughton.

KARN, M. N. & PENROSE, L. S. 1951 *Ann. Eugen., Lond.,* 16, 147.

LENTZ, T. 1927 *J. Educ. Psychol.* 18, 486.

MAXWELL, J. 1953 *Social Implications of the 1947 Scottish mental survey.* London: University of London Press.

MOLLENBACH, C. J. 1947 *Medfødte defekter i øjets indre hinder, Klinik og Arvelighedsforhold.* København: Ejnar Munksgaard.

MONTALENTI, G., SILVESTRONI, E. & BIANCO, I. 1953 *Mem. Accad. Lincei,* 14, 183.

NEEL, J. V. 1953 *Amer. J. Hum. Genet.* 5, 154.

NISBET, J. 1953 *Eugen. Rev.* 45, 31.

O'HANLON, G. S. A. 1940 *Brit. J. Educ. Psychol.* 10, 196.

PAULING, L., ITANO, H. A., SINGER, S. J. & WELLS, I. C. 1949 *Science,* 110, 543.

PEARSON, K. & FAWCETT, C. D. 1898 *Proc. Roy. Soc.* 62, 413.

PEARSON, K. & LEE, A. 1896 *Proc. Roy. Soc.* 60, 273.

PENROSE, L. S. 1950a *Lancet,* 2, 425.

PENROSE, L. S. 1950b *Brit. J. Psychol.* 40, 128.

RAPER, A. B. 1954 *Brit. Med. J.* 2, 1162.

Report of the Departmental Committee on Sterilization (Brock Report) 1934. London: H.M.S.O.

ROBERTS, J. A. F., NORMAN, R. M. & GRIFFITHS, R. 1938 *Ann. Eugen., Lond.,* 8, 178.

SUTHERLAND, H. E. G. & THOMSON, G. H. 1926 *Brit. J. Psychol.* 17, 81.

SUTTER, J. & TABAH, L. 1952 *Population, Paris,* 7, 249.

TERMAN, L. M. & MERRILL, M. A. 1937 *Measuring intelligence.* London: Harrap and Co.

THOMSON, G. H. 1949 *The trend of Scottish intelligence.* London: University of London Press.

TREVOR, J. C. 1953 *Race crossing in man: the analysis of metrical characters.* London: Cambridge University Press.

WADDINGTON, C. H. 1953 *Evolution,* 7, 118.

YERUSHALMY, J. 1945 *Ann. Amer. Accad. Polit. Soc. Sci.* 237, 134.